THE FAMILY IDIOT

Volume Two

Translated by Carol Cosman

Jean-Paul Sartre

THE FAMILY IDIOT

Gustave Flaubert

1821–1857

The University of Chicago Press • Chicago and London

Originally published in Paris as part two, book one, of
L'Idiot de la famille: Gustave Flaubert de 1821 à 1857,
© Editions Gallimard, 1971.

The University of Chicago Press, Chicago 60637
The University of Chicago Press, Ltd., London

© 1987 by The University of Chicago
All rights reserved. Published 1987
Printed in the United States of America

96 95 94 93 92 91 90 89 88 87   5 4 3 2 1

Library of Congress Cataloging in Publication Data

Sartre, Jean Paul, 1905–80
  The family idiot.

  Translation of: L'Idiot de la famille.
  1. Flaubert, Gustave, 1821–1880.   2. Novelists,
French—19th century—Biography.   I. Title.
PQ2247.S313   843'.8[B]   81–1694
ISBN 0–226–73509–5 (v. 1)   AACR2
     0–226–73510–9 (v. 2)

CONTENTS

7139681

TRANSLATOR'S NOTE

I would like to give special thanks to Françoise Meltzer,
Charles A. Krance, and Victor Brombert for their help in
preparing this volume for publication.

PART TWO

Personalization

BOOK ONE

"What is beauty if not the impossible?"

The Imaginary Child

This is Gustave as he has been constituted. Of course, any determination imprinted in an existing being is surpassed by the way he lives. In the child Flaubert, passive activity and gliding are his *way of living* this constituted passivity; resentment is his *way of living* the situation assigned to him in the Flaubert family. In other words, the structures of this family are internalized as attitudes and reexternalized as actions by which the child makes himself into what others made him. Conversely, we shall find in him no behavior, as complex and elaborate as it might seem, that is not originally the surpassing of an internalized determination.

There is an enormous difference, however, between the simple *Aufhebung* of a given and the totalizing repetition to which we subject it, in order both to integrate the *Aufhebung* into the organic unity we try to be and to prevent it from jeopardizing that unity, from sitting there like a worm in an apple and spoiling the fruit from the inside. Perpetual totalization rises like a defense against our permanent detotalization, which is less a matter of simple diversity than of shattered unity. In human reality, indeed, multiplicity is always haunted by a dream or memory of synthetic unity; the detotalization itself demands to be retotalized, and totalization is not a mere inventory followed by a totaling report, but an intentional and directed enterprise of reunification.

This reunification, however, must not be taken for a kind of Kantian unification of empirical diversity. There are no external categories being applied here to experience; it is experience itself that is unified in a movement of circularity with the means at hand—the affects and ideas that prompt one to internalize objective structures. This retotalization can take place in an infinite variety of ways, depending on the particular individual, and, in the same individual, depending on

3

his age and outlook. We must understand its dependence dialectically on the previous totalization, which is now detotalized (or threatened with being); the earlier totalization, being highly structured—even after its collapse or the introduction of a foreign element—poses a singular question to a synthetic activity which, as it is only the surpassing of the detotalized whole, can comprehend and resolve problems only insofar as it is directed and limited by the concrete totality of the determinations it preserves within it. It would therefore be more correct to say that the question and the answer are conditioned by the same "previous circumstances" and by the same options, or again that it is the question in its singularity that surpasses itself as a singular answer. Furthermore, the process of integration is permanent only because it is led into permanence by the external stimuli that are internalized as experienced determinations. Consequently, we have no difficulty comprehending that this *perpetuum mobile* is kept in motion by a relation to the world that is constantly varying in intensity and quality to the degree that the cosmic individual internalizes the cosmos and is reexternalized in it, finding himself sooner or later compelled to reinternalize the objective consequences of that externalization (in other words, its objectification).

In order to provide a few examples that are still general but will allow access to the particular case of Flaubert, we will assume that the primary effect of cosmic aggression, internalized as this or that attitude—through the contradiction it introduces into the singular, global movement of internalization—is to compromise the organic and always threatened unity that experience attains and maintains as it rolls along, like a snowball constantly increasing in size. The danger is interpreted on the basis of affective and conjectural presuppositions that the individual has collected along the way and the options that have surpassed and maintained them; according to the specific character of these options, the totalizing reaction can be effected by a transformation of the collectivity to be totalized, which is in essence an effort to reduce the contradictions by acting on the whole so that to some degree it might integrate the new element as one of its parts—or by incorporating the pithiatic belief that this transformation has indeed been accomplished. In this case, the contradiction remains real and the assimilation is *imaginary*; the consequences will vary according to the whole under consideration (microcosm↔macrocosm), but it is certain that at least provisionally, the unification in progress will comprise a structure of unreality. In such a case, this structure involves organic unity in its totality. But the totalizing reaction, in order

4

to allow the process of unification to follow its course without essential modification, can also strive to subordinate the unassimilable determination, trying not to bind it to the whole of experience, not to attach it to anything, not to allow it *as nothing* to condition the reexternalization of the internal. In this second case, the pithiatic suggestion concerns the particular element introduced and will manifest itself by a false distraction, an imaginary forgetting. If this forgetting, indeed if this distraction, were real and amounted to the total abolition of the element under consideration, it would consequently lose all its virulence; but since this cannot be the case, just because of the *ipseity* of experience, this distraction must also rest upon the modifications that the foreign body necessarily brings to the totalization in progress. In other words, the intention *to remain the same* must be blind to real changes and at the same time construct a perfectly unreal substance for this totalization, which at once becomes an imaginary totality. Sometimes the integrating movement, rejecting what cannot be assimilated, will project it or introject it onto the outside; thus, some mentally ill people, seeking to escape the guilt that torments them, contrive to make others reproach them; these reproaches, being *other*, have the double advantage of becoming *external*—the enemy is not within but can be met face to face—and *suspect*, for who can say with certainty that the accusers are not sycophants, or perhaps they are men of good faith but are inadequately informed or tricked by false witnesses? Others, projecting their guilt or their fear of doing wrong onto those around them, can condemn in their neighbor the vice they fear in themselves. In the latter two cases, the direction and identity of the integrating movement can be maintained only by making the original relation to the world an unreal one. The most frequent result, however, is that the mere presence of the nonassimilable element generates antagonistic real elements, which pounce on the nonassimilable one, attacking it and attempting to reduce it to impotence; and this cannot happen without a serious alteration of the ongoing process of totalization. These reducing agents—whose effects are worse than the disease they are trying to combat—must be compared to the antibodies that course through a transplanted heart, killing the organism they are intended to protect. *Stress* is the name we shall give to this unity of the nonassimilable element and the global defense that the totalizing process develops against it, infected precisely to the degree that it tries to neutralize the nonassimilable. In this case, neurosis is stress as much as character disorder. Of course, this totalizing effort to defuse the contradictions or to isolate them achieves its aim only at the price of dangerous divergences, which alter the totalized whole. To take only one example, the pithiatic forgetting of something inconvenient necessarily becomes a prospective and generalized forgetting; in effect, what we want to forget is not a single fact but a system of relationships of which this fact is the symbol or basis, and which can reappear at any time and in any way. Hence the "forgetful" totalization flees from all feeling and all thought, tearing itself away from other ideas and other feelings for fear of examining them too closely. Because of this, it deliberately remains on the surface of totalizing experiences; or else the forgotten element suddenly finds its freedom and is able, as an autonomous system, to structure experience its own way by provoking difficulties that will not be perceived or will be attributed to the action of other factors; as such, it will become the object of a false integration. Finally, because it is not *opposed* openly and attacked head on, the nonassimilable element becomes not only an agent of detotalization, but the active principle of a negative totalization, which develops in opposition to the other and totalizes it in reverse. Dangerous as such stress may be, however, it nonetheless offers a way of surpassing the disturbing element, especially to the extent that the totalization in progress is reexternalized and objectified through actions; in this sense we might say that every project is a flight and every flight a project. For this reason, the other name of this totalization which is endlessly detotalized and retotalized is *personalization*. The *person*, in effect, is neither completely suffered nor completely constructed; furthermore, the person *does not exist* or, if you will, is always the *surpassed* result of the whole mass of totalizing operations by which we continually try to assimilate the nonassimilable—primarily our childhood—indicating that the person represents the abstract and endlessly retouched product of personalization, the only real—that is, *experienced*—activity of the living being. In other words, it is experience itself conceived as unification and endlessly returning to the original determinations on the occasion of more recent ones in order to integrate what cannot be integrated; as if each new aggression by the cosmic exterior seemed at once a disparity to be absorbed and possibly the only chance to begin the great mixture of totalization once again, the mixture that aims to assimilate archaic, still vital contradictions—indeed, to surpass them in rigorous unity manifesting itself as a cosmic determination by being objectified through a hierarchical enterprising whole. It may be, moreover, that the spoke of the wheel lengthens; or that it remains the same and the new event does nothing but revive the "primal scene" in the same intentional unity of assimilation. From our present point of view, we might well conceive this circular movement in a three-dimensional space as a multicentered spiral that continually swerves away from these centers or rises above them by making an indefinite number of revolutions around its starting point. Such is the movement of personalizing evolution, at least until sclerosis or regressive involution sets in, which occurs at a different moment for each individual. In this case, the movement is repeated indefinitely, passing the same places, or else the higher revolution abruptly tumbles down to any one of the lower. In any event, personalization in the individual is nothing more than the surpassing and preservation (assumption and inner negation) at the core of a project to totalize what the world has made—and continues to make—of us.

Thus, while our previous descriptions attempted to leave nothing obscure, we never arrived at little Gustave's personalization, an effort made through passive activity to unify the internalized family structures. Indeed, while the two are inseparable, we had decided to limit ourselves, for purposes of clarity, to examining his *constitution* by means of a collection of testimonies. But the paradox arose from the fact that most of these testimonies *about* Gustave were offered by the child himself in his first *written* stories. We were therefore led to search for constituting determinations *through* a totalizing reaction that preserved them, to be sure, but only by surpassing them, and this we left unexamined. Yet it is obvious that any reader around 1860, if asked the question, Who *is* Gustave Flaubert?—even if that reader were miraculously privy to certain confidences—would not have replied (or not at first) that he was a frustrated and jealous younger brother or an unloved child or a passive agent (albeit an agent who had lost none of these characteristics;[1] rather, the reply would surely have been "He is a novelist," or "He is the author of *Madame Bovary.*" In other words, what was then taken for Flaubert's *being* was his *writer-being,* and if one wanted to particularize this designation, which is still too general, one would have had recourse to his particular work. In other words, in the eyes of the public, he was personalized by the novel he published. Clearly, general opinion held him first to be a cre-

---

1. Their meaning and their function have continued to vary, for each revolution forms them into a richer aggregate, more differentiated and better integrated. It is in terms of the retotalization at a given juncture, at whatever level it is operative, that the constituting determinations are themselves determined as being or not being assimilable; and in the latter case that they are seen as having a role to play—real or imaginary according to whether the integration is actual or dreamed.

ator and established an intimate though ineffable link between the pure gratuitousness of the work, an end in itself to the extent that, for the time being, beauty was an absolute end, and the author's labor; but in spite of the impersonality attached to the novelist, the public also felt that he had objectified in his work the complex of his personalized determinations. With the exception of Saint-Beuve and his imitators, no one at that time would have thought of making a spectral analysis of a text or of interpreting a work in the light of the writer's life, or vice versa; but through a style and a particular meaning in each book, readers *recognized* Flaubert the writer in what was incomparably his. In the movement of sympathy, empathy, or antipathy that draws him to, or distances him from, *Madame Bovary*, the reader places himself in relation to a man, that is, to a style of life infinitely condensed in the swiftness of a sentence, in its resonance, in the succession of paragraphs, or in their breaks. The reader does not yet *understand* this man but already *tastes* him and divines that he is *understandable;* in any event, the *flavor*, which is sensed immediately, should be reconstituted by the end of a long acquaintance or a biographical study. Yet objectification in the work is a moment of *personalization:* Gustave's contradictions and disharmonies are all in his novel, but they are integrated in an imaginary way into the unreal object he presents and are simultaneously integrated into reality through his work as the *means* of creation. Finally, by a sudden reverse movement, the reader's response ("He is the author of *Madame Bovary*") indicates that the writer must have subsequently reinternalized the external and social consequences of his external totalization—"infamous" glory, the trial, etc. And above all, Gustave must have internalized the necessity of being the man who wrote *Madame Bovary*, hence who has already written it, and who, being summed up, surpassed, objectified in a product of his labor, is rediscovered whole, after publication, with the same conflicts to integrate in another work by a personalizing revolution which must also embrace and assimilate the fact that these conflicts have already served as means in the production of an imaginary object. Thus Flaubert's reader reaches him in his being on the level of personalization and discovers his constitution only through the totalizing intention that made it the tool or the material used to elaborate the man through the work and the work through the man. We are saying that in order to resolve his inner conflicts, Gustave *made himself* into a writer. Yet from his earliest correspondence we learn that he wants to write. Was he then constituted as a *writer*? No, but little by little the meaning of that term becomes more precise and enriched: we raise ourselves from one revolution to the next on the totalizing spiral. I *will be* a writer. This is the true answer the adolescent made to his inner disharmony, this is his commitment, his fundamental option: to envelop his malady and integrate it as a means of objectifying himself through writing. We are here on the level of stress, since Gustave's malady (namely, his constitution) in turn transforms this totalizing project by thoroughly infecting it, and since the totalizing answer to this generalized infection can be furnished only by a new revolution, that is, by a new metamorphosis of personalization, etc., etc. In the first part of this work we described the malady, not the stress, because mediations were not yet given. Now we must reconstitute in all its phases the dialectical movement by which Flaubert progressively made himself into "the-author-of-*Madame Bovary*."

Gustave's answer to his illness, between 1835 and 1839, was to turn it into the means of an enterprise aimed at producing certain objects in the world. He *personalizes himself in an enterprise* in order to integrate what would otherwise be resistant to integration. The enterprise, in effect, is the reexternalization of the internalized, and such indeed will be Gustave's *person*, a permanent mediation between the subjective and the objective. More precisely and according to his own testimony, he is retotalized as the man who must achieve glory by creating centers of derealization out of certain combinations of graphemes. This definition is applied to the young Flaubert and not to all the future writers he will become—it suits him at fifteen but not at thirty-five. However, even in this limited way it is not original. At thirty-five, these three notions—glory, unreality, and language—structure a basic option, but, as often happens, before being totalized they are sometimes experienced as separate. As a child, Gustave wanted to be a great actor. He renounced that ambition—and with very bad grace—only after entering school. At seventeen, he still writes: "I dreamed of glory when I was just a child. . . . If I had been guided, I would have made an excellent actor—I felt the power within me." Thus his totalizing option was at first appreciably different from what it later became. If we wish to understand its dynamics, we must try to answer the following questions: In what way did Gustave's choosing to incarnate imaginary characters represent a totalizing surpassing of his constituted determinations? Why was this the first moment of his personalization? What did glory mean to him? Why did he abandon the stage for literature, and what remained of his first "vocation" in his second? These questions are all the more complex in that they bear on the internal temporalization of a project. But especially to the extent that they concern a totalization that is endlessly detotalized and permanently retotalized by enveloping new determinations, they bring into play Gustave's relations to *everything*, not only to his family and his friends but to his fellow students, his teachers, the culture he was taught, the institutions of which he gradually gained experience, the social environment, his own class and other classes. We must therefore follow Flaubert's evolution step by step in his human relations as well as in his relations to art, since the former condition the latter, which in turn condition the former by subsuming them. But what we must ask ourselves before anything else—since this element remains in each revolution of the spiral and is found from the first—is what is meant by the *choice of the unreal*.

Sensible children dream of their future: they will plant the flag in new territory, they will save their fellow citizens by the thousands during a cholera epidemic, they will be rich, powerful, honored. Nothing could be more reassuring: these good little citizens please themselves by thinking that they will make their mark in the world. Their desire rests on *being*, and never for a moment do they lose sight of what is real and true. In fact, things are not so simple. Even among the most realistic children, the desire does not entirely correspond to the wish-fulfilling dream, or to any other. This complex option, totalizing the earliest determinations—familial ones—through a surge of enthusiasm which they condition and which envelops them, cannot be precisely expressed by any image or discourse; in this sense, these primary imaginings harbor the allusive goal of an unreality posed as such and, occasionally, the painful pleasure of unfulfillment. Still, it is no less true that the imaginary is here experienced on the surface as heralding the real, and unfulfillment as promising future fulfillment: the child really *will be* that heroic doctor, the idol of his native city—*as though it were already accomplished*. In this sense the fiction is perceived as a postponement of what is true and as permission to enjoy it in advance. Thus, at least *explicitly*, the imagined future presents itself for what it is on the level of praxis: a mediation that is not to be found at the end of the enterprise—since it is abolished by its own realization—and that is subordinate to real goals, a systematic and interested exploration of the range of possibilities, a passage from being *toward being*.

But what if the dream turns into a dream of a future dream? What if the child were imagining a future in which he were someone unreal? What a worry for the parents! They discover that their offspring spends the greater part of his time telling himself that he will be a false physician. Not for the pleasure of imagining himself a true future charlatan (besides, charlatans are never true, even *as such*), but wholly in order to be false, that is, both not to be what he is and to be what he is not. Worse still, he feels a suspect, pervasive pleasure in the production of an appearance, that is, in mobilizing reality in order to produce something unreal that turns back on reality and totalizes it, in essence reversing the "normal," "healthy," *practical* order of things by making the real the means to unreality. Here is a suspicious character, the dismayed family will think, whose first move is to place himself *outside humanity:* he is prepared to let his prey go for the sake of a mere shadow; he prefers nonbeing to being, not having to having, an oneiric quietism. Even more serious, it is not pure nothingness he loves but the nothingness that endows being with a kind of unhealthy appearance of reality. This is the devil, lord of the trompe-l'oeil, of illusions and false appearances. From childhood on, this is Gustave Flaubert.

At the age of seven he wanted to be a great actor. Other children about that age, whether or not they might succeed in their ambition, have opted for literature. This does not mean that they were better suited to write than he, simply that they were other, and literary art was other for them, through them. It is therefore of some importance that Gustave's initial project should have been so removed from his definitive project. But if, on the other hand, the truth is in *becoming,* the writer in him must have preserved the principal features of the actor and his writing style something of his style of acting. And no one can act dramatically without letting himself be completely and publicly consumed by the imaginary.

The act of imagining, taken generally, is an act of consciousness that seeks an absent or nonexistent object through a kind of reality that elsewhere I have called an analogue, which functions not as a sign but as a symbol, that is, as the materialization of the sought-after object. To materialize here does not mean *to realize* but, on the contrary, to unrealize the material through the function assigned to it. When I look at a portrait, the canvas, the spots of dried color, the frame itself constitute the analogue of the object, that is, of the man now dead who served as model for the painter, and at the same time, in an unbreakable unity, the analogue of the work, that is, of the intentional totalization of appearances massed around this famous face. With respect to what are incorrectly termed "mental images," the image-making intention treats as analogue the partial determinations of my body (phosphenes, movement of eyes, fingers, the sound of my breath), and in this way I am partially unrealized: my organism remains an existing body which disengages from being at *a single* point.[2] It is quite different for an actor, who seeks to manifest an absent or fictive object through the totality of himself as an individual; he treats himself the way the painter treats his canvas and palette. Kean walking onto the stage at Drury Lane lends his walk to Hamlet; his actual movement when offstage disappears, no one notices it any more;[3] in themselves, the comings and goings of this nervous little man have no meaning and no other conceivable purpose than to wear out his shoes. But the comings and goings are absorbed for the public, and for Kean himself, by the Prince of Denmark strolling back and forth and soliloquizing. This also holds for the actor's gestures, voice, and physique. The spectator's perception is unrealized in imagination: he does not observe Kean's tics, his bearing, his "style"; rather, he imagines he is observing those of the imaginary Hamlet. Diderot was right: the actor does not really experience the feelings of his character; but it would be wrong to suppose that he expresses those feelings in cold blood; the truth is that he experiences them *unreally*. We must understand that his real affects—stage fright, for example: an actor "acts on his stage fright"—serve him as analogues, and through them he aims at the passions he must express. The actor's technique does not depend on an exact knowledge of his body and the muscles that must be contracted in order to express this or that emotion; it depends above all—more complex and less conceptualized—on the utilization of this analogue in terms of the imaginary emotion he must fictively experience. To feel within the context of the unreal, in effect, is not *to feel nothing* but to trick oneself deliberately as to the meaning of what is felt. The actor preserves the suppressed certainty of not being Hamlet at the very moment he publicly *displays* himself as Hamlet and, *in order to display* his character, has to convince himself that he is Hamlet. The spectators' approbation gives him an ambiguous confirmation: on the one hand it consolidates the materialization of the unreal by socializing it ("What is going to happen? *What will the prince do* after this new turn of fate?"); on the other hand, it refers the actor back to himself: he keeps the audience in suspense and knows he will soon be applauded. But from this very ambiguity he draws a new enthusiasm which serves him in turn as affective analogue.[4] Besides, a role always

2. In another sense, however, unrealization must be taken for total in each case. But this is not crucial here.

3. Of course, the general concern with *rendering* Hamlet ends by becoming an obsession in that every detail of real life is seized upon as an incentive for derealization.

4. I do not claim that the unrealization is continuous. It takes very little for it to give way to cynicism (crazy laughter on stage, an aside to one's partner in front of the audi-

involves automatic gestures (habits acquired during rehearsals) controlled by a faultless vigilance; however expected or unexpected, these are released just in time, surprising the actor himself, and are easily *un*realized as an imaginary spontaneity, provided he knows how to manipulate his gestures while abandoning himself to them. This kind of vigilance allows him to say as the curtain is lowered, "I was bad tonight" or "I was good"; but such judgments are applied at once to Kean, the individual of flesh and blood whose function is to entertain, and to a Hamlet who consumes him and who, from one day to the next, will be profound, or mediocre, or anywhere between. Thus, for the true actor, every new character becomes a provisional *imago*, a parasite that even outside his performances lives in symbiosis with him and sometimes, even in the course of his daily activities, dictates his attitudes.[5] What protects him most effectively from madness is less his innermost certainty—he is not very reflective, and if his role demands that he raise himself to the level of reflection, his real ego also serves him as analogue to the imaginary being he incarnates—than the desperate conviction that the character takes everything out of him and gives him nothing. Kean can offer *his being* to Hamlet, who will never do the same in return; Kean *is* Hamlet, frenziedly, utterly, *desperately*, but there is no reciprocity—Hamlet is not Kean. This means that the actor sacrifices himself so that an *appearance* can exist and makes himself by choice into the support of nonbeing.

We cannot say a priori that the actor has chosen unreality for itself. He may have wanted to lie in order to be true, like the actors trained by Stanislavsky and his followers, yet this desire itself is suspect. In any case, without knowing the details of his life, we cannot say anything decisive about his basic option. However, even for a "realist," his choice, much more clearly than that of the writer or artist, implies a certain preference for total unrealization. The sculptor's raw material

---

ence, etc.); but no more is needed to pass from cynicism to exaltation and its unrealizing exploitation. It all happens in the framework of a general project of unrealization in which recurrences of the real simply happen as a matter of course.

5. What supports him in his effort and is perhaps effortlessly unrealized is his "staging"—a collection of positions, movements, and attitudes indicated by the other or the director. We often hear an actor, in the course of rehearsals, say that he *does not feel* the stage direction that is provided: "Play that sitting down? Say that while moving toward the back? No, my friend, I *don't feel it*." The *feeling*—the attitude accompanying the speech—represents here a mediation between real sensations (kinesthesia, coenesthesia, postures) and their exploitation by the imaginary: if he stands up to speak, the sudden action of springing out of the armchair will dispose him to feel the indignation that has made the fictive character jump to his feet.

13

is outside him, in the world, it is the block of marble that is unrealized by his chisel; the raw material of the novelist is language, those signs he traces on a sheet of paper; both sculptor and writer can claim that they work without ceasing to be themselves.[6] The actor cannot; his raw material is his own person, his purpose is to be unreally another. Of course, everyone plays at being what he is. But Kean plays at being what he is not and what he knows he cannot be. Thus, every evening he knowingly reenters a metamorphosis that will always be halted at the same point. And it is in this very incompletion that he takes pride: how should people admire him "being" the character so well if no one, beginning with himself, knows that he is not that character in reality? Therefore, not everyone can make a career in the theater; the fundamental qualification is not talent or disposition but a certain *constituted* relationship between reality and unreality, without which the actor would never even *take it into his head* to subordinate being to nonbeing.

This relationship undoubtedly made up part of Gustave's constitution *at least after the Fall*, for he went on stage at the age of eight and did not want to leave. It may be said that his desire rested on something real, the actor's glory. But this would be to reverse the correct order: the desire for glory comes *afterward*; indeed, he did not think it was due to any special prowess on his part but rather to the good use of a technique of derealization. This can mean only one thing: discovering in himself, as a failure of experience, as his anomaly, the reversal of the "normal" hierarchy that makes the imaginary a means of realization; he tried to become personalized in the *enveloping* project of turning this deficiency to his advantage and transforming his shame into glory. But for someone to choose to endow the dream itself with inherent value, he must himself be constituted as a dream. Only an imaginary child can contemplate insuring *in his person* the triumph of the image over reality because he is constituted in his own eyes as pure appearance. Being unhappy is not enough to prompt the choice of the imaginary. Quite the contrary, the imaginary must choose you and be the source of your unhappiness. Gustave at eight years old *suffers his unreality* as an elusive lack of being. In order to understand how his *personalization* first manifests itself as a consuming integration of the unreal to the enterprise of existing, and how unreality figures in his stress under the name of a *malady* and as a *means of escaping that malady*, we shall ask ourselves, returning to the conclusions of part

6. We shall soon see that this is not true of Gustave.

14

one, what factors affected him *in the beginning* with an unreality that he was condemned to produce to the exact degree that he submitted to it. I see three such factors, each corresponding to a moment of temporalization but with effects that would make themselves felt at all levels of the totalizing spiral: his relationship with his mother (action, language, sexuality), his relationship with his father (being looked at by the other), and his relationship with his sister (specter of the epic performance).

A. Inaction and Language

The passive constitution that his mother's ministrations gave him entails the joint diminution of *Gustave's* reality and of reality *itself*. In effect, the unveiling of the real is a moment of action: it is revealed in the project that surpasses it as both practical field and permanent threat (the coefficient of adversity); its being is resistance and possibility. When perception is no longer *practical*, it turns to the imagination. Or, if you will, the difference is diminished between that which is the analogue of an absent object—hence a neutralized and derealized object—and that which seems to subsist as a simple *being-there* with no connection of any sort to our existence. In this sense, we can say that contemplative quietism *makes imaginary* what is contemplated. But Gustave is so constituted that, with his needs satisfied even before they are evident, desire is perceived in him not as a demand for satisfaction through the practical but as the oneiric expectation of a satisfaction that may or may not come, over which he has no power in any case. This means not that the impulse is without violence but that for lack of affirming itself it is without right and, indeed, its very being is in doubt—in other words, it is not *instituted*. Gustave does not know how to responsd to the external world (for loved children, that world is the mother, an always vigilant mediation between their desire and its object); so the impulse goes—by itself and fully awake—toward its imaginary satisfaction. For a desire that is violent but does not believe in itself there is not much difference between a chance satisfaction that is always unforeseen, never *obtained*, and an imaginary satisfaction. Inversely, the overprotected infant finds himself safe from ordinary dangers and does not need to provide against them. A little later, when they are revealed, he unrealizes himself by becoming derealized. It is a general phenomenon that when it is impossible for us to respond through action to the demands of the world, the world suddenly loses its reality. In a gondola one night in the middle of a Vene-

15

tian lagoon, threatened by gondoliers who were deliberating whether to take his wallet and perhaps his life, Gide fell into a mood of detached, amused perplexity: nothing was real, everyone was pretending. I recall having experienced the same state of mind in June 1940, when I crossed the central square of a village under the threat of German rifles, while the French, from the top of the church, were taking potshots at the enemy and ourselves. It was a joke, it wasn't real. In truth, I understood then that *I was the one* who had become imaginary, being unable to find a response adapted to a specific and dangerous stimulus. And at once I drew my surroundings into unreality as well. A defensive reaction? No doubt; but one that only serves to underscore a derealization whose source is to be found elsewhere. The salvation of my person no longer depending on myself,[7] I felt my acts reduced to gestures: I was playing a role; others were giving me my cue. Pushed to the limit, this feeling can lead to sleep—I have been told of soldiers under severe bombardment sleeping in the trenches they had dug. In this case, as in those I have just cited, we are dealing with a defensive reflex which can function only if powerlessness transforms mortal danger into a waking nightmare. In order to pass over into the imaginary, Gustave does not need such hazardous circumstances; his powerlessness is permanent, and the least demand from the external world, the least disequilibrium, plunges him into a daze; on this level, his translation to the imaginary and the unrealization of the world are accomplished together: the daze is understood as an analogue of ecstasy, the sea as analogue of the infinite. Let us not imagine, however, that at bottom the child was not, like everyone else, a "computer of being":[8] on the level of anchorage and of internalization, the reality of the world penetrated him and became his reality. Except that at all levels he escaped from himself—the absence of the power to affirm and to deny reduced him to believing, to believing in *himself.* And we know that belief and nonbelief are the same thing: to believe is *only to believe.* The object of the belief is therefore perceived as an unstable being that can at any moment pass from the real to the illusory, so that its reality is exposed by its very presence as a virtual illusion; inversely, illusion, for lack of being denied, is always present in his eyes as *capable* of being believed and thus containing, to what-

7. If I did not advance, the Germans would shoot; if I did, I would find myself under French fire. I made a choice, however: the danger was worse on the German side—they wouldn't miss me. But this choice, imposed by the circumstances, was so little *mine* that it seemed like an integral part of a role I had to play.

8. Merleau-Ponty, *Signes.*

ever degree, a virtual reality. Gustave does not always have the means to establish a clear-cut difference between the two.

This general lack of differentiation easily leads him from an insufficiently real world to a waking dream whose lack of substance is inadequately felt and which can always be believed if it is pleasing or reassuring. This alone, however, does not allow us to understand why the child dreamer chose to unrealize himself publicly—that is, for *others*—by playing dramatic roles. Here we should recall that Gustave's passive constitution has had deplorable effects on his entrance into the universe of language.

The cold overprotection that prevailed during his first years prevented his needs from being constituted as *aggression against the other;* he was never sovereign, never had the chance to bawl out his hunger angrily or manifest it as an imperative; he did not feel maternal love, and as the pure object of maternal care, he did not know that first communication, the reciprocity of tenderness. A little later, after weaning, when he had to express his desires in the hope that they would be satisfied, he was incapable of truly *signifying* them: the order of experience—which in him was vegetative and pathic—was incommensurate with the order of signs.

"Suffer in silence." This ancient axiom means—among other things—that we are grateful to our friends for telling us in a matter-of-fact way that they have a headache or a stomachache, without dramatizing and in a neutral voice; by keeping their distance with respect to illness, they invite us to do the same. But everyone does what he can, and there are always people who "lay it on"—their voice breaking, or faint, or falsely neutral—who identify with their suffering or refuse to retreat from it and thus make it impossible for us to distance ourselves; this is the appeal of love, of course, and we are right to say that such people want to be pitied, but wrong to be irritated by it. It is this way with Gustave. For him, language remains the principal instrument, but since he has not been initiated from birth in the myriad forms of exchange, an infinitesimal and unbridgeable distance will always separate him from his interlocutors. He thinks his pathos cannot be communicated, and above all he is unaware that every word is a right over the Other; that every sentence, even a purely informative one, is imposed as a question, a solicitation, a command, an acceptance, a refusal, etc., in the interminable conversation men have pursued over the centuries; that every question is answered, even by silence; that any two persons, different as they may be, when placed in each other's presence, carry on a dialogue, though fully intending to keep quiet, because even in the most complete immobility they are necessarily seeing and visible, totally signifying and totally signified. For the child Gustave—and later for the man—dialogue is not the actualization of reciprocity through the Word, it is an alternation of monologues. And when it is his turn to monologue, he is certain to fail before he even begins. Others can reach him through speech; they affirm in him *alien phrases* that designate him from the outside and implant themselves in his head; he cannot make them his own because of the weakness of his affirmative power and he feels, when he recites them, that they have lost their power—he will not reach his interlocutor by simple speech. To repeat the words "suffering," "love," "desire" is not enough—he must make them heard; he has no chance of convincing others unless he presents his passion to them quite naked, just as he lives it. In other words, pathos will be manifest in and through sound and gesture, but with no right, no authority; it can only *represent* his state. But for this *display* to elicit the Other's confirmation, it must not be aimed at him. Or at anyone. It is the opposite of information. Outdoing his passivity, the child must *suffer* the externalization of his pathos: the poor boy had no intention of speaking with a voice altered by emotion; as for the mimicry accompanying his statements, it imposes itself involuntarily, as though his interlocutor had surprised him in his solitude and *saw him living* his irrepressible suffering. Thus Kean playing Hamlet resolves to ignore his audience; it is the sight of the ghost that tears those stuttering words from him, that recoiling movement—and not the public's expectation. Kean and Gustave, however, through such noncommunication, aim to communicate—indirectly and without reciprocity—a pathic state; both offer themselves, *propose themselves* to impassive masters, not knowing the welcome they will receive. Will they be *believed*? Will they *move* their audience? Will they get what they are asking for? This does not depend on them—yesterday the hall was covered with gold, today, perhaps, it will be only boards. They put themselves in the hands of their judges: the groundlings are free to let themselves be convinced (or not); Gustave's parents are free to believe or not to believe, to let themselves be moved or not. In sum, the child and the actor share the same helplessness and the same goals, with the difference that Kean does not really feel the fear he *represents*, while Gustave is convinced he is expressing what he feels. When we look more closely, however, the distance that separates them is notably reduced. Kean experiences Hamlet's terror, as we have seen, unreally. At first the little boy really does experience *something*. The unreality resides, in his case, in the expression: pain or desire pretend to *escape* him and provide their own testimony uninvited. At its extreme, this takes the form of the *cry*, the cry *let loose* in order to be convincing, which represents itself as *torn* out of suffering or joy. But can we prescribe the boundaries of unrealization? The emotion Gustave expresses is not identical to the one he believes he is expressing, for his mimicry is necessarily hyperbolic: if he were submitting to it as he pretends instead of *making* it, it would correspond to an affective confusion of quite another intensity. In this sense we can say that the experienced affect, whatever it is, serves as analogue to the simulated affect.

Can we say that he is lying? Not at all. He wants to be convincing. Unable to affirm, he exaggerates. Insincere—no doubt; but only if we add that he is *affected* by insincerity—he makes too much of it because he is not capable of asking *enough* of it. Unable to discover, construct, and affirm his subjective truth all at the same time, he is certain of what he feels only after making a show of it and after receiving the approbation of others, which he internalizes and preserves within him as a hysterical imitation of an affirmation (the judicial act transformed into a verbal gesture). This means that his emotions, waiting to be instituted by his life's witnesses, escape him without being entirely destroyed and seem to be felt *in order to be represented*. All at once, pathos, instead of being the absolute consciousness of self, becomes the means of *offering-oneself-in-a-state-of-emotion-to-the-instituting-eye*. Thus the experienced affect is permeated by an impalpable nothingness, which becomes the very flavor of experience but remains inexplicable for the child because, the moment he feels he is being insincere, he feels the sincerity of what he is experiencing and trying to express. The insincerity here arises from the fact that the sincerity is clandestine. Certainly, the self-consciousness of experience—hence the permanent possibility of a reflective cogito—is undeniable, but Gustave does not consider it an *index sui:* the sentiment, projecting beyond the simple presence of the felt emotion, always entails a retrospective involvement (a decision colored by the interpretation of the past) and a vow (an involvement with the future); this is the way it escapes consciousness and becomes its quasi object at the core of the psyche, a quasi object whose likelihood increases in proportion to the subject's affirmative power, that is, to his capacity for *action*, hence to his constitution. But Gustave cannot make a vow or a decision for himself; He receives his vow from others; it is up to them to decide according to his present actions what he ought to have felt and what he will feel.

The others, however, must be persuaded. If Gustave wishes to in-

19

fluence their judgment, he must convince them; and it is fitting as well, while awaiting *institution,* that he should if not convince himself, at least become disposed to believe in what he is doing. For this reason he struggles with the constant sense of disequilibrium that torments him by intensifying the external manifestations of his state: he throws himself on his knees in order to believe, cries out to be touched by the pain expressed. If he could die of sorrow in front of his family—we know he dreamed of it more than once—this mad excess would be equal, all things considered, to the calm, assertoric judgment *I am suffering,* which is permitted only to practical agents. It would be *proof* and who could doubt it? No one, least of all the unhappy younger son, whose last breath would be a sigh of contentment: convinced at last! In sum, unable to affirm his pathos, he tries to give it the strength to affirm itself through the ravages it provokes. In vain; he fights against constituted unrealization by derealizing himself even more. The gap grows between the intensity of experience and that of its manifestations; he cannot help feeling an emotional inflation—not much gold, lots of paper money. He is irritated: whatever he does sounds false; he will soon accuse himself of hyperbole.[9] Later he dubs himself the Excessive, a name with double meanings related at once to his real "hinddignations" ("I know, I shouldn't . . . it isn't worth it, but what do you expect, *it is stronger than I am"*) and to the big words, the outbursts, the gesticulations that express them ("I know, I exaggerate, I recognize it, but what do you expect, I'm a mountebank by nature").

At a deeper level, when the child unrealizes himself in order to propose the *image* of his real state, he plays with his helplessness in order to force the Other to give him a straightforward answer: "It's your ball. I have no right to your help and besides, I am not even appealing to you; if you help me out, it will be pure generosity on your part, you will be my good lord; if you decide to abandon me, you are free to do so, but you will have chosen freedom-to-do-evil and handed the world over to Satan." To playact one's feelings is to pretend to deliver oneself to others and, in actuality, to attempt to blackmail them. But of course this violence must remain hidden, even for the one who commits it; so the unrealization grows, since Gustave seeks to conceal his project from himself at the very moment he achieves it: with all eyes upon him, he deludes himself and *imagines* he is suffering in solitude when in fact he is acting on himself in order to prompt others to com-

9. See the story told by the second narrator in *Novembre.*

miserate with him. To act on himself in order to act on others, to make a spectacle of himself in order to move them—this is the prototype of passive action but it is nonetheless action: stage actors do it every night, and they too must forget their true motives if they want to convince their judges.[10] On this level, language itself becomes imaginary. We should understand that the spoken phrases "I am ill" or "I am dying of envy" do not contain real information and are limited to commenting on the presented image, like the title of a work of art. When Klee reviewed his new works at the end of the month in order to invent names for them, a kind of osmosis was produced between the word and the painted object; the former structured the latter by pushing unrealization to an extreme, and the latter, by *appealing* to the former from the depths of the unreal, communicated to it its unreality at the very moment of verbal invention. Words burst forth that had never been yoked together before—for example, "Frog Ventriloquizes in the Swamp"—which have meaning only in relation to the singular image that called them forth. For Gustave, at least in childhood, the derealization of language was not so acute. Yet the fact remains that language appears as a verbal gesture, the integral part of a more general gesture that was intended to show hyperbolically what he was feeling.

The process of derealization does not stop there. The little boy, a slow flow of passive syntheses crushed by the weight of strange phrases that designate him, is informed by these phrases that in the eyes of others he has an *other reality*, which *they* take for his *true* reality. For them he is a person with fixed characteristics. He tries—docilely at first, then after the Fall angrily—to be this person, that is, to act it out; he guides himself by accidental successes, by his intuition, by the intentions manifested by others, expressing his desires and his pain in a certain style he thinks is *expected* from him. We should not imagine any duplicity on his part; he is not cynically trying to turn himself into what they want in order to please; rather, in the object he is for others he recognizes, as we have seen, an ontological primacy over the subject he is for himself. Gustave thinks he really is this unknown being his parents have discovered; and to the degree he thinks he has divined its features, he tries to represent it, not only to flatter

10. They don't need much time to judge an audience. Depending on the case, they act in a restrained fashion, give themselves liberties, force certain effects, etc. But for each interpretation of the role to be successful, they must not be in on the secret of what they are doing. The warning of "a tough audience" or "an inexperienced public" or "a cold crowd, look out!" remains inside them as a guiding and almost always nonverbal indication.

them but to open himself to his objective reality so that this reality, evoked by his miming and beseeching gestures, should slip into him and fill him with its density. In sum, he tries to incarnate his *other self*, to lend his living and suffering body to this collection of abstract determinations. But at every ceremony of incarnation he recognizes that he will never be for himself what he is, perhaps, for others. In other words, he wants to seduce his reality—which is in the hands of others—in order *to be* it, in itself and for itself; but as it never coincides with experience, the incarnation is perceived as at once necessary and impossible, and the child feels that he is in some fundamental way unreal. In one respect, indeed, insofar as he is his own actor, he perceives himself as a *character* and not as a *person*; in another, what he experiences *for itself* is disqualified, seems to be a lesser being, inessential, and somehow without reality. For what is felt—ipseity in its pure contingency—is perceived as a raw and insubstantial material that has no other function than to aid the public display of his character in an elaborated form. There is one standard test, however: this character will be the true one if it convinces others. But what does that prove? That Kean is really Hamlet? Or that he has played his role "well"? Yet applause is the sanction he claims. If Gustave displays himself convincingly, he receives no applause; he is treated *as Gustave*, that is, as just the person he does not feel he is. The belief of others is a prize for insincerity; it becomes constitutive in the sense that it prompts his devotion in principle to the representation of his being that gives him the double and contradictory impression of having *played well*, blindly, according to norms fixed in advance but unknown to him, and of having reached outside himself in the dimension of otherness to the objective being he is but that he cannot realize for himself. To be real, for him, is to be believed. Yet this is the thing he is never sure of; the behavior of others is obscure, unpredictable, and ambiguous. At best he will believe that they believe him; what is more, the child is never more alienated, never more unreal than when he says: "Me, I . . ." Me: the union of the innumerable profiles he unconsciously offers to others. I: the subject of praxis and all affirmation.

Gustave's defective rapport with words will end by thrusting him into an adventure that concludes only with his life: the future writer is fixed from early childhood at the oral stage of discourse. This means that he *is alienated from* his own voice, not insofar as it is the vehicle of meanings, but to the extent that it testifies, by its own modulations, to a hyperbolic pathos.

B. THE LOOK

1. *The Mirror and Laughter*

Filial love can be sincere, that is, *felt*. Filial piety, by contrast, is a "show." The child lends himself to it willingly, he says what the parents expect of him, repeats the gestures that please them—he makes a *representation* of himself. In this sense, all bourgeois children are more or less actors. But when the parents respond to this "show" with another "show" and cover the little ham with kisses, the role tends to disappear—everything takes place in the context of the intersubjective truth of familial experience. For the truth of my love is the love the other bears me. Warmly welcomed, the childish mimicry is unconscious; it goes beyond itself toward its goal, which is the response of the loved one: he *must* take the little boy on his knees, in his arms, and institute him as *his parents' beloved son*. In this response the child's playacted transports find their truth, for they were only the means to obtain that paternal smile by which love returns and is confirmed; the imposed role becomes a sacred rite, insincerity tends to disappear. In early childhood Gustave knew the daily ceremony of love; his displays of emotion were solicited so that they could be responded to. The love he then had for his parents was a passion bound to an imperative. This structure is common to most of our affections: being is duty-being, and vice versa.[11] Nothing could be more reassuring; before the Fall, the younger Flaubert son lived in security, feeling what he should feel because he was what he should be. Yet, the little boy unrealizes himself in the manifestations of his passion. Doesn't he love his father? On the contrary, he adores him. He was made in such a way that he has to "lay it on." And we know why.

He mimes *too much* what he feels, but he also mimes what he does not feel. Or at least what he does not yet feel. This is easily understandable, and in this respect Gustave is not so different from other children and even adults. Emotion is not separable from the actions that express it, and in daily relations with the "love object," actions often precede emotion and engender it. A child who is bored suddenly takes it into his head to throw himself into his parents' arms; it is not the overflowing *feeling* of tenderness that pushes him to it, but the future joy he will experience with their kisses. With lovers, too,

---

11. This is precisely what Hegel calls *pathos*. It will be understood that we have used the word *in this sense* in the preceding pages.

amorous transports are provoked more often than we like to admit by dryness and emptiness. Love is there, however—past and to come; the memory of it is a measure and a promise: if the momentarily absent but *manifested* tenderness of one of the lovers answers the real but *provoked* tenderness of the other, an event—fundamentally dual in structure—is *realized*. Of course, even if tenderness is merely produced in one lover by the other, it is reciprocal in each of them; by provoking in his beloved a true surge of emotion that overwhelms him, the lover himself feels his feigned transport transformed into the fullness of love. Gustave runs toward his father: if the father lifts him up high in the air and sets him on his lap, the insincerity is officially eliminated; what the child then happily feels is not at first his own feeling but a feeling that his lord has the goodness to nurture him; plenitude is born here from the passive internalization of paternal kisses, the externalizations of an active love. It seems to him, moreover, that in responding to his transports, his sovereign *recognizes* the truth of the vassal's love and devotion.

As long as the paterfamilias was disposed to accept his younger son's demonstrations—though hyperbolic—he validated them. The little boy believed he was raised from nothingness purposely to witness the glory of his creator, and the daily ceremony of adoration that seemed to him constitutive of his creatural being. He was not altogether mistaken: Dr. Flaubert, patriarchal bourgeois, did not deign to solicit love, but he would have been astonished not to be adored. This golden age, as we know, did not last long; gloomy, nervous, skeptical, Achille-Cléophas put an early end to the whole drama. This was his ruling contradiction: to claim the homage of his vassals on the strength of his mere existence as head of the family, and at the same time to condemn as a scientist all feudal behavior in the name of psychosocial atomism. For Gustave, this was a catastrophe. He derived his truth from the Other, having *none* of his own; when the father withdrew his credit, this second weaning created a breach in the sweet immediate confusion of intersubjective life, and such an abrupt disconnection threw the child back onto the solitude of the inexpressible, even as it made him unbearably visible. The child was still expressly invited to the ceremony of love—if only by his mother, whose statements must have confirmed his feeling for his vocation— but scarcely did he begin than he was exposed by a cold look, a hand that pushed him away, an obvious indifference, or, worse, a nasty crack, a gibe. Ham! Thrust back on himself, that is, on nontruth, Gustave was amazed to discover his unreality; unreality, indeed, which characterized his being, had been developed in order to escape the insipidness of his facticity (as we saw in part one) and to endow himself with a *being-for-adoration,* which could be seen from our new perspective as the dawning of personalization. But it is this very being that paternal rejection throws into question. Is he *devoted?* He would like to believe it with all his heart; his mother tells him so, his father denies the child's vocation without diminishing his demands. Is he doing badly what he is being asked to do well? Or is nothing at all being asked of him? Where is the proof of his mission? It must be *felt* tenderness; every time he dramatizes—which is more and more often—his transports are revealed to him in their nakedness, their insincerity is unmasked. He throws himself on his father to find in his father's arms the *warmth* of which he is deprived; in the absence of a loving response, he discovers that he himself has "acted coldly," that a futile desire to please was made manifest by an ineffectual display. Wouldn't it be the same for any child, formerly loved, whose father one day turned away from him? It all depends on the "mothering"; if the child is a practical agent to even the slightest degree, he will undoubtedly be familiar with the daze and distress, but he will break out of it—for good or ill—by playing the mother against the father, that is, by endeavoring to become his own truth. When challenged, he will affirm that he *loves,* that he has never merely *playacted* love (which will be partly false), and that he has been betrayed. This experiment cannot be performed, of course, without provoking deep wounds, but because the *trauma* is not the same the stress will also be different. Gustave's misfortune is that he hasn't the means *to be his own truth* and thereby to affirm himself against his lord and accuse him of felony. The acts of grace, consequently, remain in his eyes his constituted duty-being, which is separate from being; the little boy feels constrained to act endlessly in a drama in which he no longer believes. The memory of endured disgust, the terror of failure—daily reinforced by new failures—is enough to purge him of any tender emotion; he offers himself frozen to the warmth that is refused, he solicits it with increasingly hyperbolic actions in the name of a love he feels less and less frequently. In brief, it is his reality itself that the father's refusal derealizes; Achille-Cléophas has eyes only for the imaginary (what is *not true, not felt,* but only acted), and suddenly the child feels imaginary himself under the father's gaze. Dr. Flaubert was a highly nervous man and therefore occasionally nasty; when irritated, he managed, with a few sarcastic words, to reduce his son's "lies" to "fragments." For Gustave, called upon to weld himself to the being he must-be, it was as though he had stopped midway and, mobilizing his entire body in order to make it the analogue of a displayed but never felt pathos, he had merely succeeded in transforming himself into an *image* of love. He certainly does not think he is playing the lucidity game, which would perhaps have freed him, but believes he is affected by permanent nonbeing. He has two ways of *existing:* either he sinks into the quagmire of contingency, the wretched slough where nothing is false and nothing is true; or else he unrealizes himself as a distraught lover, and experience vampirized by nonbeing serves only to lend this minimum of being to the nothingness that allows it to appear at all. He loves, nonetheless; but love, being a duality, falls when it is not shared into the domain of *doxa,* which is in the last analysis the realm of imagination. Thus, since his sincerity, such as it is, is rejected, and since he does not recognize his own right to feel anything until adults have given their consent, he is condemned by his father's capricious mistrust never to determine whether he is feeling or just imagining his feelings. The deeper meaning of this personalizing revolution is that the child no longer knows whether he exists or is just pretending to exist. Given this option, Gustave unconsciously chooses anti-Cartesianism and, more obscurely, irrationality. If he manages only to produce images, isn't he an image himself? This might be the key to the paradox. And, if so, what follows from such an assumption is his defense: if all Gustave's feelings are imaginary (that is, true in their essence but experienced as unreal), he will be able to explore and reclaim as his own all the feelings he took pleasure in imagining. This paradoxical level, which he will later be able to use to such good effect, is intimated now without being explicit, but its very presence leads him astray. The truth exists for him, he believes in it; it's merely that it belongs to others; he has lost his truth, assuming he ever had one, but the others have kept theirs. When he compares himself to those solid persons, determined and impenetrable, he feels with terror that he is made of a diaphanous, proteiform substance that can imitate everything because it is never anything. All his life he will be haunted by the anguish that there might be people who love and suffer *absolutely for real.* We must see him at eighteen, mad with jealousy because his friend Hamard (who has just lost a brother) is overcome with grief: that cretin is suffering, and *in reality* I shall never reach that degree of suffering except through imagination! We are familiar with his defensive reaction: beginning in childhood and throughout his life he played the role of the unhappiest man alive. After the defeat of Sedan and the fall of the Second Empire, he would write—a disarmingly naive confession—that there are surely men in France who have more reason than he to suffer, but there is no one who suffers more. The fact is, Gustave suffered an extremely violent identity crisis after his fall from favor, because his being was stolen from him and he was *no longer anyone.*

For others, however, he is quite real; they see him, they know him, they have information about him that he is unaware of and that allows them to judge him. They withhold his truth and hide it from him. Since he cannot convince them to institute him as he would like to be, if he could at least see himself through their eyes and experience as a *subject* the object he is for them, he would lose himself to that being-for-others, fleeting, abstract, that is both held out to him and withheld, designated in him by words he cannot comprehend. He will be what they want, provided that he is something and someone for himself; passivity, failure, and despair lead him to submission. In his impatience to accept himself, he tries to see himself from the outside. This is less an effort to know himself than an irrational and passionate attempt; the unreal child wants to coincide with his reality. For this reason, as he says a hundred times, mirrors fascinate him. If he surprises himself in the mirror, he will be for himself the object he is for everyone else; if in the unity of a similar enterprise, he felt he were a subject outside and an object inside himself, he would recover himself entirely and would act his truth. There in the mirror, he would have the same consistency as others, the same materiality. In fact, Gustave's relation to his reflection is originally only a particular aspect of his relation to his father. At the age of five he runs to his mirror when he cries. Is this so that he can "see what kind of face he's making?" Yes and no. The grimacing itself doesn't interest him. But having shed his tears in the absence of witnesses, he is convinced—wrongly—of his sincerity. Since this is what is at issue, he longs to observe himself in action—*the way his father would if he were present*—the spontaneous manifestations of an undeniable unhappiness. He has so little confidence in himself, this unfortunate child, that he does not ask himself, "How do I look when I cry?" but, "How do I look when I am innocent?"

His misfortune is that he immediately becomes guilty and is aware of it. How do we know? He tells us himself: no sooner is he standing before his image than he starts to make faces at himself, forcing his tears or his laughter, just as the young Charles Baudelaire did at the same period and for similar reasons. Gustave is waiting for proof, and for this very reason he is disappointed: the spontaneous mimicry that ought to bear the marks of sincerity is not convincing. The image in

27

the mirror is only the vague and banal illustration of that suffering which ought to reveal to him his being-in-itself. He expected to surprise himself in *real* pain, an impervious lump outside him which is offered *to others only* as a "particular and affirmative essence," of which his inner affect can only be an internalization. In sum, he has reversed the terms and invested being in appearance—the mirror reestablishes the true order; it is the interior, so difficult, never convincing enough, that commands the visible and communicates its uncertainty to its external manifestations. And then, the child is no longer the same: he watches himself cry the way we listen to ourselves talk; indeed, he cries just to watch himself cry the way we talk to hear ourselves talk. Is he crying again? And, if it can be determined, are these the same sobs that are distorting his features? He views himself through Dr. Flaubert's eyes and observes—incredulous, scornful—the child gesticulating in the mirror in order to persuade him. Moreover, the unreality grows: the object seen is *his image*, it is not him; the reflection serves as analogue to his visible body, which eludes him; and he himself is unrealized without knowing it: a haughty observer of himself, he plays the role of the medical director. As a reaction against his disappointment and also because he is consumed—false witness to a false appearance—by the cold flames of the imaginary, he catches himself breaking through his mimicry in order to invite his own assent, which means his father's. In brief, he reverts to the only tactic he has left: convincing by performance. In this respect he is like an actor standing in front of his mirror in order to study the "impression" he makes. To tell the truth, he thought of it in the first place: when he claimed he wanted only to observe his spontaneous mimicry, he was concealing from himself his intention to learn it in order to reproduce it. How could he *see himself as innocent* without wishing to *show* himself as such to his family? He is like someone on trial working with a tape recorder so that he can let out a "cry of innocence" at just the right moment. When he runs toward his reflection, Gustave does not so much imagine he will see himself as that he will *see himself seen* so as to adjust his image *in the sight of others*. But this is what he is forbidden to do; man's relation to his reflection resembles what the psychologists call the *double sensation*: if my thumb touches my index finger, neither of the fingers is truly an object for the other since each of them is at once seeking and sought, feeling and felt, active and passive; in the same way, I can see myself smile or raise my eyebrows when looking in the mirror and at the same time I am conscious of willing these actions and producing them as a function of the reflection of my face. As a consequence, I never see *a man smiling at me* but only the image that results from the muscular contractions I have intentionally effected. Nevertheless, there is something to be learned from a reflection; we observe in it, in a certain sense, what is related to being-in-the-midst-of-the-world (relations to the environment), but never being-in-the-world.[12] The character we *see* who docilely complies with our decisions and reproduces our movements as we make them is taken in its unity as a whole, a *quasi object*, predictable and not totalizable at least insofar as it appears as an agent. Therefore the failure is total, and suddenly the little boy explicitly grasps his intentions: hamming! What shall he do? Cry with shame? Lose his temper? Not at all—he bursts out laughing. This is the second phase of the operation: unable to force others to institute him in his being as he would like, the child tries to identify with the being they would like to give him. In Flaubert's correspondence, from the first letters to the last, the mirror is linked to two different themes: laughter and femininity. Both express his submission.[13]

Gustave claims that he cannot shave in front of his mirror without bursting out laughing. To Ernest, who has become a deputy prosecutor and whom he suspects of taking himself seriously, he writes, "Look at yourself in the mirror right now and tell me if you aren't greatly tempted to laugh. So much the worse for you if you aren't,"[14] and so forth. But laughter is a collective reaction, a point we shall return to later, by which a group threatened with some danger withdraws solidarity from the man in whom the danger is incarnate. This

12. For this reason, photographs of ourselves or a film in which we appear are more revealing than a mirror. The attitude I took in front of the camera, the gestures I made, are mine, I recognize them, but I can observe them to the extent that at the moment I am *looking* I am no longer doing these very things. My image, liberated from myself, tends to become *the image of another,* and I tend to judge it through the eyes of others.

13. As we might expect, a third theme appears *in reaction:* the mirror *frees us from others,* it is our relation to our self. Our only victories, he says to Louise to console her for a failure, are those we have in front of our mirror. And to Louis Bouilhet, who was "in a depression," he wrote: "Come now, little man! Chin up! Bawl all alone in your room. Give yourself a good talking-to in the mirror" (4 September 1850, *Correspondance* 2:237). But the situations in relation to which this theme is evoked (defeats throughout the century) sufficiently demonstrate that it is prompted by wounded pride and is therefore subsequent to the other two. Of course the mirror, here, has only a metaphorical role; Flaubert says to the Muse and to Bouilhet: it is enough that we are content with ourselves; we are our own judges. But the choice of the metaphor speaks volumes: for the image of the *for-itself,* Gustave chose the object that manifests his *being-for-others.* This is not tearing himself away from the hands of others but putting himself in the hands of the imaginary "happy few" who will recognize his merit.

14. June 1845, *Correspondance* 1:182.

does not mean that one cannot truly laugh alone in one's room; it simply means that the person laughing, even in isolation, actualizes through his hilarity his membership in some community ("I'll tell them about this and they'll have a good laugh," or, "How Pierre and Marc would laugh if they were here," etc.). This behavior is not necessarily unrealizing, or we would have to believe that a priest, an officer, or a communist stop being priest, officer, or communist when they are alone. The act of withdrawing solidarity, however, is intended to break the nondifferentiation of intersubjectivity in order to constitute the compromising *other* as an object and the event as spectacle. If this is so, can one laugh at oneself? For someone *truly* capable of it, laughing at oneself would be a way of affirming oneself as an integrated member of a *current* group and of withdrawing solidarity from one's singularity insofar as singularity is perceived as a vestige of revolt against integration. At the very least it involves combating in oneself a certain integration with another—this is what Gustave expects of Ernest. He invites him to draw upon his membership in the "free-masonry" of ex-schoolboy creators of the "Garçon" in order to reject the spirit of seriousness, that is, membership in the magistrature. In front of his own reflection, let him recover the collective eye of his adolescence, and behind the magistrate he will discover the naked ape. If he is still conscious of the absurdity of this hairless beast who busies himself with judging other beasts of the same species, it will be proof that he preserves a real bond with his scattered comrades, in spite of the distance between them; if not, it is proof that he belongs fully to the constituted body of which he is a member. According to Flaubert, then, one can laugh at one's image—as a protest, a sign of youthful spirits, of moral health. The trouble is, he has long felt that Ernest is lost. He *pretends* to believe that his friend is still capable of following his advice in order to present him with an alternative (either you make fun of yourself, you great triviality, or you are a filthy bourgeois), of which the first term is annulled in advance and the second is a judgment without appeal.

And Gustave? Does he really laugh when he shaves? I do not doubt that he sometimes erupts in peals of laughter; this monster who posts himself in front of his reflection is capable of imitating Father Couillères or reproducing the laughter of the "Garçon." Does this mean that he is the victim of his hilarity, that he cannot hold it in? Certainly not; for the simple reason that it is not sincere. In fact, when he presents the "Garçon" to the Goncourt brothers, he specifies that "his laughter was not laughter" and consequently resumes his exercises in front of his full-length mirror, at the same time denouncing their vanity. Certainly the persistence of the man shaving himself can appear comic—such an explosive mixture of nature and culture—especially if we take Flaubert's point of view and judge it absurd that an ambulatory corpse should concern himself daily with mowing the grass growing on his bones. But this is comic in the realm of *ideas;* it does not incite laughter and is aimed at the species in general, not at Gustave in particular. Besides, laughter results from surprise, and our reflection does not surprise us when it illustrates the daily and deliberate actions of which it is the indispensable instrument; let us say that the young man tries to find himself laughable by making use of the other's look in order to withdraw solidarity from his own image. But all this is imaginary—the recourse to the other and the withdrawal of solidarity; indeed, Gustave reverses the terms: for him, denunciation of the self is only a means of identifying with those who denounce him. And this is his goal, pursued from childhood and later rationalized: he looks at his tears and then, disappointed, turns them into sobs in order *to be Pain;* he forgets his lines in front of himself, becomes conscious of his imposture, and quickly exaggerates his mimicry *in order to make himself laugh;* that is, he now accepts being the imposter he seems. He is judged as such, he recognizes himself as such—anything but this dreamlike lack of substance; what is unbearable to him is to remain on the border between unreality and the real. In order to become his own object, he must begin by withdrawing solidarity from himself; he will borrow *from others* the hilarious mistrust provoked by his insincere efforts to recover sincerity. He will transform the discomfort he feels before the rather unconvincing reflection of his tears into *their* derision. Now he plays the clown so that *their* laughter should come to his aid and reveal his *visible-being;* but the laughter does not come, the faces he makes do not amuse him any more than his sobs made him sad; so he laughs *to make himself laugh*—just the way he cried to make himself cry. Standing in front of his full-length mirror, then, he *plays the role of someone laughing,* hoping that the imitation will be so perfect that it will be indistinguishable from its model, just as when we want to yawn, a few pretended yawns invariably provoke a true one. What does he want? To laugh, or to become the other who is laughing at him? Both: to see himself as he is seen (therefore, according to him, as he is) and to disarm the laughter by appropriating it. For it exists elsewhere, that cosmic and sacred hilarity, that negation which *institutes him as laughable.* It is of course his father's laughter, the laughter of that sarcastic demon whose irony, by derealizing the child's behavior, made him forever an imposter, that is, other than what he claimed to be, without revealing to him what he was. If Gustave agrees to surprise his ludicrous side in the mirror, he may discover the secret of his singular essence.

What is more, to put himself on the side of the scoffers is to put them on his side. By mocking his sorrow, his agonies of lost love, his fruitless, grotesque efforts to communicate, he is identifying with the aggressor, with the paterfamilias, claiming as his own the terrible *surgical look* that never swerves away from him since the other is already inside him, observing him; in a sense he is perching above himself and *mocking* his object, the poor contemptible thing that is nevertheless necessary to his *becoming-mocker*. Briefly, despair pushes him to this harrowing and contradictory attempt: to be his being in total submission and to escape from it by becoming his executioners' accomplice; he knows the tune and sees life as a conjuror's bag of tricks. Gustave is going to become the man-who-laughs, like Gwynplaine— in other words, a man who never laughs. Obviously this new effort merely enlarges the area of unreality within him by making it part of the reflection itself. The laughter inside him is *induced:* it comes from the outside and, even internalized, preserves its transcendence; he does everything possible to give it the concrete immanence of experience, but lacking the power of suffering, he only succeeds in playacting. All his life, Flaubert's laughter *was a role he played.*[15]

2. The Mirror and the Fetish

"I would like to be a woman so that I could admire myself, stand naked . . . and look at myself mirrored in the streams." These words, written in *Novembre,* quite aptly sum up the connection between the mirror and femininity. Gustave would like to *stand naked* in front of his mirror. I have no doubt that he did so—from early childhood he would face his reflection and play the role of a woman undressing herself. Laughter gave way to admiration. However, this new enterprise has the same purpose and the same structures as the one before: since his being is in the hands of others, he tries to recuperate it by turning himself, through complaisant submission, into a fascinating object for his executioners and simultaneously for himself. The intention, however, is more complex in this case and, strictly speaking, *perverse;* its source is more distant and more profound. It is not his pathos, his

15. He said it in many different ways, and never so clearly as in a letter to Louise in 1852: "Nothing is serious in this base world except laughter." *Correspondance,* vol. 4.

passive activity that he seeks to recover; it is his passivity itself—this is what he claims to identify with if he manages to have it instituted by others. We understand, of course, that he is trying to rejoin his *being of flesh* and to be dissolved in it to the extent that his palpitating inertia itself sums up and manifests his *presence-in-the-world*, his pathic, painful, and fragile nakedness, beaten, explored, violated by overly expert hands, by an excessively penetrating look, which is none other than his constitution, an opaque core that is endlessly surpassed but always preserved by his projects. Yet this merging with the *carnal body* cannot be realized, he is convinced, except in woman. A note in his *Souvenirs*—nearly contemporaneous with *Novembre*—gives us his thought more precisely: "There are days when one would like to be an athlete and others when one would like to be a woman. In the first case it is the muscles that quiver, in the second it is the flesh that is inflamed." There is a disjunction here: either—or. Thus the two desires seem to him mutually exclusive. And surely one cannot be both a woman and a weight-lifting champion, every sex and every category. Inversely, however, in Gustave's eyes one cannot be Hercules and have pleasure. The body is the immediate means of the agent, or rather it is the agent itself; flesh, on the other hand, is pure submission—you cannot be both. The agent desires and takes—this is the male; but according to Gustave pleasure is born of rapturous abandon, of consenting and happy passivity; the woman has pleasure because she is taken. She desires too, of course, but in her own way: her flesh is inflamed *under* the other's manipulations, feminine desire is passive expectation.

The text speaks for itself: if Gustave wants to be a woman, it is because his partly feminine sexuality requires a change of sex that would permit him the full development of his resources. Listen to what the young hero of *Novembre* confides to us: "I wanted to languish to the utmost, I would have liked to be smothered with roses, I would have liked to be bruised by kisses, to be the flower tossed by the wind, the bank dampened by the river, the earth made fecund by the sun." The young man speaks in his own name as a man—it is his masculine body that dreams of these languors. And yet what is he wishing for if not to be the object of aggression, to become prey, to swoon under brutal caresses (he would be *tossed* about like a plum tree), to be dampened,[16] made fecund, therefore penetrated? And in the couples

16. A transparent allusion—which may not be explicit *for him*—to fellatio, which he was fond of, as we shall see.

he forms successively with wind, river, and sun, all the substantives that designate him are feminine, all those that designate his partners masculine. True, these are cosmic elements (water, air, fire). He himself is the earth (whether as field, bank, fecundated soil), the fourth element; and readers have cited this passage with good reason as an expression of Flaubertian pantheism. We should stress, however, that this is the *sexual* version of pantheistic ecstasy; Flaubert knows very well that the earth is woman and woman is earth in the rustic religions. The three tests are completed: constituted passivity becomes conscious of itself in erotic turmoil; it *passively* desires to become flesh under the manipulations of others, and this is a matter of a personalizing revolution—the child *sexualizes* passivity by demanding to submit to it as a *permanent passivization* in lovemaking; it will become *inflamed* if the chosen lovers transform it into burning flesh by their caresses, which are addressed to the entire body, *reducing it to helplessness*, and thus produce a retotalization of the masculine body as feminine flesh. In other words, their caresses reproduce, first through their desire, then through their energy, the primary totalization and deliver it from all frustration by pushing it to the end—to the point of possession. For this dreaming passivity, the moment of pleasure represents the perfect moment of convergence with the self. To have pleasure, for the child, is to have pleasure from the self insofar as it is overcome by the other. At once he makes his chosen master the mediation between his passivity experienced as a paralyzing lack of being, and that passivity recuperated as the joyful blossoming of the flesh in utter abandon. Certainly the role of the other is crucial since he submits the child to his desire and makes him the inert *object* of possession. But this is precisely what his paralyzed body claims. Gustave demands to identify with the *desirable object* he is for the other; his "languor" will be the internalization of his being-for-others, that is, of what he takes for his being-in-itself. In other words, *alienated on principle*, he seeks to live that alienation in sexual form in order to infuse those cold, penetrating looks with lust, to give a secret ardor to the hands that reconstitute him—then at least he would have worth as an *object of lust*. This is the desire to achieve sexual *worth* through the other's desire.

Shall we now raise the issue of homosexuality? Perhaps. But not without caution. First of all, because our preference for nominalism forbids classifications; we must understand sexual impulse—like all projects—as springing from a complex situation which is more than the sum of its elements and qualifies those impulses by its complexity the very moment they go beyond it toward their goal.[17]

Gustave needs to be caressed more than to caress; he wants to be the hare rather than the hunter. We know why. But this postulation of his passivity involves no decision on the sex of the aggressor. Rather we must recognize that it is the aggression that counts, and that circumstances alone will dictate the partner.[18] There is no doubt that

17. Sexuality, indeed, is neither cause nor effect; it is the totalization of experience through sex, which means that it summarizes in itself and sexualizes all the structures that characterize a person. Inversely, every totalization of experience, whatever its meaning, summarizes and totalizes sexual structures by surpassing them toward another end. The situation alone defines the totalizing point of view; each point of view is relative to every other within a reciprocity of perspective, and none is privileged. For example, there is no economic or practical alienation that cannot be and will not be experienced at certain moments as sexual alienation. The order of mediations, of course, is always the same; in other words, there is an objective hierarchy of structures, but this dialectic order does not by itself determine the way it is experienced. This is what Marx helps us to understand when he speaks of the reaction of superstructures on the infrastructures from which they come. Thus he can account for two aspects of the dialectic: *hierarchy* (the irreducibility of every level of being to the lower level that produced it) and *circularity*.

18. He himself wrote, during the last year of his life, to Madame Brainne: "I am not 'effeminate' as you say! Lesbos is my country. I share its refinements and its languors." It is striking that he describes himself *as a lesbian* to a woman he likes very much. And as the letter is rather gallant, this is a way of showing her that he desires her *as a lesbian*. As for knowing which of the two would have been the more active, a remark by Edmond de Goncourt in 1881 sheds some light on the subject: on 9 April he dined at the home of Madame Brainne, "whose ample beauty somewhat intimidated me, like the female giants you see at a freak show."

His best friends were certainly the objects of attachments that were homosexual in character but otherwise platonic—Alfred, Maxime, Louis. I am thinking particularly of Maxime, who admired Gustave and dedicated his first book, *Solus ad Solum*, to him. They exchanged signet rings. Du Camp writes: "We exchanged rings. We are now, in a way, engaged" (*Souvenirs littéraires*). When he made his first trip abroad, he sent Flaubert voluminous and passionate letters: "I love you, I love you; I smother you with kisses." Gustave expresses the same sentiments: "How young you were then! How charming you were! And how we loved each other!" Gustave, according to a remark of Gautier's reported by Du Camp, was insolently handsome at this time. Du Camp wasn't bad-looking either, tall like Gustave with curly hair, bright eyes, and regular features. And in their couple, he was the one to play the male role.

Enid Starkie quite unjustly accuses poor Louis Bouilhet of having had pederastic dealings with Flaubert. She relies on some unpublished passages in letters from Gustave to Bouilhet which do not seem to me entirely convincing. This, for example: "At this moment I have a vision of you in your nightshirt in front of the fire, too hot and contemplating your prick." We shall soon have occasion to speak about the general *tone* of the letters that all these young men sent to each other; we shall see that this one resembles all the others. With Laporte, in the last years of his life, Gustave behaved like an imperious and spoiled mistress. We shall return at length to these complex passions; for the moment we are studying the sexual drive in its immediate and preemptory brutality.

when chance delivers him as a passive object into the hands of males, Gustave feels deeply aroused. Yet the occasion must present itself to him—he will not look for it on his own. We have valuable information on this subject, dating from his visit to Egypt and pursued through his letters to Bouilhet in passages that the prudent Conard believed it his duty to censor but that Jean Bruneau has reinstated in the edition he prepared for Pléiade. We find the following, for example:

> One admits one's sodomy, and it is spoken of at table. Sometimes you deny it for a little, then everyone screams at you and you end up confessing. Traveling as we are for educational purposes and charged with a mission by the government, we have considered it our duty to indulge in this form of ejaculation. The occasion has not presented itself so far. We are on the lookout for it, however. The baths are where such things take place. You reserve a bath for yourself, including masseurs, pipe, coffee, linen, and you skewer your lad in one of the rooms. You ought to know that all the bath boys are bardashes. The last masseurs . . . are usually rather pretty young boys. We had one in mind from an establishment very near our hotel. I went there, and the rascal was out that day.

In the following letter he says:

> That day (the day before yesterday, Monday) my kellak was rubbing me gently, and when he came to the noble parts he lifted up my *boules d'amour* to clean them, then, continuing to rub my chest with his left hand, he began to pull my prick with his right, and bringing me he leaned over my shoulder and kept saying to me: "baksheesh, baksheesh" (which means, "tip, tip"). This was a man in his fifties, ignoble, disgusting. Imagine the effect—and the word "baksheesh, baksheesh." I pushed him . . . away. . . . He smiled a smile that meant, "Come on, you're a pig like the rest of us, but today you've decided you don't want it." As for me, I laughed out loud like a dirty old man, and the shadowy vault of the bath echoed with the sound. But the best of it is what happened in my cubicle as I was draped in fresh linen and smoking the narguila while being dried. I kept calling out to my dragoman sitting in the outer room: "Hasn't the lad Joseph, the one we've seen before, come back yet?" "No monsieur"—"Oh, God in heaven!" and that's the monologue of a frustrated man.

Louis Bouilhet's curiousity is aroused; he interrogates Flaubert: What happened on the following days? Gustave, usually so communicative, answers him briefly: "You ask me if I consummated the business of the baths. Yes, and with a merry young fellow pitted with pockmarks and wearing an enormous white turban. It made me laugh, that's all. But I would do it again. For an experiment to be done right, it must be repeated." After which he doesn't breathe another word on the subject, and his Alter Ego will remain unenlightened, at least until the end of the journey, as to whether or not Gustave repeated the experiment.

The story is simple and significant. Gustave begins by boasting of his vices; in his first letter he expresses his intention of taking advantage of the lax state of Egyptian mores in order to make love to young boys. He even has one in hand. He goes to the baths to find him—no go, the child has gone out. A few days later he returns, this time with no ulterior motive; but this time his masseur, a "repulsive man," undertakes, for professional reasons and to make some extra money, to masturbate him. Flaubert dwells complacently on this adventure and declares that at the time he pushed the indiscreet hand away—something we can easily believe if we recall his abhorrence of ugliness. Here he bursts out laughing. False laughter, to be sure, designed to show that Gustave *as an aesthete* appreciates the comedy of the situation. But he confides to Bouilhet that the best of it was that he was aroused; the hired caress of a repulsive male excited him enough for him to crave his young favorite as soon as possible. Had the boy been found, it would have happened instantly. Fortunately the charmer is out once more—Gustave's virtue is saved in the nick of time. It is clear that this phantom catamite hardly interests him. Why is he never there? But didn't Flaubert say in his first letters that the "last masseurs" were usually "rather pretty young boys"—so he has a choice. I allow that he might have his preferences, but since this is an "experiment" and must be repeated, why doesn't he select the most pleasing among them? Because he would have to *take* him. And Gustave, if he has the curiosity to do it, scarcely has the desire except in imagination. If he plays hide-and-seek with that absent rascal, it is to preserve in Bouilhet's eyes, and perhaps his own, his boasted glamor as the depraved devotee of all the vices. In sum, in this story of "bardashes" the weak element is his relation to the catamite; the strong element is his relation to the kellak masturbator. What he is looking for at the baths is not the adolescent's docility but his own submission, as an uncensored passage from the *Correspondence* testifies: "The other day I took a bath. I was alone at the back of the sweating room . . . . Hot water was running everywhere; sprawled out like a calf, I was thinking about a number of things; all my pores were dilating tranquilly. It is extremely pleasurable, sensuality with a touch of sweet melancholy, to be lost in these shadowy rooms . . . while the naked kellaks call to each other and handle you and turn you over like embalmers preparing you for the grave." [19] We note that the attendants and the clients are equally naked, but the first display a nakedness of the body, the second a nakedness of the flesh. In the hands of the kellak, Gustave feels as helpless as a corpse—his passivity is remodeled, and he internalizes it as *sensual pleasure*. A troubled pleasure, for he is not unaware that he is in the power of "bardashes." If he is to believe them, the whole staff practices homosexuality—who says the attendants don't enjoy kneading him this way? He is still young and handsome; perhaps these men desire him? If they took the least pleasure in their work, nothing would distinguish their hired gestures from amorous aggression. Raped! He reports elsewhere that he was stretched out on the floor of the baths one day when several vigorous young fellows scooped him up, as was the custom, bore him gently to the water, and energetically immersed him; this, he says, was unforgettable bliss. In this connection, Richard rightly emphasizes the theme of water in Flaubert. We might say that his pleasure here is in being *liquified*. This is true; but one of the meanings of water, for him as for Ponge, is the falling back, the sinking, and finally the teeming calm of the horizontal. When he bathed in the sea, he says, he "sprawled there," or "he rolled in the waves as on a thousand liquid breasts pervading his entire body." [20] To be changed into water is to be reduced to the boundless inertia of this element. We may further emphasize the mystic structure of his bliss; they are leaning over him, they raise him up, this is a gift, an Assumption—at least the first part; a noble power consecrates itself to the helpless impotence of a child. And of course all these impressions are experienced sexually. Indeed, there is a curious text that Gustave began and abandoned in 1840, which he prudently named *Pastiche* so that the eventual reader would believe it was a parody of *Juliette* or the *Cent Journées de Sodome* but which certainly expresses the fantasies of its author. [21] We read in it, among other things: "What would he do [Assur, the oriental prince] now that he had awakened still surfeited from the night's orgy. Would he give himself to his minions or have himself showered with praise by the seers? . . . A secret door revealed the naked minions—Assur laughed with

19. To Louis Bouilhet, end of December 1849 to beginning of January 1850, *Correspondance* 2:140.

20. *Correspondance* 2:209. Water, then, is a woman.

21. For Gustave subsequently claimed some of them as his own, in *Novembre* for example.

his eyes, embraced them, made them carry him in their arms." For Flaubert at the age of eighteen, the minion is someone who carries, who carries away, and who takes. This text does not neglect the *sexual* aspect of the ineffable pleasure he felt ten years later at the baths: in the arms of the attendants, he vaguely felt that providence was *realizing* an erotic fantasy of his childhood. Furthermore, when the kellak kneaded his proffered body the way a mother does her infants, we might almost say that Gustave's flesh was waiting for the final offer. In fact, the masturbation begins directly after the "personal cleansing," and before "pulling his prick" the masseur rubbed him down and washed his testicles. Previously withheld, now miraculously offered, after years of abeyance, the caress seems to be a natural conclusion to these meticulous bodily attentions and techniques. This dominating caress—interrupted by the client's disgust with the masseur and *not with his sex*—only makes explicit the massage ceremony's erotic meaning, which was already there beneath the surface.

It is thus permissible to ask what our little braggart would have done if the young boy had been available. Would he have taken him? It hardly seems likely; the manipulation stirred him *in his flesh* and consequently could not have aroused in him the desire to possess a young male; quite to the contrary, it awakened the desire to become completely female. If he had been able to call the young man in, it would have been to finish the job—the boy was handsome enough to be granted the right, refused to the masseur, to transform his client into an object. Disarmed, consenting, Gustave would have felt the onrush of pleasure in raising his eyes to the imperious, untouchable idol bending over his nakedness—who would have given him agonies and delights.

After that, someone will suggest, if we are to believe Gustave's own testimony, he "consummated the business of the baths." [22] *If we are to believe him*, yes. But the point is, I do not believe him at all, for the following reasons. First of all, the brevity of the account; in Egypt Gustave made love with women many times and he writes copiously of his exploits. [23] Why, then, should he remain so laconic when it comes to an experience so new and so long anticipated? And then, what does he tell us about it? That "it made me laugh, that's all." I have shown that laughter is a role for Gustave: as soon as it appears, every-

22. *Souvenirs*, pp. 74–76.
23. In other passages in letters to Bouilhet which were also the victims of Conard's scissors.

thing becomes insincere and forced. This laughter gives its tone to the entire paragraph. He laughed, *that's all*. Really? If he really had "skewered his lad in one of the rooms," he would have had to have an erection, and so he would have been moved. Did he desire the young fellow? Or was he caressed by him first? And if he had *desired a man*, wouldn't he have been quite happy to share that wish with Bouilhet and obligingly describe what he felt? Besides, his tender prey is not terribly appetizing—he emphasizes the pockmarks that "pitted" his face. If Gustave definitively renounced the handsome young man with whom he claimed to be infatuated, why—since all the attendants were bardashes—did he choose one of the most unappealing? And if he felt impelled to do it, how could this pathetic face have moved him? Perhaps in spite of the pockmarks the boy still had some physical charm? Then why emphasize his defects? Furthermore, I find equally suspect the only two details Flaubert offers: one (the disfiguring malady) is there for "characterization," and the other (the large white turban) for an "artistic touch"; the latter is much less striking since turbaned men were to be found in great numbers in Egypt. I understand that Gustave is trying to fill in the scene for Louis: the young fellow bending down, bare-bottomed, his turban on his head. But just because of this motif, the "picturesque" and "typical" evocation seems to be imaginary. As for his promise to repeat the experiment, it is hardly convincing; indeed, it seems here to be a forced effort to bring the narrative to a close. It is as if Gustave, irritated by Bouilhet's question but unable to answer with another defeat, had given him a "yes, I have consummated it" that was as close as possible to a "*no*." Yes, I have consummated the business; but I did not feel hot or cold, I laughed, that's all, and I came away with nothing but an *aesthetic* memory of a white turban on a scarred face; in short, I have not truly lived this adventure, it has not become part of my life; *nothing happened*. On reflection, however, fearing that the poorly concealed negation would be obvious to his Alter Ego Bouilhet, he resumes his boasting. Nothing happened, but I had no luck, the fellow was too ugly; with others, perhaps, I shall taste an unknown pleasure—next time I am going to do it right. If we reread the passage in this light, Flaubert's true response emerges: "No, not yet. But don't worry, I am always thinking about it and I will jump at the first opportunity." In my opinion, we have the choice of two conjectures and only two: either he invented everything, or else, to clear his conscience and without the least desire to succeed, he made an attempt that ended in a fiasco. At this point we may wonder if he did not make a show of his desire to experience "this mode of ejaculation" in order to conceal what really attracted him to the turkish baths: the wish *to be unrealized* in the bardashes' hands as a passive homosexual.

But for this very reason it seems clear, on rereading the episode of the baths in its entirety, that Gustave's homosexuality is sporadic: it is not a man he is looking for, it is domination by the other—who might just as well be a dominating woman. After all, specialized houses of pleasure exist where there are women who play the role of the kellak; half-naked, they massage or soap the client in his bath; active and compliant, they do everything, but no one has the right to touch them—this is forbidden by the management. Since what is involved is *passivization*, those young female technicians would do just as well in Gustave's case. We shall discuss his feminine relations later. But to return now to our point of departure, the important thing is that he does not at first designate the recreative valorization of his passivity as a real man but, on the contrary, as the imaginary woman he wants to be. Which means that from the start he makes his constituted passivity the analogue of a secret femininity. What is he looking for (since the autobiographical account of the first narrator reports facts that refer to childhood)? I would say that his first intention is to see himself in his mirror as a woman. Is that possible? Yes and no; certainly without faking it he cannot *perceive* the reflection of a little girl instead of that of a boy. But—the words "in order to admire myself" give us a clue—it is possible for him, at the price of a double unrealization, to imagine that he is another who is caressing a real woman, himself, on the other side of the glass. His hands are another's, they move slowly down the chest to the flanks, to the round thighs, while his eyes follow the reflection of their movement on the reflection of his body. There are two analogues here: his hands, his image. Of the image he apprehends only the flesh that is petted, neglecting meaningless details such as his genitals or his young man's chest. We shall say this is not possible. Yet, in every analogue what is inconvenient is dropped; when an old actress brilliantly plays the role of a young girl, we let ourselves be carried away, we disregard her wrinkles, we "see" the young beauty she represents; of course her age is not entirely suppressed, it remains like a lingering sadness, like a "ce n'est que cela!"— a secret disillusionment momentarily provoked not by the actress in this role but by beauty in general. Thus little Gustave's masculinity colors the desired object, through his reflection, with a certain hermaphroditism. Similarly, to give himself the hands of another he must put himself in a state of distraction in relation to the "double sensations" and to the kinesthetic data informing him that he is caressing *himself*. All this, however, remains in the imaginary child as the surpassed impossibility of being another and, at the same time, as the perfect interpenetration of the other and himself.[24] But these two resistances—the reflection, his experienced body—aid him by mutually accusing each other of making the attempt miscarry. If he were completely another, he would be a woman seen in the mirror; therefore, *she is there*, and to see her he need only unrealize himself a little more. If the reflection would let him become completely feminized, Gustave would be other than the virile hands that stroke him; he would become, *there*, the absolute object that his caresses *here* retrieve by internalizing it as *excited flesh*. A constant and swift passage from one inadequacy to the other will allow him to conceive of the fullness of illusion as accessible and even to imagine, in brief moments of tension, that it is achieved.

If I have lingered over these complicated games—which surely ended in masturbation—it was to indicate that there is no need to resort to homosexuality to characterize Gustave's sexual conduct; I prefer to call it *perverse*, a word by which I mean to designate any erotic attitude that implies an unrealization geometrically multiplied. Certainly onanism is always bound to the imaginary—scenes are invented or reinvented according to the onanist's fantasies, that is, according to the guiding lines of his imagination, which excite a child and bring him to the point of ejaculation. But if a young homosexual imagines that a friend is embracing him—and if, moreover, he is not perverse[25]—the unrealization is taken to the first power: this friend is

24. Gustave is a pretty child—they tell him so. This reputation incites him to push his beauty to an extreme in an unreal way. He turns himself into a woman, he who would have a horror of being effeminate, because woman is the object of perfect art, the desirable absolute, and the link with carnal excitement, with sensual pleasure. In fact, his young body does not lack qualities that could aid the process of unrealization; for example, his skin is still soft, his phantom hands slipping over it will lightly touch a satin skin that could belong only to the "opposite sex." Given this, what does it matter if other attributes are defective—they are *eminently* there; the child will not make the mistake of going to look for them where their absence is too obvious. He suggests them to himself, starting with the tender contact of his skin, as the implicit presence of the whole feminine organism at his fingertips. In stroking his sides, his lovely woman's breasts are abandoned in the undifferentiated carnal presence, provided they are not kept too much in mind, not formed as an explicit image which would immediately be revealed for what it is, namely for a *mental* image and not for an imaginary but concrete attribute of the handled body; in brief, for an absence and an abstraction.

25. We can say too, of course, that it is the excitement itself that produces these images—the phenomenon is circular. What matters is that the fantasies as guiding elements mediate between the affective life and the imagination.

unaware of the desires of which he is the object, and there is nothing to indicate that he would agree to satisfy them; in any case, he is absent and merely aspired to by the imagining consciousness. But in this case the gratification of desire does not require the unrealization of the subject; the little onanist masturbates while dreaming that he is submitting *as himself* to another's embrace—it is *he himself* who is mastered, caressed. It is true that the imaginary is not given its share: since his body is unreally caressed, his flesh becomes altogether unreal. Be that as it may; first of all, he need neither give himself the hands of another nor *play both roles*—a "mental" image will suffice. Furthermore, even unrealized, he passes as such in the world of images: with his build, his skin, his genitals, his desires—for he really desires his friend—and above all with *his identity*. For Gustave it is quite otherwise: the unrealization slips into the act itself; he masturbates less than he plays at *being masturbated*. For him, desire is first male, the desire to take; in the woman it comes afterward, as induced passivity, as desire inflamed. But Gustave is constrained to playact primary and inductive lust because he does not feel it; if he did, he would have to be a sexual agent, an aggressor; he would have to have the desire to take, to tranform *the other* into an object. And that would be perfectly contrary to his constituted passivity. Young males do get aroused in front of their naked reflection; provisional perversion: they want to take, and they try to see their body as if it were the body of *another* young man or, better, a young *woman;* it is only the reflection they unrealize in order to give substance to their desires. But Gustave merely wants to submit, to be reduced to slavery, in order to coincide in orgasm with his objective being. He must therefore make himself unreal to the second power—he makes the *gestures* that correspond to a desire that he doesn't feel in order to excite the beautiful body that he is *not;* acting out both swooning abandon (to whom would he abandon himself in the solitude of his room?) and virile aggression, he manages a shadow of excitation only while interpreting the role of *a couple.* Indeed, he would not even manage that if the excitation were not given in advance: the child is *really* the victim of the Other, and through his sensual awakening he is led to sexualize the primacy of the exterior over the interior. But he is so constituted that this excitation itself must be unrealized; real and experienced, it serves as analogue to the passive desire which, according to him, belongs only to woman. At the end of the drama, *his* hands finish the job and he reaches a real orgasm. But are these hands completely his? After all, Gustave is not narcissistic; it is not the beauty of his own body that

43

excites him but the excitation of his body that needs to be induced by male desire. Until the final spasm—followed by a nauseating return to the contingency of his true sex—his hands preserve a structure of otherness, which they communicate to the pleasure itself. It all happens as if the child, deprived of caresses, were wretchedly attempting to incarnate the one authorized to give them.

The *man* or the *woman?* His mother is the one who, by exploring his body, revealed it to him as a body explored; those maternal attentions, efficient and severe, constituted him as handled flesh. In the virile grip of Mme Flaubert, he knew excitation; submitting, he wished that the work of her large hands would finish with a caress. In vain; the hands awakened in him the erogenous zones of passivity, they turned him and turned him again, as the kellak's hands would do later, forcing him into sensual postures; but no sooner was he fed, washed, wiped, than they vanished, leaving him in a discomfort which he had no way to understand or explain. There was nothing masculine about the timid wife of Achille-Cléophas, however; if the child endowed her with a hidden masculinity, it was because of her imperious and cold efficiency. Everything took place in shadow—Caroline became the *agent* for him to the extent that she transformed him into a *sufferer;* this is why he had the revelation of the couple as *indissoluble unity* and as frustration: his passivity could only be *lived* as the product of permanent activity; yet, this austere activity was endlessly and inexplicably concealed, making the child into a kind of half-androgyne amputated by its other half. He was thus committed forever to an *imaginary sexual life;* he sought in onanism and later in amorous embraces to reconstitute the disjunct totality, that is, to recover the primitive androgyne. And this search only resulted in making him, each time— now male, now female—half an imaginary androgyne. When he took the role of a woman in front of his mirror and called for a masculine partner, he did not understand that what he truly wanted was to be possessed by his mother, who would be provided for the occasion with an imaginary phallus.

He knows it even less as, from the time he could orient himself in the bosom of his family, observing the relations between each member, he discovered that Mme Flaubert, honorary male, was the most submissive vassal of all: the father commanded, she bowed down and adoringly accepted the role of transmitter. A dizzying fall for the mother-goddess: she is pathos, like her younger son, and there is but one agent, the paterfamilias. We know neither when nor how nor by

whom the little boy was enlightened about procreation, but I am inclined to believe that the initiation came early. As a positivist and a
physician, Achille-Cléophas would hardly have wanted to conceal
from future physicians the processes that seemed to him *natural* or, in
the final analysis, biochemical; and then there were all those naked
corpses on marble tables that Gustave spied on, giving him a silent
and highly eloquent "lesson in the facts of life" concerning the differences between the sexes. The fact is, he was overwhelmed at the
thought that his virile half, in the course of nocturnal copulations,
was revealed to him as woman and prey in his father's arms. We shall
see later how he flew into a rage at Trouville when he imagined Elisa
and Schlésinger embracing—jealousy alone does not sufficiently explain such violent emotions. In rereading the *Mémoires*, we shall see
that he began to love the young woman when he surprised her nurs-
ing her child—that is, in the exercise of her maternal functions; I do
not think he could have thought then of possessing this gentle, strong
mother, her upper lip stitched with fine black down, who ranked in
his fourteen-year-old eyes as a grown-up. He looked at her bosom,
certainly—he says in *Novembre* that he thought he would faint the first
time he saw a woman's naked breasts—but especially at her *hands*. In
Elisa the female half of the androgyne rediscovered its male half, and
it was with the helpless infant that he was somehow inclined to identify. When he came to think later on of the pleasures she gave her husband, Gustave imagined her taking positions that were ridiculous or
degrading—or at least he thought so.[26] This was to punish her for her
imposture or her treachery; either this new goddess deceived him,
and it was only a eunuch her master possessed each night; or else she
had betrayed him, and when Schlésinger entered her, the strong
woman opened herself to pleasure and let herself be unmanned, becoming in her husband's hands the happy passivity that Gustave had
wanted to become *for* and *through* her. He then felt a strange *sexual
depersonalization*, as if Elisa were *stealing his role*; his disappointment
can be compared only to a woman in love discovering that the man she
adores is passively and openly homosexual. That year at Trouville,
something from the distant past had resurged: Gustave rediscovered
the panic and bitterness that had seized him before, when he divined
what went on in the evenings in the Flauberts' large marriage bed.

But even earlier, some of his writings—three in particular, which

---

26. He says it explicitly in the *Mémoires*. We shall come back to this.

remained unpublished until recently (Jean Bruneau published them for the first time)[27]—testify to the effect that the child was telling himself a "family romance" in the sense Freud gives to these words, an attempt to reconstruct the scandalous fact of coitus in a more acceptable fashion, one that would satisfy his fierce resentment against his mother and, in imagination, his sexual desires. The writings in question are a scenario for a "historical" play, *Madame d'Ecouy;* an outline for a drama, *Deux Amours, deux cercueils;* and a tale, *La Grande Dame et le Joueur de vielle.* We can add to these that other tale, *La Fiancée et la tombe.* Jean Bruneau believes these sketches and stories were written between 1835 and 1836. Personally, I am inclined to date them all from the year 1835, primarily because the extreme naiveté of the plots and the style would hardly allow us to place them after *Le Voyage en enfer,* and also because they all treat the same theme, which afterward reappeared only episodically in Flaubert's works. Beginning with *Matéo Falcone* we enter into what might be called the "paternal cycle"; Gustave was bent on settling his accounts with his father—and with his elder brother. But the four tales mentioned above seem, rather, to constitute the "maternal cycle." The theme found in each of them is that of procreation, childbirth, and the relations between mother and son.

In the first place, for the idea of copulation to be tolerable, Gustave has to specify that it took place without Mme Flaubert's consent. In *La Fiancée et la tombe,* Annette, Paul's beautiful and chaste fiancée, is raped by the duke Robert. Paul goes to find Robert and hurls him into the moat, but "he is immediately captured by the guards and stabbed to death outside the château." This swiftly punished murder recalls the assassination of François by Garcia; Paul is *reduced to helplessness* by the soldiers' powerful grasp, he will have time to digest his death. But if Annette's honor is avenged, the young girl is no less sullied and *guilty*—she belongs to the Devil. In fact, the condemned Paul entreats her, "if she wishes to be united with him, [to go] look for the dagger and Sir Robert's head, which is still in the moat." Annette tries to obey, "but she had mutilated the body with two blows of her sword when the weapon fell from her hands." She is either cowardly or, if you like, not virile enough to play her role as man to the end. At that moment Robert's corpse rises up and "begins dancing around her, for it was Satan who had taken on Robert's form." The Devil seeks to seduce her; "with the help of Heaven" she resists him, and he disap-

27. See Jean Bruneau, *Les Débuts littéraires de Gustave Flaubert, 1831–1845* (Paris, 1962), pp. 99–124 *et passim.*

pears. But hell and damnation! Paul's ghost reappears to curse her; she dies of shock. We see that the young lover's rancor is relentless. It isn't enough for him to have killed the man who violated his fiancée: she will be purified in his eyes only if, made virile herself, she takes up the sword (a phallic and social symbol of masculinity) to mutilate the corpse and bring Paul his dagger (another symbol). The mother is guilty of allowing herself to be raped; let her retrieve her virility by castrating the man who made her a woman. This is what the cursed son is asking. This demand will flourish in shadow until the father's death. In 1850 Gustave paid a visit to the courtesan Kuchouk-Hanem and spent the night with her. She was asleep; he stayed awake, "plunged in infinitely intense reveries,"[28] and here is one of them: "Another time I dozed, my forefinger under her necklace, *as if to retain her should she have awakened. I thought of Judith and Holophernes sleeping together.* At a quarter to three, an awakening full of tenderness." Here again, surely, we find the perverse desire to be mastered by a woman. But more than that, the desire is accompanied by fear; he would consider it customary behavior for the courtesan to avenge herself by cutting off his head and thereby recovering not her virtue but her virility. To merit his esteem, every woman must be a Judith and treat her man like Holophernes. What he demanded of his mother he now demands of the whole female sex. In vain, as he well knows: the humiliated courtesan awakens "full of tenderness." Caroline Flaubert is daily more submissive, and her platonic love, her condemned son, curses this Valkyrie who moans beneath Siegfried and refuses to rejoin the heavenly amazons.

For this reason the humiliated mother becomes the unworthy mother in *Le Joueur de vielle,* a story with a significant subtitle: "The Mother and the Coffin." This time, abandonment is the issue, and we find the same young couple as in the previous story, now called Ernest and Henriette. They sigh—fate separates them. Henriette de Harcant must marry a duke. The young lover is "tormented by a deep sorrow"; Gustave notes that the "young lady, *less sorrowfully,* looked at him with tenderness, and *yet* from *time to time* sighs and sheds tears." She is marrying Dr. Flaubert, disguised as a peer of France: "One of the most important capitalists in the realm"—in sum, a marriage of convenience. She is a whore, selling herself, an act all the more reprehensible since she is pregnant by Ernest! Seven months after the marriage

28. He says in the *Journal de voyage,* apropos of the same adventure, "nervous intensities full of memories."

"she had a son; he was thought to be a miserable specimen." A miserable specimen or, rather, a child *reputed to be such,* who will bear the consequences of the mother's unworthiness. There is no doubt that Gustave is presenting himself: here I am with my anomaly, the innocent victim of everyone's mockery. But this time he has been careful to specify that he was *not* Achille-Cléophas's son. No, he is not the product of those sordid beddings in which "a young child" is delivered to the appetites of a prominent citizen; he does not take his life—or his character—from this rich, famous man with a positivist mind. Not having been fathered by some kind of parthenogenesis—his real desire—he imagines a young and unhappy father who resembles himself. Look at him: ruined, Ernest plays the hurdy-gurdy in courtyards—"Oh, the poor man, he has such a sad way about him." Still, he is "a musician," a street performer, the salt of the earth. Like a supplicant, he approaches the mansion where the great lady lives with her peer; her son, two years old—the call of blood—comes and throws himself into Ernest's arms; the street performer "embraces him like a father." But "the mother" does not recognize her old lover: "He was chased away with insults, like a beggar." Then comes "the colossal and formidable Revolution of 1789." Ernest recovers his wealth, the peer of France loses his and dies. "His wife, having no more husband and lover, sought to lavish her affection on her son—she went to take him from his nurse." Can it be said that she had neglected him during the golden years of her conjugal happiness and that she gave first place to the fierce, hairy beast who shared her bed? Too late! "A gentleman had come for him and taken him away." Father and son are finally reunited. Behold the mother punished. But not enough. She is more and more degraded and forced at last by hunger to enter a brothel. She has been there many years (at forty she is no doubt dean of the residents), when one fine day a young man of twenty, her son— "a fine figure, noble manner, a face no woman could resist"—comes to the brothel for release and—always the call of blood—choosing his mother among the other women, sleeps with her and *"having paid,"* departs. Henriette "had never experienced such pleasure as she did with him, never had kisses been so sweet, the words of tenderness so gentle and well chosen." In brief, Gustave is triumphant. He takes revenge on his reputed father, Achille-Cléophas, now dead, by sleeping with his widow, and on his mother as well, who had neglected him in childhood, by forcing her to find pleasure such as she never had before and, since she refused him maternal love, by driving her mad with incestuous passion. And, above all, he takes revenge on all men, brutes that they are, by inflaming the senses of the whore he has chosen with the caresses of a young girl: sweetness, gentleness, tenderness—these are what transforms the expert slut, not the hired rapes to which she daily submits. We can imagine this forty-year-old leaning over the young body of her son, eager to give him at last the pleasure she had refused him twenty years earlier. These joys of renewed contact do not bring happiness to either of them, however; leaving the brothel, Gustave has himself stabbed by vagrants. Mme Flaubert runs to his corpse, "stares at him attentively for a long time," and recognizes her son. She goes mad and two days later throws herself under the wheels of the "funeral carriage that is bearing him to his final resting place."

The theme of incest is taken up again in *Madame d'Ecouy*. The treatment is cruder, since it is merely a question of quid pro quo; stripped down, however, the scenario is all the more striking. Mme d'Ecouy, a very beautiful widow, awaits her lover Monsieur de Bonnechose, who "shares the nuptial bed now draped in black." This time the woman is neither raped nor bought: she gives herself. But for this very reason it is a crime, as evidence the words "nuptial" and "draped in black." The lovers are tumbling in debauchery on a dead man's bed. They will be punished. That evening they are to meet in an arbor in the park; by mischance this is the very spot where Arthur, the widow's son, has arranged to meet Marie, the chambermaid. "He glimpsed something white and trembling in the arbor—he approached. A voice said to him, speaking very low: Is it you? And to these soft words he answered 'yes', and went into the arbor." The irreparable is accomplished. Meanwhile, de Bonnechose arrives by a secret door. Arthur confronts him—"'Who are you?' 'Your mother's lover.' 'You infamous liar!'"—and kills him. At that moment a cry comes from the arbor, and "from the other side," light and playful, runs a woman dressed in white: "It's your Marie!"—"Oh the powers of evil!" cries the unfortunate young man, "I am cursed!" This time the son, having had intercourse with his mother, kills her lover before her eyes. None of these acts has any motivation—chance alone has been the decisive factor. But the absence of motives illustrates more effectively the fantastic and dreamlike aspect of the plot. Gustave was concerned with only one thing: to sleep innocently with his guilty mother and to kill his father out of filial piety (You infamous *liar!*); the good son does not believe Monsieur de Bonnechose, he avenges his outraged mother, that is, he kills the lover he has just replaced. When the affair is over, morality reclaims its due and the younger Flaubert son cries out, as usual, that he is cursed.

In *Deux Amours, deux cercueils* there is no incest but, rather, the relentless degradation of a woman guilty of loving her husband: "a tepid union on the part of the husband, lively and warm on the part of Louise." The unhappy woman has a rival "who steals him from her little by little." Her husband "no longer takes her out into society." Every day "Amalia, the upstart courtesan and jealous of Louise, puts arsenic in her milk." The martyred wife dies; Ernest, her platonic lover, kills the criminal husband, saying: "You are a murderer. I am your executioner." The account of this demise naturally brings to mind a dream Flaubert tells us he had not long after entering school.[29]

> It was in a verdant countryside . . . beside a river—I was with my mother, walking close to the riverbank. She fell in. I saw the water foam, the circles widen and disappear; the water resumed its course, and then I no longer heard anything but the sound of the water . . . Suddenly my mother called out to me: "Help! Help! Oh my poor child, help me!" I leaned over to look, lying flat on my stomach on the grass. I saw nothing; the cries continued. An irresistible force pinned me to the earth and I heard the cries: "I am drowning! I am drowning! Help me!" The water flowed on, flowed on, limpid, and that voice I heard from the bottom of the river plunged me into rage and despair.

Gustave and Mme Flaubert are walking in a green and flowering countryside; they form a couple and this is happiness. Not for long: the poor boy witnesses the *fall*[30] of Mme Flaubert: she falls into the river, sinks, disappears, is swallowed up. The water, disturbed for a moment, resumes it course and "flows on, flows on, *limpid*." In other words, it is transparent but Gustave is unable to probe it with a look, he sees nothing; his mother *has become the river;* she was standing on the bank, she is now lying beneath it, prostrate and sleeping. The fall here represents her betrayal (she abandons her son and her maternal authority in order to dissolve into liquid docility), the brutal revelation of her imposture, and her punishment. The fact is that having disappeared, having been swallowed up, she is not dead and has not finished dying or seeing herself die; her voice still resounds: I am drowning. And this is just what Gustave feels: she is drowning in her

29. *Mémoires d'un fou,* 4.
30. *Falling:* the meaning is clearly, "Oh, never insult a fallen woman."

unconditional submission, in her thousand domestic occupations, in her innumerable concerns, which scruples and guilt push to the point of anguish; she is lost, she is no longer the strong woman of my early childhood. At once he offers himself the sadistic pleasure of making her conscious of it: the mother knows she is guilty and unhappy; she recognizes her helplessness and—marvel of marvels—she *begs* for her son's help; he alone can understand her distress, he alone can come to her aid. The entire dream serves the purpose of unreally assuaging his desire by seeing this false Penthesilea stumble and fall at his feet, recognize her fault (I am drowning), ask him for his pardon and the help of his strong arms. And *by refusing her this help,* answering, in effect: Where would I find the strength to help you? I am as you made me, inert and paralyzed. What is there to do, then? Nothing, except when the time has come to plunge in and pull his mother's body from the river.[31] But this involves becoming a male and an agent, which is what he is utterly incapable of doing: "flat on my stomach on the grass . . . an irresistible force pinned me to the earth." The force of inertia. Mme Flaubert is punished by her own sins: she sinks, claiming the protection of a son whom she could neither protect (as the mother-goddess she pretended to be would have done) nor make into someone who would one day protect her. Gustave's passivity is Caroline's crime and her punishment. The gratification is complete when the son *condemns his mother to death.* And he has unambiguously condemned her in his dream, as he has condemned or will condemn all the other members of his family, including his sister.[32] This is the revenge of inertia, the vengeance of resentment.

I have emphasized the various "maternal" themes in order to point out the young man's "sexual problematic": he somehow understands that his mother *is no longer* the active half of the androgyne whose passive half he is. She was this, nonetheless, if only in illusion; leaving her mark on him, she condemned him forever to having only an *imaginary* sexual life. An unreal woman in the hands of men, he will be an unreal man in his intercourse with women. In the first case, moreover, things are even further complicated: Gustave does not accept himself as a homosexual—rightly, since his passivity demands to be recreated by the embrace of a mother-goddess; further, when he craves a man, he endeavors to convince himself *in front of his mirror* that he is of the other sex. When his flesh does respond to the caresses of men, as at

31. We know that Gustave was a good swimmer.
32. See *La Dernière Heure,* January 1836 (he had just turned fifteen).

51

the Turkish baths, the purpose must be explicitly nonsexual (immersion, cleansing, massage "for health reasons"). If, however, he must admit to himself the nature of his excitation, he creates the analogue of an unfelt desire to possess a young boy; for pederasty (in the proper sense of the term) seems to him in a way the noblest aspect of homosexuality. One *takes;* the catamite, with his soft skin, is simply an ersatz woman; as Genet says, the male who sexually subjects another male thinks of himself as a supermale. Gustave attributes this supermasculinity to himself in imagination, while in fact he yields to the diligent activity of the *kellak:* he can only imagine himself a woman in solitude; at the baths, he cannot help it that his great throbbing body is not masculine.

With women he must certainly *play the virile role.* For this reason they scarcely tempt him. The women who counted in his life were almost always mothers (Elisa, Louise Colet, Mme Brianne), older than he (Louise Colet and Elisa were both born in 1810—eleven years' difference), and enterprising and aggressive (Eulalie Foucault—we shall return to this—*took him*). In a way this was true of Lousie Colet as well; if the love of Frédéric and Mme Arnoux—the incarnation of Elisa—comes to nothing, it is because Mme Arnoux is passive. Still, she is the one, in the end, who comes to offer herself. (Frédéric "loved her so much that he let her go.") If he feels desired by these energetic matrons and if he can see himself as their prey, his emotion is translated by an erection that has nothing "virile" about it since the sexual organ, far from being perceived as an instrument of penetration, seems to him an active passivity that lends itself to being caressed by another (fellatio, masturbation). Gustave takes this flowering of the flesh (like the erect nipples an excited woman offers to her lover's caress) as an analogue of the *phallus/sword* made to pierce and burrow. The unrealizing intention, while unformulated, is nonetheless deliberate: he *turns to account* the expression of a passive excitement in order to support the male role, to make the *gestures* of possession—in brief, to respond to the woman's demands in exchange for her subsequent resumption of the dominant role. During coitus the unrealization is increased since he tends to identify with the woman he is possessing, to steal from her the sensations she seems to feel; this overwhelmed, yielding flesh *is himself,* is the reflection he contemplates in the mirror, is his objectivity for the other. After orgasm he falls back, disarmed—it is *his turn* to be caressed. The *act* has only been the means of obtaining this.

Louise Colet was without any doubt the woman he loved best. He spoke of her to the Goncourts, six years after their break, "without bitterness or resentment." The two brothers note in their *Journal* that "this woman . . . seems to have intoxicated him with her fierce and histrionic love, with emotions, sensations, shocks."[33] They are less sanguine when they write: "There is a vulgarity about Flaubert's nature that takes pleasure in these terrible, sensual, soul-searing women who exhaust love through outbursts, rages, brutal (physical or mental) intoxications."[34] It is true that he only took pleasure in "terrible women," but his vulgarity of soul was a pose. Louise was violent, vindictive, jealous—she had stabbed poor Alphonse Karr in the back one day with a penknife. She spoke about her sexuality like a man: "A word about Louise Colet. She said to a friend of a medical student who was her lover of the moment: 'So, what has become of him, your friend? Here it is, more than fifteen days since I've seen him . . . and at my age and with my temperament, do you think it is healthy?'"[35] The "word" is reported by Gustave, as the context indicates. And we can believe he knew what he was saying. When he stayed farther and farther away from Paris and Mantes, the long period of chastity to which he had reduced his mistress drove her mad; she threw herself on him—raped! This was the accomplishment of his dream. She went still farther: she followed him, or had him followed, and burst into the private room where he was dining with his male friends, Louis and Maxime, ready to horsewhip her rival. Above all, she *beat* him: "After dinner there was a boorish exchange between Gautier and Flaubert, the former bragging with a monstrous, brutal, and repugnant vanity that he had beaten women; the latter bragging with pride of having been beaten by them while experiencing an overwhelming desire to kill them, feeling—as he finished by saying, apropos Mme Colet—the courtroom benches cracking under him."[36] There is undoubtedly a great deal of truth in Gustave's boasting since seven years earlier he had used the same formula to talk about Louise to the Goncourts: "He loved her wildly too. One day he was on the point of killing her: 'I heard the courtroom benches cracking under me.'"[37] There is no better portrayal of his sexuality: with a single movement of his great arms, without hurting her and without humiliating her, this giant could gently have held Louise at a distance. He preferred to let her

33. *Journal*, 1862 (Monaco ed.) 5:58,59.
34. Ibid.
35. Ibid., 1875–78, 15:129.
36. Ibid., 1869, 8:167.
37. Ibid. 5:59.

beat him, walled up in his passivity to the point of masochism, while in the depths of his heart an imaginary male muttered: "I'll kill her!" as he pretended to be gripped by a murderous delirium. Dramatized for the requirements of the cause, this is the very movement of his sexuality.[38]

He did love her wildly. But from afar. To tell the truth, what attracted him was also what repelled him. He wrote to her one day, "Nature certainly made a mistake in making you a woman: *you belong to the male side of things.*"[39] And toward the end of their stormy liaison: "I have always tried (but I seem to have failed) to make a sublime hermaphrodite out of you. I want you to be a man above the waist, while baffling and troubling below, where you are engulfed by the female element."[40] The virility with which he wants to endow Louise, of course, he sees as a movement toward the spiritual: "We might have soared above ourselves."[41] But the terms he uses are intentionally sexual: man above the waist—male energy, activity—woman below. Might Gustave be the complementary hermaphrodite, a woman with the sex of a man? The androgyne cut in two, unable to recover his lost half, dreams of a pair of hermaphrodites, each one provided with a real sex and an imaginary one. But what is striking is that Louise at first appeared to him to "belong to the male side": when he claims to have tried to change her, we see quite plainly that he thought not to rid her of her masculinity but to sublimate her femininity: "The Idea— this is the source of one's love if one lives by it." In fact, he dreamed of her *in advance* when he wished in adolescence "to be loved with a devouring and terrifying love" or when he dreamed of a *mistress* "who would be satanic . . . who has slaves . . . and sits on thrones." He described this mistress in the guise of the insatiable Mazza, who bites her lover until the blood flows and every day *invents* new pleasures. The most surprising thing is that he is embodied both in her, when men's hands have awakened that dormant flesh, and in her cowardly lover who, when she becomes the *subject* of the couple through her frenetic demands, is at first fascinated by this impetuousity and then

38. We find the same testimony, with very minor differences, cited by Frank: "She is strange, this woman. She is the one who has always been unfaithful and she is the one who is jealous. Lately she has even come to my home to reproach me. A log was burning in the fireplace, I was watching the log and wondering whether I wouldn't soon pick it up, smash her head in, and throw the coals on her." Bibliothèque Nationale, N.A.F., 23, 827.

39. *Correspondance* 3:328.

40. Ibid. 4:58.

41. Ibid.

flees in terror. Ernest puts the ocean between himself and the imperious Mazza; Gustave was content with fifty miles. And he actually came back. Not for long, not often, but their affair did last eight years.[42] He admired the energy of the Muse and wanted to swoon beneath the yoke when they made love. A significant sentence escapes him in another letter, during a period of relative calm: he congratulates himself on this tranquillity, which he would like to believe will last forever; you see, he says, "if *I had let myself be dominated,* our liaison would have been broken off soon enough." I very much doubt that Louise wanted to dominate him. She wanted to *have* him, that's all. But Gustave always saw in this demand, which was after all legitimate, a will to enslave. This is why he made such efforts to keep his distance: he was terrified that she might extend the domination he loved to feel in brief, dizzying moments to his whole life. Rouen was his refuge. There his mother protected him against the imperious matron; thanks to her, he could go with impunity to Paris or to Mantes once every six months and abandon himself to the turbulence of his mistress without fear of being chained to her for the rest of his life. Louise was so much aware of this that she in turn was fascinated by Mme Flaubert and was always pleading to be introduced to her. Gustave refused to bring them into each other's company, with significant stubbornness: "I find your persistence in this matter strange."[43] Not stranger, surely, than his. "I do not like this confusion, this alliance of two emotions coming from different sources."[44] "This is a tic of yours; between two affections of a different nature you want to establish a connection in which I see no sense and even less utility."[45] Certainly the "affections" Louise and Mme Flaubert bore him were, if not different in "source," at least different in "nature"; but on this level of rationalization, it could be pointed out that for this very reason there was no great risk in "allying" them and that it would have been impossible to "confuse" them. Louise was not fooled: a jealous woman, she sensed that the confusion, if there was any, existed only in Flaubert's feelings. It would be more accurate to say that this confusion had existed. And something of it still remained—resentment, regret; this is what the Muse means when, quite unjustly, she "reproached him for hiding in his mother's petticoat." This is why Louise would not stop until she had seen the other "mistress." It is also why she definitively

42. With three years of separation (1848–51).
43. *Correspondance* 4:7.
44. Ibid.
45. Ibid. 3:336.

lost Gustave shortly after the confrontation: "Once she hunted him down at home, in front of his mother, whom she detained, insisting that she hear the explanation; his mother always preserved, like a wound to her sex, the memory of her son's harshness to his mistress. 'This is the only sore point between my mother and me,' said Flaubert." [46] "*A wound to her sex*": this interpretation needs no comment.

To narrate the affair between Léon and Emma, Gustave drew inspiration from his old dream and from his memories. From this point of view, the passages he deleted from the definitive manuscript, which Gabrielle Leleu has published, are the most interesting.

He came to her deeply moved, handsome, blond, in all the candor of his lust, with the timidity of a virgin and the seriousness of a priest; Emma *savored* him[47] egotistically, in a discreet, absorbed, deeply felt way, knowing well that it was a rare thing and wanting to lose none of it, often even throwing herself on his cheek to gather, before they should fall, the shining tears that trembled in his eyes . . . This was more like *a man's passion for his mistress* than a woman's for her lover. She was *active* and *dominating*, but coquettish. She *led* him, *excited* him by all the calculated and spontaneous artifice at her command . . . Hadn't she the fantasy of wanting poetry? . . . [He couldn't even find a rhyme for the second line] Finally admitting his incapacity, he remained bitter at this little humiliation. It scarcely lasted because he had "no will but hers." He cut his side-whiskers because she preferred mustaches and even told her scrupulously all his actions hour by hour . . . He vaguely perceived *some sort of precipice in the distance,*

46. *Journal* of the Goncourts, 1862, 5:58.
47. The subject "il" [he or it] of the first sentence is ambiguous: in principle it designates Léon's love. But very quickly it appears to be connected to Léon himself as well. A Flaubertian metaphor—forced, pursued, giving the abstract a concrete shape—can present a feeling as "coming to Emma with the timidity of a virgin," etc. This metaphor can vividly show us love as "blond," since another version speaks of "blond passion." But we shall have difficulty admitting that Emma could throw herself on *its* cheek to drink *its* tears. Hence this curious hybrid—undoubtedly intentional—allows Gustave to sustain the reader's uncertainty: does Emma savor Léon's love or Léon himself? In the same sentence "il était rare" [it was a rare thing] applies both to the feeling (Léon is not rare) and to the man (the cheeks, the tears, the look are his). To savor a feeling is an accepted idea that teaches us nothing. To savor the man is something better: love devours; kissing is eating—as Hegel was the first to say. But the devouring mistress who wolfs down her lover and drinks his tears and his blood (Mazza had eaten the bewildered Ernest) suddenly becomes *the man,* according to the conception of the couple prevailing in every society where the woman is the second sex. Doña Prouhèze, desolate after renouncing Rodriguez, says: "He will not know the taste of me." Thus for Gustave, cannibalism is the logical result of "sexual possession"—it is no accident that he (unjustly) reproaches de Sade for having forgotten anthropophagy—and it is the woman, a praying mantis, who eats, the man who is eaten.

and Emma almost began to frighten him, although each time she seemed more irresistible. Where had she learned that art of *making the soul pass into flesh*, and of enchanting it *beneath* the lust that *devoured* it? One day while stroking her breast, he cut his finger on a clasp and she *plunged it into her mouth to suck the blood . . .*[48] He was revolted at this dazing of his consciousness and effacement of his personality. He wanted Emma for her tyrannies, her perpetual injustices, *her domination*. But how could he defend himself against this creature . . . she monopolized him through all his senses; she enchanted him, he was her thing, her man, her property. This was more than love, a passion, a habit—this woman *was a vice* for him.

But we also find valuable clues in the published text. We have just seen Emma loving her lover as though he were her mistress. In the definitive manuscript, it is Léon who feels like a woman: "He never questioned her ideas; he accepted all her tastes—*he became her mistress* rather than she his. She had . . . *kisses that thrilled his soul."* (Variant: "She had tender words that inflamed his flesh, devouring kisses that thrilled his soul. Where had she learned this corruption so deep and well masked as to be almost ungraspable?") The connection between the virile mistress and the mother is frequently stressed: "She called him child. 'Child, do you love me?'" and "She inquired *like a virtuous mother* about his friends. She said to him: 'Don't see them, don't go out, think only of us; love me!' She would have liked to be able to watch over his life, and *the idea came to her of having* him followed in the streets."[49] Moreover, she soon clashes with his mother: "Someone had sent [Léon's] mother a long anonymous letter to warn her that he was 'ruining himself with a married woman'; and the good lady . . . wrote to Maître Dubocage, his employer . . . [who] kept him for three quar-

48. A symbol of possession and its substitute, fellatio. But as we see, the image is turned around: taking Léon's finger and "plunging it into her mouth," it is Emma who possesses her lover; he doesn't enter her, she sucks him into her suctioning mouth (and he is grazed by *her:* this rose has thorns, whoever caresses her discovers it to his cost). So we understand that Léon's timid kisses, far from making Emma's *"soul pass into flesh,"* have the single effect of releasing in her the male desire of dominating aggression. Léon can easily be summed up in this undifferentiated blondness, his flesh. Not Emma; whoever rubs against her is stung.

49. I mentioned earlier that Louise trailed Gustave, or had him trailed. Emma thinks of it, but being prouder than the Muse, she refuses to lower herself to such a stratagem. Nevertheless she behaves like an abusive mother who wants total possession of her child, including *his life*, everything he feels, thinks, and does when she is not around. She recapitulates the other's experience, turning it into another passive manifestation of the flesh, and at the same time intrudes in order to direct him: "Don't see them, don't go out . . ." Thus she resides in Léon in the form of imperatives and affirms the primacy of exteriority and otherness.

ters of an hour, trying . . . to warn him . . . of the abyss." All these themes are present, as we see.[50]

Even the theme of the mirror: "She undressed *brutally,* ripping out the thin laces of her corset so violently that they would whistle around her hips . . . Then with one movement she would let all her clothes fall at once [published text] around her heels like a mass of clouds, and step out of it. Then she would send herself an intoxicated smile in the mirror as she stretched her arms [unpublished], and pale and serious, without a word, she would throw herself against his chest with a long shudder [text]." We can easily see why Flaubert deleted the glance in the mirror. Emma is androgynous; she melts into the arms of Rodolphe—a "true" male, empty like Genet's pimps; it is the moment of the mirror: quite naked, she contemplates her *desired* body and tries to see it with the eyes of the hunter whose prey she is. At this moment, Flaubert slips into her to admire himself and to dream of future abandon. When she is about to make love with Léon, she is the hunter. And this is not the moment, as when she undresses *brutally* like a man, to go searching in the mirror for the object of lust she was for her first lover. Even if that smile were triumphant[51]—but we are told it is intoxicated—it would hardly suit the carnivore discovering its prey and about to leap *upon* it. In fact, I am speaking here of the literary construction and not the reality. There would be nothing to prevent a real Emma, caught between carnal excitement and aggression, from looking at herself in the mirror, for she is actively engaged in awakening and guiding her lover's desire to take her. Gustave is quite conscious of this since he has been the prey, and active caressing has deliberately transformed him into the hunter. But he is afraid that in a *literary* context the finely noted contrast between the *brutality* of the gesture and the happy yielding in front of her beckoning reflection may be too pronounced, that it will disconcert the reader. There is no better indication, however, of Emma's complex character or of Gustave's dreams and experience. In this scene he is at once the man undressing, the vampire-woman "admiring herself" after "stripping naked" [52] (for the brutality of the undressing can also be experienced—unreally—as *being made naked by another*), and the young victim, already naked, who passively waits to be caressed.

50. I have italicized the words and phrases that introduce motifs already indicated in the early works or in the letters to Louise.

51. This would imply that Emma is reviewing her "charms" as the instruments in her enterprise of fascination, the means by which she holds onto her young captive.

52. See *Novembre* (cited above): "I shall strip naked."

It is especially striking that the two lovers are both conscious of the perversity of their games. Léon wonders how Emma came by her "experience"; he senses in her an "almost ungraspable corruption." These words can have only one meaning: the perversity is not in their *practices;* even if they had to make love only "in the missionary position," this corruption would remain, impalpable, unrealizable, disquieting—vaguely promising catastrophe *or crime.* Indeed, this corruption is contained for them—for Flaubert—in the inversion of their roles, in the increasing importance of the *imaginary.* Léon seeks in Emma the satisfaction of what has become *his vice,* the desire to dream himself a woman caressed by a woman. Emma too is disturbed; by the character she plays, which she cannot help playing, we could say that she hastens the unreal danger of changing sex for good: "She was suffering now or took delight in sensations that had scarcely moved her before. She had the bizarre quirks of character and depraved tastes of pregnant women. She loved spicy pickling brines, uncooked dough, and the sharp odor of burning hartshorn." He adds: "We call these strange desires the cravings of pregnant women, as if there were a need to imagine the will of an inner being in order to explain their power." In other words, these desires are imposed on the woman as *alien desires,* the desires of *another inside her.* Emma has a taste for violent sensations; she is afraid that the other, inside her—that character she cannot help playing—is beginning to impose its being on her. In truth, everything is experienced in an unbearable tension, there is something false and "distressing" in their relations. "Yet on that forehead covered with cold drops, on those stuttering lips, in those distracted irises, in the grip of those arms there was something extreme, vague, and funereal which seemed to Léon to slip between them subtly, in order to separate them." Thus the couple Emma-Léon—double hermaphrodites—reproduce the child Gustave's basic desire and his anxiety in the face of the deep-seated unreality of his being or, if you will, in the face of the impossibility of making sexual pleasure the means of merging the vague and fleeting subject he is for himself with the clear, precise—but unattainable—object he is for others.

Flaubert would have other mistresses, "actresses," Béatrix Person, or the corpulent Lagier who tells him publicly, "You, my dear, are the chamberpot of my heart." But with them, love was too real, too specific. He preferred prostitutes: you are alone because you pay them; he loved the courtesan's cool docility—they caressed him gently with their beautiful, tender flesh and ministered untiringly to his immobile body. Maternal attentions had consecrated him to impotent rages and to the compliance of mercenary mouths. When he was not constrained by the irritating demands of a mistress to unrealize himself as a sexual agent, he would get an erection by imagination. At about the age of twelve, he tells us, he wanted to know the "devouring" love of an actress—and the adjective is already to be found in *Novembre*, fifteen years before *Madame Bovary*. At the theater he is thrilled as his actress performed: "She held out her arms, shouted, sobbed, flashed lightning, cried out with inconceivable love in her voice, and when she took up this theme again, it seemed to me that she was tearing my heart out with the sound of her voice so that it could mingle with hers in a loving vibration . . . Flowers were thrown to her, and in my emotional state I savored on her behalf the crowd's adoration, the love of all those men and their desire. I would have wanted to be loved by someone like that . . . How beautiful she is, the woman so warmly applauded by everyone . . . *who never appears except by candlelight*, lustrous and singing and *set in a poet's ideal as in a life made for her! . . . If I could have been near those lips singing with such purity . . . But the footlights of the theater seemed to me the frontier of illusion; beyond* them was the universe of love and poetry.[53] He was in love with the singer to the extent that she was unrealized in the midst of an imaginary world. And in 1850 Kuchouk-Hanem provoked his desire in the same way. She was—he tells us—a "*very famous* courtesan"; she wore a tarboosh which he describes at length and which augments the impression of unreality; finally, she danced, "rising sometimes on one foot, sometimes on the other, exquisite. I have seen this dance on ancient Greek vases." Exoticism, beauty, reminders of antiquity, dance—here we are on the other side of the footlights. He decided to spend the night with her and make passionate love with this unattainable image. She fell asleep, and he was even more alone. This was the moment of "infinitely intense reveries." He tells Bouilhet: "This is why I stayed."[54] What was he dreaming about? "Watching that beautiful creature asleep (she snored, her head resting on my arm), I thought of my nights in the Paris brothels—a whole series of old memories came back . . . and I thought of her, of her dance, of her voice as she sang songs that were without meaning for me and even without distinguishable words."[55] If he is not in the mood to play the androgyne or if the situation does not lend itself, he is happy to make love in *noncommunica-*

53. *Novembre*. My italics.
54. *Correspondance* 2:176.
55. Ibid.

tion. That night he was exalted: Kuchouk-Hanem was sleeping, a "kind of death";[56] a little earlier she had been singing and speaking in an unknown language; and now he was keeping watch over her, all alone, free to unrealize himself and to unrealize the sleeper as he liked. She would be Judith or Tanit or some woman from antiquity, some image of the cruel goddess of the impossible, of beauty; he was a priest of her cult. Mâtho, tortured to death under Salambô's gaze, would later be born from these reveries.

He left Kuchouk in the morning "very peacefully" and notes in his journal: "What a lift to your vanity if you could be sure of leaving some memory of yourself behind and that she would think of you more than of others, that you would remain in her heart." Only for the sake of vanity? Since he is in the hands of others, doesn't he want to be protected *in his being* by this totally unknown woman, who might preserve—without the power to integrate it into the totality of her experience—the bare memory of what he is? He returned to Esna a month and a half later[57] and saw Kuchouk again "with great sadness," which he had probably anticipated. "I found her changed. She had been ill," and in the *Journal:* "She had a look of fatigue about her and had been ill." In brief, *she is no longer the same.* And then he knows very well that he is "not made for pleasure but only for regrets; it's over, I shall see her no more, and her image will gradually be effaced from my memory." To Bouilhet he writes: "I looked at her a long time so as to keep her image in my mind." This is the "work of mourning": with exquisite melancholy Gustave strives to transform this woman of flesh and blood into the image she will be for him tomorrow. He adds: "I intensely relished the bitterness of it all; that's the main thing, and I felt it in my very bowels."

Moreover, the image springs forth from itself and the environment is transformed spontaneously—or nearly so—into a performance. If women are involved and they offer themselves, Gustave steals away: "I went walking . . . in the whore's quarter . . . giving *baksheesh* to all the women, letting them call me and catch hold of me; they grabbed me around the waist and tried to pull me into their houses . . . Think of all that, with the sun blazing down! Well, I abstained deliberately, in order to preserve the sweet sadness of the scene and to engrave it deeply in my memory. In this way, I went away dazzled and have remained so. There is nothing more beautiful than these women calling

56. Cocteau.
57. He left Kuchouk on 8 March and saw her again on 26 April.

to you. If I had gone with any of them, a second picture would have been superimposed on the first and dimmed its splendor."[58] He makes love to make things unreal; if the woman is already unreal, why bother? She has already done the work herself, and to follow her into her house would be to risk finding reality again. Gustave calls this quite premeditated[59] abstention "stoic." It is a recognition that his purpose was to change the almehs into pure appearance. Gustave is committed to onanism by his very enterprise, which would make his constituted passivity retotalized as flesh. Most children and adolescents masturbate, *faute de mieux*; this practice tends to disappear or at least subside when they are able to have sexual intercourse (or, rather, when they take it up regularly); here again, imagination is a makeshift substitute which is cancelled out when the reality is attainable. If Gustave is basically an onanist, on the other hand, it is because the movement of his personalization makes him imaginary, first as a child and then as a man. The reason is simple: to *recover* himself as the object he is for others, he had to be both himself and the other, to carry out and at the same time experience the work of passivization, and to perceive himself in the same sexual sensation as both hunter and prey—something inconceivable except in an unrealizing tension. And the other, here, is the means; the end is the discovery of femininity in sexual excitement—if the other is too real, and therefore unpredictable, the mirage disappears. Gustave finds he is transcended by an enigmatic transcendence: he is the object for that unknown, *a* woman, and he feels once again deprived of his being because he is unaware of what she sees, of what she actually thinks of him. In order to disarm her and please her, he has to invent new roles and act them out. Then, the real being of his mistress, her breast, her hips, her truly feminine skin as well as her sex and her sexual demands, expose the unreality of his disguise. Confronted with a real woman—even a virile one— the illusion of femininity is difficult to maintain. He makes love uneasily; his partner is an intruder. Man or woman, the partner's insistent presence prevents Gustave from converting that person entirely into an image, and from unrealizing himself completely. As we shall soon see, resentment pushes him even in childhood to a sadism of the imagination, by which I mean his inert maliciousness; he is incapable of *doing* ill but not prevented from dreaming of it; didn't he call down

58. *Correspondance*, 13 March 1850, vol. 2.
59. In the *Journal de voyage*, Flaubert writes: "We turned back into the street of the almehs; *I walked there on purpose* . . . I forbade myself to fuck them."

all sorts of torments on his friends and all the members of his family? And how can we doubt that their imagined misfortunes gave him sexual gratification? This sadism, of course, is superficial and appears much later than the masochistic desire to be subjugated flesh; it is not derived from his constituted passivity, which is, on the contrary, opposed to it and contains it within the domain of oneirism[60]—and of literature. Nonetheless, Gustave's sadism exists just because it remains on the level of the dream, incapable on principle of being accomplished as an act; it is from the outset a flight into the imaginary, and can be sexually satisfied only by masturbation.

We should not imagine, however, that his mirror is enough for him or that he is content to embody the *other* through mental images. His profound masochism and his superficial sadism are in agreement on one point: the other must be represented by a *lesser being*, a minor presence that makes the other manifest as both a virile force and a tractable object. A number of paragraphs, most of them unpublished,[61] show that in the beginning of their love, before Léon's departure for Paris and the episode with Rodolphe, the clerk gradually transforms Emma into a fetish, replacing her with a glove. Léon never misses the evening gatherings at the home of the pharmacist Homais, since the Bovarys go too. "As soon as he heard the bell, he ran to meet Mme Bovary, took her shawl and put away . . . the heavy overshoes she wore when it snowed." Then, he would stand behind her and "look at the teeth of her comb biting into her chignon." This contemplation has a dual purpose: to advance Emma's transformation into a thing (and, reciprocally, Emma's costume into the living woman), and to transform the present into a memory (and inversely, so that there should be no difference between remembrance and perception). The first time: Léon—always behind Emma—contemplates her from head to foot; beneath her chignon are "curly wisps of hair sticking to her skin like kiss curls." What he perceives here is the body in its desirable and carnal life but *unknown* to the woman being contemplated. Then come the "rather thin" shoulders, the thinness being observed here as

60. The active sadist, even if he has no chance to put his projects into operation, most often imagines that he will inflict torments himself; the passive sadist is content to dream that he will witness them. As far as we can ascertain, the little stories Gustave tells himself are in the second category: he is Nero, for example; others torment *in his name*, certainly, but he is careful not to lift a finger. Inert, abandoned, he turns his back on the victims, drinking or caressing a beautiful woman, his lust fueled by their hideous, ear-splitting cries.

61. Gabrielle Leleu 1:365–95. See also *Madame Bovary* (Pléiade ed.), pp. 339, 414.

the discreet negation of the living flesh, like a reminder of the bony inertia of the skeleton, allowing the identification of the organic with the inorganic to be carried even further: "From her turned-up hair a dark color fell over her back and, growing gradually paler, was lost in shadow. Beyond there was nothing but her dress; it spread on both sides of her chair, billowing out in many folds as it fell to the floor." The folds, the "billowing" fall of cloth suggest an inorganic image of life. He can only conclude: "When Léon sometimes felt the sole of his boot poised on [her dress], he drew back as if he had trodden on something alive." Emma ends in a dress the way a mermaid ends in a fish tail.

The second moment is described in a long paragraph, which has been shortened in the published text. I shall give only excerpts:

"At that time she wore those hats in the peasant style which left her ears uncovered. They reminded Léon of ones he had sometimes seen at the theater, in comic operas and . . . this would come slowly over him, like a memory of similar emanations and forgotten feelings . . . The young man's thought would gently dissolve in these pools of memory, sensation, dream, and sometimes Emma would almost disappear in the radiance surrounding her." At this moment Léon strangely resembles Flaubert: he derealizes Emma and changes her into his "idea." What happiness to be raised above lust, *alone* and *invisible!* But the intruder arrives and plunges him back into the real: "Suddenly, when she would turn toward him and he saw her black eyes sparkling, her moist lips speaking . . . he would feel a sharp, precise, immediate desire, something piercing that shot through him all at once, and he wanted to squeeze her shoulders, to know her at least with more than his eyes." [62] From the moment he is manifest as transcendence, as looking, the sexual partner is an aggressor—he shakes off the solitude of the dream; while he is present and he can aim at *communicating,* he interrupts the process of transubstantiation by affirming himself as a sexual agent and consigning his beloved to the objectivity of the flesh. How fortunate if he could be present as object and at the same time absent as subject! What luck! This is the third moment of the operation. First, it is only dreamed: one evening, Léon finds a wool and velvet rug in his room, the work of Mme Bovary. "His heart leaped . . . He spoke of it that evening even to his employer, who sent it back with the servant who had come to look for it. Deep down, Léon found this

62. Leleu, p. 383.

procedure rather indelicate, a violation of the rug, which he would gladly have carried under his shirt, against his heart, if it had not been so big." No luck: the rug is too big. It would have been ideal, however, to immerse himself in fetishized activity, made passive by Emma; he could have been taken permanently but without any risks by this energetic woman who is reduced to the imperious inertia of the practico-inert. The poor clerk can do nothing but conclude from this failure that the mental image is inadequate: "'I never dream about her!' he noted with surprise. And every evening he forced himself to think about her, hoping that at least she would come into his dreams." What can he do? He tries to replace her with new, ersatz objects: he kisses Emma's daughter "on the neck, always on the spot where the mother's lips had rested," searching here once again for the inert vestige of tenderness. Or else he fetishizes poor Charles: "Her husband—wasn't he *part* of her after all?"[63] In a deleted paragraph, this thought is made explicit: "How often, in considering [Bovary], did he search the man's entire person for an invisible trace of the caresses he dreamed of." Charles, the fetish-husband, Emma's property, is the unconscious support of the crystallization his wife has worked on him; Léon does not attempt to identify with him as he possesses his wife; rather, he unrealizes himself as an object totalized by Emma's hands and mouth. A new failure: "This union, however, seemed to him so impossible in itself that he could scarcely imagine it." The stroke of genius comes soon afterward. From these latter words Gustave passes without transition to the line: "At the pharmacist's one evening, Madame Bovary was sewing, when she dropped her glove; Léon pushed it under the table without anyone noticing. But when everyone was asleep, he got up, tiptoed downstairs, quickly found the glove, and returned to his bed. It was a yellow glove, supple, with wrinkles on the fingers, and the skin seemed more raised around the large thumb, in the place where the hand is fleshier. He smelled a faint perfume, something tender like faded violets. Then Léon closed his eyes, he imagined it buttoned at Emma's wrist, taut, moving coquettishly in a thousand indeterminate ways. He inhaled its scent, kissed it; he put it on the four fingers of his right hand and slept with it beneath his mouth."[64] He had to dream about her; instead of looking everywhere for a trace of her work or a touch, he steals the inert effigy of the hand that does

63. Pléiade ed., p. 416. My italics.
64. Leleu, p. 391.

both, seizing the passive symbol of activity. If we read attentively, the text is eloquent: the glove is at first presented to us as *flesh;* it is Emma's whole body—the suppleness, the fleshiness at the base of the thumb, the light wrinkles (it has "lived"), a faint "odor di femina"; yes, Emma is all there, unwitting, brought down to the inferior status of an instrument. Gustave's imaginary sadism is satisfied: he has reduced a living woman to the status of a thing—she has been *delivered up.* Thus Léon punishes her for his own weakness and for the desire he feels to *deliver himself* to her. But instantly everything changes: the punishment heightens the very desire in whose name it claims to be exercised. The passive body he holds in his fist becomes an active body: under the eyes of its ravisher, buttoned, taut, it rears up; it becomes the analogue of the hand with its imperious stroking, "moving in a thousand indeterminate ways." The fair-haired boy is enraptured. What does he do? "He put it on the four fingers of his right hand." Let us say, without gratuitous punning—the word is familiar to Gustave, we've seen it come from his pen and surely it came to mind—that he *skewers* it four-fifths of the way. But this "possession" still remains imaginary. In a note attached to the plans for the book that Pommier has published, however, Flaubert writes "make it clear that he is bringing himself off with it."[65] This can be done in two different ways: either Léon penetrates the glove with his penis and then caresses it through the glove (which becomes the analogue of a yielding body), or he puts his fingers inside (a preliminary penetration but with no direct connection to the real orgasm—the insertion being for the author and his embodiment of the moment only a necessary condition of the pleasure he desires) and it becomes Emma's virile hand masturbating him, the slipping of the cool "yellow kidskin" along his member serves as analogue to the back-and-forth movement of strange fingers that conquer him and bring him to pleasure. The fetish is the female hand and the phallus merged: see how Léon sleeps with the glove "beneath his mouth," like a satisfied mistress kissing her lover's sex in gratitude. Here we are approaching Louise's famous slippers, which represented for Flaubert his mistress's embalmed virility and which he gladly used in his solitary diversions as a *transcendence object.* The slipper sums up and embodies the Muse's entire leg both as flesh and as propelling activity. Without any doubt he preferred this analogue of a "thousand indeterminate ways" to the real presence of his partner,

65. Jean Pommier and Gabrielle Leleu, *Nouvelle version de Madame Bovary* p. 63 (A).

who always disturbed his dreams. Louise was there, chastized, humiliated, reduced to the muteness of inanimate matter and at the same time active, devouring, but tractable. What pleasures he gives himself! And what perversity! A man uses in imagination an intimate article of feminine clothing the way a woman would use a dildo.

Flaubert's fetishism is the result and the summation of his sexual unrealizations, and these cannot be understood apart from the original derealization. His mother, male impersonator by imposture, woman by betrayal, constituted him such that he never stopped demanding from her a form of sexual retotalization that she had denied him from the cradle and subsequently revealed herself incapable *by nature* of giving him. He somehow feels that this gratification he demands cannot be realized at all since no one—man or woman—can give it to him. And because he nevertheless persists in demanding it (unable to desire anything else), he must postulate it *in its unreality,* not in spite of his mother but because of her. Love, like laughter, is a role he plays in front of the mirror or with a derealized instrument. And since his sexual activities have as their sole aim his realization as a carnal totality through a contradictory being who has no real existence, we must conclude that the child is committed to the imaginary to the extent that the movement of personalization compels him to realize the unrealizable—which necessarily leads him to unrealize reality.

From this point of view Flaubert's fetishism is open to a Freudian interpretation. The fetish functions as though it were at once the incarnation and the negation of the maternal phallus, except that the negation here is much stronger than it would be if he were born into a conjugal family since the *patriarchal* structure of the Flaubert group implies the wife's absolute submission to her husband. In any event, Gustave's fetishistic behavior is experienced—as Mannoni says so well—in the form of an "I know very well . . . but all the same . . ." The fetishistic object takes the place of the "all the same," which is the proper definition of an obstinate disqualification of the real and the deliberate placing of value on the imaginary. As for his relationship with the mirror, I would say that it serves him as an antagonistic reflection. We should understand that he does indeed continually reflect—he sees himself thinking, dreaming, desiring. But the reflection is generally a response to the other's aggression: challenged, I withdraw into myself in order to totalize myself against the other and dispute the vision he has of me. This is what I have called the reflection as accomplice because it can be opposed to the *alien look* only by adhering totally to what is reflected. Yet if it is true that the Flaubert parents, and by degrees all his friends, relentlessly challenged Gustave's image of himself, it is also true that he did not succeed in determining the object he was in their eyes; deprived in advance of the power to say yes or no, submissive, an accomplice to his executioners more than to himself, his reflection in the early years was merely a vague, sad estrangement that led him from amazement to daze without bringing him anything new.

We shall see later that, as it deepened, reflection would give him the means to *understand himself* better than most people do, though not better than those who *know themselves*. Moreover, he did not want deliverance because he loved his tormentors; he wanted to keep his wounds because he still hoped to be cured by the hands that made them: his wish was to find happiness in an excess of servitude. In this sense the mirror is more important for him than the reflexive movement; he seeks in the mirror *the object constituted by others*, not to dispute it but to reestablish it in its totality and identify with it. Yet this presupposes that he *might make himself other* even down to his gaze, since the other possesses him in the totalizing intuition of *sight* or *touch*. Thus both laughter and sexual excitement *fully* express the same enterprise on different planes: in his social being as in his sexual intimacy, he attempts to coincide with the other-being that others have given him, which implies that he *might make himself other* in front of his image, either by laughing at himself (identifying with the aggressor) or by desiring himself (identifying with the agent who constituted him); that is, either by becoming *his father* or *his mother*, since they and they alone know his being. And the passage from one identification to the other is made easier by the fact—taken up in the first part of this work—that he never consciously held his mother responsible for his constituted passivity and always considered the paternal curse to be the primary factor in his passivization. For this reason he has no difficulty moving from the laughter which is Achille-Cléophas's violation of his emotions to the excitation which is, he imagines, a rape of his secret femininity by a male (the practitioner-philosopher's sexual double). While dreaming of himself as a woman possessed by a man, however, he is unable to recognize his secret desire to be a passive man raped by a woman. In any event, this impossible doubling and the impossible reunification that must accompany it condemns him to be unrealized in order to be at all, that is, to pretend to be an imaginary being.

C. THE EPIC PERFORMANCE OF THE GIFT*

Gustave's relationship with his mother deprived him of affirmative power, tainted his relations to the word and to truth, destined him for sexual perversion; his relationship with his father made him lose his sense of reality. Besides Achille, who was never around, there was a fifth member of the family. She was four years old when he was seven; if she gave him the chance to love her—by which I mean a strong, simple, true affection—he might be saved. Let us see whether he was.

In a strongly integrated family, whatever the accidents of their birth, the children do not encounter each other by accident but as predestined: their feelings are anticipated, hypothesized in advance, by their differences in age and sex, their specific relationships with their parents, the prefabricated structures that form them and that each one knows in the other first. The earliest relations between Gustave and Caroline have no trace of contingency, unpredictability, freedom, that might guarantee—at least on Gustave's side—their sincerity and reality; they are preplanned by the Flaubert family's structure and history. Gustave might have been different if he had played alone in the little garden of the Hôtel-Dieu, or if two or three brothers close to him in age had shared his games. He had only one companion, three years his junior—chance and necessity comes first. It was no accident that the child had a sister—he himself was a girl *manqué*; when Mme Flaubert was carrying him in her belly, she thought she was carrying Caroline, and it was Caroline she wanted to bear. By having the impudence to be born masculine, Gustave was destined by his very gender to become the older brother of a little Caroline; indeed, Mme Flaubert pursued her enterprise, which as we know was aimed solely at reviving her own childhood. Even before Gustave was born, the little girl's name had already been chosen. The threat and the promise of a sister was contained in his organic structure, in his mother's devotion, through which the child discovered himself and was constituted; he was fashioned as the disappointing little male who would be given a younger sister preferred to him. Who knows whether, a little later, again disappointed by an infant who had the good taste to withdraw, the surgeon's wife did not drop some remarks suggesting the little boy's destiny as *future brother*. Whatever the case, he certainly knew himself

---

*"La geste du don." In what follows, Sartre plays on the different meanings of the term *la geste*—deed, exploit, legend, epic performance, even behavior. It is not always possible to render this term by a single English equivalent.—Trans.

as an *unloved-boy-to-be-followed-by-a-girl-whose-place-he-had-usurped*. We have found, I believe, the primary reason for his first personalizing option: already made passive by his mother's attentions, he wanted to take things to their logical conclusion and chose himself as a little girl in order to gain his mother's love. Such, I believe, is the element we were lacking in order to explain his sexual fantasies: he plays the woman desired by a man, unable to admit that he wants to be caressed by a woman, and this very demand masks the fundamental intention to be a girl adored by a mother. Thus from birth and doubtless *before*, little Caroline was a factor of unrealization for her brother.

After this, of course, Gustave's younger brother could have survived; if he died—unless it were by infantile depression[66]—his rapid disappearance *in relation to Gustave* was only an accident. But Gustave was born predestined, and, by a convergence of partly contingent circumstances, that predestination was realized. As a grandmother, Mme Flaubert told the story of her life to her granddaughter, who smugly reports her confidences to the effect that Caroline was indeed her favorite. If after 1846 Mme Flaubert devoted herself to her son Gustave, Mme Commanville implies that this was a last resort: "My mother's marriage and her death the following year, a little after my grandfather's, left my grandmother so grief-stricken that she was happy to have her son near her." The text is clear: it was the marriage and death of Caroline that plunged her mother into despair; Achille-Cléophas's death is mentioned only to date these painful events. In brief, the little girl arrived, much awaited by everyone, dreaded by her brother, for it was clear that she had come to claim the place he had occupied by mistake and the love Mme Flaubert had been holding in reserve for many years. This is how he *encountered* her, and as such he had to hate her or love her. His attitude toward her, whatever side he took, would lack spontaneity: it was not on the basis of the newborn's looks that he would decide but on the place reserved for her in the family hierarchy. There are now three children in the Flaubert family: the father prefers the eldest, the mother prefers the younger sister in advance. Gustave is no one's favorite. In some years, we know, he will

66. Certainly infant mortality was severe at that time. However, the death of those three young males has always seemed suspect to me. Without "mothering" an infant declines, in one month or three. Can we imagine that the virtuous and "glacial" Caroline *senior* was the cause of their precipitous retreat? Struck by the previous mournings, she would have made an effort in Gustave's case. It is to this he owed his life. Just barely. But afterward, she might have cried: "Another one!" and the newborn, in the face of such a welcome, would have beaten a quick retreat.

be jealous of Achille and wish his death. Will he be jealous of Caroline as well?

A young boy often dislikes his younger brother; with a younger sister such a dislike is rarer. In any event, Caroline's birth, so hoped for, could not be a surprise to her brother; it wasn't an *event* for the little boy, it was fate realized: "This had to happen!" Was he jealous, nevertheless, during the early years? We know nothing concrete, but it is possible that he was then wholly preoccupied with observing his father's love, no doubt realizing abstractly and without real anger that Caroline was the favorite; but as she *stole nothing* from him, if he held a grudge against anyone it was his mother. This would hardly have disposed the little boy, now an older brother, to feel spontaneous love for the intruder. From the beginning, however, he acted as though he adored her. To please his parents? Because it was expected of him? No doubt. But I see another reason too, a deeper one; since Mme Flaubert preferred Caroline, he would support this preference by disqualifying it: he would make his mother unworthy by loving the little girl more than she did and *against her*. This alone explains his effusions and his exaggerated displays of affection which were the admiration of the family. Sometimes these transports were too lavish, too public to be felt. Certainly he believed he loved Caroline, for the others said he did. But it was a minor belief, riddled with insincerity, to which he attached little importance.

When he is seven years old, everything unobtrusively shifts: the same caresses, the same kisses, but *now* the role he plays becomes essential *for him*. He needs to love his sister: "Separated by only three years, the two youngsters were scarcely ever apart; Gustave no sooner learned something than he repeated it to his sister; he made her his student, and one of his greatest pleasures was to introduce her to his first literary compositions."

Caroline Franklin Groult surveys these two childhoods rather hurriedly. It is clear, however, that the little illiterate who struggled in vain with his alphabet could not be the one who repeated what he had learned to his sister; for him to "introduce" her to his first literary compositions, a considerable amount of time would have to pass. It has been established that she took part in all the plays mounted "on the billiard table," but these performances did not begin, to be precise, until Gustave was eight years old. The relationship is rounded out, furthermore, by what Mme Franklin Groult tells us of her relations with her uncle. As daughter of the deceased Caroline, there is every indication—even her name—that Gustave and Mme Flaubert expected to see her mother revived in her: "My uncle immediately wanted to begin my education . . . As I grew older, the lessons became longer, more serious; he continued them until my marriage . . . One of his greatest pleasures was to entertain those around him. To cheer me up when I was ill and feeling sad, there was nothing he wouldn't do!" This unctuous and silly text is nevertheless significant. All the more so, perhaps, in that Caroline Franklin Groult is unaware of, or wishes to ignore, the fact that at first her uncle was indifferent toward her and, in the first years following his trip to the Orient, often irritated by her.[67] The uncle's attachment to his niece begins sometime later, from the time her intelligence was sufficiently developed for him to instruct her, amuse her, console her—in brief, for him to be bound to her by the daily ceremony of the *gift*. We have no doubt on this score: it was the big brother's gift to his little sister. We contend that he loved her from the time he could show her his generosity.

But where does this generosity come from? Haven't we established, to the contrary, that Gustave the vassal feels himself to be the object of his father's generosity? He receives it as his light and his nourishment, but his lord is the *agent* of the Flaubert history; characterized by passive activity, Gustave can only submit to the generosity; and, moreover, he is so made that he would like nothing better than to feel its effects, for it is what gives him his status and his reality. Vassal and woman in his dependence and passivity, he prefers obedience to authority. To decide, to act, to give—in short, to reign is the business of the lord; his is to fight sensual decomposition by offering to the master's male gaze the consenting unity of an abandoned femininity. Later he would dispute all authorities, though *verbally,* and he could not help resenting them for being disputable. All this is true, but before concluding let us retrace firsthand the history of the two children.

To begin with, let us note that their situation organizes itself spontaneously, and this is what governs it at the outset: when Gustave gives it a meaning, he will already have been drawn into it. The two children *play;* so we are already in the midst of unreality: there is no action here, only gesture. The difference in age only draws them closer; three years is nothing, especially when a brother nine years

---

67. The correspondence informs us that when he saw her again, on his return from Italy, he showed an almost malevolent coldness. And I will show how the fine scene in *Madame Bovary*—where Emma is seen as malicious, exasperated, pushing her daughter away with such force that she falls and hurts herself—is drawn, if not from a similar violence exercised by the uncle toward his niece, at least from a dream of violence which must often have been repeated.

older than the next child pushes the two younger ones into the same infantile behavior. The roles establish themselves within this unity. Caroline is the youngest, the weakest, and she is a girl. Here the Flaubert hierarchy intervenes, at least as Gustave represents it. He is a vassal, the object of his father's bounty—so be it. But all vassals have subvassals: in the unity of the little social cell, the paternal generosity is a *pneuma* that circulates and comes back again to the person from whom it emanates; Gustave renders to the paterfamilias some of the good done to him by bestowing it on his little sister. In this first moment Gustave himself is not the giver, he is just an intermediary; he transmits what he has received out of obedience and gratitude. There is nothing to decide, nothing to do: the bounty of the paterfamilias passes through him, animating him and giving him, through the efficacy of grace, the power to make Caroline happy. When the child pays attention to the little girl, he is no longer entirely an object, but he still does not attain the dignity of a subject; to transmit the gift is to enjoy it all over again. When his father takes him on his rounds in his carriage, Gustave tells Caroline what he saw, what happened; catching signs of interest on his sister's face, he extends his pleasure and endows it with value by sharing it with her. Nothing that happens to him is true before it is believed by another; hence, by listening to his words, Caroline confers truth. But this truth, let us not forget, appears only fleetingly, and ordinarily the pair moves in the reality of "let's pretend," or play.

Then Gustave falls from heaven, and the lord refuses his homage; the child is still a vassal since this is a fundamental intention of his personalization, but by pilfering the master he is metamorphosed into an imaginary vassal. Will he stop playing with Caroline? On the contrary. And if the game is modified, that is precisely why it becomes a necessity for him: his ludic behavior is paralyzed by an invisible urgency and, paradoxically, by a certain gravity that confines him to what is serious. What has happened? And here is what distresses him in the extreme—God has withdrawn from the world, generosity no longer exists anywhere. The golden age gives way to the age of iron: the disappearance of seigneurial love consigns to nonbeing the child's gratitude, consent, devotion—in brief, those things that were once his *real* but induced person. What is there to do but convince himself, against himself and everyone else, that generosity is not dead—and this is an impossibility unless he makes himself its depositary by playing the role of giver. He transmits the gift to his sister; he continues, but by convincing himself that he has exchanged his function of intermediary for the sovereign freedom of the lord. He will preserve his feudal universe by pushing to an extreme the perversion we have described above: he profits from the game in order to identify simultaneously with Achille-Cléophas and with Caroline. We might say that his unrealizing relationship with his reflection is bent to the breaking point; he makes himself the subject in imagination with the formal intention of becoming the object in the person of his little vassal. He takes up the torch of generosity in order to lavish on *himself* through Caroline everything he is now refused. This perversion, it will be pointed out, is quite common and found in all children who play with dolls; in fact such children usually identify with the mother, the young giant who washes, caresses, dresses, and undresses them, the doll—that is, themselves as pure objects of solicitude. Between the play-acted subject—which is the Other—and the already imaginary object with which Gustave identifies, the dialectical movement is complex: the grudges, the stirred desires, are satisfied by this far from innocent back-and-forth. I do not deny that Gustave *might have* treated Caroline like a doll when she was in the cradle.[68] But at the time of the Fall she was going on five years old; there was no longer any question of treating her that way. This vivid, conscious creature withheld *one* objective truth from Gustave. In other words, if he tried to see in her and maintain through her the object he was for others, the effort of unrealization was pushed to the limit; for now it was a matter of unrealizing a transcendence of which he became aware just as it surpassed him toward its own ends and installed him as objective reality in its own practical field. It was fitting, therefore, that he should act both *on himself*—in order to conceal Caroline's sovereignty—and *on his sister*—in order to lead her by suggestion to be affected by the docility of the reflection, all the while preserving enough independence for her to be conscious of the desires that he alone could satisfy. The enterprise, we see, is close to madness. It is proper to describe its motivations and development, for in still crude form it constitutes the model of all the relationships Gustave would establish throughout his life with those he took for his inferiors (in sex, age, talent or character, wealth, etc.).

What had he lost? The happiness of being a loved object, confidence in himself—which his mother did not know how to give him but which had just been born in the warmth of paternal love—and, fi-

---

68. At the time this might have been veiled revenge; by a reversal of the movement we have just described, he could have tried to transform the intruder into a *thing*, human only in appearance.

nally, reality. The game of generosity had to make up for this triple deficit. He had the vague feeling that he would achieve it if he could outwit his younger sister: let her believe she is a loved object, let her respond to his gifts with a permanent "femage," [69] and *in order to accept* this homage let him evoke in her the very devotion he was making a show of only yesterday, which his father, by an inexplicable rejection, struck with unreality. Suddenly we have the little feudal world restored, with Gustave both lord *for* Caroline and, *as* Caroline, vassal. The first relationship, however, is only the means of obtaining the second; thus, in his sexual relationships Gustave made himself virile only in order to experience himself as female in his partner or, after coitus, in her embrace. The lord remains the Other: Gustave is not the generous, dominating male, nor does he truly wish to be, but he compels himself to play the role. He can *do* an agent, not become one; his constituted passivity balks at that. Thus the subject dwelling within him is not himself but a secret being, impenetrable, absent, who takes shape through his gestures without ceasing to be a stranger to him, as Hamlet is to Kean. Sometimes he gets caught up in a vicious circle which partially conceals from him the unreality of his "show." He exerts himself to divert his sister; there's nothing he won't do to "amuse" her, to "console" her. It is nothing to expend himself from morning to night to coax a happy smile from her lips. He plays at giving, but by playing he gives. How could he recognize himself in this activity? Yet he makes himself generous so that generosity should exist somewhere in the world and not in order to change his constitution. We might see here a first appearance of what we will later describe as the autistic aspect of Gustave's thought: he *is* the generosity-subject because he wants to make an object of it.

What keeps him, moreover, from being entirely deluded and confusing his epic performance with an act is that epic performance, which is basically a means, also seems to be his proper end. We can be certain that the child outdid the gift out of resentment and attempted, by pushing his *representation* to the extreme, to contest the paternal attitude, Achille-Cléophas's caprice or hardness, in the name of an archetype revealed by his gesture—the total and unlimited gift of the self. Gustave cannot in any case doubt that he is *playacting:* he displays himself as the *good* lord in order to testify before heaven—without breathing a word and solely by his conduct—that the paterfamilias is a bad master.

69. Sartre's punning feminization of "homage."—Trans.

Still, his basic aim is to identify with Caroline; just as Mme Flaubert had a daughter in order to relive her own deprived childhood successfully through that daughter, so Gustave plies his younger sister with happiness in order to become through her the happy and satisfied vassal he never entirely was. The little boy had earlier experienced the humble, grateful tenderness Caroline *must* have expressed to him: now it rang false because he had been rejected; the proof that it existed, however, and depended on the Other in order to be real, that is, on his sister, rang true. When his sister blushed with pleasure and showed him her gratitude, he rediscovered the spontaneity that had been spoiled in him, and it was all the more convincing as she offered it to him peremptorily, quite independently, with the consistency of something existing *outside:* when the little girl ran and threw herself into his arms, he saw himself as he was only yesterday in the eyes of an indulgent father. Besides, he was seeking less to identify with Caroline than to identify her with himself, trying to capture his own immediate pleasure by seizing the other's concrete subjectivity. For this purpose the behavior is adequate; Gustave sketches the little girl's ravishing smile the moment he sees it; then it seems to him that he is seeing himself and feeling himself smiling simultaneously. Not, however, the way it happens when he is admiring himself in the mirror— in this case the muscular contraction is primary, the reflection can only obey; which is obvious since he is seeking the exact externalization of his emotion. But if he wants to reenter himself in the form of Caroline, he achieves it by opposite means: the visible commands and the zygomatic muscles follow. This order of succession probably suits him better; as his being is outside him, the captive of others, he is first able to see the indisputable and luminous object, *his* soul, in his sister's features. What joy to master it and feel it, fascinated, reproduced on his own face! It is not only that his rediscovered vassalage overwhelms him, it is also that the happiness he feels is in proportion to the happiness he gives Caroline.

All would be for the best if there were two of them, or, rather, if the duality that allowed Gustave to be generous did not also have the effect of making him more unreal. The primary consequence of the little boy's enterprise was to make him dependent on his sister. She was his truth, just as the Hegelian slave is the truth of his master or, more precisely, as the vassal is the truth of his lord and, better still, as the audience each evening is the truth of the actor. It isn't enough to lavish his gifts—she must still accept them. When she looks at him with what he takes for adoring submission, Gustave is compelled to think that she is *instituting* him as her lord; hasn't he done everything to persuade her that his untiring generosity ought to be repaid with unlimited devotion? The moment he tries to revive in her the child he was, Caroline repulses him by her very gratitude, *recognizing* in him the master he must represent, the *alien-subject* he neither can nor wants to be except in imagination, and then purely as a means of recovering through her his lost vassalage. And, in a way, this is what he wants. But he does not understand the contradiction at the heart of his project: if he can make his sister a true subject, her expressions of emotion and her love will go to a true sovereign. We can imagine Kean's stupefaction and discomfort if the audience, instead of being unrealized with him in an imaginary Elsinore, had suddenly taken him for Hamlet himself and refused to think otherwise. Farewell glory, farewell genius; he would be nothing but a Triplepatte who can't make up his mind to kill his stepfather. Gustave's problem is even more serious, since his ludic relationship with his sister was intentionally established and integrated into the movement of his personalization. Yet here he is, forced to live out this dilemma but unable to formulate it. Either he protests that the *alien-subject* is merely an imitated character—and in this case he confesses his imposture and as a false lord has a right only to imaginary vassals (if Caroline is truly a vassal, she must be the vassal of someone he is aping, the paterfamilias). Or else, as usual, he is fascinated by the idea that the other is made by him and, taken up by the game, demands that his sister's love should be addressed to him, Gustave, the younger son whose younger sister she is—and then how could this superfluous child, convinced that he matters to no one, fail to be amazed by the total trust he has sown in this heart that beats only for him? Then he must *in fact* be the dominating agent she loves. Yet there is nothing in the world Gustave dreads as much; this child who is inhabited, haunted, falsified by others, has neither the means nor the desire to escape them; passive and submissive as much as he is spiteful, if he could make a wish it would be that his own conduct might be determined by the depth of traditions, by cyclical time—in brief, by the density of being, of the past. Rejecting both the atomized motives of sensualism and the transcendent ends of revolt, he desires that his acts, born before his own birth, modeled patiently by history, might preserve through him the opacity of terrestrial events inscribed in objectivity. If generosity, the embodiment of freedom, should by some sudden mutation become his fundamental determination, the universe would be emptied of its substance: things, heavy poetic presences, instead of provoking his lusts would be transformed before his eyes into material to be handled; the quietism of pouting, the clammy warmth of passive recriminations would give way to the spirit of enterprise, to responsibilities. To be lord, Gustave would have to make himself his own heaven, enter the realm of unbearable solitude without support, without protection, which is sovereignty conscious of itself.

It goes without saying that the child does not formulate this train of thought and cannot even think it; he feels it as a perpetual malaise. Sometimes the game of the gift disgusts him without his knowing why—he is sickened by his imposture—and sometimes he continues to play it out of resignation—he is playing a role, all right, but it is his only means of inspiring Caroline with a vassal's enthusiasm. What does it matter if the enthusiasm is not addressed to him? The important thing is that he can internalize it in order to revive his own vassalage. In the overexcitement of the drama, illusion sometimes "takes hold," though never for long. Fear follows joy, the mirage disappears, and Gustave finds once again the brackish taste of his life and the growing feeling of unreality.

In Caroline's relationship with the person she loves, the two terms are not homogeneous: one is quite real, the other imaginary. If she experiences the happiness of vassalage, she makes it *her own happiness,* and consequently this happiness as an internalized determination is exposed as experienced by *another ipseity;* therefore it is self-enclosed and inaccessible to the young boy who claims it. Inasmuch as he perceives her, Gustave can transform the little girl into a quasi-imaginary object; he can see his own smile coming toward him. As a subject—that is, as the totalizing and centripetal meaning of this smile—she escapes him, he must aspire to her through an empty intention. And if he aspires to make his sister's *experience* his own, it will be *as an image* and at the price of almost unbearable tension, by constituting his sister's body and her actions as the analogue of his own subjectivity. Thus by an exhausting effort, the child sees his ego (one pole of the psyche, quasi object) and his *exis* coming toward him—life fulfilled, devotion—touched with nonbeing, just as imaginary experience is nonexperience conscious of being such. In other words, he sees himself constrained to imagine his own subjectivity instead of feeling it. A double failure: the unreal lord is the unreal vassal in his sister. False object for Caroline, false subject in her, Gustave feels doubly unreal: sent from one subjectivity to the other, this back-and-forth is all the more painful for him as his vassal's reality exposes his own unreality; to the extent that he intentionally provokes a *truly felt* happiness in his sister, he is derealized and exiled. The *true* love she bears him—and which he is forced to *envy her*—reveals to him his double unreality as beloved lord and loving vassal.

Gustave's derealization goes still further: in fact he *does not see* this sister made vassal, he *imagines* her. First of all, his parents take it upon themselves to satisfy Caroline's true needs: reproduction and the safeguarding of life are the true gifts of love. Suddenly Gustave's solicitude is ineffectual, transformed into a gesture. The little busybody was an actress. If the little girl can tackle that obstacle alone, does she really need a brother's help? The hand that rushes to her aid can only be in the way when the child, solemn and determined, practices walking and climbing on her own. In this case Gustave's only goal is to appear before a select audience—his parents and God—and to enjoin them to recognize his devotion and hence his reality. But he cannot fail to recognize that he is irritating or to feel the insubstantiality of his pseudogenerosity.

In the early years, however, the transformation of his acts into gestures was not so obvious; in spite of the parents' precautions and their tendency to overprotect, the brother's supervision could hardly have been considered useless. Who knows if his vigilance did not prevent falls, injuries? This little mountain dweller who battled eagles really did risk his life and really did save his sister's. Who knows if he did not irritate the little girl every morning with his useless precautions, and if his act was not simply a lucky gesture? On the other hand, who can say that in similar circumstances Gustave was not led through his dramatizing to give proof of real courage? Unfortunately, there were no eagles in the hospital garden. But he could always dream that one would come, or that his vigilance saved the little girl daily from an unsuspected but imminent death; in short, Gustave could tell himself that he too was continually creating his sister, or at least that he was reproducing her life.

But the years worked against him. As time went by, Caroline's character asserted itself. And she hardly resembled her brother—she was no wishful vassal. From before birth she was *awaited*, and knew it; her mother, out of her own desperate love, gave her that royal gift, confidence in herself. Caroline received all the Flaubert qualities, owing them not to heredity but to a happy infancy; she had her own proud reserve; knew how to affirm, to deny, to demand; and knew the difference between belief and objective certainty—it is inconceivable that she could ever be dependent on others. In brief, no one could have been less disposed to practice "the fanaticism of man for man." There was no emptiness in her to fill nor helplessness for which to compensate—that was Gustave's penury; she was formed by abundance. No doubt she was grateful to her brother for amusing her; she was pleased to share his games, to throw herself into his arms, breathless and enchanted—she loved him; but Gustave's tenderness did not make her forget her solid and deep attachment to her mother. The affection he showed her was a delicious luxury, which she would not give up for anything in the world but didn't *need*. Gustave had to muster all his imagination and bad faith to see signs of vassalage in her gratitude. This explains his crushing solicitude: he is everywhere at once; he surrounds her, besieges her, and behaves altogether "excessively," to the point that the little girl is at times discomfited. Not that he ever bores her; he exhausts her and sometimes irritates her. Two letters, written years later, bear witness to this. One is from Gustave—he is in Paris and promises on his return to smother his sister with kisses. She will protest, smiling, and push him away, and Mme Flaubert will intervene: "Oh, leave the little girl alone!" We understand that he is describing a future scene that has occurred frequently in the family past. The other letter is from Caroline herself: she openly acknowledges that her brother is sometimes too much of a good thing "for us," and we can assume that she is thinking especially of her parents. The fact is that she takes their side. These two indications, late as they are, evidently refer to rituals that were rooted in their common childhood. In order to escape the disappointment that continually threatened him, Gustave was overdoing it with Caroline.

At the time of the Fall, the assimilation of physical skills has already given the little girl her physical autonomy; and her lively mind allows her quickly to learn everything her older brother knows and sometimes even what he does not know. The boy can no longer even pretend that his generosity is a response to her need. The moment Gustave decides to exaggerate his eagerness to hide its insincerity, he finds himself driven by the independence of this decisive young person to seek another terrain for his epic performance. He has no choice: since he is generous only in imagination, he must assume the imaginary and make it a gift to his sister. He will be Caroline's jester, he will tell her stories, amuse her with his clowning, and show her the grimaces he previously reserved for his mirror. A capital reversal. In a sense his new gesture is closer than the old to a kind of praxis: its effectiveness is undeniable since it brings such joy to the spectator. In the gloomy old hospital, the only thing a passionate but somber mother and an overworked father could not give their child was gaiety. Gustave offers this to Caroline. It is a considerable gift and certainly a useful one; no doubt it allowed the little girl to live in these sad surroundings without a change in her constituted character. But the poor boy *does not have* the gaiety he gives her: so he must invent it. At the end of the process, a sad child, in order to remain faithful to his imaginary generosity, must unrealize himself as an extravagantly cheerful young man. The time is not far off when he will go on stage; by the decisive assumption of unreality he has already transformed his sister into an audience and is giving his own performance. The gap widens: previously, generosity alone was a role; to call forth Caroline's gratitude, Gustave tried to accomplish real acts; reality—a highway to be crossed, a ditch to be jumped, etc.—appeared to be a necessary mediation between the lord and his vassal, for the real made an object of the fraternal gift. When the enterprise is revealed as a *gesture*, the world is no longer an indispensable intermediary; Gustave can no longer *do* anything for his sister or give her anything *except* the imaginary; he conjures himself away in front of the little girl so that a dramatic character might be born from his suicide. Here the unreal is multiplied by itself: in order to make an appearance of generosity evoke an appearance of vassalage, the child deliberately makes himself into *an image.* The faked gift of the real becomes the gift of the self, and this is both a gift of nothing—pure appearance—and the sacrifice of the gift giver to nothingness (he succeeds in becoming appearance). Caroline's laughter is certainly real. But the fact is that the two children are separated by imaginary footlights. Earlier, when they played store and so forth, they were unrealized together and reciprocally; now the reciprocal relationship is broken, and Gustave alone transforms himself into a character. It is an invitation to travel with him, of course; the goal is that Caroline, the spectator, should unrealize herself by adopting an unreal belief in his performance. But apart from the fact that these two "flights into the imaginary" are unequal in degree (Gustave is entirely consumed by appearance; his sister limits herself to "believing without believing" in the proposed image), each takes place in solitude. Gustave the generous separates himself from his sister to the very extent that he makes her the absolute Other, the judge who will decide whether the little performer has succeeded in his enterprise. In this sense he makes her play the role of paterfamilias, but *in reverse:* the medical director's laughter exposed his younger son as a bad actor; Caroline's laughter tells her brother that he is a good actor. But if in one case the child dreaded the father's mirth and in the other he solicits his sister's, he is nonetheless offering himself to the little girl as he

81

did to the cruel father, putting himself in her hands, awaiting her verdict; with the consequence that he depends on the Other even now in his escape beyond the real. This continuing dependency could have been anticipated, moreover. In the first phase of his personalization, defending himself against the charge that he is expressing feelings he doesn't have, he seeks to recuperate his reality but succeeds only in becoming more unreal; in the second phase, the personalizing revolution leads him to internalize his permanent derealization; in the third and last phase, he assumes it. But immediately he needs an Other to assure him that *objectively*, in himself,[70] he *is* the appearance he wishes to be. Unfortunately for him, the two functions he assigns to Caroline are incompatible; she cannot be both her brother's judge and his vassal.

Here the operation is pursued on three levels of unreality, since the generous lord transforms himself into a clown in order to be reunited with his lost vassalage in another—in whom he is increasingly unsure he really finds himself. As a result, the least insincere moment becomes the moment of generosity: pretending to act was the primary lie from which all others followed; as he is no longer acting except to playact and gives of himself unstintingly, there is something like truth in his behavior. Still, he treats his sister *as a means* and not an end because it is himself he wants to fulfill through her. But he has no illusions about it; for throughout his life he will conceive of the generous act in two ways, which may seem opposed to each other but are complementary for him. On the one hand, the production of the imaginary seems to him to be the absolute gift (even if, as we shall see, it is a poisoned gift); this feeling is one of the factors in his *personalization as artist*. On the other, he quickly denounces the falsity at the source of the generous gesture. In 1837 he writes to Ernest:

Since you and Alfred are no longer with me, I am increasingly inclined to analyze myself and others. I dissect endlessly; this amuses me, and when at last I have discovered the rottenness in something previously thought to be pure and the gangrene beneath the veneer of beauty, I throw back my head and laugh. Well then, I have arrived at the firm conviction that vanity is at the basis of everything, and that what we call conscience is merely inner vanity. Yes, when you give alms, you may be moved by an impulse of sympathy, pity, a horror of ugliness and suffering, even egotism; but more than all that, you do it so as to be able to say: I am

70. I have shown that for Gustave the *in-itself* and the *for-others* are confused, or, rather, that the latter is the sign of the former.

doing good, there aren't many like me, I am better than others—to be able to regard yourself as more tender-hearted, at last to have a sense of self-esteem, which you prefer to all other kinds . . . This theory seems cruel to you, and it even makes me uncomfortable. At first it seemed false, but on closer inspection I have the feeling it is true.

Alms—an example chosen for its very banality—sums up and conceals all the actions Gustave has in mind, in other words, the practice of the Gift. Reflection, he tells us, quickly reveals that generosity is a performance organized by pride; it is only an appearance, a gesture, since the motivations for the gift are quite different from those publicly proclaimed. We act out this farce in order to fool ourselves and gain "self-esteem." In short, everything is an illusion here, including pride in self—the only kind that would count, since it doesn't come from others, if only it were possible. And what is this arrogant postulation of Gustave's if not the humble, legitimate desire to feel that he is quite real, that he truly exists? Humble and legitimate, but futile: everything the child undertakes so as to satisfy that desire is condemned in advance to being only appearance. To sum it up: generosity is but an illusion; generosity consists of sacrificing oneself in order to make the other enter the world of illusions. In Flaubert's eyes, these two maxims constitute the two terms of a false antinomy. We shall see later how he manages to resolve their apparent contradiction; I mention them here because they show that as Gustave was improvising his role as Caroline's jester, he was also conscious of sinking into the solitude of unreality.

A final question: *Who* is acting? Who is the character he originally acts out in order to amuse his sister? If we could provide an answer, we would know more about Gustave's early years. But think as we may, the information is lacking. We know only that the young boy later did not mind going on stage, pushing certain recognized features of his character to the point of caricature, playing the *idiot* because he surmised or believed he surmised that he was taken for one, exaggerating his strength or bulk to epic proportions, forcing the generosity he wanted to display until it was transformed into an unbearable exuberance. Likewise, one of his pleasures was to imitate characters—real or invented—who were not himself: Papa Couilléres, the journalist of Nevers, the Garçon. Which did he choose to do at the age of seven for Caroline's amusement? He chose to play the role of Gustave Flaubert or some strange character. To tell the truth, the two options would have to be rigorously defined in order to be set against each other. And even then their opposition is more apparent than real, for you can play the *other* and put *yourself* inside the character as well—isn't this what Gustave does as storyteller and novelist? At first, however, nothing was clearly defined; the two attitudes interpenetrated, and we can imagine that he passed from himself to the other and from the other to himself with an indifference all the greater since he was himself another—the other that others saw. We are saying, in effect, that in these early years the personalizing revolution, through a process of twinning, produced both the character and the person, and that both were equally characterized by a structure of unreality. Gustave, consequently, would never know for certain whether he was *living* the one or *playing* the other. This observation will soon allow us to discover the unity of Flaubert's unrealizing behavior, that is, the meaning of his personalization.

When the games are finished at twilight, this overexcited child in the grip of his imaginary ego once again feels saturated with himself; he wants to forget his dramatizations and become real. Yet it is time for dinner with the family. Simply by his presence, Dr. Flaubert transforms the extravagant lord into the sham vassal; every evening Gustave catches himself playing what he feels—and doing it badly. A curious actor, extremely bad at his real role, when he reveals his loves and his sorrows, excellent at "counter-roles" and "composition." In the garden, the audience is "with him." The contrast between his success outside and his failures inside among the family serves only to increase the gulf that separates him from others. It seems false to cry out when he is himself; yet he is convincing, applauded, when he passes for the opposite of what he is. So it is not surprising that in the movement of his personalization he comes to reject his experience lived clandestinely and to prefer a profitable insincerity. And Caroline's credulity leads him in dizzying moments almost to identify with his character. Noncommunication has caused his unhappiness: though this is not the obstacle, he assumes it is and no longer communicates anything of his life to anyone, except in the domain of unreality. Thus when at the age of seven he gives himself a fictive personality—which he borrows from his father—it determines his future relations with the colleagues, friends, and mistresses he will subsequently meet, with the exception of Alfred, whose vassal he will become and whom he will love wholeheartedly and quite sincerely. This is not the time to analyze his relations with Chevalier, Maxime, and Bouilhet—we shall return to these. Since we aim to bring this work only up to 1857, however, we shall have no chance later to retrace the history of his last friendship. Yet no other is more eloquent or more revealing of the relationship between the imaginary and the real in Flaubert's emotional life. I therefore give an account of that friendship here, just after the account of his "childish loves."

Edmond Laporte, Gustave's neighbor, was ten years his junior. Formerly a medical student, he left Paris, where he was living, to manage a lace factory at Grand-Couronne, near Croisset. The two men met in 1866. Tall, with light eyes, Laporte bore a slight resemblance to Bouilhet, and to Flaubert himself—he was immediately pleasing. But it was after the death of the Alter Ego (Bouilhet) and the war of 1870 that they developed a more intimate relationship. Laporte showed himself to be infinitely obliging, plied Gustave with gifts, and had the particular virtue of admiring Gustave more than Bouilhet himself had done—that is, unconditionally. Flaubert played the role of the generous lord, accepting Laporte's homage and signing himself "Your Giant." The bond of vassalage was already strongly marked by this designation. But we must read the correspondence,[71] these few lines, for example, addressed to Caroline: "No doubt you have seen the good Laporte and he will have told you his sad affairs. *They broke my heart!* The poor boy put it so delicately after telling me about them: 'This is one more connection between the two of us.' As if he were content with his ruin because it makes him like me!"

The "good" Laporte, like Louis, is a "poor boy." We have learned to recognize this somewhat condescending benevolence. But Laporte's "delicate" remark surprises us less than Flaubert's commentary; after all, the phrase itself is rather banal. We do not know how Laporte said it. But here, stripped down, reduced to its pure meaning, it seems a particular "kindness." Laporte, a little embarrassed to speak about himself—although he had underwritten certain of Commanville's debts which had fallen due and might have feared that Gustave saw in his remarks an allusion to the service rendered—cuts things short and says quite amiably, "This is one more connection between the two of us." All told, it is a small consolation and rather melancholy. It can also be seen as an excuse: "I know—we are in the same boat." In any case, the deeper intention is to cut short the discussion, for the remark is made *after* Laporte had told of his sad affairs. Not to complain to his Giant, not to trouble him, not to arouse his compassion. What is

71. The complete letters to Laporte are found in the last volumes of the *Supplément à la Correspondance*.

astonishing is that Gustave seizes on his words, exaggerates their zeal, pushes their meaning to an extreme: Laporte's simple aim was to identify with the lord; misfortune delights him because it accelerates the process of identification and he would even accept martyrdom and death, that is, the suppression of his inessential being, if in so doing he could become Gustave. We know rather little about Laporte; perhaps, after all, he did love Gustave that much. Not quite, however, since he would not allow himself to be exploited by the Commanvilles. In any case, it is Gustave who concerns us—and his promptness in inventing or recognizing the behavior of vassalage. He finds Laporte's words "delicate," he savors them—this is how he wants Laporte to be. Furthermore, this is how he describes him. Indeed, at the time of their quarrel, Commanville "kept repeating that . . . if [Laporte] had given his signature, it was in order to become more intimately involved in Flaubert's life."[72] Caroline's husband did not come to this interpretation by himself; it translates, and rather ignobly, Gustave's own opinion. In the first place, it is quite true—and this is all to Laporte's credit—that Laporte took on these commitments in order to render service to his Giant. But for Commanville to see in it the intention of becoming "more intimately involved" in his uncle's life, he would have had to overhear and misunderstand Gustave's own comments. Flaubert certainly did not present Laporte's act as a service freely rendered by an equal to his equal; he saw it as a result of feudal devotion. Not out of ingratitude, surely, but because he placed all generosity on the side of the lord. The vassal gives his goods, occasionally even his life, but out of love, in that enthusiasm which leads him to consider himself inessential in the face of his master and to destroy himself, if need be, in order to diminish the distance between them and facilitate the process of identification. Gustave explained Laporte's conduct by a permanent desire to be closer to his Giant, more intimate, and to live only for him and through him. Commanville translated this into his own language—that of self-interest—and of course the motive became absurd. What self-interest would have impelled Laporte to become more intimately involved in the life of a man who was gloomy, prematurely old, and financially ruined? And weren't the editors of the *Correspondance* (the Supplément) right to note: "Laporte could have replied that he had already been an intimate friend of the writer for ten years when Commanville's unexpected setback occurred."?[73] No; Laporte's conduct is explained by his friendship for

72. Note to letter of 28 September 1879, *Correspondance, Supplément*.
73. Ibid.

Flaubert, which he undoubtedly entered full of admiration but at the same time with a deep and accurate knowledge of Gustave's character.[74] Refracted through the feudal lens, his conduct becomes an objective and quasi-institutional bond, which, refracted in turn through the Commanville lens, absurdly appears to be a self-interested tactic based on calculation. It must be added that "poor Commanville" had the misfortune to be vain. Back on his feet after his "setback," he did not want to be indebted to anyone and thus forced to recognize his own incapacities and the fact that only the support of friends was preventing his collapse. Flaubert could *accept* the services Laporte rendered to him because they were acts of love. Commanville was certainly not a master; if he accepted the support of his friends, he *had* to attribute it to generosity (which would have been intolerable) or calculation. He opted for the second solution, basing his conclusions on anecdotes and comments of Flaubert's which had quite another meaning.

Indeed, Flaubert did not stop *demanding* things of Laporte without ever feeling *indebted*. We need only leaf through his correspondence to measure the number and extent of the tasks he imposed on "his old rock,"[75] his "collabo." Laporte arranged notes for Gustave, went off in quest of information, which he organized and submitted. He put Gustave in contact with specialists who apprised him of certain technical details. He ran Flaubert's errands, went to visit friends in Rouen who hadn't been heard from; Flaubert made him sit on the Louis Bouilhet committee so that the "old rock" could serve as his factotum and ensure good relations with the municipality. Laporte was the one who went to meet him at the end of his stay in Switzerland and took him back to Croisset; again, it was Laporte who came to sleep at Croisset when Gustave broke his leg, who cared for him and served as his secretary, and whose zeal earned him the title "sister of mercy."[76]

74. See his answer to Gustave of 30 September 1879, ibid.
75. This epithet shows clearly that Gustave meant to replace the dead Bouilhet with Laporte, for it was what he used to call Louis.
76. See, for example, 27 October 1874: "The doctor's [Devoayes] notes are excellent. I am asking him for more of this sort." February 1875: "Thanks for the little book, dear friend." March 1875: "If you have a moment . . . go to Brière's." 16 May 1875 (for his dog Julio): "Send me right away by Express the magic soapwart you promised your Excellency." July 1876: "Bring me your warblers." 26 September 1876: "See if you can find something in Arago's *Astronomie populaire* that might be of use to me." 16 January 1877 (to Commanville): "Figure out with Laporte if there is not something to be done." January 1877: "I await my Bob . . . all the more because I shall need him Friday morning for the Bouilhet business." 27 January 1877 (Laporte has lent Flaubert an anatomical piece that can be taken apart): "I commission you to dispatch to me *illico* your star-performing flunky, whose prize will be . . . your heart." The same day (concerning Commanville):

The Giant does not refrain at the time from making old "Bob" act to obtain an order for Caroline[77] or to clear up his own affairs. "Go see! Go then and see!" is the refrain. Reading the letters I cite in the notes—and many others—we find that the unilateral relationship of vassalage is evidenced by the constant and deliberate use of the *imperative.* A letter to Laporte is an order. We know, of course, that Flaubert readily employed the imperative with *everyone* (including, at

---

"I would like to talk *seriously* with you for an hour as *quickly* as possible." 29 March 1877 (again, concerning Commanville): "As for your friends in Paris, they should take the bull by the horns. Time flies! Time flies!" 11 April 1877: "If you pass by rue la Carrettes, 178 [the Dieusq residence], go in and find out what it [Philippe the Perfect's silence] means, and I authorize you, if he is not dead or ill, to chew him out for me." 13 June 1877: "I did have some jobs in mind for you, since you ask me, but the books would be lacking. You would have to get me a whole library . . . When you can let me have your Raspail and one of his *Manuels de la Santé,* send it to me." 5 August 1877: "Let the Asiatic [Laporte's nickname] offer himself to the exploitations of his Vitellius." 11 September 1877: "Have you finished working on the notes on agriculture and medicine? If you have, bring me all the papers." 1 December 1877: "The Asiatic must continue to hack away at the notes. I would like to keep you at your work." March 1878: "From now on, send me a list of reference works." May 1878: "Try to come to Croisset next Monday for dinner and the night, and bring all your notes on the Crown." July 1878: "Give me the news about Guy." Wednesday, July 1878: "Have you thought about the order for the copy of Corneille?" July 1878: "Would you mind stopping at Charpentier's [Flaubert's publisher] and telling him this for me . . ." 24 September 1878: "Bring me back two packets of tobacco from Civette at twelve francs." 28 December: "Bring me *Lefèvre et Nourrisson* on Wednesday." 4 February 1879: "If Cordier is in Rouen, you will be good enough to pay him a visit." 30 March 1879: "When you go to the library on Tuesday, *first,* get me a copy of *Ars Magna Lucis,* etc. . . . Its weight and thickness will make you look very impressive . . . To lessen your inconvenience, take my two straps to . . . quai de Havre, 7. Second, while you are at the library, find me in the 1853 issue of *l'Illustration* a picture . . . Since you cannot check out the volume, write me a description of the aforesaid drawing." 25 April 1879: "I was saying yesterday that some of the county councilmen had proposed giving me a supper in honor of Sarah Bernhardt, and someone denied it. Nothing is more insufferable than this kind of skepticism! When I state a fact, I like people at least to pretend to believe me, and I intend, my dear Bob, to prove it! Therefore, tell me *the names* of our *men-about-town* (with details) so that I can shut their traps." 27 April 1879: "Will I be angry with Tourgueneff? Four times in the past eight days he has not spoken to me . . . Do you want to come this evening and calm me down by eating the dinner prepared for that cossack?" 8 May 1879: "Go then and see Guy at his ministry and try to get some news of my business." 10 May 1879 (concerning a letter with an illegible signature to the effect that he would be offered a place at Mazarine): "Try to clear this up for me and see Guy." 11 May (concerning the same business): "Go see [Guy] today in his office and send me clarifications . . . You can go thank About for me and tell him that . . . ," etc. July 1879: "Regarding the book by *Vivier,* when you are in Paris again, take a look at that and buy it for me." All citations from *Correspondance, Supplément,* vol. 3.

Also found in their correspondence are allusions to numerous favors Flaubert asked of Laporte in person.

77. Pierre Corneille's house was being restored as a museum which was to be graced with a portrait of the poet. Madame Commanville wanted the commission. Laporte had been charged with reporting to the town council.

times, those of whom he was in awe) and that these edicts launched from the heights of his solitary room often served to mask his helplessness. But what is of primary significance for our purposes is that Gustave should have chosen the command as a quasi-universal type of relationship, which in his case remains the *unreal* formulation of a question, a request, a suggestion, or a piece of advice. When alone, he plays the great lord, without illusions but also without respite. He *knows*, in effect, the real relations that bind him to this or that correspondent; furthermore, he is artful enough to introduce his "orders" rather skillfully so as not to shock, so that they can be seen as an expression—perhaps too vivid an expression—of deep interest, true solicitude.

In his relations with Laporte, to the contrary, the command is abrupt, brutal. There is no palliative; Gustave does not bother to lead up to the command or offer compensation. When he charges his "Bob" with a frequently tedious commission, he never tempers his orders with "please" or "I beg you." [78] Better yet, he is so at ease in the role of lord that he invites Laporte to dinner most often in the form of an imperative or even a threat. I offer here a few examples taken at random:

1 March 1876: "I am waiting for you. This is all I have to say." 6 April 1876: "I am counting on you toward the end of next week, all right?" 17 July 1876: "I am expecting you on Thursday at eleven o'clock for lunch. *It's agreed*, isn't it?" January 1877: "Mme Régnier comes tomorrow at eleven o'clock. Therefore I am expecting my Bob tomorrow evening at 6:30, all the more as I will need him Friday morning for the Louis Bouilhet business." 20 August 1877: "You probably received . . . a letter from your Giant advising you to come to lunch tomorrow, Tuesday? . . . I am leaving on Thursday, so don't forget! . . . Please answer immediately, and in any case by the 9:30 boat tomorrow." 13 October 1877: "Yes, tomorrow at 6:30. But I am warning you that with a morning departure you must take precautions in advance, because this time *it would be unpleasant!* You are warned, my good man." July 1878: "You annoyed me by not coming on Monday as you had promised . . . From now on, then, choose your day and come as soon as possible." 15 August 1878: "This is what you must do, my good man. You will come Saturday by the seven o'clock boat and you will not leave until Monday . . . No excuses! You have nothing at all to do. A good grubbing and gossip session with your Giant will do you

78. Except in his two last letters. We shall come to these.

good. In other words, 'I would find it unpleasant [*môvoise*].'"[79] 14 January 1879: "Make arrangements to devote *all of Sunday* to me until Monday morning. Come on, don't play hard to get." 20 January: "Don't forget, my good fellow, that *I demand* your presence *next Saturday*."

In exchange for such devotion, what does the generous lord give in return? What he has always given his vassals: his admirable person, whose generosity basically consists of his existence. During their journey in 1874, he would play the Garçon for Laporte the way he clowned as a child to amuse Caroline.[80] This is how he invades him, dominates him, wins him over, overwhelms him with his forced, raucous laughter. Laporte presents him with a dog, with two Chinese monsters in Ming porcelain. In return, Flaubert offers him the medallion of Bouilhet by Carrier-Bolleuse. This is decorating him with the Order of the Alter Ego. A little later, Gustave makes him a gift of *his body of glory*, the manuscript of *Trois Contes* (2 April 1877) with this dedication: "You have seen me write these lines, my dear fellow. Accept them and let them remind you of your Giant." And on 11 April, in response to the thanks of the happy recipient: "You needn't thank me for something that gave me as much pleasure as it gives you. Knowing my Asiatic, I imagined the joy it would be for you to possess the manuscripts of your Giant."

That joy moves him deeply, mainly because he sees himself in it, in his vassal's house, in the form of a sacred book, obliging Laporte to be permanently grateful for this imperious gift of the self; he will be the object of a domestic cult. But, as we now know, when he was delighted to "imagine" his vassal's joy, he was living it by proxy as a happiness that had always been denied him from the time of the Fall. In Laporte he sees himself as he was before, madly in love, conquered; he once again becomes the child Gustave running toward an adored master.

Can it be said that Laporte's sincere and respectful friendship for once gave the lordly *gesture* a certain reality? In fact, he often solicited the tasks imposed on him; he loved to *serve*; his feelings for Flaubert were deep. Receiving the manuscript of the *Trois Contes*, he really did feel the joy the giver anticipated. In exchange, he offers himself completely: "What can I do for you?"—and the lord answers benevolently:

79. So it is *Laporte* who stands to profit from the "grubbing session." Gustave is doing him a favor by summoning him.

80. On this occasion he appears to have revived the Garçon—a character he hadn't mentioned for a long time.

"Stay as you are." All this is true. Yet the actual bond is, as elsewhere, tainted with unreality; the fault is not Laporte's—he is the only one of the vassals who may have played the game consciously—but Flaubert's.

Taking a closer look at their correspondence, we notice almost at once that Flaubert was not always so imperious in his relations with "Bob."[81] No doubt, from the beginning he saw their friendship as a bond of vassalage, for he immediately perceived Laporte's admiration for him. No doubt, too, he charged him with errands and commissions in the imperative mode. But the demands increase and the orders multiply from the month of August 1875. In this month, Mme Commanville—who owed 50,000 francs to the banker Faucon—asked if she could pay off her debt in annual installments over a period of eight or ten years. The banker agreed, on condition that this arrangement be underwritten by "someone reliable." Laporte guaranteed Caroline for half the sum. Raoul-Duval, deputy of the Seine-Inférieure, who was approached on 31 August, bore the rest. In September, Flaubert thanked both of them. A comparison of the letters is instructive.

He wrote twice to Raoul-Duval. On 6 September: "Therefore, my dear friend, I profit from your devotion by giving you great thanks . . . I shake your hand, thanking you again from the bottom of my heart." And on 9 September (upon receipt of a letter of guarantee that he had solicited): "I can, or rather my niece and I can only thank you from the bottom of our hearts. You have rendered me a true service which I shall never forget. I am rather sick, my dear friend, and in two or three days I am going to take refuge at Concarneau, where I shall try to stay as long as possible. I embrace you."

It's true he was sick. Sick with fear and humiliation. We can be certain it cost him a great deal to ask and to thank; his bourgeois landowner's pride suffered deeply. However, he did not hesitate to show his gratitude to Raoul-Duval: he does it humbly, "from the bottom of his heart," and, far from taking a stoical pose, he lets go, pities himself, tries to arouse pity. In a word, he accepts the role of the one *indebted*.

The letter to Laporte—sent 3 September—has quite a different tone:

My good fellow,
Faucon has agreed to what we asked.
The bankruptcy will not happen, thanks to you.

---

81. In 1873, at the time of the gift of the Chinese monsters, he still deigned to thank Laporte.

I have sold my farm at Deauville to M. Delahaute for 200,000 francs, which allows me to save my poor nephew.
So the worst is over! I long to see you to explain this whole business, after which I will leave for Concarneau. So, my good fellow, when you return to Couronne, come here so we can embrace you.

That is all. In this "thank you letter" there is *not one thank you*. Gustave waits impatiently for Laporte, not to show him his gratitude but to "explain this whole business." The tone is manly, almost military. And no sooner has he declared that Bob has prevented bankruptcy than Gustave hastens to add that he sold his farm for 200,000 francs; these 200,000 francs given to Commanville show the magnitude of the uncle's sacrifice and reduce Laporte's service to its proper value. Gustave wants to show, besides, that he is not really the one involved, it is his niece's happiness that is at stake. True, we find something of this attitude in the second letter to Raoul-Duval: "I can, or rather my niece and I can only . . ." but it is much more discreet. In other words, with Raoul-Duval he lets himself go; with Laporte he is tough and contained. Caroline adds a few words of her own:

Do not forget to come to Croisset, even when my uncle is gone.
I want very much to shake your hand and am happy to count you among our true friends.

These lines are inspired by Gustave or are in imitation of him; Caroline does not thank Laporte either—she congratulates him on his good behavior and allows him to accede to the rank of *true friend*. It all amounts to an invitation to dinner: "Do not forget to come . . . ," much like Flaubert's commands. As to the words "when my uncle has gone," they show that Gustave did not plan to postpone his departure until Laporte's return. In fact, he left toward mid-September[82] but was delayed by his affairs. On the 12th he writes to his friend from Croisset that he *has not seen him again*, promising him simply: "As soon as I feel better, I will write you from Concarneau." The promised letter is delayed—it is dated 2 October—and contains no allusion to the service rendered: "You know my troubles quite well since you have shared them." Subsequently, there was to be no mention of it except in 1879, rather bitterly, at the time of the quarrel. It may be argued that the two men saw each other frequently and that Flaubert could have shown his gratitude in person. But it was not a matter of an omission but of taking a stand. Flaubert refused to be *indebted* to Laporte. Not that he

82. He arrived at Concarneau on Thursday the 16th.

misconstrued the importance of the commitment. He simply judged that his "good old Bob" had done his duty as vassal. For this he owed him esteem and even friendship, but never gratitude. Why, it will be asked, did he show such gratitude to Raoul-Duval? Because Raoul-Duval, as someone *truly* rich, a notable, a man of political influence, impressed him.[83] Laporte, though not poor, did not have a large fortune. And he had *admired* Gustave from the beginning. Raoul-Duval *appreciated* him. What is called generosity in the latter is the spirit of sacrifice in the former. A lord honors his vassal by accepting his sacrifices.

This attitude conceals a deep malaise. We have seen Gustave playing the gift giver with his sister Caroline in order to feel through her the dazzled object of his own generosity. Caroline consequently became the independent variable and her brother put himself in her hands: $G = b (C)$. But this relationship remained *livable:* Gustave could admit dependence on an inferior because his sister's inferiority was provisional; the two children were both *Flauberts*. And, as we know, Gustave had internalized the family pride: there was the paterfamilias, his wife, his children, then a large gap, then the first of the non-Flauberts. Thus even the least of the Flauberts could look down and see his numberless inferiors swarming in the valleys below. A basic contradiction: it is not as an *individual* that he soars above them—from this point of view his constitution, the aversion he has for himself, his desire to submit in order to forget himself in his devotion or to receive his ontological status through the gracious will of others should lead him to a profound humility; he is superior to the common run of the species only as the member of a group. But as this group has rejected him at first sight and almost disqualified him, he cannot *experience* his superiority; in him, Flaubert pride is negative and other, he experiences it as a bite, an abstract and painful imperative— "Noblesse oblige"—and not as a calm certainty; in him, the duty to raise himself ever higher conflicts with the desire to fall to his knees. In his relations with Caroline, the conflict is hardly disturbing, since the brother and sister are two parts of the same whole. When this totalization of the familial dominant gives way to a personalizing revolution of the sexual dominant—as with Louise, for example—the conflict between the seigneurial imperative and the desire for submission is more acute, but Gustave knows how to exploit the situation and de-

83. The letters to Raoul-Duval, beneath the false, peevish coarseness, are often servile. See in particular 7 February 1871.

rive keen pleasure from it. Louise is inferior as a woman and as a non-Flaubert; he plays the role of the dominating male from afar, amuses himself sadistically by tormenting the jealous woman; near her, he starts by *making himself* manly and playing "the bull," but only so as to succumb all the more to the devouring embraces of the dominating Louise. With men, the contradiction is *insurmountable;* his homo-sexuality is not sufficiently developed for him to savor—to wish to savor—the perverse pleasure of submitting to his inferiors. Strictly speaking, he would accept the sexual domination of a lord, but the Flaubert pride forbids him from seeking a master among those who are not of his blood; Alfred is an exception for quite specific reasons, which we shall explain later and which are valid only in this particular case. With others, he has to dominate, to give *without giving,* to impose himself, continually to recreate the feudal hierarchy and stand on the summit. He goes against his constituted passivity, feels his insincerity; and that never really stirs the inert, dark depths of his bitter soul. Nothing can be done about it; it is stronger than he; he escapes self-disgust by accelerating his epic performance and forcing its effects.

This contradiction gives us the key to his relations with Laporte between 1875 and 1880. Gustave is clearly indebted to the man, something he can neither completely hide from himself nor calmly tolerate. The only way he manages to evade this disagreeable evidence is to carry his pretended domination to an extreme. He will multiply his imperatives and his demands, charge his vassal with a thousand commissions, constantly pester him, burden him with requests; in brief, he will force Laporte to outdo his acts of submission in order *to prove to himself* a posteriori that his friend was acting in his capacity as vassal when he guaranteed Commanville's notes, that he was obeying his duty as *debtor,* that he was simply seizing upon the first opportunity to show his gratitude for the perpetual gift Flaubert had made him of his person. And in order to thank Laporte for services rendered—large and small—Flaubert finds nothing better than to renew that symbolic gift. He claims to know that Laporte desires nothing more: "Knowing my Asiatic, I imagined the joy he would have," etc.

Flaubert's relations with Laporte (considering them at least from Flaubert's point of view) are derealized, however, because the Giant plays the giver in order to mask the fact that the only real gift comes from Laporte. In sum, Laporte must be confined within the limits of

84. Toward the end of his life, he calls Maupassant "my dear" and Laporte "my dear old boy."

vassalage, convinced—by the gruff, benevolent loftiness of the pro-
ceedings—that he was born to serve the Flauberts. In this way Gustave makes himself daily a little more dependent on Laporte; Laporte
becomes essential to the extent that he is his master's truth and must,
by his gestures, convince Gustave that this truth is nothing but *subor-
dination*. But the dependence goes still deeper: Flaubert was crushed
by his nephew's financial collapse; he was overwhelmed, he whined,
cut to the quick; he would never recover. Discouraged, aging, ill, what
was now clearly manifest was the "constitution" he was given from
infancy—the anguish and the passive sensibility. He needed to be
loved and spilled over into sentimentality; he needed to be admired
because he doubted himself; he needed to be helped,[85] to have his morale boosted; he needed someone to do all the things that fatigued or
bored him. For all these reasons he certainly needed a "sister of
mercy." Or rather—for it is still pride that reverses the roles, and
Flaubert played the woman in the couple he formed with Laporte—he
needed a man on hand to give him the strength to live; he needed a
witness so that he might hurl recriminations at his ease, and each of
his words might lose the muddiness of internal rumination by being
externalized in front of someone who finds everything that comes
from him of value. This prematurely old man, ill, passive, sobbing,
hypersensitive, both childish and womanish, goes back across the
senseless monotony of the years to reclaim the attentions, the tenderness of which his first years were deprived. He is a shabby sovereign
for Laporte. And Laporte cannot now be overwhelmed—if he ever
was—by the majesty of the master. The truth is that he loves Gustave
deeply and discovers in him—in spite of his attitude, in spite of his
groaning and his histrionics—a "parfum à sentir" which is expressed
above all in his books. Laporte's feeling might well be called *piety* (in
the sense of filial piety)—a tender and compassionate loyalty in great
part nourished by memories and respectfully drawing a veil over the
present decay. In brief, Laporte, without meaning to, exposes the
drama of the lord because he is not taken in by it. Not that he was
conscious, I imagine, of the deep meaning of Gustave's epic perfor-

85. To Caroline, 21 October 1875: "When you get old, habits exercise a tyranny you
cannot imagine, my poor child. Everything goes, everything you leave behind is irre-
vocable, and you feel death walking over you. If outward ruin is added to the inward
ruin you feel so strongly, you are quite simply crushed." Even before that "ruin," he had
feared, and now feared more and more, that Croisset would have to be sold and that he
would be driven out. This is the meaning of the letter—discrete blackmail through
despair.

mance; rather, if he took care of the Giant's commissions, it was not out of obedience to the imperatives; his real motive was a basic intuition—based on love (and retrospective admiration)—of this "hysterical old woman's" need of him. His last letter is quite clear. He did not want—and quite rightly—to guarantee Commanville's renewed notes. Caroline made her uncle intervene once more. Gustave wrote an authoritarian letter[86] in which the words "I beg you" appear, but underlined, giving them a threatening aspect: "As for me, I don't understand what is stopping you. Well, whatever you decide, my friend, nothing will change between the two of us; but before you decide, *I beg you* to reflect seriously."

"*I beg you*"; the underscoring can have only one meaning: "I, the Giant, out of generosity will go so far as to *beg* you, in your own interest, although I could command; but the exceptional, even unnatural character of this request should make you look into yourself and fill you with confusion." And why say to a friend of ten years, whose devotion is exemplary, that "nothing will be changed between the two of us"? That should go without saying. The "two of us" indicates that Laporte was quarreling with Caroline and had thus made himself an enemy in Gustave's heart as well. In other words, he had put himself in danger.

Yet Laporte was not moved. He answered Flaubert, regretful but calm:

> This is just what I was dreading, my good Giant. They made you interfere in a discussion to which you ought to remain a stranger. I cannot admit you as a judge in a matter in which your nephew, on the one hand, and your friend, on the other, hold differing opinions. If we reveal our grievances and our reasons to you . . . you will be forced to wrong one of the two and your bonds of affection with that person would be damaged. Let me therefore discuss this business with Commanville only. If a few passing vexations result from this, you at least will not have to take sides. Be assured, my good Giant, that I shall love you always with all my heart.

"Mind your own business" could not be said more gallantly. Laporte is fully convinced that he is in the right; he himself is ruined, and he sees Commanville in his true colors. If he were to renew the guarantee, he knows that it would not reverse the terms of the payment; in that case, Laporte would not be prepared to meet the commitments he had made. But he also knows that the Giant is easily fooled, under-

---

86. 28 September 1879, *Correspondance, Supplément.*

stands nothing about figures, and confuses hopes with realities. Laporte is saying to him: "Let the grownups discuss it among themselves; I will help you, I will protect you as in the past, but don't interfere in a business for which you have no taste and which you do not understand." The pretext "You would be obliged to choose between us" is merely an evasion. In fact, if Gustave were normal and lucid, he would be perfectly qualified to serve as mediator. To deny him that role is to confine him to another—precisely the role Laporte had long since assigned him: someone with a heart of gold, an old man of genius who has preserved—in all things outside of literature—his childish naïveté. Nothing of the master about him; rather, if you will, something of a mother who has remained a child-woman. Laporte does not feel *duty*-bound to his friend; on the contrary, he is conscious of *giving*. Untiringly, lovingly, but freely. Not *generously* in the aristocratic manner but quite independently, like a man who knows what he wants and does it. We can be fairly certain that Laporte *acts* the vassal out of friendship, or rather that he uses his extreme delicacy *to do nothing* that might undeceive his false master.

These nuances are subtle, for Laporte does feel love and admiration along with the piety of a Samaritan. All this is played out under cover, but it is enough to throw Gustave back on his bad actor's drama. All the more since Laporte's zeal seems to have abated a little. He remains Flaubert's faithful errand boy, but he comes to Croisset less often, stifled by the place. In the last years, indeed, beneath Gustave's arrogance we can see a lover's resentment: "You are leaving me"; many invitations, many veiled reproaches.[87] The fact is that Laporte was less

87. I cite at random: 15 August 1877: "Dear old friend, knowing your punctuality, I am quite puzzled at having no news of you . . . Didn't a letter reach you? . . . We have been waiting for you for forty-eight hours, as you promised us a visit toward the middle of this week." On Monday, 20 August 1877, Gustave imperiously invites Laporte in two notes to come "to dine and sleep here" on Tuesday or Wednesday. Laporte answers that he will come on Sunday. And Flaubert, distressed, answers on the 21st: "Be serious! You don't remember that I am leaving next Thursday and consequently cannot receive your visit on Sunday. The county council is making you lose your head!" 6 September 1877: "Here it is, eight days since I've seen my Asiatic, and I am annoyed! What has become of him!" The two friends then set off for Calvados, but Laporte left Flaubert almost immediately, recalled, he said, by his obligations as city councilman. Flaubert writes to him: "How I miss you." 3 April 1878: "What is this? What is going on with you? When shall we see you again?" and a few days later: "What is this? Why don't we see you? Why do we hear no news of Your Excellency?" July 1878: "It's been a long time since we've seen you." July 1878: "You *annoyed me* by not coming on Monday as you'd promised. It's been a very long time since you've slept here." See too the *pressing* invitation of 15 August 1878. 19 August: "I just now caught a glimpse of you on the Bouille boat . . . Not knowing when I shall be lucky enough to get you here bothers me." 1 September 1878: "Your letter vexed me—'You bastard!' I cried . . . We might have spent a few

and less taken with the Commanvilles. And, further, he was somewhat put out at Flaubert for mixing interest and friendship under his niece's influence. "Bob" had already conceded many times to Flaubert's entreaties and had renewed his guarantees, but against his will; he was afraid, and knew he would not be able to pay when the time came. And now they wanted to force him to take measures that he found repugnant. For example, he preferred to have no contact with Faucon, Commanville's creditor; Flaubert, pushed by Caroline, exasperated Laporte by urging him to take lunch with the banker. This did not prevent his showing the full extent of his friendship in January 1879, when Flaubert, one icy day, fractured his fibula. Laporte settled himself at Croisset, returned to sleep there every night, spent the first two nights at his friend's bedside with hardly any sleep, served him as nurse and secretary, answered by dictation all the letters Flaubert received. "Would you believe this of our Sister?" Gustave writes to Caroline. "Monday he left me by the 11 o'clock boat and was to come back by the 6:30 one. As the Couronne embankment was covered with water, he pulled up his trousers and walked through it barefoot to get onto the ferry. The Seine was turbulent . . . There's a real friend! who risks drowning, or at the very least pneumonia, so as not to miss an engagement, and not a very advantageous one."

Between the lines we find the well known formula: "I have a friend who would die for me."[88] And no doubt Flaubert took pleasure in exaggerating the dangers involved. Laporte nevertheless gave proof of a kind of frantic devotion suggesting a veiled intent; as if he meant: the Giant alone, reduced to his nakedness and the miseries of his great bruised body, has the right to all my time and attentions; his familial personality, created by the bonds that link him to the Commanvilles, no longer concerns me. Inversely, it might be said that he wanted to compensate for his growing reserve toward the *uncle* by becoming Flaubert's nurse. We sense in Laporte an inflexible determination to keep his distance and at the same time—both to underscore this de-

---

pleasant hours this evening, Bob! But if you really are too tired, I forgive you!" 22 September 1878: "Here I am again! When shall I see you? We find you're not exactly lavish with your visits." November 1878: "My boy, I am beginning to wonder. Why no news? What's the meaning of your silence?" 20 January 1879: "I was quite disappointed not seeing my old Bob yesterday. I am inordinately annoyed with him . . . Don't forget, my boy, that *I demand* your presence *next Saturday* for the famous lunch we have put off so many times." 19 June 1879: "What is the meaning of this? Where are you? No news of Bob for twelve days now—and Caroline writes me that not only did you fail to come on Monday, but that they had no word from you—me neither, for God's sake!"

88. Which Flaubert used in all his letters for speaking to Louise about Maxime.

termination and out of regret for having adopted it—a willingness to render *Gustave* the most compelling, the least inviting services.[89] In any event, Gustave did not miss the ambivalence of this attitude. He attempted, as we have seen, to apply the feudal grid to it. But he also felt like a helpless, wretched infant in the hands of an all-powerful adult and thus rediscovered the old frustrated desires of his early childhood: his mother was finally coming to satisfy them. So he could write to Caroline on 30 January—five days after his accident: "My morale is excellent, *better* than before [*sic*]. Laporte is amazed at my patience, at my angelic character." He abandons himself to passivity, to Laporte's overprotection. In this moment of happy quietism, the truth of their relations can no longer be concealed; for this old man prematurely "invaded by the past" and who at times, he says himself, is no longer completely lucid, childhood and femininity are reunited, the feudal *performance* is effaced. A "bewildered invalid" is all that remains.

In short, during the month of February 1879 the friendship between Flaubert and Laporte blazed up once more. In fact, it was throwing out its last sparks. The break came seven months later, on 28 September. The quarrel has been much discussed; it is commonly attributed to the "intrigues" of the Commanville household. This remains to be seen. That those intrigues took place goes without saying. But should we believe, as the editors of the supplement to the correspondence have it, that Flaubert was "increasingly dominated by his niece's authority"? We shall see later just what the Commanville's financial ruin involved and how Flaubert handled it. What must be noted here, however, is that he was deeply resentful of his niece and, more especially, of his nephew. His bitterness—which of necessity he hid as well as he could—is often manifest in a turn of phrase. In 1879 it was at its height: he accused the household—rather unjustly, we shall see—of having ruined him and, this time with justice, reproached his relatives for their negligence and bad management. In fact, in the *Supplément* to the correspondence it appears that Commanville was very irregular in paying his uncle the promised allowance and that Flaubert had to keep urging him to pay minimal and indispensable amounts, once as little as *twenty francs*. But if we know about these troubles it is *through* Gustave's letters, which means that he was highly conscious of them. The force of his bitterness is evident with even the

89. Letter of 11 February 1879 to Du Camp: "Today at last I am able to get up and I no longer use a bedpan!!"

most cursory reading. Is it credible that he should forget his niece's ingratitude?

February 1879: "Tell your husband to bring me a dozen visiting cards tomorrow." February 1879: "For the third time, I demand my visiting cards. For God's sake!" February 1879: "I am HINDIGNANT! Two white everyday shirts. My velvet slippers!"

If we are inclined to believe that this impotent anger (he was bedridden in the care of Laporte, having fractured his leg less than ten days before) was superficial and did not come from his very depths, let us read this account of a dream which he gives his niece in the same month of February: "I had a terrible nightmare last night because of my leg. I was groveling on my stomach, and Paul [the concierge] was insulting me. I wanted to instruct him in religion and everyone had abandoned me. My helplessness made me desperate. I am still thinking about it. The view of the river, which is splendid, is calming me little by little." One needn't be an analyst to grasp the meaning and import of this "terrible nightmare" nor to appreciate the real significance of remarks thrown out as if by accident, such as: "Your poor husband was certainly not born to make me happy!" But to understand the animosity hidden beneath a *playacted* tenderness, it will suffice to compare the two following contemporaneous texts. It is now the month of March. He is going "to be offered" a pension. He knows he will accept it: *"There can be no hesitation."* But he writes to his niece: "I am humiliated to the very marrow." And he adds—and this is what brings us up short: "My conscience is reproaching me for this pension (which I don't deserve at all, whatever they say). Because I had a poor understanding of my interests is no reason why the state should support me." The last sentence is a surprise: how can Gustave—who suffered the consequences of his nephew's bad luck or mismanagement—accuse himself of having had a poor understanding of his interests? He is going too far, it seems, and the phrase sounds false. As does the following one: "For you are an honest man, something rarer than an honest woman." [90] But we discover his true feelings in a letter to an unknown correspondent, published by Maxime and dated two days—at most—before the one we have just cited: "I do not want such charity, which I don't deserve either. Those who have ruined me have the duty to support me and not the government. Stupid, yes; interesting, no!" Who ruined him if not the Commanvilles? And who, then, should support him (Commanville had committed himself to paying

90. We recall that this is what he said about Louise.

Gustave an allowance) if not this couple he reckons he has saved from bankruptcy? His bitterness speaks: he was *stupid.* Which means: he "had a poor understanding of his interests." He should not have sold his farm to help those ingrates. After reading these two letters, we have at our disposal certain evidence—which a thousand other details would reinforce if need be—to the effect that Flaubert was profoundly resentful of the Commanvilles and considered they had ruined him; in the face of his nephew's and *niece's* bad management, he judged himself *stupid* to have entered into their calculations, and, indeed, they had swindled him.[91] His rage is, as always, turned against himself, and he declares that *it was well done:* I only got what I deserved. To be reduced to accept charity—we can be sure he *held that* against the niece *as well.*

He proceeds gently—agreed—but he is choking with a fury that is not far from hatred. Are we to believe that Caroline was in such a position of strength that she could cause him to quarrel with the "Sister of Mercy" he still calls "my dear" in a letter of July 1879? Furthermore, the editors of the correspondence (*Supplément,* p. 266, n. 1) admit that they don't know how she accomplished it: "Commanville and his wife convinced him—God knows by what arguments—that Laporte was remiss in his duties as a friend." God knows, indeed. *We* certainly don't. Unless Mme de Commanville had found an accomplice in *Flaubert himself* and had merely been preaching to the converted.

As a matter of fact, what can "authoritarian niece" mean? The cards were on the table. Laporte, ruined, did not want to renew his guaran-

91. Let us read, for example, what he writes on 17 February 1879 (*Supplément*) apropos of a letter sent by Commanville to Fiennes, the owner of their apartment in Paris: "They will never leave me alone! What have I done to be so persecuted? This is what Fiennes sends me. Why did Ernest have to write him insults? Ineptitude, insolence, etc. I understand that Fiennes is not pleased about it. And all that for what? I no longer understand it at all. What is the *practical* purpose of this letter? I am too enervated, exhausted, and trembling to be able to write. All this is killing me. I would very much like not to burden you, poor girl, but *I can bear no more pain.* It's too much. Go and see Fiennes. Make peace, for heaven's sake!"
Since 1875 he almost continually had the feeling that Commanville was deceiving him, concealing the true state of their affairs. "So as not to worry you," he says piously. But, himself aside, he thinks things out with much less naïveté. Compare what he writes on 1 March 1879: "I still don't understand anything about the cursed sawmill! How is it possible that its sale was estimated at six hundred thousand francs (factory and grounds) but brought no more than two hundred thousand? And how is it that I, the primary creditor, should not touch any of it? Is Ernest once again suffering from delusions? How does he spend his time? I understand that he may not be cheerful and that he may have bouts of despair! But whose fault is it? I doubt that he could hold down any job; at his age one is not about to change profession and habits." And 9 March 1879, apropos of the same sale: "Wasn't I told the truth, then?"

101

tee. Flaubert knew that. All the more so because during the winter he had thought many times he would choke with anguish imagining the fate of the poor Asiatic, ruined but constrained—by Commanville's default—to uphold his commitments when he was no longer in a position to do so. Let us read, for example, what he writes from his bed, 1 March 1879. A piece of ground and a sawmill had just been sold at a price he estimated at one-third of their value: "All I can think about is whether we shall be able to pay off *our friends!* What do *you* think? This idea keeps pursuing me as if I had committed a crime!" To be sure, Laporte had not advanced any money, but like Raoul-Duval he was one of the friends who should not have been made to pay for Commanville's imprudences. We see quite clearly that Flaubert is thinking of him when, coming back to this concern in another letter to Caroline (9 March), he writes: "You are right, my dear, we must do *everything* to avoid robbing our friends. We would both of us be miserable if they lost a sou. For in the end, we are the ones they have lent the money to. We *must not* do that. As for me, I am torn with remorse." Laporte was obviously one of those who risked being robbed if he were obliged to uphold the commitment he had undertaken. Flaubert's anguish—until the sale, he had taken his accident bravely— is translated into a nervous erysipelas whose cause he is well aware of. So in March he knows what is going on. On the one hand, the best of friends who "risked drowning for him"—on the other, a couple who had ruined him, who continually lied to him.[92]

Nonetheless, Laporte's refusal to renew commitments he could not keep was enough for Gustave to break with him. And for Gustave to write in October 1879 to Mme Roger des Genettes: "A man I regarded as my *intimate* friend just showed me the baldest egotism. This betrayal has wounded me."

The baldest egotism, the Sister of Mercy? After ten years of loyal service? And how can Flaubert write "showed *me*" when Laporte took such pains to tell him that this affair could not concern him, that he wanted to discuss it with the Commanvilles? But one turn of phrase is particularly striking: "whom I regarded as my intimate friend." What about that? Laporte *was not* Flaubert's intimate friend. All he had to do was refuse once, *only* once, to render a service—a refusal motivated by obvious and familiar reasons—for all their past friendship to seem a mere appearance. It is not even a question of a friend's behaving

92. Flaubert was so much more conscious of Laporte's unfortunate situation that he redoubled his efforts, after 1877, to obtain a paying position for him. In vain; Laporte would become inspector of works in the Nièvre.

badly but of a man whom Flaubert *wrongly took* for a friend. We shall find the last word on this incredible transformation only by recognizing Gustave's deepest intentions. The niece poured oil on the fire but she could only reinforce her uncle's mood, not change it, and it is out of reverence for Flaubert that his flatterers lay all the responsibility on Caroline. The break—desired by the Giant—is one of those exceptional circumstances that illuminate a man's "innermost convictions."

Flaubert did not want to be indebted to Laporte; when Laporte risked drowning or catching pneumonia for his sake, Gustave simply cried, "That's a real friend," which means he confined himself to letting his niece know that the Asiatic conformed to the platonic idea of friendship. When this friend, on the other hand, after spending days at a time at his Giant's bedside, felt he had to leave him for a day or two, Gustave complained with some ill humor, "My companion Laporte will not return until Monday (we must become accustomed to solitude as to poverty and old age)".[93] How dared he speak of solitude, that old man who chose to be a hermit and who had been nursed voluntarily for a whole month *out of love?* Certainly this remark must be viewed as a veiled reproach to Caroline. Gustave did not change: as in his childhood, he displays his wounds to provoke the remorse and shame of his executioners. There is no doubt that Laporte was not the target: he could not be reproached for anything; he had other obligations, which were well understood. Nevertheless, it was enough for him to cease for a moment—even for the most legitimate reasons—to devote himself to his lord for the relations of man to man to be severed. The past doesn't count for Flaubert unless it is negative, unless it is perpetuated by rancor. He doesn't count records of service except to demand even more. Gustave is content to *be*—a fixed force; this is giving, and the sacrifices of his vassals are like steps leading up to him, each of which serves solely to constrain the vassal to even greater sacrifice. The feudal bond allows Flaubert to base his harsh demands on his passivity. This, at least, is the rationalization and the drama. For if we draw aside the splendid garment, we shall discover that this passive and insatiable demanding bears a fair resemblance to what Mannoni called the "dependence complex." That author actually used this notion to explain the behavior of *colonized* peoples at a certain stage in their history. Yet, the dependence complex appears in the native the very moment the colonizer is rendered powerless. It is, indeed, the passive demand of the

93. 1 March 1879. Flaubert was out of danger—the accident had taken place more than a month before.

powerless. Or, if you like, it is a stage in the struggle of the oppressed against the oppressor. The oppressor conquers by means of weapons; a new generation is born after the defeat that continues the combat using the weapon of imposed passivity: the colonized people forever claims new favors, forcing the master to practice generosity. And Mannoni notes that one refusal is enough for a colonized native to turn away from the chosen colonizer, for him to fall back into the sly malevolence of the vanquished. Is it not something of an effort for the oppressed to force his conqueror at least to play the role of lord, to transform naked oppression into a feudal relationship, to make himself the object of the gift by offering daily greater dependence in return for the master's daily affirmed generosity? Flaubert's *constituted* passivity brings him closer to the colonial condition. His basic intention—born of original frustrations—is the inert, continually increasing imperiousness of someone powerless who seeks to humanize his fate by infusing it with a harsh vassalage. With Laporte he makes himself the intractable vassal; he makes himself utterly dependent on his friend; and we should have no doubt that he is quite aware of his ultimate claim: that the master must give his life for the slave. Gustave "is not made to live"; the ideal thing would be for a voluntary death to justify this superfluous life. In persuading himself, for example, that Laporte risked death to come and care for him, he obtains a provisional tranquillity of soul: he was not viable because he was conceived grudgingly, cared for without love, he was born a boy when a girl was wanted; but if someone gives his own life in order to perpetuate this undesirable existence, then the sacrifice is like a new birth, and the forlorn, devalued child suddenly finds himself revalued. This extreme event never occurs, of course; but any service rendered to Flaubert is experienced as a symbol and an approximation of supreme generosity. For this reason he is insatiable: one hasn't done enough unless one has done everything. He will be a morose, ungrateful, supercilious vassal. Here we have come back to Gustave's original desire. The person who breaks with Laporte is not the generous lord who ought to use his generosity to understand or, at least, to "forgive"; it is the vassal disappointed in his dependence complex, who has neither the means nor the desire to excuse his master's inexpiable crime. By refusing to renew the guarantee, Laporte is lacking in his absolute duty, which is to guarantee—and reproduce—the life of his vassal: the mother has withdrawn by buttoning up her dress; the child rediscovers his abandonment and his old rancor. He takes revenge by punishing himself; by this rupture, which wounds him to the quick, he will crush the wicked stepmother with remorse.

Let it be understood, however, that Gustave cannot define the affair for himself in these terms. Laporte is and must remain his inferior. Thus, everything is turned around: what he experiences in dependence and vassalage he expresses—to himself and to others—through the discourse of a prince. He conceals from himself the fact that his imperiousness comes from need, its sole valid foundation; he takes it for an ethical imperative. This is all the easier since Laporte comes less frequently in the evening and for some time has balked (*at his duties*) and left for Nevers, which is perfectly logical (it's his job) and nonetheless inadmissible (he is neglecting Flaubert for his own interests). Unreality slips into suffering and anger. Pride consolidates it. And Laporte's single refusal is enough to disqualify all his previous devotion. In the famous letter of 28 September which precedes and provokes the break, we find this superb remark in which the master's conceit is mixed with bourgeois vulgarity: "R. Duval has accepted this transfer and [after one letter from Gustave] is delighted that Commanville should escape from the hands of the aforementioned Faucon. What prevents you from doing as much? What are you afraid of? Until now you haven't paid anything and you are not being asked to pay now." This time, as we might have expected, Raoul-Duval, the other guarantor, is cited as an example. He is the true lord, the man of quality. Furthermore, no one need owe him any gratitude: we are told he is *delighted!* Gustave forgets only one thing, that Raoul-Duval would have the means to make good on his guarantee and Laporte would not. But what an arbitrary crudeness in "you haven't paid anything and you are not being asked to pay now"! It would be tempting to answer: "That's all we needed!" In any case, whatever the couple's "underhanded maneuvers," it is Flaubert himself who writes these sickening words; he is the one who, knowing quite well what to think, squarely refuses to take into consideration the unexpected change in Laporte's situation that took place in 1877. He is the one who—thinking, as we have seen, that his nephew is incompetent and a liar—pretends not to understand his "dear" friend's legitimate mistrust and presents as a chance misfortune what is in reality a process of deterioration.[94]

94. He adds, in fact: "Things aren't going to get any worse! To the contrary, since we have time!"

Violent anger, unjust but also unreal—or, if you will, insincere. It explodes on the surface but conceals desperate anguish. The truth escapes him in his letter of 27 September: *"These troubles are going to make me die of sorrow."* [95] In fact, he will die of sorrow. But we must understand that the real reason for the break is not Laporte's refusal of Commanville's request but the letter by which he separates Flaubert from the dispute and refuses, gently but firmly, to accept him as an arbitrator. The real and the unreal form an explosive mixture: the bitter anguish of abandonment combines with excessive rage at not being able to continue to play his role as dominator. After the break, what's left for him? Suffering and resentment. It was at this point, no doubt, that the Commanvilles intervened; they posed as stern and impartial witnesses: "After what he's done to you, you *cannot* be reconciled with him." As a matter of fact, when Laporte wrote to Flaubert for New Year's Day, 1880, Flaubert did not answer but gave the letter to his niece, in effect asking her permission to write back. She remained silent. On 5 January Gustave wrote to her: "You say nothing about Laporte's letter, of which I sent you a copy?" Not a word more. This is a timid overture; if Caroline had told him that the quarrel had gone on too long, if she had advised him to "forgive"—but the niece must have held firm, for Gustave does not return Bob's New Year's greeting. And the only further mention of Laporte is in a letter to Commanville, of 5 February 1880, consisting of the following lines: "Yesterday evening you did receive, didn't you, a large envelope containing a subpoena for the 13th of this month. I hardly read it through, but I understand it came from *Laporte*. This seems *very serious* to me . . . I am amazed that Laporte should not have given back my five hundred before claiming 13,000 francs from me. What shall I do if he gives it to me . . . We would no longer have any counterclaim." Three months later Flaubert died of sorrow, wasted by his financial troubles and no longer able to bear the separation he himself had provoked. He *loved* his "old rock," but the Flaubert pride compelled him to misinterpret that humble, anxious, and childish love, forcing it into the mold of an imperious and condescending friendship, and therefore tolerating it only after having made it unreal. But this passage to the imaginary did not prevent the experienced emotion from developing according to its own laws; it simply affected him, on the level of discourse and behavior, with a consuming insincerity.

95. His italics. The context proves, however, that this is simply blackmail.

D. He and I

The mirror, as we have seen, is a fixed, ersatz version of the other for the little boy. He seeks to surprise himself in it, transcended transcendence, with the qualities it has for one who transcends it. But he does not truly encounter the *being-as-spectacle* that he is for those around him; what he sees in the mirror is a quasi object—obviously, for how could he transcend his own transcendence? In the mirror he discovers himself as a "man without qualities," a substanceless intermediary between interiority and exteriority. His reflection merely confirms the discomfiting feeling that he is *visible;* this characteristic—common to all voyeurs—assumes a fundamental importance for him: he suffers, we might say, from an hypertrophied visibility. How could it be otherwise, since the little boy, alienated from the object he is for others, takes appearance for absolute being? Even alone in his room (he runs to the mirror when he cries) he is conscious of his *seen-being.* Appurtenances point to him, the space surrounding him has eyes, the walls have ears. The impending danger doesn't stop there: he feels as though he exists, outside, in the whole town, in what he does and perhaps permanently, for the consciousnesses that escape him and that endow him with unknown characteristics—for parents, friends of the family, neighbors, or simply passersby who have visited him or seen him and who can always compare him behind his back. He is in danger in the world, his multiple, omnipresent appearance escapes him; he is even haunted in solitude by that looming audiovisual object, his body-for-others. He must outwit all these observers; signified by the other, he must act on this signifying power, dispose his body so as to suggest favorable meanings. This leads him, as we have seen, to identify himself in imagination with the signifier itself: the person laughing that he takes into himself and the male whose hands stroke him in front of the mirror—although one refers to the paterfamilias and the other to the mother—have in common the fact that they are both semblances of the *agent* he cannot be and who decides for him.

Nevertheless, the mirror is not the other. Thus Operation Reflection is never truly undertaken; the child's intentions remain implicit and cannot be made explicit without being destroyed. In Caroline he believed he had found the signifier he needed: she would have the docility of the mirror but not its inertia. For this reason Gustave's intentions become more precise; in the course of his ludic relations with his sister, he is led to make his basic choice: having struggled unsuccessfully against derealization, he now assumes it and uses it—*he has chosen the imaginary*. With the immediate consequence that his image escapes him. In the mirror he saw a quasi object, which he tried in vain to totalize by giving himself the other's look; at least he found himself face to face with his materiality or, better, with the semblance of it. This derived from the mirror's very passivity. Caroline, a human mirror, though docile and fascinated, is active, and that is enough to make the little boy lose his reflection. All he can do now is imagine the *other that he is for others* to the extent that, refusing to submit to it, he attempts to control it. In any event, this being-for-others—which he takes for his being-in-itself—remains what it was: unrealizable. But by inviting others to realize it *as he understands it,* he becomes conscious of making it unreal *for himself.* Doubly so: first because he *imagines* the object he is for Caroline, then because the *image* he tries to purvey of himself does not correspond to anything he actually feels and thinks; the virile, laughing figure with male hands—whose shadow he sought to identify with—now takes on a strong consistency: it is the *agent.* But, as we know, activity, forbidden to Gustave by his constitution, appears to him quite simply to be the power of the Other. When he acts generously, therefore, his enterprise cannot help but be exposed in his own eyes: he is not trying to be *an* other in his singularity, even when he imitates a friend of his parents or caricatures the characteristics attributed to him—for whatever the plot of these melodramas, their aim is to manifest generosity. It is the *Other in general* that he represents, the Other-subject, of which he can be only the object. His aim is to seduce Caroline so that she might give him *there* the powers he feels he is lacking *here,* a lack that means constant frustration for him. He makes himself an object in front of his sister so that she might *objectify him as subject* or, if you will, so that she might *realize* him as generosity-object. In so doing, the contrast is accentuated between his clandestine reality, which he achieves at least on the level of experience, and his behavior toward others, which for him has the unity of a role. But we should not conclude that he deliberately pretends to be what he is not. For him, the others are *real* beings who have the power of giving things and persons their reality, of *instituting them as real.* Far from attempting to trick them, when he offers his imaginary self to others he is entreating them—at least at first—to give total reality to the proffered image. As if he were saying: I can go no farther; you go on and finish the job; let your look transform the unrealizable image I am for myself into that real totality I am through you and for you. Instead of taking pleasure in his being-in-itself, Gustave tries to direct the way others enjoy him. If the operation succeeds, if others believe and, what is more, affirm for him that he is just as he seems, he will be recreated. He does not even despair of recuperating himself; at the end of the enterprise, the subjective and the objective will coincide, not through the internalization of the exterior object but through the absorption of the *for-itself* by the *in-itself*. But *this absolute Other* that the other makes him—other than others, other than himself—can only exist, for them as for him, in the third person singular. For them because they totalize him outside themselves in his exterior being; for him because "the lord" is a role—which finds its reality only in the eyes of the spectators—and because, the very moment he wants them to realize him as *the* Generous Man, he tries to identify with the spirit of vassalage they bear toward him. The result for Gustave is an absolute priority of the "He" over the "I"; his unrealizable reality necessarily comes to him as *other than his life*. He is thus transported to the territory of the actor. For Kean, in effect, Hamlet exists in the third person; he is a certain object, created as object by his author, which presents only his exteriority, that is, words and gestures (even his famous monologue is *exterior*).[96] The spectator, no matter how empathic, can only grasp *this appearance,* and he as the actor must show the character *in its appearance* by reproducing the words and gestures that Shakespeare lent him, like a *person* whose interiority is never given but must be reconstituted. Kean comes to Hamlet as he would come to a "He" whose skin he must jump into; and for him to obtain the credence of the audience, the actor manipulates his internal self in order to give himself in an unreal way the feelings expressed by his actions. His interiority is therefore transferred to a prefabricated exteriority, and the ipseity or first person singular is simply a means for manifesting the third person. Yet Kean, even for the audience, is only an imaginary Hamlet. Gustave himself imagines that if he plays the role of lord properly, the public will reward him by recognizing his seigneurial reality. What Kean and the young boy basically have in common is that, for both of them, the intimate "you," the sign of reciprocity, is impossible; they are on stage, untouchable, separated from their audience by the blaze of the imaginary that envelops them even more than by the footlights. And how should they

96. Monologues, asides, words the character addresses only to himself, which we hear by special permission of the poet when we should not even be listening, do not truly apprise us of Hamlet's thoughts and desires, since we must take the risk of deciding whether he is expressing them truthfully or disguising them, rationalizing them, lying to himself, lying to us.

speak, if not in the third person, of someone who replaces telling with *showing?*

Caroline, however, is personally very close to her brother. The break in communication is thus not total: he exerts himself for her, he amuses her; there is some truth, as I have remarked, in their relationship. Gustave, nevertheless, is not unaware that his sister's gratitude is addressed to the character he plays and who says "I" but whom the little actor cannot refer to in the first person. So the young boy becomes accustomed to *thinking of himself* as a "He." The "I" frequently serves him only as a disguise; Gustave actually reaches himself through the mediation of others, for he attempts to bribe his witnesses by a twofold operation: the ceremony of appearance and the constant evocation of this ceremony (through commemoration or prophecy). We find a hundred examples of it in the correspondence: "Was I quite handsome?" he asks Ernest (a false inquiry, which is only a way to elicit an affirmation from Chevalier). "I'll be marvelous as an eccentric." [97] At the beginning of their liaison, he writes to the Muse: "Tell me how I look to you? How does my image materialize before your eyes?" If he reminds his correspondents of a common memory, he puts himself in their place and describes himself as they must have seen him: "Do you remember, old man, the pâté I devoured all by myself one Good Friday, the little Collioure wine I inhaled so freely?" Only an observer could speak of "the wine you inhaled so freely." By fascinating Ernest with words, Gustave is trying to force him to reinvent this memory in order to recuperate the scene through the memory of his friend; he puts himself into Ernest's skin and sees *himself* through his friend's slightly shocked eyes as a blaspheming Pantagruel. Sometimes, too, he describes himself in the present, in the future, not as he is or as he will be, but as Chevalier, if he were present, might see him. "I will do the 'Mont Doré' at my ease, smoking my pipe in the mornings on the boulevards and my cigar in the evenings at Place Saint-Ouen, and standing around waiting for the social hour at the Café National." Or, again, he presents himself as others have seen him. Apropos an argument at school: "I was magnificent. All the students in my class were stirred by the ruckus I made." To his mother he writes from Malta: "As for me, strolls on the bridge, dinners with the staff, standing about on the gangway between two drums in the company of the commander, where I posed in attitudes à la Jean Bart, cap on one side and cigar in beak . . . In the evening

97. This refers to a play by Zola; Gustave promised to be present at the premiere.

I contemplate the tides and dream, draped in my furs like Childe Harold. In short, I am quite a guy. I don't know what it is, but I am adored aboard ship. The gentlemen call me Papa Flaubert as it seems that my appearance is impressive in this humid weather." [98] Is he only thinking of reassuring his mother? This is what he claims in the following lines. But in this case we must recognize that his approach is misguided: "You see, poor old girl, that we've made a good beginning. And don't go believing that the sea had been quite calm; on the contrary, the weather was rather harsh; we were delayed twelve hours by the east wind." Mme Flaubert was happy, certainly, to learn that Gustave had his sea legs. But the last sentence was calculated to worry this nervous, pessimistic woman. And her son could not have been unaware of that: he hadn't completed half the crossing; he had to go to sea again, and between Malta and Alexandria, if it should be rough, the ship—the "poor old girl" could tell herself—would have a hundred opportunities to capsize. But Gustave, proud of being "quite a guy," cannot refrain from emphasizing the risks he is running. What delights him is to incite his mother to imagine the "He," unrealizable for him ("I don't know what it is," "it seems"), that his pluck and his attitudes have led the sailors to realize. The generous lord makes a gift to Mme Flaubert of a Gustave adored, adorable, a combination of Jean Bart and Childe Harold. He mediates between her and the "Gentlemen" on board, since through her he will resume and totalize the object he is for them.

Sometimes, moreover, when he tries to act in advance on the opinion others have of him by urging them to *expect* him to be a certain way, hence to realize him in the future in the third person, he does not even take the trouble to personalize the witness: he sketches a scene and introduces himself as well as his correspondents into it. He declares to his sister Caroline that he will be returning soon: "Be sure to have pink, healthy cheeks because I am hungry to kiss them. Indeed, I shall gobble them up! When I think of it, I won't be able to help hurting you a little, as always when my great nanny's kisses are so noisy that Mama says: 'Now leave the poor girl alone!' and you too, harassed and pushing me away with both hands, say: 'Don't be so rough!'" What is significant in this description is the objective *picture* that these three people have often presented and will soon do again. In their own eyes? Certainly not; none of them can observe the whole scene at once. Let us say rather that in this case the light functions as the look,

98. November 1849, *Correspondance* 2:105.

enfolding the trio and enhancing each one's visibility. In fact, through the mediation of the look, Caroline is the real target—she must expect herself to figure one day in this picture of two loving women beside a good giant whose love itself is devastating.

In the letters to Louise, the procedure is even more transparent. We know that he desires and fears sexual domination by the Muse—one more reason to play the dominating role at a distance. He tries to persuade her that he is a supermale, that she is receiving from him the *gift of pleasure* as an enamored vassal: "I will always remember the tilt of your head when you were at my knees on the ground, and your intoxicated smile when we left each other. I think repeatedly of our last meeting—your whole face was smiling, dazed with love and intoxication." Intoxicated with lust, dazed: Louise did not believe that such a man was possible. "You remember my violent embraces and how strong my hands were? You were almost trembling! I made you cry out two or three times." From Croisset he describes their next encounter to her in advance and takes it upon himself to reawaken this dazzlement: "I want you . . . to be amazed at me and to confess in your soul that you had not even dreamed of such transports." This promise gives further proof, if it were still needed, that Gustave's desire is insincere. He is not addressing himself to Louise's body. Not entirely, at least; by penetrating his mistress, Gustave wants to be reunited with the reflection he has revived in her and at the same time to identify with her dazzlement. His erection is itself a *gesture*.[99] Thus we have no doubt that the sexual act, in Paris or Mantes, was successfully accomplished, often repeated,[100] but altogether false—on Flaubert's side. Obliged "to take" in order to receive from her what he is really demanding—"when he had *swooned*, she revived him with little kisses on the eyes"[101]—he is excited only by his own image, which he wants to force Louise to realize; *in her* he becomes the lord of pleasure, the bull. But *in the third person*, while his ipseity tries to merge with the experienced intimacy of his "swooning" mistress.

We could cite many more examples. I will offer only one more, the most significant. It figures in the letter Gustave wrote to Ernest letting him know of Alfred's death. From other letters, contemporaneous and

99. Some actors cannot play a love scene without having an erection. We should not believe that they are necessarily excited by the actress who gives them their cue. Kean gets an erection for Juliet with Romeo's member.

100. If Flaubert's declarations were not convincing, an erotic poem by the Muse, written in the first days of their liaison, leaves no doubt on the subject.

101. Pommier and Leleu, *Nouvelle version de Madame Bovary*, pp. 18, 30.

later, we learn that he considered this death to be a deliverance for Alfred and, more secretly, for himself; furthermore, the betrayal and the break in their relations had occurred several years earlier, and Alfred's death itself had not dissolved the bitterness that Le Poittevin's marriage had occasioned in Flaubert. It is on this level that we can situate his ipseity, his experience, and that Gustave's ego, one pole of reflection, might appear to his reflective consciousness. But this is precisely what he passes over in silence or evokes by allusions that we shall have to decipher. For these emotions most often seem to him *illegitimate* determinations of his sensibility. Unable to gain official status, the subjective retains for him the profane lack of consistency of the *doxa*. In these solemn circumstances, he turns back to the Other to attribute to him the sacred feeling appropriate to such emotions, which *he* does not feel. "Alfred died eight days ago yesterday at this hour (midnight). I buried him last Thursday. He suffered horribly and watched himself die. You know, since you knew us in our youth, how I loved him and what pain his loss must have caused me. One less, one more gone. Everything is collapsing around me. Sometimes I think I am quite old," and so forth. See how flattering this is for Ernest: the deputy prosecutor, accused earlier of becoming stupidly self-important and bourgeois, is now recruited as a witness; he alone is capable of appreciating Gustave's sorrow in full measure. Nevertheless, something restrains one's pity; the same thing, I suppose, that would have prevented Ernest from relishing this mark of trust. Yes, Chevalier had known *them*. Not "in their youth" but from childhood. Only he didn't just know them; he loved them, shared their friendship; later in Paris (this is just why Flaubert reproached him) he visited Alfred faithfully. Yet even admitting that he may not have loved Alfred the way he loved Gustave, is this a reason to deny him the right to suffer at his death? Not a word about the sorrow that Flaubert ought to have considered a possibility, if only out of politeness. Had he only written: "My poor Ernest, Alfred is dead; I know what pain his loss will cause you." No; it is to "good Ernest" that his letter is addressed. Does he think Chevalier will be indifferent to the news? On the contrary, and for this very reason he does not mention it: at her husband's death, the triumphant widow prevents the disconsolate mistress from following the cortège. He was *mine*, *I* am the one who weeps. Would it be claimed that these boys formed a trio? Nonsense: Ernest had the honor of being witness to a miraculous friendship, that's all.

But suddenly the third rascal, disqualified, takes on in his new functions a considerable importance. As a witness, let him bear witness!

Since it is not his place to share Gustave's grief, let him recognize and institute this suffering in all its fullness. When Flaubert writes quickly, his pen betrays his deepest intentions: "the pain this loss *must have caused me.*" Who is speaking? It cannot be a *subject,* who, conscious of what he is feeling, would always say: "the pain this death caused me." Nor is this entirely what Chevalier would say if he were speaking to Gustave; if Ernest had written his friend a condolence letter, he too would have used a direct affirmation. In the phrase Gustave attributes to his friend there is a shred of doubt, a faint reservation: even if this slight reticence corresponded to his real opinion, Chevalier would have refrained from expressing it. "The immense pain this loss has caused you." Therefore, only one speaker is possible: if we change the "you" into an "I," Gustave's "I" is transformed by the very structure of the phrase into a "He"; Ernest, speaking to others about this Other that Gustave is for him, is the only possible subject, saying to them: "The poor boy! I know how much *he* loved Alfred. What pain this loss must have caused him." By this ambiguous turn, two meanings are introduced. *On the one hand,* Gustave is conceding to Ernest that it is impossible to guarantee unconditionally the strength and sincerity of feelings that one does not experience oneself, even when one has known since childhood the person who is feeling them: "In all probability this death *must have* been a terrible blow to him; personally I am convinced of it, but this is only an opinion, I am not inside his skin." This prudence, this restraint are proposed because they are attractive to the moderate soul of the deputy prosecutor: What are you risking? You are not committing yourself, you are conjecturing. If, furthermore, these measures persuade him to bear witness, the listener will be more impressed by Ernest's cautious affirmation than by a statement that is too categorical. *On the other hand,* a normative element slips surreptitiously into what is given out as a simple hypothetical judgment; for Gustave his pain is a duty-being: as he is, in order to be faithful to his dead friend, to himself, to their transcendent friendship, he *must* suffer hell. It is Ernest's job to realize this imaginary being and imaginary suffering. It will be enough for him to tell others; the duty-being is addressed to him too and assumes the character of an injunction: you had the luck to know us, take care: you would be heartless and foolish if you were not *assured* that I loved him more than my life and that I am dying of sorrow. Hence the flattering apostrophe—you, our unique witness—actually contains treachery and blackmail which are barely concealed. But above all it indicates the need Gustave has to feel *in the third person*—and through the mediation of another testifying before others—what he does not manage to experience in the first.[102]

Does he honestly think he is going to manipulate Ernest? Does he really take the trouble to do this? Does he even want to? He does not. He would despise, of course, what is passed along through the grapevine: Gustave struck down by a sacred illness. But what's this all about? Chevalier is surrounded at Calvi by people who do not know Flaubert and who are perfectly unknown to him; furthermore, Gustave no longer feels anything for his friend but a mixture of spiteful animosity and mistrust. Why should he try so hard to convince him? Indeed, the only importance Ernest assumes in Gustave's eyes is that he was a witness to their life. Because of this he is persuaded that *down here* at Calvi, a bourgeois consciousness—all the more valuable for having been transformed into a witness for the defense—recognizes him as Le Poittevin's inconsolable widow. And to convince himself even further, his best move is to call on Ernest to give his testimony as if its contents were assured in advance. When Gustave suborns Chevalier and summons him to guarantee his suffering, he is merely making another gesture whose real aim is less to persuade the deputy prosecutor of Calvi than to consolidate in Flaubert the belief that he *exists-suffering* there for his former friend. It is as if he were saying: my pain has been truly atrocious, Ernest knows it, *he* doesn't doubt for a moment that I have been prostrated by this death; it's obvious because I'm addressing myself to him, and his next letter will confirm that he has understood my grief. Gustave alone is the party concerned: his com-

102. We also note the surprising use of the past tense: "the pain this loss *must have caused* me." Gustave wants Ernest to witness the pain that Alfred's death *caused him.* What is this all about? Eight days after the event, is he already claiming to be consoled? Why doesn't he write: the pain it *must cause* me? Shall we say that the cause is in the past but that the sorrow still remains, as if prolonging itself through a kind of inertia, just as a moving object continues in motion as long as no external force opposes it? Nothing is further from the work of mourning. In truth the motivation for suffering is constantly present in a true feeling; it is the "never more" that matters, much more than the *passing* moment when Alfred died. For my part, I interpret the choice of the past tense as Gustave's effort to disqualify the experience: when he is writing, Flaubert does not feel this sorrow that Ernest must institute. He therefore prefers to locate it in the past, not like a certain affection that is over in a week (which would suggest that it was trivial) but like a thunderclap that did not kill him but aged him by thirty years—a familiar story. What he experienced, he seems to be saying, is a perfect and total pain, the *eidos* of pain, which will remain in him until his death in the form of premature old age. We have seen, we shall see again, that old age serves as a symbolic mediation between an unsuffered suffering and a death that has not taken place. By this means, he makes himself more vulnerable to the affirmation he solicits from others: an imaginary memory is difficult to call into question since all reminiscence, even if true, has a structure that is imaginary in nature.

rade has only been the mediator between him and himself. Flaubert imagines Ernest spreading the news—"What pain this loss must have caused him"—only so as to be able to dream about that ravaged "He" that he is for this distant consciousness. Rather than make his "I" appear to be a transcendent quasi object on the horizon of his reflected consciousness, Gustave often prefers to produce an imaginary reflection in the real but unreflected consciousness he supposes others have of him. He enters into their thought; he sees it as if it were his own and the object that appears as the transcendent pole of their judgments and their affection—it is himself in the third person. In these moments he lives his ego unreally as a "He" wholly charged with the reality his audience gives him. The reason for this, as we have seen above, is that he lacks the means to exercise what I call a complicit reflection: when he is inclined to reflect, indeed, he is already in the hands of others—of his parents, in the first place. As a consequence, his *real* ego appears to him partly as alienated, that is, as an alter ego, partly as incomplete—in many respects he is quite unaware of what others think of him—and partly as soft, capricious, unstable, idiotic. He barely distinguishes between this alienated, badly defined "I" and the "He" recuperated from others—all the more since he lacks the means to distinguish carefully between true and false. He goes from "*I am an other*," the reality that derealizes him, to "*The Other is me*," an unreal reflection on the consciousness of others and the manner in which, outwitting them by his gesture, he makes himself signified by them. In short, he deploys two synthetic unities of experience of which the most recent, the imaginary, is introduced to save him from the other. This will partly explain the importance of the theme of the double in Flaubert's works.

He will go even further: throughout his life he gives himself nicknames and keeps them, different names according to his audience. For George Sand he was the troubador, the fogey, Father Cruchard; for Caroline Commanville, the Nanny, the Old man, the Dotard, the Canon of Seville; for the Lapierres (and for Sand), Saint Polycarp; for Mme Brianne, "Excessive"; for Laporte, the Giant, etc. Each one of these sobriquets represents a role, indicating both what the chosen spectator expects of Gustave and the body of gestures Flaubert undertakes in order to represent for himself what is expected of him. In fact, he *imposes* this expectation and vows to fulfill it. It goes without saying that these variously named characters are related or complementary aspects of one and the same *persona*. For this reason there is no qualitative difference between "producing the laughter of the Garçon" (that is, projecting himself into the character so that an audience should reflect him to himself *as the Garçon*) and declaring that he is Mme Brianne's Excessive. The Lapierres, a good audience, wished him happy birthday on Saint Polycarp's day. This means that they entered into the game and that the enterprise was collective: the audience *knew his role*, just as they did at the Royal College. He plays the game *just enough* to know that they take the actor seriously, that Kean has really persuaded them that he is Hamlet: "I am still completely in a flutter about Saint Polycarp. The Lapierres have surpassed themselves!!! I received nearly thirty letters from different parts of the world. The archibishop of Rouen, Italian cardinals, floor polishers, the company of apartment scavengers, a relic dealer, etc., have sent me their respects. They presented me with . . . a portrait (Spanish) of Saint Polycarp, a tooth (holy relic), etc., and all the letters (including the one from Mme Régnier) are headed by the face of my patron saint. I forgot to mention a menu composed of dishes all named after my works. Truly, I was touched by all the trouble they had taken to amuse me. I suspect my disciple of having closely cooperated in these amiable farces." [103]

The "disciple" did, no doubt, cooperate. But the principal collaborator is Gustave himself. He took a few of the Saint's features—one in particular: excessive Hhhindignation (*sic*) against the century—and continually referred to them in his letters and in public, starting with the letter to Louise of 21 August 1853, usually in the same terms, in order to drive the point home. [104] His relation to the saint evolved slowly, however. First, he "is getting to be like . . . ," then he "is like . . ." Subsequently—a period of transition—the "like" is omitted, though the identification is still incomplete: "[I am] a *true* Polycarpian." In the end, he calmly signs his letters to Lapierre "St. Polycarp"—the process of assimilation is complete. Naturally when his friends, who are so energetically solicited, "go along" with him, when they decide to celebrate him every year under the saint's name, he pretends not to be taken in: these are "pleasant farces," they only want to "amuse" him. But these birthdays are the outcome of many years of patient effort: he wanted to be instituted as Saint Polycarp and he succeeded; his easily manipulated public signifies Gustave as being that *face of the Other* which Saint Indignant represents. And certainly he was right: the

103. To Maupassant, 28 April 1880.
104. In the letters of August 1853 and March 1854 (the night of the 2d to the 3d), the two paragraphs on Saint Polycarp are almost identical in some sentences. We shall later find repeated versions of "Hindignant like Saint Polycarp."

Lapierres *played at believing*, they unrealized themselves to the extent that they pretended to *realize* by their actions the character he suggested to them. It was food enough for him. *Before* the ceremony he was merely an unreal Polycarp for a real audience; while it is taking place, he is a real Polycarp for an audience that is suggestible to the point of becoming unrealized; the unreality thus being assumed by the others gives Flaubert a specious reality whose nontruth is sensed *there*, in those who have taken charge of it. Depersonalization is pushed to the limit this time, and Gustave no longer knows whether he is subject or object: his I is a He and his He is an I.

We shall return to this subject soon, when we study Flaubert's *persona*, the various avatars of the Garçon. It is enough to note here that the personalizing revolution creating the dichotomy of the He and the I (one, the sadistic lord, the other, the masochistic child) only aggravates the hemorrhaging of his being at this stage. The little boy became conscious very early of this leakage and tried to plug the hole by which his reality was being lost in the imaginary. This new revolution might have saved him at least some of the stress that would later make him the Artist if certain considerations, which we shall have to discuss, had not prevented him from taking his attempt to its conclusion. We shall deal with this revolution first, for despite its failure, it played a leading role in Gustave's personalization. For the first time the child takes a global view of the situation and seeks to circumvent the difficulty with the means at hand: between the ages of eight and ten he internalizes the criticisms leveled at him and takes them as the basis of a new conviction: that he *is* an actor.

From Imaginary Child to Actor

"I have nearly thirty plays and Caroline and I act out many of them," he writes on 31 March 1832, at the age of ten. When Ernest is with them, he is part of the cast. But what is striking is that most of the time the brother and sister are the only actors: the entertainer and the entertained find themselves face to face and exchange dialogue as they did when he used to play the doctor or salesman and she the patient or customer. With this considerable difference, that the earlier roles were improvised—the children were imitating adults, spontaneously—whereas in the billiard room the lines are imposed and exchanged according to a preestablished order. How did this change come about? Was it an evolution or a revolution? In my opinion, both: Gustave wanted to be an actor when he discovered himself in the process of playing prefabricated roles.

The little girl had grown; their relationship being ludic, Gustave could no longer limit her to being his audience; he had to let her enter the game and had to invent characters for her that were more complex than customer or mother. They are seen; they entertain; they *show* themselves; someone—Uncle Parain or Mme Flaubert—probably advised them, taking the opportunity to make their enterprise into an instructive entertainment, going to the library to find Carmontelle's *Proverbes dramatiques,* the works of Berquin, Scribe, Molière. Dr. Flaubert, without displaying much interest in these childish performances, nevertheless consented to give them the billiard room, and then of course he would have had to explain what a theater was, tell them about roles, productions, rehearsals, performances. In this period the little boy was familiar only with the Rouen marionettes.

The puppet theater had given a performance of "La Tentation de Saint Antoine," and the child, whatever might have been said to him, was less taken by the legend itself—although his later stubbornness

119

in giving three versions of his own *Tentation* a theatrical form that the subject scarcely required must be attributed to the persistence of a very early impression—than to the *ceremony of the spectacle*. It was a true initiation for him; he was witnessing a strange, fascinating rite, both inhuman and human—the marionette, a piece of dead wood possessed by a dream of life, has the jerky movements of an automaton and speaks with a man's voice[1]—serious and gratuitous all at the same time, since you pay to witness a completely imaginary spectacle that has no pretentions to being anything else. He easily understood that in real theaters—the kind you go to "when you are grown up"— marionettes were replaced by people; but he concluded, not to his displeasure, that these people transformed themselves into marionettes when they acted, borrowing some kind of ontological density from inanimate matter, and that at least as far as he was concerned, he would like to be an actor in order to acquire the dignity of dead wood.

So he throws himself into this enterprise. He learns roles by heart, teaches them to Caroline, rehearses every day, and when everything is ready the two children exhibit themselves before a limited, but select audience. Still, he might have gotten tired, become discouraged at the efforts demanded of his memory, or—what happens most often— given himself to the new game by fits and starts and without much enthusiasm, viewing it as an agreeable entertainment but not unique. What demands explanation, on the other hand, is his persistence and his zeal, especially the way he turned himself into a woodworker, a carpenter, a decorator, a painter, and built with his own hands a regular little theater with stage, curtain, wings, scenery, and, on occasion, "roofs"; above all, the way he amassed in two years—between 1830 and 1832—a repertory of "nearly thirty plays," that is, thirty plays already produced, which he could present to his audience from one day to the next. If Gustave threw himself body and soul into this venture, it was because it gave him something he was looking for, though without knowing it. Two moments in the process must be singled out, although only their chronological order can be determined; we do not know how much time elapsed between them. First of all, Gustave had a passion for drama, that is, for playing the roles of prefabricated characters; the reflected decision to become an actor was a conclusion that necessarily came *afterward*, when he discovered that he already was one.

Playing roles. It was time. Derealized, he unrealized himself haphaz-

---

1. Isn't this how he views life?

ardly, without success; in front of his mirror he had begun to look for that ineffable He that the others laughed at. In any event, this persona disturbed him and eluded him; variable, insubstantial, it was so diaphanous it was transparent, and then he strained and exerted himself in vain to integrate it with the self or surpass himself by embracing it. In any case, the others had its secret. Yet no sooner did he slip into a prefabricated role than he would experience a dizzying happiness, an incredible revelation: he thought he had found the ultimate protection against the fragility of his improvised persona. The difference between this improvised persona and the *character* in a written play is not substantial; in both cases a third person singular is playing himself in the first person, a He saying "I." But consistency, *Selbstständigkeit*, stability based on tradition and even being, are on the side of the character. The character hadn't waited for Gustave to be born, its words and gestures were noted and given in detail in printed books, the grown-ups spoke about it as one of their acquaintances; the character exists, it lives—that is why people say it is true to life. Since the character's affective reactions are held to be authentic when the reactions of the derealized child are judged insincere, the child need only take the trouble to express his character's emotions appropriately to prove them true. This means, first of all, that *on stage* Gustave lends his body and his blood and, in return, receives a guarantee that his conduct is justified. "Off stage" he is always criticized: his behavior is hyperbolic, insincere, unmotivated. But he finds that the spectators agree on one point: whatever the character—miser, fool, or braggart—it never does what he can and must do, which is to take account of his character and the situation. The moment the little boy puts himself "inside the role," his actions will be motivated by the passions of the character he is interpreting and will no longer need justification. And drama demands a certain excess, even vehemence, which in daily life the chief surgeon would consider exaggerated; here hyperbole cannot be imputed to the actor but only to the character, "beside himself" from blunders and misfortunes, his defects or his ridiculous qualities pushed to an extreme. The little boy is enchanted to be carried away and to shout himself hoarse *on command*: he is justified by the instructions of a dead poet; he will never, he thinks, do *too much*. He is still too new to the theater to understand the rigor and precision of the dramatic machinery as well as he might, but he senses intuitively that the sequence of gestures and lines are imposed on him as so many *imperatives*—the role presents itself as an *other-being* which he *must* internalize, something doubly seductive for Gustave. He re-

121

discovers in this obligation the very movement by which he seeks to internalize his being—namely, as I have shown, that appearance which escapes him and which he is in the eyes of others. But until now his quest was in vain; he could not *make* himself into that object he knew how to be for them because he would first have had to see himself from the outside, with their eyes. Now the character to be acted—for him as for any spectator—is first a pure *outside*, which he knows and judges as external, even as he is aware of its most hidden motivations. In relation to the character he *will be*, he is simultaneously an other and a future self; thus the apprenticeship of the role is a systematic process of reappropriation of his *other-being* through memory, intuition, and recreation. He no longer *escapes himself*, quite the contrary; in this anamorphosis he comes to himself *known*, and that knowledge continues to deepen: he must internalize his appearance in order to reexternalize it as it appears to him. Thus it seems to him that he will succeed on stage in what he so often failed to accomplish in his young life. But—and this is the other reason for his jubilation—whereas in front of the mirror or in his relations with Caroline the business of recuperation disappointed him by its very gratuitousness (no one had mandated it), he finds that as an actor he is *charged with a mission*. It is the will of a dead writer that the warmth and life of his characters should be revived, which, were it not for the devotion of specialists, would otherwise remain buried in library books, deader than stones. And if we claim to obey the playwright's wishes, we must revive his creatures exactly as he conceived them. Obviously the child's total submission to these alien demands, in spite of the narrow margin of freedom left him by the directions indicated, carries his alienation to an extreme. But he is pleased to be alienated from his being—it is reassuring and comfortable. A sovereign authority requires him to become what he is; this means that someone—even someone dead—has the goodness to care about him. As a vassal of Molière, he freely receives the bundle of rigorous imperatives we call a character; the great Molière lends weight to the attempt at recuperation (which constitutes the meaning of Gustave's personalization) by presenting it to him as his most sacred duty. Do this, say that, be the Miser, be Pourceaugnac. This mandate protects Gustave against the various contingent personas his parents impose on him with his complicity. Ambiguity, chance, contradictory qualifications will give way, he believes, to a clear, rigid array of prescriptions, a delicious and willing enslavement, at the end of which he will *show himself* as Molière wanted and as he is.

It goes without saying that when the child moves to the second phase of the process, the reexternalization of the character, he perceives, not without disappointment, that he has not left the imaginary world. Quite to the contrary, he is even more ensconced in it; he was tricked, and all his attempts to find something real to hang onto serve only to increase his unreality. He believed at first that he would realize himself through these characters; now he feels that he is unrealized in them; no sooner does he begin to act than everything that seemed opaque and dense at the moment of internalization suddenly loses its weight and substance. Even his shouts, his sobs, the gesticulation that ought to express the fullness of passions and their violence—scarcely has he lent them his voice, his limbs, than they are mysteriously reduced, secretly dematerialized, escaping gravity and threatening to waft him away with them. This is because he does not feel what he is expressing. Or at least not fully; let us say that he does not quite believe he *is* his character. Not quite—but a little, all the same; much more, in any case, than the little actors who assist him. Not used to feeling precisely what he expresses, he doesn't need to believe in a Gustave sure of his emotions who is playing Poursôgnac. Ernest is probably like this, too; certainly Caroline is—she lends herself with pleasure but without losing her inner certainties. We are not saying that the young Flaubert, who has no certainties, reproaches his character for being imaginary but, rather, that he deplores the fact that the sentiments he has a mandate to express are neither more nor less real than those he experiences spontaneously. For him, to act rage or fear is to feel those emotions to the extent that, since his derealization, to feel them is to act them. Poursôgnac, however, existed well before Gustave played the role; the character is imposed with an abstract rigor which, not being his *reality*, can be only the sign of his *truth*; yet others believe in him, for they laugh. This is enough for Gustave. To be sure, he is far from understanding what grown-ups mean by the truth of a character; rather, it is a matter of conforming to *commands* and producing a *particular command* whose objective being is guaranteed by its cohesion and unity; this synthetic unity of singular images, each referring to all the others, collectively and individually, is the source of what will later appear to him to be the *truth of illusion* and which, in fact, is less dependent on the norms of truth than on those of beauty. For the moment, the truth of the character is the little boy's reassuring allegiance to alien imperatives. His life seems to him denuded and shrunken: the words and gestures for which he takes responsibility are not dictated to him by the whim of a Great Lord; they

123

are imposed on the dramatist as on Gustave because their express function is to *advance the action*. When the words have been spoken, whatever they are, the child can no longer retreat; indeed, he is projected into a new situation and by degrees hastens the catastrophe. Until then the passive child had submitted to the vague, slack, incoherent, and monotonous sliding of a temporalization which seemed to go nowhere. Intersubjective duration was that of the family, hence of repetition, endlessly recurring seasons, holidays, and tasks; an opportunity missed soon presented itself again—you could always have another turn. But his anxiety and prophetic fatalism were poorly accommodated by that time without memory in which nothing counted, nothing was inscribed, and which seemed to be lost *to no purpose* except to be revived at a fixed and thus meaningless date. Gustave suspected a threat behind this nauseating return.

The characteristic of constituted passivity is, we know, fatalism: a passive "nature" only defines itself when it imagines that it is borne toward a cruel destiny and can do nothing to escape. Thus it is with Flaubert, who "prophesies" very early, starting from the principle that the worst is certain and, indeed, experiencing his passivity as a paralysis; when the event *shows* him a possible future, that future becomes inevitable solely because the child is conscious of being unable to avoid it. Still, the repeated and vague time of lived experience does not readily lend itself to oracles; always begun anew, stagnant or flowing slowly without visible direction, time does not allow the little boy to give his future misfortunes the clarity and imminence he would like. Furthermore, even when he prophesies, he feels insincere; not that he doesn't intuit his destiny, but the rigor of *fatum* finds no place in the contingent indolence of family life. We should add to the first maxim another which defines a directed time: "Everything I do to avoid my fate will only have the effect of chaining me to it." But from the moment he goes on stage, Gustave is intoxicated to discover the irreversibility of historical time, not as the subject that makes history but as the object that submits to it. From this perspective, the irreversible necessarily appears as a destiny. Consequently the actor prophesies: he knows his role by heart, he is aware of the sudden turn of fortune and the impending catastrophe; every line, every gesture brings him closer to the event which concludes the play and which he helps to bring about by acts that attempt to avoid it. The miser will lose his mistress, his casket—no one will give either of them back, and it will be his own fault that he loses them; Gustave knows this but Harpagon does not. Yet the actor's lucid knowledge of the future only serves to emphasize his feeling of powerlessness; not only is he unable to warn his character, he is compelled to make him act and speak in the most self-destructive way. This means that in order to play Harpagon, he must forget his oracular power and assume on command Harpagon's ignorance. An unreal ignorance, nothing other than knowledge passed over in silence, which must be kept as a guiding scheme of interpretation; skirting the illuminated zones of consciousness, the actor thus transforms this suppressed knowledge into the intuition of an ineluctable but unknowable necessity. One by one the speeches emerge from the shadows and *make themselves heard*, foreseen and unforeseen, innocent and fatal, communicating their urgency to experience. Flaubert/Harpagon rushes headlong toward disaster and *feels* it, but he neither can nor wants to know it; the wordless prophecy is the very warp and woof of temporalization. Gustave's fatalism has two sources: his constituted passivity and the paternal curse that governed his life until death. When he plays a dramatic role, he discovers the irreversible time of the curse, but an alien authority is substituted for that of the paterfamilias, the authority of the author, which is just as severe but beneficent and gives him Harpagon's destiny, pulling him out of the destiny of the Flaubert younger son while making it comply with the highest temporal moment, with the directed temporality that he needs in order to think about his life, to think about himself.

Certainly the intuition of the irreversible is given to Gustave only as long as he plays a prefabricated role. When the curtain falls, he once again recovers the slack, vegetative duration which is his lot within the cyclicality of the family. Be that as it may; this duration is *no more real* than the other since the family idiot is no more real than Harpagon. The result is that the child can refer to the character as he would to the hidden truth of the other: the dark face of cyclical time is the irreversible time of the theater. Thus he slips into an imaginary and true time, the very time he needed when Harpagon claimed his young blood and yielded him in exchange the theater's implacable duration. The child is *at home with himself* when he becomes temporalized as the miser; he admires the fatal beauty of the sequence of imperatives that are spun out one after the other, enclosing him in a destiny he *savors* as long as he plays the role—a destiny he preserves in memory when he returns to exile. Hereafter, the *category* of irreversibility permits him to prophesy more boldly; he *does not live* in the midst of the irreversible, but he can think about it since he has lived there and *can* live there over and over again. The result is that he derealizes the

125

cyclical reversibility of time and its contingency: his theatrical temporalization, which has become the guiding scheme of his thoughts, is what allows him to conceive of his life, to have "a complete presentiment" of it. It will be one of the singular and inimitable charms of *Madame Bovary* that we are presented simultaneously with two durations, one lived in its repetitive slowness, its tedious lethargy, the other utterly oracular but hidden. The theatrical temporalization sustaining the novelistic temporalization and manifesting itself to us by intersigns reveals in these striking moments that Emma is running headlong to her ruin and is bent upon realizing her destiny as one of the damned. By lending himself to this partially double temporality, the reader sometimes has the impression of rediscovering the taste of experience in Flaubert, the reciprocal derealization of time suffered and time conceived, of contingency and destiny, of ennui and anguish. When the child, in any case, engages in playacting, he creates in the realm of the imaginary a total experience of everything he is lacking in order to *be* himself at last. This means that he knows the (for him) unequaled pleasure of *forgetting himself* and *turning himself into another*, who is not, however, different from himself. Theatrical interpretation for Gustave might almost be thought of as an absence, taking its source from the child's stupors but more complex in that it is guided by remote control; he throws himself into Harpagon, surpasses himself, and rediscovers himself in the role, not as his reality but as his nominative truth. For the audience and *through it* he is Harpagon, and in this sense his being always eludes him, with the crucial qualification that he *knows* what he is for his audience and that his role is to lead that audience, in accordance with the prescriptions of a sacred will, gradually to constitute and enrich *the appearance which is his being*. He does this knowingly, with all his gestures and words: nothing is excessive, his lean, economical actions are *all* effective, all are indispensable, all are experienced at the same time by him and by the audience as solemn and sacred rites, all create him the way a dead progenitor wanted him to be. Thus in the semireal world of familial intersubjectivity, his actions, whatever they might be, are aimed at realizing him as the paterfamilias wanted him to be. But when he believes he is showing his obedience, his actions are judged inadequate either by defect or excess. Achille-Cléophas does not *recognize him*—no doubt because this terrible Moses gave life to his younger son expressly so as not to recognize him. On the other hnd, if the little boy submits to all of Molière's demands, for example, that other progenitor cannot do less than recognize his creature, saying, as if from the grave: You were what I wanted you to be; very good! By his very obe-dience Gustave is divested of all responsibility except that of clearly *manifesting* what he is enjoined to be; as for what he *is*—miser, fop, or fool—he is not held responsible. Not that he is disengaged from Pour-sôgnac or Harpagon; indeed, he is the one who cries over his lost cas-ket. But here the author takes everything on himself; Gustave will never be reproached for being *too* stingy, at the most one might say he was not being stingy enough if he were to act badly. The perfect con-vergence of the actor with his character, far from being reprehensible, seems on the contrary admirable since it is greeted with applause. Thus the irreversibility of time shows its beneficent ambiguity, for from the first lines the character ineluctably runs headlong to his doom and the actor to his triumph. But for the derealized child, an absenteeist, the character is none other than his persona created and guaranteed by the benevolence of the Other: protected by an invisible armor, he offers himself up to the blows of fate, exhibiting, without taking responsibility for it, the preestablished transposition of his ab-surdity and misfortune. In his theatrical experience the child finds ir-responsibility, submission, happy and compensated vassalage; the guarantee of the imaginary by a sovereign will, by the necessity of connections, by tradition and universal consent; a priori knowledge of his being-for-others, the ambiguity of *fatum*, the justification of pa-thos—that is, not just of his excessive gesticulation but of his consti-tuted passivity, which, by forbidding him action, encourages him to abandon himself to what he is and to show his passions through ges-tures; pithiatic belief, never total but consolidated by that of others; the ability really to feel what he expresses. The child finds all this in his theatrical experience as long as it remains in the immediate realm of unreflected spontaneity, in other words, as long as he produces himself on stage, moved only by the need to escape from his insub-stantial and tedious persona by replacing it with the being of a character.

A. To Be an Actor

Unfortunately, the passage to reflection was unavoidable. Someone might have said to him, quite casually: "You would be an excellent actor." This heedless praise had the effect of changing the objective of his quest and the meaning of the process of recuperation. Words wreak havoc when they happen to name something that is experi-enced but has not yet been named: they revive a complicit reflection

127

by proposing a meaning for something when that meaning is, in fact, only a hypothesis of the future, only an extrapolation which cannot be accepted reflexively except by a vow. I have already cited that line of Mosca's referring to Fabrice and Sanseverina: "If the word *love* is pronounced between them, I am lost." Through this expression the collectivity affirms its right of surveillance over the most purely subjective intimacy, socializing the rather foolhardy tenderness the young aunt and her nephew feel for one another. The tenderness was indefinable, not because they were afraid to define it but because they simply were not concerned to give it a status, because they were living it from day to day for the simple pleasure of living and because it was never more and never less than what it *seemed* to them when they were together, surpassed only by the looks, the smiles, the gestures they used to communicate it to one another and because it still escaped the intoxication of their encounter. "Let the word *love* be pronounced":[2] their tenderness is here endowed with a past, a future, an objective essence constituted by the historical evolution of mores, of folk wisdom, with a positive value and often an antivalue that bear witness to the contradictions of the current ideology or opposing ideologies. The development of that tenderness—first it had none, it simply *existed*— is foreseen, its end known in advance, mediocre or tragic; in brief, it is a quasi object, a product of culture that must be internalized. Reflection is caught in a trap: it confirms, and in order to preserve its signifying power it takes responsibility for the signification. The change is a radical one: Love is the aim; emotion, tenderness, desire are the means to help it be its own end; one lover smiled with happiness or enthusiasm for the other, or because the other smiled and he wanted to feel that proffered smile on his own lips. A change of perspective: love is the end; tender emotion, desire, are the means of preserving its being, that is, of remaining faithful to the vow. These are the *proofs*, the renewed promises, and at the same time the food for this abstract flame, for love—other—or love of others—which continually craves fuel because it is nothing but a vow extracted from each of them by society, with the other's complicity, which neither of the two can "betray" without denying himself. Thus we feed the vampire, we pledge ourselves to this infinite task for that final aim—or ultimate mystification—loyalty to ourselves.

Still, this is only a matter of emotion; for poor Gustave, the proposed vow will alienate him *in his very being*. Some misguided busy-

---

2. In fact, it will never be. We know how things turn out.

body thinks to please him by signifying to him *his reality*—which is, moreover, hypothetical. This is the first time since the Fall; we imagine the derealized child throwing himself into the trap they have laid for him and moving quickly from the conditional to the categorical. *You would be . . . you would do;* his interlocutor means: if your father hadn't had other plans for you; Gustave hastens to understand: if you were not lazy and unstable. From here to the simple future is only a step: if you apply yourself, you will be an actor. This is indeed what he already *is,* at least covertly. The reflection soon surfaces, working a transubstantiation during which he believes he is Harpagon, Poursôgnac—without being entirely convinced of it; in reality he is an actor, that is, a living being who has the power to animate imaginary characters. On the reflexive level, the creatures of Molière and Carmontelle reveal their insubstantiality; certainly they are imperative and true to life, but they would remain in books if Gustave did not lend them his life. Gustave: not the persona of the Flauberts' younger son but the young man who defines himself by his power to incarnate in turn Harpagon and Poursôgnac, and who consequently cannot be summed up by one or the other. Thus, he thinks, my being has escaped me; though in fact it resides in a power of mine—since others recognize that I have it. Later, indeed, when he reflects on the time spent in the billiard room, he says proudly: "I could have been an actor, *I had the inner power,*" which shows well enough that the reflexive revelation revealed his being to him as a *plenitude*—what we call in the theater "temperament," "presence." The gift reappears in its seigneurial form; he "has a gift," the gift of giving himself to the audience, of showing them a character to which he gives the overfullness of his life. To act dramatically is to practice generosity, to overwhelm the spectators, who, in return, render the actor the homage of their bravos. No sooner said than done; he has taken a vow: I will be what I am, the *Actor.*

Poor child! He's in a fine mess: some well-intentioned troublemaker made him believe that his dramatic genius was the strict consequence of natural exuberance seeking an outlet. When he perceived—between the ages of nine and twelve—that it was quite the opposite, and that the signs should have been inverted, plenitude replaced by penury, it was already too late. If he vowed he would be an actor, it was because he believed that others took him for one. We are familiar with the process: in the same way he had been a vassal, then grudgingly a lord; always in quest of his other-being, he tried to laugh at his reflection, then to steal the being of characters in classical drama. Now the unfortunate boy throws himself into a new hornet's nest and sets about making himself an actor, certainly not because he *feels his inner power* but because he remains an image in search of his reality. He believed he had found it in prefabricated roles; by complimenting him on his talent, others implied that, far from draining them of their being, he gave life to those characters, but at the price of his own depletion. He was unrealized in them, however, and the actor is at least that: a *being* who loses himself for the sake of displaying images. What he is really seeking, as he will soon understand, is not the power of the actor but that minimum of being his status as actor confers on him. Let us join in his search, and see what this last resort, being a displayer of images, can bring by way of *reality* to a child who is prey to the imaginary. Or, if you like, let us see whether it can satisfy his humble need for recuperation, his need to pass from the melancholy statement "I am nothing but the roles I play" to a proud declaration: "I am a being whose real occupation is to play roles."

A statue is an imaginary woman: the Venus de Milo *is* not and has never been. But the marble exists as an analogue of the goddess; and how can we distinguish the beauty, the purity of matter from the form that vampirizes it? The sculptor exists, or has existed, who conceived and realized it with his chisel at the cost of very real effort. In brief, Venus *is* not, but the statue exists; it is known, appreciated, has a definite value; someone or some organization owns it; if it must be sent to a foreign country for an exhibition of its author's works, we know its weight, its fragility, and will take practical measures to ship it safely. For the first time here I give this strange object a name we shall encounter repeatedly hereafter, the real and permanent center of derealization. If it has an individual being, if it has not remained stone in the mountains of Carrara, it is because someone gave it the function of embodying a certain nonbeing. Inversely, however, when that nonbeing as such is recognized as a determination of the social imaginary, the whole object is *instituted in its being*. Society recognizes in it an ontological truth to the extent that the being of this object is considered a permanent incitement to derealization by unrealizing the marble as Venus. The object is the support of the unrealization, but the unrealization gives it its necessity because it must exist for the derealization to take place. Here the imaginary is not fleeting, vague, formless; rather, it has the force, the impenetrability, and the limits of a piece of marble. The compact, inert being of the stone is there in order to be derealized publicly by derealizing those who look at it. But as a result, something of its immutable consistency and its radiant inertia is infused in the Venus or the Pièta. The woman of stone is the ideal of being—the figuration of a *for-itself* which is like the dream of the *in-itself*. Thus the sculpted stone, the mineral indispensable to a collective unrealization, surely possesses the *maximum of being* when we recall that within the social intersubjectivity, *being* is being-for-others when it is instituted.

I have taken the simplest example. Being, here, is the practico-inert of the imaginary; impenetrable, half-closed, recognized by everyone, a piece of merchandise with a *determined* and fixed flight at its center; a function, a value, a demand. But this example was meant to bring us to the status of the actor. What complicates things here is that the actor is not a chunk of inorganic matter that has absorbed human work, but a living, thinking man whose unrealization every evening is an unpredictable dosage of rehearsal and invention; at worst, he approaches an automaton; at best, he goes beyond acquired habits by "trying out" an effect. Still, he resembles the statue in that he is the permanent, real, and recognized center of derealization (the permanent here being a perpetual renewal rather than an inert subsistence). He is motivated and wholly committed to making his real person the analogue of an imaginary one named Titus, Harpagon, or Ruy Blas. In brief, every evening he derealizes himself in order to lead five hundred people in a collective unrealization. The difference between the actor and little Gustave, who also unrealizes himself all day long, is that the child does it blindly, under the influence of impulses he is unaware of, which he takes at once for accidents and for a malign inspiration. Besides, the child loses himself: as he practices imagination, imagination dissolves into nonbeing, it is a decompression of being as long as he is operating *without a mandate;* vague and indistinct despite certain reports, this unrealization is not a *ceremonial function;* he does not even know that by making a spectacle of himself he is inviting others to unmask him or to unrealize themselves with him. As we know, he acts so that the unreal—namely, appearance—should be the appearance *here,* and there the unrecoverable being he continues to set himself against. In sum, he is an actor-mythomane, conscious of casting himself as appearance so that others, more or less fooled, should take the appearance for his being and convince him of it. This unstable position involves both cynicism and naïveté, the consciousness of being that character for others in imagination, duping them in fact, and simultaneously the wild hope that through their mediation he will return to himself as really being what he acts. As always in Gustave there is a *withheld* consciousness, which he prevents from developing; for if he were to develop fully the consciousness of making himself into an appearance for others, *either* they would in fact grasp the appearance for what it is and thus not believe what he claims to make them believe, *or else* they would be duped and their testimony would become worthless. For this reason, moreover, he exerts himself before impenetrable judges: either the supreme magistrate *laughs at him*, or else the others keep quiet and watch, or else their comments are not convincing. What they say is what Gustave wants them to say, but there is no way to *evaluate* their statements. However—and intuitions such as these are also typical of him—through error he manages to further the truth: *by acting and because he acts*, he can ask others to institute his being. He is mistaken on one point only: what they declare with good reason to be real is at that moment not the character but the actor. This is what Parain, or whoever it was, meant when he declared: you will be (you have the potential to be) an actor.

Kean is *recognized* by his audience in the same way the Venus de Milo is recognized. When they think about him, it is as a real being who is the indispensable mediation between individual realities—which as such have no imagination in common—and that collective unreality which is Hamlet, for example. We scramble to get tickets to see Kean as Hamlet in the same way that tourists hurry to San Pietro dei Vincoli to see a piece of Carraran marble as Moses. The actor is created by the roles he plays just as doctors are by illnesses. A national theater has a *repertory, awaits its men:* Hamlets come and go, Hamlet remains, demanding new interpreters and sustaining them. The roles are specialties and designate their future incumbents, first in the abstract—the youthful lead, the central lead role, the three swordsmen, the fat guys, etc. To the extent that they themselves are real centers of unrealization (they are the products of effort that has been preserved and reworked from one generation to the next, and they can be deepened but not a single word changed; anyone who interprets these roles incorporates them as categorical imperatives), they designate their future interpreters, who must possess the proper voice, stature, and attitude. Moreover, constituted character enters into the game: timidity, a certain incapacity to control events joined to a pug nose, and we have the youthful comic lead, always bullied and bandied about by the course of things; aggressiveness combined with a grand manner suggests a specialization as kings or queens in tragedies. The truth is that appearance is crucial, and we can well imagine that the tragic ruler recruits his interpreters from among those who *play rulers* in life. Still, between the role and the man—we shall see this even more clearly soon—there must be appropriation; since the role requires a man with the seriousness and intransigence of the practico-inert, that is, of wrought matter, the appearance of the candidate, if he is finally accepted, receives the status of *being*. He is designated as having the "requisite *qualities*." Starting here, the laureate undertakes a long and hard apprenticeship: he *works* at it, just like a blacksmith or a carpenter; he *learns the trade*, that is, the techniques of collective unrealization—how to *produce* illusion, how to prevent it from evaporating. In sum, the imaginary is no longer the spontaneous yielding to appearance, it is the end product of a rigorous effort. Everything must be relearned: breathing, walking, speaking. Not *for its own sake*, but so that the walk should be a *show*, so that the breathing will allow the actor to modulate that other show, the voice. The apprenticeship is long; an actor's education involves a social expense that can be calculated. If he leaves the conservatory at the top of his class, the investment will be profitable: for a number of years, which can be determined as a function of the opportunities of contemporary life, he will contribute to filling the theater, to increasing the gate money, part of which will be reinvested in the same theater; in principle, therefore, he is *productive*. As a result—it happens at the Comédie-Francaise, for example—he signs a contract with the state: he will not leave the theater before a certain predetermined date. His being is here defined in advance: he is a functionary, a wage earner filling a specialized position for a certain period of time, who in exchange receives real power, the power on certain evenings to unrealize seven hundred people, by using certain techniques and directions (prescribed by the role) and by making them participate in his own unrealization. Thus he is *instituted*; the favor of the public will do the rest, and when it is great he will become an illusionist, elevated to the rank of *national treasure*. In some countries he will be canonized as a hero of work, a Stakhanov of illusion; and in others, France for example, he will be decorated or, in England, knighted. This means that he is recognized as having *real power* as an illusionist and that he is thanked for making use of it for the profit of the community. For this reason young people are often disappointed when they meet a famous actor, seeing a man of quiet elegance, severe expression, sober gestures, wearing a ribbon in his buttonhole, and quite boring in the proclaimed moderation of his opinions. Where is he hiding Lear's madness and Othello's fury? The answer is that he is not hiding them in the least—they do not exist, that's all. This evening he will recapture his loss of being.

Without risking anything, since it is calculated, contained wholly within iron-clad laws. For the moment, we let him play with his being: he *is* a member of the Comédie-Française, appreciated for his capacities and his professional conscience; he is that honorable man who belongs to the middle class and who, aside from his salaried position, receives sizable fees from the film industry; he is all the more concerned with his real being since unreality is so black and white and since he must contend with a bad reputation purveyed by certain irresponsible parties. Beyond this, of course, he is as mad as a hatter, the imaginary consumes him; the respectable bourgeois we see is his being and also *his show:* he makes a show of himself as someone who, except on stage, has a horror of making a show of himself. But this time it is *his being* he makes a show of; he unrealizes himself in the reality he has earned. Let us say that he clings to the truth that has come to him from the outside. An actor—especially a great one—is primarily a kidnaped child with no rights, truth, or reality, prey to shadowy vampires, who had the luck and the merit to be recovered by the whole of society and instituted in his being as the citizen-support of unreality. He is an imaginary who exhausts himself playing roles so as to be recognized and who is finally recognized as a worker specializing in the imagination. His being has come to him through the socialization of his inability to be.

This is what Gustave glimpses when by chance a familiar voice tells him he would make a good actor. He works within himself a veritable and, to my mind, crucial conversion: since being, in the society he frequents, is above all expressed by the profession one exercises and is measured by practical effectiveness, and since, on the other hand, he can only combat the derealization he is suffering by unrealizing himself a little more each day, he will repair this continually widening breach by making unrealization his trade. The conversion operates on the level of the *role;* we have seen that he plays his being and seeks to mystify his audience so that they will mystify him in turn by mirroring back to him the illusion he has produced. We might say that this reflection has allowed him to suppress the mystification as such, and that he begins by exposing his illusory character within the illusion. For him this is not a matter of giving up acting but of no longer cheating, of putting his cards on the table: it is not me I am playing; I am taking the role of *another,* who does not exist or who, if he exists, *is not me*—it is Papa Couillères, it is someone else, a lady who comes to visit us and says stupid things. And if by chance I become my own actor, I am not portraying myself but only a caricature of myself; radicalizing my defects, I am excessive, hyperbolic, I apply myself to making you laugh at a me that I am not. The unreal is frankly unmasked in its unreality and presented at first as such. As an actor, Flaubert deceives no one: who among the audience, then, would imagine that he is or can be Don Sancho of Aragon, Harpagon, or Alceste? A poster provides information at the entrance, and besides, it is Flaubert in *L'Avare* or *Le Misanthrope* that they are coming to see. In other words, the audience is presented with *images,* and it is these images they demand. No more misunderstandings, then. Quite to the contrary, everyone is in agreement: if people have reserved their seats, if they are moved, it is because they have some secret complicity with the actor; it seems to them, as it does to him, that it is important to present the imaginary as such. The enthusiasm of the audience proves to Gustave that unrealization, despite its inutility, remains a social need which must be ceremoniously satisfied. From this time on, by renouncing the practice of *showing himself,* by playing the mythomaniacal drama on two stages (being and nonbeing), by affirming that within certain limitations of his sex, of particular physical features, it is all the same to him whether he interprets this role or that, *provided he can act,* Gustave takes possession of his truth through the favor of the crowd. This truth does not involve the determined character he is interpreting and which consequently he is not; rather, it defines his being as the power of being all characters in the realm of the imaginary. He *is* no one because he can understand and embody anyone through imagination. He has no particular features because in his being he is a specialist in generosity. Later he will speak of his awe of Shakespeare, that genius who was nothing personally and in the real world because he imagined all passions, all situations, those of women as well as of men. We should understand that the imaginary has an analogous function to the one Husserl assigns to it in eidetic intuition. What is imagined by the actor is the man who is passion's plaything: Harpagon does not exist, someone plays him, and the actor is not miserly, or if he is no one cares; truth lies in the dialectical moments of the passional process. This naïve view, which we shall encounter later at the time of the first *Education sentimentale,* functions precisely to *confine the being* Gustave gives himself as an actor; he is nothing because he can play everything, because he can imagine all the structures of the human comedy, because he publicly produces men who are amorous, avaricious, etc. Thus he can resolve to his advantage the antinomy of experience—meaningless, irritating, monotonous—and the resplendent role he is interpreting, whatever it might be. His being is to represent all men, and for this very reason his real affections are so poor: they do him no good since they are only his, and eventually they slip into the past, atrophied. Only recently the child did not manage to justify the thanklessness of experience, which at this moment seems necessary for the feasts of the imagination: a passion, a pleasure would contain him within the bounds of their particularity—and he is happy not to be so contained. Thus, the more the actor's face is the face of everyman, the more he will be capable of expressing diverse emotions and of unrealizing himself as the analogue of diverse faces.

As we see, a complete reversal of perspective is necessary to arrive at the idea—which he does not express as I do, of course—that his objective being is that of a living center of derealization. In particular he must renounce self-expression, making a show of himself. Is this not a drastic revision? Actually not. Abstractly, this first grist of impersonalism, which implies a renunciation of living, of seeing himself, of being a person like everyone else, can appear distressingly austere. But it must be noted that it was always partial: from one end of his life to the other, Gustave played *his* character—the Garçon, Uncle Flaubert with the sea legs, the revered Papa Cruchard, the hermit of Croisset, the Excessive, Saint Polycarp, and many others. And he did so all the more contentedly because he had discovered his true status as *Master of the Unreal*. In sum, he was *reassured* by judging himself instituted in advance, integrated by the society that refused him and fulfilled by his profession; he abandoned himself to his constituted passivity which would make him all his life the martyr of unreality. The "vocation" of actor was a partial and momentary specification of his fundamental option, but it did not modify it as a whole; actor then writer, Gustave would do the Lord splendidly, as if he were saying to himself: this unrealization is utterly inconsequential; it is only an obsession with my life, and my life doesn't count, my being is elsewhere. Moreover, we must not exaggerate the exteriority of represented characters, as we shall see later; he puts himself into them, like someone who "always puts himself in other people's shoes, but he is only putting himself there"; and inversely, he provisionally allows himself to be affected by their being—let us say that he tacitly *believes* he is the character he is playing. This is not surprising; he cannot easily distinguish the real from the imaginary, any real emotion he has seems playacted, any acted emotion real. Thus, playing the passion of a miser, he is affected by it and turns himself into Harpagon. Even more important, others fascinate him without his seeking to understand them—not only because they are his truth but also because he is not theirs. His eye slides over that polished cliff, brilliant and impenetrable, so definitive, so pitiless and hermetically itself, which is a person seen from the outside. If he imitates others, it is not (or not only) to mock them; it is to try and feel what they are from the inside—even Papa Couillères, who was probably a fool but whose unfathomable stupidity had a consistency that fascinated him. He caricatures living people, in sum, in order to steal their being for a moment and know what it is to take pleasure in having an objective being. Surely he is not convinced that he is Papa Couillères while he is *doing* him, or that this theft/possession (he becomes vampirized by the being he has stolen) could be accomplished without that pithiatism that generally characterizes constituted passivities.

This said, it is still the case that Gustave, willing himself to be an *actor*, works a reevaluation of the imaginary. True, he considers it his own product, which distinguishes him from all the others—and this will be truer as time goes by. But at the same time he gives himself away: what he produces *is only* imaginary. Is this a proclaimed valorization of the unreal but a secret devalorization? We shall shortly examine the primary effect of this contradiction, which will pursue him in many guises throughout his life. For the moment it must be acknowledged that it hardly torments him, because the profession he hopes to practice can alone give him the compensation he dreams of: his father does not listen to him because he does not believe in lies; later the crowds will come expressly to hear them. Success, for the actor, preserves something that is childish, archaic, even intoxicating: the family is recreated when the child has been properly polite. The family circle alone can provide an equivalent to the moment when people rise to their feet, applaud, and cry "bravo!" In its most complex forms, notoriety is a circular challenge: it is everywhere and nowhere, it gives itself and takes flight, no one can enjoy it—you must never think about it or be alienated by its absence. For the actor, this challenge exists as well, in the second degree. In the first degree, if he succeeds, he has the full and direct intuition of his triumph. Gustave dreams of compensating for his hamming at the Hôtel-Dieu by the passionate and grateful interest his audience will bear him.

What? All Carolines, then? Yes, all. They raise their hands, throw bouquets, shout their gratitude. Since society—and no one who has been to the theater can doubt this—having a more ample spirit than Dr. Flaubert's, considers the imaginary to be a social need, and since it is grateful to the person who unrealizes himself according to certain rules, the actor Gustave Flaubert is thereby allowed to assume his generosity through these testimonies of gratitude. The gift he made to Caroline is here infinitely multiplied. He no longer has any need to play the generous man: by playing the miser he will be truly generous. The actor is glad to consider himself a lord; just listen to him treat the audience like a woman, pretending to bend it under his yoke, to penetrate it as the male does the female, to subjugate the stubbornest listener. What a mistake! To captivate the audience is to show himself as he understands one should show oneself, to intuit the audience's moods and adapt himself to them, to conjure away what might be displeasing, excise dangerous lines, erase overdone effects. In sum, he is offering himself to fascinate and produce a collective unrealization. In this sense the audience is the male, accepting or refusing the perspiring females who lavish their passive activity on the audience from the stage. This said, it must be recognized that this courtesan's work, with its thousand "accommodations," ends by drawing the male into a trap: he is seduced, he "goes along" with the actor who, during the *show*, senses the emergence and growth of a tension that can be resolved only by a triumph; he holds the audience, presents it with a gift of his body.

In fact, he presents it with nothing but the imaginary, the power of unrealization that everyone possesses virtually but seldom has the chance to actualize. This excited attention of an audience watching his gestures is something Gustave is bound to desire because of Achille-Cléophas's indifference to those very gestures; an audience will love them because they *are* gestures, whereas Dr. Flaubert held them in contempt for that reason. And by assuming his imposture, the little charlatan will gain a fervent crowd's recognition as the lord of illusion, the benefactor of humanity. In short, there is a first moment when Gustave abandons everything, acknowledges himself to be a liar and a mythomane, declares that he is nothing to anyone; and a second moment, which immediately follows the first, when everything is given back to him: the delirious audience confirms him as the master of shadows, every evening they pay him *homage;* every evening he gives himself to his vassals.

But this is only a dream. At nine years old Gustave is not a recognized, celebrated actor—he plays at being one; and from this point of view he unrealizes himself to the second degree since he imagines that he is a professional producer of the imaginary. For this reason he will abandon his own role as often as possible in order to slip into prefabricated ones. His aim? To taste glory in advance, as the letter to Ernest dated one or two years later indicates: "Victory! Victory!" etc. In order to institute against the winds and the tides that being-in-itself which he pursues and is refused, he must have nothing less than celebrity. These remarks will permit a better understanding of what the fierce desire for glory—which he often admitted to—meant for the child, and what it later became for the adult.

B. Glory and Resentment

If Gustave, from childhood on, craved glory, it was not in some abstract, uninformed manner. From the time he could talk, glory brushed him with its wing. Certainly, Achille-Cléophas was only a provincial celebrity; but a great man in the provinces is dazzling to his children, who make his relative merits into an absolute value. Glory was the daily bread of the medical director's family, the source of the Flaubert pride; you had to be famous yourself with such a father. And if you should do the impossible and beat him on his home ground, it would not be too much to expect the whole world's approbation.

We must still inquire why the child made this collective command his singular desire and his most intimate possibility. Many passages in the correspondence give us helpful clues. In a letter written in adolescence, Gustave recognizes that as a child he lived only for glory, but he immediately adds that he no longer desires it. On that day it was a passing discouragement exaggerated by a display of pessimism: "I no longer have any conviction or enthusiasm or belief." He complains readily that year: Alfred and Ernest are in Paris—and *together*, which scarcely pleases him. But when Ernest ventures to sympathize, Gustave hastens to answer: "We create imaginary evils (alas, those are the worst kind) . . . No, I am happy. And why not?" In 1846, by contrast, he is much more sincere when he writes to Louise: "Since my father's death and my sister's, the desire for glory has left me." Here Caroline is invoked to cover his tracks. It is right that Louise should understand, but only up to a point. *With* Caroline, the sentence takes on a benign meaning: I wanted to bring happiness to the two beings who were dearest to me; since they have gone, my desire has no more meaning. *Without* Caroline, it is much more disturbing: "Since my father's death, the desire for glory has left me." This sentence, however, is the true one. The young girl had another kind of pride; she felt sure enough of herself to nourish modest ambitions. When she was married, her choice was Hamard, whom Gustave treated with scornful condescension and placed below Ernest himself: a fool, a servile im-

139

itator of his friend, the great Flaubert, a halfwit. It seems that her choice—which stunned her brother—marked Caroline's revolt against this family of brains; she had had enough of them: two medical practitioners, one of them a philosopher to boot, and a future genius—this was more than she could bear. Her mother's love had given her enough strength to refuse to play the same role in relation to another brain. Deeply sympathetic to the wife of Achille-Cléophas, and to take revenge in her name on the masculine sex, Caroline apparently wanted to protect a man, to play the role of mother to him. This young girl, in delicate health but strong and rich in true generosity, had nothing of the relative being about her; she chose a sensitive, feminine husband who was ignorant of the sciences and no longer dreamed of writing, if he ever had done, and who calmly completed his studies in Paris without Alfred's noble disgust or Gustave's elegant declamations. Caroline loved her brother, but if she wished him success in his writing, it was for his sake and not for her own. And Gustave knew it; as I show later, he practically broke with his sister—inwardly at least—when he learned of her engagement. If he mentions her in his letter it is because he wants to hide from Louise the connection between his *mad* ambition and his father's curse. At the end of his life Matisse said resentfully of his father, who had been dead half a century: "He did not believe in my painting!" When the old man went to Paris, he would enter the studio of his still unknown son, look contemptuously at the canvases, speak about everything but what he saw around him, and leave quite coldly, disappointed. He died without ever being undeceived. And Matisse added angrily on the eve of his own death: "From that day on, all success was spoiled for me! I could no longer convince him and that is all I had wanted." It was not, I imagine, entirely true. But however we take it, the anecdote shows that glory is a family matter and that the unshakable obstinacy of a dead father, if by some chance it devolves upon one of the living, can spoil the joys of pride. Indeed, whom would a famous man want to convince if not a father who, out of mistrust, had pushed him into the sovereignty of genius and would rather die than confess to being beaten? Gustave felt this deeply. And of course his disappointment was more radical than the old painter's: when Achille Cléophas died, his son was at his lowest point. He would know success—thunderous, infamous— eleven years later. The younger son was struck to the core.[3] His dis-

3. We shall see that Gustave experienced Achille-Cléophas's death as a deliverance, and he even believed for a moment that he was cured of his neurosis. There is no contradiction here; or rather there is one, but it is Gustave's position in relation to his father

gust might be considered just one more drama. If you read his correspondence to the end, however, you will see that *at times* he did not
disdain the small pleasures of notoriety; yet few famous writers have
been so little satisfied by their reknown. The perfection of the work
was his unique objective. We know, we shall know, Gustave's numerous renunciations. From the age of forty-six on, one was missing: he
would never renounce glory, never renounce the figure he cut in the
eyes of his readers. When they spoke about him, even about a trivial
event in his life, he would fume with rage and terror. After his father's
death—and before beginning the first *Saint Antoine*—he doubted that
he would ever write. 9 August 1846: "It is highly problematic whether
the public will even enjoy a single line from me; if it does happen, it
will not be for at least ten years." 15 August 1846: "All that I ask is the
power to continue admiring the masters with that inner enchantment
for which I would give everything, everything. But as to becoming
one, never; I am certain of it. I am terribly deficient." 24 August: "I do
nothing, I read nothing, I no longer write except to you. What has become of my poor, simple life of work? . . . I do not regret it because I
regret nothing." 15 September 1846: "So much the better if I leave
nothing to posterity. My obscure name will be buried with me and the
world will go on its way as if I had left it an illustrious man."[4] This last
passage (we could find a dozen others like it from the same period)
clearly shows that in the period following his father's death, the il-
lustriousness of his name and his total oblivion acquired a sort of
equivalence. It all becomes clear: with the father, a loving, jealous surliness disappeared; Flaubert harbored the singular misfortune that
glory already seemed futile to him, even as he was engaged in its pursuit and was almost certain of never succeeding. And let us not believe in some compensatory negation by the other, as if the extreme
difficulty of the task undertaken and the nearly infinite probabilities
of failing should have disturbed him less because the objective had

---

that is fundamentally contradictory. And I am not speaking here only of the ambivalence of his feelings but of his situation itself. As the undisputed and shrewd head of
the family, Achille-Cléophas contributed to maintaining the young man in a neurotic
state that gave him a reason to sequester himself at Rouen and end his studies; in this
sense, the father's death certainly had the effect, if not of curing Gustave, at least of
causing a remission of his illness. But the fundamental and archaic relationship of the
child to the father (to convince him of his eminent value) was not altered, hence the
remission was accompanied by a profound frustration.

4. We understand that *posterity* has a precise meaning: Louise had experienced certain fears; she then advised him that these fears were unfounded. It is even more striking, therefore, to see Flaubert go from the refusal to have a son to the refusal of glory.

less meaning and the principal witness had taken leave. Quite the contrary: the conquest of the Golden Fleece became all the more necessary since he had built his life on it; but it revealed at the same time—certain of not being interrupted—its aberrant absurdity. This is not even nothingness, it is an absolute demand and at the same time an absolute nonsense. The conclusion is obvious: if this loner could dream of an official consecration, if the misanthrope wanted the admiration of humanity, it was primarily to dazzle Dr. Flaubert. In sum, we rediscover—in all the purity of innocence—the black dream of suicide out of resentment. From afar, glory seems to involve universal affirmation; but in the heart of the child who desires it, the universal is subordinated to particular relationships. Since no man on earth could intimidate Achille-Cléophas and confound him by saying of the younger son, "He is the better of the two!" the chief surgeon would learn of his blunder from all men together, and the silly smugness of Achille would be tainted by the judgment of mankind. "Oh, you know Achille," they would say, "Gustave's brother." But while the child appealed to humanity, present and future, they were only the means—the physician-philosopher was his end.

A letter from Gustave to Louise Colet includes a very curious passage: "My poor father," he says, "whom I so often gave cause to weep . . ." To weep? I don't believe it. No doubt Achille-Cléophas, a gloomy, nervous, irritated, overworked man, had preserved the sensibility of the eighteenth century: men wept readily until the First Empire, and certainly he may have been concerned about his son's stupors, his lack of scholarly success, and his mental health. He lost his temper a hundred times, that's obvious. But if there were outbursts, they were dry ones. Even after the uproar when Gustave was expelled from school, Achille-Cléophas must have been furious, shouted perhaps, but would he have wept? We have only to read the context to understand: Gustave plays the drama for *himself* through Louise. When he wants to convince himself of an idea that pleases him, he begins by persuading her of it. We are familiar with his favorite pleasure: presenting himself as one of the damned. Abominable sufferings—which are not specified—have anesthetized him. It was this cold-heartedness, he suggests, that prompted the physician-philosopher's precious tears. And the general meaning of the passage seems to be: "I had a father who adored me, I tormented him to the point of tears. Today you are the one who adores me—what do you expect? I was made malicious and you are going to suffer like everyone who loves me!"

142

This is the most arrant lie. Or perhaps we should put it this way: Flaubert's pen does not distinguish between fantasy and reality. Here the boaster reverses the situation, presenting his past dreams as memories. His most stubborn grievance, we know, was not to have been preferred; his father fulfilled all his paternal duties, but in Gustave's view with no particular inclination and with no tenderness. When the young man is moved by the thought of Dr. Flaubert's tears, he is playing on the candor he persists in lending, quite inappropriately, to his correspondent and using her to realize, pithiatically, a simple, deep-seated childhood desire. A positive desire, at first: Gustave would have been mad with happiness if he had seen those extraordinarily lucid eyes turn toward him, filling with tenderness. After the Fall, resentment turned that beautiful dream into a negative one. After one of his father's sarcastic remarks, after some kindness observed toward his older brother, a violent impulse shook the younger son—he wanted glory, immediately and at any price: "I shall make you weep!" From shame? From happiness? At the beginning they amount to the same thing: the docile, cunning child wants to give great joy to the author of his days to repay him for his pains; but can he help it, poor boy, if the joy is at the same time a cruel, salutary lesson? A triumph, that is what Gustave needs: to answer evil with good and to punish solely by generosity: "Here are my trophies, I offer them to you, they belong to you, to my family." This will be his only vengeance. In fact, it is exemplary. The whole little world of the philosophical practitioner is overturned: he backed the wrong horse, he was unable to understand Gustave's genius. If the old man is capable of such a blunder, what remains of his wisdom, his cynicism, his arrogant philosophy? Grateful but broken, the physician will go into retirement; he will pass on his duties and honors, appropriately, to his eldest son, but he will taste the bitterness of deriving his happiness, from now on, from the success of the son he misunderstood and rejected. Glory and suicide have this in common for the child, that both represent the murder of the father. For both, passivity is their alibi: "*I* would kill Papa? Come on! I tell you, I am killing *myself* in accordance with his prescriptions and the character that was inflicted on me!" And: "*I* should want to humiliate my father, crush him with my fame? Is it my fault if I'm carried to the clouds, if I'm so acclaimed? Is it my fault if I'm great?" In any event, when the child reacts, the father—demonic high priest, Abraham whose arm no angel stays—*has already killed* his younger son. It is up to Gustave to play the drama: either he transforms this assassination, out of respect for his father, into a suicide, taking the

143

monstrous fault upon himself; or, dead and embalmed, he finds genius in the realm of shadows, the doors of the sepulcher are torn open, he returns, gentle and terrible, to his beloved master. In the first case, Achille-Cléophas's eyes are opened and he discovers too late his accumulated wrongs, measuring in despair the depth of the love his victim bore him. In the second, he is the flabbergasted witness to the resurrection of a giant whose eyes pierce him to the core, he is thunderstruck when the giant bends down to kiss him. Thus the sweet dream of glory, quite innocent and touching to devotees, is even more perfidious than the dream of voluntary death. Suicide is only a proposition of remorse. Perhaps the father will regret his hardness of heart; perhaps, just because he *is* hard-hearted, he will not; besides, a repentant lord remains a lord. Glory challenges his *entire* being, principally the intelligence of which he is so proud: the prince of understanding is deposed; the vertical ascension recapitulates in its way the sudden mutation that made a great physician out of a future veterinarian. Achille can just barely continue in his father's footsteps. But Gustave is a true mutant, like Achille-Cléophas: consequently, he moves away from his class, he is displaced by renown. He takes flight and soars to the heights where no other Flaubert can join him: now it is on *his* renown that the splendor of his family rests, and the father is disqualified.

The desire for renown not only betrays the child's bitterness against his father, it also reveals the resentment Gustave harbored from the age of nine against all humanity. Let us reread a little-known text, his "Eloge de Corneille,"[5] which he mentions in a letter to Ernest of 4 February 1831. Gustave had few things in common with Corneille, who had no obvious influence on him. Two circumstances, however, connect him with the man he calls "my dear countryman": both were involved in the theater, both were natives of Rouen; thus we are entitled to think that the little boy writes the eulogy for his illustrious predecessor that he would like someone to write for him two centuries later. Yet in it, we find this surprising sentence: "Why were you born, if not to humble the human race?" Stylistic ineptitude? It is immediately explained: "Who dares to enter the ranks with you?" In September 1838, when he was sixteen, we find this formula echoed when he writes to Ernest: "Rabelais and Byron, the only two who might have written with the intention of wounding the human race

5. The integral text is reproduced in Jean Bruneau's *Les Débuts littéraires de Gustave Flaubert*, pp. 40–41.

and laughing in its face. What a towering position." In the "Eloge" it is not said that Corneille *intended to wound*. He diminishes by his stature alone without any conscious concern, a scornful indifference that is worse, perhaps, than the "intention to wound"—which can spring only from unsatisfied passions. The connection, however, throws into relief the secret negativity of the compliment. We see how much the child of nine finds himself estranged from all humanism: he loves Corneille *against* our species. This is exactly the reverse of the usual assumption that a worthy man does *honor* to humanity, that humanity is *elevated* by his works or his exploits. Armstrong walked on the moon for all men; all women orbited the earth with Valentina. Such works, inventions, or actions open new possibilities for everyone *in the future*, but in the present they often have the effect of diminishment. Armstrong is an astronaut for all mankind, but the majority of his contemporaries may well think: Man has taken four steps on the moon but *I* shall never set foot there. In sum, talent has the effect of impoverishing previous generations—beginning with its own—by comparison. Those the same age as Armstrong are immediately defined by his exploit as those who have not done and will not be able to do what he has done—to enrich new and future generations. These observations, however, do not always apply to works of the mind. Among Corneille's contemporaries, a number of people "entered the ranks with him"; and his readers, who reanimated the dead work by reading it, were elevated and enriched by their reading. These commonsense truths are recalled to emphasize to what degree the young Flaubert was estranged from them; in effect, it is striking that, in his eyes, great men are a race apart, despite their origins. In our century, everyone is convinced that the hero, the thinker, the artist, the politician, high as he might climb, *belongs to us;* but in Flaubert's time people were not sure of it: there was Napoleon and the "cult of personality," Hugo and his well-known dialogues with God the Father. For Gustave, the great man born in exile like Almaroës very soon notices that his outward appearance alone is human; he is shocked by it, opens his wings, and soars off to Mount Atlas. His bitterness toward our species comes from his resemblance to it. Consequently, he is not content to raise himself above it; he disparages it, pushing it beneath him. As a matter of fact, Flaubert, drawing his inspiration from his visual experience, considered the two operations inseparable and complementary; he repeated this a hundred times in his correspondence but never said it more clearly than in a note in his *Souvenirs:* the higher the summit from which one views them, the smaller men are;

145

to belittle them, therefore, all you have to do is climb a hill, a mountain, etc. For one of the elect *like himself*, it is enough to read Corneille:
for the man who embodies himself in that author or in one of his magnificent heroes, his self-styled fellow creatures seem like pygmies.
Certainly Gustave's desire for glory is *primarily* an ascendent impulse,
but, like it or not, it is immediately linked to his misanthropy.

Unfortunately for him, glory and misanthropy are at once complementary (in his mind) and incompatible. He seeks renown out of contempt for mankind, but who else will give it to him? In the same
"Eloge" he writes: "The child, the mature man, the old man, all agree
to applaud you. No one finds fault with your works." Thus glory is
founded on universal *consensus*. We ask the entire species to name its
great men. But how can this be done if the species is condemned as
abject? A choice must be made: for the consistent misanthrope, fame
is infamy; thus, to court the favor of men, one must begin by thinking
well of them. I recognize that our clever minds like to play it both
ways: one such celebrity, childish though mature, begs the indulgence
of critics by private letters yet feels free to deny them the right to
judge his works, and even to recommend them. Such writers consequently live in misery, as Gustave would do later when he grew to hate
Madame Bovary, the book that in a few days lifted him from obscurity
to the most boisterous celebrity. The admiration of the rabble did not
compensate in his eyes for the criticism inflicted by the sovereign.

Gustave—luckily or unluckily—was born into the first age of romanticism, which was, among other things, a freemasonry of young
aristocratic arrivistes and ambitious bourgeois who betrayed their
class. All of them royalists, at least until 1830, they benefited—Hugo
was the first to do so—from the favor of the monarch and considered
as just reward for their talent what was, in the king's mind, merely re-
muneration for an advertising campaign, ineffectual but adroitly conducted. This meant reviving the glorious "Old Regime," which was
not separable from the monarchical principle: the sovereign guaranteed spiritual values; they belonged to him, as did all of the nation's
goods. If he decided to elevate a Ronsard, the titles—always ennobling even if the ennoblement was not permanent (Ronsard was a
prince, the prince of poets)—that he was pleased to confer on a writer
who honored his reign were *recognized* by his successor, transmitting
to those who would come after him the mission of recognizing these
titles in their turn and preserving them. The poet was long dead; if he
was declared immortal it was because the Royal House granted him a
little of its perpetuity. God made the Bourbons reign, and the Bour-

bons, with divine right, made the fortune of poets. When Ronsard thought his name would survive, he was convinced that the French monarchy would endure until the end of time and that he would participate in its charismatic power. There is no doubt that these old ideas were seductive to the child Gustave, first because they were childish and, second, because the young and already prestigious writers had unearthed and rejuvenated them. But above all he found in them what he had sought in vain since the Fall: a reconstituted feudalism, the sovereign's guarantee of vertical ascension, a departure from his class effected from on high, a ravishment equal to what he had experienced the day the duchesse de Berry lifted him in her arms and smiled on him, a metamorphosis passively submitted to, the assurance that his posthumous destiny would be tied to that of the royal family. Who but the king, that father of all fathers, by accepting the homage of this little Ganymede, could compensate for Achille-Cléophas's injustice and compel the chief surgeon to respect in the person of his son the revered and sovereign decree that consecrated him as an artist? The medical director admired Voltaire, Helvetius, Holbach, Diderot, a couple of dozen others who had known how to express the wishes and feelings of the rising bourgeoisie. But this discreet collaborator with all the regimes was in a poor position to perceive that eighteenth-century writers had collaborated wholeheartedly with the regime they denounced. Gustave, on the other hand, even before reading them was charmed by that collaboration: Achille-Cléophas saw them as spokesmen for their class, and the little boy, consumed with envy, had eyes only for their privileges; for him, they were the darlings of the aristocracy. In other words, the little misanthrope managed quite well: he could hate the species and vindicate glory since this was obtained by the sole consent of the superior beings who ruled. Being lifted out of one's class by renown was a form of ennoblement: his lost childhood and vassalage would be given back to him. The first Flaubert mutation had transformed a country bumpkin into a bourgeois; the second would pull the son of the mutant out of the bourgeois field of gravity and give him the winged grace of an aristocrat. As we can see, this is a delightful dream of hate; for the favor of the monarch to ennoble him, to be able to pride himself on the friendship of the great, the virtue of blood and birth must be unquestionably imposed on everyone. In brief, the child wants nothing less than the resurrection of the Old Regime; he would like France to have a Sun King once again. Clearly, this bourgeois child seeks to humiliate his class, to strip it of all the advantages it has achieved and throw it on its knees

147

before the throne it had tried to overturn. Vengeance is pushed to the limit: the glory Flaubert thirsts for is not only the glory that will have the advantage of restoring the child's secret vassalage and of demoralizing the philosophical practitioner; it must also accomplish, socially and publicly, the definitive defeat of this liberal bourgeois crushed under the heel of absolute monarchy restored, provoke the disqualification of his scientific and therefore nonaristocratic capabilities by the inalienable values of those of birth, and effect the destruction of his detestable ideology by that of the restored regime.

This was only a dream. At the time the child was confusedly harboring these rancorous fantasies, the Bourbons had taken flight, the victorious bourgeoisie had put a usurper on the throne, the son of a regicide, whom Gustave would never forgive for being declared citizen-king and for sullying his crown by claiming to be only first among the French. Very soon Gustave would judge that the aristocracy, when it wasn't uselessly sulking on its lands, was dishonoring its ancestors by becoming bourgeois. There was nothing left to carry him toward the heights, no God, no king, no prince. His major contradiction, moreover, was that the bourgeoisie alone, at bottom, was qualified in his eyes to bestow glory upon him because it was from the bourgeoisie alone that he had sustained such affronts and such repugnance. Renown, for him, could only be revenge, and on whom should he take revenge if not those who had wronged him, the paterfamilias and those who surrounded and worshiped him, the bourgeois of Rouen, who, if they had put themselves to it, might have made the father take back his curse but who, quite to the contrary, took it up on their own account. It was not so much a question of *asking* them to give him glory—how could those fools, those philistines, give him such a thing?—as of *making them submit* to it like an insult. They would remain passive and Gustave's renown would enter into them; once internalized, it would become a thought that would contradict all others, producing a humiliating disorder that would make them suffer. For this reason, the child was not wrong to desire recruitment from on high: he is playing, writing, whatever, and then one day an iron fist bursts forth from the heavens and lifts him up before the stupefied populace of Rouen. Still, what counts most for him is the astonishment of this populace. Without such forced but boundless consent, he would just barely be elected by an infinitesimal minority; indeed, members of the nobility in their day had many favorites, who for all that were not honored by posterity. Thus the operation is a dual one: there is the public assumption, there is glory properly speaking, that is, the bourgeoisie's consciousness, as it raises its eyes to the zenith, of its own *abasement:* "By mounting to the heavens, he makes us understand our groveling." But if aristocrats and monarch have lost the right to *distinguish,* the question presents itself anew: who will be *qualified* to consecrate great men? In the nineteenth century, the bourgeoisie alone represented nine-tenths of the public; so the bourgeoisie was expected to be active and generous, spontaneously granting the sacred, as well as passive and parsimonious, submitting by constraint and grudgingly to the superiority it had just consecrated. Above all, in order to accord some value to its choices, it would have been necessary to stop hating and mistrusting it—and here we have come back to our point of departure. Flaubert would never break out of the vicious circle: from the Christian God, who is everything and nothing, who crowns some with his gifts and others with his curse, to the aristocracy, which embodies and dishonors the hierarchical principle, to the benighted bourgeoisie, which is the *object* of glory but not the glorifying subject—although the fame of great men is measured by the frequency and the intensity of its applause—and back to the Christian God, the young boy had to keep spinning faster and faster, passing from one idea to the other, either paying careful attention not to be aware of the changes or, on the other hand, playing one idea against the other or against all the others without ever surrendering a certain syncretistic view, the result of his passions rather than of his understanding. If he had stopped his circling, everything would have foundered in contradiction and inconsistency. I am not saying that this uncertainty is related only to his internal dispositions—subjective disorders, even pathological ones, necessarily include the internalization of an objective structure or fact; and it is a commonplace that glory is an illusion, at least in our fragmented societies. But one rarely sees a child desire it with such force, prepare himself for it with such tenacity, and systematically rid himself of all the means of enjoying it if he should ever obtain it.

As an adult, Flaubert would preserve the vicious circle of childhood, as we see from his letter of 22 April 1853 to the Muse. Louise had submitted her poem "L'Acropole" to the Académie française and had just learned that it had not been awarded recognition. Informed of this, Flaubert begins by being *indignant.* He is *disappointed:* "It's strange but yesterday evening I was full of hope, I was in a good mood." He "brands" academicians: "All of them! All of them! My old hatreds are now justified. But I would have preferred that this time heaven had not given me such good reason." We see the vicious circle:

the issue is consecration by an elite body. But he despises the Académie. Still, he is unhappy to see his contempt justified. It is true that the Muse is the one involved, not he. But he did not dissuade her from pursuing her project.[6] Indeed, he advised her, suggested a certain strategy. For example, in January 1853: "I would not urge you to irritate Villemain, and with my wily novelist's psychology here are my reasons: (1) You need him for your prize, (2) we are young, and (3) he is old," etc. On 17 February 1853: " 'Work hard on L'Acropole: . . . Pay particular attention to accuracy when dealing with these gentlemen. You know what pedants they are, and they have reason to be. If they were deprived of that, what would they have left?" On 26 March: "You can be sure that the Académie, pedantic as it is, pays more attention to the lines than to a technical description . . . If you have made the most important cuts and corrections, as you told me you did, I have hope of success. But act as in the past year, don't neglect your little details." He himself, moreover, tries to put pressure on the prefect of Rouen through his physician, a cousin of one of his friends (why the prefect of Rouen?). Does he underestimate Louise Colet? I don't believe so, and we shall see him later instructing Bouilhet, the Alter Ego, in the art of success, which he denies himself. The truth is that he judges himself superior to both of them, but in a spirit of friendship: what is good for them is not good for him, that's all. And then, he adores intrigue from afar, acting as adviser: "Action has always disgusted me to the highest degree . . . But when necessary or when I pleased, I have managed it firmly and quickly and well. For Du Camp's *croix d'honneur* I accomplished in one afternoon what five or six men of action, had they been here, would not have been able to manage in six weeks . . . The incapacity of thinkers in the world of affairs is only an excess of capacity."[7]

He is in the fray, entirely engaged. Still watchful, he exhorts Louise: "This will be your battle of Marengo." And suddenly, disillusionment. What does he proceed to do? He appeals to the public. Now it is the public who will disqualify the body of specialists and finally force their hand: "In your place *I* would remove my mask [the day of the prize giving] and I would publish my 'Acropole' revised, since only fragments of it were read; that would be a good joke. But I would not leave in *one* line that wasn't any good, and next January I would resubmit a different 'Acropole.' This time I would see to it that I would re-

6. "I have got it into my head that you should have the prize." 2 November 1852.
7. 5–6 March 1853. The whole passage would have to be cited to show the way he raves on.

ceive the prize by going about it better (politically). And then who would have his foot in his mouth? It would be a lot of fun to slap these gentlemen twice with the same idea, once before and through the public, and the second time by their own hands." But does he really believe in the *public?* In February of the same year he wrote:

> Your "Paysanne" ran into trouble when it appeared. That's justice. We have proof that it is fine . . . Anything of value is like a porcupine, people are careful to avoid it. But patience, truth will triumph. People have always inveighed against originality, which nevertheless proves itself by entering the public domain, and although they cry out against superiority, against aristocrats, against the rich, they live nonetheless by their thought, by their bread. Genius, like a strong horse, pulls humanity behind it along the highways of ideas. They pull on the reins in vain . . . for genius, with its robust hocks, always flies along at full gallop.

In short, given enough time, the genius imposes himself, is recognized—usually after his death; but during his lifetime the public only tries to restrain him and isn't capable of recognizing his worth. All glory is a rape, a direct result of genius and genius alone: it "humbles" the human species. Flaubert continues his letter of condolence to Louise after her failure: "And what does all this amount to? There are no defeats except the ones you suffer all alone in front of your mirror, in your own consciousness. On Tuesday and Wednesday I couldn't have been more depressed if I'd been hearing a hundred thousand catcalls. You must think only of the triumphs you can confer upon yourself, be your own public, your own critic, your own reward. The only way to live in peace is to leap above the whole of humanity and to have nothing more than a glancing acquaintance with them." This verbiage betrays anxiety. To leap above humanity is all very well. But if humanity does not recognize the superiority of the superman, who will settle the issue? Posterity, of course; at that moment Flaubert believes in it, faute de mieux. But most of the time he has no confidence in it because his contemporaries are *also* a posterity:

> If Tacitus returned to earth, he would not sell as well as Monsieur Thiers. The public respects busts but has little love for them. A conventional admiration and that's all. The bourgeois (all of humanity now, including the people) behaves toward the classics as he does toward religion. He knows they exist, would be unhappy if they didn't, understands that they have a certain, very remote utility, but he makes no use of them whatever, and that worries him a good deal—there you have it.

151

In short, the posterity of the classics—namely ourselves—is deplorable. Is there a historical chance that Gustave's posterity will suit him better? Here we would have to elucidate his various prophecies of the future, but this is not the proper place. Let us say in any event that nothing is less certain. In sum, the very concept of posthumous glory falls apart in Flaubert's hands. We should understand that this is not his fault; it is the regal idea of glory, gradually disappearing, that is vainly seeking a replacement of itself through him. But we have early remarked on the curious assimilation of the rich, the aristocracy, and men of genius: people cry out against them but "live nevertheless by their thought, by their bread." The conjunction of wealth with the two other kinds of "superiority" speaks eloquently about "the bourgeois he is under the skin." If necessary he would accept the support of the rich because possession refines them. But the true accord is that which appropriates the aristocracy of birth to the aristocracy of the spirit. We have returned to our point of departure. Not altogether, however; even Flaubert is less certain now even of inherited nobility. He ends with a eulogy on solitude: in the face of the deficiency of any possible reader, you must be "your own public, your own critic, your own reward." This is renouncing glory. And how could it be otherwise since the genius, the superman, has nothing "but a glancing acquaintance" with humanity? Yet one would need the inner certainty, aberrant or reasonable, of being a great man; some who have had it have ended up in an asylum, others on the throne. But Flaubert is not one of them; sick, irritable, and doubting, he flees the judgment of others because he is too sensitive to it, and in spite of his negative pride he has nothing to counter it with. It took him years to recover from the fiasco of his reading of *Saint Antoine* to Maxime and Bouilhet; of course he *rejected* his friends' judgment, but he did not challenge it—he kept it inside him like a wound without drawing any conclusions from it. We can be sure that he won no victories in front of his mirror; quite the contrary, he was looking for the reflection of a defeated man, a failure. As a child, he expected the renown he was sure he would acquire to institute him in his being as a universal singular, provided it made amends for the injury his father had done him and put Achille-Cléophas and his maneuvers to shame. At the time, Gustave did not worry much about *who* would glorify him; his success as an actor would be total revenge: dedicated to unrealization by Achille-Cléophas, he would make this paternal humiliation the very reason for his celebrity. So the circle would be closed, and this was his only concern. But in its confusion and syncretism, his desire, born of resentment, took shape: hatred, contempt, malice, all his spleen was disgorged. While his father lived, his wild passion partially masked the contradictions, or at the very least prevented them from developing: he had to convince the paterfamilias at any price, and he had neither the intention nor the leisure to reflect on the choice of means. After the medical director's death, the idea of glory, that powderkeg, exploded. Did he really stop wanting it, as he claimed? Perhaps not, but he no longer attached the same price to it; it was now only a matter of proving to himself that his father had bet on the wrong horse and of convincing the people of Rouen that they had disregarded the only great man to be born in their town after Corneille. Apart from that, if he still dreamed of attaining glory, he no longer knew what the precise object of his desire was. When it did come, like a flash of lightning, it was too late; it caused him more alarm than pleasure. It was glory, however, at least until 1846, that was the desirable absolute and prime mover of his artistic zeal.

C. On the Comic Actor Considered as Masochist

The only victories are those you win in front of your mirror. The only defeats as well . . . "Last night . . . if I'd been hearing a hundred thousand catcalls . . ." These metaphors are instructive: at the age of thirty-one, deep into *Madame Bovary*, Gustave is still using images borrowed from the theater. He looks at himself in the mirror—that is the *show;* he loses or wins battles in front of his mirror: to whom should all this happen if not to an actor peering at his reflection in order to judge an "effect" he has just developed? And what does this actor receive on the day of the premiere if not applause or catcalls? Writers are quite unfamiliar with this kind of plebiscite, at least as concerns their writing. Their works sell or don't sell, they are panned or praised by a handful of people called critics, and their friends give them their opinions more or less sincerely, that's all. It is also noteworthy that by failing to honor the Muse's poem that year, the academicians did nothing that even resembled hooting her down; on the contrary, Louise reproached them for their silence—her name was not even mentioned. This honorable failure has nothing in common with the "flop" that threatens bad actors. Once more, Flaubert's thought strays from the subject and shows us, through the free play of associations, the structures he was given in his childhood, which did not vary from that time on. From the age of eight, the theater and glory were bound together. If he speaks of glory, whatever the domain, he describes it quite spontaneously as the kind an actor might know—or, perhaps, an orator. We see here to what degree the child was haunted by the desire to recuperate his being through show or spectacle. But now, *what kind of show would he make?* What roles would he play? Had he decided on his specialty? Caroline Franklin Groult claims he had not; for in the billiard room they did tragedies too. I recognize that the pretentious niece of an actor would feel more honored if he acted in tragedies. But in the case at hand, this is pure invention. In the letters Gustave wrote to Ernest before entering school, there is no mention of playing tragic roles; all the plays named, whether "borrowed" from the repertory or "adapted"—and the difference is not very great, as we shall see—are comedies and often closer to farce. In other words, it is clear that Gustave chose to achieve *glory through the comic* and that there were not two options but only one, which was maintained all his life: from the Garçon to Saint Polycarp, all the characters he played were buffoons. Black humor, disturbing buffoonery—that goes without saying, and we shall take it up again in the next chapter; the fact is that Flaubert claimed his plebiscite through laughter.

To understand the reasons for this choice, we must ask *who* is laughing, and at what; we shall see that the two questions are really one. But this is not the place to attempt an explanation of laughter; I want only to recall some established truths—in particular those gleaned from Bergson's and Jeanson's studies—to the extent that they assist us in our enterprise. Everyone knows, for example, that laughter is an intentional behavior, a passive activity of defense, but it is helpful to keep this idea in mind in order to discover Flaubert's precise intentions. It will be pointed out, no doubt, that the phenomenon of laughter is complex and diverse; I don't deny it, and neither do I maintain that the following considerations can be applied to *all* laughter. But hilarity, like all cultural determinations, has a history that begins with the appearance of hominids; the acculturation of laughter made it a polyvalent behavior, thus we must regard its different aspects as superstructures that have produced themselves dialectically from an elementary structure, which has survived both as the hidden infrastructure of all kinds of hilarity and, quite independently, as the immediate and collective reaction of social individuals when they are witness to specifically determined events. It is this ancient, primitive laughter, old as humanity, a prehistoric survival in our historic societies, that we shall try to describe, because Flaubert sought, as we shall show, to be instituted by it.

In every collectivity, individuals share a certain representation of the human character that is born of institutions, customs, and history and defines what they are by what they ought to be, and what they ought to be by what they are. When a member of the community reveals by his conduct that this representation may well be a lie, when he voluntarily or otherwise parodies the *human character* that has currency in his community, the other members suddenly find themselves endangered. If the "French character" is but a tissue of contradictions, if it can be torn apart simply by radicalizing its principal features, I am challenged in *my* character as a Frenchman, the socialized structure of my ego, and the national order is seriously threatened since, all told, the French personality is only the syncretic condensation of the history and structures of France. To the extent that the member of my collectivity, whatever it might be, approaches me in the setting of intersubjectivity as my fellow creature and my brother, as another self, I am compromised insofar as *I* am another self, a brother, a fellow creature for *him*. If his person endangers me, I must quickly take my distance, break the ties that bind me to him. Where a social whole is involved, whatever it is, the breaking of ties is an act decided upon and executed by the majority of members present. Whether it involves pure and simple physical liquidation or banishment (expulsion, quarantine, imprisonment), the measures adopted have three inseparable features: the collectivity, whatever its previous status, constitutes itself as a group; it is unified by an action for which every individual assumes full responsibility; it purifies its intersubjectivity by the suppression of the disturbing element and for a time achieves a degree of superior integration. In any case, it sanctions anger and persecution, so that unlawful conduct is not limited to proposing an offensive image of the "human person"; right or wrong, the group judges that it has had or might have grave consequences.

The challenge to man, however, may not involve any profound disturbance. There are drunks who kill, but *this* drunk, well known to his neighbors, harms no one; he is gentle as a child. He represents no less a public challenge to the typical demeanor and standard dignity of the average Frenchman, to the upright posture of which we are so proud, and to the human voice, that sacred breath; he comes to his fellow creature as a disturbing and grotesque image, he reminds us that the "human person" cannot resist the absorption of a certain amount of alcohol. We know all that from childhood and often by direct experience; but we don't want anyone to *make us see it*. Those who have been drunk even once have felt in their flesh the sudden impos-

155

sibility of being the *average man* they were enjoined to embody; they have felt their legs stumble, they have seen the things around them waver or revolve, they have heard their own words fragmented, tumbling over each other; at the same time they have tried desperately to compensate for this decomposition, this dismantling of sequences and reflexes, by the most nobly human attitudes: distinction, serious-mindedness, a somewhat sententious gravity. These attitudes are no sooner adopted than they are corrupted, soured, or debased, demonstrating—to the drunks themselves and to others—that the "human person" is an unplayable role unless all the circumstances are favorable, or, if you like, that man exists *where and when* he is tolerated, in sum, on approval. This is what they never want to feel again (at least when they are sober), and this is what they resent in the person of the staggering drunk. But what is there to say? This good man is too loaded to act: his intoxication, begun somewhere out of sight, completes itself out of sight, in sleep. It is a pure appearance that presents itself as such, which has no past (except in the cyclical time of eternal recurrence) and no future, and which will slip into nothingness without leaving a trace. This pure representation, however, without any practical relation to our present experience, manifests itself with a force that compels our attention; the fellow rants at people, challenges idle bystanders, imposes himself, "makes a spectacle of himself." And that's as it should be, for reality here is without its usual weight; in a sense, it is not *serious*—it has nothing to do with the satisfaction of our needs, I can do nothing about it, and I am unaffected by it either for good or for ill. However, this spectacle—which has constituted itself as such—is still threatening to serious people; it exposes their very seriousness, for the drunk takes himself seriously too, splutters sententiously, and demonstrates that gravity is only a posture. What can be done about him? His innocuousness is paralyzing, conferring on passersby the status of *spectators;* in relation to him they are in a state of passive activity. We understand, of course, that they reject him without lifting a finger to strike him or drive him away. Thus, the problem is how to suppress an unpleasant spectacle without departing from that passivity which is proper to the spectator. You can turn your back, of course, but that is a losing proposition; for behind the indignant backs the ridicule of man continues. Laughter is the only suitable response.

This bundle of spasmodic, suffered, accepted contradictions is one of the most ancient forms of human behavior. It made its appearance at the prelinguistic stage because it is a signal rather than a sign, because it incarnates and reproduces the dominant structure of the laughable object by a curious mimicry, and because it is the instrument of an indirect or marginal communication and is propagated, not like a notice that is passed from hand to hand, but like a yawn, by contagion. Above all it is the stupefied internalization of an objective and scandalous contradiction that seizes the laugher, possesses him, makes itself mimicked in the form of spasms, a succession of contractions and relaxations, of inhalings and exhalings, and that he reexternalizes by projecting onto the laughable object.

In the case of the drunkard, the contradiction resolved by laughter strikes us immediately: he is both man—a human being—and not man. He takes himself for my equal and, challenging me, constitutes me objectively as his fellow creature. I reject any similarity to him, yet I am conscious of his resemblance to me; he makes *my* gestures, he speaks *my* language, but by distorting everything he seems to want to ridicule me in my role as human person. The thesis is man, the antithesis what I have called elsewhere antiman, that is, something inhuman that has taken on the external features of our species with the intention of doing it injury. Laughter is a global retort: I internalize the contradiction and free myself from it by overemphasizing the antithesis: the drunkard is neither my degraded fellow creature nor my diabolical enemy; he is a subman who takes himself for a man, and I, as a human being of divine right, witness his grotesque, futile efforts at approaching our condition. Or, if you like, the essential and particularly troubling opposition is the opposition of interiority and exteriority: internally, the drunkard takes himself seriously, he is suffused with the sense of his dignity; externally, he falls into disrepute under the effect of a poison. Laughter gushes out in the lived—but not conscious—intention to radicalize the antithesis by reducing the drunkard to pure exteriority. In this way I expel the worst of intersubjectivity, which can only establish itself among beings provided with an interiority; whoever is only an *outside*, present as a flat surface with no depth, is excluded ipso facto from intersubjective life. By taking this to its conclusion, the contradiction embodied in the spasms of laughter might be defined as the contradiction between vitalism and mechanism. The laughable person believes, according to the laughers, that he is the source of his actions, when in fact they are the result of previous circumstances and external factors. He claims to enjoy a freedom, at least a relative freedom, to be the internal unity of psychosomatic processes; the laughers, however, know perfectly well that he is being manipulated, whether the behavior he believes spontaneous is merely the reverse of an *alien will*, precise and mocking, applied to make him do everything that will lead him to the verge of disappearance without ever going farther than the manifestation of this deferred death, or whether his behavior is that of a robot whose actions can be explained from the outside as the direction, speed, kinetic energy, and internal relations of a mechanical system and whose behavior can be predicted rather precisely by the audience, though *he* believes they are unpredictable. In this sense, the quality of being laughable is a result of error: the laughable object is mistaken and takes himself for a subject. *An object that is mistaken*, a robot that considers itself a man, is an absurdity. Be that as it may, the people laughing never explain the meaning of their laughter—they laugh, that's all. It may be, moreover, that they accord the object of their laughter a limited interiority: stupidity, for example, is derisory because it acts from inside like an external manipulator, becoming an intention that at first seems human and ends by negating the human, particularly praxis. Gribouille is an example of this, throwing himself into the water to avoid the rain. He starts with the right idea: he must protect himself against adversity. But Gribouille's foolishness presents itself here as a mechanical rigidity that prevents him from grasping the totality of his intention; in brief, the idea is false, as Spinoza says, because it is incomplete: it is against *water* that one must protect oneself. Suddenly the unfortunate man's project, the mechanical application of a truncated, therefore misunderstood, precept appears to be the ridiculing of a human but not at all disreputable behavior. He is the victim of a malign power, his own imbecility, which prevents him from thinking his own thoughts and transforms them, barely generated, into inert determinations external to him, external to themselves. In brief, the laughers accord interiority only on the condition that it suppresses itself before their eyes. It is clear that Gribouille *believes* he is thinking; he imagines that he is taking a synthetic and articulated view of the situation, but in fact he is mistaken: his ideas are embolisms, clots projected into his brain. Hence laughter.

We laugh at bumblers, unfortunates, cuckolds, excrement: the scatological makes us collapse with laughter, the pornographic much more rarely unless its purpose is to ridicule the feminine body, showing beneath a woman's modesty the female who "wants to be fucked." We laugh in general at all our needs because in our bourgeois societies these needs are considered degrading to the human being. We laugh at defects, vices, blunders, failures; we can laugh at all our inclinations and all our tastes, provided they appear *in the other* as agents of dehumanization, even of death, as demonstrated in the *Famous Last Words* collected by the English humorists.[8] This means that laughter is pitiless. Or, more precisely, we have recourse to it *against pity*. Any compassion, even momentary, would be suspect and dangerous: it would prove that *we put ourselves in the place* of the scandalous individual and commit the fault of attributing an interiority to him (when this is merely the power of suffering) and, consequently, that we are not so different from him ourselves. In effect, if he sparks our compassion, he must be a man—which is sacrilege—or we ourselves must be sub-men—which is not tolerable.

Still, we are compassionate and have demonstrated it in other circumstances. And it is still true that the fundamental relationship between men—masked, diverted, alienated, reified as it might be—is reciprocity. To laugh at misfortune we must make ourselves other than we are; laughter is an abrupt mutation which affects the laugher as much as it does the object as it *becomes laughable*. In other words, to grasp the compromising person in his exteriority, we must be exterior to ourselves. This is why we internalize his profound contradiction: the spasms of laughter manifest an interiority affirmed and continually rejected. But this mutation can in no instance be the work of *one man alone*. Laughter is collective in nature; it is contagious, always arising with that intention, and when it bursts forth, it outdoes itself in order to be heard and passed on. It remains incomplete as long as it fails to provoke a collective mutation which will repeat itself to be completed, achieving the transformation of the individual into the laugher. This allows us to understand the basic meaning of laughter: instead of lynching or banishment, which are group actions reinforcing the integration of the group, laughter excludes the laughable object from intersubjectivity by suppressing all internal relations between the laughers. Or, if you like, by provisionally suspending the *category* of interiority. The connective bonds between people are severed, the scandalous object loses its power to compromise. We should not believe, however, that the suppression of intersubjective connections results in a pure molecular dispersal; rediscovering their

8. From the mouths of motorists, these "famous last words" translate that feeling of intoxication and freedom we experience at the wheel. With a better vantage point than the driver, however, we see a part of the picture he doesn't see. Hence our jubilation. For the world is a wild beast to the wary, and the road he is driving along so bravely leads to a precipice. That man is laughable because he is *already dead* and continues to affirm the sovereignty of the living. He believes he is master of the universe the very moment when the universe, which until then has tolerated him with indifference, pronounces sentence against him and makes him become his own executioner.

solitude, the spectators might cry, perhaps, but certainly not laugh. Hilarity does not disperse; it transforms one kind of society into another; the morphology of the social unit formed by the witnesses is transformed, and the group, if there is one, or the semisolitude of the bystanders, becomes *serialized*. I am not going to dwell again here on the serial structure I have described elsewhere; I shall simply point out that, in a series, each one is conditioned by all the others, but *externally*; everything that *passes* from one to the other and gradually to all seems to be transmitted mechanically, like an undulation, or blindly, like a virus. Laughter enters the ear, it is already the laughter of the other; and he whom it now possesses makes himself, by laughing, *other through all others*, the transmitter of a hilarity that has been transmitted to him from outside and consequently renders him exterior to himself, hence *other than himself*. This laughter proclaims itself in him as *everyone's laughter*, not like the common act of a group (decided in all sovereignty by each member of the group, and in full reciprocity through the mediation of a third party), but, rather, like the *index of separation*—everywhere the same—of each serial unit in relation to the one preceding and the one following. I laugh *because* my neighbor laughs and *because* we agree to renounce mutual recognition; in fact, when this neighbor is also my relative, my friend, my superior, or my subordinate, if I do not stop living in terms of the bond that unites us, if I relate his present behavior to what I know about his person and his life, the laughter will not "take"; reaffirmed interiority will prevent the contamination from occurring. If, on the other hand, I serialize myself enough to sever the bond and retain, even with my brother, nothing but the double connection of identity (as a term in the series) and *experienced* exteriority (as the alien reaction imposing itself on me the way an external power transforms me into a being without interiority), I am and I make myself a member of the *society of laughter*. This is a "collective" newly constituted which perceives, feels, and thinks *serially*, that is, according to the category of exteriority; in it, each member has become *mechanical* thanks to all the others and has replaced his ego with an alter ego in order to consider the scandalous object a machine, that is, from the point of view of the radicalized antithesis, or of mechanism.

A magistrate leading a procession slips and falls on his ass. He grimaces, picks himself up, and proceeds, limping slightly. Bergson thinks, justifiably, that if we laugh, it is because this untoward fall shows "the mechanical overlying the living." But he does not give us the social meaning and intention of this mirth. It is not certain, first of all, that the bystanders will be amused; the dignitary may be popular. Or feared. On the other hand, if he is dishonest and corrupt, if he is hated because of his arrogance, his fall may occasion peals of laughter; it is pleasant vengeance to transform the haughty and dreaded signifier into the signified. But the protective function of laughter in this example is quite otherwise. Let us imagine, indeed, that there is consternation among the spectators—the spirit of seriousness will persist along with the intersubjective setting. But at the price of a metaphysical catastrophe: they witness in terror gravity's negation of the sacred. Everything is upside down, since nature issues its commands to the supernatural, which must govern it. A president of the court of justice with his feet in the air is sacrilege committed by inanimate matter that has suddenly revolted, rejecting in the person of this "authority" the political-religious hierarchy that *this* society has established and holds to be the basis of human order. In such a case, *anything* is possible: the sacred may reveal a suspicious ambiguity, heaven may be angered and strike down the observers; in the realm of intersubjectivity, there are no innocent witnesses. To avoid such anguish they will, if circumstances permit, quickly institute the society of laughter; the crowd serializes itself in order to grasp the incident in pure exteriority, that is, through a thought whose structure and principles prevent it from conceiving of the sacred. Laughter exorcises the sense of the sacred: charismatic power exists nowhere except in the head of that old fool who believed he possessed a part of it. The fall proves to everyone except him that he never participated in the numinous and that, like everyone else, he is subject to the laws of nature; the truth of this man is gravity, he is in bondage to it every bit as much as inert matter is. The contradiction that exposes the hilarity in this example is not the contradiction that opposes nature to the supernatural, since the supernatural has hastily vacated its usual realms; it is the contrast between the dignitary's erroneous opinion of himself and his reality—a reality that his very bewilderment suddenly makes him aware of. The moment that gives rise to laughter is the breaking of equilibrium: his gestures are inhuman and too human in the sense that they are de-composed, appearing simultaneously as movements imposed by earthly attraction to a heavy object and as vain efforts to recover the upright posture that characterizes the human person; his soiled clothes and rumpled robe nonetheless preserve a derisory majesty, or rather they bear witness to the fact that all majesty is derisory. In brief, the self-styled superman collapses into subhumanity. The unhappy man's interiority is not abolished, it is disqualified; in this unbalanced mass that persists in believing it is sacred, consciousness can be only an epiphenomenon, an evil genius has ordered it such that it takes itself inevitably and on all occasions for the opposite of what it is. This animal-machine, haunted by an absurd nightmare, prompts tempestuous mirth by its groaning and limping—it persists in believing that it is suffering. The old carcass is irresistible, a provisional conglomerate of atoms joined at the moment of unjoining, which forgets that it is dust and that a cosmic shiver will suffice to disperse this bottleneck of molecules, and dreams that it is an entelechy continually reassembled and maintained by the synthetic unity of a sovereign act. Laughter is called "healthy" because it puts things back into perspective and substitutes *fact* for *right;* it is unloosed in the event of danger—a compromising spectacle—in order to disengage the spectators from the object making a spectacle of itself, and to this effect laughter abolishes solidarity. It ratifies and radicalizes the cosmic denunciation of the spirit of seriousness in a particular microcosm: the little universe that believes it is master of the world subsists only for as long as it is tolerated, and its pretended sovereignty is only the surest means of its ruin. There is nothing more entertaining in a comic film than the sage prudence, the considered maneuvers, the precautions of a conspirator who scales walls, walks on tiptoe, stops to cock an ear, in sum, whose entire behavior manifests a conscious and practiced seriousness while his enemies, invisible to him but quite visible to us, nonchalantly watch him performing all the actions that will put him at their mercy. Freedom, knowledge, self-confidence, rational organization of the means in view of a worthy end—laughter, when it does not reduce such maneuvers to mere appearances, establishes that they are bound to turn back on the one who employs them in this trumped-up world; he is a trapped man, this conspirator who has *already been exposed* but persists in playing his boring role of conspirator to the end. Trapped by his very capacities, using his own powers against himself. His sovereignty, we have seen, has the ontological structure of error, persevering in its being for lack of the knowledge that it does not exist.

After these remarks, we would be justified in believing that laughter sets itself against the seriousness of life. Indeed, we have just seen that the person who laughs, abolishing any intersubjective connection, gives himself the same structure in exteriority that he means to impose on the person laughed at. Doesn't this mean that the truth of man reveals itself only in laughter, that the "human person" is an imposture and an impossibility? Far from being absurd (the absurd never presents itself as the product of a contradiction; it is closer to nonsense), such a conclusion would have the rigor of a hoax or a time bomb. In this case, the only possible attitude would be to laugh "in the face" of all men, beginning with oneself. We shall return to this attitude and to this universal conception of laughter, since Flaubert refers to it later. But even before examining whether this position is tenable, it must be observed that it cannot exist—if it does indeed exist—except as reflexive and secondary, which means that it is basically opposed to original laughter, which is a primary behavior, spontaneous, unmeditated, immediate. Yet the purpose of this primary laughter is to save the spirit of seriousness, as we have seen: at the first threat of intersubjective contamination, society withdraws, banishes intersubjectivity with bursts of laughter, replacing it with a serial relationship. *This is a protective strategy.* In primary hilarity, laughter destroys all values and all norms; its field is an inhuman desert where you cannot breathe, where you encounter only mystified, mechanical objects; but from the moment laughter bursts forth it poses a judicial principle that did not exist in the milieu of intersubjectivity: by laughing, the laugher affirms his *right to laugh.* The president of the court of justice is *wrong* to be laughable and the spectators are *right* to become laughers; they are *right* to refuse him the compassion he demands and, when he loses his case, to find his sufferings laughable; they are *right* to exhibit stupidity, meanness, cruelty, narrowness, to refuse to understand anything, to stick to pure exteriority. By regarding him as inanimate matter, they petrify the aggressor and strip him of his human appearance; in a word, they foil the antiman; if they didn't put a stop to the shocking exhibition taking place before their eyes, it would wind up by convincing them that the "human person" is either an ignoble role or one that is impossible to play. They burst out laughing in order to bring the shocking object with them into exteriority. "Man is impossible? Of course—impossible for you." The laugher says no more—indeed, analytic thought can go no further. But the reverse of laughter is the integrated man: the right to laugh is accorded only to those who are not laughable; or rather we make ourselves unlaughable by laughing, we *prove* that we are worthy of laughing. Remember the scapegoats at school? Their comrades decreed that they were ridiculous; if there were two of them, the whole class laughed at one or the other according to its whim, but the one who was temporarily off the hook was forbidden to join in the general mirth. The law was not decreed or even formulated, but as soon as he began, the laughter would turn against him: "Think it's funny, huh? Look who's talking!" etc.

Laughter is proper to man because man is the only animal who takes himself seriously; mirth denounces false seriousness in the name of true seriousness. The scapegoat must not laugh, for he is a subman permanently affected with the illusion of subjectivity; he must persevere in his false seriousness, and he is droll when he is beaten and seeks in vain to protect himself, when he is down, when he cries, when he tries to save a little of that human dignity he wrongly believes he possesses, when he is bewildered by jokes and carefully laid traps; but precisely for that reason it would be dangerous to grant him a right reserved for true men.

Such true men are deeply serious; when they go after the antiman, they resolutely enter the ranks of humanity in order to fight the enemy on his own ground. But this metamorphosis provisionally conceals the precious bonds of interiority they share with their peers in the midst of a solemn and select society in which no one is laughable, no one dreams of laughing. The society is not named, nor can it be when its members are dehumanized, but this society nonetheless confers the right to laugh and remains present in that defensive aggression which is the laugher's way of defending the society. Fanaticism frequently generates laughter. Especially rightwing fanaticism, which is in the business of *conserving*. For it is understood that laughter is conservative. In this case, the militant mocks his profane challengers, answering their questions and their arguments with tall tales. The organization he refers to—which for him represents the society of interiority—fills him with such respect that he does not even dare to expose its program and objectives to the submen who surround him, for this would be to take them seriously. It is preferable to lead them into the arena of laughter and, with calculated clowning, publicly to expose them as caricatures of the "human person"—thus gathering the laughers on his side.

Must we admit that this society of interiority, in whose name spectators create the field of laughter, really exists? In certain cases—that of fanaticism, for example—it can be accorded a virtual existence. But most of the time it remains embryonic or perfectly unreal: the specific mission of collective hilarity is to save the "human character" which is the model for social man who presupposes its existence. But this reassuring model has never been the exclusive product of one group; it is an imperative combination of prescriptions and behaviors, some originating in the dominant ideology and others having established themselves in the setting of seriality, that very setting to which the laugher claims to descend in order to save interiority. In brief, this model is a practico-inert object whose source is to be sought in the separation of social individuals as much as in their union. In our complex societies, in which all types of social aggregates coexist, in which freedom exists only to foster alienation, and in which the forces creating a mass mentality permanently affect even the most integrated groups, the society of laughter is a permanent proposition; yet it would be difficult to say whether human relations are transparent or purely reciprocal. Laughter will not be so easy in communities that are more restrained and more integrated, and seriality will play a less important role; here the compromising outsider may risk becoming the object not of laughter but of physical violence. Still, by laughing I place *value* on seriality since I adopt or emphasize it spontaneously as a defensive weapon adopted by the group in which I claim membership. Of course, this is putting the cart before the horse: if laughter is possible, it is because seriality exists everywhere, at least by virtue of danger; and if it is contagious, it is because recurrence is the rule in serial reactions. In this sense it is a *panic* reaction, like shock, flight, terror. Except that it bursts forth in order to protect a reassuring model (which serves as security for me and everyone else), which everyone takes for his social truth and cannot defend without making it the common property of all laughers, hence the common product of a group that must have existed previously and is bound to be reborn after this measure of defensive sterilization. If laughter, by unmasking false seriousness, should not refer to "true" seriousness, those who laugh would have to draw the staggering conclusion that all seriousness is false. But that is precisely what the antiman who makes a spectacle of himself is suggesting, and it is to avoid such a conclusion that he is found laughable. Indeed, such laughter begins in panic but is quickly accompanied by a feeling of superiority: *I* don't fall on my face when I walk in a procession any more than my neighbors do and all those who are laughing with me; *I* respect the sacred and don't risk compromising it with my naïveté any more than the people around me; *I* know how to drink, I can hold my liquor; *I'm* no cuckold—like all these other men I'm one of those truly human husbands whose wives will never deceive them. It is for this reason that laughter, though born of fear, is accompanied by intense pleasure or at least by a state of cheerful excitation: both contagious and willed, it comes to me *through the other* and has taken hold of my body, meaning that it *has chosen me*; I have not produced it, I have submitted to it and adhered to it—it is proof that I have all the qualities of a man. A triumph of the "qualunquiste," laughter is a *satisfecit* that the average man gives himself. And by "average man" I mean, of course, anyone while laughing.[9]

Evoked by a *spectacle*, that is, by a *show* without practical consequences, which is therefore an incomplete reality in relation to witnesses, laughter as a passive activity belongs to the imaginary in that it succeeds in derealizing its object. In this respect it has the quality of a sanction: the unfortunate president of the court of justice must internalize the hilarity he has provoked, as though it were a judgment that tells the condemned man: you only *look* like a man! What can be done about such a judgment? An air of outraged dignity, a majestic speech would merely intensify the general hilarity by demonstrating that the old fool is hopeless. He must temporarily accept his dehumanization and the derealization of his subjective life; the moment he is driven out of intersubjectivity and would like to find refuge in his solitary interiority, the waves of laughter break over him, enjoining him not to take himself seriously and disqualifying in advance the asylum he has chosen: you aren't suffering, you only believe you are suffering, you're nothing but a haunted bit of matter. This is the moment when the laughable object, horribly bewildered yet amazed, "can't believe his eyes" and "wants to sink into the ground," lacking any other escape. In brief, he feels exterior to himself and can't get over it. The best solution in most cases—but not in his—would be to laugh at oneself first. But this would be to derealize oneself completely because such laughter is *acted*. So much for the condemned man. But the judges on their part are reassured by this condemnation to unreality: by reducing the spectacle to pure appearance, they have stripped it of any power to harm. All that has happened is that a subman has been caught posing as a man or, better still, that a subman has been unmasked as being nothing but the appearance of a man. The laugher is pleasantly surprised to see the shocking object lose all depth and all reality, becoming a flat image, invented rather than perceived by the hilarious crowd, as if an obscure divinity from time to time sent submen in disguise to our towns and countrysides to entertain us with amusing caricatures and confirm our feelings of worth. In

9. "Ignoble" laughter does exist. We laugh in a mean-spirited way when one of our fellow men, having attempted to rise above himself *in earnest*, is ruined. But here too we laugh in the name of the "human person" as our society has defined it. That means that this practico-inert entity cannot be surpassed or even reformed: the daredevil has proved it, for having (falsely) taken his dreams of grandeur seriously, he finally gets crushed under our feet. He is a subman in aspiring to be a superman. This kind of laughter conceals its baseness by referring to a rigorously conformist ethic.

this sense, what is spontaneously comic is a "happening," street theater. Serious men are amused by it for a moment and then resume
their gravity; disconcerted by the unrealism and the gratuitousness of
the spectacle, they forget they are its authors. This is because their re-
conquered seriousness begins by denying the laughter—like those
spectators at a comedy who never stop holding their sides or whispering to their neighbors: "How silly!" So we have come full circle: laughter has redeemed the spirit of seriousness, which hastens to disavow
it as soon as it reappears.

It is this "stupid and mean-spirited" laughter of conformity, however, that Flaubert has chosen to consecrate his glory. Of course, we
can assume that he made this choice for the same reasons that he
chose to be an actor: his father deprived him of reality by making fun
of his displays of tenderness. The child believed he was laughable,
and we have surprised him grimacing in front of his mirror in order to
recuperate his being-in-exteriority. This was a failure, as we have seen:
He clowns but does not *really* laugh. Nevertheless, he did his best to
be funny in order to assume his laughableness, exaggerating it in
order to take responsibility for the behavior his father denounced by
his laughter. The mirror could then suggest to him another way of recuperating: governing the laughter of others, provoking it *at will*. From
this point of view, his choice of occupation is indissolubly linked to his
choice of career: what was my constitutional vice will become the
source of my power; as a buffoon, I will liberate myself by producing
what I suffered; later, every evening before a full house, I will lord it
over others, I will chastise them for their sins, turning against them
the domination they exercised over me. The laughter prompted at my
will, when they don't expect it, will choke them; I will be king, and
they will be at my beck and call. I will make them sweat for their nas-
tiness, their vulgarity, I will brutalize them with a succession of unpredictable, necessary, and rapid little shocks, which will disappear
just when these good people are on the verge of understanding them
and taking offense. Gustave said all this to himself, certainly; he knew,
and his correspondence proves it, that laughter is spiteful; he admired
the lofty attitudes of Byron and Rabelais, who laughed in the face of
humanity. To laugh at men is good. To make them laugh at themselves
is even better; Gustave would doubly debase them: the little boy
would like to believe that man goes to the theater in order to make fun
of other men and consequently of himself.

Indeed, as Caroline's jester and then as actor in the billiard room
before a select audience, the child quickly realized the ambiguity of

his occupation. We have, in effect, just described savage laughter, a defensive reaction that is born involuntarily and ubiquitously; the comic theater is merely its institutionalization. Like tragedy, comedy has a *cathartic* function: it preserves laughter as a channel for dissolving solidarity and provides social individuals with a permanent means of withdrawing their solidarity from the absurdities and vices they discover in their fellow creatures, which compromise them because they do not always have the time or opportunity to make them objects of derision. A cuckold, of course, makes us die laughing; if he is my brother, however, and I see that he is suffering, I may offer him compassion that is insincere. The theater is there to get me out of it, for at the theater we laugh at cuckolds, and I can make fun of my brother implicitly since he shares their lot. The king of nature majestically attends the spectacle in order to affirm with healthy, masculine jollity his *racial* superiority over the submen who have the affront to imitate him. A slave would devote himself to provoking a collective laughter of self-satisfaction by publicly wallowing in subhumanity in order to take upon himself the blemishes that might tarnish the "human character" and make them appear to be the defects of an inferior race making a futile attempt to approach ours. In the darkened theater, the "human person," liberated, numberless, exults in all the orchestra seats, affirming his reign by the violence of his laughter. Unlike the magistrate who, after his untoward fall, is *made laughable* by a premature and spontaneous serialization of the witnesses, and who suffers from it, vainly rejecting the status of exteriority imposed on him, the professional comedian looks for ways of provoking the serialization of the audience by showing them the manifest contradiction of his being-exterior-to-itself and his subjective illusion. He takes himself seriously so that this seriousness should be instantly belied by a pitiless mechanism—outside him and in his false interiority itself—which reduces him to a mere appearance. He undertakes action only with the intention that his act, overturned, diverted, annulled, or turned against him by the force of things, should expose itself as a ridiculous dream of sovereignty, immediately revealing that praxis, the privilege of the human race, is forbidden to submen. His cathartic function begins where the function of savage laughter ends—laughter begins the derealization of the guilty party, the comedian accomplishes it: he unrealizes himself as *another*, an abcess of fixation for one or another of our absurdities or for all of them at the same time, and the public is solemnly informed by the advertisements that this other never really existed. It is like a warning to the public: the object of your savage laughter will never compromise you, he doesn't exist; the drunk doesn't exist and neither does the president of the court of justice who fell on his face—these are the dreams of submen and quickly exposed as such. Nothing is real that is not serious, nothing is serious that is not real. For these reasons, the comic actor appears as a buffoon who delivers man from himself by an ignominious sacrifice no one knows he has willed. He mustn't expect any sympathy from the laughers: isn't he asking everyone in the audience to break solidarity with him and treat him *as exteriority?* Above all, how could the serious people who watch him contort himself fail to consider insincere and basically *laughable* his advertised intention of provoking their laughter? Laughter safeguards seriousness, but how could a man whose profession is to make himself a laughable object be serious? How could he fail to be assimilated to the submen that savage laughter *institutes* as laughable when he does nothing but embody them? And how strange, if he is indeed a man like the spectators, that he should present himself every evening as a subman. Subhumanity must fascinate him. In this case, he is more disturbing and culpable than a drunkard or a cuckold, for such men don't know what they are doing. But he knowingly offers himself to the spectators' punishing laughter and is consequently a traitor to his species, a "human person" who has sided with man's enemies. No doubt the comic spectacle is healthy, it is reassuring and liberating; it must be approved—cautiously—as an *institution;* but the social individuals who *present* it must be vile or tainted: a man worthy of the name refuses by definition—to tell the truth, he doesn't even have to refuse—to be exiled by the laughter of his peers. Should we not despise the wretched creatures who actively seek such exile every night? Better still, should we not withdraw solidarity by laughing at *them,* since they are, after all, the most compromising of all?

It would be futile to argue that we are not laughing at *them* but at the characters they are playing. The audience scarcely distinguishes between the two. And the audience is not entirely wrong, for in order to further the project of presenting a comic character to others, you must be predestined, that is, *already laughable*—which means, as we know, already derealized by the mirth of others. In this sense, the alter ego conferred by the laughers on the laughable object and the comic actor's persona have in common the fact that they are both imaginary. The comic singer Odette Laure once spoke to this point in an interview: "To be a comic singer you mustn't like yourself very much." That is the basic fact of the matter; to deliver himself every night to the wild beasts, wittingly to incite their cruelty, to refuse any recourse to interiority, and publicly to reduce himself to an outward appearance, the actor must have been constituted for himself in exteriority at some decisive period of his life. We laugh at very young children; they know it and are pleased to make us laugh. But that laughter is benevolent, the adult is amused at seeing these submen imitate the man he is, he laughs at seeing his own gestures distorted by the clumsy little bodies that are trying to learn them; that laughter is full of good will, for the adult is aware that the little submen are men in embryo. Children exaggerate their awkwardness and their seriousness in order to please. But the comic stage doesn't usually last long; it disappears when the child acquires the inner certainty of his singularity, when he can see the difference between what he is for and through others and what he makes of himself in the intimacy of his own consciousness. The future comic is a man who is *fixed* at the laughable age. An accident or the family structure must have constituted him in exteriority: let others keep him at a distance; let them refuse to take into consideration the experienced motivations of his actions, to share his pleasures, his pains; let them judge him not on the singular meaning of his behavior but on its conformity to the demands of a preestablished model. The child will then discover himself as someone with whom no one will ever empathize; he will feel that the sovereign authority of grown-ups tends to make his exteriority the truth of his life and his consciousness mere babbling; he will perceive, without ever knowing why, that the benevolent laughter he once enjoyed provoking has turned sour. This is because, for one reason or another, his parents and his friends consider his development arrested and because his clumsiness—which a year ago they thought adorable—now means that he will never internalize the "human person" that society proposes to him; consequently, they denounce in him the impossibility of being man, which is precisely what defines subhumanity. As a result, the familial laughter is somehow an act of desolidarity: the parents show that they do not recognize themselves in their offspring, that they do not see a sign of their *blood*. A good beginning for a future comic. If the little boy, out of docility, comes to experience increasing difficulty in *putting himself in his own place*, still feeling his emotions but no longer entering into them, if he lives his suffering or his estrangement clandestinely, heedlessly; and if he withdraws solidarity from himself in the clear light of thought, if he sees it only as a way of provoking the laughter of others by an overwhelming desire to laugh first at himself in order to be united with the adults in their seriality, then a comic vocation is born and at the same time a *laughable image*—the angry subjection of the interior to the flat appearance of exteriority. Here we have that monster unrealized by the savage laughter of others: from this moment, a traitor to himself, everything is set for him to nourish the image he is for them. If subsequently he does become an actor, if he plays Sganarelle or Pourceaugnac, what has changed? These are roles, of course. But what internal certainty does he have to hold up against them? Far from being able to distance himself with respect to these characters, he must himself have been *constituted* as a character to be able to embody them. There exists in him a permanent *persona*, which is quite simply the *laughable man*, and others that are provisional, the images of an evening or a season. But we must not believe that he is unrealized in these more than in his permanent persona since by all evidence the basic unrealization is already constituted; the unfortunate fellow was condemned long ago to exploit his body and his interiority as an analogue of the fundamental *imago* which is that of the subman who takes himself seriously. Certainly the permanent persona presents itself as his own person and conceals its unreality, while the characters are given as interpretations and the audience is informed by the program that tonight they are going to laugh at Hirsch in *Arturo Ui*. But in truth the role, whatever it is, is only one piece of the fundamental persona, which will be worked, chiseled, modified in certain points, emphasized in others—nothing more. *With what* do we expect the actor to make us laugh if not with the only analogue he has at his disposal, and by what operation if not the systematic exploitation of experience in order to produce the absurd? This evening they are doing *Pourceaugnac*; he can have a hundred faces, but the one he has today on this stage, behind these footlights, is the face of Fernandel; Fernandel's body and no other lends itself to that rascal from the Périgord, his behind and no one else's is threatened by the enemas the apothecaries hold poised. And if the comedian wants to express the confusion of the poor provincial, let us not assume he will be inspired by behavior observed in others. Certainly observation helps, and he will make use of it in order to control himself. But he does not reproduce something—he invents. And in this particular case, we can agree with Wilde that nature imitates art: there are no perfect fools except on stage. In sum, he nourishes his character with his own substance. It would be inadequate to say that he *plays the fool*, that in the unreal world he becomes the imbecile he would be if he were actually afflicted with imbecility; in order to produce the analogue of the persona he represents, he becomes the fool he *is*. This

171

obscure mass of agitation, terrorized incomprehension, fear, stubborn-ness, bad faith, and ignorance, which under the name of stupidity is the index of everyone's alienation, is awakened and stirred up by the actor so that he might be unrealized through it as a magnificent idiot. What is he doing other than what he has always done, since a bad relationship constituted him laughable? To be sure, a dialectic operates between the character and the interpreter: the actor transforms the character to the precise extent that he is transformed by it. But these are relations between images. The role serves as an alibi: the actor sheds his persona, he believes he is evading himself in the character. But this is futile: in his befuddled alacrity to be nothing but a strange image there is a distinct malaise and a deep antipathy, which encourages him to revile himself so that others may triumph. He is conscious, in fact, of choosing this or that disguise *in order to make others laugh at him* as he has always done.

The public isn't fooled; when a serious passerby, alone and absorbed in his thoughts, is recognized by idlers as a famous comedian, they burst out laughing. Many actors complain of this. One declares that he cannot travel by train without seeing laughing faces pressing against the windows of his compartment at every station. Another is annoyed at not being able to enter a restaurant without provoking laughter among the diners; a third had to give up swimming in the sea except at some abandoned cove, for as soon as he would appear in his bathing suit there would be a gale of laughter from the sunbathers. We *make people laugh*, they all say, at certain hours, that's our job; but outside these working hours we are no less serious than you. From one point of view this is true: if we didn't know "what they did for a living," what would we see? Men like other men and, more specifically in our societies, bourgeois gentlemen like all such bourgeois, comfortably and smartly dressed, with inscrutable, empty faces like everyone else, an easy courtesy, affability, all very reassuring; particular signs: nothingness. As for their present concerns, they are those of all bourgeois: money, family, job, an affair perhaps, and of course a car. All the equipment for passing unnoticed. But try as they might, the crowd unmasks them: their seriousness is not a true human seriousness, it is that of submen who take themselves seriously. Something is going to happen, that's for sure: that graceful, calm demeanor, that tranquil air is going to be shattered; the crazy guy is going to fall down, his face will reflect the bewilderment and stupidity for which he is famous, a bird is going to shit on his head, the universe or his own clumsiness will reveal his hidden laughability—meaning, according to the public, his truth. The only error of these unbenevolent observers is in confusing laughability and truth. We should say, rather, that the comic actor has no truth since he sacrifices concrete existence to the abstract being of appearance, and since the seriousness he affects in town—although it may be every bit as "staunch" as that of the laughers—is distinct in that it is constituted *against* his fundamental laughaility. In this sense he is not very different from the character he plays on stage, whose function is to affirm himself against the comic, only to be conquered at last by the implacable chain of catastrophes and denounced as a falsely serious figure. With one difference: on stage the catastrophes are *certain*, the character will lose his human dignity; in town they are unlikely. In other words, this respectable and slightly intimidating gentleman will cross the street without meeting any obstacles and will soon be out of sight—nothing will happen to him. But the passersby will still consider his dignity an invitation to laugh: it offers itself *to be destroyed* in the midst of hilarity; and if heaven or hell do not take it at its word, that is their business, not his—the actor has done all he could. And this laughter bespeaks the truth: the dignified figure is a role the comic assumes in town; born of an effort to mask his laughability, it is neither more nor less true than that. Let us say that it is convenient in certain circumstances, and the actor could not live if he did not know how to affect respectability at the right moment; but in fact, he hardly believes in that respectability, which is an invented role or one borrowed from his characters—where would he take it from otherwise? It is, if you like, a thesis without an antithesis, the moment of sovereignty as it is posed for itself, cut off from him, negative, in which the force of circumstance unmasks the imposture and reveals that this sovereign being is nothing but a mechanism gone mad. In this sense it is clear that he himself invites the witnesses who recognize the actor with the hilarious expectation of a denial. The moment of contradiction that is embodied in the spasm of laughter is the moment of recognition: here is an honorable man—but hold on, no, it's Rigadin; seriousness is posed and decomposed and reborn in order to be decomposed once more, dissolved in appearance. The aggressive component of laughter here comes from indignation: you wanted to fool us, to make us take you for a man, but we are not so stupid, we know you are a clown.

A strange, determined sacrifice, to make others laugh at one's own expense. Why do it? I don't know. I believe we have established that a man could not be a comic if he had never been *constituted laughable*. But not all laughable children become comics; so there must be medi-

173

ating circumstances. Certain universal circumstances might be found if we could compare lives. But this doesn't concern me; what is important here is little Gustave's choice. He wants glory so that he can dazzle and punish his father—this is understood. But he attempts to achieve it by making people laugh at him. This is coveting the ignominious glory of buffoons. And isn't it straying from his primary intention? Does he want to be both the pride and the shame of his family or, more precisely, to make his father's name illustrious by dishonoring it? And, on a deeper level, why does he persist? *In spite* of the ignominy or *because* of it? The two questions are actually only one, as we shall see. We shall provide various answers to these questions, which are organically linked, going from the most superficial—originating in the very circumstances of the choice—to certain infrastructural givens—whose roots lie deep in his protohistory.

I have already emphasized that he set out defeated. He chose the unreal only after having been derealized; furthermore, he wasn't seeking unrealization for itself, he wanted to *realize* himself as an artisan who produces the imaginary as a profession. Wasn't this capitulating to his father well in advance and proclaiming the ethical-ontological primacy of being over nonbeing? Let us consider his choice more carefully. It may well have had the structure of a *challenge*, for such behavior is characteristic of passive activities: I throw down the gauntlet, I set myself down near that inert object and wait, motionless, impenetrable, like a dense block of inanimate matter. This common and eloquent image is sufficient indication that what is involved is a gesture, a *show*; in a challenge, it is always up to the other to act first.[10] I have described elsewhere a kind of challenge that might be called provocative impotence because it is launched when the enemy is already the victor; when resistance is impossible, the vanquished party reacts with an aggressive show of the passivity to which he has been reduced, and arrogantly takes on himself what the other did to him. We find this attitude in its pure form among colonized peoples at a certain stage of their struggle, that is, when they become conscious of their oppression yet still lack the means to drive out the oppressor; in this case, the challenge, an ineffectual ideal, demonstrates at once the impossibility and the necessity of revolt. Half a century ago, the African, grandson of the slave, colonized, ex-

---

10. To be sure, this attitude could be the first moment in a practical enterprise: the challenger's open challenge to the champion will end in combat. Only if he keeps it to himself does it have all the qualities of passivity. Most of the time, moreover, what is publicly presented as a challenge is the result of carefully calculated arrangements.

ploited, treated as a "negro" by the racist colonizers, took up the notions and words those colonizers used to think about him and to signify him. He "gathered them from the mud," a black poet has said,
"in order to wear them with pride." Negro, yes, and dirty nigger, if
you like; but by tearing your words, your concepts, away from you
and applying them to myself in full sovereignty, by laying claim to that
nature you scorn but whose originality you cannot avoid recognizing,
I recapture the initiative, I dare to think about myself, I personalize
myself against you, and I become that permanent indignity—the self-
conscious *other*. Thus was born the notion of "negritude." Circumstances alone determine a people's representatives—the African poets,
for instance—or the individuals who represent only themselves in
taking this attitude. "You call me thief," says Genet, "when it is already too late to refuse that title. It's no problem, I will be *the* Thief."
In each case, the signified attempts to become the signifier but can do
so only by assuming the imposed signification. In the realm of the
ideal, this is liberating, but *in reality* it is an internalization of the value
judgments and the Weltanschauung of the enemy. The slave, instead
of being the master's truth, accepts as a lesser evil the master's being
his truth, on the sole condition that he can internalize this truth and
throw it in the face of the oppressor: Yes, I *am* that and I *shall* be that.
And afterward? Certainly the "negritude" refashioned by the poets
was helpful to Africans at a certain moment in their history, allowing
them to refuse to be mere objects of the colonizer and to stand before
him as subjects. It is nonetheless true that the notion of *negro* has a
negative content ostensibly drawn from experience and consisting of
racist estimations of a claimed black character ("they" are heedless,
lazy, childish, thieving, lying; their brain is underdeveloped; etc.).
They are both the product of and justification for colonial exploitation. No one can take the name "negro," even in pride and defiance,
without giving assent—involuntary but inevitable—to those hostile,
deprecatory judgments born of hatred and fear, and without at the
same time consenting to the colonial system. By gathering those judgments out of the mud, all that Africans acquired was the freedom to
proclaim themselves submen. In the same way, by declaring that he
was *the* Thief and pledging himself to evil, Genet did nothing more
than recognize the absolute primacy of the values in whose name he
was condemned. In both instances we witness the development of an
exhausting dispute, a constant vigilance, a permanently watchful vul-
nerability. The colonized must never sleep, never forget the enemy—
he is everywhere, even in their room—or cease for a moment in their

effort to shame him by reclaiming in pride the insults he has hurled at them; they draw on their painful and fragile pride only in order to re-conquer their formal freedom to be—in other words, to *show* them-selves subjects, resisting the permanent temptation of shame, tire-lessly fighting the chink of interiority that never stops widening, whose source is their own courageous, perverse effort to treat the negative as positive. Futile efforts. What the poets have added with their skin to "negritude" is a certain enrichment, a lived relationship with the cultural traditions of Africa; but nothing is precise, and all this counteracculturation, because it is not accomplished in practice in the form of a revolt, remains a murky fog that barely masks the rock of internalized racist judgments. And I have shown elsewhere that Genet's colossal attempt to reverse the system of values was futile be-cause the ethic of evil presupposes the victorious universality of the ethic of good. Through the internal disequilibrium it produces, pro-vocative passivity is thus pledged to rapid disappearance when the oppressed leave passivity behind, that is, when they steal the weap-ons of their oppressor. That passivity gives way to a *practical* con-sciousness of oppression. "Negritude" has fallen by the wayside in African thought since the revolutionary battles of the Third World be-gan; now the African thinks of himself as a subject to the extent that armed struggle makes him an agent of his own history and that the colonizer becomes his object. Many people today believe the notion of "negritude"—eminently poetic and by definition impractical—was counterrevolutionary. This is unjust; it *would be* counterrevolutionary today because its effect could only be demobilizing, but it must be placed in the context of its time as an abstract movement of person-alization. Some also charge that those who elaborated the concept were objective accomplices of the colonizers, which is accurate pro-vided we add that the revolutionary process can begin only in the ob-jective complicity of the oppressed with the oppressor and that this very ambiguity permits the gradual maturation of contradictions. In the same way, Genet confirms his defeat when he personalizes him-self as Thief; but this unstable moment leads him to reverse the situa-tion by personalizing himself as the Poet of Evil—the ineffectual de-linquent becomes the effective demoralizer of his readers, who are all decent people.

Little Gustave's challenge is an impotent provocation in that he re-claims in pride what he has lived in shame. You have derealized me? Very well, I will be Lord of the Unreal. You treat me like a bad actor? Fine, I will be *the* comic, his tenderness and higher feelings so contrived that they cannot be displayed without provoking laughter. More prudent or less splendidly reckless than Genet, the child does not persist in the vice for which they reproach him, does not try to make it the pure principle of his personalization or to internalize it in order to become its subject and radicalize it by a display. *Thief? I will be the thief:* If Gustave could have conformed to this maxim, he would have declared to the paterfamilias: "You derealize me? Very well, I will be the *fool.*" We shall see that this form of abetting defiance will also be one of Gustave's attitudes and that it will lead him to the crisis of January 1844. But for the moment he isn't thinking of it, or else he is afraid of it: to take responsibility for himself as fool, that is, as completely unreal, would be to dissolve his very being into the imaginary, whether he accepts and lays claim to the nonbeing of the image or agrees only to an imagined being. In the 1830s, quite to the contrary, the little boy slips from nonbeing to being, from appearance to reality, from the disorderly incoherence of disturbed images to the profession of producer of images. Still, by this choice, and perhaps even more than the poets of negritude or the author of *Paravents*, he *begins* by justifying the enemy. In his initial project, which is to acquire being by claiming the investiture of glory, he poses the absolute superiority of being over the imaginary, as if no one had the right to dream unless society had given him a mandate to do so by charging him with enriching the collective realm of the imaginary. No doubt he sought to be instituted in the unreality that his father criticized and denounced, but at the same time he renounced it by making it the supreme value *against his oppressor:* his complicity lay in acknowledging the paterfamilias's notion of real-being as an absolute value. First, we need to reassure ourselves of our being; then we can imagine, if we like. It is on this level that we find for the first time a major and unresolvable contradiction that we shall encounter in every period of Gustave's life and that will explain his complex attitude toward "realism" as well as his uncertainty, hidden beneath his Garçon antics and his literary activities alike but constant and profound, touching on what I shall call the metaphysical value of art. To consider only the still crude form in which it manifests itself in the little boy, we might explain it in these terms: he cannot nourish the project of astounding his father with his glory and stealing off to heaven, rising above his class, and leaving the old practitioner and his eldest son climbing a mole hill, without suggesting at the same time that the imaginary—the fruit of great desire and dissatisfaction—is *in principle* superior to reality and, in short, that art, occupied exclusively with what is too beautiful to exist, far outweighs science, which is limited to verifying the vulgarities of being. At the same time, this child of scientism cannot help taking up the profession of producer of images as a last resort. The comedian's art is what he chose when all other options were forbidden him, the day he believed himself denounced as the family idiot and was forever forbidden access to the natural sciences and to his father's glory as a man of action and researcher: Djalioh is a poet because he does not know how to read, because his brain is not made to grasp "logical connections." He is destined to reign in the shadows, but that is because he is banished from reality. The real is primary, in all senses of the word; it belongs *to others*, to the true men who decipher it and rule it; the glory of an illusionist will never equal that of Achille-Cléophas, the tireless benefactor of humanity. This contradiction would never cease tormenting Flaubert. Because of it, he lays claim to his father's surgical eye and to the spirit of analysis even as he declares himself to be antiprose, antitruth, affirming that nothing is worth as much as a beautiful verse. For this very reason he will try to present the "psychology" which he claims is the lot of the novelist as an exact science and the imagination as a rigorous technique and a mode of apprehending the real. But immediately afterward, or simultaneously, he makes imagination the unique means of escaping the hideousness of the real world. Starting here, he continually oscillates between two extremes: sometimes beauty seems to him a bottomless pit, and sometimes he doubts not only his talent but the very value of literature: he is an anchorite, a saint, minister of an unknown cult of the vulgar; he is a numismatist, a philatelist, writing is his hobby; in brief, "I am a bourgeois fellow who lives in the country and busies himself with literature." We shall return to all this. What is important in this chapter is that as an accomplice to the enemy, he affirms the primacy of the antithesis over the thesis, as do the laughers: the imagination is not the domain of his sovereignty, it is the consequence of his passivity; when he takes empty pride in the images that haunt him, what is he but a dreamer who takes himself seriously, a subman who thinks he is a man? He is therefore eminently *laughable,* not only when his father laughs at him but even in the position of withdrawal that he had to adopt. We can read this between the lines of certain passages in *Mémoires d'un fou.* In the first instance, it is wounded pride that speaks: *They* are laughing at *me!* The fools! Me, with my dreams of grandeur . . . me, drowning on the edge of creation, etc. And then pride is broken: If they knew of my dreams, they would still make fun of me, they would take me for an "animal tamer," a "maker of books." Those narrow realists are impervious to his grandiose ecstasies and *they are right*—this is what he tells himself when discouragement follows his lyric effusion. They are right because their option—practical, scientific, and technological—gives them an unfair but total power over him, and he has no way of fascinating them with his dreams. He is disqualified in advance by his choice. He will never convince them, he will never convince his father: the only rapport he could have with them is the collective laughter of desolidarity which he provokes by *showing* himself in all his passionate oneirism. This means for him that the best of himself, his movement of permanent unrealization, is tainted by being laughable. And it also means that glory, if he obtains it, will be laughable as well. Later, like Genet, he will have to exhaust himself in a colossal, subversive enterprise to overturn the existing set of values. Nevertheless, although in both cases the subversion is total and has bearing on all categories (good, evil; being, nonbeing; possible, impossible; life, death; etc.) the emphasis is not on the same norms. The operation of the thief aims at constituting an ethic of evil in order to disqualify the ethic of good; that of the imaginary adolescent has as its purpose the establishment of a normative ontology in which nonbeing will have primacy over being, appearance over reality, the impossible over the possible. He will try to turn creation upside down in order to prove that a derealized child who unrealizes himself is superior to the most effective realists, and is, as he will say later, an "aristocrat of the Good Lord." We shall see that he succeeds in his enterprise, not rationally and logically and not by the "paradoxes that befuddle him," but by that leap into madness that will make him drop at his brother's feet one night in January 1844, and by the issue of that "Idumean night" *Madame Bovary*. A precarious success: he will have a terrible awakening when reality in the form of a pointed helmet forces its way into his room and sits down on his bed, destroying with one fell swoop his dreams and those of imperial France. For the moment, he is squeezed between the two edges of an insurmountable contradiction, or to put it another way, he oscillates between thesis and antithesis. In the billiard room period and during his first years in school, he doesn't know what to think of his own risibility. At times he sees it as a mark of election, and at other times as a sign of infamy.

Laughable greatness: the first archetype of the social imaginary that he knew, Don Quixote, whose adventures were read to him aloud and who was constantly laughed at, dominates the laughers with his stature. Actually, the character created by Cervantes is quite complex, but classical readers simplified him in the extreme by laughing at him unreservedly. And this was how he was transmitted, grotesque and contemptible, to the first generations of the romantics just as they were busy resurrecting the Middle Ages with their towns and their knights errant. The collective work these young people did on the comic hero was therefore to gather him up as he was, already beaten and mocked, and, while recognizing that he was laughable, to disqualify the laughers. We find the outcome of this systematic transformation in a fin-de-siècle play by Richepin, half a century later. The knight of the sad countenance frees the convicts from their chains, and these, who represent the abjection of the mob, find nothing better to do than sneer at his stupidity; they spit in his face, jeer at him, and, if I remember correctly, pelt him with stones. Never is the hero so great as in this moment when, without hatred or regret, he prepares to die in the midst of laughter he himself has provoked. The seventeenth century ridiculed the character because he took himself for a valiant knight of the Middle Ages at a time when chivalry no longer made sense and when the deeds of solitary men were impossible; from romanticism to symbolism, by contrast, the greatness of the Don of La Mancha derives from the fact that, living in a time of impossible chivalry, he turns himself, to the great detriment of his body and his unsatisfied heart, into the *impossible knight*, meaning the knight of the impossible. With his reasoning and unremitting madness, he outshines the most famous paladins who, no matter how courageous, undertook only what promised at least a chance of success, for he commits himself when there is every chance of failure so that the pure image of the gallant knight might exist beyond the real, proof that man takes full responsibility for himself only by first accepting his own unsurpassable impossibility.

As we see, these well-intentioned authors have fixed the poor knight in the typical attitude of provocative impotence because they immediately recognize that this seeker after the absolute, displaced on earth, perplexed, strange, is an object of permanent hilarity *for the realists*. It is easy to see how the imaginary, laughable child who later, at the critical point of the century, will be claimed as a precursor of both the naturalists and the symbolists, might have seen in this pitiful but sublime hero his model and his consolation. In his eyes, Don Quixote is also an imaginary: he encounters windmills, believes they are giants, charges with his lance lowered, and falls on his face like a common buffoon. But is he not inspired, this wondrous gentleman who lives day and night in a world where giants and captive princesses are found at every turn? What stirs Gustave above all is that this Galahad, this Roland, this Lancelot is not truly talented—talent in this case being physical strength and facility in the handling of arms, indispensable to anyone who would take on twenty men single-handed. One breath is enough to topple that old clumsy carcass who spends half his time with his feet in the air like a common president of the court of justice. Inopportune, anachronistic, called by a myste-rious and perhaps diabolical voice, he perceives what doesn't exist, and never does what he means to do. Gustave recognizes himself in Don Quixote: isn't he pledged to glory, yet—if he believes his family's opinion on the subject—deprived of all the talents that would allow him to achieve it? *Therefore* he *must* be comic, this child without quali-ties, since like his master he will be a laborer in the impossible. He will be comic because he will fail in all his efforts for lack of particular propensities. And because he will persist in beginning all over again. That will be his genius: he will play the subman who takes himself for a man, the coward who thinks he's a tough guy, the little shrimp who acts like a bully, drawing his talent from his awkwardness and signify-ing by his greatness that beyond the ridicule attached to dreamers, it is beautiful to take oneself, in the face of all disappointments, for some-one one knows one cannot be.

Signifying—that's all right. But to whom? Not to the ferocious laughers who mock him in the name of realism or, what amounts to the same thing, in the spirit of seriousness, common sense. Nor to the nobility or the monarchy: they have become suspect, and besides, they hardly respect comics. There is still God. He is the best witness, he is the loving father; he will see everything, the laughter, the suffer-ing of the object of mockery, his sublime and ignominious sacrifice, *he* will recognize Gustave's greatness, *he* will reward him with eternal glory. *On condition that he exists.* We recognize here the vicious circle formed by the two ideologies clutching at each other. When Gustave feels within him what he called the "dawn" of faith, he is not far from believing that his sacrifice ennobles him: offering himself to the laugh-ter of others is, in sum, equivalent to the feudal gift. He feels guaran-teed by the absolute. But the dawn doesn't last long: night closes in and crushes it; the Great Witness never existed. All is suddenly re-versed; Gustave once more finds *his* world, that is, his father's world—where the worst is always certain. In this world you are punished in proportion to the nobility of your ambitions; the desire for glory, the noblest of all, must be only a trap and must lead to the most exem-plary chastisement. A child would give his life to be a Talma, a Frédérick Lemaître, if only for a day. What will happen? Will he remain un-known or fail miserably and die in despair? For God's sake, that's not the worst thing that could happen. The worst is what sometimes oc-curs in the sketches of Mack Sennett and, in a slightly different form, in some of Charlie Chaplin's films: the tragedian takes himself seri-ously, gets up on the stage, declaims his part, and, far from failing miserably, achieves unequivocal success with *laughter;* the director im-mediately engages him to keep on playing his part with the utmost seriousness, which has triggered the audience's mirth. Glory will come, but it will be a nightmare; and this *achieved* glory will be the exquisite punishment for the desire for glory, since it crowns the un-happy actor, not for what he claims to do in his sovereignty as man, but for what he does in reality, which is exactly the opposite. The lau-rels go to the worst tragedian on earth, to the man who takes himself for Augustus or for the aging Horace when all his attitudes, at once forced and vulgar, expose him as a comic valet who has mistaken his job. He provokes laughter because the spectators know his true nature and anticipate it while he totally lacks self-awareness and because his very undertaking to impose himself as subject is grotesque. If laugh-ter stigmatizes the massive error of the subman who takes himself se-riously, does he not figure as the prototype of the laughable man who is comic in spite of himself by taking himself tragically? The punish-ment of his noblest dream is that it is granted and that its object is revealed to be ignoble: theatrical success, a strict reversal, passage from the positive to the negative with no previous warning—these farcical traps are common in the worst of possible worlds. And this time God is away: no one is there to witness that the tragedian is right in spite of what people think; they laugh at him, that is his only truth, and no one finds greatness in this execrable actor who persists in his error. Furthermore, after the ignominy comes voluntary debasement; engaged by the director, the comic becomes a comic quite consciously in spite of himself, and to increase his reputation or simply to earn a living he is base enough to disavow himself completely and—an ab-ject sacrifice—to reproduce on stage his grand attitudes in order to amuse the public at his own expense. Gustave senses this; he might have been able, he may have hoped, to compensate for his primary derealization by unrealizing himself in the roles of kings and warriors. Later, in solitude, didn't he like to imagine that he was Nero or Tam-berlaine? But Achille-Cléophas's denigrating irony slipped even into the compensating dream and disqualified in advance all the child's at-tempts to escape his father; these attempts will be *entirely* laughable and the more so the higher they are aimed. He has a single resource: to get there first. Instead of resigning himself after the fact, basely, to being a laughable object, he will get the jump on the others and deliberately provoke their laughter before they realize what is happening. It is not just the theater and glory that are involved; Gustave is one of those Gribouilles who deliberately and constantly make others laugh at them in order to be sure that at least no one is making fun of something absurd about them that they are unaware of. As an adolescent, a young man, an adult, he insists on making people laugh at him—and at others, as we shall soon see—people being his friends, his parents, his schoolmates. He likes to recall that he made Ernest or Caroline "roll with laughter," he invents the Garçon (we shall return to this), he does an idiot's dance in front of the Goncourts, he portrays himself as a dual personality—a bookworm in private, a traveling salesman when he has an audience; for the moment he enters a gathering, whatever its nature, the participants are *primarily* spectators for him. This means he is afraid of them, and for fear of being mocked behind his back he immediately dons his comic armor: there he is, playing the subman who takes himself seriously in order to show everyone that he *doesn't take himself seriously*. At the same time he delivers himself to their laughter as he is, in his suffering and his basic gravity, and by a complicitous challenge caricatures himself as ignoble so that in his degraded state he will be at least sovereign.

This is what he is trying to express by the often misunderstood formula: "The ignoble is the sublime below." Certainly by its very structure it recalls the antitheses and rhetoric of romanticism; but it bears a specifically Flaubertian meaning. Hugo goes as far as slipping a great soul into a grotesque body; he lets us see the power of paternal love in a professional buffoon. But God's favorite interviewer is not subversive, or at least not in that way. The ignoble for Hugo is merely the ignoble, and great emotions, even if they are awakened in the heart of a buffoon, remain great; far from being made ridiculous by the person who feels them, such emotions transfigure him. With Gustave it is quite the opposite, as we quickly perceive if we try to construct the symmetrical and complementary maxim which seems to be implied: "The sublime is the ignoble above." This sentence—which is nonsense if taken literally, proves to us *in any case* that the elusively evoked symmetry does not exist. Certainly, there is an "above" since we talk about a "below"; furthermore, we have seen that Flaubert's mental space is structured according to the absolute vertical. Yet we find nothing above but the bitterest disillusionment: above, the sublime,

183

the object of the most legitimate desire, is revealed to be a diabolical mirage; he who wants to be an angel becomes a beast; he who aspires toward the "noble" region, missing a firm foothold, trips and falls, breaking his neck amid laughter. *Suffered*, this fall is merely ridiculous; it will be ignoble and sublime if the victim knows how to transform it into a spectacular plunge into the mud. Ignoble—it is the radicalization of baseness, of cowardice, of sadism, of a flabby and cruel cynicism; it is the deliberate choice to be a subman out of a hatred of the human condition, the decision to portray great emotions in order to ridicule them one by one, either by showing that they are impossible—and grotesque in their serene seriousness—or by exposing the stupidity and egotism concealed by their boasted idealism. For Gustave, the ignoble is *a show*, a trumpeting of vice which the public confirms by its laughter. The ignoble actor provokes laughter when acting love, generosity, suffering, because he ridicules these emotions in his own person; for he has a grievance against them and against himself. Flaubert loved *showing* he was ignoble, indulging in vulgar talk, laughingly recounting medical student stories to make people sick; he made the Garçon a touch vulgar, he enjoyed the company of low women who, in their conversation and their manners, revealed the shamefulness of their sex and consequently of love itself. The actress Lagier, whose company he enjoyed, was not ignoble in herself; it was he who forced her to play the role of an excessively lewd woman; she did it, moreover, quite consciously. It is on this level, the lowest, that one encounters the sublime. The truly sublime, since heaven is empty. And what is it, then, if not the self-destructive fury, the anger against himself that finishes the job begun by the paterfamilias without the least hope of recompense? He makes people laugh at him out of disgust with himself and humanity; he destroys in his person, and publicly, all human values in order to show that he is unworthy of them and, at the same time, that they are unworthy of his immense, grotesque desire. His sole purpose is to provoke horror and contemptuous, condemning laughter: if *that's* all the world is, I'll show what I think of it by becoming filth myself. As a misanthrope, I claim the solitude of the hermit or the infamy of glory: I will show my hatred of men by throwing myself at their feet to make them withdraw their solidarity from me through laughter and spit at me out of a sense of superiority. Sublime, I choose to proclaim publicly the realists' justified triumph over my dreams; I assume this loathsome triumph in order to push my despair to the limit even as I refuse to take it seriously and bear witness *for everyone*—this will be my ultimate ridicule—that all nobility in this

184

base world is nothing but the grotesque dream of a visionary, though a world without nobility is in itself shameful.

The sublime below, after all, is absolute negativity; Gustave is not trying to use his negations to suggest something positive. Quite the contrary, he begins by recognizing the vanity of his dreams. The imaginary man, having no more at stake, sinks into nothingness. Without God, Don Quixote is only a senile old tale-spinner, his absurdity not the measure of his greatness but the truth of his being; Gustave is only the family idiot, and if he dreams the impossible it is because ungrateful nature and the paternal curse have deprived him of any real possibility. If he rejects *himself*, if he invites others to reject him, if he wallows in shit in front of serious men, provoking them by his very defiance to strip him of his rank and dignity, it is because he takes enormous, miserable pride in that pure passive sovereignty, the free assumption of the rejection others have offered him since his birth. The negation comes from them, but by taking responsibility for it—on his own, we know, he has no way to affirm or to deny—he radicalizes it and makes himself its martyr. Thus the noble impossibility of being a knight errant becomes, from this new perspective, the ignoble impossibility of being Gustave. There is nothing besides the real world, but the martyrdom of young Flaubert points an accusing finger at all of reality because it reveals in him that its products are flawed, that man is not viable since he evaporates in laughter while denouncing the whole of reality, the realm of Satan, as an impossibility ignorant of itself. Nothing more: his only freedom, the sole sign that he is something different from and more than a quivering and laughable lump of flesh, is the horrified negation of himself and everything else.

Whether he plays the role of Don Quixote or the role of an infamous and scurrilous buffoon, we again find ourselves at opposite poles of the primary compensatory project: the Knight of the Impossible and the impossible Gustave are both objects of universal derision. Gustave is lost without compensation, Don Quixote is the chosen of the hidden God, but both are the despair of their families. A little while ago, Achille-Cléophas, dazzled by the glory of his misunderstood son, wept with happiness and, more secretly, with remorse. Now, remorse is no longer in season: the medical director can congratulate himself for having accurately judged his younger son; if he weeps, it is from rage and shame. Let us observe, however, that these two contradictory projects have some basic features in common. In both, Gustave is famous: as great man or as buffoon, the whole world whispers his name. In both, pride remains. And the sullen intention to chastise the father who has cursed him. Hence it is not surprising that the little boy oscillates between these extremes; the reason why must be sought in the particular structures of resentment. His vindictiveness, pondered by a constituted passivity, obviously intends to punish, but never by an act or directly; the victim—without knowing how or why, poor thing—in a situation he has neither brought about nor foreseen, except by "gliding," finds himself by his existence alone acting as the executioner of his own executioners. Starting here, the project of vindication can be envisaged in two opposed but complementary scenarios. (1) Condemned, the resentful man counts on the course of events to reveal to the judges that they have committed a monumental judicial error: the accused is in fact an angel; not only is his innocence manifest but it has been established that in any event he was not within their jurisdiction. Obedience for this unfortunate angel consists in accepting the sentence, stifling his cry of innocence, and, though still not admitting guilt, sanctimoniously purging his pain. He counts on the indignation of others to carry out his vengeance against the bad judges: they find him in prison, throw themselves at his feet, kiss his hands, and the members of the tribunal take flight without his even thinking to blame them. And so little Gustave, scorned, ridiculed by the paterfamilias, gives his hand to everyone, bows down, and sets to work in the unpleasant domain to which he has been relegated. He will be the first to be surprised when ennobling glory crowns him before the eyes of the confounded medical director. (2) But in resentment, as in Kafka's penal colony, the sentence is internalized, sewn into the skin of the condemned man, who is inclined to grant the correctness of the judges' decision, yet never ceases to regard them with rancor. Obedience, manipulated differently, becomes pitiless and black, it becomes a complicitous challenge, the victim assumes the sentence, and radicalizes it out of rigid respect for the judiciary; punished for a crime he isn't certain he's committed, he zealously sets about making himself a criminal and ends by assassinating his judges in order to justify their sentence. Gustave dreams naïvely of innocent glory in the immediate circumstances, as long as he believes he is living in a feudal world and as long as he does not question the value of the imaginary and his role as public entertainer. As soon as he starts to question, under the influences of the paternal irony, the meaning and importance of unrealization—which he takes for his lot—he rushes to radicalize the sentence, supposedly to conform to his father's will but in fact to steal the father's laughter and turn it against him by making it universal: laugh at me as much as you like, I will make myself laughed at by everyone on earth. If you are unhappy about it, what can I do? I am only what you've made me: humanity's clown. In this second project, Gustave becomes the ill-natured fellow he believes he is; in a fit of rage he wants to do evil and wants the greatest evil done to him so that the insults and laughter will reach his father through him. Whatever his shame, he will never pay too dearly for the bitter and delicious pleasure of making that honorable man of science the famous progenitor of an illustrious derelict. "Yes," he would then cry out in a paroxysm of pride, "I enjoy universal scorn, I am the lowest of men, they call me freak when I go by and I'm proud of it. But you, unworthy father who made me so abject, you are worth less than I am since you haven't the courage to face dishonor."

The independent variable here, in short, is the idea he has of the public and consequently of himself. Sometimes he thinks that the public, full of gratitude, respects him as a professional, a psychologist who knows how to pull the strings and knows the laws of laughter; and sometimes he has the feeling he is offering himself up defenselessly to practical jokers who come to the theater to see him abase himself. In any event, we shall be justified in believing that the original proposal was optimistic at first: the child believed he had found an escape in glory; the black project of abasing himself could only have come afterward when, upon reflection, he saw the imaginary being stripped of its value before his eyes. The vicious circle that keeps him spinning endlessly from white to black and from black to white, from divine glory to infamous glory and the reverse, was constituted between his ninth year of age and his first years at school. He dreams of happiness and money, of sweet revenge, of exercising a mysterious power over the crowds, and then the dream turns into a nightmare; when he has touched the depths of disgust, when he is persuaded that the laughable subman par excellence is the man who takes images seriously, he must try again or die; he comes back to glory and desires it for itself, prudently, without specifying in what area of expertise he will merit it. Little by little he regains confidence and hope, and it is in the midst of optimism that his usual rancor is reborn: the worst is certain, men are vile, the realists are right. The wheel is turning. It will never stop.

Until this point the child was merely unlucky, but now, as Jung said, the birds have really bitten him: when he comes to choose infamous glory, it is because he cannot do otherwise. If he refers to it, if he indulges in hyperbole, it is because human reality—for him as for everyone else—can comprehend a situation only by surpassing it. We need not content ourselves, however, with this analysis. Certainly we have left surface motivations behind, but for the moment we are swimming between the surface and the depths; by enlisting Gustave's constituted passivity to explain the vicious circle of glory, we have surely addressed ourselves to the basic issue, but we have only used it to gain a better understanding of the meaning and function of certain emotions and of already elaborated notions (glory, actor, comic and tragic, etc.) corresponding to them. In this chapter we have not yet envisaged that fundamental *en soi*, not so much as an abstract quality but as lived experience itself in its primary savor and basic exigency. This exigency, however, we know: it is the *flesh*. We have seen little Gustave caress himself in front of his mirror *with the hands of another* in order to try to become that heavy sweetness, satiny and mysterious, which exists only to give sensual pleasure to the warrior and is achieved only through the pleasure he takes in manipulating it. What does he want in this case if not to reproduce, by modifying it, what may be called—by slightly distorting the meaning of a current analytic term—the primal scene. He discovered himself, around the age of first weaning, as an object molded by the beautiful, insensitive hands whose perfect efficiency reduced him to helpless nakedness. It is in this form that he experienced his sexual attachment to the mother and that his sexual desire was structured: for him, desiring the other is swooning before a severe beauty so that expert, manipulating hands should restore him to an infant's nakedness. Even if he wants to recover this primary state, it is surely not because it exists in his body as a vague recollection of fulfillment; quite to the contrary, he was constituted both passive and frustrated. And if in physical excitement he aspires to revive this state, it is to receive from the other what he was not given by maternal care. Is this love? In theory it is. But if it is true that he lacked love, we must also understand that this very lack constituted him such that he was incapable of claiming the real object of his frustration. What he in fact desires is a replay of the primal scene, this time with his mother taking sexual pleasure in transforming him into a malleable object. Logically he should complain that a certain coldness in her manipulations prevented him from being constituted as a subject; but precisely because the very notion of a sovereign subject remains atrophied in him, like the notion of affirmative power, it is quite impossible for him to claim a sovereignty whose meaning escapes him. This is nonetheless what is at issue, but his need for love, refracted through his passive constitution, is transformed into a desire to be *radically an object*: the other must play with him, treat him as a sexual device, and take pleasure in the carnal bondage into which he is plunged. Thus the primal scene is corrected, ameliorated. The maternal hands had a *practical*, utilitarian goal; the child's bondage was only a means—digestion, attentions, hygiene were the ends. In the sexual scene as he dreams it, the effect is just the opposite: he thinks the manipulations which reduce him to a sensuous passivity and make his body vulnerable to the will of others are *useless*. Useless *to him*, of course; the manipulator has only one goal: his own pleasure. Insensitive to Gustave's desires—and he has none except the specific intention that they should not be granted—the other will therefore reawaken the attitudes imposed by the mother: lie still, yes, like that, it won't be for long. But the other's aim will be more radically alien to the caressed body of the grown man since it makes him a means of pleasure. The meaning of Gustave's passive desire is that his mother, by preserving her admirable severity—the little child felt his body to be a means chosen by her to accomplish tasks he did not recognize as his—made him the means of her pleasures, and that she deigned to take pleasure in him. We have understood that the caresses he dreams of are hostile: maternal indifference—which as such is unbearable—is transformed into sexual violence. The partner plays at being indifferent, that is part of his role: it pleases him to ignore the thoughts, the feelings, the desires of someone he is transforming into a thing; more precisely, he pretends to neglect them because in fact his pleasure is partly in his contemptuous refusal to take them into account, while his knowing hands stimulate them, transform them, whatever they may be, into somnolent excitation, carnal acquiescence. For Gustave, pleasure[11] will come when he feels entirely possessed *against his will*, with his rapturous consent, by the pitiless *activity* of the other. To be subdued by a vanquisher who acknowledges interiority only in order to reduce it deliberately to pure carnal exteriority through a gradually imposed excitation; to submit in a state of sensual intoxication to being dehumanized and reduced to the status of an inanimate thing; to recognize, swooning, the racial superiority of the manipulator—what is this if not behaving like a masochist in bed, a comic on stage?

At certain levels of his experience Gustave tries to accept the second

---

11. Sexual but not genital.

weaning, or the curse by laughter, in order to fight it. This is his complicit defiance. But on the most basic level he clings to it because his flesh is fully in accordance with it. He dreams of being an actor and laughable because laughter is a sexual punishment: the child may well tell himself that he *will make* the spectators *laugh* by manipulating them with tried and true methods, but he is warned by his very masochism that this language, born of the bravado of comic actors and of their misery, presents things in reverse: the actor offers himself as a woman, the audience is male in its sovereignty. If it consents to be amused, its laughter strips the "laughable" actor bare: Gustave will be utterly naked, manipulated by the laughers, reduced to his pure exteriority; violence will be done publicly to his intimate life, for the laughter bears witness to the fact that others refuse to take it into account, that they deny the claimed sovereignty of the subject and enjoy reducing it to a mirage. The child will experience the delights of being transformed into a *thing;* reduced to impotence, he will feel the bitter pleasure of giving joy—he, a subman—to men who watch him kicking helplessly and who, by his useless attempts to take himself seriously, are confirmed in the triumphant sense of their own superiority. In this sense, we recognize an exhibitionistic fantasy at the basis of his "vocation." Rousseau showed the washerwomen his "ridiculous object"; there is nothing surprising in this, since the memorable spankings of Mlle Lambercier had, if I may say so, eroticized his backside. So it is with Gustave: this tall, handsome boy turns his "ridiculous object" toward the spectators. But while the lower back takes on particular importance in farces (kicks in the behind, enemas), the ridiculous object is here none other than his entire person. At the same time, his deep desire to acquire a real status and his effort to unrealize himself by appropriating the imaginary world is what makes him offer himself as fodder to the public so that they might disqualify both by their laughter; he enjoys exhibiting himself like a ridiculous woman, yielding himself to these pitiless observers and swooning in their brutal grasp. At the source of this obscene *show* is the dizzying temptation of acquiescence: all right, I admit it, I confess publicly, I am a subman, I am a robot, I am a thing, I will find peace only when your crazy laughter, internalized, has at last taught me to break solidarity with myself and, still panting, to become wholly *your* object. When he debases himself so that derision may be coupled with blame, and his companions may break solidarity with his repulsive bag of bones, leaving it naked and rotting but still encumbered, there is no doubt that he is aiming to satisfy his masochistic impulse by radicalizing his exhibitionism. We shall see more than one piece of evidence to support this in the following chapters.

Nevertheless, while the masochistic impulse may be at the most basic level, there is no cause to give it special status in relation to the attempt at recuperation and compensation that pushes Gustave to lay claim to glory. In other words, it does not represent *the* truth about Gustave, the recourse to glory being only a pretext, the veil in which it is wrapped, but rather *a* truth dialectically linked to all the others. Without any doubt it represents a protohistoric determination of his sexuality and, as such, is a latent or actual dimension of all his behavior. This doesn't mean that the masochistic impulse produces his behavior. What is basic must not be confused with the infrastructures, and we would be wrong to apply to persons the schemes that are imposed in order to understand social reality. The external conditionings are the same, but personalization internalizes them and totalizes them according to a singular order, which is moreover variable from one moment to the next, depending on the circumstances. Gustave's masochism is a certainty, but his sadism is no less so; he may advertise it a little too complacently perhaps, but it is born of his negative pride and the reckonings of his inflamed resentment. We shall come back to this. Let us simply note that he willingly embodies, for himself alone and in silence, all the historic roles of conquerors and destroyers; he gives himself omnipotence and is pleased to turn it to *evil* uses, whether to consummate a genocide or to kill an individual by the most ghastly slow torture. And naturally this is a matter of role playing: he is in the midst of depopulating France or hacking up a senator when the bell rings, he gets up, follows his comrades into the yard, and becomes once more the peaceable giant who "never abused his strength to humiliate those weaker than himself." How could he be otherwise since the models he takes are all involved in action, pure subjects, agents of history? In fact, sadism is an activity; I would even say it is—among other things—the project of achieving *absolute praxis* through the full use of the other and through his transformation into an object. For this reason, Gustave's passivity can only be haunted by cruel dreams or, if you like, he can only dream that he is *other* and play the role of *man of action* for his own satisfaction. And when he imposes himself everywhere, shouting, gesticulating, drowning out the voices of others or interrupting their speech to importune them, he is perfectly conscious of not really dominating them—none of them would let themselves be dominated—but of playing the dominator, of pretending to be first. In brief, Flaubert pride, born in Achille-

191

Cléophas from his practical success, necessarily leads to an imaginary sadism in the humiliated child; it becomes an image of pride and at the same time a powerful agent of unrealization. In this sense, even the positive glory Gustave claims is conceived as imaginary; later he will incarnate Attila, Nero; now he plays the role of an adult actor solemnly bowing before a delirious public that is giving him a standing ovation. Glory, omnipotence, praxis: it is the same sadistic dream of the vanquished, who impotently take their revenge *in imagination*.

From this point of view, masochism will seem more consonant with his true constitution—indeed, what is it if not Gustave's acceptance of his passivity? As a sadist he unrealizes himself as his opposite; as a masochist, he makes himself into what he is. To this proposition I answer that *he is nothing* and that when he radicalizes his constituted passivity, he must also unrealize himself, both because he resurrects the primal scene *in order to modify it*, hence to live it out as it did not actually happen, and because the *masochistic idea* in him—to be an en-soi-pour-soi *inside out*, to become *through others* a pour-soi completely engulfed by the en-soi but preserving enough consciousness to take grisly pleasure in the metamorphosis—can be manifest only in imagination. We can see that this subject, paralyzed by his own hyperobjectivity, is just as *impossible* as Don Quixote. The missile has been launched; let us watch it orbiting. First, pride (not that it *is* first; I start with it for convenience—the movement is entirely circular). Gustave plays the role of Kean, of Frédérick Lemaître; "Some people's teeth will be set on edge." Then the catastrophe: the laughter is debasing, the child reddens with rage, and in complicit defiance and resentment begins to wish for infamy in order to dishonor his family. When he takes pride in his frenzied self-destructiveness and in what I have called his pitiless obedience, he is no longer a masochist; rather, this is a form of secondary sadism which aims at punishing others through systematic self-destruction. At this moment, as Odette Laure says, the child seems not to like himself very much and somehow to be punishing himself sadistically too, but *as other*. I would call this self-punishing rage voluntarist if Gustave were capable of volition; let us say, rather, that the voluntary aspect is part of the role and that the child plays the character sincerely, his angry passions serving here as analogue. Still, acted or not—in any event he tries to believe in the character—that violence breaks him; he does not *see* the abjection he seeks at the price of extreme convention, it is not imposed and remains an abstract end which has no real consistency of its own and would evaporate if he did not persist in supporting it. But while he is absorbed in finding the sublime in the ignoble, something like an opaque substance, a call for consent, awakens within him; the end he has been maintaining by force suddenly escapes him, is concretized, and, offering itself spontaneously, becomes sexual vertigo and temptation. All he has to do is abandon himself, abjection will invade him like an unforeseen product of his spontaneity. The other has simply reclaimed his primacy. The child wanted to subdue the other, or at least to tear himself away; then, judging victory to be impossible, he made the other the means of torturing himself and punishing his father. This is how the project, by a foreseeable dialectic (he has restored his powers to the Other in order to recruit an ally against his father, and in so doing has yielded and sooner or later submitted), resurrects the old dizzying hold, the frustration and profound desire of his passive flesh. The desperation to *make himself* an object becomes passive and is transformed into pithiatic belief: horribly and deliciously, he feels like *the other's thing*. The constrained, forced movements by which he tried to achieve the grotesque, even while rejecting it, disappear, useless, from the moment acquiescence is substituted for refusal; an almost lethargic immobility replaces these movements, an abandoned, breathless torpor which is sometimes accompanied by gasps of pleasure. Has the boy perceived the transformation? He must have done, since he has *lived* it. But he easily manages to keep quiet about it—even if it results in masturbation—for it enables him to achieve his end. He wanted to be ignoble and he is. Is he really? In no way: he has done nothing but abandon himself to the Other's mastery and claim his laughter as a form of fierce embrace. He has been invaded not by ignominiousness but by his own passivity as constituted by another; it has served him as analogue in playing the role of inanimate object at the mercy of a cruel lord. He gets a *hold* on his new character—going beyond his body toward the impossible—he *feels* it, as the actors say; in short, he believes in it. He is no less an imaginary for all that. Everything as the Other, in this circumstance, is unrealized, whether or not he is present at the comedy; Gustave has done nothing but fob his sadism off on the other. Nero indulging in the pleasures of the table and of love while listening with voluptuous indifference to the cries of some unfortunate being tortured: later, Gustave would play this role, but now the part is acted by the Other, and Gustave plays the role of tortured victim. The imperial indifference that disqualifies the painful interiority of his victim becomes in the other the cruel laughter that reduces the buffoon to his exteriority. We may readily conclude that, when playing Nero, Gustave must sometimes have slipped unconsciously into the skin of the tortured victim; and, inversely, when he cries out, powerless before the hardened gaze of the spectators, he never forgets to hide in their midst, if only for a moment, in order to see *himself*. Sometimes, however, the emphasis is on one of these two characters, sometimes on the other.

When Flaubert is at the height of willed humiliation, especially if he can satisfy his overwhelming desire, he winds up horrified with himself; he suddenly discovers that his self-indulgent humiliation risks turning into *real* resignation. He is mistaken, of course; at this level of unreality the imagination never refers to anything but itself. Nonetheless, he feels as though he were going to attain his *reality* and find his being in a real assent to the intolerable condition that has been imposed on him from all eternity. But his masochistic behavior, like his sadistic behavior, is in fact a means of evading that reality. Should it be seen, *before all else*, as the choice of the imaginary? It is one thing to unrealize oneself as an abject monster, an object of universal scorn, that is, as an unloved infant; it is quite another docilely to accept being the least gifted of the Flauberts and to recognize the superiority of a despised older brother. For certain men there is some pleasure in abasing themselves at the feet of a Venus in furs, the implacable beauty who treats men like slaves, and all the more easily since she doesn't exist;[12] there is no pleasure for anyone in recognizing mistakes, errors, a modest mediocrity. Masochists are mad with pride, as is well known—Gustave especially since he is infected with family pride. It is the Flaubert pride in him that falls into a panic when the child becomes confused and acts out submission. Declaring oneself infamous out of rage is acceptable; but isn't it dangerous to submit all at once to the vertiginous joy of infamy? After the delights of the fall, what would happen if the little boy could no longer rouse himself? What would happen if Gustave, in order to push the pleasures of shame to their extreme, humiliated himself in front of Achille and told him in a sincere voice: you are more intelligent than I am? It would take next to nothing, he thinks; it is playing with fire to renew endlessly the *gesture* of a consent one doesn't want to give *as a real act* for

12. The women who whipped Masoch or, at his request, let him act as their footman consented to it only out of a submission far removed from the contempt he asked of them. He was handsome and they loved him, so they were prepared for his caprices, as no doubt they would have been if he had been a sadist. He was not unaware of this, and I imagine it didn't much displease him. Those trembling women with whips plunged him into the imaginary; they *were playing the role* of the cruel Amazon, which he only wanted to dream through them.

anything in the world. Flaubert's masochism is more profound than his sadism because it goes deeper and conforms to his constitution; moreover, it can be called his permanent temptation, a constant appeal to that great overburdened body—which later, at Croisset, will leave the writing table a hundred times a day to fall onto the couch. But for that same reason, he is disgusted by it: no sooner does he let himself go than he jumps up in a state of savage and exasperated pride, a state of nervous sadism that exhausts and overstimulates him but gives him back his pride. The missile has made a complete orbit, for Gustave recovers both his optimism and his ill nature; in a word, the imaginary *object* recovers himself as imaginary *subject*, and we understand that the little boy oscillates from one dream to the other since in reality he is neither subject nor object.

A closed circuit: glory, the theater, laughter, everything in its place; the sadistic character is a "composition," Gustave endeavors to make himself the wicked lord. The role of the masochist is more in his line; it's no strain for him to act the derided vassal on tenterhooks, rejected but faithful. A single vexation: these perpetual revolutions increase his derealization; within his perpetual circuit, the child deals only with images. Since his sexuality was unrealized in the decisive years, we shall see later that his sexual relations would remain unreal *for him:* he would have relations with women of flesh and blood only through the mediation of the imaginary, making them play roles without knowing it so that they would permit him, willy-nilly, to play his own roles.

TEN

From Actor to Author

Gustave, an actor in order to recuperate his being, was led to act in plays written by others, which was appropriate to his dream of vassalage. But about the same time he also began to write plays for the purpose of acting in them himself. Isn't this behavior the opposite of submission? The imperatives remain, but he is the one who has chosen to impose them on himself. How can this be explained? Should we assume that his true "vocation" was finally awakened? It will suffice to consult his earliest letters. They allow us to see how the little boy passed imperceptibly from theater to literature and how the writer would always feel that he was born of the actor.

He has just turned nine. He writes to Ernest Chevalier on 31 December 1830: "The friend you sent to see me seems like a good fellow although I've only seen him once. I will also show you some of my plays. If you want us to do our writing together, I would write plays and you will write your dreams and as there is a lady who comes to visit Papa and tells us stupid things, I would write them down."

But on 4 February 1831, he has changed his mind: "I'd told you that I'd do plays but I won't, I will do some novels I have in mind . . I have put aside the billiard table and scenery . . . In my *Proverbes dramatiques* there are several plays we can put on."

At that time he had just written the "Eloge de Corneille" and the "explanation of the *famous* constipation" that Mignot would autograph the following year. On 11 February he urges Ernest to collaborate with him. "Please answer me and tell me if you want to get together to write stories, please tell me, because if you do want to, I will send you some notebooks I have begun to write and I would ask you to send them back to me, if you want to write some things inside that would make me very happy."

On 15 January 1832, after eleven months of silence (or are the letters lost?—in March 1832 Gustave mentions his letter of the previous January, calling it "one of *my* letters"), Flaubert informs Ernest that he is taking notes on Don Quixote. He adds: "The billiard table is deserted, I'm no longer doing any plays as you're not here . . . I forgot to tell you that I'm about to begin a play to be called The Miser Lover, it will be about a miser lover who refuses to give his mistress any presents so his friend gets her away from him . . . I'm also going to start a History of Henry IV, Louis XIII and Louis XIV."

Two and a half months later: "We've been busy on the billiard table again. I have about 30 plays . . . I have written a poem called "a mother" which is as good as "the death of Louis 16." I have also done several plays, among others one called The Ignorant Antiquary which makes fun of stupid antiquaries and another which is called "preparations to receive the king," which is a farce" (31 March 1832).

And in the following letter, which the Conard edition dates approximately 3 April 1832 (he is ten and a half and already in school): "Victory, victory, victory, victory, victory, you'll be coming one of these days, my friend, the theater, the posters, everything is ready. When you come, Amédée, Edmond, Mlle Chevalier, two servants and perhaps some students will come to see us act. We'll put on four plays you don't know, but you'll learn the lines quickly. The tickets for the first, second, and third performances are done, there will be regular seats, there are also galleries, and decorations. The backdrop is ready, perhaps there will be 10 or twelve people. So you must be brave and not be afraid."

At the age of nine, then, he had already *written* plays; so he must have composed them at eight. This was not, however, his only literary activity. In his letter of 31 December 1830 he adds: "I will send you my political and constitutional speeches." Highly serious speeches. He calls himself a "constitutional-liberal" and an admirer of La Fayette; there is a notable relationship between the "genres" he has chosen in that they are written to be recited or declaimed. The actor and the orator are two branches issuing from the same trunk.

His "Eloge de Corneille," written in the same period, is also meant to be spoken aloud: the child summons the author of *Le Cid*, addresses him familiarly, and crowns him. He doesn't hesitate, moreover, to put himself on stage, speaking in the first person and denigrating himself to get a laugh: "I am only a kid—excuse me for wanting to speak about Corneille, but let's forget the compliments, my friends, just wait for something tasty to put on your shelf," etc. This eulogy, further-more, does not issue from his usual preoccupations; its object is the dramatic author of Rouen; by celebrating one of the glories of the the-ater, the child is putting himself under the protection of his illustrious predecessor and fellow citizen.[1]

Gustave needed more plays for the theater in the billiard room. In-forming Ernest of this, he proposed that they pool their resources, though not by collaborating but by writing in the same notebook. The child defines their respective roles with complete clarity: Ernest is not to compose so much as a comedy; he has the right only to interpret Gustave's plays, but he is requested to write *his dreams*—gently but firmly confined to Lamartinian reveries. The younger Flaubert son as-sumes the role of director; it is up to him to invent the argument and put it on the stage. The "stupid things" said by the lady-who-comes-to-visit-Papa (why not "to visit us" or "to visit my parents"?) will per-haps be transcribed without comment in a collection of nonsense, but in any event these are spoken things, transmitted orally; they are thus within his province and it is his job to write them down.

The letter of 4 February 1841 bears witness to an abrupt change. He has "put aside the billiard table and scenery" and will no longer write plays; if by chance they should go back to acting plays, the *Proverbes* of Carmontelle will do. What is the source of this change? Spite, of course: Ernest is never available, or perhaps someone has "vexed" Gustave by criticizing one of his dramas. The fact is that it is the *author* in him who bows out, not the actor; the actor will play Carmontelle wholeheartedly while the other transforms himself into a novelist out

---

1. "The elegant explanation of the *famous* constipation," which has been preserved for us and which Jean Bruneau has reproduced in its entirety, dates from 1830–31. I tend to see it only as a "joke"—the kind many children write without any aspiration to literary glory. However, it underscores Gustave's puritanical horror of the natural func-tions and—the necessary counterpart of his disgust—his sadistic and masochistic in-clination (cf. the preceding chapter) for the basely *scatalogical*. We shall again find that attraction to the "sublime below" for which shit, according to him, is the best symbol. The influence of Molière is certainly present: a Diafoirus is speaking here. In other words, this is Gustave playing the role of Diafoirus in order to ridicule himself by ridiculing medicine. *Of course*, his father is not the target, his father is a *great* physician, etc. Nevertheless this is the first of numerous writings in which Gustave reveals the ambivalence of his feelings. I point out also the comparison—which would rightly strike an analyst—of "the sea that produces no surf" and the mother who makes no more children, a double metaphor signifying the body that can no longer defecate. No-where is the relation of reciprocal symbolization of "mother" [*mère*] and "sea" [*mer*] more evident; but here a third term must be added, which is shit [*merde*], for the cursed child is avenging himself by assimilating *noble* childbirth to *ignoble* defecation. And of course he is assimilating himself to a turd that has been "made" and abandoned.

of spite. Indeed, the titles of his future works are significant: "La belle Andalouse," "Le Bal masque," "Cardenio," "Dorothée," "La Mauresque," "Le Curieux impertinent," "Le Mari prudent." Bruneau has remarked that four of them are taken directly from certain episodes of *Don Quixote*. We should also note that the two titles "The Curious Impertinent" and "The Cautious Husband" have a similar structure to "The Miser Lover" and "The Ignorant Antiquary," which are the titles of plays. In both cases we have the presentation of a "type" character whose chief fault pits him against the other characters or the general mores and puts him in a situation that prompts him to bring about the final catastrophe himself; in brief, behind these labels we sense the necessity and irreversibility of time in classical farce. The curious impertinent will be punished by his curiosity or by his impertinence, or by both together. The cautious husband is comic as a husband, that is, as a probable cuckold. Is he *too* cautious and will his precautions simply precipitate his conjugal misfortunes? Or is his prudence a virtue, like that of the married couple in "The Enchanted Cup" who refuse to acknowledge their fate? In this case the wife is the figure of fun and also, perhaps for the sake of contrast, some imprudent fellow oversure of his wife who, as in La Fontaine's play, is about to drink when the water jumps out of the cup into his face. In any event, we are dealing here with the strict time of dramatic machinery and not with the "apparently" less predictable time of advent or of "adventure." We might say that the spiteful little boy selected certain subjects he had first conceived as dramatic plots and decided to treat them as "narratives." None of these novels was ever written. When Amédée Mignot was publishing the "Eloge de Corneille" in 1832, he found "in the two children's desks . . . "The Miser Lover" . . . and certain lucubrations . . . several of which were signed." He himself admits to having left aside the "Epitaph to M.D.'s dog" in verse "of brilliant poetry and romantic freedom," but he makes no mention of the stories Gustave proposed to write. On the contrary, he indicates that "The Miser Lover" is "a play in seven scenes with four characters." The sudden adoption of the novelistic genre as a means of expression thus seems to have been a bad-tempered whim, a makeshift chosen because the child wanted to go on writing; for a moment, literature posited itself independently because his dramatic art and his vocation as an actor had been challenged.

Something doesn't fit, however, for eleven months later Gustave solemnly declares that he is deserting the billiard table. Is this definitive? It isn't clear: I am not *acting* anymore, he says—and not "I will not act anymore." Still, his tone makes us feel that some failure is involved. He gives only one reason for his decision, disguised reproach: "You aren't here." Is there another motive? When he is "busy on the billiard table again," Ernest is still absent and "the two of us are acting, Caroline and me"; why couldn't he reconcile himself to this single but privileged partner two months earlier? What the reader will have noted is a curious reversal of his projects: in February 1831, spite made him abandon *all* theatrical activity—he is no longer going to be an actor or an author. On 15 January 1832, on the other hand, he seems to dissociate the actor's art from the art of the dramatist; in the same letter in which the former takes its leave, the second affirms itself: "I have begun . . . the Miser Lover." We know that he finished it. Are we to understand that he was writing for other actors, for posterity? This would involve the assumption that he had renounced the pursuit of glory on the stage for good. Besides, the information furnished by Mignot—and given by Gustave himself—indicates that this piece was chiefly a simplified version of Molière's play; so he was still thinking of acting it with his usual partners. Here we discern only one new form of behavior: "postponement." Gustave shows himself capable of writing a play *for a later time,* uncertain when it will be performed; thus, although the two moments of the operation are not detached from one another, the ties that bind them are somewhat loosened. The Gustave of today is writing for a future Gustave who will not be entirely himself, yet not entirely other; and the first enterprise, without ceasing to be the means of the second, immediately gains in importance and value.

Starting in March 1832, his mood changed; he was "busy on the billiard table again," he had "done" several plays, one of which was a farce, and he reveals to Ernest that he has a repertoire of "nearly thirty plays," which implies that he was working despite all difficulties and discouragements. Three days later everything is explained: what Gustave did not say to his friend on 31 March is that he had engaged in delicate negotiations to obtain authorization to produce his plays before a wider public, that is, before at least a dozen persons. Easter vacation had begun, he begs Ernest to join them. It seems he may have been rather sly in dissembling a project that surely kept him busy for more than a month; if he resumed his activities as builder-carpenter-painter-decorator, if he began to act again, even with Caroline alone, if he spilled so much ink, it was with the sole purpose of giving a public performance. At the end of January or in February he glimpsed the possibility of realizing his grand project during the spring vacation, and this hope was enough to throw him furiously into his work.[2] His letter of 3 April is nothing more than a victory cry: he exults, he rejoices. There is no mistaking it: his purpose, carefully concealed from everyone, perhaps even from Caroline, never wavered from the time he appropriated the billiard table: to exhibit himself to real spectators and, by so doing, to become a real actor. All his efforts, often rebuffed but untiring—as author and as actor—had this single aim. Whatever his spitefulness and his sulking, he continued to regard writing as one means among others and performance as his absolute end. That the performance of April 1832 may have been the result of two years' work and may not have been preceded by any other of the same scope (there were sometimes two or three grown-ups in the room, relatives, friends of the family, domestics—Dr. Flaubert apparently never came), is indicated by Gustave's enthusiasm and stage fright. Curiously, this apotheosis seems also to mark the rapid decline if not the brutal liquidation of the entire enterprise. Gustave would write other plays—few in number—and he also left plans for melodramas, but we find no further mention of the billiard table in his correspondence except much later when he is recalling an already quite distant past. The only allusion he would make to it is reported by the Goncourts, and their memory may have betrayed them. In any event, it concerns a later period: Gustave was fifteen, the Garçon had just been invented; the small group of initiates were gathered in the deserted room during vacation to pass judgment on the clownish pleadings, the funereal and grotesque speeches. If this testimony is accurate, the billiard room had changed functions: it had become the site of collective improvisations with no spectators present. Nothing indicates more clearly that, at some point between 1832 and 1835, Gustave *must have* renounced the career of actor once and for all.

We are not there yet, however, and I have brought up the performance of Easter 1832—about which we know nothing except that it *probably* took place—only in order to recreate the process in all its phases and to reveal its true orientation. We must encompass it all if we hope to answer the question we posed at the beginning of this chapter. Many children who dream of acting dramas, and some who *do* act them, still feel no need themselves to fashion the characters they will play. Why is Gustave, noted at first for his passivity, so different?

The first explanation that comes to mind is circumstantial: the plays

2. He probably wrote at school during the week and rehearsed on Sundays.

in the repertoire were too long and too difficult and required too many actors. Ernest was seldom available; Caroline was five years old in 1830—not much could be demanded of her. We may wonder whether Gustave's plays were not, in the main, *necessary* arrangements, adaptations. Take a look at "The Miser Lover." It is a shortened version of Molière's play, which involves a dozen characters, not counting the commissioner and his clerk; Flaubert kept only four of them: the skinflint (the ridiculous lover who is punished for his stinginess)— the starring role, which he reserved for himself; his fickle mistress, played of course by Caroline; the friend, which Ernest would play when he had the time; and a minor character, whom one of the three actors would play in disguise. The scenes too are reduced in number: Gustave, I imagine, could have played twenty without tiring, but his partners—especially his sister—had less stamina; they had to be spared. Consequently, the plot is simplified: Gustave would keep only Harpagon's love affairs. The only modification that seems not to have been prompted by the need for economy, for cutting and condensing, is the young author's judgment not to preserve in his play the amorous rivalry of father and son. But this is because it might have been shocking—indeed *did* first of all shock him; it might have transformed the production—did he vaguely sense this?—into a sort of psychodrama in which he would take the role of his father and would be revenged on the black lord by covering him with opprobrium. The wound was still too fresh, the ambivalence of his emotions too strong: the paterfamilias was all the more sacred since he had cursed and renounced his son.[3] This transformation is not basically different from the others— only that the others were quantitative and this one is qualitative. It is not a question of some positive need to *ameliorate* the plot but, rather, of self-censoring: the author's work is not only aimed at essential cutting and compressing; it also consists in giving an expurgated version of its great model.

And *Poursôgnac?* He doesn't claim that it is original. Molière's play, however, involves at least twenty characters and could not be performed in the billiard room without cutting half the scenes and four-fifths of the characters, which implies considerable rewriting: when ten consecutive lines of dialogue are deleted, the cut will be left bleed-

---

3. He makes fun of medicine in "The elegant explanation . . ." but his intention remains shrouded, since Achille-Cléophas must not have spared bad physicians within the privacy of his family. The child could therefore persuade himself to some extent that he was imitating the philosophical practitioner. Above all, he was not aiming at him in particular in his role as father. It is all benignly obscure—nothing is black or white.

ing unless a sentence can be found to replace them. But *Poursôgnac* is one of the first plays he includes in his repertoire; he is nine years old, wholly consumed by the desire to be a celebrated comic actor; he is aware that the piece is unplayable and, attracted by the role of the provincial numbskull, he supplies in all innocence and awkwardness the changes that allow it to be played. The result, certainly, is not a new comedy but a collection of thoughts and observations: "on the billiard table" they will give "selected scenes" from *Monsieur de Pourceaugnac;* the child is conscious of the fact that *Poursôgnac,* a badly managed arrangement, is not his work; only the mutilations are his; yet he doesn't judge himself responsible for them since they were forced on him. What escapes him is that, playing fast and loose with his scissors, he has begun his apprenticeship as author; he will pursue it, will become more and more adept, and with more experience will progress from hack to adapter; one more step and he *discovers* he is a dramatist, just as earlier he discovered he was a comic actor by surprising himself in the midst of playing comedy. This evolution involves three phases: *Poursôgnac* marks the first; *The Miser Lover* the second; *The Ignorant Antiquary* and *Preparations to receive the King* the beginning of the third. It is not impossible that these two last "works" may have had unknown sources, but we cannot doubt that Gustave was emboldened to the point of taking great liberties with his models and that he made changes in the plots, not demanded by the penury of the actors or the paucity of means, for the simple pleasure of appropriating the plays of others for himself. The author remains in the service of the actor, but he has grown conscious of his powers.

This interpretation of the facts seems right *on its level,* that is, on the surface: *this is how it happened.* But it would become false if we were to content ourselves with that; Gustave could remain at the stage of arrangements, improving them from one play to the next, without giving the final push that transforms an adaptation into an original work. Or, rather—and this is the crux of the matter—he could make indispensable modifications in the works of others without *taking himself for an author.* Taking yourself for an author is, as I have shown in the preceding chapter, *deciding that you already are one and vowing to be one.* The *intention* here is at one with the *discovery:* this is what we must bring to light and describe.

Here we find something that will facilitate our approach: although Gustave may not have seen it immediately, he was not at all surprised by this new avatar of his personalization; far from hurling himself into the unknown, he was following a great example. His notion of the actor/author was not yet Shakespeare but Molière; an indiscreet copyist, Gustave pillaged Molière's works, massacred or plagiarized them—excellent reasons for imitating his life as well or, better still, appropriating it. The imaginary child wanted to *be* Molière—this was the new role in which he unrealized himself. Corneille, to whom he played homage, was an eponymous hero for the town of Rouen, a tutelary hero for Gustave, who nonetheless did not want to identify with him; in his eyes his fellow citizen's hidden weakness was that he had his plays acted by others; this tragedian reduced the actor to the rank of means, the *written* tragedy became the end. Molière was the absolute actor: by no means was he an actor merely to serve his plays, but he wrote his plays, the child thought, to provide fine roles for himself; inventing Tartuffe, Argante, or Monsieur Jourdain in terms of his own temperament and with the avowed intention of deploying all his resources in these roles, he created his "characters" by guiding himself with the requirements of his "inner power" which demanded to be externalized in its totality. And this is precisely what Gustave wanted to be. The model of Molière was all the more fascinating in that he was a *comic* actor who, in order to get laughs, did not hesitate as an author to prepare the ignominious mudhole in which as an actor he would wallow. It was also to Molière, certainly, that the little boy owed the calm audacity with which he presented his plagiarisms as original works. Someone could have told the child that *L'Avare* was first written by Plautus and then rewritten by Molière; was Gustave doing anything very different when he gave it a third reworking under the title *L'Amant avare?* To tell the truth, when children take it into their heads around the age of eight to compose plays or novels, they never produce anything but servile imitations, and believe they are writers when they are only copyists; but most of the time this is because they don't really understand what they are doing. Keeping company with Molière gave Gustave, on the contrary, a lucid and cynical arrogance that allowed him in full knowledge to consider himself a creator. He would persist in this attitude for quite a while; his first stories are imitations: the subject, the plot, the construction, even the style, and sometimes whole sentences are borrowed. However, the child was right to affirm his originality; what belongs to him is the *meaning* he gives to his borrowings, the way he experiences the story he seems to be copying. In brief, his illustrious predecessor was not only an example to follow or a role to play; he was an inner light; when Gustave put himself in Molière's place, he seemed to understand himself better, his obscure impulses were deciphered and rationalized. Furthermore, he *chose* this new character and played him with passion. There must have been some affinity between them, or at least the little boy thought so; and it is on this level that we shall find the intention that transforms the lived situation by going beyond it with a vow. Molière gave him the simplest means of recognizing and thinking about his long-standing and deep-rooted project of totalizing the world and life in his own person.

For a long time this passive agent, in his stupors and ecstasies, felt himself visited by the universe and at the same time diluted in the infinite, lost in it. Later he would repeat—in a different way—that there was a reciprocity of perspective between the microcosm and the macrocosm, as if each were the totalizing reflection of the other. We know where he derived this impulse toward the All that later, in *Madame Bovary* as much as and perhaps more than in the three *Saint Antoines*, would make a cosmic writer of him.[4] Originally this child, poorly anchored in language and in his family environment, attempted to escape from them; his pride pushed him to soar over the reality that imprisoned him; his estrangement compelled him to turn back in midflight and try to embrace reality whole through a comprehensive intuition that would finally totalize and decipher it: only a complete intellection of reality could reveal to him what he might well have tossed aside. For this reason we shall soon find him again on the summit of Mount Atlas dreaming of the world stretched out below him. I say that he is dreaming because his constituted passivity prevents him from reaching any conclusions; in *Le Voyage en enfer* it is the Other who will give him the password, and even then he remains skeptical and puzzled in the face of this other-knowledge, unable either to reject it or fully to internalize it. But this passivity, we know, is active in the sense that it cannot even exist without becoming a surpassing of the given. Which must be understood in two ways at once: passivity has its own method—gliding—for achieving its objectives, but it is also haunted by the phantom of praxis, which is perceived at each surpassing as the thing of which it is apriori incapable. This is the source of the passive agent's ambivalence toward action, properly speaking, which he would like to be capable of exercising and which he despises to the extent that this capacity is denied him. What haunts the cosmic child is the Act in its highest form or, if you like, its achievement, synthesis, restoration of the unity of the multiple, or, better, the articula-

4. I don't mean a thinker or philosopher but, quite precisely, an author whose permanent subject is the world. Victor Hugo and Jules Verne are such authors, among others.

tion of the parts according to the strict rules governing relations established by the All. This instrument was lacking in his father, his milieu, his class, his time; his constituted passivity does not prevent him from having a presentiment of it. Quite to the contrary, because he is not a practical agent he skips to the moment when the enterprise is achieved without passing through the various moments, often posed for themselves, which mask the moment when the operation turns back on itself and is reassembled, totalized; but the same passivity allows him neither to accede to it nor to conceive of it with any precision. Inactive, he dreams of shutting himself within the macrocosm by an act that would reveal it and would fully constitute its unity. In a way, this is putting himself in the place of the absent Creator in order to deny mechanistic dispersal. For the little boy, totality is not a notion; it is the matrix of his entire affective life, the fantasy of a creation that would allow him to produce the All that is crushing him. We shall see that from adolescence he would understand that this demiurgic production can be only imaginary. At eight years old it is a need that is *lived* but can be neither known nor pondered. And if at first he wants to be an actor, we know that it is for other reasons, which are in fact not without connection to this cosmic postulation since glory, all other reasons aside, appears to him as the unification of the human race through the common admiration of all for one. But the pursuit of being and the escape beyond the real, while dialectically linked, are nonetheless aimed in opposite directions. When he approaches the work of Molière, he has already promised himself fame through his talent as actor; but from the moment he is told about the life of the author/actor, it is a new revelation—he becomes conscious of his totalizing impulse and believes he understands its meaning: Molière is great because he made a *total work,* and this is just what Gustave in his enthusiasm finds himself attempting two centuries later. Gustave is mistaken: he cannot yet know that the total work aims at the derealization of the All; chiefly, as we have seen, he is in search of his *reality,* so he takes this revelation in the most realistic sense: a work is total if it contains in itself the material conditions of its realization. Molière took on everything: he was company director, administrator and manager, dramatic director, author, actor. The actor embraced everything: in the sublime moment of performance, he appears as Sganarelle, as the imaginary invalid; gathering his work and his troupe around him through his acting, he offers the public in the space of one evening everything, the All, the months of labor and difficulties from the humblest to the noblest tasks; he, the campaign manager, can say with pride: I have done everything with my own hands. Gustave will do the same: of course he doesn't use the words *total work,* and for good reason, since the notion itself in the abstract remains alien to him; he wants to be Molière, that's all, but in the passion he invests in this enterprise we discover the totalizing option in its crudest form. The autonomy of his work, in the craftsman's sense of the term, *for the same reason* demands the arrangement of the billiard room as a theater, the invention of a scenario with characters whose gestures and words are to be established in advance and fixed in writing, appropriate scenery that he will choose and paint either himself or with a team under his direction, the distribution of roles, rehearsals, the deployment of the actors, and finally the performance, which will be no more than the unification in action of all these efforts, in the sense that the end is the synthetic unification of the means used to achieve it. The totalizing impulse is ubiquitous from the beginning to the end of the enterprise, in hammering nails into boards, in the words he traces on paper, in his bellowing before the spectators: his creation will be entirely his if he starts from nothing and fabricates everything himself.

Acting comedies is giving: he will show the public his generosity-object by sacrificing himself to make them laugh; this is all the more generous in that the object displayed, with its infrastructures and superstructures, is spun wholly out of himself. As lord he will make his little vassals experience his generosity-subject: he cuts and stitches their roles, he makes them gifts of the roles; these gifts enclose the beneficiaries and confine them. They are obliged to learn and recite the speeches he imposes on them "with the proper intonation." Gustave subjects them to his fatalities, he becomes a categorical imperative for Caroline and Ernest, as Molière and Carmontelle were for him: "Express yourself on stage as if the character invented by the author were your objective truth." This is another aspect of the total work, to transform the troupe's director into the other actors' fate. If he chooses to play a "dramatic proverb," their destiny will be Carmontelle; if he mounts one of his own works, he is making his friend and his sister enter his own world; he captures them in order to recreate them according to his general plan; they will be charged with tormenting the grotesque monster he embodies, he will make them the means of aggravating his vices and absurdities. By involving them in the total work, he affirms his omnipotence by a miracle: the creative resurrection of the human race.

I say resurrection and not unrealization because it doesn't occur to the imaginary creator that he is only leading Caroline and Ernest into his unreality. Indeed, the ambition of the total work is *also* to mitigate the deceptive derealization that Gustave cannot help experiencing when he gives himself over to his role but inadequately feels what he is expressing. When he turns himself into upholsterer, carpenter, author, he would like these practical, real enterprises (he really does hammer real nails into real boards) to provide some ballast of reality to the final unrealization. He tries to give a *genuine background* to the performance that will include all these means within it, as if the performance were only the surpassing of this real given, as if these worked materials taken as a whole constituted its *being* and, as a consequence, as if these artisan's activities constituted Gustave's practical being. The truth of the actor would be this labor crystallized in the wrought objects that make it possible and at the same time engender it ex nihilo. Finally, that truth is also an object to be presented to the public.[5]

The moment of writing, therefore, appears to Gustave as an inessential stage in the total work he wants to produce. And yet, considering it objectively, one cannot help seeing a radical reversal of the ongoing process. A passive agent leaves his role as the one guaranteed to become his own guarantor; in other words, the guarantee the actor needs when he acts continues to exist, but now Gustave himself has established the imperatives in a phase that precedes the operation. He has within him, then, a *natura naturata* and a sovereignty *naturans;* the latter guarantees the former but itself seems bereft of any guarantee. But isn't this kind of free activity forbidden to Gustave? Isn't the author an agent, a lord deciding the destiny of his creatures in the same way that Moses-Flaubert has decided the destiny of his sons? And Gustave can *act* the lord, as he did to amuse Caroline, but he has neither the desire nor the possibility to be that lord in reality—furthermore, sovereign activity and full responsibility frighten him. If he were placed at the top of the hierarchy, he would dread having nothing but the empty sky above his head, and all he counts on, in his heart, is holding the place of first vassal. To build a stage and scenery is just

5. He couldn't be more mistaken; not that these activities or the objects in which they are exercised are illusions. But these realities are the means of unrealization; the backdrop will be an imaginary "*house.*" It does not lend its being to appearance; rather, appearance affects it with nonbeing, the entire enterprise is derealized. On condition, of course, that the total work is the product of one man. The division of labor in real theaters introduces zones of reality into the very enterprise of unrealization; the stagehands collaborate in an operation whose purpose is a showing of the imaginary, but this aspect of their work is quite marginal for them—they are workers who have a manual task to perform and they execute it for a certain fee.

fine, this is obeying; there are hypothetical imperatives that incite the little worker and support his zeal: if you want the floor boards to hold together, they must be solid and well anchored, etc. These are the prescriptions of the profession, the advice of grown-ups; alienated from his enterprise, Gustave acts without giving up his passivity—there is nothing to decide, the rules impose themselves; he serves the future requirements of his characters, whoever they may be, without thinking for a moment of imposing his law on them. But what happens to him then? When he becomes an author, isn't he conscious—while believing that he is simply continuing his work—of an abrupt break in continuity, of a temerity he thought he was incapable of? How does he *experience* this reversal? We must try to find out, for these literary beginnings will determine all his subsequent works.

To begin with, let us say that at the outset his audacity escapes him in the same way as his sovereignty *naturans*. This is because, initially, creating is only imitating: he trims, recasts, patches, but even when he gives his imagination a little rope, the model is there, like a guiding scheme and guarantee. In writing *L'Amant avare*, Gustave becomes his own future fatality; in a sense his voice is decisive—the role is a string of imperatives, but Harpagon has slipped into the invention of the role as an imperative of the creation. In this form, the function of author cannot frighten him: he makes himself the mediator between two orders, obeying one he produces the other and transmits it to the actor. Furthermore, the classical conception of creation is, as I have said, highly reassuring: one must imitate the ancients or rework them in an attitude of humility. This idea cannot be displeasing to children, who see with new eyes their parents' *dejà-vu*. In brief, the boy makes little distinction between the old and the new, between adaptation and original work, for in all domains he is at once an apprentice, repeating what has gone before, and a newcomer whose experience cannot be reduced to that of preceding generations.

When he discovers he is a dramatic author, he must become conscious of his audacity. But in the final analysis, is this audacity really his? It has happened to him; he made no decisions about it but simply finds himself *in a state of suffered temerity*. In other words, writing for the purpose of acting and not for writing, he cannot be afraid of freedom: it is strictly limited, on the one hand, by the models that still serve him as guiding schemes and on the other by the secondary role he assigns to the author. What is more, composing for the purpose of recitation, he alienates himself forever from his own voice. This means that he subordinates the act of writing to a passion for "mouthing" and that the passion for reciting is the final purpose and present inspiration for his literary activity. This amounts to saying—and we shall have occasion to come back to it frequently—that literature from the outset seems to him a passive activity.

In societies that possess writing and for everyone who knows how to read, determinations of discourse are always audio-visual. The emphasis, depending on the case, is on one or the other of these two components, and the one that is neglected tends to cancel itself out. In the seventeenth and eighteenth centuries, for example, the principal concern of essayists and writers of fiction was to appeal *to the eyes;* if their prose is harmonious, it is certainly not by chance, but the music of their sentences is only the object of a marginal intention, the essential aim being to condense the greatest amount of information in the clearest form with the strictest economy of means. By moving his eyes, the reader reawakens the words articulated on paper by the movement of a hand. The verbal body, here, is the grapheme: it represents verbal materiality, that is, the *living presence* of the sign. This has its own transcendence; it goes beyond itself toward an absent object which is the signified, but as signifying matter it refers to no other form of materiality, not even to that of the sound to which it corresponds—although it is sometimes accompanied, in the reader, by inner resonances that add nothing to it. As a result, everything is in action in the classical reading: while reconstituting the words, the reader's eyes hold them at a distance and scrutinize them. Nothing in the hands, nothing in the pockets; trickery is not possible; there is no physiognomy, no mimicry, no tone of voice to capture one's consent—the writer must convince the reader word for word, without *moving* him, by rational argument.

With Gustave, at the age of nine, things are the other way around: he writes his plays not to be read but to be heard. I am not, of course, claiming an opposition between phoneme and grapheme *in general,* like that between passivity and action. Oral language can transmit orders, commands, information, affirmative or negative judgments, decisions, arguments—this is, indeed, its *practical* function. You can read a classical text "aloud" and render its intentions perfectly, although the author may not have intended it to be transmitted orally. Still, our voice is ourself as other. Visual inspection discovers the signs but holds them at a distance, whereas in oral communication the speaker enters the listener's ear; in one sense, he offers himself up as sacrifice, and in another sense he first compromises, then loses himself. The voice is the whole person, since a gesture, an attitude can always replace a word without interruption to the discourse. But that voice is our body *for others*, since we neither hear it nor know it completely, and it remains a quasi object; we scarcely *recognize* it when we hear it on a record or tape in all its objectivity; it acquires its objective consistency only in the ear of the hearer, and at the same time it escapes us and is lost. When I offer an argument to a stranger, he may be thinking: "What a disagreeable voice!" and I may sense his impression from his manner without ever being quite sure of it; in any case, I know he will assimilate his feeling to the argument I am putting forward, and its logical power will thus be weakened. Against my situation of "transcended transcendence" I will defend myself by the use of parasemantic auxiliaries, such as intonation, timbre, facial expression, charm, authority, etc. I will lower my tone, make it less pointed, I will avoid anything nasal or speaking from the chest. On the other hand, if I have a fine voice, I will use it quite deliberately to convince; in consequence, I will be more concerned with the *show* than with the demonstrative force of my discourse. In effect, it is less a question of *proving* than of fascinating and seducing. In other words, whatever the message, oral transmission always involves one part performance, therefore pathos: speaking is often an act, but this is transformed into a *gesture* at the first sign of difficulty.

For Gustave it is pure pathos—he never uses his voice for reasoning but exhibits himself in it as *constituted passivity*. Either he must abandon himself to it, or, what amounts to the same thing, it must *escape from him* and deliver him. We know why: he has suffered from infancy from a verbal malaise; he *is spoken*; the locutions deposited inside him do not designate him to himself but are turned toward the outside, he is their *signified*, but for others. He wants to be an actor in order to assume the situation and reappropriate—or appropriate—his being by fascinating others with his voice. This "loudmouth" knows the strength of his vocal chords—they allow him to impose himself by unburdening, by imperiously making a spectacle of himself. He aspires not to become something different from what they see but to compel the audience to see him as they have made him. He will speak *himself* as they speak *him* by radicalizing speech. When he writes *L'Amant avare*, the significations produced—or reproduced—become sticky with their future sonority. He is inspired during the moment of composition, which means that others speak into his ear—he abandons himself to that voice and writes under its dictation. He is familiar with this romantic conception of inspiration—his letters testify to that; it serves his purposes, writing under the dictation of his own voice, listening to its future sounds and fixing them on paper so as to reproduce them, then rereading each of his sentences out loud in order to control their vocal power. Thus, in this earliest period, it seems clear that creation is a form of gliding for the child; the hierarchy of classical objectives is reversed: meaning is the object of marginal intention since it is the means of declamation. Meaning is preserved only to give unity to the vocal inflections and to the parasemantic auxiliaries that will give them value—this will be the rule imposed on the gasping, the roaring, the stammerings of rage or torpor that Gustave already hears and will soon produce in front of an audience. It is not an act; the present pathos is a simple prefiguration of future pathos. The graphemes are merely abstract indications that will later allow him to modulate his voice in the same way that it resounds today, still unreal, in his ears. As long as they exist only on paper, *L'Amant avare* or *Les Apprêts* are like orchestral scores, notations without any inherent value or substance which refer to the musical execution. Writing, which is simply meditation, will be effaced when the speech learned by heart is imposed on the actor's body in a performance. Whereas in classical literature the grapheme represents the verbal materiality to itself alone, here it refers to the materiality of the phoneme, conceived as an "intelligible mouthful." During the process of composition, concern with understanding, with making oneself understood, is secondary: signification is deferred to the day of the public performance when the Word will gain its fullness of being, that is, its sonorous materiality and its surpassing toward an absence. On that day, a vocal event supported by the appropriate expression will fill the ears of the audience, revolve in their heads, and explode; they are being counted on to *hear* it, in every sense of the term, and to confer on it a meaning that partially escapes the actor. For Gustave, the master of words is the other; it is up to the other to give them their truth.

There are many actors like this, who don't understand what they are saying and don't act any the worse for it; they take into consideration only the affective meanings of their role. Often that is enough; they would be wasting their time to try to decode the other semantic layers that compose their character, and so they leave this to the audience. Yet those layers should have been preestablished (at least partially) by the author. Flaubert's originality, as a child, is that he is never entirely privy to the secret of what he is writing, not out of heedlessness but because his first concern is to employ his constituted passivity in order to give vocal expression to passion. What we are talking about is *comic* passion, the passion of the robot who takes himself for a man, a passion characterized by error, nonknowledge, and incomprehension. By his very situation, therefore, Gustave is committed not to understand what he is doing; in order to play *Poursôgnac* or *L'Avare*, he abandons himself to the meaning that occurs to him, that travels through him, and is allowed to be deciphered only by others. Thus the man who would later become a zealous stylist, who would call himself a craftsman, a chiseler, a worker of art, etc., began by affirming the insubstantiality of the written thing, an inessential means of vocal expression. At first he relied, quite literally, on inspiration: the original material of his art was that "tree of life" rooted in his lungs, the respiratory system. Yet we shall find him again, two or three years after the performance of Easter 1832—if it really took place—wholly occupied with producing a "total work"; but this total work has changed in nature. Around the age of thirteen, he decided to edit and distribute at school a weekly paper for which he—with one exception[6]—would be sole contributor. Here we encounter once again the totalizing creation, the enterprise that pulls its object out of nothingness and includes phases of manual labor: making copies,[7] distributing them. Only the end pursued has changed, since it is now written discourse that is involved in all moments of the enterprise, becoming at once its source (in the moment of writing) and (in the moment of reading) its essential objective. How should this sudden primacy of the visual over the auditory be interpreted? How was this "reversal of praxis" produced? How did Gustave experience it? What will be its impact on his ongoing personalization and on his first works? This is what we must now examine.

Such a change cannot be considered the result of simple evolution. Certainly we shall see that words eventually consume the voice, but that would not suffice to explain this abrupt about-face—something external must have intervened. I do not mean that *someone* need have explicitly intervened to discourage him or that some event may have deflected him from his first choice. Achille-Cléophas forbade nothing. The Easter performance was not ridiculed. What does Gustave himself say on this subject? Very little. But we find in his correspondence two allusions to his rejected vocation: the first in a letter of July 1839 to Ernest, the second in a letter of 8 August 1846 to Louise Colet, which are mutually illuminating. "If I had been properly guided, I would

6. Ernest wrote for it at least once.
7. Perhaps Caroline performed the function of copyist.

have made an excellent actor," he writes to Chevalier. And to Louise, seven years later: "Deep down, whatever people say about it, I am a performer. As a child and a young man I had an unbridled love for the stage. I might have been a great actor if heaven had made me poor." This second text corresponds curiously to a remark of Stendhal's that dates from 1832, which Gustave could not have known: "Kean seems to be a coffeehouse hero and a fellow of little breeding. I excused him easily: if he had been born rich or into a good family, he would not be Kean but some frigid fop."[8] This comparison clearly indicates the contempt in which the profession of actor was still held. Kean was occasionally the nighttime companion of the Prince of Wales; but this did not prevent the newly arrived gentry, cold and puritanical, from judging him ill-bred. Actors had gained the right to be buried in sanctified ground but not the right to be invited to dinner at the home of a bourgeois family. Achille-Cléophas, in any case, would not have admitted them to his table, for reasons less of disgust than of utter indifference. He went to the theater from time to time—when he passed through Paris with his family—but the world of the imaginary was perfectly alien to him, and, as we have seen, he would not attend the performance of April 1832—he had other things to do. No doubt he would not even have been shocked if Gustave had dared to confide to him his ambitions: he simply wouldn't have believed him. And if, as is more likely, the child kept quiet, the paterfamilias would not even have suspected that his younger son hoped to practice so discredited a profession. He listened with one distracted ear to the reports of Gustave's and Caroline's activities; to his mind, these children played at being actors the way they played at doctor and patient, but with the difference that their new game—and for this reason it was not disadvantageous—gave them access to classical culture and developed manual dexterity. It never even dawned on him that the son of a scientist might be *inclined* to go on the stage; if he had explicitly tried to dissuade him, Gustave might have persisted; what discouraged the child was the feeling that no one even feared he would dishonor the family. When you are a Junior Flaubert you do not become a buffoon, that's all. It is not something to dread or to forbid—there is no need, even, to say it isn't done. The *fact* is that a chief surgeon's son becomes a physician or a lawyer *by force of circumstance*. In vain did the little actor "gather out of the mud" the word "ham" which had been thrown at him not long before: *he wasn't taken seriously*. Was the boy aware that he

8. Stendhal, *Souvenirs d'egotisme*, in *Oeuvres intimes* (Pléide ed.), p. 1443.

would not go far without advice or "guidance"? Did he ask to take acting lessons? In this case his demand was quietly but decisively rejected by rather surprised parents, mildly amused by what they would have considered a bit of childishness. Thus his very attempt to give real status to his derealization was itself derealized. No one believed in it, no one recognized him as *being* an actor. In order to resist this nonreception, in order to reenter himself and declare to himself, "We shall see what we shall see," Gustave would have had to extricate himself from the hands of others. We know that he was incapable of doing so and that others had even suggested his vocation; its origin was that compensatory sentence pronounced by someone else, "You would make an excellent actor," which, out of misunderstanding, he latched onto with passion. *Another* may have suggested to him a way out, but it was a false window since *the others* did not believe in it. For him to have persevered in his enthusiasm, his father would have had to cry out in horror, "That brat is going to dishonor the family; I'm afraid he's got the makings of an actor." But Gustave couldn't even manage that. It is true, to *institute* him against his father required universal consent; so it mattered little at the outset, or it was even preferable, that his father belittled him. But in the absence of any public consecration, in order for him to believe sufficiently in his "inner power" to launch himself in such an ignominious career, the paterfamilias would have had to give him an initial investiture. Lacking this, he was defeated in his challenge. Treated like a ham, he cries out: "I will be an actor." They answer him: "More hamming; you make a *pretense* of wanting to act, but the Flaubert nature in you has other aims." Both glory and ignominy instantly fall into the imaginary: he used to believe in them, now he can only dream of them.

How did he take the blow? Very badly. He was still smarting when he wrote *Un Parfum à sentir;* one of the themes of that story is the unjust contempt in which performers are held. Gustave's bitterness becomes understandable when we remember that he considered himself a performer whose basic instinct had been repressed and falsified. As I have shown, he experienced his "vocation" in the negative form of an appeal to being; but we have seen him a few years later presenting it to Ernest and then to Louise in a positive light, as an excessive, overflowing generosity ("inner power"). The signs changed the moment the vocation was derealized and Gustave had satisfied his desire for glory by daydreaming. He "sees" himself on the stage, he endows himself with incredible power, the audience rocks with laughter beneath his clenched fist. Suddenly the vocation is born of a gift: the brilliant actor needs to spend *himself.* The basic intention here is to conceal his ruin from himself: he has lacked the power to maintain his belief toward and against everyone; in the world of the imaginary, everything is reversed: he had genius, inner power, and it has been broken. "If I were born poor" clarifies the "If I had been properly guided." This last statement only functions as a cover; it hides an "if they had not done everything to discourage me," which the child prefers to imply and which is expressly conceived to disguise a confession he doesn't want to make *to himself:* "If they had given me the least encouragement." This is how the blame is entirely shifted to others: on the one hand, an unbridled love for the theater, a performer's nature, genius; on the other, chance, which caused him to be born into an honorable family. Blind chance, unjust, idiotic. But chance takes the blame, and Gustave evokes it only out of prudence—blindness and cruelty are charges he brings against the family, against the idiotic conformity of those bourgeois who have *clipped* his wings; it is as though Gustave, by accusing his parents of depriving him of his power, sees in his rejected vocation the symbol of an earlier castration *begun again* in 1832. It is permissible here to use the vocabulary of psychoanalysis and to describe as castration the constitution by maternal attentions of a passive activity that would always prevent the younger of the Flaubert sons from showing—in any area—a "virile" aggressiveness. And it is familial indifference that causes his constituted passivity, crushing in embryo his first attempt to take responsibility for himself by surpassing himself.

The importance of the consequences of what we shall call his "thwarted vocation" cannot be exaggerated. They will be developed in three different directions, which I merely indicate here because we shall have occasion to speak of them again. Indeed, we find those consequences at every moment of his life, in all his letters, on every page of his work.

1. If he renounced the *career* of actor, he still could not curb his "unbridled love for the stage." He would never stop *playing roles in public.* What is at issue here is something quite different from his insincerity, which can be defined as his *experienced* derealization, that is, his incapacity to distinguish what he feels from what he expresses. This insincerity is therefore *at the source* of his thwarted vocation, and the new castration can only reinforce it; to the extent that it is part of the very fabric of his life, however, it is done and suffered but never named. The *roles,* on the other hand, are explicitly perceived as such: Gustave acts the part of the journalist of Nevers, Papa Couillères, the

Garçon, Saint Polycarp, etc. Sometimes these are imitations, some-times creations; in any event, he states their names and titles; he does not claim to *be* the Garçon—whatever the close ties that unite creature and creator—but to *do* him:[9] "I am *doing* the laughter of the Garçon, the Garçon's entry," he writes. He cannot stop himself from making those around him—family, friends, contemporaries—his audience or his partners. Suddenly, unrealizing himself in front of them, he im-poses the status of spectator on them and undertakes to make them "rock with laughter" whether they want to or not; he entreats, he im-portunes, he intoxicates, but since he cannot become professional, he makes them institute him as an amateur comedian. Or else he im-provises, challenges his audience like music hall singers who call on the audience to join in; he transforms them, makes them his "cues," and involves them in the clownish and dismal "happenings" from which he exits in a daze. Now buffoon, now stage manager, the Flaubert younger son takes revenge for not being able to go on stage by *turning life into theater.* He was forbidden to derealize himself at a set time in front of a paying public, and was thus made into an exhibi-tionist of derealization; an actor by profession, he might have satisfied his "unbridled love for the stage" every evening and shown himself, he thought, to be a good citizen, a good comrade, the rest of the time. The theater might have played the role of an abcess of fixation. But the wound was lanced too early and the infection spread; in other words, the *spectacle*—whether he exhibited himself or invited the people around him to join in the show—became *in the banal course of daily life* his most frequent way of relating to others. Speaking to *one* other per-son, he is merely insincere; two are a virtual audience or a potential troupe; the theatrical demon torments him and he rarely resists the temptation. Unspoken insincerity or proclaimed drama are the op-tions; except perhaps with Alfred, as we shall see, he will have no other human relationships.

2. The brutal disappointment of 1832 resulted in a fixation. Without this renewed castration, he might conceivably have abandoned this *oral* phase of discourse; frustrated, dispossessed of his being, he would always remain alienated from his own voice. We need only go back to his correspondence. As a correspondent, Voltaire is perfectly conscious of addressing himself to people who are absent. Better, he takes advantage of this absence, he uses it to take his time, to reject

9. It may be said that the Garçon is a collective creation. True enough. Still, we must know—and we shall come to this shortly—what that means.

the first impulses of his pen, and to write only those words that most clearly reveal his explicit intentions, deleting his "unspeakable" ones; in short, he is on his guard and makes his letters, like his works, a means of *controlled* communication. Flaubert *speaks* to his correspondents: he writes to them at night, when they are sleeping, in absolute silence, and the movements of his pen are unrealized as the imaginary movements of his glottis; he *writes sounds,* summoning his interlocutors by his incantations in order to transform them into an audience. Denying time and distance, he summons them by feigning uncontrolled abandon—which he took for the *exis* of the actor. As in the period of *L'Amant avare,* written discourse *remains the analogue* of oral discourse, the thirteen volumes of his correspondence seem to be the tape of a conversation taking place over half a century. This is what makes them so valuable. His letters are striking because of three singular qualities combined in a unique fashion.

The first is what I earlier described as summoning his correspondent. I cite at random. Here is the opening of a letter to his sister: "You, my old rat, annoy me! Come on! You are trifling, making small talk. Say instead that you are annoyed at having to write me." Another opening, to Caroline: "How I miss you, my poor rat!" To Ernest, who has just lost his father: "Poor dear Ernest, what can I say? There is no consolation for such pains." To his niece Caroline, the opening of a letter: "How are you? Chat with me a bit." To Ernest on the death of his mother: "My poor old friend, what do you want me to say! I've suffered the same loss." To the Goncourts, the opening of a letter: "Don't beat around the bush, fellows!"

We could cite numerous examples of these abrupt, rapid-fire openings, these rhetorical questions, these bits of advice which, at least formally, demand the presence of the interested party; but we would also have to examine, in the continuing paragraphs of the respective letters, the attacks, the willed oversights, the grand oratorical flights.

There is more. In his epistolary attitude, as in his *exis* as author/actor, meaning is the object of a marginal intention; Gustave is quite aware of this: he abandons himself to pathos, meaning will be born—*for the other*—of the words that are set down, roared out, on paper. On 5 July 1839, after several rather obscure lines—obscure by omission rather than excess—he writes (to Ernest): "All right, here I am shooting off my mouth, flinging words around; scold me roundly when I start affecting style. My last sentence, which finished with 'misty,' seems rather hazy to me, and the devil take me if I understand it myself! After all, I don't see what's so bad about not understanding yourself; there are so many things we understand and would do quite as well not to know about, syphilis, for example; and besides, does the world understand itself? Does that stop it from going on? Will that stop it from dying? For God's sake, I'm stupid! I fancied some thoughts were going to come to me, and it was nothing at all, nonsense! It upsets me but it isn't my fault, I don't have a philosophical mind."

It is remarkable that in this passage, style—taken, moreover, in a pejorative sense—is assimilated to "shooting off my mouth," that is, oral discourse. It is even more remarkable that Gustave cannot resist falling into his "vice" just as he is asking his friend to correct him. Indeed, at first he denounces his tendency to prefer "shooting off his mouth" to meaning: he talks for the sake of talking, for the pleasure of emitting fine sounds linked *at least* by syntax, but he doesn't understand what he is saying. Then suddenly, referring to his first statement, he says, "I don't see what's so bad about not understanding yourself." This reflection, quite interesting in itself, might if taken further lead to a more precise *understanding* of himself inasmuch as he doesn't see what's so bad about *not* understanding himself—or, rather, not understanding what he says. But he breaks off, interrupts his thought, and launches into pseudophilosophical verbiage, false analogies, metaphors—the statement is lost.[10] He realizes it and by a new reflexive reversal comes back to making fun of himself. Nevertheless, the theme of reflection has somewhat changed: this time he reproaches himself for relying on words, for throwing them around as they come to him, sure that they will produce a meaning that the Other can decipher (or that he can decipher himself—as other, that is—when he rereads himself). In brief, he lets himself be possessed by his sentences, by some passive synthesis that articulates the words within him, in the shadows of memory or outside on the white sheet of paper, in the hope that these harmonious combinations will *also* produce an idea, just as the actor lets himself be possessed by a coherent role without seeking to understand it. Can we say that he had no signifying intention to start with? That would be a mistake, since he tells us himself: "I fancied some thoughts were going to come to me." He seems, on the contrary, to have intuitively grasped an abstract scheme

10. The sentence concerning syphilis is meaningless, properly speaking. The first half of the one about the world is vaguely connected to the proposed theme (the world does not need to understand itself to "go on"; the cosmos obeys strict laws it knows nothing about), but an unbelievable flight of thought (will that stop it from dying?) leads Gustave to contradict himself—at least apparently. He is so conscious of this that he stops short: "For God's sake . . ."

which was then buried beneath speech. Let us say that he glimpsed an anti-Cartesian theory of language—for him, conception does not precede expression; rather, the reverse: we speak, and the meaning comes through the words. An inadequate thesis, taken in isolation, but a proper corrective to classical intellectualism: we are spoken to the extent that we speak—and vice versa; thus meaning comes to us, *other*, to the extent that we make it. We say more than we know, more than we understand, even when we force ourselves to express only what we have clearly conceived; so that the *thing said* is both *before* speech (as it is known by the speaker) and *after* (as it comes from speech itself) and appears at first only to the listener. There is no doubt, however, that this ambiguity appears especially in oral discourse. Writing, in general, reduces the amount of meaning that has occurred by *chance*: there is control, correction, voluntary omission, especially in classical writing. A unique feature of Flaubert's letters is that he exaggerates the oral attitude to the point of grasping only one of the two complementary aspects of spoken language.

This directed noncontrol not only breaks all logical connections between propositions and leaves to naked language the task of producing meanings; its effect is also to relax the writer's vigilance and to let slip into the discourse confessions and confidences that Gustave doesn't want to make, truths he would like to hide from himself, without his even perceiving that they have escaped from his pen onto the paper. I have remarked on this tendency already, and we shall have a hundred other occasions to note it: what makes his letters an unparalleled testimony is that Flaubert wrote them by abandoning himself to pathos, and the sentences arrange themselves on the model of free associations. I do not wish to return to this here but only to give one of the reasons for it. "Free association" is conceivable only in oral discourse; you have to speak quickly, take yourself by surprise, unburden yourself in your own voice, let it speak. If Gustave crams his correspondence with such associations, it is because he writes the way one speaks on an analyst's couch—with the qualification that the patient, while letting himself go, never loses consciousness of the fact that he is in quest of something and that he is revealing himself to a witness in order to be revealed to himself, while Flaubert wants to produce "thoughts" for the other but does not want to seek himself, or find himself. Still, the results are the same: he never ceases to betray himself by his outbursts. This means that he puts himself in circumstances that promote free association: urgency and rapidity, the irreversibility of time, the impossibility of taking something back, of retracting what has "escaped" from him; in short, he talks fast on paper.

The disappointed actor finds another way of using his voice: eloquence. His letters are speeches: he doesn't write them to enunciate them himself but to produce a resonance in the ears of his correspondents. He dreamed of being an orator, of that we have proof: he lends several of his characters—Frédéric in particular—the ardent desire (quickly spent) to move crowds with his words and be acquitted by the jury. In his adolescent letters he is more explicit: he will never defend, he says, the widow and the orphan. He is a misanthrope—why should he? We can hardly picture him exulting at the idea of saving the innocent. If he should plead, he tells us, it will be to acquit the guilty. The very guiltiest, of course, someone whose crimes will be obvious and proven. We quite understand that for Gustave this isn't a matter of demolishing the battery of proofs like a Perry Mason by refuting them one by one, by producing other clues and reconstructing the crime in such a way that the accused could no longer have committed it. Instead, he will stimulate the jury with paradoxes (of the kind he tried unsuccessfully to establish in the letter I just cited) and will then abandon himself to pathos, to flicks of the wrist, to his own voice, and will cause a flood of tears to be spilled for the monster who is his client. I know; his resolve at the time was to demoralize; he meant to ridicule justice—what is more amusing, he asks, than one man judging another? This is what he would demonstrate by systematically acquitting the quilty and—I wouldn't swear to the fact that he never thought of it—condemning the innocent. But beneath this explicit and published project, a simple dream, there is another dream: he wants to give the word the terrible power of changing men in spite of themselves. The attorney for the defense, as he sees him, has an audience just as an actor has: he too must fascinate his audience by voice and gesture; he doesn't tell the truth any more than an actor does, since by striking grand attitudes and abandoning himself to pathos, he tries to acquit a man he knows is guilty. Nonetheless, he cannot convince his audience without being convinced himself, that is, without *unrealizing himself* in the role of the orator who believes what he says. The difference? When he wants to be a demoralizer, Gustave not only pretends to make a spectacle of himself; as a rejected actor his resentment is radicalized, and he means to exercise a negative influence on his audience and use his powers to *pervert*. He will become a lawyer since that is what his father wants, but his *being as attorney* will be *instituted subversion*. As a comedian he might have made others

221

laugh; as an attorney he will reclaim their laughter and make them laughable by systematically making them believe the moon is made of green cheese. These two attitudes—that of the comedian and that of the orator—illuminate each other: the second, glittering with malice, gives us a better understanding of the secret danger of the first. By making people laugh at him, he tinges the laughers with baseness, sacrifices himself to make them ignoble, forcing them to reject all compassion. Inversely, the first reveals to us the meaning of the second: the comedian unrealizes the spectators, he is a center of derealization. The orator is no different: the jurors hand down a verdict contrary to their deeper feeling to the extent that the eloquence of the attorney for the defense derealizes them by affecting them with an unreal belief in the innocence of the guilty. Sganarelle is transformed into Scapin, the man we laugh at into the man who makes others laugh. The essential thing in this new dream of glory is not so much that it makes us see the radicalization of resentment in the spiteful little comedian but, above all, that it shows us the child's creative project as a polyvalent relationship with his own voice.

3. From this perspective, it is no surprise that Gustave's earliest works should have been conceived on the oratorical model. We have seen that from the age of nine he was offering to show Ernest his "speeches." It is neither by accident nor caprice that he calls his first nondramatic works "Narratives and Speeches" (1835–36).[11] The word "speeches" was added as an afterthought—the writing is more formed than that. Gustave reread his notebook, no doubt at the end of the school year, and judged that the general title would be completed by this term. It is all the more significant that no actual speech is included. Perhaps he thought of writing one; in this case he was equating the story with a piece of eloquence which—like the actor's couplet—was made to be spoken. Or else—and this seems to me more likely—he was struck by the oratorical aspect of his first narratives. Indeed, the epilogue of *Un Parfum à sentir* shows, some months later—he was fourteen—that he was conscious of writing his works the way he wrote his letters: at the mercy of pathos, without always understanding what he was saying, by summoning an imaginary audience: "So I have just finished this strange, bizarre, incomprehensible book. I wrote the first chapter in one day, then I didn't work for a whole

11. The words traced on the cover of the notebook containing *Matéo Falcone, Chevrier et le Roi de Prusse, Le Moine de Cartreuse, Mort de Marguerite de Bourgogne, Portrait de Lord Byron, San Pietro Ornano*.

month; in one week I did five others and in two days I finished it. I will give you no explanation of its philosophical thought; there is some in it—look for it. I am now exhausted, harassed, and I fall wearily into my armchair without having the strength to thank you if you have read me or the strength to get you not to do it (if there is still time)."

The future dogmatist of impersonalism could not, at this time, resist *showing* himself. He didn't have to write this epilogue except for the pleasure of talking about himself. He makes a spectacle of himself, puts himself on stage: he is in his room and falls wearily into his armchair; in front of him, on his writing table, are sheets of paper on which he painfully traces the last words of his "book." It will be noted that the story he just finished is intended to be cruel and sinister; no one should laugh—except the malicious characters who people his narrative—at Marguerite's misfortunes. But as soon as he makes himself visible, the tone changes: he is imperceptibly but intentionally comic, this harassed author who falls into his armchair. At the same time he summons his public, as he did Ernest or Caroline in his letters, but aggressively; there is some philosophical thought, look for it! I am too exhausted to thank you for having read me, and besides, you will have done better not to, etc. This is how he exhibits himself, aggressively clowning without giving up his passive negativism (I will not explain, I will not thank), half comedian, half orator, as we find him *in life*, at school, and later at the boulevard du Temple or at Mathilde Bonaparte's.

There is more. This valuable epilogue gives us information about the way Gustave composed at the time, and it is clear that it is very much the way the actor/author, some years earlier, wrote his plays. Inspiration seized him, then left him the same day; he writes the first chapter and leaves everything unfinished, out of disgust no doubt— we know his great enthusiasms and his disillusionments. Dead calm, a month passes, and suddenly the wind rises: five chapters in seven days; new disgust, which keeps him from his writing table for an unspecified length of time, then new flight—he finishes his narrative in two days. *Un Parfum* was written in February and March, during the last part of the second trimester. At this time of the year, as all teachers know, exhaustion has accumulated among the students. Yet the teachers must be even more demanding as these last two months are decisive; in the third trimester, with rare exceptions, the chips are down, and there is room for nothing but recapitulation. For a student fully engaged in scholarly competition to produce a work of about sixty closely printed pages,[12] including many long paragraphs, would be a real tour de force, if everything did not come rushing out in a stream whenever he sits down to write; as it is, Gustave abandons himself to the text, his pen speaks, he never goes back over what he has said, corrects nothing, and at the same time reveals himself, as in his letters, through the numerous *lapsus calami* which are, in fact, *lapsus vocis*. Does he fully understand what he is writing? No more than he did as an actor, no more than he does as a correspondent. He says so quite literally: I have just finished this strange, bizarre, incomprehensible book. Of course he is addressing himself to readers, and at first we understand this to mean: incomprehensible *to you*. But should we stop there? It is rare that an author judges himself unintelligible; rare too that he should discourage the reading of his works. Yet on this last point we know that Gustave, at least during his adolescence, was as sincere as he could be: he was afraid of being unmasked—we shall return to this in a moment. It is as if the child himself sensed the bizarreness and incomprehensibility of what he had just written and was alarmed. In other words, he is surpassed by his work; when he rereads it, it seems strange to him: he abandoned himself to inspiration, and what has been set down on paper is his "particularity" insofar as it is visible to the malevolent eyes of others, but escapes *him*. He knows very well that he has invented Marguerite's misfortunes out of his own, and yet he does not recognize himself in this ugly, deserted wife. What did he mean, then? He no longer knows, but he is afraid that others do, or, at least, that they see the absurd bizarreness of his own person in the strangeness of his work. The object is there *as other;* the young author verifies in this other the otherness of his inspiration, which has projected on paper his incomprehensible *anomaly*. There is no question that his narrative contains "philosophical thought," but he doesn't really know what it is; others will have the job of making it explicit. Thus, in the letter cited above, "I fancied some thoughts were going to come to me, and it was nothing at all," the discourse produces its own meaning, and it is up to Ernest, to his readers, to arrive at it. There is one difference: in the letter, the "thought" burst like a bubble and Gustave perceived it; in *Un Parfum*, he is convinced that it can be read between the lines. And this is just what worries him. In the preface, however, he seems certain of what he wanted to do: the anecdote should give us a glimpse of the inflexible and unrecognized power of the goddess Ananke. We are told the "philosophi-

12. Edition Charpentier, pp. 42–102.

cal" meaning of the narrative *in advance* and with utter clarity. Why does he claim in the epilogue that the meaning is hidden? No doubt he felt the idea was distorted and embellished by the discourse that should have illustrated it and thus, as far as he was concerned, it was obscured. The importance of the epilogue is that it translates Gustave's *estrangement* from his product. Indeed, as we have seen, inspiration seizes him, overwhelms him, and leaves him as though it were an *alien* force. He is at once responsible and not responsible for the objectification of his anomaly.

To understand Gustave's complex relation to *his* inspiration, we must go back to the notebook of "Narratives and Speeches." In these very early works too we find the methods of the author/actor; the child reveals himself a copyist of genius. We have noted this in connection with *L'Anneau du Prieur.* Jean Bruneau has reproduced the argument and the model as they figure in *Nouvelles Narrations françaises* by A. Filon.[13] The reader may check for himself: he will see that Flaubert closely followed Filon's "narrative"—the sequence of events is respected, there is a close correspondence between paragraphs, and many of the sentences are identical in both texts. I have pointed out, however, that Gustave's originality is complete, for he makes the copied narrative serve an obscure underlying purpose. He does this by making a few changes here and there—so subtle and discreet that they escaped Bruneau himself. But it is striking that in order to explain himself the young author should have needed a prefabricated text—just as he needed a preexisting role when he was an actor. It will be said that a child making his debut as a writer inevitably leans on something—and imitates far more than he creates. That is true. But Flaubert is thirteen. It is rather late for *copying.* Especially when such a powerful personality is already in evidence. If at this age Gustave still uses models, he does so deliberately: he wants to internalize an objective and rigorous order so as to reexternalize it, modified, through the subjective movement of an inspiration based on memory. The young author writes the way an actor acts: he recreates an inflexible, learned scheme; the only difference is that the actor interprets— that is, he submits his passive activity entirely to an objective rule— while Gustave learns to change, to betray elegantly, imperceptibly, the imperatives he imposes on himself by making systematic alterations: vassalage and deception. Originality—hence the beginnings of literature—is on the side of deception. This will be explored later. What I

13. Bruneau, p. 59, etc.

want to stress here is that the inspiration in *Un Parfum* seems *other* because Gustave wanted it to be other when he first adapted *Pour-sôgnac* for his own theatrical purposes. At thirteen, writing for his voice, the child is not yet certain whether he is an author or an actor.

Later we shall see that the secret of style in Flaubert's great works is eloquence *rejected*. And rejected *by the other*. Gustave wrote *Madame Bovary* in a state of oratorical abandon, then cut and trimmed under Bouilhet's influence. The orator is there, everywhere, but censored, rejected, painful; he is hounded, compromised, but he returns *in the very compression* of the prose to lend a strange, sonorous vibration to even the most stripped down sentences. All we need to indicate here—and we shall take it up at greater length later—is that the *voice* remains to the end *the completion of the writing*. Not that the style of the great works is oral—quite the contrary. Rather, the writing itself is double-faced and becomes an audiovisual means of communication—otherwise how are we to understand that he "needs to shout out" all the sentences he writes?[14] The true conclusion of his works is surely the moment when he reads them before a chosen circle of friends or colleagues. It is at this moment that the word takes its fullness and borrows its singularity from the particular timbre of the voice that forms it. Public readings were certainly the fashion; in the salons of the Arsenal, people were always declaiming their works. But usually these were poems or plays. Gustave, on the other hand, invited Maxime and Louis to Croisset to subject them to *thirty-six hours* of performance, *interpreting* his first *Saint Antoine* for them. Even more distressing, he sought their judgment on the basis of this single, tedious audition. As if the words pronounced by him, articulated into sentences by his breathing, should instantly acquire complete intelligibility, as if it were possible to judge a large work full of paradoxes, each of which should be the object of lengthy reflection, on the basis of a single test-run. Naturally the listeners' verdict was negative: the work should be put in the closet. Was he not conscious that he had done himself a disservice? He was and he wasn't: he had a vague presentiment of it but he persevered in his error. Not only because he loved to be unrealized in his voice but because he could not conceive of the beauty of a paragraph without its musical organization. Or without its meaning, which, according to him, becomes clearer to an audience through the articulation of intelligible mouthfuls of sound.

14. We shall see later that the audiovisual aspect of language is the source of his taste for puns.

The ideal thing, then, would be written words spoken with his voice in the heads of unknown readers. And since that cannot be, the real celebration must be the public reading; the moment of publication—even if the book were to be read by every Frenchman—must be something of a letdown. Testimony to these complex and contradictory sentiments is found in a note he sent to the Goncourts to invite them to hear *Salammbô*, which was to be declaimed before his friends "from 4 to 7 o'clock and after coffee until the listeners croak." You might say he does everything to ensure his failure and that he is aware of it but cannot prevent himself; he knows very well that he will make his public "croak." Not, of course, from cardiac arrest but from boredom, by demanding of them an almost intolerable effort of attention which will end, sooner or later, in a sort of tetanus of the mind. He knows this but goes ahead anyway: he is the good giant, the giver (this is a new myth, which we shall explore in a subsequent chapter), and so much the worse for the recipient if he is crushed by the bounty of this Pantagruel. The essential thing is the *giving* of his work and its transformation into a performance in which Gustave is the only actor. Here we find him, then, in this last phase of creation, become once more the author/actor inhabited by the imperatives he has given to himself as other. Still, this return to dramatic interpretation is quite rare: to give himself one evening's pleasure he must put himself out for several years. And he knows very well that reading aloud—which *for him* is the conclusion of a thankless labor—represents only one inessential moment of the literacy process. The book will be read by thousands of *eyes*; for these readers, the sonority of the text, if it exists in some dim way, is only a pleasant remnant—silence is its essential quality. Not only the silence of the study, but, even more important, the meaning beyond language which is the mute totalization of the written work, that is, of everything that is expressed through words. Put differently, while the audiovisual aspect of the word is always present for him, it is merely a rather futile attempt at recuperation; thrown back on graphemes, Gustave submits to a net loss for which he will never sufficiently compensate.

Can we say he is aware of this loss? Absolutely. From the age of fourteen, he is quite explicit about his dissatisfaction with the written word—a dissatisfaction that will persist at least until the crisis of 1844; the written word is clearly inadequate as it can render neither feelings, sensations, nor ecstasies. This denunciation is his recurrent subject, and, as we know, the deepest reasons for it lie elsewhere; but if he slips it into most of his early works from the age of fourteen on, it is as an occasional yet crucial motif. He was forbidden the career of actor; hence, words were deprived of their ordinary accompanying gestures, mimicry, and intonation; they were suddenly mutilated, became little more than inert scaffolding—how could he give them back their former fullness? Deprived of his old sound tools, he had to replace them by crude, mute instruments which, because they were not heated by his breath, would never express his animating pathos. Of course, he would read his text aloud, interpret it, giving a singular aspect to the universal vocable through the *timbre* of his voice, and hence would be able—on rare occasions—to preserve the illusion that he *was giving birth* to it by expectoration. But he knew very well that reading is not acting. Even the ludic aspect of literature has nothing to do with acting.[15] Above all, *writing* for unknown readers is an attempt to captivate and seduce them by defenseless graphemes, which they interpret as they like. He is vulnerable—nothing in his hands, nothing in his pockets; the writer traces his scrawl and goes away, leaving it to the most malevolent inspection. It is one of Flaubert the *stylist's* deepest intentions to find a written equivalent to oral seduction. As an actor he could have fascinated, he thinks; therefore, he must find a *trick* for fascinating by writing. But this search will come later, after a great deal of anger, and will involve sacrificing the already precarious health of his mind. For the moment, he is thrown into a contradiction from which he cannot escape: while writing, he keeps within him the dream of an oral conclusion to his literary work, but at the same time he discovers what would have remained hidden to the author/actor: *that we do not write the way we speak.* I do not claim that this banality is true. But neither is it completely false. Certainly an apprentice writer is often unequipped; I have known some, among my old friends, whose conversation was seductive and whom we never tired of listening to—their physical and intellectual charm was communicated in words that issued from them and came to us as their image in sound, whereas in writing, much to our surprise, they faded before our eyes. If they made progress, it wasn't by bringing their works into relation to their oral discourse but—as Gustave would do—by making *some other use* of language and by inventing *written* equivalents for their gestures, their voice, their style of life, directed to the eyes of their readers. We do not write the way we speak, and yet we write, at least in the course of life, when we cannot speak. This is the antinomy the child ran up against. What is writing, then? He will give an answer to

15. Though of course they belong to the same category.

that question and we will eventually learn what it is. For the moment, disgruntled and anxious as he is, writing strikes him as an austere last resort.

In any case, his desire for glory fades and gradually turns into a refusal of all notoriety. As an actor he would have brought honor to his century—he was certain of it; the vicious circle of sadomasochism could function only on the basis of this certainty. Now he no longer knows what to do: How is he to play this inferior instrument with half the strings broken? And when others know how to use it, they are simply demonstrating that they had a vocation to write. Despite his pride, Gustave cannot convince himself that he is dedicated to writing, for he is sure that his genius disposed him to dramatic art; he imagines he is exercising an inferior activity for which he has no gift. And so he is plunged into doubt and rage; his mental state is revealed to us in a letter—no doubt a little tardy—that he wrote to Ernest on 23 July 1839, parts of which I have already cited: "I might have been . . . an excellent actor, I felt the inner strength, and now I declaim more pitifully than the worst bungler because I have gratuitously killed my zeal . . . As for writing, I have completely renounced it and I am sure that you will never see my name in print; I have no more strength, I no longer feel capable of it." Later we shall see the incidental causes of these complaints. But the text is revealing; he speaks *first* of his talent as an actor, a talent botched by others' rejection and his own self-destructive tendency. Yet his talent is himself. And from the way literature is introduced into the paragraph, we understand that it is only a secondary activity, a last resort that hardly concerns him. He *might have been* an actor, but he has not tried, according to him, to *be* a writer; he has written, that's all, no doubt to conceal from himself the loss to which he was subjected when others refused to sanction his true vocation. The prepositional phrase "as for" indicates clearly that the information following is of marginal importance, inessential; it merely completes the picture and answers Ernest's possible objection in advance: "You declaim like a bungler, all right. But what about your writing?" For Gustave, the important information is given in the first sentence: from the moment I could not become what I am and study drama, I gratuitously killed my zeal. My heart is ravaged by a mass of artificial things and endless clowning—and nothing will come of it! So much the better! As for writing, etc. The essential thing is said, the totalization done: I am cold and dry, I read nothing, I write nothing, I am nothing because I have destroyed myself with my own hands to finish the work of the executioners who have deprived me of myself. I had the *"inner strength"* of a great actor: others did not want to recognize my inclination, and suddenly I lost it, I am a shorn Samson. The word "strength" is repeated when there is a need to explain why Gustave *also* renounced writing: "I *no longer* have the strength for it." So he had it in the past? Certainly he believes he did, but he does not claim to have possessed at any moment of his former life a special gift for literature or any mandate. He quite simply refers to that zeal, that inner strength which dedicated him to the theater; even after he was forbidden access to it, he retained enough of the old fire, he thought, to throw himself into eloquence and writing. It is true that artistic choice is often polyvalent in the early years. Yet a hierarchy exists in each individual case, conditioned by familial structures and early history. Ravel might *also* have been able to write and paint in his youth, but he became a musician. Let us imagine the impossible: no sooner had he caught a glimpse of his principal vocation than he was forbidden to compose; he would have painted, no doubt, or written. But we can imagine his rages, his regrets, and his bitter conviction—without any real basis—of being inferior as a plastic artist to the musician he might have been, and of persisting in doing something for which he was not entirely suited.[16] Gustave had similar frustrations in his adolescence. Kafka said, "I have a mandate but I don't know who gave it to me." As a writer, Flaubert did not have this good fortune. We shall see him haunted all his life by the disturbing question, Do I even have a mandate? Aren't I "a bourgeois who lives in the country and busies himself with literature"? If we want to understand the reasons for the insistence with which he repeats Buffon's saying, "Genius is but extended patience," we must remember that he did not "enter literature" by the king's highway but by the narrow gate, and that, not being one of the *chosen* in this domain, he was compelled quite early, from the age of fifteen, to find a replacement for inspiration—those sure of their election have only to abandon themselves to it. In others it is a trick, a malicious joke played by the devil; they think they are singing and are merely braying—by *labor improbus*. We shall return to this.

Certainly we should not push this interpretation too far. Indeed, the letter of 23 July 1839 can be understood quite differently: if Gustave decides to give up writing—quite provisionally since a month later, in August, he produces *Les Funérailles du docteur Mathurin*—it is because he is unhappy with *Smarh*, which he finished in April; we

16. The basic choice of artists is polyvalent in childhood because it is above all a choice of the *ludic* and of derealization through the imaginary. External circumstances, internalized, make that choice specific and orient it but it always remains *plural*.

shall see in a subsequent chapter what great hopes he attached to this work when he conceived it. Rereading it one year later, he would be highly disappointed: "It is all right to turn out drivel, but not this sort." And we know that from April on, afraid to reopen his manuscript, he was troubled, sensing that "the famous mystery is bereft of ideas." [17] So he should have reversed the exposition of his motifs as he presented them to Ernest: a *literary* failure is the basis of his decision to renounce literature. If he mentions his thwarted vocation, it is in order to blame others for that failure: it wouldn't have happened if they had encouraged me to go onto the stage. And it is also to escape the temptation to deny his own worth: better to be a comic genius stifled from birth by his family than a nothing, pure and simple, without vocation or mandate, "an imbecile," someone merely "taking up space in society." In the same letter he prophesies that he will be "a respectable man, dutiful and all that . . . I will be like the next man, proper, like everyone else." But while he is thinking that others have misunderstood and broken his "inner strength," and that his literary failure results from the fact that *his mission was different,* he remains superior to the mediocrity they inflict on him. The center of his preoccupations, then, the *essential* thing, is literature; and in his usual fashion he invokes his first choice only in order to conceal from Ernest and from himself the true direction of his thoughts.

This interpretation is quite valid, and I believe it is as true as the other. What is more, while the two seem incompatible at first sight, I am convinced we must adopt both. At seventeen, Gustave accommodated to the substitution that was imposed on him. At first he was merely resigned to writing, but he eventually became *invested* in the enterprise: he understood, no doubt, that the glory of Molière crowned the creator rather than the actor. In the hierarchy of his personal op-

17. To Ernest, 15 April 1838: "Yesterday I finished a mystery that takes three hours to read. Only the subject is worthwhile." 13 September of the same year: "The famous mystery I did in the spring takes only three hours' reading, continues with an unbelievable rigamarole [*galimatias*] or, as Voltaire would have said, pompous nonsense [*galiflaubert*]."

We note the importance of oral reading: Gustave has *timed* his text. He adds: "(for your next visit) . . . I have enough to bore you with my productions for a long time, more noisy than agreeable." Unbelievable rigamarole, a reading more noisy than agreeable—these words shouldn't fool us; we are accustomed to Gustave's insincerity, his false modesty. After all, he was not so disgusted with *Smarh* at the time since he envisaged reading it to his friend. Yet these words, this time particularly violent, nonetheless betray his fear of having failed in his work. No doubt he was counting on Ernest's admiration to convince him that he had succeeded.

As we see, Gustave's great disgust with writing is proclaimed in the month of July, sandwiched between two other letters that shed light on it.

tions, the actor precedes the writer, there is no doubt of that; in the social hierarchy—on which he is more dependent than others—the situation is reversed. He would be greater as a novelist than if he limited himself to playing Sganarelle. Tension is established between these two scales of values, both of which are internalized: troubled, he is going to attempt to write, *scripta manent;* he will mark his century, and his work, less ephemeral than the *flatus vocis* of the actor, will long outlive him. He thus accepts doing what he likes least. *On condition that he excels in his art:* if he takes pen in hand, he must become at the very least the leading writer of his time. When he is able to believe, to convince himself—at the moment of conception—that the scope, the richness, the beauty of his projected work will equal the greatest of the classics, he forgets or renounces his first vocation and throws himself into writing with enthusiasm. At this moment he is not concerned with the path that leads to celebrity; *renown* is what counts, this alone will satisfy his pride and his resentment. But as soon as he attempts to realize his work, he is disgusted with what he writes. Obviously; he has only one subject, the world, and his art is not yet equal to his ambitions. Suddenly he rediscovers his folly: what need did he have to impose this *pensum* of writing on himself when in his heart he felt the zeal, the inner strength, of a comic actor; he is punished for listening to others and betraying his vocation. *Pensum* is what he will later call his novel about la Bovary. But he must rise even higher and convince himself that this word—except when he abandons himself to eloquence—designates in his eyes the whole of literature, that abstract and sustained work he does so joylessly. For this reason we are not surprised by his confession in his letter of 23 July, "By wanting to climb so high, I have torn my feet on the rocks." He played *Poursôgnac* happily, abandoning himself to his "nature"; in order to produce *Smarh,* he toils and misses his mark ("I could have made myself miserable, I could have made everyone around me suffer," 23 July); so he furnishes himself with proof that he was not made to write. Later he will talk once again about glory. But never as he did before. First, he is convinced that it will forever elude him, and besides, intangible literary renown, lifeless and diffuse, has nothing in common with his childhood dream, the intoxicating pleasure of immediate success, an entire audience on its feet, applauding and shouting "bravo."

There is more. As a comic actor, Gustave gives himself to everyone sadistically, masochistically; in the billiard room he plays the buffoon and bares his bottom for an enema—he is not afraid of suffering as an ignominious martyr and of provoking laughter. He could well be called an exhibitionist. On the other hand, he hides his writings. Aside from Alfred and Ernest—who is still not always admitted to the private readings—no one knows anything about them. Until the publication of *Madame Bovary*, writing seemed to him like *sinning alone*.[18] At the beginning or the end of a story, he often challenges unknown readers who might try to open his manuscript: *"Do not read me!"* Look at the beginning of *Agonies*—he is sixteen: "The author has written without pretention to style, without desire for glory, the way one weeps without affectation. . . He never wrote with the aim of publishing later; his belief in nothing was too real to him, too devout, to be told to men. He wrote for one or two people at most . . . If by chance some unfortunate hand should discover these lines, let it beware of touching them! For they will burn the hand that touches them, exhaust the eyes that read them, murder the soul that understands them." We could cite many such warnings. Furthermore, he "dedicated and gave" *Mémoires d'un fou* to Alfred, which means that he wrote for him alone and arranged that he alone should read the work. He repeats a hundred times in his correspondence that he will never publish. To Louise, in the epic-oratorial style he is fond of employing in the early years of their liaison, he declares that he will be buried with his manuscripts unviolated, like a warrior with his horse. And this vow is continually repeated: to leave no trace of himself on earth, to erase his footsteps, to be forgotten, twice dead, as if he had never existed. Thus the passage from dramatic art to literary art seems to be similar to the passage from *social* being to secret singularity. Let us not, however, jump to the conclusion that he breaks the hold others have over him; as an actor he delivers himself, as a creator he writes in fear and resentment, he disguises himself; but in both cases he continues to be dominated by the Other—isn't hiding oneself an implicit recognition of the primacy of the person one is hiding from? What is the difference, then, between the two attitudes? First, as always, it is the material conditions that surpass and structure the praxis. To play comedy *implies,* whatever the actor's feelings, that he is *representing* a character to an audience: theater is collective. To write the role one is going to play—as does the author/actor—already entails a certain isolation; while he is composing a role or inventing dialogue, the author/

18. A comparison between the artist's work and masturbation is often found in his written remarks: "Let us masturbate the old art to its deepest joints." "The erection has finally come, Monsieur, by dint of beating and manumauling myself," etc. Cf. Roger Kempf: "Le Double pupitre" in *Cahiers du Chènevis*, October 1969.

233

actor must physically or mentally retreat, distance himself in order to have the leisure to envisage the dramatic situation as a whole. But this retreat is *passed over in silence,* and the author/actor is only half aware of this because he is writing for performance and for the actors in his troupe; he is therefore *in the midst of the crowd,* even in the silence of his study, imagining the reactions of the public and trying to utilize his comrades to the best of their abilities. If, on the other hand, the work being written is destined for a purely *optic* reading, the retreat is fully conscious; it becomes the object of a formal intention. And certainly an author is in the midst of his characters, he is always wondering what reactions best suit their natures—"can I push this blond's passions to their extreme? After what I've said about her already, can she have such strong feelings?" Which amounts to asking: "Is she a well-made character?" But this is living with the *author's* creatures, remaining in *his* imaginary universe. In this case there is no longer that osmosis which makes the author/actor continually compare his fantasies with the capacities of living persons, inventing—sometimes improvising on stage, in the course of rehearsals—dialogue suggested by the actors' particular way of interpreting their roles, or revising a couplet the actor cannot manage to "get out" the right way. In this sense the writer, even when he envisages one or another of his characters *objectively,* remains alone with himself. Not that it would be impossible—as bourgeois subjectivism has too often claimed—for him to speak of someone other than himself, or that his creatures are necessarily projections of himself in the milieu of otherness; the question is more complex and we can answer it only by a dialectical treatment of its primary data—in this chapter we shall have occasion to study the crude and archaic aspects of Gustave's first creations. In any event, to the extent that the author invents, he ultimately deals only with himself: his fictions are not always himself as other, but they are always *his; he* always smells, as he creates, the "bad odor" of his imagination.[19]

By the same token, we don't mean to deny that in writing he pre-

---

19. I am not saying that solitude is imposed *by definition* on the writer; *social* forms of literary creation exist—collaboration is one such form. There are others: the cultural revolution can lead to the collective production of a written work (as well as to the challenge of art in the name of practical creation). I am describing the situation most common in the nineteenth century, symbolized by the fact that many writers, in order to find extreme isolation (like Balzac or George Sand), worked *at night,* when sleep abolished the society around them (Stendhal, by rising at dawn, demonstrated that he still belonged to the classical centuries and that he brought the literary attitude of the eighteenth century into the era of "romanticist" solitude).

served a direct bond with his public. But this bond, at *that* time and in *that* society, could only confirm him in his solitude. Not only, as we shall see, because he was doing his work at the time of an unreachable public. But also because the reader, while reading, was—as the custom of the time dictated—as alone as the writer was while writing. I have shown elsewhere that certain works break the barrier of seriality and create, even in the most complete isolation, a kind of appeal to the solidarity of the group. In that postromantic period, however, reading obviously serialized the reader and returned him to his serial individuality. Thus, even though an author might have his public constantly in mind and attempt to foresee its reactions to every word he wrote, he would have only a confused impression of juxtaposed solitudes, which would necessarily confirm him in his own. Thus, the literary relationship between members of the creating couple at this point in time can be qualified as *nocturnal:* Gustave falls back on masturbation because this relationship seems to him like onanism for two. He reacts against it by imposing on his friends those sessions of reading aloud which were "more noisy than agreeable." But his attempt at socialization merely increased his loneliness: by reserving his work for two, or rather only one *listener,* he forced himself to reject all the unknown readers who might have liked what he produced. Anyway, how can you write without wanting to be read? The consequence of these contradictory postulations is that Gustave established his rapport with the public beyond its radical negation. This is marked by the naïveté evidenced at the end of *Un Parfum,* when Gustave pretends to discourage from reading his work those who, by necessity, have already read it from beginning to end. He is aware of it, and tries to correct his false candor by an ironic "if it isn't too late." In *Agonies* he guards against making the same mistake and this time begs the reader at the outset to put down this "book" whose lines "burn one's eyes." But why? Isn't it already a *book*? Isn't it already "in circulation"? Can Gustave help wanting to be published? The last words of his first chapter prove that "when he is in despair, he is still hoping" to find an unknown alter ego who, despite his prodigious warnings, will go past them and "thank him . . . for having brought together in a few pages an enormous abyss of skepticism and despair."

We can now understand the clandestine aspect of writing for the young Flaubert. As an actor he wanted to make people laugh and so was not afraid of ridicule. From its conception to its realization, comedy is entirely a social enterprise: it is born of a collective fact, laughter, and results in the comic, a proposition to the audience of the laughable thing *reworked*. The child makes himself comic because he discovers that he is laughable; in this sense the flight toward the role is ambiguous: he yields to it, certainly, when he plays the buffoon, but at the same time he controls the laughter; and then, too, the character he interprets is, in spite of everything, other than himself. In short, he reveals nothing to the honorable company other than what they knowingly made of him. Socialized by derision, he attempts to institute himself as the qualified representative of all who are laughable. The *social* aspect of the enterprise protects him against any temptation to reveal himself in his solitary truth; on the level of the comic, such truths have no currency; no one can even conceive of them, since the actor makes people laugh only by breaking solidarity with himself. From start to finish, everything is public. It begins with the others' "impact" on Gustave and ought to end with Gustave's "impact" on them. An ignominious triumph, certainly, but one in which the child has nothing to lose. Suddenly the enterprise is *denied:* the little boy is still laughable, but they deny him the right to make himself comic, which casts him back into his solitary truth—or, rather, reveals to him his *nonsocialized* subjectivity. In fact, as we have seen, even his interiority at its most profound has been shaped by others, and the awareness he now has of his anomaly was triggered by the fact that others have refused to allow him to elaborate socially the risibility they have given him. Since literature, for the child, is primarily dramatic art *denied*, it seems to him to embody his unsociability—his exile in himself. The denial circumscribes and sanctions his *anomaly:* he is already laughable—hence the object of a minor disgrace—but by forbidding him to exploit his social character, the others force him to defend himself *by taking himself seriously*. He was expecting comedy to institute his other-being, meaning his being-for-others; this denied, he expects literature—against his social dimension, which remains but which he is forbidden to exploit and must suffer in humility—to institute his being-for-himself, which until now he was living in the whirl of the immediate. The result: set against laughter, he weeps through his writing. His early works, with few exceptions, are grim. It will be pointed out that they were written under the influence of romanticism, of his unhappy life at school; and, in a sense that we shall explore later, this is not incorrect. But let us not forget that the author of *L'Amant avare* had already read tragedies and dramas and was not particularly happy; at that time, however, he wrote only comedies. His relations at school could not have been so unpleasant for him at first since he invited school friends to the billiard room so as to clown for them. The main reason for his change in outlook is that he was thrown back on his interiority, which appeared to him for the first time in his life as it really was: a nest of vipers. What he surpassed in the comic parade now becomes impassable; not that interiority is self-affirmed—it is the outward rejection that reduces Flaubert to a state of thankless misery and resentment. If chance had at least made him a narcissist. But he scarcely likes himself. His "written cries," in the service of the impassable, can only be cries of hatred against others and proclaimed disgust for himself. At the same time the sentences he writes satisfy strange, dark desires he knows nothing about firsthand. Perhaps the most striking texts from this point of view are not those we interpreted in part 1 but the plans for "melodramas" that he conceived without ever giving them finished form. Through the fabulations of his despair we glimpse the "family romance" of which I spoke earlier: his mother is raped or seduced and abandoned. In any case, deflowered in duplicity or horror, the wretched woman gives birth to him, the child is taken away, and she wallows in the gutter. In the end, Gustave has her for a hundred sous at the brothel. Having recognized—too late—her lover as her son, the infamous creature throws herself beneath the wheels of the hearse that carries him to his grave. Who is this weeping woman, this victim, this creature whose most sublime feelings are brutally mocked? As we have seen, she is both Mme Flaubert and Flaubert himself. But how could the child move from light comedy to these perverse and morose lucubrations? Quite simply because he does not give himself a role in the plays he aspires to write. The author/actor could do only farces, since he had to reserve the "starring roles" for himself; the actor having taken leave, the author dreams of writing for the theater, but since he is no longer constrained to do comedy, there is a change of perspective and the plays in hand take a definitively dark turn. They are no longer—to the same degree that his other writings were—a social means of visually presenting his executioners with the monster they made him, but rather a nocturnal and masturbatory effort to give substance to his rancorous dreams, his forbidden desires, his moods, by *setting them down* on paper.

For this reason his attitude toward his new state is ambivalent: he wants to be there and at the same time he doesn't. Let someone else masturbate at night if he should chance to find one of Gustave's manuscripts and read it by candlelight, hiding from his family, finding there the confirmation of his terrors and the disturbing satisfaction of his desires. The writer-in-spite-of-himself certainly wants this, and indeed such a reader is by definition the opposite of a mocker—he is disarmed by solitude. Yet the young Flaubert has only a minimum of sympathy for this alter ego: too close, during his nocturnal orgies, to confer a true *objective-being* upon his creations, he is liable from one moment to the next to join his comrades and deride the fool who moments earlier moved him to tears. The best thing would be to kill himself, as was the fashion after the publication of *Werther*. In any event, the danger of literature is here: by expressing his inner feelings in written words, Gustave the laughable gives laughers new occasion to laugh. If he spoke to them, his presence, his force, his conviction, his voice might restrain their hilarity; but he has slipped into the inert graphemes that are only what they are. Here he is quite the opposite, completely naked, defenseless, the prisoner of these soiled pages, which readers can interpret as they like, a cold surgical eye can size up, or a group of young jokers can read aloud for their amusement. Later, Gustave will try to provide against these things by his stance of "impersonalism," a set of operations aimed less at suppressing the author's *presence-in-person* than at concealing it from the suckers who read his books. In the meantime, throughout his adolescence he writes only to unburden himself and is terrified lest someone make fun of his complaints.[20] This is the source of his double writing, aggressive and disagreeable: he abandons himself and takes himself seriously only to turn around and be *the first* to mock himself. He who breaks solidarity with himself first, as we have seen, has some hope of escaping collective laughter or, at least, of getting the laughers on his side. But if it isn't a matter of chance, of an unexpected circumstance that made him momentarily laughable, what a painful position to be in! He is constantly being waylaid, analyzed, his speech is scrutinized, his unintended puns and involuntary and unfortunate allusions to well-known events are exposed, etc., etc. He is like the school scapegoat: forbidden to laugh at others though they are free to laugh at him, arousing in the pharisees around him the contempt a respectable man feels for a fellow who makes himself absurd—"in order to seem interesting," say these fine pricks, while for such unfortunates the only

---

20. "If I take the risk of showing [these pages] to a small number of friends, it will be a sign of confidence" (*Un Parfum à sentir: Deux mots*). "Perhaps you will laugh afterward . . . looking back on a poor child who loved you more than anything else and whose soul was already tormented with such foolishness" (*Agonies*: dedication to Alfred). "And then Christ wept . . . and Satan, laughing more horribly than one of the dead . . ." (ibid., conclusion). Etc., etc.

issue is to avoid the grinding scorn that would isolate them and compensate for it by denouncing it when it manifests itself.

This is Gustave's state as author during his adolescence. He abandons himself to his complaints and hastens to break solidarity with those complaints by declaring them laughable. In short, his writings are clandestine from the beginning: he protects them from the Other by locking them away in his drawer and, in the text itself, by recourse to laughter. This new avatar will provide a better understanding of the evolution of the comic for the adolescent, and of the way he moves from being a laughable object to the subject of laughter (no longer controlling the laughter of others but appropriating it in order to transform it into a trap, enticing others to laugh at him so that they may be constituted as laughable by their very laughter and revealed as the pure objects of his derision)—in a word, the way he passes from *Poursôgnac* to the god Yuk. At the present moment he borrows the laughter of others to forestall intolerable mockery, to proclaim before and after his complaints: readers, these are jeremiads; don't worry about making fun of them, I transcribed them for your amusement and I don't take myself seriously. But *he does take himself seriously;* his irony is only a precaution—it clenches its teeth or, rather, it is acted. In this way it reveals to him that it is otherness, the others' view of him, and that somehow he stole it from them, that he knows their motives and turns their hilarity against them. From Gustave's point of view, the procedure is the chief thing. But we can also see in it—we shall return to this soon—the *purposely worked* transformation of the primary comic (the buffoon offers himself to men who take him for a subman) into one of its secondary forms (by laughing at himself the comedian laughs at his human nature, and the laughter he deliberately provokes in others throws into derision, by them and through them, the whole human race). In this period, the combination of candid abandon and black humor is unique to Gustave.

We must still explain the nature of the passionate and grim interiority into which he was plunged in his thirteenth year by a sovereign rejection. Does he discover it or create it? Both. In truth, it already existed implicitly as what he tried to surpass in the being of the actor, as the deep but unknowable humus from which he drew, through confident inspiration, his most comic effects; in other words, as what *he should not have taken seriously.* He wanted, we know, to flee his derealization by *realizing himself as actor.* A rejected actor, he finds himself again in his *constituted dereality* as imaginary child. But since his games with Caroline, this imaginary child has been enriched with negative content; in the beginning this was merely love refused, pathos lived but denounced by the outside world as a lie. Now the original castration is twice repeated: there was the Fall, then the opposed vocation; resentment raises its head and does its work, all the lived experience we described in part 1 becomes explicit, affirms itself— wasn't it by reading his early works that we were able to decipher the underlying intentions of this sundered heart? Jealousy, envy, bitterness, misanthropy, fatalism, skepticism, the conflict of two opposed ideologies, it's all there; at the age of thirteen, "the worst is always certain," he won't give that up again. But this induced pathos, developed and made more openly explicit, remains nonetheless *derealized*. He suffers, he despises, he is enraged, certainly, but he never manages to convince himself fully that he feels his passions *for real*. First of all, they do not contain affirmative power; they run rampant and carry him away like natural forces, but his constituted passivity deprives him of any possibility of assuming them or combating them. By this means—and by the surgical look that disarms them—he submits to their violence as in a dream, without being able to recognize them or ordain their reality. Here we have the primary insincerity: he is incapable of knowing whether he is suffering for real or playing at suffering, and at the same time he crams this felt but unvalidated pathos with imagined feelings—such as the Great Desire we spoke of earlier—by which he is affected but to which he does not submit, or, more precisely, with feelings he isn't certain are his own or someone else's and which he is only attempting to experience properly in all their phases, but *in imagination*. In other words, after this new banishment, thrown back on an *autistic* solitude in which his thoughts develop without any reducing agent, the social buffoon, far from finding himself in these thoughts as a *person*, sees himself plunged into the pitiless, dark world of the imagination; this world, interior and exterior, subjective and objective, consists of the shifting relations of an illusory macrocosm with an illusory microcosm where everything is experienced "between the lines" by a *He* and an *I* indistinct from each other. Formerly, I have said, this muddy business was submerged in dramatic *interpretation;* now that is forbidden. Certainly he will not stop *playing roles* before his peers or showing himself to his intimates by means of what I have earlier called *epic performance*. But pride prevents him from giving himself to others in all his dereality: as vassal, he displays the lord's *epic performance;* at school he plays the *role* of the Gargantuan naughty boy. For the rest of his life he has but one means to express all his misery and shame: the word. His insubstantial emotions will take on substance only when he puts them down on paper; the pen alone transforms his dereality into unrealization. Reduced to monologue, speaking alone and knowing neither *who is speaking* in him nor *to whom*, nor what this *in him* means, he will escape total disintegration only by personalizing himself as *at least* the one whose duty is to transcribe the voices he hears.

Here we find a new option; we can say it was developed under the pressures of constraint and urgency. Thrown back on derealization, the child is concerned not with *expressing himself* but with personalizing himself through words. He will be an *author*, fine. But this choice of an imposed mutilation must surely present the *literary thing* to him as a confused jumble of contradictions. Objectively, an author has higher standing than an actor; for Gustave, subjectively, it is the other way around. These two axiological systems are purely and simply incompatible. But their antagonism is not experienced openly. In the first place, the Other is sovereign; he is the one, in the child's eyes, who holds the keys to reality; if the move from dramatic to literary art is held to be progress, it must be so; *true* glory is the glory of Hugo, not of Kean. This affirmation of the Other in him is all the more striking as it is deep down and surreptitiously denied by experience: Gustave *falls from above* into literature, he suffers it, he harbors a secret resentment against words. In consequence, the literary object first appears to him as ambiguous, or as singularly deceptive. Gustave's ambivalence concerning his new enterprise is marked by alternating moments of enthusiasm and disgust. He glimpses a subject that seems to him grandiose and is nothing less, as we know, than totalization. On this level of abstraction, it matters very little whether the totalizing enterprise is undertaken by the author/actor or the writer; whatever the approach, the work—this is the essential thing—will be nothing less than the All caught in a trap. He is burning, with his cheeks on fire he throws himself into writing, and the disillusionment comes with the very movement of his pen. This isn't what he wanted; he had hoped to cry out, to faint, and what does he have to do with these silent daubs drying on the paper? It is at this point that he abandons the work. Let us recall *Un Parfum*, taken up, dropped, taken up again: one day of work, a month without opening his notebook, a week for the five subsequent chapters, and then, after a new silence of undetermined duration, two days for writing the last seven chapters and the conclusion—rushing at the end, it seems, in order to be rid of a disheartening task. This is not entirely the case; let us say that he abandons himself to inspiration to the extent that it is oratorical and that words disappoint him to the degree that they detach themselves from his interior monologue and become—by a transubstantiation that never fails to surprise him—the black shells of dead insects. We know the reasons for this ambiguity. He gets pleasure from pushing his eloquence to an extreme *even as* disillusionment invades him, and he takes the bit in his teeth in order *to have done with it* sooner, before he is overtaken by ennui and forced to throw in the towel, leaving the work unfinished. It is not a question of dissatisfaction stemming from the author's inadequacies; the disgust comes afterward, when he rereads his work. What he feels deeply, without ever articulating it, is the inadequacy of written language: on paper every sentence seems to be an impoverishment of what he imagines he conceives or feels, which is in fact only the sonorous—and imagined—richness of his eloquence. Upon rereading, he verifies his defects; it is as though, while working, he were somehow thinking: this instrument is not made for me; and later, avidly rereading his work in order to find traces of his talent, as though he had concluded: I am not made to play this instrument. Let us not imagine that he hated writing; on the contrary, he took pleasure in listening to the words bubbling up in his head; rather, his pleasure is continually spoiled by the necessity of *transcribing*. And he preserved, at the time, a secret animosity toward his own enterprise. Animosity, a malaise hidden beneath the exuberance of inspiration—this is how he first *lived* his relationship to literature.

There is another contradiction which, like the last one and for the same reasons, is by no means a confrontation of opposed principles but manifests itself as an objective ambiguity: his style *roars*; in other words, his sentences have persistent sonority. We have enumerated above the chief consequences of this *superaudibility*; but at the same time he is not unaware that his task as a writer is to favor the *visible* in order to compensate for the disappearance of sonority and its accompaniments in the way of gesture. There is more: the primacy of the phoneme is maintained on the sly, muted as it were, with all the immediate sociability it implies for Gustave—it is his rejected *public-being*—while the structure of the grapheme necessarily sends the young author back to a solitude he cannot assume—in effect, the solitude of dereality and not a *real* isolation. On this level we might say without exaggeration that the ambivalence of his enterprise is translated by what fascinates him (the vertigo of the soliloquy or of masturbation; a perpetual temptation to leave the "Rabelaisian laughter," his new public role, for the dismal and sordid comforts of sadness and to push his anomaly to the extreme in the imaginary), and what frightens him (just as onanism and sinking into a narcissistic bog can frighten a bourgeois child stuffed with prohibitions).

What further contributes to veil these antinomies is that the paterfamilias has scarcely more indulgence for men of letters than he does for actors. Certainly the profession of writer is not dishonorable, but it is nonetheless unworthy of a Flaubert. On this point Achille-Cléophas's thought was probably more complex: he admired Montaigne, I suppose, since he cites him in a letter to Gustave. And Voltaire. If by some supernatural premonition he had known that his younger son would later equal either of these great men, he might have softened. But he was only too certain of the contrary: his son didn't have much of a brain, he would never rise to the level of these moralists. The philosophical practitioner, who prided himself on writing well, as the applied elegances of his thesis demonstrate, judged both that literature is within everyone's reach (a good mind, cultivated and with a solid knowledge of its mother tongue, is always capable of dispatching a missive or spinning out an argument) and that one must have a powerful mind and keen intelligence, be a brilliant observer of human mores, to dare to be a specialist in it without seeming ridiculous. Gustave was perfectly informed on this point. His father was not unaware that he wrote and did not see any harm in it, provided the young man's studies did not suffer. He would undoubtedly have accepted the idea that this son, having become a physician, subprefect, prosecutor, or notary, might publish at his own expense a slim volume of verse written at idle moments, but for him it was inconceivable that anyone could devote his life to so futile an occupation. Thus the prohibition remained, and the child, who was conscious of it, felt clearly that by writing he remained on the level of the imaginary, that he was merely playing at being a writer; the ludic aspect of this activity deterred him from examining its contradictory nature. As he did not encounter the same inflexible denial to which his family had subjected his true vocation, Gustave felt neither the passion nor the sadomasochistic emotions that had earlier tormented him; he no longer dreamed of affirming himself against them through the "glory of the good-for-nothing." At first, in any case, he confined himself to living with literature without deciding whether he was made for it or whether, as he would soon say, Art is the most sublime and the most disappointing of illusions; nor was he much afraid that he would one day be forbidden from consecrating this union. In any case, if there is a prohibition, it will not have the character of an anathema; it will be possible to combat it or get around it (later we shall see Gustave pitted mercilessly against his father, the passive activity of the former against the voluntarist activism of the latter). Less threatened, this new occupation lacks the rending fragility of the earlier one; he is less tempted to cling to it in desperation. For these reasons he is in no hurry to throw his second challenge in the face of his family—"*I will be a writer*"—and to commit his whole future with a precipitous vow. He writes between parentheses, casually, without being much concerned with why he does it or with forcing his immediate intentions. Literature is a dreary and solitary game, he plays at it faute de mieux, without true pleasure but with the awareness that while he merely pretends to write, someone or something deep inside him takes it seriously—which gives him no joy but profound anxiety.

Here we have a child, then, who launched himself into a formidable enterprise to which he believed he was destined. It was dismissed, and he was forced to specialize in an activity that corresponded, according to him, to an inessential phase of the earlier one; he wrote the way he hammered the boards of his theater together: in order to go on stage. This means of a means becomes his unsurpassable end; the shock would scarcely have been greater if, for having hammered nails before playing *Poursôgnac*, he suddenly turned out to be a carpenter. The metamorphosis is more radical in any case, for he is sent from sociability to autism and discovers in himself, without knowing very clearly *who* is thinking them, a confused swarm of thoughts that horrify him. At the same time his essential problem seems to lose any chance of being resolved: he must have himself instituted by others as a center of derealization *in his body*. Finished: the body is rendered to its animal reality, the unreality remains in his soul. He is stripped of his comic voice, of his clownish gestures; he feels his frustration in the disgust of every word he writes. Discontented, anxious, he keeps thinking they made him drop his substance for his shadow. If this is how it is, one question arises: Why does he persist in writing? Why all that labor? All those passionately scribbled pages? If literature is an imposition, why does he do it with such avidity? Others, no doubt, would have dropped it, or else have gone mad. By what sublime or stupid heroism does Gustave persist in following a path he thinks will lead him nowhere? How, in the same work, can he clearly express his disgust as a writer and suddenly cry out: "Maybe you don't know what a pleasure it is to compose! To write, oh, to write is to seize the world, its prejudices, its virtues, and to sum them up in a book; it is to feel your thought being born, growing, living, standing on a pedestal, and remaining there for ever!"[21] This cannot be understood unless the second castration was the source of a progressive *conversion*. This we shall now examine.

21. End of *Un Parfum à sentir*.

Scripta Manent

In this case, the conversion seems to be a phase of personalization. It is no longer only a question of internalizing what is suffered or even of assuming it in the unity of stress; in Gustave's case it is also a matter of *going with* the impulse to make a brutal about-face, of gradually guiding it and, after a rotation of 180 degrees, of assuming his situation by surpassing it toward an *elsewhere* defined and posed by a new and spontaneous option, as if it were the chance of a lifetime.

But first, a cautionary word: for Gustave, literature was born of a thwarted vocation, and it would always bear that mark. I would recall, however, that the original vocation was no gift, in the ordinary sense of the word—it was neither plenitude nor capacity but a need. As an actor, Gustave was not *gifted;*[1] he acted so as to launch an appeal to being by exploiting the means at hand, that is, his very derealization. But can we say that he himself did not regret being discouraged? Properly guided, couldn't he have gone on to act before the public and known glory in the theater? I answer that the question is meaningless. Gustave is *not* Kean, and he knows it very well: the son of a respectable family, his first vocation was born *to be thwarted.* And if he had rebelled? If he had fled the paternal domain? Then he would not have been *that* Gustave for whom, as we know, all active revolt was forbidden. We can ask only one meaningful question: Having *been* an actor—in front of his comrades, his family, his peers—when he played his favorite *roles*—the Garçon, the Idiot, the good Giant, the Excessive, or Saint Polycarp—was he any good? Was he convincing? To find out we must examine the testimony of those who saw him. The testimony varies from one witness to another and, for some, from one moment to the next; occasionally he fascinated or disturbed. The Gon-

---

1. No one is.

courts were stupefied by the Idiot's carryings-on; his father took fright when he imitated the Journalist of Nevers. Sometimes he won people over—witness his influence over his schoolmates—but chiefly he was irritating. And then he was quite transparent: Jules and Edmond were quick to sense something forced and false in his game that shattered the illusion. Later, neither Laporte nor Lapierre believed in Saint Polycarp or the Giant: they played at being believers out of friendship, to please him. The main thing here is that he is destined to incarnate a *single* character—for all his avatars resemble each other—not entirely his own character but the *persona* he wants to appear in the eyes of others, which we will describe in the next chapter. Thus his first vocation seems scarcely more than the simplest and most immediate reaction to his derealization; and I mean that this, as well as his constituted passivity and his pithiatism, would have served him if he had gone into the theater. But aside from the fact that these determinations would not have been sufficient, each one of them is, above all, negative. For this reason the rebuffed actor in him could not thwart the budding writer, the way a congenial exuberance, an overflow of directed energy might have constantly obstructed or diverted his inspiration or his literary effort. There is nothing there: simply a void, a lack to fill, a nostalgia. The new solution contains in itself the rejected solution, it makes itself a negation and thereby has a better chance of approaching positivity. While it *subsists in* this surpassing which changes the very terms of the problem, the first vocation *coexists with* it, without institution or visa, as a fierce need to play roles publicly, which in a sense gives license to the writing to be more rigorous, less eloquent, since Gustave's improvisations allow him to desublimate with his voice.

Originally, then, literature seems to be a solution of replacement, at once urgent and doubtful. The problem remains the same: this child is unsure of everything. Perhaps he imagines he exists—how can he give the imaginary a consistency that approaches the real? Something has changed, however, in the givens of the situation: the castrating rejection has relegated Gustave to another sector of the unreal, that of images we improperly call "mental," which romanticism called the realm of the "dream." Until this time, obviously, he had already been dreaming, but without giving his dreams any particular status; caught between ecstasies[2] and histrionics,[3] the fleeting, fragmented images

2. Or stupors.
3. The entire epic performance, which attempts to make himself feel in extremity what he does not feel sufficiently on his own.

surfaced and slipped into oblivion at the mercy of an interior mono-logue (we shall return to this) which remained rather meager. In the beginning he doesn't dream of making this imagery the stuff of his art. He is an actor. On the contrary, he quite willingly leaves these written exercises to Ernest: "If you want, we'll write things together and I'll write plays and you will write your dreams and since there's a lady who comes to visit Papa and always tells us stupid things, I'll write those." The division of labor is clearly indicated: to me, dramatic art, to you, literature.[4]

It is striking that the dream—which must be taken here in the sense of poetic revery—does not at first seem to him worthy of being tran-scribed except to the extent that it is someone else's. Ernest undoubt-edly shared with him his future projects, his hopes, his regrets; per-haps he went so far as to invent gentle, melancholy stories in which he was always the main character. We know that he was a little older than Gustave, and ten is not too early to dream of tender passions, chivalrous love. Was the young Chevalier at this period more novel-istic, more "romantic," than Gustave? In 1831 Gustave already gives evidence of a rather extensive education, though an exclusively *classi-cal* one. May we suppose that his friend confided his youthful agita-tions to him? Probably. It is clear that the burlesque satire of shop-keepers in uniform that Ernest would write a little later under the name of *Soliloque d'un Garde national*—and give as a contribution to the tenth evening gathering of the journal *Art et Progrès*—does not evidence a strong propensity for poetic meditation. But although the character speaking in the first person is a ridiculous *composite* and not a lyric projection of the author, Ernest's *I* seems more structured, more affirmative than Gustave's (as it appears in *Le Voyage en enfer*), and more limited as well. This *I* is quite capable of abandoning itself to a directed oneirism without ever losing its vigilance. Moreover, it seems very likely that between 1839 and 1840 the future prosecutor

4. On the basis of his letters and his writings in that period, we can say that Gustave divides prose into five areas: *discourse*, ("Eloge à Corneille," "Discours politiques"), *his-tory* (in 1831 he presents his mother with a summary of the reign of Louis XIII), the *human document*, originally oral (the transcription of things overheard: the lady who says stupid things . . .), *drama*, and *dream*. To be sure, he also wrote poems (Epitaph on M.D.'s Dog . . . ," etc.), but these are in general circumstantial and certainly do not inspire the *Meditations poetiques*. The letter of 31 December 1831 tells us that of all the five, two are privileged in Flaubert's eyes: *drama*, which in its way includes the docu-ment and discourse since he regards it as the result of oral literature; and *dream*, which, on the contrary, comes directly from the heart—the words rise to the pen from the depths, without necessarily passing through the oral stage.

abandoned himself to the melancholies of bourgeois romanticism: he read Rousseau,[5] admired George Sand, experienced religious effusions,[6] sobbed noisily, shocked Gustave by sending him solemn, poetic epistles on friendship,[7] and, curiously, after an interval of ten years, returned the proposition Gustave had made him in 1831: "You tell me to tell you my dreams."[8] During this period, Gustave reproached him haughtily for the elegiac tone of his letters: "What was going on with you the day you wrote me? Don't you know yet that according to the poetics of the modern school (a poetics which has the advantage over others of not being one at all), all Beauty is made up of the tragic and the comic? The second part is missing in your letter."[9] We shall learn later, through a letter Gustave addresses to his mother in 1850, that "Chevalier too has been an artist—he carried a dagger and *dreamed*[10] dramatic schemes." "Like Anthony," specifies the *Préface aux Dernières Chansons*. In short, it is quite likely that Ernest moved from a sensuous, somber sadness to an ironclad seriousness—a perfect example of what Drieu calls the "dreamy bourgeoisie." The important thing is that Gustave, a clandestine dreamer, discovers the dream through the spoken confidences of another, as if the abandonment to the self, the bittersweet intimacy with the self, came to him from the outside, through speech—as if the light of otherness had revealed to him his own damp recesses and sordid promiscuity with himself. It had to be that way. His ego was not strongly enough structured to assume the anonymous speech that went on inside him in the words of others. The fact is that the child in 1831, while recognizing that the dream provides the material of literature, does not intend to cultivate his dreams or, more particularly, to set them down in writing, whether because he doesn't believe he has any, judges them unworthy of transcription, or holds this literary genre to be inferior. We might call this a dialogue between deaf people, between Gustave the extravert, solely concerned with discovering "the world, its prejudices and virtues," and Ernest the introvert, attentive only to the movements of his heart. We know that this appearance doesn't bear examination; Ernest will adapt himself quite well to the realities of his life, and Gustave's extraversion is merely the imperialism of a triumphant

5. *Correspondance* 1:35. The influence of "the Savoyard vicar" is evident.
6. 15 April 1839.
7. 19 January 1840.
8. 14 January 1841.
9. 19 January 1840.
10. My italics.

introversion. Nonetheless, in the 1830s the younger son of the Flauberts wanted to conquer objectivity, through the theater, and left it to his friend to account for his soul, in other words, his subjectivity.

Nevertheless, after the castrating rejection and his beginning school, Gustave, who had been literally *silenced,* found himself condemned in spite of himself to the inner life, that is, to derealization, which could be externalized neither by gestures nor by voice. The family refused to allow his vocation, and, as we know, he submitted to its decision resentfully: within *himself as well,* his derealized universe no longer demanded expression by noisy outpourings; between interiority and externalization the flow was interrupted. As for his comrades, he imagined they were spying on him; if stupors or ecstasies should take him by surprise in class and they were to find out, they would burst out laughing—paternal derision pursued him even to the benches of this old place. The inversion was complete: his futile desire to realize his unreality pushed him to communicate what he resented and, in direct consequence, *to resent in order to communicate.* Universal ostracism, now internalized as a major prohibition, forces him to consider the movements of his heart or his mind as uncommunicable. In fact this is merely a hypothetical imperative: if you don't want people to laugh at you . . . But the pride and the radicalism of this ulcerated soul soon transform it into a categorical imperative—we know the story, how the victim wants to push his cruel obedience to the limit in order to become his executioners' executioner. Gustave goes still further and through resentment transforms the prohibition into an impossibility; what he resents is unspeakable *in principle*—men cannot communicate among themselves. This is affirming the internal imaginary for itself, for Gustave, although turned in on himself, nonetheless remains derealized. But at the same time, by an intentional process of self-defense, it is valorizing the imaginary as nonreal and nonbeing against the vanquishing enemy. For the little boy, to withdraw into the self does not mean to find his truth against the universal lie, to put an end to doubt by the affirmation of a *Cogito;* rather, it is to flee the real that withholds itself, to flee the four walls of his prison by attributing value only to the phantasmagoria that haunts him to the extent that it is not susceptible to being transmitted by expression. Until now, the imaginary child has been seeking to give substance to his imaginations of objectivity by socializing them; after his resounding failure, he reverses his movement, he gives himself imaginary affections, or else satisfies his desires through images *in order to assume his exile,* in order not to be like the others, to be no longer completely real, to escape the reality enclosing him. This is his way of avenging his anomaly and of transforming it into a mystery. Nonreality terrified him; now he is delighted to become unreal, invisible, inaudible, in the midst of the "fools" who surround him. But since his private games are by definition *unvoiced*, and he has cut the tie that binds them to his act, the obvious result is a modification of their structure. The image— what I call elsewhere the imaging consciousness—is no longer the anticipation of the role or its product, it is no longer related to the public *game*. And if the analogue surpassed toward . . . still exists—as it does in everyone—in the movements of the human body, these become imperceptible, or barely outlined, and, what is more, they rarely engage the whole body but only certain organs: the eyeballs, the extremities, the vocal chords. There, precisely, is the analogue of images called "mental." But it should be observed that the imaging intention is reversed: it was centrifugal, offering *to others* a scene with Gustave on the inside. It becomes centripetal. Not that it does not aspire to an absent or nonexistent *exterior*. But it aspires to it *in order to engulf* the imaginary child, to build a fortress around him, to surround this fictive ego with fictive presences homogeneous to him. We might say that intentionality is seen here to be double: the imaginary object having lost its social dimension (and at the same time *rejecting* it) is posed in its objectivity only in order to confirm the derealized ego in its fictive subjectivity. This is precisely what we call autism, that affinity of the silent phantasm and of all phantasmagoria with the phantasmatic witness found at the center of the show, so that by reciprocal expedience the images confirm their imaginary producer *in his unreal being*, just as he confirms them in theirs. In this circuit, reality as the negation of the unreal is totally discarded, and the *appearance of being* comes to the phantasmagoria from the fact that its witness exists only in appearance and consequently cannot confront them with his real being at the very moment he is producing them.[11] Let us say, to be concise, that the question of being *is no longer posed* to the extent that the child is resolved to consider only the *being of appearance* in this universe of which he is the center. He nonetheless suffers from a very

11. To imagine is at once to produce an imaginary object and to become imaginary; I did not stress this adequately in *L'Imaginaire*. But if the person who produces an imaging consciousness has not had difficulty adapting himself to the real, he retains the nonthetic consciousness of making himself unreal in an unreal universe. The self-conscious reality of this nonsituational consciousness suffices to reduce its productions to their true ontological status of pure appearance. In the case of a thought even slightly tainted with autism, this nonthetic consciousness remains, but its admonition is not heeded; the reasons for this deliberate deafness are different in different cases. In Gus-

real malaise, and it is only by constant tension that he is able to maintain the fiction against an omnipresent and protean reality. Let him *imagine himself* in India, a fabulous rajah, an emperor of ancient Rome, or a barbarian horseman galloping after Attila, or simply the beloved of an exotic lady; he needs to shore up this evanescent imagery with solid, material elements through which he produces the imagery and which are like the roots and trunk of this riotous and fragile blossoming, now serving as analogue, now inciting him by their ambiguity to go beyond them toward the visual or auditory image, and at times, when everything falters, supporting the edifice with their consistency as things. We have understood that for him these supports can be only the *words of others* or, if you like, language *as other* which others have placed in him, the heavy, learned vocables that present their signification to the Other and turn toward Gustave their opaque materiality. Yet we must understand that the reversal now extends itself to the Word. An imaginary actor, the child imagined—before the public performances—that his voice would make itself heard by the audience; he took their ears in order to listen to himself, he borrowed their eyes to see himself—in short, imagination was governed by passive activity. Now the *visual* is suffered as well. Gustave is in India, he no longer makes himself a spectacle; it is the people, the temples, the mountains that *offer themselves to his eyes*; he takes them in, he delights in them. And similarly, words are introverted: he does not summon them as *said* and aimed toward the other but as heard and seen by himself, as *suffered occupants*. In the *vocable-pathos* there is a contraction of the audiovisual dyad, and the two aspects interpenetrate; indeed, in the little actor's audiovisual dyad, the separation chiefly had to do with the *audible* being aimed at the other as the result of an activity, while the *visible* aspect of the word was only the *suffered means* of future declaration. Since the contact points are severed, the flow of lived experience conveys words as they have been *received*, beautiful and impenetrable, *speaking by themselves* as they have been read by the child or pronounced in his hearing: memory reconstitutes both dimensions in an indissoluble unity—a true "sight-

---

tave, we know, it is explained by the "impact" of the Other, who has deterred him from early childhood from heeding the intimate and permanent evidence of his ipseity. In other words, constantly *warned* of the unreality of his dream, he puts this warning in parentheses because the inferred characteristic of his being-for-itself is devalorization and being-in-defiance-of-self. Thus, paradoxically, it is the Other's suffered primacy that inclines the child to go in search once again of the fables of autism, that is, of a solitude that tends to become extreme.

sound." The ear sees, the eye listens: this is the "mental" structure of the suffered word, which will be broken only at the moment of praxis when Gustave must write or speak.[12]

It is only proper to let Gustave speak for himself. He explains himself perfectly on the question of these mental exercises in *Novembre:* "At school," he tells us, "I dreamed of passions, I would have liked to have them all."[13] The autistic nature of these ruminations is undeniably confirmed by the following lines: "No one has ever known anything about what follows, those who saw me every day no more than anyone else; they were connected to me like the bed I sleep on, which knows nothing of my dreams."[14] This *reifying* image says a good deal about Gustave's attitude toward the people around him; it will be noted that he compares his waking dreams to those he has in his sleep: to daydream is to be half asleep. Further on, he insists on the paralysis that shackles him in these moments of directed oneirism: "I was a dormant chaos of a thousand fecund springs that did not know how to manifest themselves or what to do . . . In the variousness of my being I was like a vast Indian forest . . . perfumes and poisons, tigers, elephants . . . mysterious, misshapen gods hidden in the crevices of caves . . . a great river . . . an island of flowers . . . corpses discolored by pestilence. I loved life, nonetheless, but expansive, radiant, radiating life, I loved it in the furious gallop of the chargers . . . and in the midst of everything *I remained immobile; amid all the action that I saw, that I even prompted, I remained inactive, as inert as a statue surrounded by a swarm of flies buzzing in its ears and running over its marble surface.*"[15] Thus the wildest phantasmagoria has as its indispensable correlative the most absolute immobility: he abandons himself to his constituted passivity. Deaf, mute, blind, and firmly bound, he severs contact with the exterior world and lets himself slide into a solipsistic intimacy with his life, his bodily warmth, his flesh. Moreover, he presents night as the achievement of this retreat: "And when evening came, when we were all lying in our white beds with our white curtains, and the *maître d'études* alone walked up and down the dor-

---

12. Let us not imagine that audiovisual teaching reconstitutes this unity of interpenetration *in perception.* To hear a word while seeing it is, of course, to be informed simultaneously of its two inseparable aspects. But the rational synthesis that operates here has nothing to do with the syncretism of memory. Rather, it ought to be compared with the condensations of memory and dream that frequently offer us several persons in one.

13. Edition Charpentier, p. 311.

14. Ibid.

15. Ibid., p. 327. My italics.

mitory, I curled up even more inside myself, delightedly hiding in my breast that bird beating its wings, feeling its warmth! I was always a long time getting to sleep, I listened to the hours toll; the longer they were, the happier I was."[16] Looking at these passages, we are forced to acknowledge that Gustave does not intend to describe to us the tame, continually interrupted reveries of a "well-adjusted" adolescent; rather, he depicts an almost neurotic state, intentional, certainly, but outstripping his clear intention and yet suffered to the same degree that it is produced. When he emerges from this state, moreover, his dumb bewilderment is described in the *Mémoires:* it seems as though he has been pulled out of a deep sleep—he doesn't know where or who he is. For when he "curls up inside himself," meaning inside his internalized dereality, he executes in resentment the sentence others have passed on him; the *bed,* which is at the center of all these descriptions, is the symbol both of this escape through self-hypnosis and, curiously, of his hatred for the people around him. Not only does it represent family and schoolmates abruptly transformed into a pallet, but at the same time the young boy, in his oneiric moments, is making a doormat of those closest to him and stepping on them: human consciousness is dream; on those who do not dream, Gustave confers the shadowy opacity of inorganic matter. We can only applaud this conjuring trick, the prelude to a still more radical reversal of which we shall have to take account in the third volume of this work. What Gustave is fleeing, in fact, is the derealizing gaze of others—of *an* other, especially—in short, an acute consciousness that makes the sovereign decision as to what is real and what is not. Scarcely settled into his soliloquy, however, he transforms this lucidity in imagination into obtuse unconsciousness and the real into accumulated torpor—and behold, the philosophical practitioner is disarmed. Not without exhausting tension: the child is *invaded* by the imaginary, and yet it is too much, even with all his efforts, to maintain himself unrealized: "Not wearing out existence, existence wore me out, my dreams tired me more than great labors."[17] What is involved is both abandonment to passivity and a mental exercise: for the imaginary to triumph, he must preserve himself in a state of *permanent distraction* in relation to reality. And above all he must surpass by assuming his dereality in order to transform it into *unrealization.* The *self* that he rejoins when he "curls up inside himself" is indeed, as Gustave is aware, a pure image: "I imagined I was great, I imagined myself as a

16. Ibid., p. 313.
17. Ibid., p. 326.

supreme incarnation whose revelation would dazzle the world, and its discords were the very life of God that I bore in my entrails." Here we have the ego he so often encounters: a supreme incarnation of the God who incarnates it, both of these august characters being attainable only by an effort of unrealization. When he grows weary, when the thread breaks, he falls back into distracted mediocrity: "I am emptier, hollower, sadder than a battered, empty barrel";[18] and after a pantheistic ecstasy: "Quickly I remembered that I was living, I came back to myself, I got myself going again, feeling the curse take hold of me once more, feeling that I was reentering humanity; life returned to me, as it does to frozen limbs, in the feeling of suffering."[19] In this fine text, Gustave is explicit: to rediscover life is to rediscover the curse of Adam, to reenter his human envelope. The boy hesitates between two interpretations of this nauseating return. The first, which is intolerable, is closer to the truth: he falls back into his "anomaly"—which is nothing more than the mass of his personal deficiencies—into his subhumanity. In this case the dream is an evasion and a compensation: he flees from his interiority by unrealizing himself as a god incarnate. The other interpretation is the whispering of pride: these sad awakenings make him fall back *into humanity.* Had he left it behind? Yes, because he is master of the Imaginary. Here we must assume a reversal of the ordinary scale of values: the child will be a superman, he will tear himself away from the species if he radically devalues the reality others deny him and if, assuming his dereality as the condition of his greatness, he makes the unreal the supreme value. Such is one of the aspects of the progressive conversion which, from this point of view, will not be completed until the winter of 1844; we shall return to this. But from the time he entered school, his pride was in feeling *other:* "I saw other people live, but with a life other than mine: some believed, others denied, others doubted, still others did not bother about any of that and went about their business, selling their wares, writing their books, or preaching from their pulpits."[20] In short, men are defined by their practical contact with the real: their inexcusable fault is in not *challenging* it. In this curious passage, Gustave speaks in the same breath of the "shopkeepers" for whom he has such contempt and writers, his future colleagues, dogmatists—believers or atheists—and doubters (whereas in his *Mémoires* he spoke of pushing skepticism to the point of despair). He envisages everything from the

18. Ibid., p. 323.
19. Ibid., p. 338.
20. Ibid., p. 329.

point of view of the imaginary: the doubters and the devout, atheists and believers, confront each other on the question of the *reality* of the Almighty. At least they share this great preoccupation with the real—no Christian will answer the arguments of the libertine with the statement, "What does it matter to me whether He exists or not since I imagine Him," or, better yet, by restating the ontological proof: "Since I have inside me the idea of a perfect being and since the Imaginary is more perfect than reality, the essence of that Being implies that he exists only in my imagination." And if the writer of books resembles the shopkeeper, it is in the measure to which he exercises a real activity by communicating to real readers true (or so they are thought to be) ideas about reality. In his adolescence, Gustave is "antiprose" and "antitruth." He judges himself to be a poet, and poetry, as we now know, he sees as a fabulous opera being performed in his head, which he often thinks he could not write down without degrading it. In this period, radicalizing his option, he tells himself that it is better to dream of writing a sublime poem than to attempt to write it—which betrays the uncertainties and repugnances of the disappointed actor faced with literature. What matters to us here is that after the castrating rejection, Gustave persists in unrealizing himself as a character. But—and this is another aspect of the conversion—this fictional character is not conceived as a *role to play;* it must no longer be externalized for others but internalized against them as the guiding scheme of his imagery. In other words, Gustave must give himself in imagination the heroic and sublime subjectivity of his fictive ego—fictive to the extent that it is noncommunicable.

Nothing demonstrates this better than the study of the contents of his fabulations. Since the character is by definition a superman and he is the one dreaming, his dreams must obviously in themselves manifest this superhuman grandeur; and since Gustave has long felt that a creature's value is measured by the abundance of his unsatisfied demands, the dreams of his imaginary ego will present themselves as the fictive fulfillments of his infinite desires. But the logical consequence is that these infinite desires will themselves be imaginary. An appearance of appetite receives an appearance of satisfaction: what is the real basis for this game of illusions? The desire for these desires. On this point Gustave is perfectly lucid: "I dreamed of passions, I would have liked to have them all." "I was immediately gripped by the desire to love, I wished for love with infinite greed, I dreamed of its torments."[21] "In his thoughts" he takes the first woman to come

21. Ibid., p. 316.

along—provided she is beautiful—and wants to be persuaded that he is smitten: "But I felt that I was forcing myself to love, that I was merely playing a role that didn't fool my heart at all . . . I regretted loves I had not had, and then I dreamed of others that I would have liked to fill my soul with."[22] He recognizes that "the aim in which these vague desires converged . . . was, I believe, the need for a new feeling and as an aspiration toward something higher whose summit I could not see." At bottom it is a "desire without object"[23]: "I vaguely coveted something splendid that I could not have formulated by any word or given precise form in my thoughts, but for which I nonetheless had an incessant, positive desire."[24] This uncertain aspiration— more negative than positive, despite what he says—is the desire for All, therefore the desire for nothing, and is in truth only the wish to break the monotony of a dull and utterly regulated existence, to fill the infinite inner lacuna with some kind of infinite plenitude. It is this desire, however, which in its *reality* will serve as analogue to the imaginary passions of the "incarnation." See how he describes his frenzies of imagination: "Sometimes, exhausted, devoured by limit-less passions, filled with the ardent lava that flowed from my soul, loving nameless things with a furious love, regretting magnificent dreams, tempted by all the sensual pleasures of thought, breathing in all poetries, all harmonies, and crushed by the weight of my heart and my pride, I fell into an abyss of sorrows . . . I no longer saw any-thing, felt anything, I was drunk, I was mad, I imagined my own greatness." Let us read carefully: can this furious love of nameless things be real? It is the object that defines love. The fury here is only the savage intensity of an empty heart that wants to invent passion. As for the magnificent dreams, why doesn't he dream them again in-stead of regretting them? Regret of a dream, for Gustave, is merely the dream of a regret. The sensual pleasures of thought, likewise, only tempt him, but not to the point of trying to exercise his understand-ing. As we know, affirmation and negation are denied him; so what he feels is a vague longing to exercise some kind of judgment—an ac-tivity he is aware of though he has never experienced it and which, in his eyes, represents the intellectual powers of the other. Does he set so much store by these things, then, analyzing, deducing, drawing *conclusions?* No; but the character, the one who contains within him the All in the form of desire, seeks to retotalize the cosmos through a

22. Ibid.
23. Ibid., p. 326.
24. Ibid., p. 311.

synthetic flash of intuition; rather, he retotalizes it constantly through meditation, that empty imitation of thought: "And I was at the top of Mount Atlas, and from there I contemplated the world and its glitter and its mud, its virtue and its pride." Such is our imaginary Gustave: perched on a summit, head hollow, he pretends to contemplate the universe in order to taste the joys of the intellect in the midst of the unreal. At this moment, his heart is bursting: he is caught up in his role, inhabited by such great thoughts, such magnificent desires, even if mere appearances, that he must surely be a giant himself. "Oh, how I would have loved if I had loved!" he cries, naively.[25] But here is the counterpart: "I have loved nothing and I would so much have liked to love . . . I was neither pure enough nor strong enough."[26] He experiences "indifference toward the most enticing [things] and disdain for the most beautiful."[27] He admits: "I saw nothing that was worth even the trouble of a desire."[28] And: "Those passions I wanted to have, I studied in books."[29] In other words, the real is never desirable. This same child, panting with love for an infinite, invisible, nonexistent object, is cold and dry when he comes in contact with individual beings, specific and living. Is this not the deepest meaning of *Rêve d'enfer?* Almaroës, the Robot, desires nothing. It is not for lack of trying: "I attempted to imitate men, to have their passions, their interests, to act as they did, but it was in vain," says the Iron Duke. He gives two reasons for this, which are mutually exclusive: the first is that the things of this "small, miserable" world hold no attraction for creation's latest model: "Our poor pleasures, our paltry poetry, our incense, all the earth with its joys and its delights, what did all this have to do with him, who had something angelic about him?" This explanation *by excess* is found again in *Novembre:* the cosmic child does not love because nothing of what *exists* is worth the trouble of loving. The explanation *by default* is found in both works as well: Almaroës is attached to nothing because he has no soul, in other words, because of the coldness of his heart. And this is repeated, in a whisper by the hero of *Novembre:* "I am empty and hollow." Or again: "I lived in a higher atmosphere where my heart was filled with pure air, *where I shouted with triumph to enliven my solitude.*"[30] These shouts of triumph cast out into

25. Ibid., p. 327.
26. Ibid., p. 323–324.
27. Ibid., p. 321.
28. Ibid.
29. Ibid., p. 319.
30. Ibid., p. 321.

the void to lessen his boredom are the imaginary flashes of great desire and mad love. When the games of his imagination are over, Gustave—he dates this break around his sixteenth year—will still preserve that sublime and sacred image of himself, the Personage, which Flaubert pride would support. But he recognizes that it is a container without contents: "I had made myself a temple to contain something divine, the temple remained empty."

The adolescent makes no choice between the two interpretations of his generalized anorexia. But knowing that unhappiness, humiliation, and resentment uprooted certain desires very early, we are forced to accept the second interpretation. For Gustave, debaucheries of the imagination are doubly compensatory: they compensate for his burning failures by inventing a sublime ego, for his bored indifference to everything by inventing the grandiose desire for all, and by affecting all passions at the same time without feeling any.

He is a prisoner who hates his prison and escapes it each day by jumping through time to land on the threshold of his twentieth year. With all the seriousness of the Flauberts, he generally refuses to pretend that he is not at school; it seems preferable to tell himself that he has already graduated. This is a tacit acceptance to expiate his suffering to the very limits: he must do it, mustn't he, and when you are the son of a celebrated surgeon, you must pass the baccalaureat, *noblesse oblige*. So he is twenty years old, he is starting out in life, leaving Rouen and his family behind. On this premise the young dreamer strains to compensate for his vexations as an unloved child by wallowing in foolish indulgences: "I invented stories for myself, I built palaces, I lived in them like an emperor, I dug out all the diamond mines and threw the diamonds in torrents on the road I had to travel."[31] He is "loved with a devouring and fearsome love, the love of a princess, of an actress, that fills one with pride and makes one *the equal of the rich and powerful*."[32] In this last scenario, moreover, the compensation is manifest. The unloved child avenges himself for his family's indifference by being adored by a great lady, a famous actress or a princess. It is always the same plan for ennoblement: a royal woman raises him to her, makes him the equal of the rich and powerful; glory does not come to crown his efforts this time, he receives it through an intermediary. He changes his skin, if the occasion presents itself, or his sex. Here he is as emperor: "for absolute power, for the number of slaves, for armies wild with enthusiasm." Here he is as a woman: "to

31. Ibid., p. 313.
32. Ibid., p. 315. My italics.

be able to admire myself, naked . . . and see my image reflected in the streams." As king of India he mounts a white elephant; as Caesar he attends ancient festivals; as a member of the triumvirate he flees in Cleopatra's galley. What does not change from one narrative to the other is his passivity; he is never an *agent* in his dreams: he *receives.* He is the object of adulation, idolatry, his subjects obey him, his armies are fanatically devoted. As for women, when his temperament is awakened, they cover him with kisses and he abandons himself, swooning, to their arms. In any case, in whatever form he imagines himself he is the passive center of a fabulous and submissive universe that is made only for him. And this passivity of the hero surfeited with honors and tender gratifications merely reflects the passivity of the dreamer abandoned to his dream. These compensatory *gifts* obviously exist to introduce us into the universe of dark desires and their oneiric gratifications. There are other dreams that the "broad river" brings with it, "corpses turned green by pestilence," but we will grasp their meaning only if we first investigate Flaubert's technique of unrealization, for his passive activity demands mental exercises and workable instruments. He is open about it in *Novembre:* "I hurried to do my homework so that I could give myself over at leisure to these precious thoughts. Indeed, I promised myself in advance that I would do so, thinking of it as a concrete pleasure, and began to force myself to dream, like a poet desiring to create something and prompting his own inspiration. I entered into my thought as deeply as possible, examined its every aspect, I went to the end, I came back and began again; soon it was an unrestrained plunge of the imagination, a prodigious leap beyond the real, I made up adventures, I invented stories for myself . . ."[33]

This text is very important: it shows that Gustave achieved the unrealizing ecstasy only by a sort of self-hypnosis. He "forced himself" to concentrate on an object of meditation; the "prodigious" leap beyond the real will have taken place only afterward. In other words, there must first be something for Gustave to fasten his attention on, but the young boy in this phase of ascesis does not yet consider that he has gone entirely outside reality; it is at the end of this long pithiatic meditation that he abandons himself to his provoked and suffered state as imaginary creature. We have yet to discover *on what* he fixes his inner gaze, what kind of object revolving "in his head" produces his self-hypnosis.

33. Ibid., p. 313.

In the *Mémoires d'un fou* he seems to imply that he entered directly into the universe of palpable images: he thought, he tells us, about "the most sublime thing a child's imagination can dream of."[34] He adds: "I *saw* the Orient and its vast sands . . . I *smelled* the perfume of those tepid seas of the Midi . . . some brown-skinned woman with an ardent gaze took me in her arms and *spoke to me* in the tongue of the *Houris*." A festival of the senses, then: he sees, he hears, he smells; without any mediation he conjures up visions that are barely weakened perceptions. To tell the truth, the passage is hardly convincing. First of all, Gustave's proposal is something different: he is not simply describing his practices but comparing his "sublime imagination" to the narrow realism of his fellow students. And then, this is already a "scrap" of literature, for his visions are written and generalized. What makes his confidences suspect is not only that they do not mesh with what must certainly be called the *essential poverty* of the image, but that they replace sensation, continually escaping anyone who wants to reproduce them, with a visual organization Gustave delights in, where words play the role of analogue to imagined objects. And what he neglects to say in the *Mémoires* he has no difficulty telling us in *Novembre:* the mediators between the derealized child and the unreal world into which he is transported by his own unrealization *are words*.

In the first place, in the text cited above he emphasizes the narrative structure of his oneirism: I made up adventures, I invented stories for myself. No longer does he invent naked sensations, or produce totally new perceptions for the gratuitous and esthetically pure pleasure of contemplation: Gustave now recognizes that he constructs "adventures" with the intention of giving himself in the unreal world the benefits—riches, power, love—that he was denied in daily life. And certainly he does not write: "I told myself stories," no doubt to avoid the pejorative nuance of this locution. But it is evident that such a structuring of the imaginary cannot even be attempted without the good offices of discourse.

He pushes sincerity much further, for it is from his own mouth that we learn the incantatory role of words in his enterprise:

> Certain words dazzled me, the word *woman* and especially *mistress;* I searched for the explanation of the former in books, in engravings, in paintings in which I wanted to tear off the carefully draped cloth and uncover something . . . As for *mistress*, to me this was a satanic being, the magic of the noun alone threw me

34. *Mémoires d'un fou*. Charpentier, pp. 90–91. My italics.

into prolonged ecstasies . . . I had so often read the word love in the poets and so often repeated it to myself just for its sweetness, that for every star that shone in a blue sky on a gentle night . . . I would say to myself: "I love, oh, I love!" and it made me happy, proud, already prepared for the most exquisite devotions . . . For me human life revolved around two or three ideas, two or three words; and all the rest turned around them like satellites around their star . . . tales of love existed in my head side by side with beautiful revolutions, beautiful passions face to face with great crimes . . . I dreamed of the suffering of poets, I wept with their most beautiful tears; pages transported me, made me as wild as the pythoness, my spirit was ravaged with pleasure, I recited those pages of poetry to myself as I walked by the sea, head lowered, walking in the grass, repeating them to myself in the most amorous and tender voice . . . It is beautiful to live this way ("by repeating stanzas of love poetry") in eternal beauty, to assume the air of kings, to have passions in their most elevated expression, to love the loves that genius has rendered immortal . . . From this time there was one word that seemed to me the most beautiful of all: adultery. An exquisite sweetness hovers over it. It is fragrant with a strange magic; all the stories we tell, all the books we read, all the gestures we make say it and speak of it eternally to the heart of a young man; he drinks of it joyfully, he finds in it a supreme poetry mingled with malediction and lust.[35]

Nothing could be clearer: the mediating object is the word. He meditates on the word, he is fascinated by the word, it is the word whose "every aspect" he examines and which, after holding him in its spell, will be the springboard for imagination. We can apply to Gustave at this period what would later be said of Gottfried Benn: (for him) . . . "drunkenness and the dream are concentrated in certain privileged sounds which act on the deepest levels of the self just like hallucinogens." And he might have written these lines of Benn's and laid claim to them for himself: "I wrote [in a story] 'then the olive tree came to him,' not: then he stood before the olive tree, not: then his eyes fell upon an olive tree, but: then it came to him, the disappearance of the article being still better. Therefore, 'olive tree' came to him, and the structure in question provoked a torrential irruption which recaptured the silver of the fruit, the light rustle of their grove, their harvest, and the festival of olive pressing."[36] Except that the verbal "structure" does not at first seem for Gustave to *recover* sensual

---

35. *Novembre*, p. 311, 313, 314, 317, 319, 340.
36. Jacques Bouveresse, "Gottfried Benn," in *Critique*, August–September 1969.

significations but rather to represent them; these significations are at once *within the structure,* indistinct givens, and outside it, aimed at through the material. For Gustave, the word seems to be literally a hallucinogen, but not by acting on the deepest levels of lived experience; on the contrary, it is the deep forces that raise it in order to be resumed by it and surpassed toward the object. Here the word has a double function: on the one hand, it arrests and mirrors back real or pretended passions, which it engulfs as though it were their flesh-and-blood object; on the other hand, it offers itself as the outstretched finger pointing to the horizon, like a signal orienting and defining a quest. See how Gustave uses it: the term *mistress,* for example, possesses no conceptual signification, primarily because the word is a mutant and retains a double meaning. When he read Corneille, when he wrote *L'Amant avare* ("he does not want to give a gift to his mistress"), the name read or penned designated—as in the seventeenth century—the beloved woman and neither implied nor excluded sexual relations between the woman and her lover. At this point it often served as a synonym for fiancée. But from the middle of the eighteenth century, without entirely losing its first meaning, it was joined to another, which soon became dominant: a man's "mistress" gave herself to him outside of marriage. Gustave learned the second meaning without forgetting the first, and no doubt at an age when he was rather far from having a clear picture of the "work of the flesh"; for he tells us in the same paragraph that he still did not know how women were made. For these motives, the word, while closing around these two accepted and intermingled meanings, invited pursuit, referred to a mystery beyond what Gustave could conceive, to a beyond of kisses and caresses. Yet the word takes on a very strong emotional coloring as a consequence of bourgeois puritanism and the religious injunction against illegitimate relations. "Mistress" thus becomes for the child a synonym for a cursed woman. In other words, he accepts the familial taboo: forbidden loves, lost and venal creatures who destroy households, he takes all that at face value. With this reservation, however, that the femme fatale, enemy of all husbands and wives, does not altogether mask the platonic love object, the radiant fiancée of former times. Even in his worst confusions, then, "mistress" preserves the purity of a sword of Toledo or a Malayan dagger. It is naked evil in its satanic splendor. And the child, full of secret bitterness, loves to spill tears for the evil that is in her. A typically Flaubertian reaction: he begins by obedience to the bourgeois norms—*he* is certainly not going to break any swords defending women who lead irregular lives;

263

they are she-devils, set on dishonoring the respectable family man. After which, precisely for the crimes imputed to "mistresses," he falls in love with them. This word—like the word adultery—takes on for him a poignant charm, "an exquisite sweetness hovers over it, it is fragrant with a strange magic." Everything is turned around. Venal? Yes, but what grand and terrible demands: "It was for their mistresses that kings sacked and won provinces; for them . . . they fashioned gold, chiseled marble, moved the world." The hyperbolic Gustave pushes the bourgeois condemnation to the limit: these terrible ghouls are the demons of useless expense, they consume in order to lead the whole world into the abyss of the unbelievable dominion they have over the powerful. *Mistress, luxury,* and *gold* attract each other and form a dazzling constellation. In fact, it was from his first years in school that the child discovered these "magic" words. And eight or nine years later, the young author of *Novembre* claims them for his purposes with all the themes associated with them when he declares, this time in the present, like a universal maxim and at the same time like a confession: "One who is not sufficiently wellborn not to want a mistress because he could not cover her with diamonds and house her in a palace . . . guards against loving like a weakness." In his twelfth year he has no idea of such proud resignation; besides, it is a dream; so he is allowed to dream of mistresses whom he showers with his largess; he gives himself the most fabulous riches for the joy of uselessly squandering his wealth; all the gold of his father the rajah will be spent, he will make his subjects sweat blood; what pleasure he will have in squeezing his people like lemons to satisfy the caprices of his favorite. As for the cursed woman, indifferent and cruel, she will live "on a throne, far from the crowd for whom she is an *execration* and an *idol*." [37] The cursed son's sweet revenge: the infamous crowd that caused him so much suffering cannot help worshiping the very favorite it execrates; the wicked boy gives himself the exquisite pleasure of imagining Evil revealing itself with impudence, its demonic beauty forcing those it crushes to venerate it. Add to this the third determination of the word, which easily extends through the other two: a mistress has slaves over whom she exercises the right of life and death. And this is how the courtly lovers of the Pleiade are to be understood: their mistresses are cruel, making them pine away, giving them barbarous orders. Flaubert's masochism is satisfied here as much as his passivity: he will obey, feminine hands kneading his flesh will chain him to the chariot of a

37. *Novembre*, p. 314. My italics.

"dame sans merci" who will drive him straight to his ruin. We have come full circle: raised above other men by the favor of a goddess, he will use his power to ruin them and at the same time ruin himself, throw himself at the feet of the triumphant she-devil. What pleasures he promises himself!

But if the word resonating in his head or vaguely pronounced functions as a hallucinogen, why does Gustave need to put it through his pen, to write it down on paper? The answer is that he wants to *materialize* it and at the same time push to the end the process of *imaginarization*. The words he repeats in his head, which no one hears too clearly, resemble images, in a sense, to furnish the imagining consciousness with good analogues. Fugitive, inaudible, they glide away; despite their fascinating *otherness* they seem to belong to lived experience in its pure subjectivity. Even when little Flaubert pronounces them aloud in solitude, they are still too much *his* to impose themselves on his oneirism and sustain it to the end, for they exist in their sonorous actuality only for the time that *his* voice is declaiming them. *Scripta manent.* Certainly *his* hand traces the graphemes, but they survive the movement of his fingers, become isolated, self-sufficient, and when the ink has dried they take on an independent, objective existence. Indeed, this cannot happen, even when there is subvocalization, without the visual component's becoming dominant, which immediately implies distancing and perspective. But in the case at hand, visualization clearly appears as an enrichment: what was inside me, a mute, shapeless vibration, is perceived outside me as a beautiful, discrete object, splendidly material and real, full of dreams yet without losing its mute, sonorous presence in my head. Completely other, irreducible, and always full. Gustave writes, at this moment of his life, to push *verbal satisfaction* to its extreme.

In order to understand what this must mean it would suffice to open at random the first volumes of his correspondence—examples abound. But I prefer, by skipping ahead a few years, to give the most typical examples, which are found in *Novembre:* "Oh! to feel bent on the backs of camels, in front of you a red sky, brown sands, the shimmering horizon stretching into the distance . . . Oh, India, India above all! White mountains filled with pagodas and idols . . . If only I could perish while rounding the Cape, die of cholera in Calcutta, of the plague in Constantinople! If only I were a muleteer in Andalusia! And trotting all day in the gorges of the Sierras see the Guadalquivir . . . running . . ." I cite five lines—there are five hundred. We see the process at work: the sentence is only optative, but the words are so rich that they fulfill the wish (unreally) while claiming only to express it. A desire is exposed by fashioning real material and is unreally gratified by this same material. India! The Cape! Calcutta! Constantinople! Andalusia! Guadalquivir! The visual beauty of these words serves as analogue to the beauty of the towns and sites they designate; rather, they gather up that beauty and totalize it unreally in their simple *physiognomy*. I did not yet know the Dalmatian coast when I learned to my great disappointment that the beautiful and proud Ragusa (pride, beauty that were suggested by the name) would from now on be called Dubrovnik. This was treason, sleight of hand; vanished from the universe was not only a registered trademark but an entire city, white and shining, that I would never see.[38] And what would India have been for Gustave if it were not called India? Let us reread the text cited above; we see that it conjures up false desires in order to set up the word which, visibly unrealized, will gratify other desires unreally without making them manifest. "To die of the plague in Constantinople, of cholera in Calcutta"—this is the type of false desire obviously modeled on the popular slogan "To see Naples and die!" This wish, however, contains some probability of real gratification. The accent is on "To see Naples"; the "and die," which comes afterward, has two overlapping meanings: (1) "And if one must die for it, so be it;" (2) "Naples being the marvel of the world, you must give up your life after seeing it rather than pollute your sight by letting it rest on vulgar spectacles." But the young Flaubert is saying nothing of the kind; the object of his wish is quite precise: to die of the plague in Constantinople, of cholera in Calcutta. The interchangeability of the places clearly indicates that the goal is death—one can also drown rounding the Cape—and that the beauty of the sites is not without equal; it even seems that we could draw up a list of what might be called addresses of death. And certainly in *Novembre* Gustave insists particularly on his desire for death: "I want to perish, but in glory in Calcutta, in Constantinople," etc., and something like this would therefore be the correct formulation of his wish. Unhappy as he is, the young man chooses ghastly deaths which have nothing voluntary about them. To kill oneself in Calcutta would be the ideal; he takes a long walk through the city, a new Werther, looking once more at the streets and the temples he has loved, goes home, and at dawn, after a night of meditation, calmly blows his brains out. The city is a constant presence un-

38. Having seen it since, I can no longer imagine any other name for it than Dubrovnik.

til the last moment. In the agonies of the plague or cholera, on the other hand, it has retreated; the fever mounts and makes him lose his mind. What good is Calcutta if you go there only to die, mad with suffering, or to fall comatose on a miserable pallet? On the same page, moreover, he choses life as well: as a muleteer he "trots" along the Guadalquivir. The essential thing, then, is not to perish but *to be another*, a dying Indian, an Andalusian muleteer, anyone but the tourist Gustave Flaubert. He must in some way belong to the landscape, be born in the Indian city, take the place as the material of his work, be ravaged by the sickness of these unhealthy countries. From this point of view, and *at the moment he expresses it*, the desire for death is a false desire; there is even a contradiction between the choice of suicide (if he has to kill himself, why not do it in Rouen without so much fuss?) and the nomenclature of addresses of death. Indeed, the advertised option conceals another, more truthful one: "I do not want to die before having seen Calcutta," which itself is determined by the profound desire to give birth to a word-fulfillment. To produce "Calcutta," to write it, to see oneself write it, to reread it when the ink has dried, is to produce himself as other and imaginary in the center of Calcutta. The real desire is not even to live in the distant city but to trace the eight letters of the master word and enclose himself within it.

This is what "writing his dreams" means: making the optative a means of unreal pleasure, projecting one's imaginary self into the grapheme and at the same time making it imaginary while preserving its sumptuous materiality. In a sense, this could be seen as a case of desiring only in discourse and being satisfied only by the nonsignifying portion of the terms of discourse. We must still be more specific: in the text already cited, the enterprise consists of using the signifying function and the imaging function of the written word simultaneously; explicitly, Gustave is concerned only with the first—he is informing us of his desires. But if it stopped there, the five lines would be reduced to this single sentence: "I want to be another somewhere else." The signification—without the statement's being lost—must serve as pretext for the choice of rare and precious materials that symbolize the desired object. This is choosing the word for its physiognomy, as I have said. But what is this physiognomy?

All graphologists are sensitive to the physiognomy of a word written by hand. I have seen them visibly disgusted by letters in handwriting that betrayed baseness or "perversions"; they were reacting to the graphemes as they would to faces, or as they would to suddenly

267

exposed genitals. I only mention the fact to shed light on the singularity, the individuality, of the *read* word. But in the case at hand we are not concerned with personal handwriting: when Gustave traces his letters, he does not recognize himself in them because through them he is aiming at printed characters. This means that he grasps "Calcutta" in its universal and objective form, going beyond the idiosyncratic form his hand gives it. Printed language is Platonic in the sense that there is only a single word "Calcutta" run off in a hundred thousand copies but entirely present and manifest in each one; on this level, every vocable, including all others in its differential determination, appears in its true individuality, totalizing and totalized, which is that of a singular universal. To apprehend it as sign is a related and complementary activity of perception. To grasp its material singularity is to imagine it. Its "physiognomy" is revealed only in certain circumstances, which expose structures that are nonsignifying but closely tied to signification at different levels.

1. The graphic configuration of the word. This is revealed only by the general relation of the term to the sentence conceived as an organism. And the sentence itself exhibits its organization only if we place it once more in the unity of the context which—functioning as *contingency*—gives it its real function beyond signification. If I say: "My cousin from Bombay was just named consul to Calcutta," or "If only I had been able to die of cholera in Calcutta," the two sentences are equally signifying. But it is the context that determines their *meaning*, that is, their particular essence,[39] their impenetrable presence of structured individuality. The first might be strictly informative: it may be that one wants to convey the information that the cousin has finally found a job. In this case, Calcutta does not unveil its marvels. The second sentence, placed once more in the long list of Gustave's desires, is provided at once with a signification and a symbolic meaning: its configuration functions as analogue. If you read: "perdus sans mâts, sans mâts" ("lost without masts, without masts"), the poetic organization animates the word. Barred like a cross, the *t* rises above the other letters like the mast above the ship; the letters are clustered around it: there is the hull, the bridge. Some people (I am one of them) perceive this white letter as if the vowel *a* were crushed beneath the circumflex like a collapsed sail beneath a low and cloudy sky. The negation expressed by *sans* (without) acts chiefly in the signifying universe: the

39. Of course, the context also defines and refines their *integral* signification. But this obvious role does not interest us here.

268

boat has lost its mast, it is lost: this is what we *learn*. In the obscure world of meaning, negation cannot destructure the word *mâts*. Let us say that it *fades* the word to the point where it becomes the analogue of a kind of photographic negative. The ship *has* a mast in my eyes, although I know it no longer does: it is transformed into a ghost ship. Moreover, this is what Mallarmé expressly wants: quietly to ruin sumptuous words, to provoke the collision of sense (a surpassing of the physical presence toward the unreal) and signification to the advantage of indeterminacy, and finally of a subtle nothingness on whose surface being glides. In truth the word *mâts* has no objective and real resemblance to the object it designates. But the art of writing, here, consists precisely of constraining the reader, willingly or forcibly, to find a resemblance, to make the object descend into the sign as an unreal presence. It will be said that in this case, any word—despite its conventional character—can have an imaging function, and I answer that this is obvious: indeed, the question is not one of a chance resemblance between the signifying material and the object signified but of the felicities of a style that forces us to grasp the materiality of the word as an organic unity, and this as the very presence of the object in question. No doubt, the feverish rhythm of the hemistich and the repetition of the two words *sans mâts* gives the second *mâts* a particular intensity, as if the phrase, continually increasing in volume and speed, did not find its unity in this last word; and as if the word, the last level of a passionate ascent, the rampart against which it is broken, had gathered into itself all the expressed meaning. But as the first *sans mâts* conveys by itself full signification (an unmasted ship), the second, thus exalted, cannot be useful *as a sign;* readers, assured of its importance by its place and emphasis but finding in it nothing more than the first, are led by this contradiction to grasp it *differently,* that is, as unrealized materiality or symbol, as a transmutation into presence of the designated object. Moreover, we should not imagine that this derealizing construction is proper only to poets. All prose sentences have their own speeds: we pass into the imaginary as soon as we yield to the movement. "The self is hateful, you cover it, Miton, but you don't get rid of it." Here we have rapids running between high banks. There are also long majestic rivers. Semireal movements, making present to the eyes the so-called movement of the mind. Carried along by the more or less lively course of the sentence, the word stretches or contracts, the allegro is astringent—the derealized vocable presents its materiality in the form of a small, hard pebble, a dense presence; the adagio, on the contrary deploys the sumptuousness of a word. And which words, someone will ask, have this sumptuous character? All of them. See what happens to three letters and a circumflex, *mât*, according to how it is used. It is a question of how you treat the sounds—their place in the sentence, its rhythm, the organization of the paragraph, a hundred other familiar procedures; if the treatment is appropriate, the reader will take any grapheme for the analogue of the signified object. To show the artist at work, let us return to the five lines from *Novembre: peste à Constantinople. Choléra à Calcutta.* In the first example the two key words share a common internal structure—the presence of the two consonants *st* which are so noticeable (especially if there is subvocalization). In the second example, each word has three syllables, both beginning in the same way in both words (*ko* and *ka*) and finally becoming assonant with each other. It is likely that the choice of these vocables was not deliberate; nonetheless, it remains intentional. And the intention, obscure as it may have been to Flaubert himself, is no less manifest to us: through internal similarities—nonsignifying in themselves—through assonances, through a symphony in *A* major (O-e-a-a-u-a), the verbal material is exalted and imposed on our attention. If it were not preceded by cholera, Calcutta would have less opacity, less mystery (by which I mean the unreal and paradoxical presence of the signified in the signifying, as this signifier is *also* nonsignifying). The basis of all this is, indeed, that the visual weight and consistency of any printed word are qualified to *represent* the impenetrable consistency of any object encountered in experience. The secondary graphic structures are therefore only modulations: well guided, the reader will know how to exploit them.

This, however, would not suffice to nourish the dream. It is often the case, to Flaubert's supreme happiness, that the physical configuration of the grapheme, *before any treatment*, awakens certain resonances. It contains in itself, as an organism all or part of other verbal organisms. To cite the first example that comes to mind, the château of Amboise is linked for me—and for a great many people—to *framboise* (raspberry), to *boisé* (wooded), *boiserie* (wainscoting), to *ambroisie* (ambrosia), to *Ambroise* (Ambrose). These are not idiosyncratic relationships that have grown up in the course of my personal history[40] but of

40. Obviously, these do exist. An analysis would reveal them. They constitute, in each of us, the singular and incommunicable basis of all apprehension of the Word. But though the poet—choosing semicommunication—can use them in his poems, the prose writer cannot make use of them. For this reason it would be useless to speak of them here.

objective and material connections accessible to any reading. As they have not been established by an act of mind and nonetheless impose themselves in an indissoluble unity, we can call them *passive syntheses*. Indeed, the more one abandons oneself to the dream, the more they stand out. Here, however, the significations of associated words, although introduced by their materiality, are integrated to the "dominant" signification (Amboise). But scarcely have they flowered on the surface of the "visualized" word than they lose their transcendence (or their *aim toward the signified*) and remain within the "dominant" in immanence as simple material qualifications. The château Amboise has no significant connection with raspberries: it isn't a nursery of raspberry bushes, raspberries are not sold there, it isn't painted raspberry red; and if we did not know its name, no one would think of comparing that powerful edifice to this sweet, fragile fruit. In other words, the signification of the associated vocable in no way alters that of the dominant signification. Let us say that it slips into the "visualized" word as an internal qualification of its materiality. Or, if you like, as a material factor of unification. It remains *within the grapheme*, incomplete (two letters—*fr*—are missing) and yet whole, passed over in silence yet sensed, like those half-buried memories which play such a role in the perception of new faces; in brief, it is "unsayable" information from the materiality of the vocable about itself. Almost unperceived when the sentence tends to reduce it to its role as sign (which never entirely happens)—"I was telegraphed from Amboise . . . ," etc.—it is exalted and enriched when, by contrast, the style aims to make the word imaginary so that the verbal material may be grasped as the analogue of the château itself. Then the unreal presence of the château is found, in language and *in language alone*, before experience or despite experience, to be structured materially by the complex materiality of the vocable, by some organization of "*framboise* minus two letters" which extends to the totality of the construction. If you wanted to rationalize it, to change this obscure immanence into a signifying transcendence, you would have to say that the object made present unreally, a luxury building rather than a military construction, is meant to be a tender and beautiful flowering of the Renaissance. But this would be only an approximation. Primarily because the passive synthesis is by definition irreducible to signification. Then *framboise* itself contains other passive syntheses which qualify it in its material and qualify Amboise at the same time[41]—those I cited above: *boisé,*

41. It can happen that certain of them, unperceived when the dominant is "framboise," are actualized when the master word is "Amboise."

boiserie, etc.—so that the qualification by the name of the fruit is never complete; it is opposed, crossed, arrested, enriched by something beyond itself made of overlapping resonances which, once mingled, confer a marvelous, inexhaustible density to the imaginary presence.[42] The construction of the sentence, we have seen, disposes the reader to open himself to its riches, a gentle force inclines him to unrealize himself. Inversely however, the words sometimes have so many overtones that they become imaginary under our very eyes and at the same time produce the unrealization of the entire sentence and the person who reads them. These are metastable organisms, always ready to spill from one side or the other—reality, unreality—and the young Gustave cherishes them above all else. From this moment, he chose— he would understand his choice only after 1844—to treat written discourse as a massive analogue of all the absences he wanted to make present, all the knowledge he would have liked to possess.

As I have just shown, the material structures of a sign, by making a thing present, give it *their* physiognomy, which becomes its *sense*. But this physiognomy, constituted only by relations that are internal to the discourse, is purely verbal and gives an insubstantial image of experience. The reader encounters Florence, woman and flower, at the turning of a page, thus he fashions events or objects. But to the extent that this word designates a city and unrealized, makes it present, the *sense* of the word is only a pretense, for the city of the Medicis, hard, dry, virile capital of the Bank of Florence, has nothing to offer its visitors but its thankless and splendid beauty. To choose the sumptuousness of names is to prefer the universe of the Word to that of things and to prefer satisfaction through words—or false satisfaction—to the real pleasure of the things of this world. This will not be easy, for we cannot compel discourse to exercise the semantic function and the

42. Let us note, for example, the feminine ending that constitutes both fruit and château as women or *womanly things*. And that absence of the *fr,* rather hard consonants in *framboise,* gives the château transmuted into presence an "incoyable douceu" [*incroyable douceur* (incredible sweetness) with the *r*'s dropped] as fops would say. I have no time to linger here over constitutive relationships. But it is certain that even this graphic materiality functions on the basis of totalized language, thus in tandem with other words that are absent but shape it from a distance: there is no doubt that the feminine sweetness of Amboise is deeply accentuated by its *verbal* relation to Blois. The two words seem to be two variations of a single sound unit: Boise, Blois. And because of this they are opposite to and differentiated from each other as masculine and feminine. There could be no better demonstration that these secret and imaginary differentiations operate in discourse and with no relation to experience. Indeed, two facing or juxtaposed buildings may sometimes present themselves *to the perception* as opposite sexes (the austerity of one, the charm of the other, etc.), but this is certainly not the case with the two châteaux I have cited here.

imaging function *at the same time.* Writing—and reading, which is inseparable from it—imply on this level a subtle dialectic of perception and imagination, of real and unreal, of sign and sense. In order to transmute into presence an imaginary Calcutta embellished with all the charms of its name, we must at least have a rudimentary knowledge that it is a city in India and that its inhabitants are Indian. But if we subject words to the appropriate treatment, at the very moment of being rendered imaginary the signification becomes an implicit structure of the verbal sense. This dialectic and this treatment are none other than *literature,* at least as the nineteenth century conceived it. In any case, it was the literature that Gustave chose in his adolescence. See what he writes at seventeen, striving to define the "needs of the soul," precisely those needs that writers and especially poets have a mission to fulfill: "an immense thirst for the infinite, [a need] for dreams, verses, melodies, ecstasies."[43] It is clear that little Flaubert came to literature because the written word, an inert permanence, an object of mediations that can unceasingly be returned to, is a better agent of derealization than the "intelligible mouthful."

3. I should add that the constant passage from sign to image and vice versa would not even be possible without mediation. And I refer here to what I have said above about the words "woman" and "mistress," which Gustave took such pleasure in repeating. For him, as for all the adolescents of his age, these words have a conceptual signification—which he sensed long before he knew what it was—and an "unsayable" sense made up of overlapping notions under the control of an inarticulable desire. On this level the syncretic richness is the intermediary between the sign as transcendence and the unreal presence of the thing as immanence. In a sense, of course, there is *designation:* woman is meant by the term "woman" which Gustave murmurs to himself. Yet that meaning comes not from knowledge—in the beginning, at least—but from ignorance. Flaubert expressly says so: until his adolescence, it was the mystery of the sex that he designated by this word; as for female organs or sexual relations, he had a presentiment of everything without knowing anything. Woman is the black and fascinating void that draws his desire. For this reason she is also in the word as an immanent expanse, as *sense* or, if you like, as a materialization of significations as quality. This metastable characteristic of semantic syncretism—woman, that unknown, is aimed at all women, she is what persists in the word that embodies her—allows the contin-

43. *Les Arts et le Commerce,* January 1839.

uous dialectic of sense and sign: always ready to evaporate toward the object, to be surpassed, to be forgotten so that the object may be manifest, the syncretic aim is, at the same time, always rejected and consequently tries to be fused in the materiality of the grapheme, which becomes the cipher and incarnation of femininity.

Thus we have uncovered three levels of the process by which the word is made imaginary. And the third refers us to the true motivation of style, *desire*, which literature—such as the adolescent Flaubert conceives it—gratifies in the unreal by means of its very inarticulability. These remarks lead us to formulate two essential problems: in what sense is literature gratification? What desires are gratified in Gustave's early works?

We have already given an answer to the first question: *scripta manent*. But at this point such an answer seems inadequate, or at least inadequately elaborated. Indeed, if it is true that the writer, incomparable and totalizing, comes to this encounter with that incomparable and totalizing idiosyncrasy, the word, it is just as true that he creates and has a presentiment of the encounter, that he prophesies the word that rises to his lips before he even knows the word, so that it is always a matter of a quasi-encounter, of a pseudo-experience, appointed, attempted, which collapses in too much familiarity. Before tracing the letters, I did not know precisely what this word would be; in tracing them, I perceive that I have always known it. The reader is the one who has the real experience: the word jumps him like a thief. It is the reader who will suffer the shock of imaging, the passage to the imaginary. It is for him that the word will function as a "hallucinogen." Is writing a way of being a stranger's cat's-paw? Yet Gustave is explicit: "I write to give myself pleasure."[44] And he adds: "If I write, it's so that I can read myself."[45] And: "I am dying to tell me to myself."[46] The real problem is knowing what this ego is that reads. It is evidently posterior to the one that writes; therefore its meaning must be: I make my books for the future reader I shall be. Indeed, when Dr. Cloquet "engages him to put down in writing in the form of aphorisms all my ideas, to seal the paper and open it up again in fifteen years," he accepts with enthusiasm: "That may be very good advice, I am going to follow it." But visibly, what interests him most is Cloquet's next remark: "You will find another man." In other words: in fifteen years you will be other than you are now, and you will look at yourself with

44. *Souvenirs*, p. 103; 21 May 1841.
45. Ibid.
46. Ibid.

the eyes of another, *truly* deciding on your present being. The advice was given in the summer of 1840. If Gustave was so intrigued that he set to work and produced thirty-six aphorisms between 25 January 1841 and the first days of February,[47] it was because for a long time—in fact since he had begun to write—the young man had been "dying to tell me to myself." In this light the unrealizing utilization of the grapheme takes on another meaning: to write in order to read oneself (the same advice that Monsieur Lepic gives Poil de Carotte) does not necessarily involve the supposition that the two operations must take place fifteen years apart. You can become your own reader fifteen days from the moment you become your own writer. In this case, everything is changed: for the adolescent, the adult Gustave was the Other himself, mysterious, enviable, and terrifying. To address himself was not to seek to please himself, for he did not know his future tastes, his preferences, his vision of the world—he was submitting to his future judgment. Suddenly the words lost their sumptuousness: this unknown, future gaze tarnished them. But if you write to read yourself the following week, you address yourself to an ego which is "neither entirely another nor entirely the same." It will be the same Gustave, other only in that he will no longer enter fully into his work. He must forget his work sufficiently, and it is enough for him to have done so, to become estranged from the written words. He will encounter these quasi objects again in a quasi experience (the entire process might be called quasi reading). He will know, of course, the general sense of his work, he will recognize whole pages in passing, but words and certain strategies of style that make them imaginary will rise from oblivion,

47. After the last aphorism, and at the head of a kind of Journal, he writes: "*set down on 8 February.*" It is not impossible that he may have written all these aphorisms in one day. In any case, this is one of the admissible meanings of the parenthesis that ends number 36: "Oftentimes when I see passersby whose looks I don't like I would like to blow their brains out (some other day I will finish these formulas)." In fact, he never took up this "formula" again. But we are used to these abrupt abandonings, the counterpart of his enthusiasms. The genre of the "maxim" attracted him—although he did not really know how to use it and put himself in most of his maxims—probably because he had a taste for "paradox," which in one brief sentence can expose an outrageous contradiction. And then he was disgusted with the genre, suddenly realizing the profound stupidity of Dr. Cloquet and his advice. Cloquet, in fact, as the context proves, irritated by Gustave's pessimism, was always repeating to him: You will change (which in his mouth meant: you will become bourgeois, you will become a contented father), and his famous counsel is marked by a certain hostility: Go on with your gloomy ideas, write them down, put them in a sealed envelope and don't mention them to us again. In fifteen years you will laugh at the young braggart you are today. In sum, Cloquet sought the complicity of the adult Gustave against the adolescent. He could not have made a worse calculation; few mature men have been so faithful to their youth.

totally new, and take him by surprise. In this sense the inert perseverance of the grapheme is a promise of future delights, whereas the vocalization of the word, always instantaneous, can only be repeated and is always subjective, incapable of being modified or enriched. It is the written word that produces this reversal: Gustave the author becomes a quasi object for himself inasmuch as he is there, exposed on the pages of his notebook. In truth it is not so simple; it will be years before he can get outside of his work and look at it with the surprise of a stranger. And, as we know, such returns are often distressing. Even so, at the very moment of writing there is a *postponement*, the surprise he is preparing for himself, and this is enough to give the grapheme—at least in the form of a presentiment—its future color. I am not saying that Flaubert delights in it beforehand but that he enjoys the word insofar as he sees in it the promise of a delight. In this he is like graffiti writers who, as they trace their inscriptions on the walls of urinals, are exquisitely excited by the shocked reaction they hope to provoke in others—with this slight difference: for Gustave, the other is his future self. Unknown readers,[48] however, are not absent from his concerns: we know they are inessential. Nonetheless, to the extent that, while fearing them, often even wishing to conceal his works from them, he knows—*scripta manent*—that a drawer can be forced, that a manuscript can *always* fall into the hands of strangers, their presence has the effect of marginally consolidating the future objectivity of words. When he returns to what his pen is now tracing, he must recognize the fact that he will see it not only as the result of a forgotten act but also as a collective, escaping him by its structure of seriality but for that reason fulfilling him by its otherness. "The future ravished me":[49] that says it all. When he writes to his future self, already entirely imaginary, he takes pleasure in the unreality of his *approaching* unrealization *through the process by which the graphemes are made imaginary.*

Is there not, however, in the very act of composition a still unreal but more immediate gratification? Yes: a gratification of the desire to desire. 8 February 1841:[50] "I wrote a love letter[51] for the purpose of writing, not because I love. Yet I would like to delude myself that I do: I love, I believe while writing." He came back to this idea several years

48. And known: Alfred and Ernest have reading rights. But Gustave does not write *for them.*
49. *Souvenirs,* p. 103.
50. Ibid., p. 99.
51. To Eulalie Foucault.

later in a letter to Louise Colet, on which we shall comment in due time. Here we see the passage from phoneme to grapheme: shouting to the night winds "I love! Oh, I love!" may be charming but in the long run it becomes less and less convincing. And the text cited above makes clear that what is at stake for Gustave is the credibility of language: in what form will discourse—his own discourse—be most likely to engage the pithiatic adherence of the boy? His answer is precise: writing. The reasons for this are apparent: writing seems like a passage to action, like an externalization as well as a composition. It is not a matter of copying "I love you" a hundred times; that would be a schoolboy's punishment. You must *invent* love, do something original, come up with passionately authentic phrases, *put yourself in the position* to recognize them from the inside. This means you must imagine you are in love. In sum, the order of means and ends is apparently reversed: orally, Gustave speaks of love in order to imagine he is in love; writing his letter to Eulalie, he imagines that he loves her in order to be able to play the lover. But this is only appearance; he knows quite well that at bottom—indeed, he says so the same day—his goal has not changed: "to make myself believe that I love" in order to feel the painful delights of passion. Of course, on the surface the pithiatic aspect of the enterprise is undeniable: it isn't only a game (it is *also* a game), it is a successful attempt, at least as far as his pen is concerned, at autosuggestion. And there is no doubt that the receiver must be reckoned with: once again it is the Other who will definitively judge his sincerity. If Gustave convinces her of his feelings, he will really experience them—we are familiar with this scheme. But Gustave is not worried; his words are born of flights of imagination which are nonetheless *accurate*, meaning that they conform to the descriptions which, as we have seen, he "learned from books." She is going to weep for joy, good Eulalie, she is already weeping: "You love me so much?" "Ah yes, I love you, and even more than you think." His pen runs on, a sweet emotion grips the young letter writer: I believe, my God, I believe, I *feel* desire for her, regret, the sad melancholy of separation. How happy I am! Eventually he has to sign the letter, his happiness fades, but every day he can begin again. And then, must his letters really have a recipient? Can't he write to himself, "telling himself his dreams," consolidate his oneirism? I will do plays and you will write your dreams, he proposes to Ernest; a little later, no doubt out of spite, he changes his mind: I will write novels. And what do these novels, which to judge by their titles bear a strong resemblance to the plays he abandons, represent if not his written dreams? In this sense, writing, while it saves him from autism, is the objectivization and materialization of autism. Writing, for Gustave at this time, is a role which, without ceasing to be an unreal determination, persuades the actor who plays it that he *is* truly the character. And by means of this never quite complete belief, the player enters fully into the world of imagination. The young Flaubert's literature is the imaginary materialized.

It is not true, however, that he becomes a writer only to satisfy his desire to desire. This is why we must return to the second question we have asked: *what* is gratified in his early works? We shall be able to find the answer, I believe, if we examine an obvious paradox. When Gustave reports his mental exercises to us in the *Mémoires* and in *Novembre*, he has them begin from the time he entered school and implies that he pursued them long after he had begun to write. And he gives them to us for what they doubtless are: reveries directed and organized around certain "magic" words and whose end is the gratification of certain very simple desires: the child would like to be an exceptional person whose merits place him above others, he would like to possess the rarest things and the most beautiful women, to roam the world, to see legendary countries and cities. He speaks of poetry, of ecstasy; he drowns in the infinite, declares himself to be antitruth, assigns to literature a single function: to supply and sustain the lovely reveries of the advantaged. Nothing more; these, it seems, are the innocent desires of a precocious adolescent. But in his written work, and particularly in the narratives contemporaneous with these noble aspirations, all is blackness: horror, misery, suffering, an iron law ruling that virtue must always be punished and vice rewarded; it is hell, and the damned, suffering and cruel, are each other's demons. The change of signs is rigorous, automatic; I will give only one example, but there are a hundred. Flaubert loves to repeat that "there is something of the strolling player in him." This gives a kind of romantic and *positive* aura to his unreality. *Saltimbanque* is a beautiful word: if it remains in Gustave's head, it will allow him to gratify his dream of being a nomad. And it is true that the theme of the strolling player— from Hugo to Mallarmé, and including Baudelaire and Gautier— marked the sedentary poetry of the nineteenth century. Little Gustave saw some of these traveling showmen; he tells us that they fascinated him, as much by their adornments as by their incredible freedom. He wants to write about these whimsical, penniless bohemians who dazzle him and for whom he feels a kind of kinship. But it overwhelms him: the moment he speaks of them *with his pen,* what is positive becomes an absolute negative. In *Un Parfum . . .* these players become the most wretched and despised of men; their work is hard and thankless, they die of cold and hunger, dragging themselves from town to town, objects of universal contempt. To be sure, this is a slightly blackened version of the truth. But Gustave does not write out of a concern for objective truth; rather, he is seeking certain gratifications. How is it that in his inner dream, the players are knights of the imaginary and he is full of pride at being one of them, whereas when he writes about them he burdens them with misfortune and assigns a ridiculous dancer, an ugly woman, obscene and jealous, the task of representing him among them? What has become of their freedom? What has become of that supreme insouciance he so admired in them, that contempt for the bourgeoisie? That proud cry, "I am a strolling player," with which he broke the boredom of his lofty solitude—why has ink turned it into the self-debasing complaint, "I am only a strolling player"? Or, as he will say in the *Mémoires:* "a displayer of dancing bears"? This child who dreams of being a beautiful woman in order to admire himself naked in the fount, why, the first time he dares to make his dream concrete, does he give himself the repulsive body of poor Marguerite? How can he both "invent marvelous stories" in his head to compensate for the Fall, the castrating rejection, and use his pen to invent others, perfectly ghastly, which lead him without compensation to despair?

Is it that he tells himself the first stories in order to flee from a truth that the second group of tales tries to encompass? The answer is hardly satisfying: in both cases we are dealing with fictions, and what proof do we have that in his written narratives Gustave seeks *his* truth in order *to express it through words?* We would be closer, I believe, to Gustave's intentions if we said that the desire to desire—which impels him to build an imaginary world first inside himself, then outside—is the only explicit intention but not the only real one. All told, assuming it is not entirely played out, it is the one that possesses the least reality. So that if the sorcerer's apprentice sits down at his work table, his demons are at work, everything is turned upside down and he has an unreal but *material* gratification of his black desires. Furthermore, are those desires he dwells on daily at his studies and in the dormitory so innocent after all? In the first place, they are often born of wounded pride: "The fools! *They* laugh at *me?* They, so weak, so vulgar, laugh at me whose spirit reaches to the limits of creation." The revery is thus a defense against and a condemnation of the other the moment it is produced. On a deeper level, it bears witness to passive aggression. What does he want, the good little subject? Travels, glory, love? Nothing could be better. But "it was Rome I loved, imperial Rome, that beautiful queen wallowing in orgies, soiling her noble garments with the wine of debauchery, prouder of her vices than she was of her virtues." In this world capital, what role did he want to play? None other than that of Nero. "A tiger's loves . . . vast, sensuous pleasures . . . bloody illuminations . . . amusements that make Rome burn." His Neroesque character does not even know what the love is that Gustave wants to experience; he takes women or men while some unfortunate who has displeased him is being tortured in the very same room. What, then, does the boy dream of? He tries, by autosuggestion, to persuade himself that in a splendid and corrupt city he is the emperor, most corrupt of all, and that he sets the city on fire for the pleasure of seeing the *beautiful* flames devour it and roast his fellow citizens. He comes back to this in *Novembre* and once again crowns himself emperor: "for the sake of absolute power." And what will he do with this power? "I would have liked to annihilate creation . . . Oh, that I could wake in the glow of burning cities! I would have liked . . . to gallop over the backs of the people and crush them with my horse's iron hooves, to be Genghis Khan, Tamberlaine, Nero . . ." No doubt if we read the autobiographical works attentively, we can distinguish certain periods; the furies that gave rise to these genocidal fantasies were, according to him, much later than his first reveries: "I was against life, against men, against everything, in a nameless rage." All right. But in the *Mémoires d'un fou* he situates at a much earlier time—his first months at school—that "nervous irritation that made [him] vehement and carried away like a bull driven mad by the sting of insects." He had then, he says, "terrible nightmares," and he describes one of them whose contents, to which we shall return, obviously refer to memories from his early childhood. In short, he is faking: his splenetic humor—we know all about it—was manifest *before* entering school, although contact with his peers and his professors may have exacerbated it. And when he dreams of being loved—very early, if we are to believe *Novembre*—we know that he wishes for a mistress, a "satanic being," who will love him with a "*devouring and frightening love . . .* that makes you the equal of the rich and powerful." Thus the cherub's naïve purity conceals a will to power, resentment, and hatred. The innocent desire—love of love—exists, no doubt, it is not just a pretext; it represents a repeated attempt to escape the dark forces, to escape his misanthropic and solitary destiny. To love, to be loved: to communicate outside himself, to forget forever his "awful shadows," to escape the world of fear. Nothing doing; no sooner is it formulated than the innocent postulation veers off into darkness. Let us recall Calcutta, Constantinople: here we have the poisoned mirage. To round the Cape, yes; but this wish dies, the behavior of failure becomes dominant: he will fail at this enterprise as he does at all the others and will lose himself at large *before* completing the voyage. Is this not the "supreme poetry" which he himself defines as a "mixture of malediction and sensuality"? The innocent desires have an *unreal* existence; it is the task of words to awaken them; the dark desires are perfectly real; it is the task of writing to gratify them *unreally.*

Let us not believe, however, that these desires reveal themselves to him in the act of writing; he has long had the habit of satisfying them through the drama of internal language. In the drafts for novels published by Madame Durry there is a very instructive notation. Flaubert—he has already written *Madame Bovary*—sketches in a few words the story of a couple. The character of the woman is already more elaborated than that of the husband. We learn that she is humiliated by him, that she hates him but is constrained to tolerate him out of a love for luxury. This feminine condition is precisely Flaubert's situation within the family: though humiliated, he cannot break with them—not out of a taste for luxury (there is no hint of that in the Flaubert family), but out of a taste for comfort and the fear of being without it. Once more, Flaubert *sees himself as a woman.* And he is speaking for himself when he says of his heroine: "She avenged herself through monologue."

This brief sentence is not followed by any commentary. The author, writing here only for himself, has no need to develop the thought— he knows what he is talking about. The "monologue" is purposely devised not to be heard, which is enough to alert us that the vengeance is unreal. This voiceless discourse would have a real impact only if spoken aloud: "Drop dead then, you bastard. My God, make him drop dead," or: "You are a turd, you manage to hide it from others, but I know it and you do not know that I know it." The mute speaker takes pleasure in reading the characters of the people around him, enumerating their base actions, predicting their destinies, pledging them to the worst misfortunes. Or else he describes his misery, the awful fate they have arranged for him; he makes them touch the unhealing wounds their hardness of heart has caused him. Of course, no one must divine any of this. Far from provoking uneasiness or dissatisfaction, the monologuist finds advantages in the unreality of his behavior. First of all, for various reasons he needs his vengeance to be unreal: if the wife leaves or kills her husband, the hen that lays the golden eggs dies as well; Gustave cannot live outside his family, he could not bear being driven out. So the monologue is complete as it is. And then the mute reverses the situation: he is not the one who remains silent: the others simply don't hear him, he is shouting at the top of his voice among people who are deaf. And they are all the more ridiculous for not knowing that someone has unmasked them and is telling them the truth about themselves. Isn't he comical, that gentleman who smiles affably to someone throwing in his face an "old turd" that he doesn't even hear? Finally there is God. God, or the ontological power of the Word. God listens to these unheard words, he takes good note of them. Or, if you like, things that have been said remain, they are stones; some change in being must result. And what pride there is, when one still respects one's father, in feeling reproved, cursed, for having treated him mentally like a swine. The act—there it is, thinks the monologuist with a bitter joy: I damn well said he was a swine, my father, and if I have done nothing else I have called down upon myself the thunderbolts of the Almighty. This is how bitter and passive souls, racked with resentment, amuse themselves.

By itself, the monologue tends toward fiction, both because it is imaginary and because wishes, when taken for realities, readily turn to prophecy. According to the character of the speaker, words will gather in his head to inflict the worst misfortunes on his intimate enemy, that is, to tell the story of his life as it will be in the future, or to tell the story of his victim in order to measure his guilt by the anticipated results of his wickedness. Or, as Gustave does, to interweave the two narratives and repeat them a thousand times. In his early works—in which his heroes are bold monologuists and talk into their hats just as they have arrived, needled by suffering, at the height of wickedness—we can see the internal dialectic of the Flaubertian monologue, the reciprocal conditioning of the two types of narrative. "'Oh!' he said to himself, sobbing with rage." This is Garcia; after such a fine start, we see him push his unhappiness to an extreme *through words*, predict the worst, recount his future humiliations in detail, and take pleasure in giving them the inflexibility of fate: "'Me, his brother, *forever* poor and unknown . . .'" Sadistic and masochistic at the same time, he first gratifies his desire to punish his executioners by turning on himself, and as soon as he is justified he moves on to a dream of active vengeance: "'Ah! Now I understand the joys of blood, the delights of vengeance and atheism and impurity!'" So finally this *aside*, placed at the beginning of the tale,[52] seems to be the matrix of the entire story: Garcia, crazed with anger, in effect kills his brother and knows both the joys of blood and those of impurity. But, as we have seen, the murder of François is something less than convincing. It is thus fitting that the violence should be maintained on the plane of language; everything happens as if Garcia were incited by his internal narrative to *write the story* of the murder he is quite incapable of committing. Or, better yet, as if Gustave's monologue had required transmutation into the written story of Garcia. I think, in effect, that the child makes the transition to literature on two levels: the unreal desires are gratified on the level of the isolated word; the real desires, expressed by the monologue, are gratified by the written fiction. In other words, Flaubert's first narratives are the materialization of an unreal vengeance. Why does the monologue require transcription, and why does this transcription undergo a metamorphosis into pure fabulation in which even the characters are fictive? These are the questions we must now address.

The first is an easy one to answer: to the extent that the monologue is made into a *story*, it soon reveals its inconsistency. Autistic thought assembled around one or two words is self-sufficient. But, once spoken, it becomes organized and rationalized. On this level, deployed as narrative, it demands an internal temporalization. The sugar must dissolve, the unnatural father must take his time dying of shame. And in this specific case,[53] real temporalization, far from sustaining imaginary duration, plays against it: it disperses and overturns the narrative. It is not true that the monologuist can dream *in detail* of the tortures he will inflict upon his brother; no sooner has he set the scene than it vanishes into oblivion, must be retrieved or reinvented, and despite what Loyola believed, such scenes lack the solidity required for actors to make their entrance. More generally, the story can be told schematically but not developed: no moment, no episode can serve as a springboard for the following episode, each marked by the essential paucity that characterizes the mental image and internal speech. Above all, none of these episodes has any impact on those that follow because consciousness produces them in isolation; they *replace* each other instead of being mutually enriching, and their inert succession is sustained only by lived duration. A synthetic

52. In chapter 2 of *La Peste à Florence*.
53. The reader's own time is rightly lost in the service of the novelistic duration.

act can certainly bind them to each other, but it is *from the outside*, and then when the present event is joined to anterior facts, these *no longer exist*, meaning that they have slipped away, bearing with them elements indispensable to the continuation of the narrative: "I'll slaughter you, you will bleed like a pig." Very well, here is the floor red with blood. "You will cry for mercy and I shall laugh." The mouth opens in the darkness, the cry escapes from it but quickly fades—this is happening nowhere, the floor with its blood has disappeared. As for the laughter, that is something else: by prophesying laughter, the avenger finds himself all alone *today*, laughing up his sleeve at *future* events that he predicts. What is there to do but begin again? There is a profound monotony to this discourse which never reaches an end for lack of a stable platform to lean on. This platform is the written artifact: once again, *scripta manent*. He will make progress, he will enrich the story with its entire past only by registering everything; as soon as it is conceived, the invention is fixed; he can return to it endlessly, the bloody floor is solid now, it will pass from one episode to the other, it will be integrated—a reminder, an allusion will be enough to make it a constant of the narrative. From this point, vengeance, which is meticulous, can delight in detailing the tortures it contemplates: the victim's spasms, his proud face now distorted by terror, the instruments of torture, the delight of the executioner—all of it can be described and summoned since *writing is accumulation*. For Gustave, who as author-actor already has the habit of the pen, the thing is accomplished without his perceiving it. Especially since writing, after the public games of the theater, is a kind of solitude, almost clandestine—therefore homogeneous in nature to the monologue. Born of a castrating refusal, it will tell of the sufferings and the revenge of the castrated. Rather, it *will be* that revenge itself. Reduced to silence, the great voice still speaks internally, and the mute words it engenders somehow find a way of becoming externalized in the words silently traced by a hand.

We must here give an answer to the second question. If literature, in its primitive form, is a means of articulating and organizing Gustave's vindictive monologue, why do we find nothing in his notebooks of what we ought to find: diatribes against his father or falsely resigned complaints, denunciation of the usurper Achille and complacent enumeration of his future misfortunes? In *Matéo Falcone*, the most primitive of his vengeances—and the most elementary—instead of reading lamentations, "Father of unjust justice, you crucify me, my mother will die of it," why do we find the dry narrative—a borrowed subject besides—of a family drama in Corsica in which a certain Matéo kills his son with his own hands? If it is true that Flaubert is avenging himself, what pleasure does he find in developing the character of these foreigners in an unknown country and in extreme circumstances of which he has no experience? For anyone who seeks to know Gustave, it is of the greatest importance to find a solution to this problem, for what is at issue is nothing less than the conception of the novelistic as the child formulated it in his earliest works and as the adult preserved it. Let us quickly note that little Flaubert had certain knowledge and models: *Don Quixote* was read to him, and later he got to know other novels. This knowledge facilitated the passage from the monologue to writing, but it could very well—and we shall have to decide about that—have concealed its true significance from him. We should note that the boy did not move from reality (his *real* sufferings, his *real* projects of vengeance) to fiction but from one fiction which concerned him (he is the subject) to another which to all appearances did not. I have said above, in effect, that his soliloquy was an unreal gratification of his resentment, by which I mean that its function is particularly to satisfy in the unreal a desire that we realize can never really be satisfied. In brief, we remain in the imaginary; in this light too, mute speech and the grapheme are here homogeneous. This much said, we must be careful not to accuse Gustave of cynicism, as if out of prudence he had disguised the facts, changed names and places. It is true that his prudence is extreme and that his first fictional writings are tied to a universal mistrust. We have seen his contradictory relationship with readers: he repulses them, horrified, while wishing they would read him. Hence the double nature of his first works: they are readable and therefore open to everyone, *offered up;* because of this they are by nature *hidden.* This means that he locks up his manuscripts with a double lock; and he knows quite well, alas, that he is taking this precaution against an imaginary danger: neither Dr. Flaubert nor his wife would force open drawers in order to control their son's production; they have other fish to fry. On the other hand, I have shown above that in the same narratives themselves, when the story risks being too evocative, certain disguises may be perceived. The young writer seems to insist on the differences that separate real events from the recounted event, as though he were concealing the true meaning of his work. Who is going to believe, however, that he consciously adopted the novelistic form to cover his thinking and satisfy his vindictiveness safely? Some people have done so, perhaps, but if they have used literature as their means, they are not likely to have gone far with it—literature insists on being an end in itself. There are others, too, who monologue by pen and in their private journals tell everything quite openly—at least everything of which they are explicitly conscious—at the risk of carrying vigilance to an extreme; such persons want not so much to be gratified as to know themselves, and we are not speaking of them. Gustave, indeed, autistic from the start, thinks not of knowing himself but of dreaming himself through writing. Everything is there. For this reason we should not fall into the opposite error. Certainly the adolescent says much more than he means to; he offers himself up without knowing it—with a little analysis we can glimpse his "disturbing depths." This is what I am attempting here. But he has some kind of presentiment of it, and the security measures he takes are aimed at diverting the penetrating reader rather than the members of his family (here, too, such measures remain merely symbolic, ineffective); we shall see later that he understands himself admirably without knowing himself, hence that fear of unwittingly revealing his miserable nakedness. But what betrays him, and he is not unaware of it, is the manner of telling the story; in this sense it matters little whether the hero is Gustave in person, or a mouthpiece, or ten contradictory and simultaneous mouthpieces. But if he is afraid of offering up to an eventual reader the dusty corners of his soul, which are not legible even to himself, in other words, of giving advantage to the enemy, he is highly conscious of writing in order to broadcast his despair and satisfy his resentment. In his case, then, doesn't literature spring from the monologue? Let us reread the first pages of *Agonies* or the preface and conclusion to *Un Parfum à sentir*; we shall see that while cursing his potential reader—or mocking him—he claims full responsibility for the pessimism and misanthropy manifest in the works. He knows what is there and to what he is committed; what makes him afraid is not what he is supposed to be hiding (the names and private status of the real protagonists of his family drama) and not only what he is unaware of and fears expressing inadvertently, but above all *what he says*.

If we try to explain the passage to the novelistic by avoiding both these perils—the interpretations of cynicism and of absolute unconsciousness—we quickly realize that the monologue in general allows fictions not only of the first degree but also, at moments, in outline, of the second. This is what Freud calls the "family romance." The child tells himself a story in order to satisfy in his imagination desires that are otherwise variable: his parents are not his true parents, he has other, secret ones; he himself, as a result, is not what others believe him to be; or else the parents are the same but their condition is different and thus his relations with them, his daily life, his aspirations are different as well. He still says "I" but sees himself from the outside. We find numerous traces of these ruminations in Gustave's first works. First of all, there are the sketches for melodramas: his mother is a whore, his father a great lord who does not keep his word; as for him, for his twenty years, the poor guy in all innocence screws the whore who has given birth to him. Or else the unhappy woman is a black slave raped by an orangoutang; his father is at once a savage beast and an enlightened man of learning who ordered the experiment out of scientific curiosity. These are not, of course, the boy's first "family romances"; these writings are too elaborated, too suffused with knowledge. But at the least they let us glimpse a very archaic taste for this kind of fabulation—which certainly characterized his monologue.

In this, however, Gustave is no different from other children who will never write. His "anomaly" is that his desire to be other is confused with his desire to be real. I have spoken enough about this not to recapitulate. I want only to note that with his objective being in the hands of others and his subjective life unrealized, he would have to surprise himself as the other he is for others in order eventually to enjoy his reality. For him, "I" is present but unreal. "He" is real but aimed at emptiness, absent. He tried through comedy to make himself for others that other the others see. Now, when he projects himself into written language in order to read *himself,* he offers himself as *other* to an observer who is *none other* than himself; in other words, he incorporates himself into the materiality of the grapheme, and instead of reality he will give himself material weight by making himself an *other object* in his own eyes. The subjective "I" remains where it is, but in the word he traces, "I" turns into "He." Transformation at sight: to gratify not the desire to know himself but, quite simply, the desire to exist. It will be many years before Gustave conquers the literary "I"; and often it will still turn out to be only a "He" in disguise.[54] This

54. In the *Mémoires,* when Flaubert recounts his love for Madame Schlésinger, he says I. And in principle it is indeed *I* who is speaking since he shares with us a real experience and feelings he truly had. However, he cannot help changing the age of the narrator—intermittently, it is true—and from pretending to be an old man evoking a childhood memory. Inversely, of course, there are "He's" that are "I" in disguise. More complex still is Fromentin's procedure in *Dominique,* the narrator speaks in the first person; he meets the protagonist, whom he describes in the third person; one day the protagonist lets himself reveal confidential matters to the author; here he is, then, speaking of himself in the first person while a time lag (he is evoking his past) prevents a perfect convergence of the speaking I with the I about whom he is telling the story. Thus the broken, past, surpassed I of the stranger confessing himself is that of a He whose state-

spontaneous change is clearly intentional. But we should not assume that it is explicit and deliberate—Gustave has no sense of it. He wants to speak of *another*, who attracts him by his quasi-real consistency (the grapheme's, in the final analysis), who lived in the sixteenth century, and is *himself at long last visible to him*. Not the poor schoolboy who wouldn't know what to say about Gustave because he doesn't know him and has been deprived of his reality,[55] but a dense and vivid being who has nothing in common with him except that he has a mandate to satisfy in himself and through himself the untamed rancors of his creator. Of course this creator does not explicitly recognize himself in his creature; or, if you like, he has no clear, conscious knowledge that it is himself—as objective presence—that he fully possesses: how could the nebula identify with the burning rock that spins off from it? The identification takes place silently, however; desire is the operative element: the sufferings, rages, pleasures of his characters move Flaubert in a peculiar way because they are his own. And his gratification will be all the more violent for taking place *out there* in a character external to him who tends to become self-enclosed, affirming his independence from his author. Gustave as an imaginary child "is not enough to have"; he doesn't know what pleasure is. But Mazza, Marguerite, Djalioh—hard, and dense, variegated little statuettes—are something else: without being more real, they possess enough materiality to embody the vague feelings that cross the *animula vagula* of the little boy in all their flamboyant violence, so that those feelings can become what they are. Djalioh is not created and put into the world to symbolize the young Gustave's sufferings; on the contrary, Gustave made this monster so that he could suffer the sufferings of Djalioh.

Hypostasis is finally rendered unrecognizable by the organization and rationalization that writing introduces into the dream. While he is enclosed in autism, the child can satisfy his desire to be a woman in imagination without being affected by otherness. Whether he quietly pronounces the key word "woman" or repeats to himself "I am a

---

ments a narrator who says I reports to us (one might go on infinitely and place in the stranger's narrative other strangers he has known and who one day shared their worries with him in the first person), and this perspective "en abîme," as we so prettily say (the cow carrying in its mouth a box of cheese with a label that represents a cow carrying in its mouth a box . . . etc., etc.) could not prevent Fromentin from being the only narrator, since it is his own story he makes the stranger tell—with a few slight modifications. Yet this triple internal distancing in the narrative is not a purely formal artifice; it somehow expresses the *distance from the self* that characterizes lived experience for Fromentin (at least during one period of his life).

55. "I am so difficult to know that I do not even know myself." *Souvenirs*, p. 100.

woman," the result is the same: he is transformed without losing his identity. He *is* female, always has been; he caresses his cool, soft, adolescent skin and *imagines to himself* that he Gustave, provided with female sex, is the object of male desire, and he writhes with sensual pleasure in his lover's grasp. Hooray! In this unstable and fleeting image, which, at the price of exhausting tension, can last for the time it takes to masturbate, other and self interpenetrate without opposing each other. As soon as he writes, otherness is what comes to the fore. Certainly he can scratch on a bit of paper—he's done it before—"I would like to be a woman," but that doesn't get him very far. How can he possess the "second sex" unless he recreates himself as a woman through words, with a woman's name, life, manners, condition, and destiny? Hence his metamorphosis: she is called Marguerite or Mazza. He could certainly give himself the pleasure of saying, "I." And afterward? This is what Maria will do a little later—inspired by Eulalie but especially by Flaubert's desires: "I am a country girl, my father was a farmer . . . For [the one who will be capable of making himself loved] I shall twist and turn like a snake, in the night I shall have wild gyrations and rending spasms." But despite the "I," or rather because of it, Maria becomes *the other;* she steals the first person singular from the author and affirms against him her illusory consistency as subject: it is *a* woman who says I, therefore an *object* for Gustave. This is all the more inevitable as his sexual desire is contradictory. Roger Kempf, in an excellent article,[56] found exactly the word to define it: androgynous. The woman he is describing—Maria or Mazza—is at once the woman he would like to be and the woman he would like to possess. Therefore, *the other and himself* constitute the core of his creatures. At an even deeper level, his original desire is not so much to be penetrated by a man's sex as to yield to the hands of a woman who is manipulating him. But at the same time he has the male desire to enter this strong woman, with the hint of a mustache on her upper lip, older than he, if only to legitimate in his own view and his partner's the dominating embraces to which he aspires; or he has this desire in order, as lord of the drama, to identify (as he did with Caroline) with the humble vassal swooning in his arms. At the very heart of the female character he invents there is a perpetual vicious circle, what Picasso calls "desire caught by the tail." This woman is Gustave's object only insofar as he aspires to become her docile object as quickly as possible, and for this reason the I and the He—in Mazza, for ex-

---

56. Cf. "Le double pupitre," *Cahiers du Chènevis,* October 1969.

ample—are swept up in an unceasing circular movement. Through her he enjoys, he describes, infinite insatiable lusts that elude him but that he would possess if he were a woman; through her he satisfies his resentments by means of monologue and crime. But suddenly she rises up *before him*, the Mother Goddess, devouring, satanic: he becomes her object; ungratified, she demands of him endless gratification; he will leave her his hide. Ernest, suddenly green with fear, flees to the ends of the earth; Gustave has made himself into Ernest in order to become the object of this imperious claim: in Ernest he admits that the love he wants to inspire in a "mistress" *frightens* him. The dominated woman interests him only to the extent that the dominating woman is awakened in her, an infinite *black* power that fills him with sensual desire until the moment he yields to her embrace. At this moment the creator, terrorized, is the object of his creature; he creates her such that she might satisfy that terror he both dreads and covets. But at the same time, proud, tormented, wicked, she becomes his hypostasis: in her monologues, which he wants to make delirious and sublime, she becomes his mouthpiece—once again we find the "mise en abîme" mentioned in an earlier note in connection with Fromentin, for the *I* of this She refers to that of the author. At the moment of her creation, Mazza is the author frightening himself. How should he recognize himself in this complex figure—not by her character but by the circularities and the "mise en abîme"—that is *himself and the other, himself as other*, and *the other as himself?* So unlikely is it that he does not hesitate—as we shall see below—to exercise his sadism on the *object* Mazza, thus making her the *absolute Other*. Yet how is it that he does not recognize himself in her? He loses himself in her, and at once his character appears to him as a disconcerting and unstable mixture of transparency and opacity.

What is more, the "unspeakable" complexity of his impulses cannot be summed up in a single protagonist. First of all, the narrative itself, if only formally, demands a number of actors: how can one describe the victim's sufferings without speaking of the executioner who inflicts them? What would Mazza be without Ernest? Or Garcia without old Cosme and François? Furthermore, written vengeance assumes the punishment of the wicked: the family drama is reorganized—unrecognizably—around the unhappy hero. Except that Gustave—and this *too* is his revenge—enters into the minds of these substitute henchmen and lends them thoughts purposely in order to give himself the pleasure of deciphering them. But as soon as he puts himself in his characters' place, it is *himself* he puts there: himself and something else; thus each of these characters is plural, for as they meekly play the role attributed to them, Flaubert slips into them, and it is as Flaubert that they think what, as the other, they actually do. Look at Isambart, who embodies gratuitous cruelty: he tortures Marguerite because, like Gustave, he hates ugliness; or, rather, Gustave inside him motivates his sadism by the hatred of ugliness. So Gustave needs Isambart in order to express *himself* fully; but as *that* character acts according to the nature assigned to him as torturer, the cringing hostility of a bewildered child toward everything that disturbs him is presented to us in an ignominious light. One in many, many in one. Dr. Mathurin is surely Father Flaubert and younger son at the same time. If we consider the syncretism of *Quidquid volueris*, we recognize that two fundamental themes have been skillfully woven together. We have long been familiar with the oldest of them: the father's curse, the *unjust* triumph of culture over nature and science over poetry; the other Gustave associated with Trouville: sexual jealousy, Schlésinger's *unjust* possession of Elisa. The two motifs work quite well together: the pivotal point is still usurpation, but it has doubled in volume—the usurpation of honors in the name of false merit, the usurpation of women. Monsieur Paul is charged with playing the role of double usurper, which indicates that he is produced by telescoping Achille and Schlésinger. At the same time he is the incarnation of the pater-familias who has cursed his son by engendering him and condemning him to be neither man nor beast. Can we say, then, that Gustave has given his character the explicit task of representing all these people at the same time? Certainly not. The unity of the character—which is undeniable—his subtle way of escaping all definition, lies primarily in the fact that he has been created by the plot itself, and that, within the plot, the second theme has served mainly to rejuvenate the first. Nonetheless, it is Monsieur Paul's essence to be double or triple, like the visitors of our dreams, not only because he is executioner and usurper twice over but because, in him, Gustave's impulses enclose real and various people, all equally guilty in his eyes, sometimes over-lapping one another and sometimes merging to reveal their variegated wickedness in a single denunciation. It should be added that Gustave would not be above slipping into the skin of this character from time to time: young and already famous, a man of science, an explorer, an adventurer, intelligent, insensitive, loved by women without having to pay for it, Monsieur Paul embodies everything Gustave lacks, every-thing that would make the little boy the happiest of men. And of course we know with what vengeful irony the author has invented this "marvel of civilization": he is everything Gustave detests. Yet he is also everything he envies: we are not unaware that at times he yearns to "shine in the salons" and that he is devastated not to be a millionaire. And he sometimes transfers himself to Monsieur Paul, his worst enemy, so as to enjoy for a moment the advantages he fears he will never possess. Gustave is like this in all his stories: omnipresent, unrecognizable. He is an accomplice to every one of his creatures, and there is not one who does not horrify him.

This is necessary if he wants to carry his hatred and his bitterness to the point of paroxism. As it progresses the written discourse must gradually disguise itself as something alien, as if it were produced by automatic writing. The monologue was his, was him, and for this reason it could not go as far as the examples given above; in other words, respect—or its appearance—remains, and hatred is hidden; various interdictions repress or distort his sexual impulses. For him, writing is the process of freeing himself of repression. When the ink is dry, the signs no longer belong to him: something has been set down that will belong to the first reader who leafs through those pages. It is of little importance that this first and only reader should be none other than himself; besides, all he can do with the writing now is to *read* it, passively lending himself to the resurrection of meanings. But *above all*, if these inconstant and diverse characters confront him with an irreducible materiality, if he *feels* that they are his images but doesn't know them at all, if he is never the one who tortures and punishes, if the cruelty takes place within the story and without any deus ex machina, solely through his creatures, if he can kill François only with Garcia's dagger and Garcia only with Cosme's sword—and Cosme only with the inevitable consequences of his conduct—Gustave is able to sidestep all possible censure. He is not responsible for anything: a tragic and bloody story is written through him and goes beyond him. Perhaps he pities Garcia, perhaps he would like to stay Cosme's hand; in vain, for these men have decided their own destinies. Thus, when a timid sleeper dreams of *murdering his father*, he arranges for it to be accomplished by someone else, whom he futilely attempts to restrain: all he can do is to throw himself weeping on the corpse. Little Flaubert, however, unlike the dreamer, is conscious of surreptitiously directing his oneirism. But he does not articulate it to himself; he has no words left to tell himself—they are at the end of his pen. It may be, for example—for all I know—that Gustave was never in on the secret of his fratricidal intentions, or that he deliberately saw only rhetorical figures in the imprecations of his internal monologue

("I'll kill you! I will!"). But scarcely has he conceived poor Garcia than the written words lead him on: the thought of the younger Medici son or his materialization becomes a decision, which leads inexorably to its execution. Gustave himself is only the historiographer: he tells the story, nothing more, and any enjoyment he may feel is just part of the bargain. In order that he might in particular satisfy his sadistic masochism and his masochistic sadism on all these unfortunates, he must be both the I and the He of each of them.

Masochism comes first: Gustave embodies himself in Marguerite, in Garcia, in Mazza, in Djalioh, all of them quivering and tormented. He enjoys suffering a million deaths through them. Resentment, pride, passivity. The primary and arousing pleasure is submission. The curse of the father and the insertion of the member—it's all the same: he is skewered by his destiny. If he pushes his misfortune to the extreme by writing, it is to denounce the infamy of his executioner by means of that inflexible obedience we discussed in part one. If Mazza sufers infinitely, it is because she is possessed by the desire for the infinite—with which Gustave endows her to the extent that he himself is quite incapable of feeling it. We are here at the stage of dolorism, that arrogant and vindictive masochism. Here, harsh pride—I am the greatest lack—is combined with powerful rancor—they have deprived me of everything.

But to the extent that the character, self-enclosed, dense, and secret, becomes an object for Gustave, to the extent that Mazza, through the very words he uses to describe her, is presented in her own right as a beautiful young woman with a splendid body, he pursues her with angry cruelty—no longer to condemn the world and his father through her, but for the exciting pleasure of becoming one of the pack, of doubling the suffering of the poor abandoned girl, of tearing apart her sumptuous flesh, and, by leading her to her death, of symbolically annihilating the universe in this singular disappearance. He will not spare her even afterward: she is naked and dead, therefore more than naked; the commissioner, who has come to take a deposition, will further besmirch this obscene abandon with the scrutiny of a voyeur. Marguerite—as he projects himself into her—is "sentient fragrance"; but it has also pleased her demonic creator to make her an ugly, unhappy woman—everything he abhors. What pleasure he takes in tormenting her! Isambart, instantly summoned, certainly represents human wickedness: he is there, as we can imagine, in a purely representative capacity. But suddenly Gustave gets inside *him*—without even knowing it, I suppose—and makes himself the executioner of his own base works. We know the results: how the little boy, "sweet as a bad angel," will lead his victim from disgrace to disgrace and finally to the dissection table. He takes a sadistic pleasure in detailing the misfortunes of virtue in order to give substance to his masochistic belief that the worst is always certain. For us as readers who are *strangers*, this double satisfaction by martyrdom and viciousness results in the profound, and surprising, ambiguity of his characters: they are wicked as hell, we are told, but they are never to blame; they are the best sons of the earth since they suffer, and their infinite suffering demonstrates the immensity of their desires, so the author affirms, but he never evinces his solidarity with them. Hernani too is one of the damned of the earth, bringing misfortune to everyone around him; but Hugo loves himself and puts himself into his character with such complacency that we immediately put ourselves there as well; banished but splendid, we weep for ourselves. What reader could identify with the disastrous Marguerite, the wretched Garcia, or even with the disturbing Mazza? They inspire neither respect nor pity but, rather, intermittent irritation, which is exactly what the young writer feels for these creatures who are not sufficiently himself and not sufficiently other. He created them in order to see himself as other, and their otherness excites him now, for their relative independence is combined with total dependence and he can dispose of them at will, provided he does this through the mediation of other characters. Can we say that they are presented to us as pure objects? That would be inaccurate since we are constantly entering into them and are constantly invited to be caught up in their monologues. No sooner have these eloquent complaints drawn us into the heart of these martyrs, however, than we are driven out; on the other hand, as executioners we are bidden to enjoy their sufferings. At this moment their very subjectivity becomes (or rather would become, if the child's writing ability equaled the richness of his intentions) an *object of pleasure* for the sadistic reader: again he can penetrate the victim at will so as to feel as nearly as possible what the victim feels—without leaving the comfort of his otherness—or pretend to be unaware that the character has a human consciousness and suffers in order to affirm all the more his own omnipotence. But these very conditions and the perpetual reversal of outside and inside make the victims' objective status uncertain: we enter into them, we *are* their suffering and their unreflexive discourse, we leave them, we enjoy the delectable sight of their throbbing bodies, we enter them again, we become the *reflection as other* of their consciousness, which becomes reflected consciousness, the quasi-object of a reflexive subject that escapes it. In brief, we can never situate ourselves comfortably in relation to these creatures because the author has created them in discomfort under the dictates of multiple and contradictory desires. Such as they are, however, their pendular movement—an unrelieved oscillation between the subject-martyr and the tormented object, which corresponds to their author's oscillation between doloristic resentment and viciousness—gives them a suspect presence and a grating ambiguity never before encountered in the European novel. From his first writings Gustave permanently structured his creative intuition, which would later give birth to Emma Bovary. Unloved, scarcely loving himself, he invented a new discomfort for the reader: he gives his characters the task of making material and individual, beyond the words that describe them or report their acts and thoughts, what is inarticulable in his fundamental desire.

We have not yet reached the stage of true conversion, which is characterized by a complete reversal and a decisive assumption. And our descriptions have shown only the phases of a process of internalization: Gustave has been reduced to talking to himself in silence, writing to himself. Literature seems to him a means of escaping from autism by materializing and rationalizing the imaginary; at the same time it allows him to satisfy unreally his desire to desire as well as his actual desires. But it is still only a means: he uses it morosely, regretting the sonorous power of spoken words; he is afraid to commit himself to a dead end. Suppose he is not gifted? He "will enter into literature" definitively when he comes to consider it his absolute end. Indeed, on the first of April 1836,[57] in the postscript to *Un Parfum à sentir*—he is fourteen years old—he cries: "To write, oh to write is to seize the world . . ." and we can consider the conversion complete. What has happened? In order to understand, we must reread the entire paragraph I cited at the end of the preceding chapter.

What strikes us first is the highlighting of the totalizing intention. "To write is to seize the world and sum it up in a book." And, especially, it is to transform it radically. Gustave had long harbored the ambition to totalize: in the "billiard room" we saw him become a jack-of-all-trades for the ultimate purpose of producing *out of nothing*, ex nihilo, the final object, namely the public performance. But at the time

---

57. We do not claim that the conversion took place that day, or that it came like a thunderclap. We say, rather, for reasons we go into later, that Gustave became conscious of what the fact of writing meant for him *at the earliest* during the school year 1834–35, *at the latest* on the first of April 1836.

he conceived of totalization in exteriority, like those vertical concentrations which allow certain companies to control a product from the extraction of raw material to the ultimate stage of manufacture. I call these totalizations "exterior" because they may allow costs to be lowered or productivity to be increased by eliminating middlemen, for example, but they do not necessarily improve the quality of the product or substantially reduce the number of work hours necessary to produce it. In other words, it is *a priori* a matter of indifference to the producer and the consumer whether or not the paper manufacturer owns the forest that provides the raw material. Of course, in the context of a national economy such concentrations will have important consequences—which can even turn a society upside down—but this is *a posteriori* insofar as they accelerate the process of integration that characterizes today's capitalism, or insofar as a consequence of possessing mines or forests abroad is the sacking of underdeveloped countries;[58] with regard to the paper, it is difficult to decide if it would be better or worse. The same goes for Gustave's plays. It is true that he did everything himself and was rightly proud of it, but the extensive totalization was to result in the production of that *singular play, L'Amant avare,* which would show us the comic misfortunes of a highly "conventional" *individual:* the moment he slips into this epigone of Harpagon, does it matter that Gustave rather than some other household member or family friend has nailed the boards he is standing on? The play must go on. And it must be good.

From the moment he writes, everything changes: the totalization is internalized within the finished product. *Le Voyage en enfer* dates from 1835; it was no more than eighteen months earlier that Gustave had "put aside the billiard table" forever. And no writing will show more clearly, more naively, his new totalizing intention: the subject of the story is nothing less than the world; after traveling through it quite exhaustively, the child discovers it is hell. In short, he is totalizing an infinite but imaginary experience. The objective and subjective aspects of that experience are highly noticeable, for on the one hand it "sums up" the world and on the other it "constitutes" the author. Gustave will be more explicit a year later when he writes the postscript: "To write is to seize the world . . ." Concomitantly, "it is to experience one's thought being born, growing, living, standing upright

58. But this heavy exploitation and pillage would be no different in nature if a foreign company were to buy the soil or the subsoil of the country in question and to limit itself to extracting a material, which another foreign company would then take over and work into a product.

on a pedestal, and remaining there forever." The objective totalization of the cosmos can be done only in the subjective milieu of the totalization of a *person*. Eventually both merge in the work, which is thought objectified, raised up forever on a pedestal, that is, separated from the author. The book is simultaneously the subjectivization of the objective and the objectivization of the subjective.

In *Le Voyage en enfer*, however, while the totalizing ambition is very pronounced, the boy is far from being fully aware of it. It is not the author who does the totalizing but Satan. Gustave does not take sides: after all, isn't his guide often called "the Deceiver"? Yet the relation of the literary object to the subject who composes it is given *in the writing:* for hell is not simply defined as the place of ultimate suffering, it is Satan's *realm:* he is the one who doles out misfortune and makes sure that the worst is always certain. Thus the unity of the world and the sinister coherence of the movements that traverse it reflect the will of the devil and his malign intentions: the world is his product, it is the objectivization of the Accursed One or, if you will, his objective being. Satan is a novelist; the cosmos he governs, subject to general laws and particular decisions, is a singular universal, just as a book is. Inversely, the author is a devil—Gustave will say it himself soon enough, and he will not refrain from pushing his creatures into the infernal cauldron.

For the moment, he makes a pretense of harboring a creative freedom that frightens him. He copies and betrays, as he did in his heyday as author-actor; the paradox is that he has taken *Paroles d'un croyant*[59] as his model. We note the decided unreality of the author: "And I was on Mount Atlas," etc. Who is speaking? The little boy who, a year later in the postscript to *Un Parfum*, will say: "The first chapter *I* did in one day?" Certainly not. The *I* of *Le Voyage en enfer*, Flaubert's first literary *I*, is that of Lamennais or, rather, Gustave posing as Lamennais. Furthermore, the young author borrows the themes of his elder and goes so far as to copy his style: *Le Voyage* is written in biblical verses, which nearly all begin with the conjunction "and." Lamennais's inspiration temporarily finds its source in revolutionary optimism. Gustave knows this so well that at times he cannot help imitating that optimism: in the course of his journey, the narrator sees Liberty triumph over Absolutism by beating him over the head with the club of Reason. Liberty, moreover, is also called Civilization. Here

59. Published in 1834. Outraged by the attitude of Gregory XVI, Lamennais had abandoned the (hidden) pessimism of theocracy for democratic optimism.

297

we have pure Lamennais. This society of free and reasonable men predicted by the young author: is this hell? Not hell, but the result of Progress, that bourgeois utopia which Flaubert will soon view with horror. Gustave nonetheless remains unperturbed: what does it matter to him if a few remnants of his model crop up here and there in his manuscript. The essential thing is the transmutation of the positive into something negative: the religious and biblical majesty of *Paroles d'un croyant* is used for the hidden purpose of expressing a grinding despair. In this sense Flaubert in his youth is much like the devil: like the spirit who always denies, he needs Being and the positive in order to vampirize it and turn it into negation: as an author he becomes the parasite of an already written text which he bends to his own ends by making it say the opposite of what it says.[60] His procedure here consists of giving himself over to an alien totality whose structures and rhythms he learns by heart so that he can then fuse recitation and inspiration. Inspired, he reconstitutes his lesson through writing and limits himself to reversing signs with a snap of his fingers, so that the conclusion, a totalizing negation, imposes itself on him in all its rigor. This paradoxical choice of models allows us to understand that in 1835, at least, Gustave was not fully aware of the consequences of his literary option. What has obviously happened is that language *by itself* has revealed to him totalization in interiority. The moment one enters language to cultivate it and not to use it for one's own purposes, there is no way out again; the work is its own foundation: being a determination of language, it finds within it its material and its instruments. What need have we of nails and boards when we have the *words* "board" and "nail," and when the justification of a literary work can be provided only by another discourse, which is also dependent on literature?[61] In short, language is a conventional totality; as soon as we accept the substitution of words for things, as every writer does,

60. We already encountered this process in our discussion of *L'Anneau du prieur*. J. Bruneau gives an excellent demonstration of it in his work, *Les Débuts littéraires de Gustave Flaubert* (pp. 235–36), when he recalls the parable of the traveler in Lamennais and the use Flaubert makes of it in *Agonies*. Lamennais: *a number* of travelers; a heavy rock blocking the way; uniting in their efforts, they move it and resume their progress. Flaubert: *one* traveler confronted with the same rock, which he cannot move; he tries to scale it, falls back exhausted, cries for help, no one comes to his aid, tigers devour him.

61. Unless, as in *La Modification*, the interior discourse of the novel takes account of *everything*, including the novel itself: the character is led to the point where it becomes necessary and urgent for him to take up the pen; that is, the last page of the narrative justifies the first and vice versa. It must be recognized, however, that this attempt at circularity—which has numerous precedents (*Werther*, for example)—is not one of the happier features of this in many ways remarkable book.

as Gustave has just done, then the word is transformed into the world or, if you like, being-in-the-world appears as a being-in-the-word. The immediate result for a mind bent on totalities is that totalization can only be intensified. When words symbolize as much as they signify, they refer only to words, for two reasons: because the grapheme with all its signifying functions is already the totalization of an absence, of language as a whole; and because, when language is taken as an analogue of a signified, this semantic totalization has the effect of making its materialization stand out as display. In other words, the unity of language as perpetual totalization gives the dispersal of the real universe the imaginary unity of a *Creation.*

Gustave does not of course *know* any of this when he begins to write. Words are what lead him into the interior of language, words are what fulfill him such that after a brief attempt—in publishing his school newspaper—to find a graphic equivalent of extensive totalization, the child no longer feels the need for it and reduces the material work of the laborer in art, as he will later call him, to simple writing. It goes without saying, however, that he would not have submitted to being led in this way if he were not in search of a *Nature-organism* inside and outside himself to pit against the mechanism of his father. In making a work, he becomes *his* work; the creation of the imaginary world by words cannot be done without his constituting himself, against molecular dissemination, in the indestructable organic unity of the creator. In fact, the totalizing character of the word has often escaped the best writers, whether they wish to produce merely singular determinations of discourse—which happens with those I would call anecdotal in character—or whether they aim for the signified in its reality—which is the case, for example, with pamphleteers. This totalizing character is manifest to Gustave to the precise extent that the imaginary child comes to terms with the unreal presence of the totalized.

Flaubert, however, might have spent a good deal more time thinking about it if the ideology of early romanticism had not itself been totalitarian out of abhorrence and scorn of bourgeois liberalism. We do not know when he read *Faust,* that magnificent "mirror of the world," which was to have a decisive effect on him later—because the subject of the drama was none other than the *All.* Maynial dates this encounter at around 1834, but without convincing evidence. Besides, the German author's ego is not visible in his work to a very young boy. Flaubert did not know Quinet's *Ahasverus,* it seems, before 1836. But Lamennais was sufficient. Without *Paroles d'un croyant* he could not have made the leap; what he found in it—along with the universe—was the possibility of making an unreal world totalized by an imaginary subject. Not that in Lamennais the subject is not *real*: indeed, it is the disappointed theocrat who expresses himself in his book. But when the child abandons himself to his inspiration-recitation, he *plays the role* of a sententious biblical prophet. In this way there is perfect homogeneity between the speaking ego and what he says: both are imaginary. This was necessary at first; only an unreal author can attempt the panoramic—therefore unreal—totalization of the universe. Gustave, however, consumed by imagination, could not have conceived on his own that his magnificent project of seizing the world and annihilating it by unrealizing it demanded of him the simultaneous process of his own unrealization. Lamennais offers him his self and a text to consume: the child seizes both. In the text, totalization is presented as already accomplished; the false Lamennais need only remake it in the negative: the world of God is the little world of the devil. We can easily imagine with what fascination the little boy read *Paroles d'un croyant*: to escape his condition as an inexperienced child whom adults refuse the right to express his "full presentiment of life," to borrow the knowledge and voice of a fifty-year-old and at the same time wrench himself out of the human condition, perch like some giant on a summit, and from this height survey the entire planet. We know that his family history had long prepared him for vertical ascension, so to speak, and that verticality finally structured his stupors, transforming them into imaginary ecstasies. Later, in *Agonies*, he would reproduce the *Voyage* episode. But—and we shall get a fuller view of this in another chapter—the narrator, who speaks in the first person and whom the devil has spirited away in the folds of his cloak, is a desolate child. Or rather, he *was* a child: his adventure has already taken place, he is retelling it. This is because, in the meanwhile, Gustave has seen things clearly, as the postscript to *Un Parfum* demonstrates: in order to be unrealized within his panoramic ego, there is no need to transform himself into a colossal Memnon; the process of totalizing is enough. The entrance into literature is like entering a religious order: one devotes one's life and soul to the imaginary to the degree that it is given form through words. For Gustave, literature has only one subject, *everything*, and every work, long or short, must say *everything* in its own way. This involves a total requisition of his person.

Let us not imagine, however, that even at the time of writing *Un Parfum* Gustave was aware of the extreme implications of his option; he would not reach this awareness until the crisis of January 1844.

What struck him above all in April 1835, when he reread the story of poor Marguerite, was that he had captured the world and human society in his vignette, and that at the same time he had gained *his own person:* the book-becoming of the world could not be accomplished, in effect, without the *world-becoming* of his thought—which must be taken here in the largest sense (sensibility, affections, imagination, understanding). This thought, at first hesitant—it has just been born— seeks itself, deepens and amplifies itself until it embraces the infinite universe. What triumphant joy! We are not far from Mallarmé's orphism. And what a will to power: *to seize the world!* His power surpasses Nero's—that emperor reigned over Rome but not over the sun. Flaubert reigns over everything, even the stars, provided they descend into the words used to designate them. Here we have the revenge of the disinherited child: he was nothing, had nothing; now he is everything, has everything. In one sentence he makes ten heads fall and can make worlds collide; and when he returns to his manuscript as a reader, he eventually extracts from it something that is at once the objective sense of being and the fundamental character of his own thought. It is in his work that he will make himself into Tamberlaine, Genghis Khan, and all the other famous ravagers; in his work he will make apparent the relation of interiority that unites him, a microcosm, to the macrocosm he describes. At once the conversion is accomplished: it is a new moment of his *personalization,* he has found his *being;* since his ego is nothing other than the world totalized, he will be the one who captures the infinite in words and constitutes his own person. This is what might be called the demiurgic temptation; he gives in to it, his pride stops at nothing. And in that instant he wants to forget that his omnipotence exists only in the realm of the imaginary and holds sway only over word-images. In the "strange, bizarre, incomprehensible" work he has just reread, he has found something consistent, the impenetrable residue of a forgotten thought, of *his* thought, an autonomous life that suddenly refers him to the impenetrable consistency of *his* person, that is, of the builder who never shows himself except in the singularity of the structures he erects. It will be noted, indeed, that nothing in the postscript indicates that this totalization is born of the reciprocal unrealization of the producer and his product. Gustave *knows* it, however; at least, he is conscious of it. But in these moments—so rare for him—of intense jubilation, when he finds himself face to face with the quasi object he has pulled out of nothingness, he strives—the way he did as an actor—to pretend that his discretionary power over being is only the unreal reverse of his absolute impotence. After 1844 everything will become clear: genius and fool, the family idiot will have become Gustave Flaubert; until then he will continue to vacillate between truth and antitruth, between the real imaginary and the imagined real. A passage from *Mémoires d'un fou* clearly indicates his uncertainties: "There are poets with souls full of fragrance and flowers who see life as the dawn of heaven; others have nothing but gloom, bitterness, and anger . . . Each of us has a prism through which we perceive the world. Happy is he who sees pleasant colors and cheerful things in it . . ." This text in its benign tolerance offers the view that everyone, according to his personal history and temperament, has his particular weltanschauung, and that the world is rich enough to support them all; he who would claim to reduce the world to what he sees through his own prism would at once drift, by his exclusivity, into the Imaginary. The universe would therefore never be "summed up" in a book; it would appear only in the colors that characterize him who depicts it. But there is not one line in the *Mémoires* that does not belie this feigned tolerance: evil, that is the secret meaning of the world; and Gustave uses the diversity of opinions to justify his despairing skepticism. The worst is always certain—is this *true* or is it *imagined?* He does not yet come to any decision, for he lacks the power of affirmation. But he is not unaware, at bottom, that in choosing words he has opted for nontruth, for appearance and nonbeing; better, that he has somehow confirmed his absolute impotence. Witness, in the *Mémoires*, his cry of rage: if they knew, the fools, what is going on inside me, they would take me "for a carnival showman, for a maker of books." If he does not want to collapse, he must not limit himself to imagining the world; he must also imagine to himself that he imagines it as it is. For the moment at least: as long as he has not firmly established the imaginary's absolute superiority over reality.

In any case, if he seizes the world so as to put it into those little herbariums, books, we know that it is not so as to know the world but to possess it and abolish it—doubly: by reducing the world to the universe of words, which he knows how to use, and by permeating it with the negative principle, evil, which if it alone governs the course of things can only mean the systematic self-destruction of being. We can see in these conditions how the conversion issues dialectically from the unreal fulfillment of singular desires through the materialization of the word, encloses those desires, totalizes and surpasses them. What are those desires, indeed, if not destructive impulses born of resentment and of Gustave's need for compensation, and cast by his passivity into sadistic and masochistic dreams? Each of them represents Gustave's being-in-the-world. Left to themselves, sometimes they isolate themselves and affix themselves to one word, and sometimes they interpenetrate and indulge together in a syncretism without real unity. Literature offers itself, therefore, as their unification. Not in the sense of a rationalization or an articulation but, quite the contrary, insofar as in its original statement it develops and renders hyperbolic the negative ferment that is the same in each of those desires. Literature presents itself as an enterprise of possession (compensating omnipotence) and of radical extinction (words substituted for things, imaginary substituted for real, denunciation of evil), since its object is explicitly the *All*, that is, all forms of being which are drawn into Gustave's poisonous dream. What is obscure in his impulses, at the first degree, becomes perfectly clear in the second degree, in the literary project. The literary project, however, far from replacing these primary desires, allows them to *organize themselves* freely at the heart of a story, determining its episodes as they will, a story upon which the literary project itself imposes nothing other than the totalizing unity of a narrative, that is, a succession of events apparently linked, whatever their underlying sources. In short, the hidden postulations, those that dare not speak their name and those that stammer it, continue to be gratified oneirically, beneath a disguise: in a Marguerite, in a Mazza, the young author can ruin himself without recognizing himself. Still, the literary intention being a totalizing one, his desires are satisfied *as if in the real world*, and each desire in the story is expressly charged with revealing the being-in-the-world of the character in whom it finds satisfaction. Furthermore, each is exalted by the fact that it is felt to be involved in a vast enterprise, the total gratification of hatred through the extinction of being. Each desire is recognized in this enterprise, and vice versa, just as the place of each desire in the narrative is marked by the total enterprise as both an *inessential moment* (I am quite willing for Isambart to torment Marguerite, but let him act quickly) and a *necessary phase* (since the global enterprise of abolition is at the heart of each anecdotal enterprise, just as the whole is present in the part). Thus the moment it is satisfied within the narrative, shamefully, behind a mask, each desire feels eminently gratified by the construction of the literary object in which it participates. The superior, total gratification happens this time without a mask, since it is the author who satisfies himself in and through the project of denouncing the world. To tell the truth, the author remains an imaginary figure, but he is still Gustave the pup-

303

peteer as he is unrealized in himself. So the work, taken as a totality, finds its confirmation and its density in the satisfactions of detail which are its episodes—and each of these finds its deepest meaning in the totality of the work. Thus the author is at once outside, constructing his trap for the world, and inside, experiencing suffering and pleasure in all his characters.

Gustave, between the ages of thirteen and fourteen, was converted to literature when he understood that he could use it in an attempt at countercreation, which would make him the imaginary equal of God, and that the enterprise of writing would at last give him his *being*—that he could construct himself in the process of constructing. At a deeper level, literary work offered itself to him as the highest form of suicide. I am not claiming that this child of thirteen could already have understood all that Mallarmé develops in *Igitur,* which we might call "On literature considered as suicide." But I would recall that at this period he was almost continually tempted to end his life. We have seen to what extent this temptation involves bitter humility and insane pride. Gustave sees dying as a way of eliciting the ultimate consequence of the paternal curse, and thus turning it against the one who pronounced it; it is also a way of *making himself the equal of the Creator* by annihilating His Work in the person of His witness. If he dies by his own hands, the flame that kindles being is extinguished, and the creation is engulfed in darkness. We have noticed the strange arrogance betrayed by this suicidal project: is Gustave indeed the only witness, the only flame? And what about the rest of us, his grandchildren? And our great grandchildren? And what of God himself, who sustains the world by continuous creation? At this moment it becomes apparent to us that through God the little boy was pursuing the unique paterfamilias: you made me; all right, I am worthy of you since I destroy myself. This is the meaning of all those raging suicides that people his early works. The murder of François is self-punishment: Garcia doesn't even take the trouble to hide from it. But above all, as we know, it is the punishment of the father: by forcing Cosme to kill him, the younger son sovereignly destroys all the father's work, a quarter of a century's efforts to raise his elder son to the rank of cardinal. All these considerations were and remain valid, provided we take no account of the literary project. Because this project is essentially *totalizing* for Gustave, it naturally becomes a project to capture the world in a mirror—something that cannot happen without a general derealization of the cosmos. And this in turn requires that the operator derealize himself, first in a single stroke, if only to conceive the enterprise, then more and more as a direct function of the panoramic view that tears him from his anchorage and from the universe. Once again we find very specifically the dialectical connection that the suicidal Gustave has established between his own extinction and that of the macrocosm: in order to destroy the world it was necessary and sufficient that the child destroy himself; in order to derealize the world, that is, to draw it into words, it is necessary to make himself the imaginary lord of language. Is this enough? We shall soon answer this question. But we cannot doubt that the metamorphosis is indispensable: a detached consciousness, imaginary master of word-images, *this and nothing more*. This is dying: the author denies *real* needs (or satisfies them without noticing), he abstains from *living his life;* lived experience, however, does not cease sliding confusedly toward real death, but it is reduced to an anonymous flow by the systematic absenteeism of the living person. Passions themselves are no longer *felt:* they may roar, but the master of words is in a state of permanent distraction where they are concerned, unless he gives them imaginary gratification through language. There were, then, two stages: before the conversion, unreal satisfaction was the aim; at the moment of conversion, the bewildered child glimpses that, in a later phase, the sought-for satisfaction will become a means of writing. The artist will produce the countercreation only if he becomes a conscious corpse and if he considers all life, including his own, from death's point of view. Before 1844, Flaubert is entangled in his own ideas. He even rails against art and artists who ape the divine work, the creation. But this is because he has lost his grip: what the "Artist" wants, what Gustave wants deeply but without being clearly conscious of it, is not to *produce being* but, quite the contrary, to reduce being to an immense mirage, which will self-destruct in the process of totalization. He will give being to nonbeing while intending to make manifest the nonbeing of being. The supporting structure of the work is of course material—these are printed words; but the use to which they are put unrealizes them, and the printed book becomes a permanent center of derealization. To kill and be killed simultaneously in a frenzy of enthusiasm which screens an already sepulchral calm: this, in a word, is what proposes itself to the child.

I say distinctly, *proposes* itself, since it is his totalizing ambition that comes to him through the symbolic structures of language. He does not *know* it, he *feels* it: it is the summons of death. For this child "born with the desire to die," indeed, there is true being only in the permanence of nonbeing: "Man . . . loves death with a consuming love. He gives it all that he creates, he leaves it, he returns to it, he does nothing but dream of it while he lives, he has the germ of death in his body and the desire for it in his heart." Life is a brief convulsion, a fixed grin, a provisional status. True being is that "of the long stone effigies lying on their tombs," inorganic, eternal images of the perishable human organism. And when he defines life beyond the tomb: "If one still must feel something, let it be one's own nothingness, let death feed on itself, admire itself; just enough life to feel that one no longer exists." Isn't it clear that this is precisely the kind of existence literature offers him—no longer to *feel* anything but that one no longer feels anything, to imagine everything and deposit word-images in the eternal materiality of the book? This is what he desires when in the postscript, he rejoices to see his thought "being born, growing, standing on a pedestal, never to descend again." The succession of these verbs is revealing: in them we see thought, at first *organic*, transformed into a public being, like the stone effigies in which it is petrified in the process of totalization, surviving everything, as it stands on its pedestal, in the inert insolence of its minerality. Literature offers itself, therefore, as a prefiguration of death: if one enters it, one is a living witness to the mineralization of one's Idea, that is, of one's own person. To make a book is "to give death what one creates," to become, while alive, something nonliving that belongs to nonlife, to the inorganic, all the while reducing the totalized world to its pure appearance. For Gustave, writing is the refusal of anchorage; but at the same time, as an impassive worker of language, it is the attaining of the incorruptible being of matter through the perpetual transformation of subjective "thought" into written words, beyond the games of the being of nonbeing and the nonbeing of being.

Thus Gustave, around 1835, had a double conception of literature: on the one hand, insofar as it proceeded from the interior monologue, it appeared to him as a totalizing gratification, unreal but materialized, of his rancors and desires—a virulent frenzy that would be calmed only when it had put the world in a cage in order to denounce its unreality. On the other hand, it was an appeal to calm, an invitation to rejoin, while still alive, the eternal ataraxia of the dead. These two aspects of art are not really contradictory, for the second requires a murder-suicide to begin with, which the child often dreamed of accomplishing out of pride and retribution in order to punish the unworthy father and all his infamous partisans. In any case, the sacrifice accomplished, it is the extinction of desire—except what is imaginary—that proposes itself. He who "makes Art," as Gustave will say later, "is not born for pleasure." In both cases the choice of the imaginary is vengeance and compensation, which explains the audacity with which Gustave will soon be able to leap from one conception to the other. For the moment, the first is predominant: this oversensitive boy has amassed too many rancors, humiliations, affronts; he feels frustrated, anguished, his own enemy and everyone else's; writing is his imaginary revolt. Yet the second conception is not absent here; Gustave already has an inkling of it as it emerges through the first and motivates it. For the countercreation *must* be totalizing. And totalization as a task to be accomplished and forever begun anew, to the extent that it is the rule of appearances or, if you like, the norm of the imaginary, suddenly reveals its true face: it is merely the other name for Beauty. We will return at more leisure to Flaubert's idea of the Beautiful. For the moment it remains embryonic. Let us note, however, that, from this time forward, it appears to the child as the only justification of unreality. Even in this still crude form the conception is richer and more original than the one he saw paraded in the manuals, which made beauty "multiplicity in unity." That notion, which remains strictly formalistic, provides us in effect with an entirely abstract means of judging *Don Quixote* and, quite as easily, an occasional poem on the death of a parrot. Kant, whatever one may say, establishes this definition on a philosophical foundation but adds nothing to it when he presents the Beautiful as a finality without end. The mark of finality is the integration of diversity through *praxis:* take away the end, and what remains is the integration, which is posed for itself but has lost its meaning. Thus, in the eighteenth century the aesthetic object was determined by means of the narrow but external relations of its parts to one another. A hundred years later, Valéry went no further when he demanded that each element in a work of art should maintain a multiplicity of relations with all the others. Running through the nineteenth century is a strong current, born in the classical centuries, that goes against romanticism, symbolism, and Mallarmé, and aims to explain works of art by analytical reason.

From the age of thirteen, Gustave is protected from this error by his hatred of paternal mechanism. He is not at all concerned, at least at the outset, with unifying diversity by whatever means. He begins with a totalizing intuition, as suggested by this well-known passage from the *Mémoires:* "I had an infinity more vast, if that is possible, than God's . . . and then I had to descend once more from those sublime regions toward words, and how can we render in speech the har-

307

mony that rises in the heart of the poet and the gigantic thoughts that bend a sentence, just as a strong, swollen hand bursts through the glove that covers it?" This infinity, "more vast than God's," makes us smile despite the disclaimer "if that is possible." Nonetheless, these are not hollow words: certainly Gustave "has" nothing at all, but the intention is clear: he plays at embracing God's infinity, which is none other than Creation itself, from the point of view of nothingness, which, according to him existed before Creation and will survive it. Nothingness: *its* point of view, the very seat of panoramic consciousness. Nonbeing surrounds being on every side, slips into it, circulates through the porosities of the macrocosm; suddenly nonbeing is the substance; and movements, lights, sounds are only accidents. This is where the totalization of appearances should take place: the Creation is offered to Gustave, who hovers above it; he discovers it as an All whose secret he knows, or, more precisely, it is the secret that totalizes Creation (the world is hell). And totality is a very specific form of unity: in it, the All is the synthesis of all the parts and *their relations of interiority*, but it is also fully present in each only by their singular determination, by the nothingness which is in them and which prevents the whole–part relationship from being reciprocal. As this part of nothingness is capable of being only *appearance*, the parts are distinct from one another *on the surface* but bear witness to the same essence which produces and informs them. Far from diversity unifying itself, therefore—or being unified from the outside by some demiurge—it is the original and synthetic unity that is diversified without ceasing to be unity; nor does it cease to manifest itself simultaneously in each of its hypostases as their fundamental meaning and the mysterious yet perceptible affinities that unite them, establishing harmonies among lights, scents, and sounds, revealing through diverse lives the same misfortune belonging to all men, the same curse of Adam. This will be beauty for Flaubert, this is what will now overwhelm him when he thinks of it. And, since there can be no question of finding it in the real universe, which is probably the effect of chance, it must be seen as the fundamental claim of the imaginary. Art, like the countercreation, aims at producing centers of derealization where nothing is to be found but a universe-image born of a vivid and totalizing intuition present in a work in every single detail and in all of them together, just as the whole is present in the part. In short, this universe-image is understood everywhere as the secret and mutual appropriation of words or colors or sounds, as the deepest essence of any element taken in particular, and as the *unsayable* meaning of the entire work in which it is manifest and which it overflows with its infinity. For example, if the world-image is like hell, there must be an affinity between the torments of the damned and the objects that surround him: not that this environment is necessarily sinister; yet the splendor of the forest or of the ocean must by some sorcery express the same unsayable idea as does human suffering. Is this to say that meaning must be a thesis and that the novel, for example, must be written in order to demonstrate that we live in the realm of Satan? Not at all; we shall see in another chapter that Gustave's "idea"—the world is hell—is not only unsayable but unthinkable and, consequently, unthought. It can only be suggested as immanent and transcendent as a whole in relation to all the connected episodes in which the young author seeks to satisfy himself in the imaginary. And, indeed, when we recall that Flaubert's desires are inarticulate, that the characters in his early works[62] are at once lyrical subjects and the objects of his sadism, that he totalizes from the first words (*ananke* in the introduction to *Un Parfum*, the prophecy in the opening chapter of *La Peste à Florence*) in order subsequently to unfold this "summing up" of the world in an adventure and fold it up again in the final conflagration—which is what gives novelistic time the circularity that is the very image of temporal totalization—then we perceive that the totalizing unity is too rich and too complex to be contained in a formula, and we can only *live* it in imagination by unrealizing ourselves in the reading of the story.

Such is beauty, then, dimly glimpsed by Flaubert as the supreme end of his totalizing impulse. He can dream of it in certain moments of ecstasy as a self-enclosed infinity which is present even in a blade of grass. He can come even closer to it in certain of his stupors. This can be seen clearly in a passage from the first *Tentation:*

The Devil

Often, for no special reason—a drop of water, a seashell, a single hair—you are brought up short, your eyes fixed, your heart open. The object you were contemplating seemed to gain ascendancy over you to the extent that you yielded to it, and bonds were established. You were pressed together, you were joined by innumerable subtle strands; then, by virtue of looking, you could no longer see; listening, you heard nothing, and in the end your very mind lost the notion of that particularity which had held its attention. It was like a vast harmony swallowed up in your soul . . .

---

62. And also of course in the mature novels, but with more art and artifice.

> You felt in its plenitude an *unsayable*[63] understanding of the unre-
> vealed whole . . . because of the infinite that bathed you both (you
> and the object), you interpenetrated equally and a subtle current
> passed from you to matter while the life of the elements slowly
> overtook you, like sap rising; one degree more and you became
> nature, or nature became you.[64]

This passage has multiple implications, and in the following pages
we shall often return to it. What interests us for the moment is the
aesthetic project manifest in it (which finds its issue in the first *Saint
Antoine*). Every object is evidence of the infinite because it bathes in it
and contains it; the same is true of every subject, despite its particularity. Consequently, the relation of subject to object is not unity but,
on its deepest level, identity. Contemplating a "drop of water" Gustave finds in it the whole of creation as well as his own existence: he
becomes a drop of water, and the drop of water is transformed "by the
subtle current that passes from him to matter." At the farthest limit,
Gustave is the totalizer totalized: he becomes nature—a pantheistic
ecstasy—he abandons himself to divine totalization, he is nothing
less than the presence of the All here and now; or nature becomes
him: he enfolds and totalizes the infinity of creation in his particular
determination. And this second metamorphosis—compression, condensation, a "summing up" of the universe—can happen only through
unrealization; the artist will unrealize himself in what Hegel has
called the *absolute subject*. In these moments when Gustave scatters
himself[65] in order to be caught up again into a vast synthesis, the scat-
tering is real, the synthesis is a proposition of the imaginary. Further,
he must distinguish between the ecstatic experience of the totalized
and the task of the retotalizer. Gustave makes the distinction *himself*:
the former he names *poetry*, and the latter, literature (or art, as you
like): "I had to descend once more from those sublime regions toward
words . . . and how can we render in speech the harmony that rises in
the heart of the poet?" In other words, how can the infinity of things
be totalized through the infinite totality of verbal combinations? Beginning in his fifteenth year this problem appears, his enthusiasm—
so spontaneous, so jubilant in the postscript to *Un Parfum*—is damp-

63. My italics.
64. Edition Charpentier, p. 247.
65. Saint Anthony answers the devil: "It is true, often I have felt that something larger
than myself was mingled with my being; little by little I lost myself in the green of the
meadows and in the current of the streams I watched passing by; and I no longer knew
where my soul was to be found, it was so diffused, universal, expanded." Edition Charpentier, p. 247.

ened, but it has revealed to him his literary project. No, he has not seized the world, he has not summed it up in a book. But that is precisely his task: beauty is, in his eyes, what we might call in the Kantian sense of the term the ideal of the imagination. It is not given in ecstasy: it will give itself to him who has known how to render ecstatic totalization through words.

At this moment the conversion is achieved: fired by the infinite task required of him, the child who "wrote to please himself" finds himself confronted with a strange purpose, which is nothing other than the projection of his totalizing intention outside himself as an *imperative*. Since he has direct access to the All through intuition, his sublime mandate will be to retotalize that vivid intuition through language. To sum up the world in a book—what more could he dream of, this little ham starved for glory? The countercreation will put the reader suddenly face to face with a terrifying immensity, unbearable and beautiful, affirming itself in the imaginary by a "vibrating disappearance" which will be completed only with the book. A gigantic work, it would magnify its author. And what a compensation for all those mortifications he has endured! To play the clown before a gallery of fools, that's good, it's very good, in fact. But it only amounts to denouncing one absurdity among many. To recreate the world—or to create a counterworld—and make it visible through words, that's even better; what fascinates the little totalizer is that no more exhaustive enterprise could be found. Outside of this, indeed, any human occupation is contemptible. The engineer, even the scholar, aims at obtaining finite results and thus determines himself as a finite being; but the true creator—or countercreator—wants nothing less than everything. For this very reason we demand of him that he be nothing in particular, nothing real, but only a total unrealization of his singularity in relation to a cosmic creation. How could the most overweening pride refuse this mandate? Gustave will be as great as the world. Writing is the most beautiful delirium.

Especially as all the moments of the process are preserved: by writing for his own pleasure, in order to satisfy his desires and his desire to desire in the imaginary through words, by allowing his resentment, his masochism and sadism to guide him, Gustave increases the likelihood that his books will unveil the terrifying muzzle of the cosmos and its cruel beauty. The subjective motive that led him to write his first works is surpassed but preserved in the impulse that carries him toward his new, objective aim. Should we call this "sublimation"? I don't think so—that would still be a matter of interiority. The truth is

311

that the project, being the externalization of the interior, finds its concrete efficacy only by stating clearly what it is *through the exterior;* and this exterior, having its own qualities, structures, and dimensions, changes the form of the project, *externalizes* it, and reflects it back to itself as a requirement of objectivity. Literature is not a deserted beach, it is a region of the objective mind elaborated over millennia by specialists; Flaubert's conversion leads him to define himself in relation to his colleagues, predecessors, and contemporaries as one pioneer among a thousand in the literary field. He will have models, examples, guides, an *exis* to internalize, an apprenticeship to complete. At the end of his conversion he finds himself *outside* again, in the midst of others, and it is the others who lend him his status, even though he would like to surpass them all.

We shall see in a coming chapter how, sometime later, Flaubert becomes alienated from his goal, that is, he sees it return to him as a categorical imperative which demands the sacrifice of *everything.* Let us note here only what is at the source of this alienation: the contradiction persists in Gustave between literature as a last resort and literature as demiurge; the conversion has borne him to another terrain, but nothing in him has changed. The contempt for written words has turned into mistrust, but it persists: Gustave claims to have "gigantic thoughts that bend a sentence and burst it." In other words, the grapheme, dry and closed, without auxiliaries, allows the major part of the idea to escape, provided it doesn't burst the sentence that is supposed to contain it. This mistrust is at the source of the problem that will soon be his chief concern: how to treat written discourse so that it might be fit to suggest the totalizing idea in its confused richness? It has been said of Hugo that his work was a form in search of its content; it might almost be said of Flaubert that his is a content in search of its form. But his discomfort does not stem solely from the inadequacy of words to render intuitions; it also expresses Flaubert's doubts about himself. He was certain of his vocation as a comic actor; he was prevented from pursuing it. After some hesitation, here he is face to face with a formidable and fascinating task: to create a countercosmos out of words. But who says he is capable of doing it? Who has given him a mandate? His arrogance only masks his humility. He questions himself: how could I, unworthy as I am, be capable of writing the Book, that book for which it seems the universe has been created? And if I don't write it, isn't it a crime to have "gone into literature" when I wasn't made for it? Alain said: we have been promised nothing. And this is particularly true for the apprentice author who abandons or rejects his works in a rage, telling himself: I am not gifted. But then, Gustave thinks he has been promised the worst. Wasn't the devil playing him a trick, giving him the inner strength of an actor in order to deny him the glory merited by his innate talent, and then diverting him into an enterprise so madly ambitious that it would break his back? After all, this is the general scheme of things: a soul is great through its infinite desire and punished in proportion to its greatness. He repeats this in *all* his youthful works: how can he, as an author, hope to escape the common fate? He is hesitant about the very meaning of what he is doing; sometimes he glimpses the grandeur of his project, which is to totalize the imaginary, and at other times he no longer understands it—for example, when he falls into eloquence—and believes that he is supposed to put reality on trial. We shall have reason to return to the double aspect of this ambiguous work. The paradoxical consequence of his doubts is that he predicted his own destiny as a failed writer *from the day* he was converted to literature. But he has a tendency, as we shall see, to generalize his case; furthermore, at times he is grieved by his own mediocrity and at others declares that art is a snare. Since beauty is the imaginary totalization of the world through language, and since language by its nature is incapable of performing this function, the conclusion is self-evident: "What is Beauty if not the impossible?" Beauty, beyond reach, suddenly gleams in a well-turned phrase—it's a trap; turn toward it and it disappears. At such moments Gustave takes advantage of his misfortune: if it is true that he is forbidden by the nature of things to succeed in his enterprise, and if it nevertheless makes its presence felt through language, like light glimmering through the trees, if he takes it as a summons addressed to no one in particular but which he alone has heard, if man is defined by the greatness of his enterprise, and if Gustave, perfectly lucid, calmly despairing, persists in his own while knowing it to be impossible, then the adolescent, a new Don Quixote, finds his truth in the choice he has made: disdaining his own possibilities, it is he who has chosen impossibility as the only thing possible for him. And as existence manifests itself in the project, as he cannot be Gustave Flaubert without attaining the objectives he proposes for himself, he becomes—by his own choice and, perhaps, by some grand, Satanic election—a martyr (in the double sense of witness and victim) to *the impossibility of being man*. Indeed, all his youthful works give evidence of this impossibility: in them we find nothing but incomplete if sublime submen, who are either torn apart or simply robots.

This hyperbolic and grandiose conception of his choice sustains him and consoles him in his moments of confusion; above all it caters to his profound taste for failure. It will travel the length of the century in order to be given its perfect form by Mallarmé. Perhaps at the same moment it was being born in Gustave's twin brother, the young Charles Baudelaire. Just now, in the crude form the little boy gives it, this conception can be expressed thus: a work of art is the only surviving relic of an endless shipwreck in which the artist and all that belongs to him has been lost. But Gustave does not always avail himself of this comforting pessimism. The reason is that he has predecessors and peers. Homer, for example. Or Shakespeare. When he thinks of them, he falls back into doubt and once more asks himself if beauty is impossible only for him.

In short, at the age of fourteen Gustave was converted. But it was a stormy conversion. He would never disavow it and would never stop questioning it. We shall see how his confused ideas, which contradict each other and interpenetrate in a primitive syncretism, are given a notable and necessary clarity by the crisis of 1844. Is personalization, then, achieved with conversion? Certainly not, but the totalized kernel is firmly implanted. Gustave the imaginary has turned himself into Gustave the writer. But the totalizing movement is not arrested for all that. Before our eyes the little boy has integrated his relations with his family, with his friends, with a public, with words, with himself, and with the world as totalized unreality. But during these same years and those immediately following, he would be *confronted with the real* for the first time: in 1831 or 1832,[66] Flaubert entered school. He left in 1839: for eight years he submitted to the rather rough discipline of the little community, shared the eventful life of Rouen schoolboys, formed bonds of antagonistic competition or of comradeship. We must retrace the history of those years—decisive, according to his own testimony—if we want to understand this new circuit of his personalization. But before entering them with him, we should determine the importance of the role played at about the same time and at the same level of integration by his new lord, Alfred Le Poittevin.

66. There is uncertainty about the month, not the school year, since we find him anyway in the sixth year class beginning in October 1832.

From Poet to Artist

Of the various ideas that emerged from this slow maturation, one—
which matured in other minds as well around the same time—would
strike it rich in the century as it progressed: if beauty as totalization is
an absolute end in itself, art is not in the service of man but is only the
means of attaining the beautiful. This idea declared itself against utilitarianism as a pure imperative: in other words, it is man who is in the
service of art. In this case Gustave's personalization had to integrate
the new norm, whose influence on the *being* of his person cannot be
overestimated; indeed, his very being was in question, the inessential
being that had to be sacrificed *in vain* so that the essential might exist.
Conceived in this way, the impossibility of the artist was not merely a
choice or a destiny, it was his ontological imperative. He had to lose
himself as man in order to give pure gratuity a chance to be glimpsed
through a work that was imperfect and served the purpose of nothing
and no one.

Although these determinations are implicated in the young boy's
quest, however, they would become explicit only gradually, beginning
in 1835. At the outset, as we have said, he is a *poet*, and this means that
ecstasy counts more for him than the words that express it, although
in the decision to transcribe the poetic state all future requirements
are already contained syncretically. What masks them is that he has
structured his stupors in a compensatory intention and that he regards himself above all as the man who *receives* these ecstasies and
who, through this imaginary gift, finds himself placed above the common herd. Gustave could not *by himself* have moved from this conception, optimistic in spite of everything—the poet is fulfilled, even by
horror, since it is in him and through him that the macrocosm is totalized—to that profoundly dark conception of the artist as a kamakaze
pilot. The field of the practico-inert (the objective spirit is part of that)

reveals its requirements only to the extent that directly or indirectly it refracts and charges with its inertia the intentions of *others*. Gustave began his personalization against his family; now he continues it through his friendship with Alfred, for and against him, and simultaneously through his life as a schoolboy. First we shall see how the influence of Le Poittevin the son, integrated and transformed, pushes the poet toward his condition and being as artist. It will then be fitting to examine how that personalizing stress is transformed by school life—the imaginary child's first contact with reality. We shall then be able to resume our primary study and show the passage from poetry to art in the works that Gustave wrote at this time, between 1836 and 1842. In other words, lest we fall into hopeless confusion, we must deal in three successive chapters with the liaison between Alfred and Gustave, his school life, and the transformation of his writings (especially the passage to the autobiographical cycle). But we would quickly fall into abstraction if we were to forget that these three processes are *contemporaneous* and, far from being isolated, are dialectically connected to one another. It is the same man at the same moment who gives himself to his new lord, plays the Garçon, and drafts *Agonies*. At the end of the third chapter we shall try to restore the unity of his development.

> *I have loved only one man as a friend and only one other, my father.*
> Gustave Flaubert, *Souvenirs*, p. 52.

From the time he was ten until he was twenty, Flaubert loved, admired, and imitated Alfred Le Poittevin; he gave himself to Alfred as a disciple to his master. On the surface, Alfred is a piece of unbelievable luck: thanks to him, Gustave might rediscover the steep path of feudal ecstasies outside the Flaubert enterprise. But if we study the actual history of this most unusual liaison, we shall see that luck turns into bad luck in a doomed life. This childhood friendship is a mystification: born to compensate for Gustave's exile and estrangement, it only—seen as a whole—increases them.

For the child to have loved this companion—five years his senior,[1]— as he did, Alfred had to fulfill three conditions, of which the last two seem contradictory.

1. I shall pass quickly over the first, which is obvious. Besides, we

1. Born 29 September 1816.

shall return to it: the older boy had to be, or had to appear to be, someone whose vassal the proud young Gustave could call himself.

2. There could be no blood ties between the child and the adolescent. Had he been born a Flaubert, Alfred would have been defined like the others by his relationship with the paterfamilias; as a relative being he could not have delivered the younger son from his relativity. Above all let us not imagine that the young man represents a substitute for the father: he is too young and the medical director too old. No, he is an Anti-Achille, he plays the role in Gustave's life that might have been filled by an older brother. In other circumstances indeed the difference in age—even a considerable one—can be a powerful bond: Edmond de Goncourt, born in 1822, was eight years older than Jules; nothing would disturb their loving brotherhood—their father, having died, was no impediment. In the Flaubert family, Achille saw himself as charged by the father with barring the younger son's way: he was the militant angel surveying the plain from halfway up the hill; in order to reach God, one must first rise up as far as this guardian of Paradise. Yet he could have played the role of guide, intercessor, *daimon*. But the medical director's unjust preference made him incapable of it. In Gustave, however, the existence of the false archangel stimulated the need for a true older brother, superior by nature and sacred tradition, worthy of adoration, and generous, who might give *value* to his younger brother simply by smiling. If he were to exist, this miraculous brother, radically *other* than Big Brother Achille, would have to escape the zone of paternal influence, that is, the Flaubert blood, entirely, so that the child might love him for himself and for his singularity outside paternal commandments and, in a sense, against that abusive father. A brother removed from the start from Achille-Cléophas's jurisdiction and who quite independently dares to determine good and evil—for himself and for his younger brother. A brother who is neither from the same mother nor, above all, from the same father.

3. And yet—this is the third condition—Gustave could not have loved him if he were merely a chance friend. He had contempt for the schoolboys his own age: they were not Flauberts. Gustave was interested only in his own prison galley: the others could go to the devil. Unless, of course, they were the products of the same deep past, unless they had the same "sweet mother tongue," unless they took part in the same private ceremonies and were bound to the Flauberts by consecrated bonds.

The Anti-Achille did exist and he fulfilled the required conditions.

Madame Flaubert happened to have a childhood friend, this friend was reputed to be very beautiful, and she had married a wealthy textile manufacturer, Monsieur Le Poittevin. Boarding-school friendships quickly fade; the young women would have forgotten each other if the frail bond of affection were not at once sustained by an objective bond, solid in quite another way, which became established between their husbands. I do not think that the friendship of the liberal industrialist and the analytic surgeon was exemplary; but it was a marriage of reason in which the egos of these gentlemen had little place. There was conformity of opinion: each found in the other his own opposition to the regime, his prudence, that depoliticization accepted with good grace and a cynical smile that saves face in private—and saves only that—in short, what can equally be called wisdom or cowardice. There was still more: Doctor Flaubert lived a life of dependence on the rich; he needed connections in Rouen's high society, which was closed and fearful, not to mention miserly, and so hardened to pain that even the wealthiest hesitated to call a doctor in case of illness. Le Poittevin was an entrance ticket. As for the industrialist, although mechanization was practically nonexistent in France, he respected the man of science in Achille-Cléophas. To what degree I am unaware—that depended on his capacities of foresight. But the time when they knew each other was not long after Saint-Simon—damning politicians, sovereigns, and their prelates—had shown that thriving national economies would not be affected by *their* loss, but that the entire life of society would immediately break down if industrialists and scientists were to disappear. This idea was ubiquitous during the Restoration: these two types of *new men* were brought together: an enlightened Fronde was pleased to regard them as builders—which indeed they were.

Nothing then could be more solid—it was cement. They even went so far as to give the connection between the two families an appearance of kinship. Doctor Flaubert became Alfred's godfather, Monsieur Le Poittevin Gustave's.

These godfatherships were the consecration of a quasi-familial bond. Neither of the children remembered his baptism. But like everything that happened in Gustave's life, their future friendship was preestablished; its place was marked in advance by a kind of quadrille, the fathers pretending to exchange their younger sons. To be sure, the friendship was not inevitable; but the two baptized children were predisposed to it by the fathers' friendship, of which their own, if it happened, would be a direct product and repetition. Gustave would never *meet* Alfred: he was part of the prenatal reality—men and things—that surrounded Gustave and which, as he would know all his life, had existed before him and was arranged to drive him to despair. For Gustave, Alfred was, in a word, a factor in his destiny. If they should love each other, moreover, it would not only be as individuals; the parents would congratulate themselves at seeing the representatives of the coming generation carry on the friendship and thus contribute to tightening the bonds between the two tribes. It was a union strongly encouraged, as we see in the correspondence: the boys saw each other freely in their respective homes; the two families welcomed them, and the intimacy of the women as well as the fathers' solidarity appeared to be reflected in this burgeoning affection.

All of this is enough to make one feel repulsed, even by the best of friends. Recall *Si le grain ne meurt* and young Gide's rages when his parents took it into their heads to offer him the sons of their friends as comrades. Such rages, such obstinate refusals, are typical of individualism. For the young André, those children were disqualified in advance because he had not *chosen* them. He stubbornly repulsed these protected, gently directed relations, since he would never know if they were truly his own work or that of the adults. He did not want to pour the spontaneity of his feelings into the mold of a friendship that was *other* and—like the marriages of the period—"arranged."

Gustave was not concerned with all this: we know that he was not an individualist. Naturally, his friendship for Alfred would be *elective*, meaning that he would choose to love him and to love in him what others were unaware of or ignored; he would discover in his own way and from his feudal perspective the role that the other had to play in his life. But his choices would seem to him all the more right, his inclination all the more sacred in that their framework and object were predetermined. And what joy for the resentful man to discover in all his truth, and to *oppose* to his family, the very friend they had *imposed*. Always sacred, the new lord passed into the black world and became the accomplice of the wicked child. Yet the situation had to lend itself to this, the elect had to possess demonic capacities. We shall see that Alfred was not lacking in this respect.

He was four years older than Gustave. For a long time it was the Flaubert children—the younger son and the lastborn daughter—who paid visits to the Le Poittevin children at the textile manufacturer's fine house that faced onto the Grand'Rue and had a large garden with an aviary. The Le Poittevin children went less frequently to the Hôtel-Dieu. So it was at the industrialist's home that their relationship would

319

be formed and would soon constitute an imperishable childhood memory. When he entered the house on the Grand'Rue, Gustave slipped into the bosom of a magical family. The aviary was a sign: this improbable cage contained living objects that served no purpose. The Flauberts took great care never to bring into the Hôtel-Dieu such useless curiosities or anything expensive and frivolous. There is no doubt that at Alfred's home Gustave made the enlightened discovery of pleasure, of that happy gratuitousness which he would soon contrast with utilitarianism. The aviary was beautiful and served no purpose; Madame Le Poittevin, more beautiful still, served none either. As the oppressed offspring of a semipatriarchal family, Gustave was enchanted by the exoticism of a conjugal family. He needed only to cross the Grand'Rue to reach another continent. Of course, he understood nothing of all this: who indeed could have grasped the changes in progress? But he saw very clearly the contrast in mores, in family economy, in the style of living. There the mother's personality effortlessly balanced the father's authority.[2]

To tell the truth, this doubling of values and powers, which would be the rule in the second half of the century when the conjugal family would attain its full development, occurred in the Le Poittevin's home in 1820 only by a remarkable accident. Madame Le Poittevin, thanks to her "rare" and universally recognized beauty, assumed in the eyes of Rouen high society the intrinsic value of a jewel; she became the least precise but surest sign of her husband's wealth and, above all, the most glittering and functionless ornament in his salon. The most discreet as well: she knew how to live, and we have no reason to doubt her virtue. But beautiful women cannot be understood without reference to the proposition that they give themselves over unconditionally to beauty. Often this passes for character: beauty has its norms, like

2. On what Gustave thought of his godfather we have only one piece of information: his letter of 24 March 1837. Ernest wants to read Byron; he answers: "I could take Alfred's but unfortunately he is not in and his library is closed. It was still open yesterday, but just imagine, his father, who left today for Fécamp, put away the key along with the others to his rooms; so, *Amen.*" Nothing more. But the "just imagine" lets us know that the industrialist's avarice and bourgeois meticulousness were the subject of jokes between the two comrades. Or rather, *among the three*—how could Gustave know the father's faults except through the son's confidences? How would he dare make fun of him without the son's authorization and even encouragement? How, *at this period* (of the vassal's ardent and unqualified love for his lord), would he permit himself to seek Ernest's complicity against a member of the Le Poittevin family without Alfred's being party to it? In other words, Alfred discreetly imposed on his disciple his personal preferences for the feminine elements in his family: his mother, Laure. Of his father, the least we can say is that he did not respect him.

truth, and when one is *oneself* someone that others take to be an incarnation of Platonic beauty, one internalizes aesthetic norms as categorical imperatives. Madame Le Poittevin introduced the Other into private life: her power came to her from public consent. She was other, therefore ungraspable; her husband's caresses slid over her; Le Poittevin had to become accustomed to this. He even demanded that his wife preserve that singular universality even in the nuptial bed—it was good publicity. Thus, in the Le Poittevin family, fundamental gratuitousness was woman. Everything else follows: the gratuitous engenders the gratuitous. We say of a room or an apartment that we sense it has "a woman's touch"—by this we mean contrivances meant only to please; an order that is intuitive, unjustifiable, and charming; a taste for detail for its own sake; and a certain narcissism revealed smilingly in things. Nothing of this sort was found at the Flauberts', and yet the feminine presence was indisputable. Madame Flaubert, as present as Madame Le Poittevin, was not narcissistic; running the household absorbed all her attentions; she felt herself to be, if not her husband's associate, at least a junior working partner. She was a relative being and wanted it that way, drawing her legitimacy from her works: indispensable as much as she was inessential, she put things in order, restored, conserved, fought against profiteering, and, since she *earned* nothing, tenaciously sought to reduce expenses. The apartment of the Hôtel-Dieu was a house of men with a woman in it. The "feminine presence" in the house on the Grand'Rue was more than discernible, it was intoxicating. First of all, the Le Poittevins were freer than the Flauberts. And I am not speaking here of political or philosophical freedom but of the simple fact that they were much richer: with essentials assured, enough was left over to portion out at will for unproductive expenses and even for invented needs. In 1830, however, despite its economic progress, members of the bourgeoisie were not ready to make disinterested acquisitions; they accumulated. In the Le Poittevin family, disinterestedness, minimal as it was, was introduced a decade earlier by a creature who was a luxury in herself, since her highest and least contestable quality made her necessarily a "finality without end"—that is, in the eyes of her admirers and hence in her own, a useless bit of splendor. That she loved her children, that she turned her attentions to raising them, that she—like her boarding-school friend—supervised the management of the household and servants, I have no doubt. Nor that she did her best "to make herself useful." But these family duties are not comparable to those imposed on her by social and, through internalization, subjective determination. Chosen for her beauty, she put pictures of herself on all the walls, forced the whole house to reflect her; she contrived at once to be the bourgeois Wife and to have her narcissism projected all around her in the furnishings. Flowers, knickknacks, shawls: we have no details but no more is needed to date Gustave's first encounter with that searing, inaccessible beauty that gives nothing and takes all. This was a personal contact and took place the first day the child took it into his head to raise his eyes to his godfather's wife. He liked the house on the Grand'Rue more than any other place: there he found the lofty gratuitousness of this woman *on the surface of things!* From the moment they entered, Gustave and Caroline were set free; strangled by paternal omnipotence, these children escaped from a masculine society and instantly entered into one ruled by femininity. They not only gained entrance to the world of liberal spending, they experienced a family organization in which the mother played the central role; far from wanting—like Madame Flaubert—to be only a one-way intermediary, communicating the father's orders to the children, Madame Le Poittevin drew her authority from herself and gave or withheld the keys to a realm to which her husband was not admitted.

It is in this realm that Alfred, the dearly loved son of "the beautiful Madame Le Poittevin," shines sweetly for little Gustave. Their relationship is usually thought to have begun very early, and that is certainly true in the sense that they met early on and often in the garden of the aviary. But there is nothing to suggest that they shared anything more than the reciprocal and familial affection of adoptive cousins at that time. It is similarly claimed, without proof, that at the time of the "billiard table" Alfred had deigned to write a few plays for the repertory and to "supervise" their production. I don't believe it. It is most unlikely that Gustave's letters of the time should have made no mention of it. And, as we have just seen, the first time Alfred's name appears in the correspondence is on 24 March 1837, when Gustave was fifteen years old. Furthermore, it was not the boisterous interpreter of *Poursôgnac* that young Le Poittevin was interested in; his sympathy could go only to the solitary and lost schoolboy. One cannot imagine their relationship beginning before 1835: at that time Alfred was about to finish his secondary studies. He was possessed by what he would later call the literary *rage;* in *Colibri* the following year he was going to publish poems that were resolutely Byronic and revealed a kind of inner anguish—it was as if he were suffocating. *Satan* offered young Gustave the metaphoric articulation of his own underlying thematic. The black archangel is jealous of Adam, the "favorite of the God he detests," and promises his Fall. "Your days of despair will be my feast days." Adam is going "to roll in the abyss," carried off by Satan. "Eternal confusion will burden (his) race." Christ will expiate his sins in vain. Here we have Gustave's "curse of Adam." The end of Alfred's poem depicts the same kind of defiance in evil-doing that we find in Gustave's youthful works: it is to God that the Demon addresses himself, this time to scoff at the entire Creation:

> Tu descendras alors sur ton splendide trône,
> Quelques justes épars recevront la couronne
>   Pour avoir pratiqué ta loi.
> Mais frémissant de rage et chérissant leurs
>   crimes,
> Le reste des humains roulant dans les abimes
> Viendra t'y maudire avec moi!

We recognize the theme: God the Father has failed in his work, and man, damned for eternity, is the accusing witness: I curse you for having made me guilty and damned.

A little later Alfred refuses to use any mouthpiece—he himself challenges the Creator:

> Dieu nous fit pour souffrir, et sa jalouse haine
> Nous frappe sans nous écouter . . .
> Ouvrez de nos aïeux l'histoire lamentable
> Vous y verrez partout la trace détestable
> De notre malédiction.
>
> Les plus justes frappés par le céleste glaive . . .
> . . . C'est en vous frappant que Dieu se fait
>   connaître . . .
> Assouvis donc, ô Dieu, ton éternelle rage.

Two stanzas at the end of the poem do, it is true, reestablish the Almighty in his goodness:

> Ainsi je me plaignais dans les heures de doute
>   . . .
> Mais un éclair d'en haut vint calmer ma
>   souffrance.

But the least one can say is that they are neither convincing nor convinced: having formulated specific accusations against the eternal Father, he should at least take the trouble to refute them specifically. But he doesn't. A lightning flash calms the poet down; God pours a

323

soothing balm on his wounds—nothing more. This false ending is hastily tacked on to permit the poem's publication. The two exchanged godsons, confederates in satanism, were ripe to *recognize* each other. Furthermore, the elder, impelled by anxiety and pride to reject both perfect solitude—he will come to that—and the indiscreet reciprocities of a friendship between equals, found himself disposed around this time—we shall deal with this at length—to choose the company of a child. That a nineteen-year-old graduate should have chosen him, Gustave, the family idiot, to listen to *himself* talk out loud in front of him, and that this new lord should have made him the gracious gift of his Byronic poems in exchange for his homage, this is what overwhelms the boy: two cursed sons, proud and melancholy, unite against Gods and Fathers. What a blessing for the embittered heart of the younger son! Unfortunately, neither their pride nor their curses were of the same nature, as Gustave would discover at his own expense.

Indeed, it seems that for the older boy the desire for glory had neither the barren frenzy nor the compensatory violence that it had for the younger. The beloved Alfred had nothing for which to compensate. Why run after glory? By the time he was twenty he doubted that the game was worth the effort. At this time he still believed in the fatalities of genius:

> Fardeau que ceux qui l'ont portent en
>   gémissant
> Et que pourtant la foule envie.

It is a scathing vanity:

> Un besoin de sortir de vulgaires sentiers
> Pour frayer devant soi des routes inconnues
> De quitter les humains qui rampent à nos pieds
> Pour s'aller perdre dans les nues.

Naturally it is also an irrepressible force:

> Les volcans en travail peuvent-ils contenir
> Leur lave qui veut se répandre?

The theme of the Cursed Poet (*Poète Maudit*), which will have such success throughout the nineteenth century, as we all know, is amply developed in his verse.

> C'est le sort du poète . . . sur la terre
> Il est né pour souffrir jusqu'à l'heure dernière

324

> . . . Je dois pour que la fin à mon passé
> réponde
> Mourir désespéré.

Not only in his past nonchalance but even in his present, Alfred sees a slow work of unconscious assimilation:

> A ses impressions son âme abandonnée
> Sans travail et sans but laissait couler l'année
> L'heure de l'avenir en lui se préparait
> Sans que de ce travail son âme eût le secret.

Every great man's life is a destiny, powers of transcendent origin are at work in him accumulating the riches he will one day put to use. Is this a divine plan? Does Alfred already possess the principles of his future doctrine based on metempsychosis? In any case, he is convinced well before Rimbaud that "I is an other": that soul in which the future prepares itself without its knowledge, that transcendence hidden in immanence, is the first casting of the poetic unconscious. Alfred always thought of himself—we shall see—as much richer and more profound than his immediate consciousness could know.

But his meditations on death soon reveal to him the futility of literary work. In "Le Tasse," a poem published in *Colibri* in 1837, he writes:

> Oui, je suis insensé d'avoir perdu ma vie
> A composer ces vers que déjà l'on oublie
> D'avoir eu la petite et sotte vanité
> D'arriver comme un autre à l'immortalité;
> D'avoir vécu pour ces quelques grains de fumée
> Que l'on appelle honneur et gloire et renom-
> mée . . .

Doubtless this is Tasso speaking: he misjudges himself, the verses "that are already forgotten" will be immortal. But what's the difference? Doesn't he die in despair?

> Il ne vit pas briller la divine auréole
> Et lorsqu'il s'en allait monter au Capitole
> Il tomba mourant à ses pieds.

If God does not exist, if the soul dies with the body or survives it by losing its memory, genius is nothing but a trap, a useless passion; his certainty about himself cannot serve as a judgment on his works. In other words, inner experience is not comparable to its objectification in language. Alfred reaps what he has sown. If art is not a reciprocal relation between author and reader, nothing can support it, it collapses on itself. Already the poet is asking himself: wouldn't it have been more worthwhile

> . . . dans un calme dédain
> Mépriser tout cela; puis attendre la fin
> Aux lieux où j'étais né, dans un modeste asile
> Suivre une route enfin moins haute et plus
>   tranquille?

In plain terms: wouldn't it be better to stay in Fécamp, in Rouen, within my family, to take a position and a wife, and to replace the praxis of the artist with the "calm disdain" of the aesthete? Alfred makes no decision in 1837; he still believes that his unconscious impulses have decided for him. He will be a genius, he *is* one. He doesn't know how

> de comprimer ce feu (qu'il) voit s'étendre . . .

He will be a poet *in spite of himself.* Yet at this very moment he stops writing, pursues legal studies, becomes a lawyer, renounces literature *forever.* We have proof of this in a letter to Gustave dated April 1845: he had just finished the first part of *Bélial*, and had told Gustave about it a few days earlier. Returning to this happy news, he speaks of his astonishment: "I do not know what I could have been thinking, but when Germain told me two years ago that I would come back to the literary *rage* I scarcely believed it. Events have realized the prediction . . ." In short, from 1837 to 1845: eight years of crisis ("It was around eight years ago I posed to myself the problem of my existence") during which he is bored to death: "I'm wearing out my shoes in an attempt to distract myself, and just because I had an exclusive vocation for Art I become more and more estranged from it."

In fact, between 1840 and 1845 he is still writing a few poems but does not publish them. The tone has changed, however: irony replaces Byronic satanism, the challenge to God is substituted by a rather lewd "carpe diem" and conceals a painful skepticism. In "Le Poète et la jeune fille," the poet cries out:

> Muse! sois ma seule maîtresse . . .
> Laissons l'imbécile vulgaire
> Aimer sous sa forme éphémère
> L'Eternelle et pure Beauté!

Such is the religion of which he is the "neophyte." A young girl passes by. He immediately leads her into a grotto and promises to imitate the sage:

> Quand Plutus vint lui offrir ses dons
> Lui qui dédaignait la richesse
> Ouvre les deux mains and s'empresse
> Confus à demander pardon.

In a word, art and the Platonic mystique of the beautiful are being abandoned for simple lust.

We still have several of his manuscripts; the numerous revisions to be found in them indicate that, despite his reputed laziness, he worked hard. To no avail: his poems are flat; it is as if some sort of return to order were accomplished in him and expressed literarily in the form of a return to the eighteenth century.

We can conceive of Gustave's growing discomfort: the cursed archangel, his lord, who introduced him to *Lara*, to *Manfred*, and no doubt to *Faust*, and who seemed to share his burning passion to write, is suddenly renouncing literature, and if he still deigns to compose a poem now and then, his *excessively light* verses have a double and contradictory flaw—they smell of effort yet seek facility. The disciple felt he had twice lost his master: he could no longer understand him and no longer sufficiently admire him. To this disappointment, which he dared not admit, were added the pangs of separation: from 1838 to 1841 Le Poittevin lived in Paris while studying law. In 1842 it was Flaubert who left: Alfred was in Rouen, apprentice lawyer and assistant to the Attorney General; he was overwhelmingly busy and thus lacked the time even to see his friends or write to them. In 1844 Gustave suffered his nervous attack; in 1846 Alfred married. But as I shall soon demonstrate, their correspondence indicates a definite cooling of the friendship from as early as 1842, for which the master was entirely responsible, as if with the same gesture he had detached himself from art and from the adolescent who still believed in it. Hence, the master's marriage, which so pained the disciple, seemed to Gustave an ultimate and conclusive betrayal. But also a revelation of Alfred's true "nature." To understand the "influence" the elder exercised on the younger, we must never forget the ambivalence of their relations: it explains, in effect, how Gustave personalized himself at once in accord with Alfred and—sometimes wittingly, sometimes unwittingly—against him.

What do we know about Alfred? Very little. The first of his letters published by Descharmes dates back, the postal stamp tells us, to 1842: he will soon be twenty-six, Flaubert will be twenty-one. Le Poittevin is in the midst of a crisis but his personalization is complete: four years later he will marry Mademoiselle de Maupassant; two years after that, he will die, thus becoming what he was, for beginning in 1842 marriage and death were his two secret and contradictory postulations. Thus his attitude as revealed in his letters is but the culmination of a long history: what would we know about Gustave if we possessed neither his childhood letters nor his youthful works? There is one fact, however, that we cannot doubt: even in the golden age of their friendship, the disciple was afraid of the master. Doubly so; because his satanic skepticism knocked everything down, and because Gustave suspected his elder of a secret conformism. If not, would he have written, in *Agonies*, in his dedication to Alfred: "Perhaps you will laugh later when you are a married man, dutiful and moral, when glancing over the thought of a poor child of sixteen who loved you more than everything and whose head was already tormented with so many foolish things"? Let us note that these lines *end* the dedication: no optimistic consideration is inserted to revise or soften them. See too in the same year, 1838, the lines in italics which precede the first chapter of the *Mémoires:* "To my dear Alfred, these pages are dedicated and given . . . You will perhaps believe there are many places where the expression is forced and the canvas darkened at will; remember that it is a madman who has written these lines . . ." This precaution would seem futile if one did not feel that it issued from a certain mistrust: the boy is afraid of making his elder smile, whether later, *when he is married* (could he have foreseen Alfred's evolution so clearly if it had not already been evident in some fashion?), or at the present time, in which case the elegant skepticism of the master would be shocked by the incongruous violence of the disciple. Even in the dedication to *Agonies* he takes pains to mark his distances: for him, *pathos*, for his friend, intellect: "This mean gift will remind you of our old talks of the year past. No doubt your heart will swell when you remember that delightful aroma of youth which embalmed such despair." It could not be better said: Alfred *amused himself* with despair or, at least, took an intellectual pleasure in his enterprise of demolition; as for Gustave, it only caused him suffering. We shall examine in detail the twin terrors Alfred inspired in Gustave. For now, we can see that, in spite of their apparent opposition, they may well be subject to one another: to take skepticism to its extreme is to justify the worst compromises of principle by claiming to denounce the conformity of nonconformity. When Alfred speaks, Gustave feels threatened by both nihilism and the pressure to become bourgeois; he suffers from confusion: what if becoming bourgeois were the final purpose and strict conclusion of nihilism? Furthermore, it is in 1838 that he remarks in his notebook of *Souvenirs:* "I have loved only one man as a friend and only one other, my father." A strange sentence, whose incorrectness is significant. First of all, it shows the underlying connection between the new lord and the old. In addition, the use of the compound past—that accomplished past which nevertheless preserves some tie to the present—manifests clearly that Gustave loved Alfred, claims to love him no longer, and in all evidence loves him still. If he were not attempting—out of anger and discomfort—to reject this friendship from the very depths of his memory, he would write: "I will have loved . . ." etc. We can therefore localize the high point of their liaison in 1837. After that it declined. There would be a renewal of the friendship, however, in 1840, to which Flaubert's correspondence bears witness; speaking in July 1845 of the sadness experienced five years earlier upon his return from his travels in Corsica, he adds: "Do you remember the state I was in all of one winter, when I would come to you Thursday evenings . . . with my big blue overcoat and my feet wet with snow, which I warmed at your fire?" At this time he seems to have sought consolation in the company of his former lord. But neither of them had the heart to resume the nihilistic games of 1837; now, moreover, it is Gustave who goes on Thursdays to Alfred, and Alfred who stays home, debilitated and gloomy. They were to have one last rapprochement in 1844.

We shall attempt to explain this evolution in detail. But it is fitting to remark at the outset that Le Poittevin's letters fully justify Gustave's mistrust. What is immediately striking about them—that is, on the most superficial level—is surely their conformism: "It is infuriating that we should not be freer, for your part as well as mine, to make our encounters coincide, but we are both submissive to customs and habits." We note his concern to associate his friend Gustave with this submission. It is important to Gustave too that the other is his father's godson: they curse their families—gently—but without leaving the interfamilial setting. In 1842, Alfred goes as far as to be delighted by Gustave's evident sadness at leaving his family in order to study law in Paris: "Thus we find ourselves weak men with the same weakness as our peers . . . It's not, after all, that I'm inordinately surprised. I knew you were not a man of steel and the temptation was strong. These are powerful feelings the family develops. When our fathers have lived out their time and our brothers and sisters each have their own house *to themselves,* I imagine it will create a strange desert around us. Solitude is good for the strong, but provided you grow into it. If it comes too late, a man . . . eventually dies of it . . . My mother . . . spoke again (of your sadness) at dinner. Lengliné . . . whispered in my ear that the *little girls* would cure you. He laughed a lot, making fun of you, but I laughed even more, it must have been bizarre laughter, for it covered and extinguished his—you will understand that."

Alfred triumphs: Gustave shares his weaknesses. Lengliné reveals his baseness by comparing the deep family attachments of a young provincial to the easy pleasures he will be offered in the capital. Suddenly Le Poittevin confesses the anguish he would have felt to leave his people: outside the family is the desert and you can die there. Indeed—except for the years that he too spends in Paris studying law—he leaves the house in Rouen only to accompany his parents to their property in Fécamp. He is certainly not forced into this since it is he who twice asks to be registered at the Royal Court of Rouen: the first time, in 1842, with success, for he would be a probationer, then a lawyer; the second, in 1846, without success, for he would not attain the rank of deputy in the jurisdiction of the Rouen magistrature. He occasionally dreams of travel, of the Orient. He writes: "I lead a very irregular life . . . I am suffocating . . . I needed to travel, to move about; not to stay here stagnating by the hearth. There are people around me who say they love me and it is true; these people have the means to save me, but they will give it so ungraciously that I hesitate to ask them for it." This is an admission that his father would give him permission to travel if he begged him for it. And yet *it is true* that Alfred is suffocating in his family, though it is also true that he does not want to be separated from it.

What does he do? He cloisters himself most of the time, but he is present at the parties his parents give and, not infrequently, he "makes calls": "Yesterday I made 'my calls.' Do you feel the plastic beauty of the man in his black frockcoat who makes calls from one o'clock till seven and then goes home to his hut to dine?" This passage sufficiently indicates that he loudly advertised his contempt for social obligations so as to avoid withdrawing from them. Besides, he reserved his irony for Flaubert alone; he writes to him in May 1845: "We are two Trappists who speak only when we are together. Do you know that it is hard never to think out loud?" Within the family, in society, he uses the same language as others and limits himself to "bizarre" smiles, addressing to himself signs of imperceptible connivance. When the scene seems *too* comic, he lets nothing show but tells himself that he will report it to Gustave. This salon life—in which no doubt he shone—did he really dislike it so much? We do not know. What we do know, on the other hand, and what René Descharmes has certainly brought to light,[3] is that even though he made fun of the Civil Code, he was not insensible to the tiny satisfactions of amour-propre that the intermittent exercise of his duty brought him: "I received many congratulations, twice those of the presiding judge of Beauchamp in his résumé. For which I don't give a damn, incidentally!" But he does, so much so that other letters—particularly that of 14 December 1843— show he can be quite vexed when a defendent prefers another lawyer to him. One day he writes to Gustave: "Do you feel the beauty of the punished man and of the magistrate who does the punishing?" But at another time he says that one must humor "the amours-propres of the magistrates" if one wants to "enter that fucking club," and, indeed, after his marriage he solicits a position as deputy in Rouen. In other words, he refuses men the right to punish, but if the body of magistrates accepts him, he will be one of those who mete out punishment.

In Alfred's case, certainly, there is a great deal of suppleness, too much perhaps, as well as a rather lively taste for compromise. Would we have believed, for example, that we could find from the pen of Flaubert's master: "I have put off the play on Emma Caye; I scarcely occupy myself now with things that are not immediately publishable. Perhaps even what seems so to me will shock the public taste a little. This solid hypocrisy will be alarmed at the freedom of my Muse" (13 September 1845). The two last sentences are clearly written to make up, in Gustave's eyes or in his own, for what may have seemed shabby in the first. It is nonetheless true that he does what his disciple will never do: he abandons a work—perhaps obscene, but so what?—in order to work at others which will give him, he thinks, immediate satisfaction and will "place" him in the running. Taking Alfred objectively, we find a gifted young bourgeois, brilliant, perfectly adapted to the "customs and habits" of his milieu. In his fashion he even goes so far as to take up "liberalism," the ideology of his class. See the first

3. René Descharmes notes that beginning in 1842 he was both lawyer and third assistant to the attorney general of the king attached to the royal court of Rouen. And Flaubert writes to Chevalier on 24 February of the same year: "Alfred works in the office of the attorney general and spends his time writing writs of accusation." On the 25th he made his debut as attorney for the defense, this time "in a theft case in which an adolescent stole a few five franc pieces." But arguments for the defense are of no more interest to him than those for the prosecution: "We shall never despoil the widow and the orphan, but we shall scarcely interest ourselves in them."

lines of his *Essai sur la Revolution française:*[4] "The human race finally wanted to exchange the tunic for the virile toga. England and France set the example, the whole world hastens to follow. Let us not doubt that liberty will be the fruit of this noble impulse. But to obtain it, constancy will have to finish what enthusiasm has begun. Since men wish to govern themselves, they must prepare themselves as soon as possible by serious, strict study for the role that awaits them." In short, the bourgeoisie has taken power: let it base on reason the institutions it will gradually create for itself. Written under Louis-Philippe, this text, no doubt more republican than monarchist, merely radicalizes the paternal opinions. In any case, politics do not interest Alfred; and this very conformist life leads naturally to its end, which is marriage. He never ceased to scoff at this "establishment." As late as May 1845 he writes: "Lengliné gets married tomorrow. Baudry on the 31st. Dénouette is married. Here are all our friends falling in line. We too . . . but elsewhere! Do you see my *Father-in-law* from here? I wager you don't picture that face to yourself any more than that of the 'Garçon.'" Fourteen months later he married a nobleman's daughter, Aglaé-Julie-Louise de Maupassant, and immediately afterward gave her a child. Previously, even while deriding marriage, he took pleasure in teasing Gustave, predicting to him that this would be their common destiny. A strange sort of joking, which Flaubert frankly detested, proving that he took it seriously. When in 1842 Gustave communicated his sadness at leaving the Hôtel-Dieu, Alfred, as we have seen, gently triumphed and took advantage of the situation by adding: "You were indignant, earlier, when I said you would someday have to deal with a civil registrar; *qui vivra verra*, let us wait and see!" The meaning is clear: you have family feeling, therefore you will one day take a wife. This statement partially explains the preface to *Agonies;* it is true that Gustave, like Alfred, is like a fish out of water outside the family setting, in which he suffocates. But his relations to the Flaubert enterprise, his sulking, his violent refusal "to create life," have greater depth than his friend's comfortable bourgeois skepticism. To show the trajectory of this life, let us recall that Le Poittevin, after staying several months in Paris alone with his wife, was to go to La Neuville-Champs-d'Oisel to die at the home of his father-in-law, whose face he had challenged his disciple to picture to himself four years earlier.

Such is the objective truth of this young bourgeois, slightly in advance of his peers but not an abnormal product of his class, neither

4. Published in *Colibri* in 1837.

economical nor spendthrift, taking care not to ruin his father as other sons would do—less often than is said—in the Second Empire, but scarcely interested in succeeding him as head of his factory. For reasons that we will attempt to unravel, Alfred could see himself only in the role of pure consumer. It would be unjust, however, to limit him to that role, since very early on he chose to write. Must we conclude that his real unhappiness came from not being gifted? That this was the real motive for eight years of silence? That would be meaningless. His misfortunes as a writer proceed visibly from a poor relation to literature.

Or rather to art, that passive activity whose function—as we know when we leaf through his letters and find on every page that irritating formula "Do you feel the beauty of . . ." (which Gustave, incidentally, takes up on his own account)—consists of compensating for his submission to bourgeois mores by derealizing the society that surrounds him. This is what he writes, for example, in a letter that Descharmes dates June 1844: "I have to tell you about an extraordinary scene. A man like you would have paid 10,000 francs to see it and that would not have been too much. I did not laugh because, at its most elevated, Art arouses neither sadness nor gaiety. One contemplates and one *casse-intellectualise-jouit.*" [5]

The scene is one that took place in his family or in the close circle of his acquaintances. The episode is clearly grotesque (as is emphasized by the "you would have paid 10,000 francs," which furthermore, although Alfred is ironic, remains decidedly suspect—what is bred in the bone will out in the flesh). At the same time it touches something vulnerable in the young man, who, if it had not, would have reported it in his letter: Alfred is prudent, as we see from his correspondence;[6] it is out of precaution (as well as laziness) that he waits to share it with Gustave orally. Therefore, scarcely has the event been announced than Le Poittevin puts on airs so as not to be compromised: he now has only an observer's relation to those who will be the protagonists of the story; he even forbids himself to laugh—laughter is at once rejec-

5. This play on French idiom is not translatable, but its component parts suggest, respectively, all-out effort, intellectualization, and the intensity of sexual pleasure. See Sartre's note 7 below.—Trans.

6. 11 September 1842: "I have begged you to destroy the letter that contained the changes in my dythyrambe. I beg you to please tell me in your next letter whether you have executed your promise in this regard." 8 December 1842: "It is needless to remark to you that these pages cannot be communicated to anyone." Undated (around 1844): "If you read this to Monsieur Beaudry or to anyone else, let it be only once, so that no one could make a copy or even commit it to memory. This is a strict order."

tion and complicity, as we have seen. A condescending look, that's all. At the root of the aesthetic attitude that he has chosen we discover a need to reject the purposes of his class all the more radically while reproducing its behavior all the more docilely: "I see the carriages of the Barbets pass by my window on their way back to Valmont; and the landowners of Abbaye! Do you feel the beauty of *ladies* in the country? Of strangers? Of all that poor sort who shiver in Paris during the winter and sweat during the summer in the country? How asinine it all is!" But what does he do that is any different—except that he shivers in Rouen more often than in Paris? And isn't his mother a *lady?* Precisely for these reasons he demolishes the values and purposes of "that poor sort" (actually the bourgeoisie) and reduces this coming-and-going of carriages to the most absurd restlessness. I admit that he is also expressing, almost unwittingly, the provincial's contempt for the Parisian "stranger." But we know too that when the occasion offers itself, he is able to look down at himself from above and contemplate himself "as artist": when he "makes his calls," isn't he inviting Flaubert to join him on the heights in order to admire—without sadness and without laughter—the "plastic beauty" of a man in a black frockcoat who is none other than himself?

Don't these flights strongly resemble the resurgent pride we have discovered in Gustave? From a certain point of view no doubt: verticality is common to both the flights and the pride. But in the disciple the vertical goes in two directions: the ascent is produced after the fall and against it and often ends with another tumble; in the master it goes only in one direction—there is no descent after the climb. Beloved Alfred does not know the shame or the anguish of sinking, of losing favor. It is tempting to believe that he very early accomplished the economy of ascensional movement and that he was established on his aesthete's perch, which finally became his natural habitat. What does he do up there? He *"casse-intellectualise-jouit."* In this expression, the *casse* often used by Gustave ("je casse-pète d'enthousiasme," "I explode-fart with enthusiasm") is merely a verbal prefix whose job is to intensify;[7] it marks the *explosion.* The association of words that draws our attention is *"intellectualise-jouit."* The muddy tide of the everyday is not of itself organized to offer the observer the unity of an essence or a type: experience presents only rough drafts; it is the art-

---

7. Grammatically, *casse* is the third person indicative of *casser* [to break]. We must take it in the familiar sense of "at top speed" (*à tout casser*) and conceive its syntactic function as "back-breaking effort" (*casse-tête*) or "heart-breaking" (*casse-coeur*), although the second term is a verb and not a substantive.

ist who extracts its *eidos* by a triple elaboration of these givens, isolating, unifying, and radicalizing the empirical contribution. We are not, it is understood, on the level of painting, drama, the novel—it is the look that works *on itself* in order *to see* the object in its naked perfection (discarding annoying details, glorifying those that serve its design) by detaching it from its human meaning. A man in black on a sunny day, knocking on every door, going in, coming out, taking up his futile course as his shadow lengthens at his feet: that is "plastic beauty." These retouchings, solicited by the object itself—if the young aesthete is to be believed—are of an exclusively *intellectual* order: a matter of abstracting, of generalizing, of "typing." And this plainly shows that Alfred, despite his momentary Byronism, was not deeply touched by romanticism; he would appear to be a pure classicist, in fact, if the "intellectualization" of experience were to operate materially in the conception and production of a work of art. The naturalism of the "Great" century is the rationalization of nature by palette or pen. But what prevents us from seeing in him a tardy disciple of Boileau is that he presents aesthetic intuition as a *selbständiges* whole; the aesthetic pleasure which—according to classical norms—the work alone gives when it is completed he says he feels in the *preparatory* moment of contemplative organization, as if the immediate elaboration of his perception instantly produced a spectacle *for him alone*, from which he draws intellectual pleasure, grasping, for example, in his father's precautions of "hiding the keys" before leaving on a trip the *idea* of avarice as it is manifest in Harpagon. From this point of view, Alfred's attitude closely approaches that taken unwittingly by a number of his contemporaries. One thinks in particular of the moment described by Schopenhauer when, the will to power suspended, the Idea becomes visible to the imagination. It must not be forgotten, however, that Alfred's conduct is doubly negative: first he *derealizes* what he sees, even himself (the man in the frockcoat or the ladies traveling by carriage are pure appearances); then, decisively severing himself from all human purposes, he reduces the actions of men, whatever they may be, to aimless agitations. In contrast to the Schopenhauerian artist who grasps the complex ramifications of the Idea and its meaning as a singular universal, young Le Poittevin always comes back, no matter what he does, to the same abstract conclusion: man is absurd.[8] How could it be otherwise since his premises themselves are absurdities? The greatest stupidity of the human race in his

8. *La Promenade de Bélial* is in a different key—we shall come to it.

eyes is to persist in living. Why do it? What's the point? For him, then, *beauty* is nothing more than this absurdity revealed: the judge who punishes is *beautiful*, but no more so than the starving wretches who beat each other to death for a piece of bread. It is clear that this haughty verdict, exercised nonchalantly by one man alone, who claims to be self-sufficient, has nothing in common with the activity of the artist; on the contrary, it defines the quiet malice of the aesthete.

This is why Alfred has such difficulty writing. In fact, his pleasure is complete when he contemplates the family circle or his mother's salon from above; a tiny shove and the ladies are transformed before his eyes into archetypes. What need has he of words to fix these metamorphoses when he can reproduce them at will and each time *casse-intellectualise-jouit?* His relations to writing are complex. One might say that he is compelled to write from a sense of duty so as not to remain bound to a quietism to which he could easily accommodate himself but which he judges to be sterile; he never feels that quasisensual bond with language that makes true writers, nor the feeling that whatever happens in his mind achieves its fullness and its ontological consistency only when it is objectified outside him and against him on a sheet of blank paper. To translate his intuition is only a matter of duty, for it is already complete, just as he is concerned less with finding the unique expression to complete it, to enrich it, and to reveal it in his own eyes than with pouring it into a neoclassical mold that will be its embellishment. Reread *Bélial:* the style is dry, airless, not without a certain bourgeois affectation or those deliberately obsolete graces that serve to elevate the author to the rank of a *well-bred* narrator in good society. Despite some successful formulas, what dooms Alfred is that he attaches style to his idea as though it were an elegant ornament.

This said, at a deeper level he is impelled to write and deprived of the means of succeeding at it for the same reason. He expresses it in these terms: "I must have been a statue in a past life," and its source is his relations with his mother. One is not the son of the beautiful Madame Le Poittevin with impunity. Alfred lives a somewhat oedipal situation simultaneously in two ways, and we shall attempt to recover the original situation through his two ways of living it. We might say, reading his letters and poems, that he regards his impotence as a suicidal anorexia and at the same time as a superb ataraxia. Anorexia or ataraxia: these are the two panels of the diptych. What joins them?

1. When he *complains* of his immobility, two other themes always appear, which are negative and organically linked: that of a slow

death knowingly brought about by excess, and that of resentment against his parents and particularly against his mother. During those eight years—especially between 1843 and 1845—his anorexia devastated him. He writes in "Comme a dit le vieux Dante":

> Mais, vers aucun désir ne me sentant porté
> Dans mon inaction je suis toujours resté . . .
> La route qui s'offrait, je ne l'ai pas suivie
> Mais pour me diriger, voyageur incertain
> Je n'eus pas avec moi le poète latin
> Et sa main . . .
> Ne m'a pas comme but, au loin montré la
>   Gloire.

At the same time, in "A Goethe," a fragment of verse that is nearly contemporaneous, he is distressed about what one might call his *instability:*

> Dès que je me connus, je me sentis mobile
> A toute impression comme l'argile . . .

Desires and emotions follow each other and dissipate—no constancy, no consistency. Mightn't these verses have been written by Gustave himself, who some years earlier showed us the unstable Djalioh overwhelmed by violent and fleeting passions that afterward vanished "like lightning in a puddle"? No doubt: neither of the two friends can "stick" to a feeling very long, by reason, as we shall soon see, of the constituted passivity that characterizes both of them. But it is not the *same* passivity; its origins are distinct, the functions and meanings different. It should be noted that pathos in Gustave, inconsistent and partially insincere as it may be, is at the same time almost unbearably powerful and acrimonious. He leans, he pushes, I admit, but he is often submerged. And we have already identified some of his constants: resentment, the desire for compensatory glory, resurgent pride all deserve to be called passions; all Alfred has is a vivid and colorful sensibility, which can bind him neither to a woman nor to art.[9] As he says in his letter of 28 September 1842, "Passion is a beautiful thing, but it takes more than will to have it." Yet Le Poittevin, like his contemporaries, thinks suffering and passion are the apprenticeship of genius. The true elect are "initiates in human existence":

> Quand la passion, précoce à les blesser
> De ses mille replis vient à les enlacer.

9. He is mad with pride as well, but his pride is different.

And further:

> Pour atteindre au rang que le ciel leur destine
> Il faut à tout jamais quitter la Fornarine
> Et ne gardant au coeur que le culte du Beau
> De ce qu'ils ont senti retracer le tableau.

In short, the artist "intellectualizes" his sorrows; breaking those all too human chains in the name of a nobler passion, he raises himself from pathos to his Idea. In addition, it is necessary to have known the common attachments that result from "ardent sensual pleasure." Alfred confesses that he has had no such experience, nor has he felt the more voluntary impulse which aims to build work on renunciation. I intentionally employ these two conflicting words because Alfred, when distressed, explains his immobility sometimes by his coldness of heart and sometimes by his lack of will.

"Strong enough not to act against my will, I was not strong enough to act as I should have. I needed to travel, to move about . . ."

"I had a singularly fine and delicate nervous organization. I might have been able to do something *if I had known how to be an artist.* What I have always lacked is *will*, I sensed it before knowing it and for that reason, perhaps, I have never believed in free will."

It is no longer a question, as it was when he wrote "Le Tasse," of presenting his own genius as a volcanic exuberance and a fatality; now it is rather an incomplete state that must be acknowledged. Something is wanting—affect or will—which prevents genius from manifesting itself. The result is the *common shipwreck:*

"The wave I thought I was controlling sweeps me away and the triumphant course I had thought to achieve is transformed into a common shipwreck whose very site no one will ever know" (1842).

He *suffers* this impotence, this abulia. "My inertia has grown to such colossal proportions that there is no longer *the principle of the least action* in me." And: "What is there to say about a needle always pointing at zero?" Or: "If the supreme good is action, I am devilishly far from it." Around 1844 he had, no doubt for reasons of health, given up the practice of law and was living with his parents, doing nothing, sometimes at Fécamp, sometimes at Rouen.[10]

The result was boredom. That "colossal" boredom which he passed on to Gustave as though it were an illness. It must be said that his disciple offered particularly fertile ground. In those moments it

10. His attempt to reregister in 1846 was probably occasioned by his marriage.

pleased Alfred to kill himself in small doses: whores, alcohol. The suicidal intention is evident.[11] Especially when he drinks: "I lead a highly irregular life and am much weakened; I am stifling" (March 1845). "I always take a bit too much of the old rotgut. I got so sick from it the other day that at midnight I threw up out the window . . . It is troublesome that my stomach is worn out with fatigue, and decidedly it does not seem to me I am destined to attain old age" (September 1845). But it can easily be seen that this self-destruction is tinged with rancor. At Fécamp he gets drunk *all alone* and *in his parents' house;* he vomits out of one of their windows while they are sleeping. The will to sully the paternal residence is even more obvious since he adds: "What do you think of the gay blade (*understood: that I am*)? And of the bourgeois opinion on the morality of such a sly dog?" Where would he encounter bourgeois opinion if not at the family table, at his mother's salon, at the homes of the notables of Fécamp when he dons his frockcoat to make "his calls"? He vomits *against* his friends and relations, certain of the scandal he would provoke if it were known that the Le Poittevin son was a drunkard, yet prudent enough to get drunk in secret in the middle of the night. And of course he accuses his family; this day-by-day suicide—they are responsible for it: "These people have the means to save me, but they will give it so ungraciously that I hesitate to ask them for it. And yet they will weep over me when I am dead—stifled to death—without their having done anything or known what to do" (March 1845). Implacable, mellow resentment: Alfred—as we learn from his correspondence[12]—loves to imagine his future death and burial; with a highly aesthetic satisfaction he imagines his family all in black, red-nosed, walking behind his coffin. In order to be sure of dying and of poisoning them with remorse, he is careful to ask nothing of them. He could save himself by traveling: this is not revealing a desire but offering a diagnosis; he no more wishes to change his place than a sick man wants the painful operation that will cure him. In this latter case one *submits* fearfully to the surgical intervention because it is the sole means of recovering health; Alfred does not go even this far: he recognizes that he would have to be torn away from his family, which is a pathogenic environment, and, *deciding* that this is impossible, he feels himself led by them voluptuously to his death.

11. He knew his health was delicate: "Always being ill, I am beginning to tire of the life I lead" (28 July 1843). And the following year he had to give up his profession. This is precisely the period when he got drunk or ran to brothels in order to destroy himself.
12. "Do you see from this distance the day of my burial? Euh!"

Voluptuously? Not always: it *seems* from reading his letters that this feeling of oppression is at times somatized as respiratory distress.

Whores: another instrument of suicide. More pleasant than rotgut? Hardly: "I have rude senses, but I cannot give a kiss that is not ironic." This is the period when he writes "A Flora," "Le Poète et la jeune fille," "Quand des femmes de Tyr," and, most important, "Les Lotophages." In these ambiguous poems we find a pungent mixture of sensuality and misogyny. He preaches the hedonistic *carpe diem* and at the same time condemns it: one must divide one's life between boredom, which is death, and "orgy," which is resurrection:

> Ainsi dans un esprit que la souffrance brise
> Se réveillent souvent, par une étrange crise
> Les instincts de la chair
> Et l'homme, dans les feux de la brutale orgie
> En son corps défaillant sent renaître la vie
> Prête à s'en détacher.

Above all, in spite of the muses' exhortations, one must gather the fruits of the ancient Lotus, which bring both drunkenness and oblivion:

Choeur des Femmes Lotophages
> Cueille, étranger, cueille avec confiance . . .
> Son suc est doux, il endort la souffrance . . .
> *A ton foyer* si des peines sans nombre
> T'ont fait des morts envier le repos
> Si tu fuyais quelque souvenir sombre
> Cueille les fruits de l'antique Lotos

Choeur des Muses
> Songe aux projets mûris dans ta jeunesse, etc.
> [Songe] à la postérité.

Le Naufragé
> De l'avenir qu'importe le suffrage
> De vains projets pendant le souvenir
> Je veux puiser aux fleurs de ce rivage
> L'enivrement qui ne doit plus finir.

But the "Chorus of Serpents" has the last word:

> Encore un qui tombe
> Femmes, par vos mains

> Poussez à la tombe
> Les troupeaux humains.

These human herds are composed only of males. Woman, accomplice of Satan who gave her the apple, is excluded from the species.

> Féconde en artifices
> Elle a dépassé les malices
> Du Dieu rampant.

And her aim is to damn men by debasing them. Thus when Alfred, failed poet, succumbs to feminine charms, he does it knowingly; he knows that the enchantress desires his doom and that she will deprive him even of the consciousness of the "common shipwreck" which, lacking grandeur, had allowed him to preserve at least the negative dignity of regret. But it is precisely from this regret that he intends to free himself; he abandons himself to the claws of a wild beast because he is seeking self-destruction, but he does not forget the fundamental wickedness of the female animal.

We shall understand his phantasms better if we read the poem "A Flora," addressed to a young girl he seems merely to have glimpsed.[13] At Caesar's orders, a young Christian is tied to a bed. A female slave is ordered to make him sin:

> Aux regards du jeune homme elle offre sa
>   poitrine
> Et sous ses deux bras liés passe ses deux bras
>   nus
> Elle étale à ses yeux ses formes magnifiques
> D'un doigt luxurieux elle parcourt son corps
> Et, sur son front collant ses lèvres impudiques
> Veut de sa nudité lui livrer les trésors.

In order to preserve his virtue, the catechumen bites off his own tongue and spits it into her face. He is, says Alfred, a "perfect fool."

> Que n'étais-je moi cet heureux néophyte
> Que n'étiez-vous Flora, l'esclave du préteur
> A vos empressements j'aurais cédé bien vite
> Et vite des chrétiens renié le Seigneur.

13. "Why did this young girl I hardly know remain in my memory like this? I don't know, and after a few hours more I probably would have become disenchanted with her as I did with the others. But as it is, I do like to think of her from time to time. Is it because I have addressed two poems to her? And isn't this memory of her only a new form of vanity?"

One is struck by the similarity of this erotic dream and those Gustave nurtured at the same period. Alfred has seen from afar a young girl who seemed to him desirable. What does he want from her? To take her? No, rather for her to take him. He feels immobilized, lying on his back, and Flora comes to him, naked and lascivious, animated by criminal intentions. She will awaken his desire *in spite of him* by skilled, specific caresses. And then—in fact, how can she do it without climbing on top of him, since he is tied down?—she will yield the treasures of her nakedness to him: we understand that she herself is charged with managing the details of the intercourse. In effect, the young man is saying to this unknown girl: artful and malign creature, if you take it upon yourself to excite me by caressing me as if I were a woman, then "play the man" and finish the job alone; I will be happier to be taken by you than by anyone else. Isn't this what Flaubert asks of his imaginary mistresses? In fact, it is not. The passivity is the same, but, despite appearances, Alfred's masochism is not very well developed. What he expects from Flora is what he arrogantly demands from the young prostitutes he pays—Descharmes's sense of decency has deprived readers of numerous passages in his letters where he regales Gustave with accounts of his "priapism." Happily, they have been preserved: Madame Théa Sternheim possesses the original letters, and Roger Kempf has been good enough to send me the photocopies. And from their reading it emerges that Alfred had only a moderate taste for coitus, to the point where he occasionally harbored anxiety concerning his virility. He clearly preferred fellatio and enjoyed cunnilingus. During these sessions he demanded that his partner satisfy him in "the style of Alcibiades." Here is one description—among others—of his pleasures: "While her tongue excited this old Priapus, her finger worked inside my ass, I gasped for eight or ten minutes, legs outspread like swooning Dorothea, or rather like an honest whore, and I ended by discharging as I swooned. All this is quite literal." And he adds in the margin: *De Sade, Volume III.* The reference is there so that Gustave might understand the allusion to Dorothea, but, as we shall see, it seems to relate to the entire letter, and shows him in his true colors whether he intended it or not. It is true, Alfred unrealizes himself as a woman under these caresses, he is Dorothea, he is "an honest whore," he gasps, he swoons, and later, writing to Gustave, he takes pleasure once again in the memory of his femininity. But his "androgyny" has different sources from Gustave's—we shall try further on to spell them out—and another meaning. Gustave dreams of being kneaded by the authoritarian hands of a dominating woman. Le Poittevin, however, abandons himself to the docile and bought attentions of a slave whom he scorns. There is no doubt that he deliberately chooses these "vile creatures":[14] they are not witnesses, he can shoot off into the air in semisolitude. No communication: what matters is himself and the intensity of his pleasure.

I recognize that a young bourgeois in 1840 was in most cases constrained to satisfy his sexual needs with prostitutes—the women of his milieu were inaccessible to him; as for the young women, they were untouchable and well protected besides. To the same extent that he respected his sisters and mother, he despised the "slut" whom he made the instrument of his pleasures; the sexual act seemed to him a satanic caricature of the conjugal duty he would soon fulfill and whose sacred purpose was procreation. So he hastened to laugh about it *with his comrades* in order to dissociate himself from it as quickly as possible. Lost creatures, cursed, and *dangerous*, nearly all the "girls" were likely to be sick and contagious; one screwed them in fear, which provoked ill humor. And then, above all, the girls were poor: as they gave themselves for pennies, the student begrudged them their low price for reminding him of the modesty of his allowance; he was angry with them for not being like the high-class "demi-mondaines" frequented by young society men with money. In contrast to this hostility, young men under the July monarchy gave platonic love a place of honor; to atone for their venal loves they would nurture a tender, respectful, and asexual feeling for a friend of their mother or sister. This dichotomy—the hot, black Venus of the streets; the white, cold goddess of the marriage vows—is to be found in the literature of the time and is the social source of the Baudelairian dyad—the trivial whore, "the horrid Jewess," and the ice maiden.

Rare, however, were those who, like Alfred, satisfied real misogyny in their venal affairs. The haste with which he recounts his prowess and the care he invests in reviewing the details are striking. Roger Kempf has noted that in his impatience "he even . . . scratched out his story in pencil." Should we conclude that the young man was eager "to tell everything immediately afterward, as if the proximity of pleasure still allowed him to share it with [Gustave]"?[15] In certain cases this is not in doubt, and we shall come back to it when we examine the

14. "Have you been to Delille's? Have you seen Madame Alphonse again? There are precious acquaintances to be had there: one goes only when one likes, and without their taking it into their heads to return the visit." So much for the truth of that "philosophical love of whores" that Gustave attributed to Alfred.

15. Roger Kempf: "Le Double Pupitre," *Cahiers du Chènevis,* October 1969.

homosexual component in this unusual friendship. But most of the time there is nothing to share: the dryness of the accounts scarcely invites daydreams. The tone is deliberately crude and betrays a deprecatory intention; the pursuit of the base and the grotesque is deliberate also, the chief point being to provoke laughter at the coupling, to devalue it, to reject its moist intimacy and offer it publicly as a spectacle to a society of little bourgeois males. It is clear indeed, according to certain passages, that Alfred did not reserve his confidences for Gustave alone; his former friends and the young men of his circle were entitled to them as well. Since all these bachelors visited prostitutes, exchanged addresses, passed the "little girls" they had used back and forth, this publicity was not at Alfred's expense but at that of the women he mentioned. His narratives betray sadism as well. "Having picked up a slut on the sidewalk, I did not hesitate to follow her home. I made her strip naked but like a worm, and promised her five francs if she would swallow the discharge after sucking me off. We must encourage these propensities . . . I didn't stop at that, and my piggishness was such that I skewered her on Charlemagne's sword. Naturally I banged her. Despite my fear of syphilis, I shot off and without a condom . . . My prodigality was such that I gave the bitch 25 francs . . . Coming home I rubbed myself with *eau de Saturne*, amazed at my own imprudence. I then wrote to the Flaubert I mentioned. Adieu, old pederast. Are you happy with me (Hernani)— Alfred Caligula." Le Poittevin's son, the bourgeois who dons his frockcoat to make his calls at Fécamp, takes pleasure in forcing the "slut," the "bitch" he has "picked up," to submit to his caprices for money. See how he makes her the slave of his "piggishness" and how he enjoys his omnipotence: "I made her strip naked but like a worm." Like a worm: what is a whore but a long white worm? And what contempt in the "Naturally . . ." Read: Obviously, since I was the master and she was my *thing*; he depicts himself, in short, turning and manipulating this living body as though it were an inert instrument. Fear and disgust follow: he rubs himself with *eau de Saturne* and worries: and what if that drain-hole were syphilitic? The unfortunate woman is definitively destroyed; she was the tool of his pleasures, and in his memory she is tranformed into carrion. The tone of the letter, bantering and supercilious, is unbearable, and we would find his sadism rather repugnant if it were not, taken at face value, incomprehensible. Why would this son of a good family be set upon debasing a whore that he already regards as debased? And what was the great achievement in obtaining from her, for ready money, "fantasies" she has given to others for the same price? Alfred's boastings are comprehensible only if in his imagination he has debased *woman* in the person of this prostitute. That is, the bourgeois woman. His mother. If his passive flesh darkly craves the repetition of maternal caresses, he expects such caresses not from a sovereign genetrix but from a guilty and humiliated mother. The reason seems clear: loved as he was, Alfred had not had Flaubert's sad childhood; male and firstborn, he had known a golden age of childish loves whose unique object was the textile manufacturer's wife. Until the age of five he was an only son—Laure was born in 1821; that is, he had his ration of tenderness. The rancor came later, we do not know why: a mother who was *too* beautiful, too attached to her beauty? Too worldly? Or was his sister preferred to him? In 1827, when he was sent to boarding school, the break was completed. Descharmes himself recognizes this when he writes: "The years he spent on the school bench *completed* the plunge into a vague and incurable sadness." [16] In any event, it was between 1821 and 1827 that he felt *betrayed* by Madame Le Poittevin. Another letter—this one published—shows quite clearly that his taste for "bitches" was linked to his desire to defile his childhood. He writes in May 1845:

> I was raised in that region. Le Havre and Honfleur for many reasons still give me a peculiarly tender feeling. There I dreamed of love when I was very young, of that love which I would reject today wherever it came from, whatever it was. Today I have the final word on this foolishness, exquisite among all others, but I love to return to the past when I believed! . . . Of those women, some are married, others are still available. I wonder what you will think of a project that I shall realize as soon as I can: I am going to spend three days at le Havre and Honfleur with a bitch I shall choose ad hoc; I shall make her drink, eat, stroll with me, we shall sleep together. I shall have great joy taking her to the country where I believed when I was young! . . . I shall dismiss her when we return. I am like that Greek who could no longer laugh after descending into the cave of Trophonius.

The pretext is purely formal: I believed in love; disabused, I want to ridicule my naïve beliefs by taking a whore along; our grotesque

16. My italics. Descharmes believes the "crisis" of 1840–45 can be explained by an unhappy love affair. A purely gratuitous hypothesis and one which becomes comic when the good man, in his desire to justify at any price, advances that *la belle sans merci* was none other than Flora.

frolics will destroy what remains of my former naïvetés. But who can believe that a man of thirty would want to avenge himself so childishly for an amorous disappointment—especially if that disappointment had to have taken place ten years earlier? It is fitting, moreover, to note Alfred's insistence on the fact that he was "very young." We know that in 1827 (at eleven years old) he became a boarder at the Vallée school, whose students took courses at the *collège* in Rouen, and which he left only in July 1834 at the age of eighteen. As he spent his holidays at Fécamp during this period, we must conclude that he is referring to his first ten years. Is it credible that he could seriously have dreamed of love at that time? This man who never left his family—wasn't he wholly taken up with family affections at this early age? Of course he does add: "Of those women, some are married, others are still available." But what is this all about? These were his playmates, whom he pushes to the fore in order to conceal the true protagonists. What resentment would sufficiently warrant returning to his childhood haunts—which he still loves, he says—with the intention of sullying that childhood forever? As if it had been nothing but a fraud, a vile illusion, as if it still clung tenaciously to the places that had provided its setting. As if in order to conjure it away, an act of magic were required—in other words, making love with a whore. As if he were angry with himself for still feeling some tenderness for that childhood and were condemning himself to fornication in order to ravage his heart and replace those naïve emotions with cynicism.

This bitterness appears still more clearly in a passage from *Bélial*. When he was working on it, Alfred knew that he was condemned; he had taken his suicidal enterprise to its conclusion. And here is what he writes:

> Descending from her carriage, Madame de Prival found herself at Père Lachaise cemetery . . .
> "Take my arm," said Bélial, "and let us take a turn through these tomb-lined paths."
> "See that old lady," said the duchess. "She seems quite desolate. One would believe she is made of marble, clothed in white as she is and motionless in front of that mausoleum."
> "It is her son's," observed the devil; "he was a brave soldier who was killed in a rout. But this little gentleman you see down there. Do you know who he is?"
> "No," answered Madame.
> "Our soldier, already come from the other life. That young woman he is holding by the hand is his new mother."

346

"What are you telling me?" cried the duchess. "I imagined that if men are reborn, they return to find life in the womb that bore them. Do the names of father, son, wife, have no more meaning, then, beyond death? You smile? . . . You must know that my heart is trembling and that your hard knowledge frightens me."

The devil then gives a rational explanation of this law of metempsychosis: "Taking their existence from the same sources, children would return the same as they were without ever improving themselves." But this is hardly convincing: first of all, the parents themselves, we are told, progress from one life to another; character, as Alfred himself says, depends not on heredity but on one's former life. And, what is paramount: we accept everything in this loosely constructed fable without believing in anything. The author invents myths and symbols at will, we follow him out of simple amusement: it is absolutely meaningless to us whether souls are reincarnated in the same families or in others.

It is not meaningless to Alfred: this dying man does not want to be reborn to the Le Poittevins. He imagines an eternity which allows us to bypass parental relations: the belly from which he came will be only one receptacle among thousands of others—there is no more *genetrix*. We note the duchess's curious omission: "Do the names of father, son, wife have no more meaning, then, beyond death?" But it is a mother who is weeping on her son's tomb; and the duchess, a future mother, ought to be indignant at being denied that maternity *ad aeternum* which most women at the time claimed. What is striking is that the old lady dressed in white and whom "one would believe . . . is made of marble" (we recall: "I must have been a statue") is mystified before our eyes: she weeps for her dead son, and he, revived, holds another mother's hand. The sorrow of the first has no more meaning, it is born of simple ignorance: if she knew the truth, she would no doubt suffer but for good reason: jealousy, the rage of the dispossessed owner, would torment her without respite. Alfred has been amusing himself. To illustrate his thesis that "parentage ends with death," he could, as he often does, show us in Bélial's mirror several incarnations of the same soul and each time to other parents. He has preferred to conjure up the ex-trooper in the very places where someone is weeping over him: this way he can savor at his ease the spectacle of the Mother-Goddess duped. An eye for an eye, a tooth for a tooth: he will betray her by his death as she betrayed him when he was alive; in the image of the little boy who goes off with a younger woman, leaving the old woman to her desolation, I find an underlying intention: Alfred wants

347

to have another childhood, or, more precisely, he wants to relive his own by eliminating the guilty woman who spoiled it for him.

Here we have the first panel of the dyptich: Alfred, who is anorexic, considers himself a pure lacuna; what is he lacking? Transcendence in all its forms: a desire that might propel him out of himself and into the world, an enterprise, any form of pro-ject, the will to participate in praxis. "If the supreme good is action . . ." This hypothesis, prompted by the reading of *Faust*, is revealing: when Alfred judges himself *from the point of view of action*, he regards himself as an invalid. Sexual desire—the only desire he feels, born of anguish and boredom—leads him back to immanence: he hires a woman, enters with her into a free contract for work, and, once relieved of the wages he pays her for services rendered, can close up on himself, attentive only to his pleasure as the pure subjective quality of lived experience.[17]

2. *Ataraxia.* In order to reveal and assess himself, Alfred makes use of another point of view, that of *being*. He has recourse to it in 1843–44, then in the midst of his crisis, and his poems reveal that his knowledge of its use dates back to 1836—and probably earlier. As soon as he puts himself in an ontological perspective, the signs are reversed, and negative is changed into positive, pessimism into optimism, resentment into tender indulgence. This attitude was consolidated increasingly as his health declined and he felt death drawing near; it is the counterpart of his self-destruction and in one sense its meaning and explanation. Here, especially, he differs from Gustave, who sought his real being but encountered only the imaginary. For Alfred, on the contrary, the renunciation of action seems to be an ascesis that reveals to him his essence, whereas in truth he never doubted the underlying bedrock that constitutes him, in his eyes. At the time, he loftily writes: "I have absolutely banished from any future plan whatever is not *myself.*" Can we imagine Gustave taking up this Barresian maxim as his own? To cultivate one's self is all very well—still, you must have a self and like it. Flaubert's bad luck—the good luck of his readers—was that he was thrown unhappily into the minipraxis of literature, his passivity already constituted, because he found himself intolerable. Alfred's bad luck, perhaps, was his nar-

17. It goes without saying that when two partners *communicate*, pleasure is a fact of intersubjectivity: the desire of one is nourished by that of the other, and the same is true of orgasms if they are synchronous. Alfred is so inattentive to his venal mistresses that he thinks he is capable of making them come if he deigns to do so. Doesn't he write that he swoons "like an honest whore"? Whores are not honest (this is certainly not what is asked of them), and their swoons on command are generally faked. The cynic Le Poittevin falls into naïveté out of indifference.

cissism. He felt a tenderness for himself, for his memories: "From the height of the hill I had climbed I seemed to see us both clearly on that already distant day when we came there together . . . What was this gloomy and anxious *self* who was looking at that other, *if not* gayer, at least younger self? . . . I am sending you half of this memory so that you must thank me for this letter if it gives you pleasure." [18] The movement of the thought is clear: he knows very well that Gustave will be thrilled to receive his letter. But he wants to specify the reason he is writing to him: it is not so much that he is moved by finding Gustave again in one of his memories but rather that he is enchanted to find *himself* again. The recipient owes his unexpected [19] luck to the revery of an ego developed on the ego he was. Half a memory: the half in which Alfred is the protagonist with Gustave at his side, the tragic confidant. If it is Flaubert who plays the primary role in the other half, it is up to him to revive it. In any event, the emotion that inspires Le Poittevin's message is not a renewed warmth for his former vassal but a tenderness prompted by his own youth. There is surprise in this reflexive contemplation but no sadness, still less judgment. In a general way he is intrigued, interested, and pleased: "I had the idea . . . for some poems, some modest, others ribald!—Odd individual that I am." He loves to enjoy this oddness through the eyes of others: "I just had a visit from a relative . . . who is a notary in Cherbourg. I think he finds me *droll.*" He is complacently surprised at his own "obscene and modest" nature, and it is to Gustave himself (to whom he nevertheless writes: "We are something like the same man and we live the same life")[20] that he declares: "I love you very much but I must sometimes seem to you bizarre. It is an oddity of very happy or very unhappy people." [21] The reader will doubtless be annoyed by this fatuousness, this affected reserve which can be felt in the same letter when he writes: "It is infuriating to be born not thinking like anyone else. As weary of the self as of others, seeking ordinary happiness and being unable to find it. There must be something, however, beneath all that . . ." False discretion, false complaint: Alfred is enchanted with his *difference.* I have reported elsewhere the proposition of a young bourgeois of 1925: "To act like everyone and be like no one"; the young bourgeois of 1840 says nothing very different, submitting quite docilely to the conformity of his milieu and not afraid to preach an esoteric ethic, valid for

18. Fécamp, 28 September 1842.
19. We shall see that Alfred hardly ever wrote.
20. 7 June 1843.
21. Published by Descharmes, *Promenade de Bélial*, p. 218 and dated by him 1843.

himself alone (and out of courtesy to his correspondent): "We would be ungrateful for our own if there were not a separate morality for such natures as there is for kings."[22] The visitor in his frockcoat does not have to justify his earthly actions—on this level he observes the "morality of men," but his true morality is *other* and *elsewhere*, and it is to this morality alone that the *royal nature* he so eagerly attributes to himself is answerable. Far from basing his value on the all too human actions he performs without deigning to think about them, he derives that value from *his quality*, in other words, *from his being*. He is an aristocrat who says, *noblesse oblige*. And his major obligation is simply to become what he is. Look at his civility: he does not claim that "his own" (his family, his friends) are submen; on the contrary, they are men, and he would reproach himself for seeming ungrateful to them. But while he sends his hypostasis to be present at his mother's receptions or to draft writs of accusation in the prosecutor's office, he is working on himself above it all, on his peak, until he can finally cry out in triumph: "I have killed everything in myself that was human."

The ethic of being, in effect, requires that he renounce the aims of the species and all forms of praxis: *being*, as he understands it, is the opposite of *doing*. The imperative of the *other* morality: be the one who is. Nothing more, nothing less. Realize *for yourself your being in itself*. I have shown elsewhere the attraction that this unrealizable (the in-itself-for-itself) dimension has for men. But it can present itself in infinitely varied forms, many of which do not exclude praxis, quite the contrary, but limit themselves to directing praxis toward ends it cannot attain. The specific aspect of the *ontological ideal* for Alfred is that it presents itself as an imperative and that it is manifest in its perfect nakedness, as we can see in this frequently cited passage from a letter to Gustave that Descharmes dates back to 1843[23]: "It was around eight years ago that I posed for myself the problem of my existence: life accepted as an enigma, which is a polite way with respect to the eternal Father of not calling it something else, reduces itself to im-

---

22. He returns to this in *Bélial:* "'There is the morality of men above,' observes the Devil. 'Then . . . there is the other.'"

23. For reasons which do not appear to me to be decisive, nor does he offer them as such. It seems more probable—as Descharmes first thought—that it was written in 1845. In any event, the question seems to me unimportant. I am far from claiming, as we shall see, that Alfred's positive attitude appeared at a precise date and that from that moment on he constantly maintained it. Optimisim and pessimism would alternate until his death and certainly did not wait until 1843 to do so. It does show that the young man *on the whole* was oriented toward a positive intepretation of his experience, which seems to be confirmed when one reads *Bélial*.

passive immobility. One might believe that, the premises being posed, the conclusion would follow of itself. But in practice this is not so easy. To live without living and to have developed only one faculty—that of feeling—was something arduous for everyone, for a poet perhaps impossible. I am wearing myself out in the pursuit of this harsh ideal, but Prometheus feels the vulture and the flesh still throbs."

To live without living: to be without acting or suffering. The problem is not completely resolved, but he adds: "I am more peaceful, nonetheless, than before. Experience has cost me dear, but it is complete. I would not sell it so easily if such a trade were possible." Here he is, presenting to us as dearly acquired wisdom what he was yesterday calling a "common shipwreck." Let us keep in mind: it was a *shipwrecked man* who craved the oblivion of his projects and traded his future against a perpetual present: the poet closed himself up in a brothel, abandoning his "vocation as artist" at the door; the chorus of serpents then concluded that this was a bad bargain. Today the metaphors have changed: no shipwreck but a slow ascesis. The follies of his brothel days are passed over in silence; anorexia becomes a providential sign, the beginning of an ascension that will end with complete ataraxia. Formerly he wrote: "My inertia has grown to such colossal proportions that there is no longer *the least principle of action* in me." This inertia he was suffering, which "was growing" in him like a cancer, becomes here, under the name of impassive immobilism, an ethical end—*the* end—which he deplores having not yet completely attained. Earlier, the waves were carrying him away; he now claims that he was steering his boat and knew where he was going. To be sure, the contradiction is not total: surprised by a universal disgust that leads him to apathy, to abulia, he could straighten the rudder, use the winds and currents to go toward what he suddenly discovered was the true purpose of the voyage. Yet these are two hardly compatible interpretations of the same experience; we shall see that the primary aim of *La Promenade de Bélial* is to reconcile them. How can one remain passive and work on oneself at the same time? How can one *suffer* one's life and take all the credit for progress imposed by circumstance? How can one achieve transcendence of being without leaving the immanence of subjectivity? Such are the questions this reversal poses to him. It will be noted, furthermore, that Alfred is approaching a Kierkegaardian "repetition": he has lost everything and everything is given back to him; indeed, in the same letter he writes: "I believe that I would understand the practice of Art and its theory better today than formerly; but the faculty has developed only in company with disdain, and I no longer want the glory that I would possibly gain by lifting my hand." Here he is then, perched so high that even art is beneath him: an artist chiefly by virtue of his ataraxia, it is that very condition that deters him from writing. He *knows* that he can write masterpieces, and that is enough for him. No matter how naïvely full of self-conceit this declaration may seem to us, we must beware of seeing it as mere boasting. It corresponds exactly to his aestheticism: to him who cuts himself off from the world and "dehumanizes" himself, the movements of the species appear as pure spectacle; the lightest push is enough to organize the perceptible universe, which reveals its beauty to the *imagination*. Let us make no mistake about it, in fact, when the young man flatters himself on "having . . . developed only one faculty, that of feeling," he is certainly not referring to affectivity—how could anyone practice both *pathos* and *apathy?*—nor can he be referring to pure sensation. For him, every spectacle has a meaning, even if only reduced to the unveiling of human absurdity. In order to understand "feeling," we must go back to the "*do you feel* the beauty of . . ." that embellishes his letters: impassivity releases the aesthetic aspect of the exterior object to the same extent that it derealizes it. Starting from this principle, Alfred believes he has a greater understanding of the nature of art: the work must have this contemplative gratuity. But at the same time he wonders what good it is to *transcribe*, since Beauty gives itself entirely to contemplation.

These remarks will allow us to come closer to the object of our search: what is this being that Alfred already is when he is still striving to attain it? Isn't impassive immobility simply the inertia of a stone? Well, actually not. Alfred says so clearly in a letter written before 1845: "I had a singularly fine and delicate nervous organization. I could have done something *if I had known how to be an artist.*"[24] What is of importance here is not the part of the sentence that is underlined; on this point the young man's opinions vary, since he writes in 1845: "How shall I succeed? To me this is a secondary question; the primary one is to be an artist," which seems to indicate that he once again had the hope of being one. It will be noted, however, that the two passages are concerned not with "making art" but, indeed, with achieving an ontological transmutation. This is what gives its importance to the first sentence: "I had a singularly fine and delicate nervous organization." Here is Alfred's *being*, that royal nature of which he boasts; the subjectivity of lived experience, of what is *felt*, is effaced before the

24. Alfred's italics.

objective structures that condition it; immanence discovers ontological transcendence, ungraspable and omnipresent. Alfred is certainly not an organism: if he is entirely reunited with himself, he will have the haughty inertia of an *organized* object. That he feels himself to be such there can be no doubt. He writes: "Why am I not that cock who crows, fucks, and doesn't think at all rather than your servant's sacred monad(?)"[25] A monad, a closed totality with neither door nor window; nothing enters it, nothing leaves it; created by God, it is merely a formula that develops and produces its consequences according to the principle of identity, and its apparent changes cannot mask its perfect simplicity, which is always identical to itself; yet the Creator has constituted it such that it is a mirror of the universe. But we shall come closer to his feeling if we bring to mind a sentence cited above: "I have quite a few subjects in mind but unbelievable bouts of laziness. It goes well once I get moving, but how can I get myself moving? *I must have been a statue in some past life.*" When he seeks to explain his inertia, it is indeed something mineral that he is comparing himself to, but a mineral that has been *worked*. He thinks he has the singularly fine organization, the delicacy, and especially the gratuitousness of marble: sculpted by an artist, receiving nothing, giving nothing, useless to everyone and above all to himself, he defines himself against utilitarianism as a finality without purpose. He might say, *he does say*, that he is beautiful "like a dream of stone," that he "hates movement that shifts lines," that "he never cries and never laughs."[26] At least Baudelaire made Beauty speak these words, whereas Alfred speaks in his own name; Baudelaire created works of art, Alfred claims *to be one*. Let us not confuse him with those who, toward the end of the century, wanted "to make their life a work of art"; Alfred lets his life flow with the current and prefers his being: by means of an entirely negative operation, he intends to clear his very substance of any human undergrowth in order to bring it forth in its insolent, aesthetic perfection. It is primarily for this reason that he is deterred from writing: the function of a work of art has never been to produce other works of art. That is the business of the artist, who is a man. In attempting to give himself the superhuman impassivity of a stone Venus, Alfred, confident of the beauty of his inner being, is transmuted into a statue dreaming of being a sculptor.

25. *Id.* And the question mark is his.
26. Letter 33, p. 212: "I did not laugh because art at its highest level excites neither sadness or pity."

Naturally, this is an *imaginary* transmutation: the substantial being that is Alfred's aim through immanence has no reality. The young man has chosen to identify with his organization; if he succeeds in doing so, he thinks, he will grasp the beauty of the spectacle of the world, and that alone. He counts on perceiving the universe through the delicacy of his own substance—meaning, through *his own beauty;* he intends to apprehend things the way an art object would if it were conscious, that is, through the categories of gratuitousness, finality without purpose, uselessness, etc., which have presided at its *making*. Beautiful—if not in his perceptible appearance at least in his pure being—Alfred turns himself into a reckoner of scattered cosmic beauty; this means that by him and *for him alone*—but does he know this?—the environment is unrealized by the very movement of his own unrealization. Here we see him, then, aiming at becoming a permanent center of derealization, which is the very definition of the art object—except that in the object everything is organized so that the derealization takes place in the interiority of him who contemplates it, whereas by unrealizing himself in the impassive object-subject (in-itself-for-itself), the young man himself effects the derealization of his surroundings. Indeed, he takes his real anorexia to be an analogue of an imaginary ataraxia; immobile impassivity is the meaning it sometimes pleases him to give to his apathy. Is Alfred then an imaginary man, like Gustave? Not at all. In the younger boy the unreal is there from the beginning: he was *constituted* that way. In the older boy, it comes at the end: he was loved, cherished, too much perhaps, enough in any case for him to have acquired a solid sense of his reality. The imaginary appeared in him only later, as a defensive reaction: it is at once the ascendant movement that allows him to conform to the mores of his milieu while detaching himself from it, and his own optimistic interpretation of his troubling inertia. He never succeeds, moreover, in maintaining an attitude *for long*. We have seen him go back and forth, often in the same letter, deplore his apathy or boast of having nicely progressed in his enterprise of dehumanization. In 1847, one year after his marriage, he still writes: "Like people who have been at sea and who have brought back with them only a great repugnance for returning to it, I feel utterly antipathetic to the least disturbance since my return from Naples. A few strolls close to the house, in the vegetable garden, and less frequently to the edge of the woods. This is the daily round of the body it pleased divine providence to attach to my mind. Moreover, it isn't that the mind works much—

they simply each sleep on their own side."[27] His regrets and his lucidity prevent the imaginary aspect of Alfred's being from truly becoming integrated with the synthetic movement of his personalization.

Further, both interpretations—negative and positive, realistic and derealizing—coexist in him: "Is there a meaning? Half the time I believe *there is* and the other half that there *isn't*."[28] That his optimistic belief in the meaning of the universe is inseparable from his leap into the imaginary is demonstrated in his letter no. 35, undated, the last in the collection. He has just presented his ontological morality—"To live without living"—hence his preference for unrealizing himself; he suddenly falls again into disillusionment without losing his arrogance ("It is infuriating to be born not thinking like anyone else, as weary of oneself as of others," etc.), and then rises up again with a beating of wings: "There must nonetheless be something beneath all this . . ." In other words, my melancholy, my weariness, my anorexia, my singularity *have a meaning.* And this meaning is tied not to some mandate delivered by the god of the Christians but to the ataraxia that is made explicit through its ennui. Nor is there any doubt that the ontological dogma, despite his constant oscillations, gains in importance. We should therefore account for the recourse to the imaginary—whose intermittence is compensated for by the frequency of its repetitions—with as much care in Alfred's case as we did in the case of Gustave, in whom the unreal is integrated with his person. We should, that is, if we had sufficient information—as we know, this is not the case. We shall therefore be content to indicate the directions which such an inquiry could have taken if the circumstances had been more favorable.

Self-destruction is a kind of passive vengeance here: it is turned against others but is never accompanied by the least self-disgust. Alfred loves himself because he has been loved. At the deepest level of ennui, his pride remains whole. Gustave's, as we know, has "come afterward"; it is a negative principle, a wound, a counterattack bound to fail. Alfred's lordly pride, as empty as his disciple's, is entirely positive for having *come first:* that calm certainty of self is nothing other than the confidence of the Mother-Goddess internalized. He does eventually grow weary of himself, but never to the point of challenging his own validity.[29] He sticks with himself, whatever he does; but, not

27. 14 April 1847.
28. 23 September 1845.
29. It is striking that even in the worst moments of his short life he never doubted his genius. His self-assurance appears clearly in each of his letters. Here is one example.

being in on the secret of his earliest frustrations and of the resentment to which they led, he observes himself as a "strange" object, something that disconcerts him while continuing to charm him. It is primarily, though superficially, for this reason that he is led to assume that behind his behavior, behind the ego itself, pole of the reflected but *quasi object*, there is an Alfred-object, a "delicate nervous organization" that produces this behavior according to certain rules and which—his pride is certain of it—possesses a metaphysical meaning. Let us not stop here, let us go one step further: we can do this because other young men of his time, his contemporaries within five years, other sons of conjugal families, some of them also victims of a thwarted love for an excessively pretty mother, are prepared to publish their fierce refusal to serve, their firm intention to be of no use to anyone, for anything. Perhaps the contradictions of the bourgeois family, by partially freeing them from the paternal yoke, have made these young men particularly sensitive to the social reality of alienation. They start life with the feeling that "others have had them"; and in order to avoid being *used*, that is, being made instruments, being drained of their particular substance and given another way of doing things as a substitute, they devote themselves to the service of *uselessness*. For them, the beautiful is *primarily the antisocial*.

Such is Alfred: he has chosen his mother against his father, as his energetic refusal to further the family enterprise clearly establishes. Inherit it, yes; work for it, no. His father's fortune gives him an advantage—or a disadvantage, if you like. Others must produce and *sell* what is useless—they have to live; it produces capital for their publishers. He, however, can escape the tyranny of profit and remain totally unproductive: he doesn't have to *make* useless works since he himself is perfect uselessness. Between the gratuitousness of the art object and that of the pure consumer there are such affinities that it is hardly surprising if the latter sometimes takes itself for the former. A man of superfluity and a chiseled object are the *luxuries* of working society: by wanting to be a man of superfluity, Alfred transforms him-

---

On 13 September 1847—he has gone back to *Bélial*—he writes: "I do hardly any reading, of course. Composition excludes this diversion, and when one is planning literary works one can hardly be occupied with those of others. Each in its turn: the models we admire have proceeded as we do, and we, *still by analogy,* certainly have the right to proceed as they do when we are concerned with posterity." Translation: Hugo, when he was writing *Les Feuilles d'automne*, which I particularly admire, did not divert himself by reading the works of his predecessors; and I, the future Hugo, have no time to read Hugo's new productions when I am composing.

self into a superfluous man. What is real in him is the oedipal choice: against the textile manufacturer who incarnates Action, he opted very early for total inactivity, and that ancient choice is decisive since it paralyzes him to the end, despite his passing whims. But it only actualized, in the person of a young Oedipus, the *possibilities of class* that the work of fathers brought about for their sons. The Le Poittevin son prefigures in his person a particular phase of bourgeois evolution: in him, industry is freed of its primitive austerity. Having chosen to be superfluous, he will live the whole of his brief existence on the *superfluous* part of the paternal profit. And certainly it is up to the proprietor to decide what to reinvest, what to deposit, what to devote to unproductive expenses; but by investing his luxury in his wife's beauty, the textile manufacturer was unwittingly preparing to define the superfluous by the demands of his son. Alfred pushes to the limit this slight decompression, this precarious dawn of freedom, which benefits his class, but this is because he himself is its product; it was in the upper middle classes that the domestic structure of familial relations gave first place to conjugality. The New Gentlemen began to refine themselves; money gave them manners.[30] These crude refinements of the newly rich, purloined and radicalized by a child, led him to reject utilitarianism. But once again it was wealth that made this rejection possible: Alfred has property, therefore he lives *by others*—he does not even see his needs and naïvely believes that he continues to exist

30. To be sure, we are at the dawn of primitive accumulation—very soon the competition will become more serious. But at this stage a manufacturer aimed at maintaining his enterprise rather than enlarging it. Mechanization of the textile industry came about in many cases in spite of the owners, prompted by crises (1827, 1832, 1837, 1847). Furthermore, Normandy lagged behind Alsace and even the north: 3,600 spindles in Rouen for a middle-sized factory in 1834 as against 4,000 in Lille. It is true that the "spinning jenny," invented by an Englishman in 1826, appeared in Normandy (1836) sooner than in the Lower Rhine. But few models were built. The industrialists also mistrusted machines: they were afraid of increasing unemployment, which foments social unrest. In France, wages remained very low, and the economy of manpower was rarely sought; in addition, the spinning jenny required a good deal of power. But in spite of the crises, money flowed. The progress of industrialization, real but slow, could not absorb the whole of the profit in the form of reinvestments. In this confused period the manufacturers, to the same extent that they resisted mechanization, had the very limited power to devote a portion of their surplus to unproductive expenses. Most of the time they would limit themselves to creating, through an increased demand, new but nonetheless useful positions, which would have the effect of promoting and increasing the middle classes. Be that as it may; between 1820 and 1830 the future ruling class slowly became conscious of its power of choice. It would no longer be quite the same under Louis-Philippe, when accumulation and concentration would destroy family capitalism and replace it by limited liability companies. But the "freedom to choose" would gradually return at the beginning of the Second Empire.

simply because he began. With needs satisfied, what is there to do? One spends oneself: *living is spending one's life,* slipping toward death. And if dying takes too long, you take it in hand, and to speed things up you use all the money necessary to destroy your youthful health. The advantage of pleasure is that it is sterile, costly, and ruins the body. In other words, the man of superfluity is the man of expense and receives life only *to spend it;* indeed, before being buttressed by a fundamental intention, Alfred's quietly suicidal attitude was prescribed by his objective situation. He was to some degree conscious of this—undoubtedly his greatest merit—and wrote in his brief essay on the French Revolution: "We do not explain things by men but men by things." To tell the truth, this is still a form of mechanistic materialism: the time is not far off when in the unity of a similar dialectical process men will be explained by things and things by men. What matters here, however, is that Alfred never believed in free will and felt that he was the product of his milieu even more than of the couple who had engendered him. Taking things once more in their basic order, we discover a spiraling process in which the inner choice actualizes the possibility offered by wealth, and wealth, in a second movement, inclines that choice toward a radicalism for which it alone can provide the means; this enables wealth in its turn to be supported and exploited by an ever more rigorous desire for death, which contains all the preceding determinations and defines Le Poittevin's attitude, but which would not even be manifest if the father's revenues had not become the son's immediate possibility. We can see that on this level Alfred declares through his fundamental choice both that he is, like everyone else, a unique person and that in his body he realizes the general possibility for sons of good families to destroy simultaneously and mutually the inheritance and the inheritor. It is on this level that he *imagines* the beauty of his soul, the invisible transcendence of immanence, in order to justify his gratuitousness: the alibi will be his genius, finality without purpose, splendor folded back on itself, producing nothing and serving nothing. This affirms his right to inaction. If he sometimes regrets not *being* an artist, it is only in those moments when he believes he *has* to materialize the beauty that is his particular essence. He puts the cart before the horse; in his eyes, the artist is not the one—neither beautiful nor ugly—who creates a work of beauty *outside* himself; rather, he is someone who has received a mandate to externalize his inner beauty. But he does not really want "to work": his works, the mere hypostases of his being, would bring him nothing more than he imagines he already possesses.

The reasons I have just advanced cannot adequately explain Alfred's unrealization as a work of art in its constant, defensive repetition. Pure consumption is a convenient springboard for a leap into the imaginary; still, one must want to make the leap. To understand what impels him, we would need to know about the childhood of our Impassive Man, and we are ignorant of almost everything about it. I am therefore going to risk a conjecture, knowing quite well that there is nothing to support it but the fact that it integrates and totalizes all my previously argued reasons. It is not with impunity that, as I have said, one is the son of the *beautiful* Madame Le Poittevin: one runs the risk of developing a hyperoedipal complex (in the sense that we speak of the hyperexploitation of colonized people). During the precious years for which he still feels a certain tenderness, Alfred confused the development of his person and his taste with his apprenticeship to maternal beauty. Or, if you like, beauty was revealed to him as being wholly embodied in his mother. Not only does he cherish her in her physical person but at Honfleur, at Fécamp, in the mansion at Rouen, he makes a catalogue of the young woman's preferences. The movements of this charming body have left their mark everywhere: in the choice of a knickknack or a piece of jewelry, in a flower arrangement, in the harmonious folds of a drape, the child *recognizes* her. Madame Le Poittevin, a good mother and a good wife, passed nonetheless in her husband's eyes, in the eyes of the people of Rouen, even in her own, for a useless marvel—a housewife's work is scarcely noticed since it consists of restoring. How could her elder son have failed to be proud of the admiration she inspired? How *too* could he have failed to see her through the eyes of others and discover through them what they took to be the singular essence of this very beautiful woman: that her being resided in her appearance, in her austere futility (let us not imagine a woman dripping with diamonds; she was without any doubt *economical*, but in this epoch of utilitarian puritanism, the differential is what mattered) and in her femininity, which she manifested by the choice of objects that reflected her image. Here she is then, at the same time lively, gracious, and utterly inert, dispersed in the environment that reflects her. In Alfred's early childhood she was, like all good mothers, a carnal and sexual presence that at times seemed to him of such closeness that he was simply at one with her: at this age we know neither beauty nor ugliness, and besides, we have no use for it. But when the child learned to talk, when he discovered *through others* that his mother was beautiful, he must have been both pained and dazzled: this adored beauty was the first maternal betrayal. It seemed to him both that she *gave him more*, in her inexhaustible generosity, and that she leaped backward to an infinite distance; for one can appropriate the breast one sucks, the silky skin one caresses, warmth, a sweet animal odor, but never *pure appearance*. I have written elsewhere:

> Someone "beautiful" . . . is a being who is incapable of giving himself to perception and is in his very nature isolated from the universe . . . At times, however, we take an attitude of aesthetic contemplation in the face of events or real objects. In such cases everyone can verify in himself a kind of retreat in relation to the contemplated object, which itself slips into nothingness . . . It functions as an analogue of itself, that is, an unreal image of what it "is" becomes manifest for us through its actual presence . . . Extreme beauty in a woman kills any desire for her. In effect, we cannot place ourselves at the same time on the aesthetic level on which the unreal "herself" appears that we admire, and on the realizing level of physical possession, . . . for desire is a plunge into the heart of what in existence is most contingent.[31]

Therefore it is Alfred who effects the real "distancing" when he contemplates his mother aesthetically; let us say, he tears himself away from desire. But because this desire, momentarily suspended, is still not suppressed, the child feels the inalienable appearance of the imaginary as a frustration for which his mother is responsible. She was his most intimate possession; his painful dazzlement forces him to understand that she has escaped him. All the more since this discovery is doubtless contemporaneous with the second betrayal—which we have glimpsed through the young man's resentment but know nothing about. What we can *suppose* is that *through* Madame Le Poittevin's beauty he grasped her worldly life; in this sense, by the perfection of her forms and features she belonged *to others* more than to her own child. This at least is what he believed. If around the same time he saw her giving her love and attention to Laure, the newcomer, he must have desperately tried to possess his mother *in that beauty* by which she escaped him, and to transform himself in order to recuperate the love of which he felt deprived. In any event, he had long since chosen the maternal world; presently, it no longer sufficed, and he recognized that he had never entered it. In order to gain admittance, he will try to identify both with his mother and the trinkets she has chosen in which she mirrors her beauty. In a desperate effort to recap-

31. *L'Imaginaire*, pp. 243–46.

ture her lost love, he becomes the art object she is *and* the object she has produced as flesh of her flesh. He seeks on the one hand to recapture the indivisible unity that preceded weaning, and on the other to share the condition of the objects she lightly caresses and seems to love. This is a way of making his being out of internalized appearance, of giving lived experience the inertia of fashioned things or, rather, of imagining behind his apathetic stupor the splendid passivity of a chiseled jewel. He *is* his mother—hence his particular "androgyny," and she wears him on her finger like a ring, on her neck like a necklace. She loves herself in him, the most precious of her products; he roots himself in her, he is dissolved in her, he will be her ornament: his soul will be beautiful and mirror her beauty. The tenderness she lavished upon him, the words of love she spoke to him must have facilitated the task: the objective essence of his soul would be the inactive magnificence of the maternal body. It seems, however, that the second real or supposed betrayal may have caused him too much suffering; for this reason the identification with the mother and her beauty would remain on the level of phantasm—always recurring, never integrated. Sometimes he forces the guilty mother, embodied in a whore, to caress him as she would a beautiful vase; at other times he believes he has found the secret of his inertia in his *aesthetic* nature as a finality without purpose, that is, in his secret identity with the woman who bore him. As we see, this conjecture merely summarizes our previous descriptions and the motivations we have proposed. It respects, as it must, the priority of infrastructural and conjunctural conditionings since it presupposes the mode of production, class, family institution outside of which the endeavor of identification could not even be conceived. Nevertheless, it is undemonstrable and I offer it up for what it's worth.

In any event, when Alfred took up the pen once more in 1845 to write *La Promenade de Bélial,* it was not so much, I imagine, that his taste for literature had returned—even though his old hope of "being an artist" had been revived—but rather to *materialize* his phantasms and give them through writing a consistency that would allow them to explain his real state enduringly and completely. For several years he thought to contemplate his being, always ungraspable, and found himself each time plunged into an ontological revery that quickly unraveled, betraying its oneiric character. On the other hand, he often imagined that if he should succeed in concentrating himself, in assembling and organizing his ideas, in totalizing the perceptions he flattered himself he had as he meditated, and above all—*verba manent*—

in objectifying them in imperishable graphemes, he would establish once and for all the *meaning* of his being *in its truth*. From this perspective, *Bélial* seems to be a response to the question that tormented him for eight years: under what conditions is a being like myself possible? Or, more accurately, because he had to satisfy his pride: what sort of universe would require my existential attitude, which is hardly the result of pure chance? This means: how can determinism be reconciled with a transcendent finality such that the words *cause* and *effect* become equivalent? (In fact, Alfred considered himself to be the exclusive product of previous circumstances, but he meant to prove that these circumstances had fashioned him in his being the way a sculptor makes a piece of marble submit to the Idea.) How can my marblelike inertia *suffer* an ethical progress that is continuous, incessant, and yet claim credit for it? How can I reconcile my slipping toward death and the slow maturation of my inner beauty? Is there a point of view from which one might grasp optimism as the necessary outcome of absolute pessimism? Here we have the origin of those "ideas" of Alfred's that elicited Gustave's dazed admiration and fearful mistrust. We must recognize that they proceed from a certain philosophical astonishment that puts the self at a distance as an inexhaustible object of contemplation, always examined, always hermetic or ambiguous. Moreover, the young man reads Kant, Hegel, Spinoza, Darwin, and many others with the sole aim of finding answers to his endlessly considered questions. Yet the result can be only a pseudophilosophy since his problem is not to understand the world but to justify himself; and Alfred's "ideas," produced to satisfy the demands of a comprehensive defensive strategy,[32] are organized rather like a handy pocket *ideology*, issuing from an adroit exploitation of the ideology of the bourgeoisie. Besides, whether they are spoken or written, they remain imaginary: *images of ideas* which, like those of a dream, have no other purpose than to gratify the dreamer's desire, meaning in this case that they are assembled and externalized so that the pseudophilosopher should be persuaded of their truth. Le Poittevin is not wrong, moreover, in calling his work a "philosophical tale." We see the ambiguity of the label: are we dealing with a philosophy expressed allegorically through a tale, or does the fable reside in the philosophy itself? The author hasn't decided.

We shall see that the chief reason he adopts the theory of reincarna-

---

32. The intermittent recourse to the imaginary had been, until that time, merely a tactic.

tion is that, when reworked, it best corresponds to the questions he poses. It should be noted, however, that he is inclined to this choice by a sort of "lived experience." One evening in April 1845,[33] he clowned around for quite a while, "imitating a woman having an orgasm," and then walked with a friend "down the boulevards" to shock the passersby. After this charming exploit, he came home "weary of the present, of the past, of the future." But he immediately adds, barely taking the trouble to begin a new paragraph: "There is also something in me that has never been satisfied, I am not sure what. Reminiscence? Or a vague perception of the future?" Nothing more, but it is clear that although these two sentences follow one another, they are not referring to the same future, and that the "reminiscences" of the second are not to be confused with the memories he is weary of. We should not, however, try to find in this unemotional and modest complaint the grand Baudelairian theme of dissatisfaction. To be sure, it involves a closely related motif and Baudelaire also believed he had memories of "previous lives." But Alfred's dissatisfaction, if we are to believe him, does not come from the yawning infinity of his soul—otherwise why attribute it to reminiscences, to presentiments? These words seem to indicate that the deprivation bears on precise and limited objects of which he is deprived today but which he has enjoyed in the past and will enjoy again. This means that his *being* is not *totalized* in his present existence: he escapes himself through the quite vague reminiscence of what he *has been*, meaning *that other* which he still is— without being able to define it—at the heart of the *self;* but he also feels, like some vague future summons, an invitation to some *other passage beyond*. These lines offer us the most precise formulation of his experience. He already holds his theory of metempsychosis at this period, but he has alluded to it as early as 1842. He is quite serious and quite disgusted when he writes: "I believe indeed that if we are of this world, we are not of this century. Do we have something to expiate? I do not know, but the crime must be great if it is in proportion to the tediousness of our lives." Elsewhere, he recounts with poetic complacence that he was strolling by the sea and, as he notes, "found in myself a son of the North crossing the light mists of the heaths, and I felt inside me something of the ancient life of the Scythian nomads."

In *Bélial*, this is what becomes of these foggy perceptions: "Have you sometimes seen . . . great bulls bellow and stallions gallop across the prairies? Have you not perceived in their eyes the flash of thought

33. He was in the midst of writing *Bélial*.

and something like a majestic hope? Another life is preparing itself in silence beneath those calm brows. Come what will. The hour is approaching when the animal, casting off its hide, will raise itself to human thought and the speech that communicates it." The same thing holds for every creature; for man, too, future being already exists, though it may be grasped only in the form of a lack, a subtle torment. We know that later, after reading *Louis Lambert*, Flaubert would write to Louise: "This Lambert is for all intents and purposes my poor Alfred." Lambert too is impelled by strange and irrational events to pose philosophical questions: he has a prophetic dream, he affirms an instance of "thought communication" produced in his family; he sets to reading Swedenborg and receives intuitions whose objects are inaccessible to the senses. Prying into the mysteries of being, he cannot bear his amazing discoveries and goes mad. Indeed, the similarity of the two men is not immediately obvious: narrow, prudent, skeptical, and at least externally conformist, Alfred was certainly far from madness. For Lambert to have reminded Alfred's ex-vassal of his ex-lord, Alfred must have taken his minor troubles seriously and must have used them in Gustave's presence as the basis for his doctrines; his recollections and his prophetic intuitions prove that Alfred's life and his organism were but a means—secondary at that—of apprehending his being in *this* time and in *this* world. Being is imperishable substance, and its eternity is sometimes palpable to him—although in his intuitive confusion he may not be able to recognize it—not as a summons from on high (the word *reminiscence* must not deceive us despite its vague odor of Platonism) but through the vague remembrances or unintelligible oracles that relate to other appresentations that take, or will take, place in the same world, to other moments in history. For us, these two series of illuminations without contents are mutually conditioned: he was frustrated but first he had been passionately loved, and the contrast between Alfred's present destitution and his former princely condition makes him fall occasionally into an unsatisfied stupor;[34] at the same time, this indecipherable past guarantees the future: the prince that was will no doubt become a prince once again. Alfred would not accept our interpretation: if he wants to give optimistic solutions to the problems that plague him, he must interpret his troubles as the sure signs of his multiple reincarnations. A few readings on Brahmanism no doubt helped him make the leap. Here he is, theorizing:

34. I would also attribute Baudelaire's *poetic* and intermittent belief in metempsychosis to the memory of a "paradise" lost.

"The memory does not survive death; but the soul in creating itself a new body takes from the conditions of its past life the aspirations of its new life." Of all the examples that Bélial will cite, the clearest is certainly that of the orientalist: "In his past life he was a celebrated orientalist. Now he studies his own grammar, not suspecting that he is its author." This is what has to be demonstrated: Alfred suffers himself, yes, but such as he was made in a previous existence; other than self, he derives only from himself; his arrogant doctrine rejects heredity—parents are just material causes. On this basis he jumps into optimism with both feet. Here is a glimpse of the future: "The soul cannot die, it renews the body it inhabits at each phase of its existence. Only each phase brings it nearer to the Ideal, the ultimate development of worlds . . . The circumstances vary, the result is the same. The unbridled rule of Matter calls forth the reaction of the Spirit. In order to emancipate itself, [the Spirit] condemns [Matter], seeing in it the ceremonies of Hell. But later, from the ideal heights, man perceives wider vistas; knowledge makes him impartial. After setting the Spirit free, he rehabilitates Matter and grasps their identity beneath their apparent opposition."

Hence we have three phases or hypostases: "Captivated by the unknown marvels Nature has been so generous in bestowing, [the Spirit] will first become Nature's slave, will then deny it in order to free itself, and finally, returning to it, will bring it under the sway of its Empire. *To the infinite aspirations we feel confusedly welling up in ourselves there are, then, when they are ripe, correspondent realities*[35] . . . [In the third phase], beyond humanity, there are upper regions to which . . . geniuses . . . will one day be elevated. It is sufficient for such a progression that a new sense should awaken inside them and open up to new needs a whole world of new emotions."

Despite his eclectic and sometimes neo-Platonic vocabulary, Alfred is inspired chiefly by Hegelian optimism. We recognize the movement of consciousness which becomes estranged, recovers itself, and opposes itself by the negative principle in order finally to reestablish the unity of the subject and its objectification in the absolute. No doubt these three moments—in which, moreover, we recognize the celebrated trinity—also vaguely reproduce the three kinds of knowledge according to Spinoza. Finally, we recognize at a superficial level the influence of the first evolutionary doctrines and, at a deeper level, the bourgeois ideology of progress. Here it is simply a question of spiri-

35. My italics.

tual progress: like Gustave, Alfred condemns material progress and the social progress it is supposed to engender.[36] But for all that, the ideology of his class is inside him, he has merely displaced the point of application. The myth of reincarnation is not necessarily linked to a progressivist evolutionism, as witness the Hindu religions from which Alfred borrowed it. For him to have taken the step from one to the other, as if he had deduced the second from the first, the ambiguous notion of perfecting and unlimited expansion must have been bred into him from an early age, and he must have believed in it implicitly without even being aware of it.

In the uninterrupted chain that goes "from worm to man" and from man to superior spirits it is easy to mark the place the young man attributes to himself. There is no doubt that he judged himself newly arrived at the frontier that separates the second phase from the third. A genius pushing at the limits of the human, already a superman by his "infinite aspirations." In one movement he reconciles the sharpness of his sensual appetites and his spiritualist quietism: "He fell back into the phase of passions but promptly came out of it again . . . Relapses . . . are in the order of things . . . [One] falls back into the previous state only to emerge from it very soon." Things couldn't be better: the brothel is no longer the abode of the lotus eaters but the place where Alfred, a superior spirit, is conveniently and briefly going to backslide; women preserve their malignity, but for great souls they become inoffensive. Of course they make men "fall," but what does it matter if, once they've shot off, they bounce back up to the "cold ceilings" of humanity. These regressions, normal and increasingly rare, prove that in previous lives the young Alfred was subjected to the inflexible yoke of the senses, the "reign of exterior things and of lusting eyes." One must pass this way, as demonstrated by the fact that the evolution of the soul through its incarnations is reproduced in the very life of each particular reincarnation. Alfred explains with a great deal of clarity that—as people have said for some time—"ontogeny recapitulates phylogeny." Materially: "The infant in the womb does take on the attributes of its own species right from the start. Its soul, having become human, reclaims with its new body the types of inferior species . . ." Spiritually: "As high as the spirit may have reached, at each of the creative crises that renews its outer covering, it sets out again from the lowlier degree through which it has already traveled." These remarks allow the author to find once more inside

36. "Have you been . . . to compliment Gautier on his increasing exasperation with the progress of the human race?" 6 August 1842.

himself the "three phases" as moments of a continually renewed dialectical process. He yields to matter, disgust jolts him into a condemnation of the senses in the name of an abstract idealism, his premonitions warn him that he is very close to the superior state in which the senses and the spirit will be reconciled. Behind the philosophic reconstruction we find once more the history of this conflicted consciousness, oscillating ever more frequently between the two terms of its underlying contradiction and dreaming of a future synthesis.

La Promenade de Bélial could be called Alfred's *apologia pro sua vita*: it's true, once I was a brute, but it sufficed that amid pillages and rapes I experienced certain anxieties and that "I, whose force was law, sometimes glimpsed the existence of another." My subsequent life was that of a monk who died a virgin, and after other avatars I was reborn a philosopher: "I had emancipated the spirit, I was rehabilitating matter and teaching . . . their absolute identity."[37] Dissatisfaction based on the vague intuition of some incompleteness, the simple consciousness of an empty state, the muddled aspiration to totalize—in short, the Hegelian negation *lived in passivity*—this is what sufficed to prevent being from coinciding with his present life and to confer upon the individual the *merits* that will allow him to ascend to a superior stage. In his present existence Alfred *capitalizes* on all the malaise that previously, intermittently, detached him from the immediate—from accumulation, profit. All is well since, as Marivaux says, he prefers his being to his life. At once this life in its present particularity justifies his pessimism—it is a necessary evil; one must *abstain from living, live without living*. And Alfred's aesthetic amazement at the movements of the bourgeoisie is easily explained: it is not so much *what they do* that provokes him, it is the seriousness with which they do it; these people, submerged in the immediate, never have the slightest doubt, they certainly never put their enterprises and their purposes in parentheses. They are in no way condemned for that; less advanced than Le Poittevin, they still remain on the lowest rung of the ladder, tied to their pure materiality. Our pseudophilosopher thoroughly enjoys himself, he will make explicit the meaning of his suicidal enterprise: isn't this the only concrete and practical way of realizing his detachment? What can we hope for, then, except to die, since we shall be reborn closer to the Ideal, and since this anticipated, desired death itself becomes a merit, an excellent investment? One must kill oneself slowly, with alcohol, with prostitutes, *with the ennui* that is the necessary conse-

37. Descharmes, p. 222. These lines figure in a version of chapter 4 that Alfred rejected in the definitive manuscript.

quence of the stubborn refusal of all human aims; one must "live without living," and this means to die one's life. Dying is Alfred's intimate future, impatient as he is to become other; it is also his present: that clear, transparent lagoon lacks only the consciousness of itself to be transformed, finally, into the nothingness that it is. Time slides over him, time without content; only the orientation of temporality remains palpable to him. He wrote to Gustave: "Everything is uniform except time, which marches on; it's almost like being in a tomb." Now he has resigned himself to the inevitable: dead, he wants to die; conversely, he realizes his future death by his daily ataraxia and sees his mute life, an ungraspable confusion, *in the repetition* of three temporal ek-stases, as the reflection—continually reborn, continually jumbled—of eternity.

This lofty, morose Catharism is nevertheless a kind of optimism. Pessimism condemns life *from the point of view of life;* Alfred scorns it *from the point of view of death.* For in the end, although death is only a prelude to birth, so that *La Promenade* might be considered a hymn to universal Eros, to cosmic fecundity, Death retains the advantage. How can we fail to recognize this in what Alfred takes for his being, an ungraspable transcendence that is recapitulated in no particular existence and manifest in all by disqualifying them through the revelation of their futility, that announces their finitude, their coming death, and that suffers transformations of which it preserves no memory from one hypostasis to the other and is consequently itself pure absence? We can look forward to it: death's point of view on life is aestheticism; it will be art for the postromantic generation. And so, at least *on paper*, the various interpretations Alfred offers of his fundamental attitude are found to be reconciled. This inanimate art object first believed himself to be the pure product of maternal beauty; out of resentment he now refuses to be the flesh of that flesh but retains the status of precious, artistically worked matter. Inert, he will be his own goldsmith; he will have the inorganic being of a rare and dead stone encased in a ring that was engraved in the course of previous lives and whose magical power is to derealize its surroundings; in other words, he releases the beauty of things and events and also—which amounts to the same thing—holds it suspended in the infinity of nothingness. A dead man exalts and kills all living things by communicating his murderous beauty to the objects that surround him. A ritual, secret assassination, of course: the victims persist in living because they don't know any better. But the process is no less valid metaphysically:

a deceased prince detaches them from their lives as they will detach themselves from it after several hundred reincarnations.

The Le Poittevin son has reestablished everything in an instant: "There is a meaning," life is no longer an enigma; he believes that on the basis of a rather dry rationalism he has constructed an axiological system and a cosmic hierarchy in which he occupies an enviable place. He progresses toward the Ideal, the "ultimate development of worlds," where Matter and Spirit will reveal their underlying identity which is none other than beauty—their double and simultaneous abolition. Aristocratic, spiritualistic, quietistic, individualistic to the point of solipsism and vaguely satanic around the edges, this ethic was the only one that could have suited him. It does save everyone; one is struck, however, by something callous about it. Alfred took eight years to go from Byronic pessimism to this smiling pantheism (worlds have one soul, it seems, and according to him individual souls end by merging into it). But just as a sense of disillusionment lingers in *La Promenade*, one feels from his first known work—he was twenty years old—that he already bears within him the principle of his later optimism: in *Satan* we see the Accursed fall prey to infinite sufferings, but he stands up to God and makes himself the master of the human race. Alfred has the pride of one who, like the Master according to Hegel, for having risked his life is placed above it and puts his highest certainty in an ego void of content, the simple "I think" as the vehicle of all thought; or perhaps it would be better to say here, an empty "I imagine" as the matrix of every possible image. He has maintained his loyalty to Satan since he has invoked Bélial, a fine little devil, to give him authorization to articulate his theories. But what a difference between the cursed archangel and that smiling character who declares he has been slandered by the Christians, adding: "This is what was understood by the Hussites, who called [the Demon], contrarywise, *He who was wronged*." The contrast between these two characters allows some appreciation of the distance he has come during these eight years. At first Alfred rebelled, something Gustave would never do; but the rebellion hardly suited his supercilious, conformist, and cavalier nature; that may be the reason his lyricism was so quickly snuffed out. From this point of view we shall hardly be mistaken in considering *La Promenade* a theoretical justification of a *return to order*. In the course of his long silence this ambiguous young man has aimed at only two objectives, which appear contradictory but which he certainly did not take to be so: to destroy himself, and to be reintegrated with his class, with the society frequented by his family. *Bélial* provided him with a double solution: one must die to the world—ataraxia, or death of the soul; suicide, or the slow deterioration of the body. But precisely for that reason nothing one does has any importance—rebellion is as vain as utilitarianism; one might as well stay where one is and do as everyone does—all that counts is detachment. Let us understand, of course, that Alfred could neither tolerate bourgeois life nor refuse its comforts. This can be plainly seen when we note that he began *La Promenade* in 1845, "fell into line" in July 1846—it was on the 6th that he married Louise de Maupassant—took the book up again and finished it in 1847, and died in April 1848. As if his theory of reincarnation had no other purpose than to convince him to "make an end of things," as they say, or rather to make two ends as quickly as possible by assuming the roles of husband and bourgeois father, and by ducking out immediately afterward.

Such is the new lord that Gustave has chosen. At first glance, the young man and the adolescent are joined by a number of affinities: both have extraordinary parents—Achille-Cléophas is Science; Madame Le Poittevin is Beauty; both, the victims and the accomplices of their families, received in their earliest years a passive constitution that led them to scorn all forms of action, to condemn bourgeois utilitarianism, and to profess quietism; both are tormented by chronic dissatisfaction. In addition, each of them has a taste for history from which—for lack of personal experience—they draw their "knowledge of the human heart," but they still prefer poetry and the imagination; disturbed by the discomfort of their agnosticism, they each try to remedy the situation by an effort of cosmic totalization which sometimes verges on a kind of pantheism; both are impelled by an overweening pride to perch on summits, from which they contemplate the bustle of men below with scornful irony not unmixed with malice. We understand why, under these conditions, Alfred should have written to Gustave: "We are something like the same man and we live the same life."[38] Does he believe what he says? That is another matter. This sentence is part of a letter of excuses: Alfred begs his friend to forgive his "long and reprehensible silence"; in such circumstances one often overdoes the protestations of friendship. And Gustave? What does he think of their relationship? Does he judge it to be solid and flawless?

38. 7 June 1843.

We have a curious letter on this subject. On 9 September 1852, Flaubert had just read *Livre posthume* by Maxime Du Camp, published by the *Revue de Paris:*

> Contemptible, isn't it? . . . *our friend* is ruining himself . . . One senses a radical exhaustion in him . . . I do not know if I am mistaken . . . but it seems to me that all of *Livre posthume* is vaguely reminiscent of *Novembre* and that a fog of my making hangs over the whole of it . . . Du Camp will not be the only one on whom I will have left my imprint. His mistake was to accept it. I believe that he acted *very naturally* in trying to disengage from me. Now he goes his own way; but in literature he will remember me for a long time. I have also been fatal to that unfortunate Hamard.
>
> I am communicative and exuberant (I was, more truthfully), and although gifted with a great capacity for imitation, all the wrinkles I get by making faces do not alter my appearance. Bouilhet is the only man in the world who has done us justice on that score, Alfred and me. He recognized our distinctive natures and saw the abyss that separated them. If he had lived, it might have become ever greater, he by his clearness of mind, I by my extravagances. There was no danger that we were becoming too closely joined. As for Bouilhet, we must both have been worth something, for in the seven years that we have been sharing our plans and our words, we have kept our respective individual physiognomies.[39]

This text offers a typical example of the progress of Flaubert's thought. The publication of Maxime's book irritates him deeply. For good reasons and bad. The good ones: the work is bad, lacking personality and facilely executed. The bad ones: *Novembre* is still in my drawer. Du Camp cut *Saint Antoine* to pieces and now they've published *this*. In fact, it was Flaubert's *inflexibility* that was responsible for his refusal to look for a publisher for *Novembre*, but that refusal was not without its cost; there is a very understandable contradiction between the honorable ambition of a young man who would like his manuscript transformed into a printed book, and the collection of prohibitions—the most important of which are aesthetic—that prevent him from submitting it to public judgment. So when he notices that Maxime has had the nerve to present a mediocre work to the *Revue de Paris* and that it was immediately accepted, his ethical disapproval—art is *also* a kind of ethic—is exacerbated by a jealousy he dares not admit to. With what alacrity he transforms this modest suc-

39. *Correspondance* 3:56–58.

cess into a shipwreck: "*Our friend* is ruining himself!"[40] His wounded pride is immediately evident: at bottom *it is not true* that Maxime has been published and that Gustave remains unknown; what has been published is a lesser *Novembre;* if the *Livre posthume* was pleasing, it was to the extent that it was reminiscent of that work. It is not fitting, however, that Gustave's influence should have beneficial effects on a friend who has turned away from him: if Maxime by virtue of that in-fluence should achieve glory when the younger Flaubert son despairs of ever attaining it, that would certainly be hell. Hence the sly repeti-tion of the romantic theme so dear to Gustave: "I bring unhappiness to all who surround me," which explains the unexpected allusion to poor Hamard (Gustave indeed believed that he had gone mad trying to imitate him).[41] Certainly, the *Livre posthume* was published because its first readers had a foretaste, in reading the manuscript, of the work they were unconsciously waiting for, which Flaubert did not deign to give them. But this unexpected luck turns into a disaster for Maxime: now, with the novelty worn off, everyone can discover the ass hiding in the lion's skin. In short, it is Gustave who *has ruined* (without want-ing to, of course) poor Du Camp, it is he who has put his brother-in-law on the road to the asylum. Hence a new delusion of grandeur: "I am too strong, I, the excessive, bring unhappiness to him who tries to imitate me"—which is masked and rationalized by this passage to the universal: no one ought to imitate anyone. This allows him in passing to put balm on another wound to his self-esteem (Maxime no longer admires him, Maxime goes his own way): Du Camp *acts as is proper* when he tries to disengage from me; his mistake was to accept my imprint.

And here, quite suddenly, with no apparent connection, he goes on to the next line and starts talking about Alfred. Immediately, as always

40. *Our friend:* Louise detested Maxime; Gustave hadn't forgiven him for criticizing *Saint Antoine*—this is the meaning of the italics. It will have been remarked that the young man is taking his revenge: an eye for an eye, a tooth for a tooth; you have con-demned my work, you have forced me to bury it; all right, I'll sink yours. But he cannot prevent himself from altering the truth. In the same paragraph he writes, in effect: "If he ever asks me what I think, I promise you I will tell him exactly what I think, and it won't be pleasant. Just as he didn't spare me *his* opinion *when I didn't even ask for it:* this will simply be tit for tat." The italics are mine. Certainly Maxime gave Flaubert un-solicited advice. But the main "opinion," for which Gustave harbors a simmering ran-cor, we know *had* been asked for in due and proper form: Du Camp and Bouilhet to-gether had been summoned to Croisset to be subjected to the reading of *Saint Antoine* and to communicate to the author their judgment on his work.

41. Let us say he *wanted* to believe it: it would be his revenge on the criminal friend who had stolen Caroline from him.

when he touches on a sensitive point and increases his customary in-sincerity, mistakes abound: first, the cascade of *il* (he or it) which des-ignates sometimes Bouilhet, sometimes Alfred, sometimes the gulf that separated the two young men. Then the astonishing "he by his clearness of mind, I by my extravagances," which is not part of the structure of the sentence and seems to assume an active verb ("we would have widened it") when apparently it was a *suffered* event to which Gustave refers: given the distinctive natures of the two friends, the abyss would have continually widened. It is true that the passive and active can be used interchangeably since constituted characters are expressed by actions; what is surprising is that the young man cannot entirely formulate his thought and passes over the verb that would express a reciprocal and disjunctive action by the two friends. Finally, we note the omission of two negative elements [*ne* and *pas*] which the publisher had to reestablish for the sake of the text's intel-ligibility. These are signs of great confusion: if Flaubert were speaking instead of writing, we would say that he was stammering. At this point he comes back to the subject of Bouilhet; he calms down and everything becomes orderly again.

Why mention Alfred? There is still some connection between his thoughts, but it is affective and not logical. It is as if someone had in-terjected this troublesome question: "You say that it is always wrong 'to accept another's imprint': well, what about Alfred's imprint? Didn't you accept it? Didn't it mark you forever?" Who is speaking here? Who is asking these questions? Who is forcing Gustave the braggart onto the defensive? The chorus. One word tells us: "Bouilhet is *the only man in the world* to have done us justice." The only one: therefore, the gen-eral opinion—that of his parents, his friends, friends of his family— was that he submitted to Alfred's influence. Yet Gustave doesn't ven-ture this opinion without disguising it. He writes, "do *us* justice," as if in the eyes of their circle the influence was reciprocal. All told, this is a position of withdrawal; if pushed, he could always exclaim: Well, yes! We marked one another reciprocally, no one dominated in this couple, we worked out our ideas together, etc. It is of this that he post-humously convinced René Descharmes, who speaks of the younger's influence on the elder during the last years of their friendship. Nothing could be more false: Alfred followed his path with inflexible rectitude from birth to death. Furthermore, when he writes this letter, Gustave intends to stick to his first line of defense: it is others who imagined this reciprocity; it matters little to him that Alfred may have received his imprint; what he defends himself against is having received that of his friend. Is this not a total disavowal? Compare these two statements: "We are something like the same man," wrote the elder; and the younger, four years after Alfred's death: "An abyss separated us that would have become ever greater . . ." Between these two "distinctive natures," separated by an abyss and always growing farther apart, no communication was possible; like ships on the high seas, they may at best have signaled their positions to each other by flares, flags, and searchlights, but these exchanges of information could not alter their solitary courses. This is not convincing, however; the facts are there and Gustave knows it quite well: he *imitated* Alfred and everyone could see it. All right, he is going to disqualify their observations: "I imitated him, of course! But who didn't I imitate, from the journalist of Nevers to Papa Couillères? There is in me, you see, something of the itinerant performer, the inner strength of the actor, and thus a great capacity for imitation. So there you are, I aped him. For laughs. And our fine folk took it seriously." A great capacity for imitation—precisely. Or rather—and this is not a reservation but the indication of a lack, since we do not know whether he had any talent for it—a constant impulse to imitate someone, a need to get hold of the being of others in this way, to steal their reality from them. This is a recognized sympton of hysteria.[42] But it must be understood that imitation involves belief; what Gustave wants to forget in 1852 is that he imitated Alfred with the deeply serious intention of *identifying with him.* Did he run away from it? This is another matter and we shall come to it. But for now, the harshness of his denials seems to indicate that the enterprise was doomed to failure and that he understood that it was. See to what degree he presses the denial: "All the wrinkles I get making faces do not alter my appearance." When he seized on his friend's attitudes, when he tried to adopt his thoughts, these were only passing grimaces, and the grotesque wrinkles that creased his face disappeared without leaving a trace; we know the man he is describing here—the comic who would make all of France laugh and dishonor his family by getting slapped and kicked in the ass on stage. Couldn't it be said that he is trying to debase his past? At least, someone might propose, he is going after himself, he is ridiculing his love for Le Poittevin and Alfred is left untouched. I am not so sure: if the copy is faithful—and it is, in his opinion, since he possesses the "capacity for imitation"—and makes faces, it is because the model makes faces. Moreover, he indicates briefly but specifically what distinguished their "natures," and it

---

42. Freud to Dora, in *Five Psychoanalyses:* "Who are you imitating?"

is certainly not his friend who comes out on top: "he by his clearness of mind, I by my extravagances." Of course, an extravagant person is a fool, an excessive, a dreamer; the word is chosen for its pejorative brutality. And "clearness of mind" is a positive quality, isn't it—who wouldn't want it? But we are beginning to know Gustave: the faults he attributes to himself are often disguised virtues. The word he uses here we shall find again later in his *Préface aux Dernières Chansons*, where it takes on its full meaning: "Our schoolboys' dreams were superb examples of extravagance . . . We deserved little praise, certainly! But what hatred of all platitudes, what aspirations to grandeur!" Such was Flaubert, according to his own testimony, at the period when he frequented Le Poittevin: his excesses testified to the fire that burned in him and—why should he hide it?—to his genius. Poor Alfred cuts a sorry figure by comparison, with his "clearness of mind": he isn't even granted that exceptional intelligence that would later be recognized when the myth of their friendship will have prevailed over its truth. He has clear and distinct ideas, an enviable facility in an engineer or a professor of mathematics yet one which at the same time marks their limitation; this quality is valuable in practical life, scorned by Gustave, and goes against "reasons of the heart," which it rejects without knowing them. Dryness, abstraction—these are its consequences; indeed, it will have been noticed that if Gustave differs from Alfred by his extravagances, it is because Alfred, limited by his intelligence, is sadly incapable of excess. A reasonable and prudent bourgeois: like Monsieur Paul, after all, or Ernest, whose moderate perversity was terrorized by Mazza's infernal passion.

Why does Gustave so stubbornly reject the fact of Alfred's undeniable influence over him? First of all because he scarcely believes in influences: at the age of eighteen months a man is made; thereafter he only develops his essence, that is, it unfolds; nothing and no one will prevent him from following his destiny. If by chance he is derailed by some external action, he will lose his life or will doggedly return to follow his path. We find here once again the old bourgeois idea of the "impenetrability of beings." And these maxims, repeated a hundred times, serve mainly to hide his fear of being influenced: this is one of the explanations for his unsociability and his voluntary sequestration. How could it be otherwise for this imaginary who depends on others even in his being and is never very certain of his reality? In the letter cited earlier he describes himself as exuberant and communicative. Wrongly. Exuberant, yes, to the point of glutting his listeners. But this is precisely *in order not to communicate:* he thunders, bellows, loses his breath, and leaves them no time to make suggestions, to slip in advice. With Le Poittevin, however, things went differently: Gustave recognized and accepted the ascendence his friend had assumed over him. Let us simply recall that dedication: "Think of me, think for me." It is difficult to find a greater testimony of trust: you find the ideas, you expound them to me, I adopt them. It is love, at this period, that explains such total abandon. And this love was betrayed: in 1846 Alfred was married, and all of Gustave's previous rancors (we shall see that he harbored some) crystallized around that ultimate betrayal. We shall return to that. It is therefore perfectly comprehensible that his resentment should prompt him to say: I owe him nothing, he never gave me anything; I took him for someone else and we had no common taste. But there is something more in his violent and stammering disavowal—he is disturbed by an emotion that comes from a more distant source: Alfred was a bad master, and where would I be now, he thinks in terror, if I had followed his teachings? And what if something should still remain in me of his fascinating and pernicious ideas? In fact, during that year Gustave was rather tranquil; he had begun *Madame Bovary*, and although he sometimes had suspect bouts of disgust ("la Bovary irritates me"), he was determined to follow the enterprise to its conclusion. But his fears remained; two years earlier, during his travels in the Orient, he had been afraid: "from the past, I go dreaming of the future and I see nothing there, nothing. I am without any plan, without ideas, without any project, and what is worse, without ambition. Something, the eternal 'what's the point?' is the constant refrain and its bronze wall blocks every avenue I open for myself in the land of hypotheses . . . I wonder where I got the deep disgust that I feel now at the idea of stirring so as to have myself talked about."[43] In fact, he is "ill" from the awful blow of the reaction to *Saint Antoine*, and the reason he no longer dares undertake anything is that he is haunted by the fear of risking a new failure! Note this confidence that escapes him *in the same letter*: "It seems to me that if I misfire again with the first book I write, I can only throw myself into the water. I, who have been so daring, am becoming timid to the point of excess." In this universal disgust, however, this ennui that envelops him even as he sails up the Nile, he recognizes the disgust and the ennui that led Alfred to his death. We find evidence of this in a new letter to Bouilhet dated 4 September. It seems that the Alter Ego is at this time undergoing a crisis of the same sort in Rouen and believed he was au-

43. 4 June 1850.

thorized to share it with Gustave. He goes so far as to echo Gustave's "What's the point?" from the month of June. He'll have cause to regret it: in the meantime Gustave has been cured, and violently upbraids him; yes, during the preceding four months he too had "repeated the *inept phrase*[44] you send me, 'what's the point?'" but *Saint Antoine* was to blame. He was "disappointed," that's all. Never in his right mind would he have condemned the artist's effort. Bouilhet must not take it into his head to confuse him with Alfred: Gustave's disarray was entirely accidental and in no way resembled the arrogant, disdainful indolence of his former lord. And here he begins a thorough criticism of Le Poittevin's attitude:

> If you think you are going to bore me for long with your boredom, you are wrong. I have shared a more considerable weight; this sort of thing can no longer frighten me. If the room at the Hôtel-Dieu could tell of all the boredom two men stirred up at its fireside over a dozen years, I believe the household would collapse onto the heads of its bourgeois inhabitants.[45] That poor idiot Alfred! It's amazing now that I think of it, and all those unshed tears that still remain in my heart on his account. How we carried on together! We looked into each other's eyes, we soared so high! Take care, it's amusing to be bored; it's a downward slope . . . All right, little fellow! Bawl all alone in your room. Look at yourself in the mirror and pull your hair.

This text clearly outlines the ambivalent feelings Gustave had for Alfred. First of all, it is an energetic rejection of "boredom" in all its forms: it was the master who suffered from ennui and pulled the disciple into it: "I have shared a more considerable weight." Fascinated, Gustave was nonetheless dying of fear: if "this sort of thing can no longer frighten [him]," it is because he has the experience of some memorable terrors that have hardened him. What was he afraid of? Of too successful an identification of the vassal with the lord. He even says so here: "It's a downward slope." It would take very little for him to add, like Joseph Prudhomme: "A slippery slope! A fatal slope!" Which is to say that he dreaded joining Alfred in his dreadful anorexia; convinced of the vanity of everything, even of art, he dreaded reaching a point of no return, the inertia of the needle always pointing at zero. Furthermore, Le Poittevin's ennui was not without its pleasure: "Boredom is amusing." Where had this directed boredom led him? To

44. My italics.
45. That is, on Achille's household.

marriage and to death. Suddenly Flaubert realizes that he is going too far; without transition he returns to his customary refrain: "How we carried on together! We soared so high!" The reference is to the famous Thursday conversations. But Gustave exaggerates: those conversations, begun in 1834 or 1835, did not last a dozen years, for the lord went off to Paris around 1838, and, when he returned, the vassal was on the verge of departure. Around this time, they began to see each other less frequently and their relationship slackened. This simple remark suffices to make it clear to us that Flaubert is preparing to intensify his insincerity—we know the tune. He certainly isn't lying when he writes: "We soared so high,"—he believes it, or he wants to believe it. But these words, added in haste, nonetheless serve to correct the bad impression Gustave feared he had made on the Alter Ego. In point of fact, can one soar so high when one stirs up boredom at the fireside of a small room? Conversely, weren't the philosophical discussions, if the speakers were fired by the same enthusiasm, of a nature to diminish their boredom? In truth, these three lines, which have no logical connection with the general statement—and which appear here just like clockwork—reveal to us Gustave's real thought, unbeknownst to him, though that is precisely what they are supposed to conceal: the high-flying ideas that were born of boredom—and continually increased it—all ended with the "inept phrase" that Bouilhet sent back to him. The general and systematic reviews undertaken by the two friends were contrived such that they led inevitably to the same conclusion, to that inept and monotonous "what's the point?" which came from the elder and was imposed on the younger. Gustave had a narrow escape: a perverse archangel—who idly challenged the whole universe for the sole purpose of justifying his idleness—completely failed to drag him down in his scandalous fall. What revenge: to survive! The master was mistaken, his cavalier and panoramic views were false since they led him to marriage. To Bouilhet, the little frog who wants to make himself as big as Alfred, Gustave flatly declares: "How I wish I were there to kiss you on the forehead and land a couple of hard kicks on your backside." And it's as if he were saying: "A couple of kicks in the ass, that's what my ex-lord deserved; that's what he needed to cure him." From this point on, we understand his relief when in 1852 he could declare to Louise, though still not quite certain of it: we had two distinct natures; an abyss separated us. In other words, he was delivered from Alfred's grip, and, *quite naturally*, like Maxime, "he is now going his own way."

These two letters are masterpieces of insincerity: Gustave conceals and reveals his feelings by turns. But when his thought allows itself to be intercepted, its rare lucidity must be acknowledged. It is true that the two friends did have distinct natures, and everything that seemed to bind them together did in fact estrange them from one another. Alfred's influence on Gustave was deep and would be lasting, but far from transforming him into an epigone of his elder, it would succeed in changing him in himself, through the double frustration we are now going to examine.

A. FRUSTRATED FRIENDSHIP

Just what does the young man ask of his elder? A *gift* that allows him to pay homage; in other words, enough love for the child to be justified in loving Alfred to distraction; a *valorization*, enough esteem for the unloved child who has scarcely any self-esteem to be justified in having a little more. *Being:* we know that Gustave's being is in the hands of others; and, being an imaginary, the younger Flaubert has reality only for them and through them. The sad thing is that they are often hostile toward him—or at least he believes they are—and clearly display their aversion to him; and they are secretive as well, so that Gustave can neither feel nor know what he is in their eyes. If he gives himself entirely to Alfred as Achille gives himself to Dr. Flaubert, if he lives from Alfred's life, if he serves him, and if his new lord *looks at* him, the adolescent thinks he will finally have the intuitive joy of his being and knowledge of his truth; above all he will climb up and sit above those who debased him. This is what he hopes; will it be given to him? In order to find out, we must go back to the beginning of their friendship.

We know that their relations became intimate around 1835, when the younger boy was thirteen and the elder eighteen, and that their friendship was never livelier than in this period. The difference in age is of great importance. First, it adds a striking trait to Alfred's character: it is rare for a very young man to choose a child for company. This child was Gustave Flaubert, someone will say. But that's just the point. If we are not to yield to retrospective illusion, we must recognize that this boisterous and yet withdrawn schoolboy, in spite of obvious qualities, bore no mark of election. We are in the position to know that bitterness, rage, and despair were overwhelming the boy's profound sensitivity. He said so himself later on: "The secret of everything you find surprising in me . . . is in that past of my inner life that *no one* knows. The only confidant it might have had has been buried for four years."[46] This means that the child did not reveal himself easily; for him to have opened up to Alfred, the elder had to have taken the first steps, to have discovered passions in him, a very lively intelligence despite the mediocrity of his scholarly achievement, and, to use an expression of the day, the tragic beneath the affected grotesque. Above all he had to have loved this little boy *against men*. Against their bustle, their vivacity of mind, he enjoyed immersing himself in this gloomy and violent soul still obscure to itself. Against knowledge and culture he sought in Gustave the virginity of thought.

How about Gustave himself? Can we imagine the intoxication of the unloved boy who sees coming toward him a prince of this world, a *man* nearly as old as Achille who detaches himself from the world of adults in order to seek him out among the children, him, a younger son scorned and frustrated by his elders? There was no doubt this time that he had been *chosen*. We know that he defends his hypersensitive pride against a painful feeling of inferiority; yet now someone comes to him and loves him *for what he is*. With what mad enthusiasm he gives himself to his new master. To what extent is the love he bears him homosexual? In his excellent article "Le Double Pupitre," Roger Kempf has very ably and judiciously established Flaubert's "androgyny."[47] He is man and woman; I have specified above that he wants to be a woman in the hands of women, but it could well be that he may have experienced this avatar of vassality as an abandonment of his body to the desires of the lord. Kempf gives some disturbing citations, the following in particular, which he finds in the second *Education*: "The day of Deslauriers's arrival, Frédéric allowed himself to be invited by Arnoux"; perceiving his friend, "he began to tremble like an adulterous woman under the gaze of her husband." And: "Then Deslauriers thought of Frédéric's person itself. It had always exercised on him 'a nearly feminine charm.'" Here we have a pair of friends between whom, "by tacit consent, one would play the wife and the other the husband."[48] Rightly, the critic adds that "this distribution of roles is very subtly demanded" by Frédéric's femininity. And Frédéric in *L'Education* is the chief incarnation of Flaubert. Conscious of this femininity, we may say, he internalizes it by making himself Deslauriers's wife. Gustave very skillfully shows us how Deslauriers is excited by his wife Frédéric, but we never see Frédéric enraptured

46. Early November 1851.
47. This is the term used by Baudelaire to characterize Emma Bovary.
48. Kempf: article cited. Let us recall Gustave's and Maxime's "engagement."

with the virility of his husband.[49] Alfred's letters sometimes sound a curious note: "I will come to see you on Monday without fail, toward one o'clock. Are you getting a hard-on?" "Adieu, old pederast!" "I embrace your Priapic splendor." "Adieu, dear boy, I embrace you in the style of Alcibiades."[50] It seems to me that the epistolary use of these "turns of phrase" is a clear indication that they did not refer to any real practice. The usage was, indeed, generalized and seems to have been adopted, between 1842 and 1845, by the whole little band of Flaubert's comrades. Gustave informed Alfred that Du Camp saluted him in the style of Alcibiades (which was no doubt the equivalent of that other formula: "Maxime wishes to be remembered to you"), and Alfred answered: I sodomize him. Pleasantries, if you like. But not innocent: between bachelors in their twenties, such pederastic jollities are not customary. Furthermore, although they tended to become the common property of the group, they were introduced by the couple—chiefly by Alfred, one could guess. It will be remarked that he gives himself the active role: he is the one who does the caressing and the sodomizing. Isn't it because he is conscious of the feminine excitement he provokes in Gustave? Or, rather, that he *has* provoked? By the time they exchange these letters, the two friends are quite distant from one another. And somewhat later in Flaubert's correspondence we find this disclosure: "Could [David] resemble the musician king of the Bible whom I have always suspected of having an illicit love for Jonathan? . . . Such a serious man, besides, must be slandered. If he is chaste, he has the reputation of a pederast, that's the rule. I too had that reputation at one time. I have also had a reputation for impotence. And God knows that I was neither one nor the other."[51] In this text it is not the disavowal that matters (Gustave was, by his own admission, well and truly impotent for eighteen

---

49. Except perhaps in an ambiguous passage that Kempf cites although he considers it unconvincing: "A man like that [says Frédéric of Deslauriers] is worth all women." Should we see in this remark Frédéric's unconditional "virility" or this confession: to be the mistress of a man like that would give me more pleasure than the possession of all other women, my sisters? It must be noted that in *L'Education sentimentale* Deslauriers seeks to possess the women who Frédéric loves. He fails with Madame Arnoux but succeeds with Rosanette (Frédéric had given him permission to try). And it is quite certain that Gustave was fond of this kind of trio. Unpublished letters of Bouilhet prove that he slept with the Muse and that Gustave knew about it. In the same way, Maxime slept with Pradier's divorced wife, who only loved Gustave—who gave Maxime permission to do so.

50. These citations are made from the photocopy of letters that Roger Kempf kindly sent to me. They will also be found, along with many others, in his article already cited.

51. To Louise, 1 September 1852. *Correspondance*, 3:11.

months),[52] it is the information he gives us: he was believed to be a pederast. When? "Old pederast," Alfred says to him just when Flaubert, running to whores and brothels, means to prove that he is neither impotent nor homosexual. In other words, it is certainly not his chastity that is the source of this slanderous reputation. Unless it dates back to the time of his adolescence: in *Mémoires d'un fou* he tells us that his first sexual experience took away his taste for carnal relations and for himself; under these conditions, might he not have resisted being dragged to the whorehouses of Rouen? But since Alfred, his sole confidant, echoes this rumor four years later, we can easily imagine that he knows what he is talking about. It therefore seems likely that the younger boy more or less explicitly desired to complete their friendship through a carnal union in which Alfred would play the role of the male, and that if Gustave had the "reputation of pederast" at the time it was because of his attitude toward his friend.

Let us say it at once: by all appearances, his passive but aroused expectation was disappointed. Certainly he was handsome in those years—he had the ambiguous charm of adolescence; Alfred was at the age where desires are still uncertain: for all we know, he too might have been attracted—as Deslauriers was by Frédéric—by the feminine charm emanating from Gustave's young body. But if there were touches, sexual contacts, a few sessions of reciprocal masturbation— which I doubt—they lasted only briefly. For Alfred had too much virility to be interested for long in boys and too much feminine passivity to take pleasure in playing the role of an active homosexual. Beginning in 1838 at the latest, he discovered his true tastes: to receive the caresses of a venal and humiliated woman, that was his specialty. His homosexuality, if it is indeed pronounced, was also entirely passive; his letters prove it, he wishes Gustave could see him when he swoons with delight, and wants to know that the spectacle of his rapture gives the voyeur-in-spite-of-himself a hard-on. But this is no more than a mere fantasy: he describes his sensual pleasures in order to complete them by the excitement they will provoke two days later in the provinces. It is an act of isolation; he neither gives nor shares anything, quite the contrary: he frustrates, offering himself while he slips away.

In spite of Roger Kempf's ingenuity and the number of his citations,[53] we remain in the realm of conjecture. But it doesn't really

52. We shall return to this further on.
53. Kempf acknowledges it himself, in fact, for the title of his conclusion is, "After all, why not?"

matter that much. The fact is that for Gustave the friendship is total-itarian and not reciprocal. It begins with a vow (in his adolescence he planned to write a story whose title we know: "Le Serment des amis," "The Friends' Vow"), which is nothing if not homage, implying the lordly gift and the loyalty, body and soul, of the vassal; to be complete it should also imply cohabitation,[54] common work if not collaboration, celibacy, and so forth. If Gustave sexually felt these requirements as a desire to be possessed by Alfred, it was only the carnal totalization of their liaison—not by any means its truth but *one* of its truths. And the amorous frustration translated into corporal terms a general frustra-tion. This general frustration could be embodied in terms of this amo-rous frustration and quite as easily in a hundred others. Gustave cer-tainly wants to be the lover; yet the beloved must have some need of him, if only in the way that we say God needs man. At the very least he doesn't want to feel that in Alfred's eyes Baudry, Boivin, Chevalier, and he himself are interchangeable. After all, it is the lord who has *distinguished* him. And it is here that the misunderstanding begins: what the younger boy demands, the older one is constitutionally inca-pable of giving him. I was particularly struck by a passage in their cor-respondence. We are now in 1842, 23 September, the Le Poittevin fam-ily is at Fécamp for their annual visit, Flaubert's family is in Trouville. Gustave has been trying to imitate Alfred; he writes to him proudly that for the whole of the vacation he has been keeping company only with a child and an idiot. We already know his reasons: childhood fas-cinated him—and so did idiocy and "bestiality"; in these states he re-covered the rough and earthly world of his former reveries. And it also pleases him to imitate his master and to establish these affections *against men*. If he still remembered the time when, at thirteen, he be-lieved himself to be the object of attachment—perhaps even fascina-tion—of a big boy of eighteen, what must he have thought of Alfred's gently implacable response: "If you keep company in Trouville with a stupid sailor and a child of eight years old, that's fine but beneath me, who keep company with no one."

Is Alfred joking? Hardly—he says humorously what he thinks. To spend time with a child is a moment of ascesis whose result must be total solitude. It is true that the letter is written five years after the *intense* period of their friendship: the fellow who around 1835–36 at-tracted Gustave as a permanent disciple was the Byronic *poète maudit*; and what can one expect now from a stylist who has opted for im-

54. Cf. the first *Education:* "We should stay in the same house," etc.

passive immobility? Still, some sort of self-sufficiency is to be felt in this jocularity—and which dates back to an early time. Alfred esteems Gustave, there is no doubt, but with a very obvious feeling of superiority. This feeling is to be found everywhere. Of course, there are declarations of friendship, uneffusive and infrequent. For example: "Come back then, I am thirsty for you; we are two trappists who speak only when we are together." Or again: "I have a great desire to see you again; in spite of everything there is something that bleeds in us when we are separated for long. Distraction at first prevents our feeling it, but we are not *distracted* for long and the habit is reawakened." We note the *in spite of everything* and the *for long*. If the separation doesn't last too long, distraction suffices to mask what is only a habit. If this habit is finally reawakened, it is because Alfred is never amused by anything, is "not distracted for long." And this strange reservation—in the same letter, one of the friendliest:

> When will we be able . . . to chat a little *like two old friends* . . . ?
> I have a great desire for it on my part. I love you very much, but I must sometimes seem bizarre to you. This is an oddity of very happy or very unhappy people.

Why this "but" if not to respond in advance to an accusation of indifference? In fact, Alfred scarcely writes. Of the thirty-seven letters that remain to us, nearly all—except the first five—begin with excuses:

> No. 6: I beg your pardon a thousand times, my dear friend, for the neglect in which I seem to have left you . . . [8 December 1842]

> No. 7: I am truly ashamed, my dear Gustave, of my tardiness in answering you; but I am very busy, very lazy, very bothered . . . [30 December 1842]

> No. 8: I am truly ashamed of my behavior toward you . . . We make promises but we have difficulty keeping them . . . [*and after four or five lines*] I would write you at greater length but . . .[18 March 1843]

> No. 10: I have just learned that you are furious with me . . . [15 May 1843]

> No. 11: I must truly beg your pardon, my dear Gustave, for my long and reprehensible silence . . . [7 June 1843]

> No. 12: If I did not write to you sooner, carissimo, it was not exactly that I hadn't the time: strength alone was lacking, as usual . . . [25 July 1843]

He also uses the excuse of his illness ("being always ill . . ."), but Flaubert scarcely believes it; on receipt of the letter of 7 June 1843, he writes to Caroline with a mixture of anxiety and suspicion: "Hasn't Alfred been ill? Was he really ill or simply indisposed? That scoundrel writes me so rarely that one never knows how he is living or what's become of him." [55]

No. 15: Pardon me for this brief letter, my dear Gustave, but . . . [23 September 1843]

No. 18: Whatever the pleasure I usually feel in reading your letters, I truly felt a moment of remorse in reading the one I just received. It is not that I don't think of writing to you . . . etc. [14 December 1843]

No. 19: If it has seemed to you, my dear child, that I have turned away from you for some time now, it's that . . . [no date]

No. 23: I have been a bit tardy in writing to you, old friend, because I have done a great deal of work . . . to make Art is also to think of you.[15 September 1845]

No. 25: I have thought of writing to you for a long time, my dear Gustave, but it's not only my well-known laziness that prevented me, I had to write to my two families at the very least a few lines and several times . . . [9 September 1846, Florence]

No. 26: You must have a little indulgence for a lazy friend . . . [17 April 1847]

No. 27: It would be a great shame, then, dear friend, to delay sending you the promised letter (if I had not begun work again on *Bélial*).[13 September 1847]

The following undated letters from Descharmes's collection are of a piece. When they are both in Rouen, Alfred often writes to cancel a meeting:

No. 28: I couldn't go to see you today . . . it's impossible for me tomorrow . . .

No. 29: I was indisposed all these days . . .

No. 30: I see I am forced to leave you without my company tomorrow . . .

No. 31: I have delayed a little in writing to you . . .

55. *Correspondance*, Supplement, 15 June 1843.

No. 32: . . . I was all set [to hear your novel] . . . Friday something unexpected happened to my father. Yours saw him and knew about it, I thought he would tell you.[56] I went to Monsieur Sénard's, but he wasn't there. I had to come back on Saturday . . . Sénard put me off until today . . . I will come tomorrow but with Levesque and Boivin. Wednesday I am booked, I will only be free, then, on Thursday, and again can promise you only my good faith for Friday or Saturday; I don't think, however, there will be any problem.

And what condescension when the unhappy Gustave allows himself to protest! 15 May 1843: "I have just learned that you are furious with me, that you are mailing to Déville whole volumes of curses aimed at me; such a thing is ludicrous and merits explanation . . ." (There follows an "explanation" which is hardly convincing but has the merit, in Alfred's eyes, of laying all the blame on Gustave). He adds: "As for myself in such a case, if I had something interesting, as you must have, to write to you, I would have delivered a rebuke later, but I would have given you some sign of life. I believe that in not giving me one, you were in the wrong and that you were quite silly to blow your stack; I very much want to forget about it, but it is rather like something one might expect of a man besotted, no doubt by excesses which I hope you'll make up your mind to tell me about."

A little later, 8 May 1844, a new explanation, a new rebuke: "If I have seemed, my dear child, to turn away from you a little for some time, it is because it seemed to me that on your side, on a recent occasion, I had found less frankness than I expected. That had made me hide various things from you which otherwise I would have been quite ready to tell you. It had made me sad to act this way, but I shall be happy to have been mistaken."

The tone is striking, all the more because Gustave's "crisis" had occurred three or four months earlier and he was far from being cured. Moreover, Alfred adds matter-of-factly: "Send me a prompt account of your state. I hope that the country and the sea will have almost restored you." The end of the letter is colder still: "Adieu, my dear Gustave, get well and always count on me *et nunc et semper.* News of your sister who was still unwell when she wrote to Laure.[57] But regards to your family."

56. In other words, Alfred did not even think of purposely asking his godfather to deliver the message. He was expected and didn't come, without canceling the engagement.
57. This is equating Caroline's ailments (of which the gravity was not yet known) with Gustave's illness.

Condescendence, severity: no real concern for Flaubert's illness. Gustave, however, had certainly spoken about it to Alfred when he felt it coming on, or at least had told him his subjective state; the Master doesn't even allude to it—he wants a health bulletin. He does add, however: "I do not know what fatality follows us, but you would think something was trying to throw obstacles between us, yet it all amounts to a straw meant to stop two seas from reuniting. Why have we never found ourselves together in Paris? You would think the city does not want to shelter us together until the hour is come when it will have no choice but to receive us. Let us at least hope so."

But the whole passage rings false, unpleasantly so. The first sentence is a literary convention: nothing could be less comparable than the two friends and two seas reuniting. Gustave, strictly speaking, might compare himself to a torrent in the height of passion. But the calm quietist of Fécamp lacks the violence of a body of water in movement. Unless one would want to call that immense gap an ocean.

No; reading carefully, we perceive that Alfred rejects reciprocity and seems to avoid it all the more as the friends advance in age. Thirteen years old, eighteen years old: this is the basis of a hierarchy. Twenty-three years old, twenty-eight years old: the bond of vassalage tends of its own accord to be transformed into a democratic relationship. Yet a bond of equality is something the elder does not want at any price. From pride? Certainly. But not only for that reason; this man of expense and superfluity, this pure consumer, this schizoid is simply not made for communication: he has nothing to receive and nothing to give. The reserves and the avoidance of 1842–48 permit a better understanding of what he sought in Gustave around 1834–38.

He favored the little boy not *in spite* of his young age but *because of it*. Let us recall that one day he would tell him: "Do you know, it is hard never to think out loud?" The sentence is clear: Alfred might have written: "not to talk to anyone," "not to communicate one's thought to anyone." But he doesn't go that far. What he wants is to talk out loud in front of someone who is sufficiently conscious to give his *consistency* to the proffered word, but sufficiently lost so that there is no danger of his becoming a judge or even a full-fledged witness. At the time of the famous conversations at the Hôtel-Dieu, Gustave fulfilled both conditions to perfection. He was what I shall call the *minimum witness;* he listened, enthusiastic and passive, without ever contradicting or modifying Alfred's mental exercises with his own preconceptions. If he intervened, if he sometimes surpassed the older boy, it was in passion: the master disdainfully put the world on trial and the disciple cried out with rage and disgust. That was just what Alfred wanted. His cold heart had no need to love—he had heaped all the love he had on his mother and buried it. He wanted to be loved by a child, as if the vampirized sensibility of another could become *his* sensibility *as other*. He took pleasure in provoking shock and sorrow in the young heart as if he were thus endowing his own thought, pure and empty, with an affective profundity it had never had. Alfred, a nonchalant Narcissus, loved himself through Gustave's mediation; he had no need to *test* his ideas, to confront them with the ideas of others simply because they were his and the only ones he could produce. He was not concerned with passing from subjective certainty to truth: he charged Gustave with consolidating his certainty through admiration. In other words, he only half relinquished the subjective: what charmed him was to feel the *weight* that the least of his maxims had *for another*. Half understood, adored, he took on in his own eyes some sort of reverend mystery; the master's stoicism, an abstract and sterile negation of life, always needed to dissimulate its formalism. Gustave loved a figure of flesh and blood, with a voice, a face; through this love the master felt *his* voice, *his* face as the concrete material of the Idea.

In this friendship—which Alfred alone could *determine*—I also see a certain amount of prudence, for we know that this aesthete, because of his identification with his mother, is constrained by worldly compromises. He dreads being judged because he vaguely fears that someone might uncover the contradiction between his principles and his actions or, more profoundly, that someone might reveal the partial truth that his universal contempt serves to justify his conformity. Gustave is naïve, stifled by his family—the child will not discover the real meaning of the master's activities. When it pleases him, Alfred is willing to mock or blame his parents—he has put them in parentheses and so spared them. He needs a friend who does not push the enterprise of subversion to the point of challenging his life within the family. When Lengliné makes fun of Flaubert and whispers that little girls will console him in Paris for his exile, Alfred himself feels attacked: he defends family ties against the stupidity of a brute. Here again, it is the vassal's *limitations* that he values.

This is the source of the mystification: chosen, the child feels *valorized*. Yet Alfred saw in him only a virgin and limited disciple, whom he would form before interaction with others had deformed him. For the lord, Gustave is only half a man: Alfred loves him only for his receptivity, meaning that he is attached only to himself. Narcissus can examine his visage in a young river. For this reason, the golden age of their friendship dates back to Gustave's early years. From the moment he becomes a worthy interlocutor, he loses all charm in his friend's eyes. Chosen *against* communication, the disciple gradually becomes more demanding, and in the name of this very choice he demands to communicate with the master. Alfred rejects this: having no progress to make, he judges any challenge useless. By now the younger boy knows the older by heart and perfectly comprehends his ideas; no more mystery. He doesn't argue yet, it is true; but he might start, who knows? Does he judge? Alfred could not tolerate anyone judging him, even in the name of his own principles. He distances himself. In a sense, he spends his time escaping. This is the source of Gustave's painful impression that he loses value as the years go by. Alfred loved the child *for his childhood* and against adults; to the extent that their difference in age becomes less important, he increasingly sees in Gustave the future adult and tends to love him less. It is both to summon Gustave back to his lost childhood and to keep him at a distance that in his last letters, when Gustave had long since reached his majority, Alfred persists in calling him "my dear child," a formula that had to be extremely unpleasant to the addressee and which, in the eyes of a witness who is neither a judge nor party to either side, betrays a very unpleasant state of mind. Not only does Alfred have no *need* of Gustave, but he distances himself more and more as if from an accomplice who knows too much about him. In the end he prefers solitude or anyone other than Gustave; in his mother's salon, he tolerates Lengliné, Boivin, and Ernest. Not that he finds them of any interest, but because they *do not* matter. With them he can stay on his own, playing the woman who has orgasms, picks up men, drinks, listens to their idle talk, laughing mysteriously, and doesn't give herself. What separates him from Gustave is both the memory of their past intimacy and his friend's strong personality, which affirms itself a little more each day. From the moment Gustave ceases to listen passively to Alfred's monologue, we have a dialogue of deaf men. Here, for example, are Flaubert's exhortations, fierce, plebeian, practical: "Think only of Art, of it and it alone, for everything is there. Work, God wills it: it seems to me that this much is clear." [58] "Think, work, write, roll up your shirtsleeves to the armpits and fashion your marble like the good worker who never turns his head and who sweats, laughing, over his task." [59] "Send everything else packing, and yourself as well,

58. Genoa, 1 May 1845, 1:167.
59. Milan, 13 May 1845, 1:171.

all except your intelligence."[60] And here are some of Alfred's "answers": "I have perfectly separated from every future plan whatever is not myself . . . The chief question is *to be* an artist. I admire your serenity. Is it because you are less distracted than I, less assailed by the *external*, or is it that you have more strength? You are always happy to save yourself by a means that I too would have and which until now I have had no desire to cling on to. I no longer want the glory that I might gain by lifting my hand."

Obviously, the two men no longer understand each other, although they both still use the key words that charmed them in other times. Flaubert is irritated: it seems that his friend has affirmed his value only to devalue him all the more. The adolescent believed that the master's gaze conferred upon him at last his true being; now he perceives that Alfred looks at nothing and no one, has perhaps never looked at him, and has eyes only for himself. In the face of this blindness, Gustave, stripped of his reality, feels himself falling back into the imaginary. His profound disappointment was certainly not unrelated to his crisis of 1844—as we may surmise from Alfred's letter of the following 8 May; it indicates that the two young men were blaming each other for their lack of frankness. But we can understand their growing divergence only by examining the other frustration their flagging friendship imposed on Gustave.

B. Negation Frustrated

Unlike his master, the younger boy is not a "man of superfluity"; indeed, superfluity does not exist among the Flauberts—any more than pure consumption. Gustave was embarked on the family enterprise from infancy. This was enough to give him basically the structure of a "man of the necessary." We shall begin by elucidating this situation.

From the beginning of the century, the middle classes were increasing their numbers: they began to weigh indirectly on the decisions of the ruling class, and the consciousness of this nascent power made them bitterly aware of their political impotence. The most radical of their number would be republicans from 1830 on; the majority remained cut off from politics. Their problem was socioprofessional: set apart from the masses by the rich, the middle classes could preserve their privileges only by consolidating and continually augmenting them. Midway between the "disadvantaged" and the dominant

60. Croisset, September 1845, 1:192.

classes, born of the currents that drew them upward without allowing them to reach the top, they recognized both their *dependence*, hence the ambivalence of their relations to the advantaged, and their *quality*, hence their hatred of manual laborers. I call the representative of the developing middle classes a man of the necessary in order to distinguish him from men of need. These last are the slaves of hunger, whereas he, thanks to the increasing accumulation of capital, is put in possession of the means to assuage it. This man *has the necessary*. But for this very reason he is alienated from it: in order to avoid failures and setbacks, to distance himself from that constraint of the body which is physical need, he finds his necessity in the social. His task, rather, his categorical imperative is to obtain confirmation of his granted status. But there is no goal involved: he ameliorates certain positions, he places markers for an ulterior and more solemn confirmation, which will itself be only a springboard. *Sociality*, in the man of the necessary, overrules everything else: he eats to work, works to save, saves to move upward, moves upward to work still more. He never stops to enjoy; luxury and the goods of this world are not his affair: he refuses even the pleasures within his reach; but he is stingy with respect to needs as well, not only for reasons of economy but to demonstrate that he has raised himself above a purely natural existence and no longer shares the gross appetites of the masses. And it's true: satisfied in advance, his needs are dulled, and in any event he is proud of not being concerned with them; in one fell swoop he has rid himself of those urgent, encompassing aims that impose themselves on the starving man and lead him to combat. As for eating less than a laborer, the man of the necessary can easily manage that, especially when he is practicing his profession, as he so often does, in his shop or office. He is *L'homme moyen* par excellence: the man of means, the man of the mean, the average man. As much a stranger to the real aims of the possessing class, whose principle is the accumulation of capital, as to those of the exploited classes, whose most imperative end is *in this case* the satisfaction of needs, he is never an end in himself in the social process (as is somehow the man of need when he fights the exploitation that tends to reduce him to being only the essential means of accumulation) nor—like the capitalist in his own eyes—the essential means to an absolute end, namely profit. This auxiliary of the bourgeoisie lives on a minimum part of the profit that the bourgeoisie concedes to him in exchange for specific services. In other words—whether he is a lawyer, a doctor, or a notary—he is a means to means: his own end is to restore social means or regulate their relations. Thus he will not abandon his function as administrator or clerk, and he will be constituted by the internalization of his duty. The initial terms and, quite as much, the ultimate terms of a *practical* series elude him for the very reason that his social reality is never at either the beginning or the conclusion of an enterprise; on the other hand, he clearly grasps the intermediary means, means of means, appearances of ends which become means when one attains them—because his very condition is that of an intermediary. Not a breath of freedom: he is paralyzed by all the systems he has constructed to dissolve teleology without losing instrumentality; hence, we could formulate his major imperative as follows: "Act in such a way that you treat the humanity in your person and in others as a means and never as an end." With this, the man of the necessary takes pride in becoming the best possible means; with open eyes, he makes *l'être-moyen* his absolute end, and aspires to rule the instrumental world.

This was the ethic of Achille-Cléophas: he held his children to be the means with which he had provided his family. Certainly he made the family a means of progress for science and, conversely, made science a means of existence for his family. I am sure that the pride of knowing, the curiosity of singular and intense research had pulled him out of the dirt, and that as a man of science he had known absolute ends, such as knowledge, the pleasures of luxury, discovery. But his deepest reality remained conditioned by the *mediocrity* of the unproductive.

Gustave could not escape his conditioning any more than Achille. With all his own gravity he supported and nourished the morose seriousness of the family. As a child he believed in everything, he gave himself over fully to the austere games of economy; there is no doubt that he was impressed with his fundamental responsibilities. Provided he could draw a smile from his father, the little boy asked nothing more than to become the most decisive of means, the most deprived of ends—in fact, he was that already. The drama came from the "law of primogeniture," from familial "sarcasms," from school: Gustave had the bitter revelation that he *was not a good means*. This discovery distorted, falsified, led him astray, but the stuff he was made of, the Flaubert substance of which he was a minor and monstrous mode—how could that have altered? It was that substance that made his contradictions so acute. You can put up with being a bad means if you take yourself for an end. But if you are made a means from the outset? Gustave asked only to be a first-class instrument: *this* is what he was denied, nothing more. From his earliest years he was already structured by the common enterprise; by the father's alienation he was alienated from the Flaubert organization: vassalage—his first impulse—introduced him through feudal enthusiasm into that working microcosm; utilitarianism, the lord's style of life, was revered, the child internalized it, and he would make it the deepest, the most extended, the firmest of his submerged foundations. All this, of course, was done without words: even now the adolescent has no words to designate the foundation on which the entire edifice rests, which is anterior to all else, even to the "ambitious jealousy" that torments him. In fact, he is not jealous of a woman or of the glory of a captain or a writer; he is jealous of an honorific responsibility and of the money indirectly connected with it. He is in agreement with the Flaubert imperative: this organization must be able to furnish the best and most expensive physician in Rouen; in case of unexpected death, again the family must be able to send another of its members to replace the deceased member instantly. His unhappiness therefore starts *at the beginning* of this original agreement—his rages and his despairs are fueled exclusively by his primary frustration; we have seen that they are extreme—for frustration itself has extraordinary force.

Gustave, of course, does not see that this "ambitious jealousy" and the tendencies that support it are practical determinations of utilitarianism: vassalage, feudal impulses, the desire to believe are sufficient to mask in him the Flaubert arrivism in its heavy reality. When he becomes conscious of his jealousy, everything is already disordered: the arrivism is seen but sublimated in despair; indeed, the child is set up in his instrumentality and discovers himself to be a poorly made tool that will be thrown out with the garbage. Starting here, his conflicts—internal—with the family will depend on the exile in which a child who did not ask to be born is maintained; his feelings for his brother will express his bitterness in the face of universal injustice. Rejected impulses, an exacting sense of justice: this is what he will see in his heart, what we shall see at the front of the stage. But the background is an infinite absurdity: ends-means becoming means-ends. He was carefully fashioned, he claimed it all as his own doing; and *it turns out* that no one wants to make use of this conscious and organized means. He discovers uselessness, but not like Alfred as an arrogant gratuitousness; rather, as a lesser being, as an objective refusal to make use of him. Sharing the principles and passions of his tormentors, he cannot free himself by revolt; a negation that is unformulated, unformulable—and consequently without real effect—suffocates under the fantasmagorias of resentment. Let him seek God, let him denounce the aridity of paternal certainties, let him dream of glory or suicide, whatever the child works at until the time he leaves school, his efforts are disappointing, repugnant, pigheaded: he wants to be at least Achille's equal, and at the same time his body resists and betrays him. All of Gustave's actions, all his attitudes, all of his dreams are strictly determined by his *Flaubert being* or, if you like, by his character as means, and by his singular *lack of being*—that is, by the verdict implied by the father who does not find him *enough* of a Flaubert and at once designates him a second-class Flaubert. The austerity of his family life rested entirely on utilitarian passion, but at the same time it hid it from him: it was "virtue by disposition." In the same way, the physician-philosopher's Learning clothed the enterprise with an almost disinterested dignity: Science devotes itself to universality. Thus the social progress of the Flauberts was linked to the progress of Thought; the child can even imagine, without obvious bad faith, that his family's social progress is merely the reward for that other progress, and that the researcher, impelled solely by concern for knowledge, accepts the distinctions or the money without caring for them, out of modesty. This is a theme we sometimes encounter from Flaubert's pen—but rarely: in his works, knowledge enriches. And we find no real concern for knowledge of the world, either in his early tales or in his letters. Strangely, this adolescent of fifteen acts as if the universe of knowledge were *already known.* He has no curiosity: what good is it to dwell on detail since the principles of the whole have been established? Everything being known, it is incumbent upon the flights of the poet and the philosopher to sum it all up. In other words, Gustave's ambitious jealousy impelled him to covet money, honors, a certain *quality* that marked the superiority of the Flauberts over other men; but—disgusted by the father's aphorisms and the older brother's success—he was never concerned with *knowledge for its own sake.*

To grasp the underlying state of affairs, we must regard his ascents, his contempt, his appeals to God, his misanthropy as attempts at diversion and compensation that remain, despite everything, peripheral—at least at this time. This boy wants to get ahead; the excesses of his black romanticism must not—as I have said—be taken lightly. But neither must they obscure the fundamental seriousness of a boy who dreams of becoming a noteworthy means, a notable of his good city of Rouen. He grumbles, often tries to disqualify these means-ends, which he knows in advance he will not attain. But these dodges, the recourse to pride, to ecstasy, far from proving his nihilism reveal to us from the beginning a "lost utilitarian." If he wants to force his family and his schoolmates to pay more dearly for the bad turn they've done him, if he detaches himself from their crude interests and sees them collapse at his feet, it is *precisely* because he is incapable of detachment. This supernumerary vassal, in order to pull himself out of the world of interests *from above*, began by devoting his rejected vassalage to those great absentees—God, the spiritual nobility, nobility plain and simple—whose nonpresence appeared to him as a very mild regime of nonbeing. To add to his misfortunes, however, this solitary elevation is pure unrealization. The result could have been a cycle of brief but languid periods, a return to imaginary ascents followed by new falls moderated by automatic breaking devices, if envy, jealous surliness, the terror of dying like a rat in a trap, exasperated arrivism countered by its inevitable consequences, fratricidal hatred and shame, total submission to the family and unquenchable repugnance for the fate it had dealt him—in brief, all those passions issuing from his social condition and his particular situation—had not fanned his defensive system to a white heat, making the ascents more ambitious and the falls more brutal every day, yet without giving Gustave the negative power that might have allowed him to revolt. When Alfred took a liking to him, the younger Flaubert understood that he would die if he did not learn to say no, to challenge himself, to challenge everything he still respected.

The little boy is dazzled by his future master: he sees in him the archangel of refusal. Le Poittevin, indeed, is in his Byronic period: he defies God, the eternal Father; in Gustave's eyes he is the invincible loser. Loser: nothing could be more pleasing to the child, victim of a curse that forced him to lose from the very beginning. Invincible: this is how Alfred would function as a model; the Cursed one, a magnificent theologian, has the strength to confront his Creator with an indestructible No. Negation is the absolute weapon: Flaubert wants to enroll in Satan's school so that he can learn to use its methods.

This is where the misunderstanding begins: Alfred is a secondhand Byron. It pleased him at the time to express his malaise, his bitterness and pride, by condemning the "work of God" and reprimanding the Creator for it; we know that his inner certainties, born in his protohistory, gave him the strength to affirm and deny categorically. But the position of loser hardly suits him—for he quits writing. Certainly life is a defeat *in principle*, but only for those who agree to live it; Le Poittevin feels the strength to refuse: "To live without living." He will kill "all that is human" in himself; Gustave is unaware that there are two negations, that of the master and that of the slave. Alfred attempts to practice the first: he puts himself above his life and simultaneously seeks to destroy it. He replaces revolt with a global, calm negation: the world of labor and struggle collapses at his feet, the young man will be at once an empty "I think" and a superfluous jewel. Gustave, however, aspires to a patient, laborious, and corrosive negation that will attack details one by one, directly, without questioning inculcated principles or fundamental impulses. A man of the necessary, he needs to challenge the situation that is made for him in the milieu of necessity in the name of the very values this milieu produces. No doubt he harbors some vague hope that a reversal will occur at the end of this progressive dispute, which will provide his reward. But he does not yet know if his victory will allow him to escape the enterprise of necessity or to reestablish himself within it with all the dignities he deserves. To tell the truth, if he had to choose, he would opt for the second solution: he would like to have the strength publicly to denounce the injustice of which he believes himself the victim, but such a denunciation would have real meaning only if it were addressed to men of the necessary. Thus, negation must be internal to the system. The ideal thing for the unloved boy might be to demonstrate, by stating his case, that the world is bad but that there is no other, and that consequently it would be vain to attempt to escape it or to exchange it for anything else. For two reasons: this world has wounded him, this world alone will have the power to cure him; besides, the child, whatever he might say, has internalized certain norms which are now part of him: he respects the work of the "professionals"—knowledge, money, property. His first works offer proof of this: Garcia faints with rage but does not dream of denying the importance of honors and wealth—he wants them for himself, that's all. What Gustave asks of his new master is to transform his fearful resentment into limited revolt.

But it doesn't take long for him to discover that beneath a borrowed Byronism, Alfred is set in a universal and fixed negation of life, and that he looks at everything from the point of view of death, or nothingness. But, his lord tells him gently, it is also the point of view of being. Alfred holds out his arms to him, smiling, gracious, patient, and so handsome;[61] he wants only to raise his vassal up to him. The child is

61. To my knowledge we have no portrait of him. But Gustave felt such disgust for ugliness, such attraction to *visible* beauty, that he could only have devoted such love to a good-looking young man. Did he not say later that Maupassant was the living image of his uncle? And the nephew, as we know, was extremely handsome.

fascinated but anxious; he wants to identify with this marvelous grace—he *loves;* he asks only to abandon himself to the hands of the beloved, physically, no doubt, and certainly morally. The elder is *animus,* the younger, *anima.* To identify is saying too much; Gustave more modestly asks to be engulfed by Alfred: he *will be* his master—and that only in part—only to the extent that he roots himself in him. Fascination or confusion? He does not know; is he going to fly or fall into a pit? By letting Alfred swallow him up, will he at last find *being* or be annihilated? The lord wants *nothing;* from his philosophical abstention he derives a radical condemnation of reality; disqualified, the universe is nothing but a shower of confetti, a shimmering of reflections, nothing worth lifting a finger for; the young Oedipus makes himself useless in order to identify with the being of an extravagantly beautiful Jocasta. Now Gustave understands: if he ever rejoins the master, he will find eternal snow up there, anorexia. He is gripped by anguish; his passions are narrow and fierce: he nurses the bitter desire to become a *great* Flaubert in order to bring a smile, perhaps tears, to his father—he wants to lead his family in its assault on Rouen society, to *arrive,* to get the better, one way or another, of the brilliant Achille. How could he fail to see that these human, all too human, aspirations are decisively condemned by his beloved's philosphy? Alfred in his lordly way despises such wretched aims. Gustave, a man of the necessary, feels crushed with others of his kind by the pitiless nonchalance of the man of superfluity. To the shame of being a bad means is added the shame of wanting to be a good one: here we have the middle class stripped naked; beneath the gaze of an aristocrat, Gustave discovers with shame that he is part of it. The sole salvation: climb up to this rich man who awaits him. But that would be tearing out his heart, and he clings to his desires, his resentment, his despair, his vain and conscious hopes of being—what will he be offered up there? Not even a return match—oblivion. He will act on himself, on himself alone, he will empty himself of everything, and during this ascesis the wicked will pursue their triumphant career with impunity. The little victim will not even escape their "sarcasms," he will simply become immune to them; but the executioners will not know that. Yet Alfred need only appear: his superiority proclaims itself. Over everything. Even over the philosophical practitioner. For *he* is the true philosopher. He has "ideas." Dazzling. Irrefutable. Gustave hasn't any: can we use the word "ideas" for his obscure, singular aversions, born of necessity or desperation? This captive thought, pondered, obsessive, uncertain, these intimate impressions that vegetate in their darkness and mutely seek a language? None of it is "reasonable" or reasoned, these are defensive movements. Ideas are a luxury; to have them is to become one's own heaven, with all the anguish that goes along with it. Alfred can allow himself a few: this beloved boy has rights to the world. For him, truth exists. He often confuses it with his whims—because he is sovereign. He does not verify: he invents, and his inventions have the force of law. Gustave cannot allow himself to affirm, to deny; he knows that his barely formulated ideas, if he even had any, would become false. He imitates his friend, borrowing his power of negation, adopting his language, but Alfred's paradoxes have no guarantee for the disciple but the principle of authority and the love he bears the Master. Does Gustave believe in Alfred's theories? Yes and no: they fascinate him, he convinces himself for a moment by autosuggestion, but that doesn't prevent him from endlessly touching the Other's certainty without ever sharing it. If he wants to make it his own, it becomes in him an *alien conviction*, a malignant conviction that terrorizes him because it inhabits him without fulfilling him. "Alfred had ideas, I hadn't any." This amounts to saying that he never *shared* his friend's opinions: Le Poittevin's thoughts filled Flaubert like the devil's coins and changed into dead leaves when he touched them. Even their intellectual agreement was fragile and deceptive. Gustave is conscious of being the passive element in the Thursday dialogues ("Think *for* me"); Alfred himself does not claim to be a Socrates, an intellectual midwife—he "thinks out loud." At once he throws his friend back into pathos; Gustave has nothing left but excess, passion, hyperbole, "extravagances"; shocked, he takes these summary executions to extremes, this game of Aunt Sally that ravages his heart while satisfying his rancors; he drags himself groaning to the feet of the unfeeling Almaroës, who tells him with a somewhat scornful smile: "That's how it is; it's not worth building a cathedral over it." To which the bitch Flaubert, with "pendulous teats," humbly replies: "Remember that I am a madman."[62] In short, if it is true that the possibility belonging to another whom we love becomes, when we discover it in him, our most intimate impossibility if it was refused to us a priori, Gustave has seen himself *denied* by Alfred the right to form rational thoughts. Certainly we cannot say that the adolescent was inclined to have them. But the beloved "philosopher" has formally excluded him from the "reign of

62. Dedication of *Mémoires:* "Remember that it is a madman who has written these pages."

the mind" by the apparent care he took to bring him to it. For this reason the proud disciple, after 1847, would attempt to give feeling a depth and universality to match those of the Idea: we have Charles Bovary saying to Rodolphe: "It's fate!" He attempts to equal the dead master and perhaps surpass him. There are two ways of thinking, with the heart and with the head; either will ultimately reach the same truth, and the first way is better than the second, since it adds to its richness the concrete intuition of lived experience in its singularity. Besides, in spite of the mimicry that makes him claim and radicalize the theories of the lord, he remains mutely convinced that "real" truth rests in the hands of the paterfamilias: there is none outside of science and mechanistic philosophy (which in its way, too, is a despairing nihilism but one that leads to utilitarianism). He is mistrustful of Alfred, so dazzling, so sure of himself, too convincing: who knows if what is good for him will be good for me? And what if these ideas are false? And if I embrace them lovingly and can then never get rid of them?

How Gustave *lived* the Thursday dialogues we know from an almost contemporary testimony, *Les Funérailles du docteur Mathurin*. Flaubert recounts the final conversations of a master and his two disciples—two: no doubt Ernest was sometimes admitted to the Aunt Sally game. "If you had only seen them lay waste to everything, drain everything . . ." And it is clear that the three confederates, like sorcerer's apprentices, are terrified at what they've done. Alfred certainly was not; so it was Gustave alone, torn between enthusiasm, iconoclastic zeal (symbolized here by drunkenness), the frightened consciousness of *doing ill*, of blaspheming, and finally of selling his soul to the devil, in short, of deliberately choosing the dark side, and a growing anger against the acknowledged values (acknowledged by Gustave himself as well) that could not be defended properly.

> In their heart was a living power, an anger they felt gradually climbing from the heart to the head, their movements were jerky, their voices were strident, their teeth chattered against the glasses; they drank, they were always drinking, holding forth, philosophizing, seeking the truth at the bottom of the glass. Happiness in drunkenness and eternity in death. Mathurin alone found the latter. That night, among the three men, something monstrous, magnificent happened . . . everything passed before them and was greeted with a grotesque laugh and a grimace that frightened them . . . They resumed drinking . . . It was frenzied, a fury of

drunken demons . . . Mathurin now a cynic . . . will march in with all his power, he plunges in and dies there in the last spasm of his sublime orgy.

Mathurin was first father Flaubert—as we have seen above—and then Gustave himself. Now he is Alfred[63] "thinking for" Gustave, who is at once embodied in the "disciples" as well; but *he is also* Gustave straining furiously, "monstrously," to merge with Alfred and reach "eternity in death." In short, *Animus* thinks, *Anima* throbs: these rather general surveys ("metaphysics treated in depth in a quarter of an hour," morality by "drinking a twelfth glass") are only the *still bound* disciple's *access route* to a demonic Virgil. At each step of the way the child sheds a belief or a hope (in fact he doesn't shed anything, for he will have to begin again the following Thursday—let us say he is wounded and bleeding); he must do it, for it is written above: "*Lasciate ogni speranza.*" Alfred awaits him, fascinating and deceptive, warm and frigid. Above? Below? It's all the same: the reverend master is none other than Satan. And Gustave damns himself by the love he bears him.

Le Voyage en enfer was published in 1835 (in *Arts et Progrès*) and *Satan*, Alfred's poem, in the first half of 1836. The two writings, then, are contemporaneous, and as there is little likelihood that a boy of thirteen could influence a young man of eighteen, it seems infinitely probable that the myth of the fallen angel, so dear to the romantics, touched Alfred first and, through him, Gustave. For Le Poittevin, as we have seen, this is a period of pessimism. From the outset he identifies with the Accursed One, and this first poem is nothing but a long apostrophe to the Almighty. The younger boy seized the occasion at once: Alfred is the Demon. *Le Voyage en enfer* recapitulates, after a fashion, the first conversations at the Hôtel-Dieu. Gustave raises himself with his own strength to the summit of Mount Atlas: this is the ecstatic elevation, the first intentional transformation of his stupors. *By himself,* however, he is incapable of rising above a vague meditation: "From there I contemplated the world and its gold and its mud, and its virtue and its pride." In other words, he is incapable either of "analyzing"—as he would say—human behavior or of drawing the appropriate conclusions from his study. It is on this summit that Alfred awaits him: "And Satan appeared to me." The older boy takes

63. Has it been noted that Mathurin in his last hours strikingly embodies Alfred's two complementary attitudes: knowing that he is going to die, he kills himself with alcohol and professes a grim hedonism that is simply a justification for suicide, even as he "pushes his cynicism to the end" and reaches eternity through death? Sensual hap-

the younger one away with him. "And Satan took me away with him and showed me the World." In brief, the demon somehow makes the young author come down again. But he does it to make him see in all their individual details the large entities—gold, mud, virtue, pride—that he had grasped as wholes. It is simply a question of providing him with a greater variety of experience; but this empiricism ("He showed me scientists, men of letters, fops, pedants, kings, and sages") is only fictive: Satan was operating in a closed field, in Gustave's room. The scientists, kings, sages were invoked *by words:* through words they were submitted to the vitriol of *negation* and did not resist it. In brief, the devil fertilizes Flaubert's passive meditation by teaching him the use of the negative principle. After the enumeration and the dissolving analysis comes the final synthesis: Alfred *concludes;* Satan, gathering up all acquired knowledge in one phrase, declares: "The world is Hell."

In a sense, this is just what Gustave asked him to do. He charged *another* instead of himself with the task of drawing conclusions from an *alien thought.* But the child's caution will be noted: while he uses Alfred's negativity for his own purposes, he leaves him with the responsibility. He doesn't claim the Devil's procedure and the final formula as his own idea; he merely *reports* it. This is evidence enough that he is *mistrustful.*

Smarh will allow us to understand his reasons better. Alfred plays the same role. And this is how Gustave sums up his story to Ernest:

> Satan leads a man (Smarh) into infinity . . . discovering many things, Smarh is full of pride. He believes that all the mysteries of the creation and the infinite have been revealed to him, but Satan leads him still higher. Then he is afraid, he trembles, the whole abyss seems to devour him, he is helpless in the void. They come down again to earth—there he is on his own soil; he says that he is made to live here and that everything in nature is subservient to him. Then comes a tempest . . . He again admits his weakness and his nothingness. Satan is going to lead him to men . . . Here we find Smarh disgusted with the world; he would like it all to be over with, but Satan, on the contrary, is going to make him experience all the passions and all the misery he has seen . . .

---

piness through the demonic and sublime orgy, the calm ataraxia of the heights: the ephemeral and the eternal mirrored in each other, isn't this a portrait of Alfred as Gustave might have painted it in 1839—that is, with one year's distance from the talks at the Hôtel-Dieu? What properly belongs to the younger Flaubert is the pathos of the character and his "grotesque" style.

This time the ascent is led by Alfred: Flaubert manages to get up as far as Mount Atlas on his own, but no higher. The younger boy, clinging to the coattails of his elder, believes he will find knowledge and encounters only the void. He hastens to redescend to *his* ground. But Alfred then demonstrates to him the vanity of every enterprise. Once again Smarh/Gustave spins around in the void. In truth, what he asked for, to file his chains, was the patient negation of the slave. He hoped at bottom that he would be allowed to condemn the family organization, to disqualify the paternal enterprise, in which he plays a secondary role, in the name of another enterprise for which he would be solely responsible.[64] He will do nothing of the sort: Smarh will spin around in the void indefinitely; he will have tried to be a poet, but the vanity of the enterprise becomes evident to him when the woman he loves (Truth) leaves him for Yuk, the god of the grotesque.

These remarks allow us to give a new meaning to *Rêve d'enfer.* Almaroës, as we know, is in part Gustave, but *he is also Alfred.* Nothing very surprising; the theme of the double, whose source lies deep within Flaubert, is nourished by everything he encounters; later Frédéric and Deslauriers will represent, before all else, two possible attitudes towards life, but Deslauriers will be Maxime *as well.* Almaroës represents matter but also a creature deprived of a soul and hence of desires; in contrast to Satan, whose role Gustave assumes for once and who is a cursed younger son, Almaroës incarnates the "living without living" of the Le Poittevin son, and this sentence from letter 35 might be perfectly applied to him: "It is a pity to have been born not thinking like anyone else, weary of oneself as of others, seeking common happiness and being unable even to reach it." Here is another (April 1845): "I have killed in myself all that was human . . . Perhaps I have resolved the problem like the tyrants of Tacitus: '*Solitudinem fecisse pacem appellant.*'"[65] What is striking in this philosophical tale is the inversion of roles and the reversal of the meaning of their conversations: Gustave/Satan wants to lead Almaroës back to human

64. Alfred knows this so well that he writes to Gustave on 7 June 1843: "What do you say to following in the Flaubert footsteps and promising your father a rival to his name in some other branch? What do you say to the Penal Code!" Naturally, the intention is ironic. But in a double sense: father and son are discretely mocked on two different levels. In fact Flaubert scorns the law, that "other branch," but it is true that he hoped to rival his father and even to outdo him. For him, the "other branch" is art. Art—and not the law—is opposed to science. Of course, the young man is careful not to present things from this angle.

65. The Latin citation is inaccurate but nonetheless significant.

life, to desires, to love—for he himself is nothing but desire. But the master triumphs: nothing will make him abandon his "impassive immobility." More striking still is that the confrontation of these two beings is *agonistic*. Satan hates Almaroës and tries in vain to strike him; this passage speaks volumes about Gustave and the ambivalence of his feelings for Alfred: the younger boy was afraid of his elder, he loved him certainly—as much as he could love—but he resented his iciness, his indifference; the frozen lover displays his bitterness and his admiration together. At the same time the man of desire is terrified by the idea that he should sever himself from the passions and misfortunes he cherishes.

At the end, as we have seen, the Devil, vanquished, changes into a She-devil: he crawls, crushing his heavy breasts against the earth, as if their battle had *also* been an amorous joust and in defeat he were revealing his femininity to the handsome, indifferent Almaroës. Julietta was but a semblance: it was Satan, beneath his disguise, who wanted to be taken by the Iron Duke.[66]

For the first time the term "temptation" is encountered from Gustave's pen. It ends in absurd frustration: if the younger boy offers himself to his elder, if he wants to "lead him into temptation" by the beauty of his young body or the submission of his soul, he can put his clothes back on—Alfred will not emerge from his benevolent coldness.[67] But isn't this a reversal of the terms? At bottom, isn't it Almaroës who tempts Satan? In the later narratives the Devil is reestablished in all his power: he is a sheik, Smarh is only a poor man, Saint Antoine offers only passive resistance. If we read the first version of *La Tentation* without keeping in mind the talks at the Hôtel-Dieu, we may understand nothing of the title he gives it.

I know what someone will say: Antoine is the artist; he is attracted to the goods of this earth and finds in his cult of Art the strength to refuse them. But this interpretation, while highly accredited, doesn't resist scrutiny. Flaubert often said that he could not write unless he

66. Roger Kempf rightly shows that Frédéric, Deslauriers, and Madame Arnoux at one point form a triad in which the pederastic element is dominant. But this time the relation is reversed: Deslauriers, sexually aroused by Frédéric's femininity and jealous of the love he bears the young woman, tries to seduce her. If Deslauriers possesses her, he will possess Frédéric carnally. This reversal of roles changes nothing of the phantasm: it simply expresses Flaubert's inner vow. It is this kind of dominating jealousy he had hoped to provoke in a virile friend.

67. Which can be understood in two ways: either, "I moaned in his embrace," but he did not seem excited by it; or, "I offered myself and he pretended not to notice."

was living like an anchorite; but he never claimed that such a life was painful to him or even difficult to lead; it was the presence of men, not solitude, that brought him to the edge of fury. When he writes the first *Saint Antoine*, he never tires of portraying himself to Louise as a supplicant, aged from infancy by the sufferings that have drained him; he has an aversion to the world and often declares that he doesn't even want to leave a name behind; in any case, he misses no occasion to signal to his mistress that terrifying but undefined misfortunes have rendered him forever incapable of loving. And then, on close reading, the first *Tentation* offers this oddity, which the two others barely attenuate: the Saint does not seem to be *truly* tempted: scarcely has one of Satan's demons gone about trying to seduce him than another arrives who sabotages the work in progress; Antoine has only to leave well enough alone, they will devour each other. The vices conspire together to scoff at the virtues; but when they are alone they make an uproar, each claiming to be superior to the others, and their babbling deafens us without managing to fascinate us. The only attacks being conducted vigorously are those of logic and science against religion, but they do not prevent the rebirth of faith. In any event, it would have been better to entrust the task to a single demon than to surround Antoine with this ineffectual pandemonium.

Nevertheless, we must trust Gustave: if he affirms that he was tempted, he must have been convinced of it. What should we understand by *temptation*? I see two principle structures. One is the system, both axiological and totalizing, that itself defines the nature and importance of denial. The other is the instrument of disgrace: passion. But we would be quite wrong to see passion as only a spontaneous product of the sensibility. In fact, Eve is tempted by another or, more accurately, by the Other—isn't this the name reserved for Satan? The apple is the operational means. It may be that it is in itself desirable. But what matters is that the sensibility of the victim who is *led* into temptation should be fertilized by the Other, and that from this coupling a monster should be conceived within it, an *other* desire. Tempted, I find the Other again as the basis of my desire. This enticement, which touches us deeply without ridding us of our responsibilities, is grace against the grain, a black grace, a demonic replica of efficacious Grace, transcendence in immanence of affectivity. It leads us to sin, that is, to commit an act that refers to a system of norms strictly opposed to that which governs us, or, if you like, temporarily to adopt as one's own all the system's antivalues. This means turning oneself into another, passing through the looking glass. We understand that the tempted victim regards the fruit ripening in his soul with horrified fascination, which is merely the negative aspect of religious terror: the alien temptation-determination of himself is revealed for him as a determination of his profane affectivity for the sacred. The transcendent, recognized at the deepest level of my intimate experience as the ungraspable truth of that experience and as my own existence having escaped into the milieu of otherness, is precisely the sacred in its ambivalence: white if it conforms to dogma and is valid for everyone, black if it reaches me in my noncommunicable singularity and incites me to deny the system that supports and nourishes me, to prefer the solitude of sin, closer to black masses and blasphemies than to our wretched little daily crimes. This satanic election provokes a leap of pride: pitiless Grace has touched us, made us sacred.

From this point of view, the young Gustave's temptation was real; the axiological system in him is that of the average man, his *reality* is the collective and domestic being of the Flauberts. His article of faith: we are on the earth to serve some purpose; there are *serious*, essential objectives, man is the inessential means of achieving them. And misfortune demands that he meet a lord who denies both the means and the ends of the human race. This lord makes *negation* appear at a distance within his vassal, but it is transformed into an immobile nothingness. Flaubert feels his desire to deny as something that is his own and also as other: it is his own to the extent that Le Poittevin has only made explicit an implicit negation, it is other to the extent that the negation is transformed under Alfred's influence into a fixed nonbeing that presents itself as being. If we now reread *Saint Antoine*, we shall find the temptation that had escaped us until now and we shall see it developed from the first page to the last. It is the temptation of the artist, certainly; but not by the goods of this world: by nothingness. With this veil of appearances burned away, what remains? Nothing, that is obvious. In this case, the absurd project of making himself into an artist. Art is a nothing that depicts nothings. Literature? Inanely sonorous bric-a-brac. Isn't it better to know one's own nothingness and stay there in the lofty boredom and perfect inaction of the sage? When Antoine turns his head and lets himself be fascinated, the fantasmagoria will fall into ashes; the Night of Non-Being will be found once again and that asphyxiation by the void that Smarh so dreaded. In a curious passage that would later disappear, Satan/Alfred carries Antoine/Gustave off "into space":

ANTOINE (*borne on the Devil's horns*)
Where am I going?

THE DEVIL
Higher.

ANTOINE
Stop!

THE DEVIL
Higher! Higher!

ANTOINE
My head is spinning, I'm afraid, I'm going to fall . . .

This is a new reworking of the page from *Smarh* that I already cited. As in *Smarh*, he discovers the universe from above. But the moment the saint is gratified by contemplative pleasure, the Devil, a dry and logical mind, ruins everything by revealing to him that this plenitude of being is illusory, that nothing exists except nothingness. What is striking here is that this revelation is presented not as an abrupt and terrifying shock but, *on the contrary*, as a delicious temptation:

The Devil's body, losing its proportions, is penetrated with light and illuminated; his immense eye becomes all blue like the sky, his wings disappear, and his increasingly blurred face becomes ravishingly beautiful.

THE DEVIL
. . . These moments of clarity that filled you with such joy, you were the one who saw them. Who told you that they are?
(. . . *Frozen, awestruck, bewildered, Antoine comes closer and closer to the Devil* . . .)

THE DEVIL
. . . and if that world is not, if that spirit is not . . . ah! ah! ah!

ANTOINE (*Hanging in the air, floats face to face with the Devil and touches his forehead with his own*)
But *you* are, nonetheless! I feel you. Oh, how beautiful you are!
(*The Devil opens his enormous maw.*) Yes, I'm coming, I'm coming!
Etc.

We note the strange connection between beauty and nothingness. The moment Satan uses the arguments of a wornout skepticism to question the reality of the world, Antoine, more susceptible to appearance than to reason, is fascinated by the physical aspect of his companion, by his "ravishingly beautiful face." As if Beauty itself were only a trap in the service of the Demon, and as if Gustave wanted to recall the attraction he had felt for his friend when he was alive. In any case, this is the only moment the saint finds himself in danger: fascinated by the sumptuous beauty that presents itself as a *being* ("But you *are*, nonetheless! I feel you"), he gives in to the temptation to let himself be absorbed by it, and the author would have us understand that if the unfortunate Antoine were not saved by a miracle, he would be swallowed up into nothingness. This allusion to the beauty of the Devil leads us back to the status of art object that Le Poittevin claimed to give himself. No doubt Flaubert in his love for Alfred, the prestigious heir, had been strongly tempted in his adolescence to raise himself to that status. No doubt he understood, already at this period, that his social condition made such a metamorphosis impossible for him, or rather that he could attain it only by slipping into madness, like the hero of *La Spirale*.

One must *have* in order *to be*: if Gustave *possessed*, he *would be* that marvelous indifferent one and could *casse-intellectualise-jouit*. The younger boy recognized early on that no moral ascesis could bring him near his elder—it would take a material change. In fact, it was already too late; he would have had *to be born rich*. Lacking that, Alfred would remain an inaccessible lord; and it would be impossible for Gustave to unite in himself the necessitous asperity of the Flauberts and the ataraxia of the Le Poittevin son. Alfred, whether his idleness expresses itself in debauchery or quietism, differs from his friend in a *quality* which the unhappy disciple has understood is but the dialectical product of quantity, that is, of his fortune. Beginning with this assertion, we can determine Alfred's precise influence on Gustave, namely the role he played in Gustave's personalization. It seems that the disciple, asserting both his desire to identify with his master and the impossibility of joining him without seriously damaging his ipseity, had wanted to go beyond this contradiction by developing himself in two different directions: he integrated the superfluous in his person as an unattainable ideal, and gratuity in his work in progress as an absolute imperative. It goes without saying that the two movements were related by reciprocal conditioning.

1. The Superfluous as Infinite Lacuna

More lucid than his master, the slave gets to the bottom of things when he defines "real life" by the possession of the superfluous. But let us make no mistake—it is not things he covets but the quality of soul that makes it possible to covet them. A vicious circle: that same quality comes to the wealthy from the wealth that frees them from the reign of necessity. Abundance allows them to stop considering objects solely in terms of the function of their instrumentality. Gustave understands the secret of Alfred, the ineffable heir, since he very early assimilates wealth and sensibility, reducing the one to an internalization of the other. Provided it is enormous and due to an inheritance—which presupposes a suitable education—wealth prompts an authentic conversion in its new owner. In other words, give the Flaubert son the treasures of Golconda and you will make him into the Le Poittevin son. Gustave is so convinced of it that he expresses one day this extraordinary wish: "I would like to be rich enough to give the superfluous to those who have the necessary." We should not be too shocked; it is true that the sentence reveals profound insensitivity—Flaubert does not like the poor: they are ugly, dirty, envious and thieving. But this misanthrope is not claiming to make a charitable gesture, he is merely indicating to us on what condition he would tolerate the dealings of men: people of need should be left as they are, except for getting them drunk from time to time. One needs them for lowly tasks. But those of the necessary are to be elevated by abundance: the middle class is suppressed by a shower of gold that transforms all its members into nabobs. Man is at last possible; and society. Nevertheless, despite the universal twist he has given it, his wish concerns only himself. By writing it, he seriously examines his austere childhood: if only someone had given him the sense of the superfluous *in time*. Instead, they worked on him from the very first day; his flights of inspiration notwithstanding, he knows that they turned him into a *means*. When he later denounces "the bourgeois under his skin," we shouldn't imagine he is accusing himself: he is rehashing a grievance—one of the oldest he harbors against his family. And "bourgeois" is not directed here against the rich but rather against the average man and, through him, against the petty bourgeoisie as a whole.

He goes still further: wealth is ascesis. It delivers the wealthy from necessity; Gustave sometimes dreams that it can deliver him from need itself. If he were the possessor of an oriental palace, reclining on a "divan of swan's skin," surrounded by works of art, he would forget to eat and drink. The contemplation of precious stones would nourish him, desire endlessly revived and endlessly fulfilled would take the place of hunger, thirst, sleep. And—without a doubt—sexual need. Thus, living without living, he would reach the level of the supreme species, characterized by the atrophy of animal impulses and by the hypertrophy of the "faculty of feeling"—the second, moreover, being the reason for the first. Immobile and fulfilled simply by the sight of *aesthetic* appearances, useless and solitary, he would realize the slow, systematic annihilation of his body and at the end of his ascesis would become, like Alfred, an appearance.

We might take this mysticism for a writer's pose if we did not know that Flaubert, unable to crush his needs by the massive irruption of the superfluous, often resorted to abstinence in the vain hope of strangling them. As an adolescent he fasted out of a hatred of all material servitude. Here again we find the first strata of his memory, the dead of the Hôtel-Dieu, the feeling that he carried a corpse beneath his skin; he had a horror of all that is *organic*—the demands of the body and biological development as well, the movement of life. Alfred was sure of finding an echo in Gustave when he wrote to him: "I no longer love [women] except in statuary or painting;—man can be beautiful in that form too, but those who have said it is wrong for sculpture to represent life have spoken more truly than they might have thought, and more profoundly. I believe that life, so beautiful everywhere, is not so in man." [68] Gustave's early experiences combine with the good lessons of his master to show him the absurdity of his tenacious will to live: must we heed the claims of our carcass? Gustave was to have little respect for the base materials of which he was made; through pure desire, through trading jewels and marble, he wants to incorporate into himself not only his lord's calm emptiness but the inorganic as well. An inert lacuna in a body of granite—this would no longer be living, thank God, but *being*.

In order *to be*, we must *have*; and we *are* what we *have*: that is the metaphysics of the man of property, and of Gustave, the man of property manqué. Here he performs an extraordinary about-face. The younger boy, being deprived of that *being-beyond-life*, that finality without end which characterizes Alfred, will adopt them negatively as a continuously felt lacuna. He will internalize this lack as the *painful consciousness of lacking*, though it must be understood that this purely *external* negation becomes, in his hands, constitutive of his being, and that through dolorism he makes himself the unconditional refusal of this negation. *In his being*, therefore, he styles himself as a negation of negation, or as impassioned revolt against the impossibility of being Alfred. And as the impossible identification must occupy itself primarily with the means of realizing itself—were it only to discover that

68. 8 May 1844. Alfred feels revulsion for whores. Hence this rather stupid line that might serve as epigraph to a handbook on bourgeois "distinction."

these means are inaccessible—it will manifest itself in the first instance as a vain desire for wealth. Alfred himself desires nothing. He *has*, he *is*. Where Gustave is concerned, it is not so difficult to recognize that this infinite desire is *imaginary*. The letter of 20 September 1846, in which he articulates to Louise the governing imperative of his sensibility, ought to be read in its entirety. I shall cite only the essential passages:

> Here lies one of the hidden but enormous wounds in my nature. I am immeasurably poor. When I say this to my mother . . . she . . . who does not understand that the needs of imagination are the worst of all, it offends her; she thinks of our father, who acquired for us a sufficient fortune by his work. Well now! I maintain that it is an immense misfortune, one you are conscious of each day, to be born into mediocrity with the instincts of wealth. You suffer from it every minute, you suffer from it for yourself, for others, for everything . . .
>
> I am full of excessive cupidity, even as I value nothing. Someone could come and tell me that I haven't a *sou* left, I would not sleep any the worse that night[69] . . . But my weakness is a need for money that frightens me, it is an appetite for splendid things, which, being unsatisfied, grows, sours, and turns to mania. You asked me the other day how I spent my time with Du Camp? For three days we worked out on the map a grand tour through Asia that would last six years and cost us, as it was conceived, three million six hundred thousand and some odd francs . . . We were so carried away that we got sick; he even came down with a fever from it. Isn't it silly? But what can I do about it if it's in my blood? . . . Yes, I would have liked to be rich because I would have done beautiful things. I would have made practical art, I would have been tall and handsome . . . Axiom: the superfluous is the primary need . . . Do you know what I thought about during these last days? Two pieces of furniture that I would like to devise; the first would be designed for a drawing room with a blue dome: it's a divan of swan's skin, and the second is a divan of colibri feathers. That was enough to keep me busy for a whole day and make me sad that evening. Don't imagine that I am lazy—I am naturally active and hard-working . . . But things leap up inside me and carry me away in spite of myself.

Here we have the theoretical articulation of Flaubert's most famous fakery. But for the moment let us take it seriously and see what it

---

69. Nothing could be farther from the truth: he was tormented by the fear of want. Furthermore, we are acquainted with his despair of 1875.

offers. First of all, the man of the necessary begins by denying himself: he is born into mediocrity, but this accident of birth does not prevent his "nature" from escaping utilitarianism on principle—he has the instincts of wealth. He repudiates the honest living acquired by work; "valuing nothing," he raises himself above the reign of means. In short, he is not the product of the middle classes, he has fallen among them by mischance. What characterizes him is an "appetite for splendid things." However, these "splendors" are not—or not always—works of art. He covets neither paintings nor statues. Palaces, yes. Furnishings. Above all, jewels. We might say that this hired laborer of art recoils at finding the traces of other hired laborers on the goods he demands, the fixed substance of their work. He dreams of a quasi-natural beauty, a finality without end, based on rarity. The reader will have noted the curious phrase "I would have made practical art." He means that he would have created aesthetic events: "to get the rabble drunk every night . . . fling the superfluous to those who have the necessary." He would like to produce a radical transformation in the subjectivity of his fellow men that would bind them more closely to the superfluous while curing them of their utilitarianism. At the same time, through the power of his gold, he would organize "street spectacles" that he might "*casse-intellectualiser-jouir.*" In addition, as the context adequately indicates, he would have introduced some order into his possessions. He would turn himself into a decorator, a landscape gardener, a dress designer, etc. Gustave would like to dispose his goods around him and be objectified *for himself* in the unity he imposes on them: the ordering—always revocable—of superfluous objects surrounding him would reflect his superfluity, *would affect him* with a finality without end. He would internalize the palace, the gems, the blue salon with the divan "of swan's skin"; it would be *him*, useless at last, characterized in his being by the merchandise around him.[70]

In a word, since he does not define himself by possession, Gustave will define himself by *desire,* that is, sumptuously and universally by everything he does not have. With this, he surreptitiously makes himself superior to Alfred: Alfred is sated; Gustave will be insatiable. In the former, the void is calm; in the latter, it will be a screaming deprivation. In sum, the son of the chief surgeon is an honorary rich man.

70. Cf. also 7 December 1846: "We spend our time (Maxime and I) in conversations I'm almost ashamed of, in foolishness, in imperial daydreams. We construct palaces, we furnish Venetian villas, we travel to the Orient surrounded by our entourage, and then we fall flat into our present life again and grow as gloomy as cadavers."

He raises himself above the middle class by his innate passion for the superfluous; he also triumphs over the great landowner by the suffering born of frustration. We have already encountered this in him in the course of our regressive inquiry. The *mad desire* begins early in his sixteenth year; we now understand the *historical* reasons for this quintessentially Flaubertian motif: insatiable desire is a deconstruction of the average man [l'homme-moyen]; it is the negative equivalent of the Le Poittevin ataraxia. This young man knows opulence only by hearsay; that doesn't matter—he desires it as a ruined nabob might regard it with regret. With the same *enumerated* bitterness. The external signs of wealth, sole objects of his lust, must be as familiar to his imagination as to the saddened memory of those who have lost everything after having possessed it all. This is what he is telling his mistress. He tells others too: we shall soon see him, during his travels in the Orient, justify his indifference by a curious paradox: the imagination of artists is prophetic; all that he sees in Egypt, in Greece, he had known through specific images he had formed at home in his room before having any experience of them. He takes this idea to heart; we shall find it frequently in his writings and we shall see that it has complex origins. But there is no doubt that he needed it to guarantee his sumptuous lusts. When the desirable is unknown and the desire would be as poignant as a regret, the imaginary must present itself as an anticipated memory.

This is not enough: one must aim at the infinite through earthly goods. In what would it be manifest? In gold. It is not a question of envying Alfred or even the richest of bankers. The desire-regret is addressed directly to the fabulous resources that ancient Creosuses amassed by slave trading, that Oriental princes owed to serfdom, or the exploitation of peasants. One must be a Monte Cristo or nothing; French capital, revenue, stock—all these are constantly *defined* and *limited* by economic laws of which he is ignorant but whose inflexibility, therefore, he does not doubt. But these treasures—distant, fabulous, antique, accumulated over the centuries, stand by their own strength; without limits, without laws, they increase by themselves, the wild infinity of the innumerable.

This is still not sufficient. The high quality of desire rightly preserves it from organic impurities; but this sytematic search for the *gratuitous* should not in itself be gratuitous—it would at once lose its seriousness, its dramatic tension. Nothing would then distinguish it from simple caprice. The need itself is measured by death: one must breathe or die. Can one find in desire a similar guarantee? Yes: in the novels, Mazza, Emma—in a way it is their demands that kill them. But in the letters to Louise it is Flaubert himself who is at issue. Flaubert, who does not mean to die despite his infinite frustration. There remains another aspect of need: radicalism. One must eat—everything is fine when one can eat. But when the shipwrecked on their raft have exhausted their supplies, the need remains: *eating is impossible* and yet one *must* eat. We know from *La Méduse* what survivors have done, and how they have transformed the universal impossibility of feeding themselves into the impossibility of living limited to a few. Sustained by all the violence of an organism that wants to persevere in its life, unweakened need maintains its exigency when its perfect absurdity has long since been demonstrated. For the starving there can be remission; but thirst never releases its man, nor does asphyxiation. It seems that life in these extreme cases affirms itself, furiously and spasmodically, as an absurd flame already extinguished by the universe and as each member's permanent right over the whole species.

Flaubert can complete his apparatus: he will give desire this contradiction of need pushed to the end. Alone and poor, in his own room, he burns with lust for an extravagant palace: it is absurd and he knows it. And yet the desire is there, raising its head *with good reason*; it poses *of itself* its impossibility, he is torn apart by it, there is nothing to be done—the wound embitters but inflames him. Better still, he would quickly calm down if the thing that is so desirable were readily at hand. *It is the essence of infinite desire to desire the impossible.* Or, if you like, self-conscious impossibility awakens desire and exalts it; impossibility endows it with its rigor and its violence, and desire rediscovers impossibility outside in the object as the fundamental category of the desirable. At the same time, by its very necessity the absurd demand is affirmed as a right. If Gustave, conscious of his impotence, is thrown into lust by impotence itself, it is because man defines himself *as a right to the impossible.* There is neither misunderstanding nor caprice in this strange determination: it is a fact of our human reality; man has only to pass into this world and the world must recognize his right. I said the world; the man of need addresses himself to other men—a kind of humanism will be built on this postulation. Yet the man of superfluity is not a humanist; in any case, Flaubert is not. But his universe is so charged with meanings, with his dead God, his loquacious Devil, and his mystifying ascents, everything seems so fabricated, so permeated by nearly visible intentions, that the substance—being or nothingness—of the macrocosm seems to reproduce in its underlying unity the principal characteristics of the human microcosm. Matter, of course—nothing more. But if man is pure matter, we must recognize that, in Gustave's eyes, matter is anthropomorphized. Thus, as the shipwrecked slip under, all their absurd and sublime affirmations allow them to inscribe or reveal in the heavens a metaphysical jurisdiction whose first principle is that the desperate love of the impossible bears in its very nature the right to obtain it.

No trace of optimism here; in the realm of Satan, everything happens in reverse: rights exist, but only in order to be violated. The young Flaubert cared only to prove his singular quality by the grandeur of his desire: unable to identify with Alfred, he made himself the *negative* of his lord; the impossibility of merging with his friend presents itself as his particular merit and singular essence. He himself recognizes it, however; this painful gap of the soul is purely imaginary. He is certainly not lacking in "bitter passions," but in order to make himself Alfred's *black double,* he must do his best to decipher them otherwise. In whatever jealousy, in whatever fleeting or lasting fury, the point is *no longer to see* the product of particular and finite frustrations, themselves determined by the structures of a certain Flaubert family; with the aid of the new grid he strives to seize upon each felt deprivation *of something* as the sign of his election, that is, as a quasi-religious deprivation that extends to everything. Thus for certain Christians, the love we bear all creatures is aimed through them at the absolute Being who created them. The scheme is an old one, we know, since Gustave bears the ineffaceable traces of feudal ideology. But here it takes on all its power: the least desire, the most banal envy will be once and for all interpreted as a manifestation of the negative and devout bond that unites too demanding a microcosm with too evasive a macrocosm. In his youthful letters, we often see him transforming on the spot a disgust born of some vexation into an infinite appeal; here is the procedure: "I am more afraid of a pinprick than of a saber's blows . . . I feel the truth of this very cruelly in my family, where I am now subjected to all possible irritations, all possible discouragements. Oh, the desert! The desert! A Turkish gallery! A mountain pass and an eagle crying in the clouds!" Mount Atlas? Mount Ararat? Asia? Africa? It doesn't matter: Flaubert's nostalgia is cosmic; he takes the opportunity of a pinprick (Hamard invites himself to Croisset, Achille has not invited his brother to an exclusive dinner, Madame Flaubert has been nervous and meddlesome, etc.), which makes him want to leave his family and get out, to dress this negative and defensive reaction in sumptuous finery. Besides, mad as they seem to him, his own wishes disconcert him by their inner poverty, by an innate dryness. When he speaks of the objects he covets, the same phrases always come up: divans of swans' skin, of colibri feathers, hammocks of colibri feathers. What are these things, in fact? Nothing at all. Or else disguised utensils, rather ugly at that, whose sole interest for him comes from their function as *signs* of rarity and, consequently, of his refinement. The same is true of the "gems" he claims to covet. But Flaubert was *not* refined. Later he will bring back from his travels worthless trinkets from the "*gros Orient*," the Goncourts tell us. He is merely playing at covetousness, "making noise" about objects he is ignorant of—for lack of training and curiosity—that can neither be conceived nor imagined, and that would be indistinguishable, were the occasion to present itself, from the products of "mass-produced folk art."

He hardly bothers, furthermore, to conceal the incoherence of his declarations and his behavior. In his letters to Louise he alternates contradictory declarations according to the needs of his cause: sometimes he is simply moved by an unspeakable and painful covetousness, and sometimes he writes that his soul has fallen into an incapacity to desire anything whatever for having formerly been too covetous. To tell the truth, in both cases he is "posing"; he switches from infinite deprivation, his own role, to perfect ataraxia, Alfred's role, as if after their estrangement and then the death of his friend he were successively playing out their two characters. But there is something more serious: even as he wants to dazzle Louise by these bits of eloquence that describe his insatiable appetites—gold, palaces, precious gems—he is quite simply telling her that his desires are drained, and that he wants nothing more than to live in Paris with an income of a hundred thousand francs, "like everyone else." His passion for luxury makes transparent his real taste for comfort.

From time to time, however, he desires the superfluous concretely. But what a contrast between the modesty of his desires and the air of gravity he assumes when he mentions them. On 14 September 1846, for example, he writes: "I was told today that fifteen days from now I shall receive some silk belts from Smyrna—that pleased me. I admit this weakness. For me, you see, there are any number of inanities that are quite serious." This foible, this detachment so full of irony, this pretended shame which makes him describe as "weakness" the very *quality* he glorifies in himself, allow us to feel the astonishing crudeness of the milieu that conditioned him. Are so many words needed to say that you are expecting some belts from Smyrna and are pleased about it? Yes: the words as well as the irony are needed in 1846 when you are twenty-four years old and disengaging with great difficulty from the family utilitarianism; to love a silk handkerchief, an oriental foulard, is a matter of defiance. Let us reinstate the affirmation disguised by these flimsy negations: for me, the superfluous is a serious business; I am capable of waiting impatiently for exotic trinkets that will serve no purpose. We might call this a distant echo of Alfred's haughty confession: "I have memories of insignificant facts perhaps because I have always forgotten the important things."[71] In Gustave's eyes, Le Poittevin represents *the man of taste*. To the extent that the younger man wants to be the negative of the older one, taste is indispensable to him: otherwise, how could he be frustrated by a lack of *aesthetic* treasures that the rich possess? Yet taste is something unknown in the Flaubert family, and, as we shall soon see, beginning in 1838, Gustave bemoans the fact that he has none. For this reason he will play the "cursed aesthete." In this sense Alfred's influence effectively leads his friend to push his unrealization to the extreme; in other words, in Gustave's case the personalizing movement encloses a new sector of the imaginary. We have seen him as a child assuming unreal desires or, if you will, delightedly imagining lusts he didn't at all feel. At that time, it was a spontaneous reaction to his situation. Now the effort becomes systematic and thought out: he no longer dreams of some small happiness but structures himself *in his person* as an enlightened art collector and—the other side of the same role—as a man damned by infinite desire. When he writes, "What is Beauty if not the impossible?" his words have a double meaning: Beauty is what one cannot make, but it is also what one cannot have.

2. On Gratuitousness as Categorical Imperative.

Doing is essential for being. Even as the adolescent is immersing himself in the imaginary in order to be reunited with his lord or to make himself into his negative, he turns Alfred's dubious influence to his advantage by at long last establishing what will become his own *reality*. For some time Gustave had decided that he was a poet. But he takes poetry to be a mental attitude; it is a process of derealization that is nearly always manifest as a defensive reaction: pursued by the real, the child escaped into unreality. This behavior resembles a mystic elevation and Flaubert knows it, describing mysticism in these terms: "I

71. 15 September 1845. The insignificant facts he reports in this letter naturally constitute an aesthetic spectacle: an old fiacre on the road, friends singing, "meadows covered with water."

would very much like to be a mystic; there must be such sensuous delights in believing in paradise, *drowning* in waves of incense, *annihilating oneself* at the foot of the cross, *seeking refuge* on the wings of the dove . . . I would have liked *to die* a martyr."[72] The words he uses are significant, poetry is an escape, deriving from his stupors, and can verge on a loss of consciousness. Certainly he is proud of those "states of the soul" whose specific *quality* raises him above the vulgar. However, he is not unaware that they never go beyond the stage of subjective determination and, being imaginary, will never give him the least chance to realize himself: "I knew what it was to be a poet, I was one inside, at least, in my soul, as all great hearts are . . . All my work was inside me and I have never written one line of the lovely poem that I delighted in." Ecstasy is felt for itself, it is the forgetting of the self, an exquisite death; Flaubert knows that it represents only a certain way of living his failure, hence he does not really think of externalizing it; *writing* the "lovely poem he delights in" cannot constitute the object of an imperative in his eyes. And even less so because he is convinced that words would betray him.

In the same way, his writings of 1834–37, born of a transitory "inspiration," of rage or bitterness, seem to him merely an extension of his subjective turmoil. He finds release in them, avenges himself, tortures himself at will; these consolidated dreams replace an impossible revolt; in them he satisfies his sexual impulses unreally; the work emanates from a masturbatory autism from which it partially frees him. It is striking that Gustave should have preserved to the end of his life his mania for comparing "composition" to onanism. Something comes out of him, as in sex—one cannot write on command any more than one ejaculates voluntarily. Until the age of sixteen Gustave prefers "improvisations" to anything else; he writes: "There is something superior to reasoning, and that is improvisation."[73] To be sure, he did not write in obedience to a transcendent demand but from exuberance. Sometime later, moreover, when he had already profoundly modified his point of view, he returned to the idea of improvisation: "Day of lassitude and anguish—it's a need to write and be expansive, and I don't know what to write or what to think."[74] No mandates: a need he also calls a "confused instinct"; a *vis a tergo* impels him to write, even when he hasn't a subject in his head. It is like some vague

72. *Souvenirs* pp. 60–61. My italics. Cf. letter to Louise Colet 27 December 1852: "Without the love of form, I might perhaps have been a great mystic."
73. Ibid., p. 54.
74. Ibid., p. 102.

germination, and from this perspective the work, the viscous fruit of his entrails, extends him though it can give him no new ontological status. And in a sense he is right: the materialization of the imaginary is not its realization.

Yet, beginning in 1837, everything changes. Slowly, of course, but continuously; the process will continue until the crisis of 1844, through the hesitations and contradictions we must later specify. Here we are concerned with locating its beginnings: "At fifteen I certainly had more imagination than I have now. As I advance I lose in verve, in originality, what I perhaps gain in critical perspective and in taste. I'm afraid I shall reach a point at which I shall no longer dare to write a line. The passion for perfection makes you despise what merely approaches it."[75] Fifteen years old: he turned fifteen in December 1836. The transformation began then, at the time of the conversations at the Hôtel-Dieu: the regression of imaginative power, the appearance of "taste." Around 1838 he begins to talk about art.

It is now that Alfred's influence, or rather Gustave's bitter reflection on their half-hearted friendship, becomes decisive. Gustave wanted with all his heart to imitate his lord, to be himself the man of superfluity, that graceful finality without end who seemed to him to escape the laws of the species and glide above it. He could not do it. The spirit of seriousness was quickly reawakened in him; the son of the chief surgeon was brought up with a respect for intellectual work: he would not be an idler for anything in the world, a man who does nothing. And yet how beautiful he is, the incomparable Alfred! All the more cruelly beautiful as he is inaccessible. He has just slipped away, and Gustave, lacerated but still in love, has not stopped dreaming of an impossible identification. It is now that the idea springs forth, muddy and confused, which he will gradually clarify: for the dialectical connection between having and being he will substitute that of being and doing. Until now he has written without difficulty, like Milton who, if we are to believe Marx, produced his poems the way a bird produces its song. Yet his painful liaison with Alfred and the fear that Alfred's suicidal immobilism inspire in him throw him back on the ethic of effort and merit. Gustave is a *worker*, work is isolated and affirmed for itself: "Nothing is continually satisfying but the habit of persistent work."[76] He sees *labor improbus* not as the only possible means of reproducing his life but as an enterprise one owes it to

75. *Correspondance*, 1:17, September 1846. To Louise Colet.
76. Ibid., vol. 2, 26 July 1851.

oneself to bring to completion, by the sweat of one's brow, in tears, in order *to gain merit*. Only by strenuous and successful effort, in whatever the chosen field, can the crude labor of Achille-Cléophas and Achille be outclassed. That's all he has to do, the songbird will turn himself into a "worker in art"; he will put the austere morality of the scholar, the professional conscience of the physician, at the service of pure gratuitousness. Alfred taught him to reject human aims without tearing himself away from his condition as an average man. A means he will remain, then, but not the means of a means: he will escape the infernal round of means-ends and ends-means if he turns himself into the unique and essential means of an absolute end—an inhuman one since it has no other end than itself. Gratuitousness imposes itself, then, as a categorical imperative: for the work to perfectly contain Alfred's impassive immobility, the artist must have no *human* motive nor reason for producing it. This means that great suffering and great anger are not good counselors when artistic creation is at stake—we shall return to this at length; they can draw forth glorious outbursts, a movement of the pen, but they will be out of tune in a work which demands a retreat on the part of the author vis-à-vis himself, a partial disincarnation. Just as, for Kant, every act born of our ordinary motivations, even if it seems to conform to moral law, falls outside morality, so any invention that might be inspired in the artist by his lived "pathos"—and even the need to dream—falls, in fact, outside the realm of art. The parallel can be extended: for Kant, the sole ethical motive must be determined *a priori*, namely, the respect that moral law itself inspires; what Flaubert himself begins to understand is that the sole motive of the artist must be an *a priori* determination of pathos, that is, the desperate love that impossible beauty arouses in him from a distance. Is this not a sublimation of his desperate love for Alfred, the impossible friend? Is this not a new effort to get closer to him? Art, as he conceives it, demands in effect an ethical effort for it to be raised above the passions. God knows, however, they are violent and overwhelming: Gustave is not unaware that it will be impossible for him to suppress his passions and that he differs in this—profoundly, definitively—from his elder, who does not feel them at all. But beauty's exigency comes to extricate him: for the moment he no longer has to operate on his passions;[77] he is being asked simply to put them between parentheses when he works so that inspiration should never come from them. Thus in the moments of conception, composi-

---

77. He will return to them in 1844.

tion, and execution he *must* regain Alfred's ataraxia. And of course that ataraxia can only be intermittent. The pen is scarcely put aside when the pathetic returns with a vengeance. But if the love of beauty remains the essential and constant determination of his affectivity, if the adolescent never forgets, even when his heart is in total chaos, that he is totally and desperately pledged to beauty, if when grinding his teeth, taking his pleasures, or sobbing he never stops thinking about his work, the savage impulses, without losing their force, are affected by a certain inefficacy; they remain, but devalued, and he submits to them as to inevitable evils without letting himself be possessed by them. One admires his resilience: he rejoins his friend on the heights, for love *a priori*—which is basically the love he bears Alfred—confers on Gustave a kind of *honorary ataraxia*. But since gratuitousness presents itself as an imperative, demanding of him the sacrifice of his self, that ataraxia takes on in the eyes of the Flauberts' younger son the same seriousness that characterizes the actions of the paterfamilias, the "sacrifices" he imposes on himself in order to protect his family, to invest some of his profits in property. For Alfred, who *is* a work of art, ataraxia is its own end—to attempt to justify it would be to revert to the level of his species; precisely for this reason it remains suspect in the eyes of the disciple: an average man, an homme-moyen, must be able to *justify his actions*. So by wrenching himself away from romantic lyricism, by making gratuitousness a demand of the object, Gustave gives himself a justification for ataraxia: it reenters the universe of means since it is the necessary means for the work he would produce. At once Gustave's indifference to his own emotions seems, from the perspective of necessity, to have a sounder basis than Alfred's anorexia, which after all is merely a fact; Gustave's indifference is a policy, directed toward an end. Besides, Flaubert's attitude does not retard the process of self-radicalization: ataraxia, by putting the totality of his affective life in parentheses, necessarily engulfs the artist's ego, which is its opposite pole. Hence the counsel given later to Le Poittevin, when Gustave has reached the end of the metamorphosis: "Send everything packing, everything and yourself as well, all of it except your intelligence." [78] A precept whose passionate urgency must not conceal from us its condescension. Gustave cannot be unaware that Alfred courts the self: the younger man feels real joy at the thought that the disciple has surpassed the master by deeming his own person inessential and by disqualifying it in favor of

78. September 1845.

FROM POET TO ARTIST

work. Now he too wants only to be an "I think," but while the ex-lord, practicing the stoicism of the masters, makes this "vehicle of categories" an unsurpassable end—one must reach it, and when reduced to being only that, one contemplates the world and one's own navel—the former vassal makes the "I think" (send everything packing . . . except your intelligence) into a synthetic activity guiding and controlling the work, in short, the means of producing the work. In this way he feels he is escaping quietism: he will toil more than those who "serve" ("Think, work, write, roll up your shirtsleeves and fashion your marble like the good worker who never turns his head and who sweats, laughing, at his task"),[79] he will totally commit himself to a transcendent end, he will rediscover the project and the surpassing, but the very uselessness of his labor allows him to accede, in good conscience, to the forbidden universe of unproductive expense. Alfred expends part of the paternal profit and his own life *for nothing;* Gustave will expend his powers and his life producing splendid inanities at great cost *without the least profit to anyone.* It is not an accident that the words "good worker" come so often from his pen: literature is a craft, writing is assimilated to a physical effort: the writer fashions with his chisel the marble of language. And what is the result? An object that is its own end, as Alfred claims to be *his* own end. Thus, not only does the patient negation of the slave penetrate and transform the master's ethic, but on a still deeper level the slave *produces* the master.[80] Gustave will never identify with his friend—in this regard he feels inferior to him—but each of his works will be like the symbolic re-creation of Alfred, which is a manifest superiority: I cannot *be* you but I can *create* you, ungrateful lover! Your immobile and arrogant impassivity I internalize, not as my essence but as that of the unnecessary objects that will issue from my hands; I lack your "singularly fine and delicate organization," since I am a Flaubert, but I have loved it enough to internalize it: it will be the guiding scheme of my enterprise, the matrix out of which my works will issue. You have taste, I do not; but I will acquire it: *labor improbus vincit omnia;* I lose myself so that you might be *ad aeternum.* Perhaps this explains Flaubert's insistence on presenting artistic invention in the guise of erection: the disdained lover takes his revenge by making himself his beloved's progenitor: writing is Gustave's virility.

79. 13 May 1845.
80. This is truly Hegel's idea transported onto a level of idealism and sexuality: by his work, the slave reproduces the life of the master.

Unfortunately this fine construction leaves aside the chief questions: if the artist's inspiration comes neither from God nor from his passions, where does it come from? And if we reject the whole idea, what is a creator who is not inspired? We needn't worry, Gustave will rediscover them on his way and they will lead him to the brink of madness. For the moment, of primary importance to him is the metamorphosis of the literary object: it was lyric *translation* put in the form of his dreams; now it is born ex nihilo from a goldsmith's work executed in those precious gems, words. No springboard, no momentum: tenacity; perhaps at length a form will define itself outside, product of the chisel. His pride comes from having chosen the most difficult way: to produce an object "made of nothing." He now allows himself the aesthetic intuitions of his ex-lord: we find many an allusion, after 1842 and especially after 1844, to the "artist's vision." But there, where Alfred *casse-intellectualise-jouit*, Gustave feels he is practicing his profession: by putting his passions aside in order to reduce the world to a spectacle, he creates the materials for his art. The attitude of the aesthete is a necessary means of the artist: perhaps this is where we should look for the replacement of dethroned inspiration.

Be that as it may, beginning in 1838—thanks to his resentment, which allowed him to disengage a little from the master and step back from the magisterial teachings, Gustave gradually discovered his *reality:* he would be the Artist. Certainly he would not so easily abandon the drama of infinite desire—for it was prompted by his original dissatisfaction and by his love for Alfred. But the movement of his personalization now closes around two postulations: one leads him once again to *imaginary being,* since hysterical desire to imitate the beloved and an acknowledged incapacity to raise himself to Alfred's level make Gustave try to base his being on *not-having;* and the other, prompted by love but also by rancor and the need to surpass both the beloved and the self, aims at giving him an absolute goal, which, by its exigencies, might define his work and hence his real being. He will be the worker of the imaginary—for the unreal alone can be pure gratuity—he who gives his life to establish permanent centers of derealization. We envisage here only the subjective motivations of the second postulation; in a later chapter,[81] we shall observe motivations which are directly *social.* Yet it is not, nor can it be, a question of acting only from a *demand:* Gustave postulates the ontological status of the artist; he will not reach it before being *recognized* (by whom?—another

81. "From Poet to Artist" (sequel, in part 2, book 3).

unasked question) as the *real* producer of objects that are *unreal* and *beautiful* (or approaching as nearly as possible to perfection). Therefore we have the assumption of a new figure in the ballet of being and nonbeing: since he wants to arrive at being through doing, and since he is conscious of having done nothing yet, the adolescent is led to *play* the artist in anticipation and at the same time *really* to suffer not being one (what is there to prove he *will become* one?). But this evolution concerns Gustave's dialectical relation to the works in which he objectifies himself; his liaison with Alfred plays only an indirect and secondary role here, which will diminish and finally disappear. We shall not speak of it here.[82] What matters is that in spite of the ludic aspect of this anticipation, it rests on a firm and specific project whose foundations will no longer be subject to change and will continue to be enriched.

From this point of view too, Alfred's influence is undeniable: because of him the turbulent Gustave is led to amalgamate classicism and certain aspects of romanticism in order to forge a new idea of beauty. In his lack of emotion, in fact, Le Poittevin is related to the writers of the eighteenth century, as much in his post-Byronic verses as in his prose. Because of him, no doubt, Flaubert discovered Montesquieu's *Essai sur le goût;* without him Gustave would probably not have known Boileau's *Art poétique,* which was "explicated" at school and doubtless suffered from the abysmal tedium that textual commentaries and recitations[83] so effectively exude. And it was certainly Alfred's instruction that accounts for Gustave's vigorous collegiate defense of classicism against his schoolmates who were still taken up with romanticism (this according to Du Camp's testimony). Taste, work, the art object as end in itself ("Every poem shines with its own beauty"), condemnation of pure lyricism and naked inspiration,[84]

---

82. Cf. book 3: "Preneurosis," which is entirely devoted to retracing it.

83. Gustave always had ambivalent feelings toward Boileau, as he did toward Voltaire. In the *Souvenirs* he grants him "Attic taste" (refined taste) while much preferring Racine, who is a creator. In 1843 he becomes indignant at the "cold-blooded fart" who "did in" Ronsard. But when he gives advice to Louise, it is Boileau whom he cites as an example: "That crusty old Boileau will live as long as anyone because he was able to do what he did" (18 September 1852). He enjoyed rereading "that good Boileau, legislator of Parnassus."

84. An excellent Poem . . .

> Is not one of those efforts produced by a caprice
> It wants time, care . . .
> But often . . . a Poet without art
> Sometimes by chance heated by a fine flame . . .

Art poétique, canto 3, Pléiade, p. 176.

willingness to nourish his talent by reading and so to reconnect with the Ancients, to produce the work as the quintessence of a culture more than two millennia old: this is what the classics brought to Flaubert. But he rejects their naturalistic humanism; for this he substitutes the misanthropy of "Young France" and the pure gratuitousness of the beautiful, an inhuman end, an idol that devours its priests. Besides, as we know, putting his passions between parentheses would allow him to make them the raw material of his art: the *distancing*, though provisional, gives him the right to reproduce them. Which leads Gustave to this definition of the perfect work: "It must be cold like Boileau and wild like Shakespeare." [85] Cold like Alfred, wild like Gustave. Frozen ardor. Congealed by language. Romantic furies transformed into pure appearances by the impersonal, impassive look of the classic. On the level of cultural rationalization, such is the program that corresponds to Flaubert's second amorous postulation.

Does all this bring him closer to his beloved Alfred? No: he is moving farther away and knows it. It is not without malice that he advises this narcissist to send his ego packing. Both of them lay claim to art, but for the one, who is merely an aesthete, the Ariel of family capitalism, the artist is he who *is;* for the other, he who *does*. We may surmise to what point, around 1845, Flaubert's advice must have irritated his ex-lord. For the latter, works—if he should attempt them—will never be more than the byproducts of his *artist-being*, and though the birth might be painful, he prefers to pass over the moment of work in silence. Gustave on one occasion elicited this lofty reply: "I no longer want the glory I might perhaps gain by lifting my hand." By these words—which were not chosen to please—the elder attempts to reestablish distances: he glides above art and scorns it. The younger boy remains below; moved by who knows what vulgar passion, he struggles in vain, and will just barely attain—at best—the trivial condition of goldsmith. But for Flaubert it is now the reverse: the ex-lord is at fault for *not using* the gifts nature gave him. Even worse, his writings, when he takes it into his head to do something, are not good; and if he talks about publishing them, he betrays a malleability that Gustave hardly looks upon with favor: "[My novel] will not be as long as I had thought because I first want to sound the public's taste, then perhaps do a second *Promenade de Bélial*." What's this? He wants to *please*? If he pleases, he will finish the work, and if not he will drop it? What kind of servility is this? Gustave never dreamed of flattering the

85. To Louise. *Correspondance*, 3:46. (1854; no month or date given.)

reader—he is shocked, afraid that Alfred is bringing to literature the same spirit of compromise he manifests in his family and worldly relations. "Take care with your novel," he answers; "I do not approve of the idea of a second part: while you're at it, exhaust the subject, condense it in a single work." For the younger man, of course—who is at the level of doing—there is no place for concern with public approbation; in his view—contrary this time to classical thought—the reader's pleasure is a subjective determination and therefore without much importance. What he wants is to *objectify himself* in a work conceived and executed according to the *techniques of the beautiful*, which he will have tested and sharpened himself. The elder, aristocrat of being, that is, of death, basically asks nothing of his writings save that they give him the accessory satisfactions of vanity.

Suddenly the young writer sees only anorexia in the ataraxia that put his friend above other men. Alfred's reality is laziness. Worse: perhaps he is simply a bourgeois, as Gustave had always feared? Then, in 1843, he betrays Alfred with a new friend, Maxime Du Camp, whom we have mentioned and shall mention again. There will, however, be a last rapprochement between Gustave and Le Poittevin beginning in May 1844, when Maxime makes his first trip to the Orient. Flaubert writes to Alfred: "We would really be wrong to become estranged." Alfred acknowledges that he has been hurt by Gustave's friendship for Maxime.[86] Maxime, informed of current developments, is mad with jealousy. He writes from Constantinople: "You have seen beauty where there is none. You have been enthusiastic over trivial things whose artistic side ought not to obscure their horror and absurdity. You have lied to your own heart, you have unpityingly mocked sacred things; you, who have a superior intelligence, you made yourself the ape of a corrupt being, a Greek of the *lower Empire*, as he himself says; and now I give you my solemn word, Gustave, he is laughing at you and doesn't believe a word he said. Show him this letter and you will see if he dares deny it. Forgive me, my very dear child . . . but friendship is relentless and I had to speak to you this way."[87]

One Sunday in May 1846—the flame of 1844–45 was already extinguished—Flaubert learns the news: Le Poittevin is getting married.

86. Unpublished letter, Bibliothèque Nationale, Paris N.A.F. 25 285.
87. Unpublished letter of 31 October 1844, Spoelberch de Lovenjoul collection, library of the Institut de Chantilly. This letter weighed on Flaubert. It explains in part why, in his letter to Louise, cited above, he passed so quickly from Maxime to Alfred and why he recognized in himself a great talent for imitation: Maxime reproached him for *aping* Alfred.

He is deeply saddened. Should we believe that he sees his old lord's decision as an "apostasy" and that it seems to him like "the news of a scandal surrounding a bishop to the ears of the devout"? This is what he would later write to his mother, adding: "Alfred's death has not effaced the memory of the irritation it caused me." But I don't believe a word of it. In 1846 Gustave was quite lucid; besides, we have seen him already suspicious some ten years earlier in his dedications: "Later, when you have got married . . ." On that Sunday evening, he takes his pen in hand and writes to the apostate bishop: "Unfortunately, I have long seen it coming—I believe that you are suffering from an illusion, and a big one, as always when one effects an Action, whatever it may be. Are you sure, great man, that you will not end up a bourgeois? In all my hopes of art I was united with you. It is this aspect of things that hurts me . . . You will always find me again. It remains to be seen whether I shall find you . . . Will there still be between us those *arcana* of ideas and feelings inaccessible to the rest of the world?" Obviously these interrogatives are disguised negations. Doesn't he say at the beginning of the letter that he had "premonitions" about Alfred's future? And he adds: "Unfortunately, I have long seen it coming," which means both that he is certain of Alfred's action and had always feared it. I will not find you again! You are lost to Art and to myself! Little by little you will lose those *arcana* of ideas that I admired in you, you will turn into a bourgeois! These are the prophecies and curses hidden beneath this anxious solicitude. And, more deeply: "I discovered today that you are bourgeois, that you have always been bourgeois, and I perceive that I have known it for a long time." No, for Gustave, Alfred's apostasy is only the last of a long series of betrayals that began in 1838; from that date they had become continually more estranged. Yet Gustave's "irritation" is such that it will not be effaced even by his friend's death. In 1868 he reveals to Laure the real cause of his fury: *jealousy.* "When he married I had a profound attack of jealousy; it was a rupture, a rending! For me, he died twice . . ." In fact, he still loved Alfred, without illusion. But the blow was of such violence that it provoked an inner rupture—this was Alfred's first death. Gustave even attempts to despise him: "Sire Alfred is at Neuville doing nothing much and always the same being you know;" and on 28 April: "I saw Alfred last Thursday . . . [he] is always at the same game, he vegetates as in the past, and even worse than in the past, in a profound laziness. It is deplorable." A commentary followed that must have horrified the editor, for he omitted it. Happily the text is clear: at twenty-six, Gustave stands in pitiless judgment of the beloved master: to live without living is quite simply to vegetate. The condemnation is retroactive: it extends, if not to his whole life, at least to Alfred's youth. Even more, it is an ontological verdict: Alfred wanted only *to be;* very well, it is his being that Gustave attacks. Is it such good luck for this "poor guy" to have received, or to have given himself, the being of a vegetable? Some years earlier, at Achille's marriage, his younger brother pronounced sentence on his elder with lively satisfaction. Yet aren't his alarming predictions—"He will become a dutiful man and will be like a coral stuck to the rocks"—the same as those he takes up to describe Alfred's future? And isn't it revenge to demand Ernest's complicity against his former lord? Isn't he *too certain* of finding an ally in this assistant prosecutor—a pompous fool whom he scorns and envies with all his heart? Doesn't it delight him to have the verdict he pronounces against his best friend in the name of art confirmed by someone else in the name of utilitarian morality? And isn't it *intentional* that he imposes this complicity on someone who dared, in Paris from 1838 to 1840, to replace him in Alfred's affections?

What is certain is that this lacerated soul suffered too much in 1846 to feel his friend's second death deeply. His letter of 7 April 1848 bears witness; he announces Alfred's death to Maxime in these significant terms: "*I* buried him yesterday." [88] The abandoned mistress exults: she has regained her faithless lover. "When daylight came, around four o'clock, *the nurse and I* [89] set about the task. I lifted him, turned him, wrapped him. The impression made by his cold and stiffened limbs remained in my fingertips all day. He was horribly decomposed. We put two shrouds on him. When he was arranged in this way, he resembled an Egyptian mummy bound in its bandages, and I experienced I cannot say what an enormous feeling of joy and freedom for him." *For him? Are we sure?* Of course, in a letter to Ernest of 10 April, Gustave writes: "He suffered horribly and saw himself dying." [90] We might therefore be tempted to interpret the last sentence in the most banal sense: he is finally delivered from his suffering. But beside the fact that the interpretation would not account for his "enormous" joy—it could only be a matter of simple relief—it was *at Alfred's death,* Monday evening at midnight, that he should have felt this deliverance. Observe, on the contrary, that the conjunction *and* in this sentence links together an action and a feeling that are at first in conflict: *after*

88. *Correspondance,* 2:81. My italics.
89. Ibid. My italics.
90. The repetition—at three days' distance—of the formula "I buried him," which also figures in this letter, testifies well enough to a deliberate intention of recuperation.

having bound him like a mummy—or an infant in its swaddling clothes—*after* having symbolically reduced this still too living cadaver to impotence, to the organic inertia of the *thing*, Gustave suddenly experiences an "enormous feeling" of freedom *for* Alfred. He is free, then, this corpse Gustave has just trussed up like a sausage? "I repeated to myself this line from his *Bélial:* 'Joyous bird, he will go to greet the pines in the rising sun,' or rather I heard his voice repeating it to me, and I was *deliciously* obsessed by it all day." Yet if Alfred's soul exists, it was certainly not while being wrapped in the shroud that it left his body but much earlier, on Monday evening. Why is it that Gustave, who sat watch for two nights beside the mortal remains of his friend, reading and meditating, should not have perceived this in the course of his meditations? The truth is that the joy and deliverance, dedicated perhaps to the dead lord, are Gustave's alone; this is why he feels them *after* the operation he carries out on the cadaver. In so doing he *fashions* Alfred and renders him symbolically into his condition of pure object. Like a mother—was he not himself the object of Madame Flaubert's ministrations?—and also like an artist creating an *art object,* by fashioning life in the black light of death. Through the actions he performs he effects in himself an interpenetration of two symbols: Alfred leaves himself unreservedly in his hands, Gustave finally possesses him; gone is that cold nonchalance, that "clearness of mind" that separated them, as well as those dubious affections of which the disciple was so jealous (has it been noted that neither in the letter to Maxime nor in the letter to Ernest does Gustave breathe a word about the *wife?* [91] Where was she, then?). Now the male, the master, is the former slave girl who acts upon the sleeping lord, drunk with the elixir of the lotus eaters; a single consciousness keeps watch, his own. On the other hand, like the psychagogues of certain societies, Gustave feels charged with the task of leading Alfred back to his true being, which is nothingness; by so doing, the "good worker" makes these remains *his work:* wrapping the shroud is a rite of pas-

91. With what pleasure, on the other hand, he speaks of her remarriage in 1853. He recalls a trip by boat from Rouen to Andelys with Alfred; then, without transition: "She was at Trouville, Alfred's wife, with her new husband. I did not see her." *Correspondance,* 3:332. We note the passional structure of the sentence, and the "She" that suddenly surges up undetermined, which Flaubert will determine specifically only in order to be understood by Louise. For him, Madame Le Poittevin, née Maupassant, is *"she."* Nothing more. And what he wants to show the Muse is that this whore is unfaithful to Alfred (she should have remained a widow all her life), as Isabellada was once to Pedrillo. A final vengeance: even *that,* the lasting love of a wife, Alfred will not have had.

sage; without it, Alfred would have been only a very ordinary corpse; by wrapping him in bandages, Gustave has consecrated him, the artist has made himself priest without ceasing to act as artist. Then suddenly freedom bursts from his heart: he is delivered from his jealousy, if not from his rancors,[92] delivered from his bitter passions, from his still vivid suffering. Alfred's death *makes him right:* the path he followed could only lead to catastrophe. Gustave has *won,* the triumphant slave buries his master: here is proof that *he* is the true artist.

Even so, we should not assume that Gustave is ready to forget Alfred. Not at all. In him, the work of mourning is done quite differently. A dead Le Poittevin passes into his friend's *imaginary world:* he will obey its governing laws and bend himself to the whims of the new creator. Already in the *Mémoires* he had remarked how he "amused himself, in hours of boredom," with his memories: "At the evocation of a name, all the characters come back with their costumes and their language to play their role as they played it in my life, and I see them act before me like a God who would amuse himself by looking at his created worlds." And in the same work—we shall return to this—he recognizes that he did not love Maria (Elisa Schlésinger) as long as she disturbed his dreams by her inopportune presence—he was too fiercely attentive to them, then, really to feel his love. But two years later, when he returns to Trouville, she has the discretion not to be there. "It was now that I loved her, that I desired her; alone on the river bank I created her there, walking beside me, speaking, looking at me." Thus it is with Alfred: Gustave takes possession of him and unrealizes him; he "creates" him to his taste; Lord of the Imaginary, he will give the beloved image the necessary finishing touches without fearing any objections from the interested party. Already in the triumphant letter of 7 April one feels the work has begun: Le Poittevin, from the depths of his nothingness, sends Flaubert messages to assure him of his love and to charge him with representing him on earth. First of all, the dog: "She had become attached to him and went with him everywhere when he was alone." And "Wednesday I walked all afternoon and [she] followed me without my having called her." Then the books: "Last night I read *Les Feuilles d'automne.* I always came upon the pieces he loved best or were relevant for me to present things." And as if these admonitions were not enough, the dead man himself takes on speech: Gustave hears his voice, a "delicious obsession," repeating to him a line from *Bélial.* And, since he is already

92. Partially assuaged by the reifying manipulations he performs on the beloved.

there, why not let him enter the holy fraternity of the Flaubert dead; we need only look at this significant "coincidence": "[When I sat watch over him] I was wrapped in a cloak that belonged to my father, which he wore only once, the day of Caroline's marriage." Caroline's marriage, the first betrayal, the origin of all subsequent catastrophes: Achille-Cléophas wore that cloak and then he died; and Caroline died; and Gustave wraps himself in it in his turn while Alfred decomposes. Mission accomplished. We understand why Flaubert has spent "two long days" there and that he has had "astonishing perceptions and dazzling intuitions of untranslatable ideas." On returning to Rouen, he falls on his bed, sleeps all night and the following day. As he did after his baccalaureate; as he would do after his voyage to Carthage—this is his way of drawing the line.

From this time, Alfred—disembodied—passes in effect to the rank of myth. Gustave writes in 1857: "I never knew anyone (and I know many people) with so transcendental a spirit." In 1863: "No day, and I dare say hardly an hour goes by when I do not think of him. I know now what is meant by saying 'the most intelligent men of the time,' I take their measure by him and find them mediocre by comparison. None of them has ever dazzled me the way your brother did. What journeys into the blue he took me on . . . I recall our interminable conversations with both delight and melancholy . . . If I am worth anything it is no doubt because of that . . . We were so beautiful; I did not want to fall from those heights."

As we see, the scheme was set quite early and would not vary: in 1857 Gustave, despite what he says, did not know many people; he meant, however, that his friend was superior to all other representatives of the species. In 1863 he did know the "representative intellectuals" of his time; I admit they were pedestrian—one has the intellectuals that one deserves—but the Saint-Beuves, the Michelets, the Renans, the Taines were certainly worth as much as the Le Poittevin son. Never mind; they were bound to his conqueror's chariot because *it was understood in advance.* We note that the awesome course "through space" has changed over time into "journeys into the blue." The Devil redeemed becomes once again the Archangel. Could it be that Gustave is turning him into a cult? Not at all. Merely reread the last citation: "*We* were so beautiful; I did not want to fall from those heights." Who could suggest, knowing Flaubert's first twenty years, that he wrote in order to remain at his friend's height? The truth is that he swallowed and digested the dead master to the extent that he could no longer distinguish Alfred from himself. We find evidence of this in the famous letter of 2 December 1852 that he sent to the Muse "five minutes after finishing *Louis Lambert*." Summarizing Balzac's novel in his own way, he writes: "It is the story of a man who goes mad thinking of intangible things." Only to add: "This Lambert is almost my poor Alfred." This is to forget that "poor" Alfred *never* went mad and, furthermore, scarcely thought of intangible things; and also that Balzac specifically says Lambert is mad in the eyes of the world but not in those of his mistress; for her, "living in his mind, all his ideas are quite lucid. I follow," she says, "the road made by his spirit, and though I do not know all its byways, yet I know how to reach the end with him . . . content to hear the beat of his heart, and all my happiness is to be near him. Is he not everything to me?" Finally, Gustave seems to forget, or *feign* to forget, that the narrator in this story presents himself as a former comrade of Lambert and his intimate friend; he speaks in the first person, and he is the one who has the honor of rescuing from oblivion this "flower born on the edge of an abyss, who would fall back into it unknown." And during their school years, the fraternal feeling between the two boys was so great "that our comrades put our two names together, the one was not pronounced without the other; and to call one of us, they used to cry, 'The Poet-and-Pythagoras.'"[93] In short, a single boy in two; a single life: except that the Poet survives and testifies for Pythagoras, thus realizing *to his profit* the symbiosis he describes—two men in a single one, himself; a single life for two, his. From this point on, Gustave as reader could enjoy himself to the full: in 1836 there was only a single being and that was Gustave-Alfred, Pylades-Orestes, the Poet-and-Pythagoras. Let us read his letter. He begins by situating Louis, who is Alfred. Third person singular; Alfred is the object. From here, slipping into the first person plural: intersubjective unity. "I found *our* words there . . . [their] conversations are those we had, or their analogues." How his androgynous side must have been struck by these lines of Balzac's: "No distinction existed between things that came from him and those that came from me. We mutually forged our two handwritings, until one of us by himself could do the school work for both." A single handwriting—isn't this the best symbol of carnal union? And besides, doesn't Balzac say, in order to define the relationship between the Poet and Pythagoras, "the conjugality that bound us to each other"? Nothing could speak more to Flaubert's heart: isn't conjugality the

93. Two nicknames, rather, each of which suffices to depict the character of the child to whom it is applied.

bond between Henry and Jules, between Deslauriers and Frédéric? And here too, of course, *Anima* belongs to the poet, *Animus* to the intellect. But what enchants our reader Gustave is that this symbiosis enables him to nurse the old wounds of pride. One word surely bowled him over: "stupor." He read, dumbfounded: "And everyone laughing, while Louis looked at the professor as though in a stupor." Here in a flash he recalled the schoolboys' laughter when the study master caught him dreaming. But what enraged him then—we shall return to this in the next chapter—was his radical incapacity to prove the superiority of the dream over reality. Here Lambert is misunderstood, laughed at, for an incontestable quality: like Alfred, he has it over the others by virtue of his intelligence. "We acquitted ourselves of our schoolwork as if it were a tax levied on our tranquillity. If my memory is not unfaithful, often it was of a superior quality when Lambert did it. But both of us being taken for idiots, the professor always analyzed our work under the sway of a fatal prejudice and even retained our papers to amuse our comrades." *Therefore,* when they laughed at Gustave, it was *for his intellectual superiority:* he was not an idiot of genius, as they made him believe, as Alfred himself by his simple existence made him feel. But simply a genius—in breadth of imagination and depth of thought. The words he read, of course, served only to gratify fantasies: Alfred and Gustave did not keep company at school but at the Hôtel-Dieu, and they did not know that delicious and clandestine union of two lovers united against public opinion. Yet the shock must have been great, for in the letter to Louise, after noting the resemblance between Lambert and his friend, Gustave passes from "he" to "we" and suddenly from "we" to "I." Lambert is now he himself, Flaubert in person: "There is a story of a manuscript stolen by schoolmates . . . *that happened to me,* etc., etc. You recall that I spoke to you about a metaphysical novel . . . in which a man, by dint of thinking, ends by having hallucinations, after which his friend's phantom appears to him to draw the conclusion (ideal, absolute) from his premises (worldly, tangible)? Then . . . this whole novel of *Louis Lambert* is the preface to it. In the end, the hero wants to castrate hmself in a kind of mystic mania. At nineteen I had this desire . . . add to this my nervous attacks, which are only the involuntary downswing of ideas, of images. The psychic element then leaps above me, and consciousness disappears with the feeling of life." [94]

94. Nothing could be more dubious. Gustave, except in this passage, always maintained that he remained conscious during his crises.

And in order to complete the identification with Louis: "Oh, how we sometimes feel near to madness, me especially." But no more than he explicitly affirms this identification, does he abandon the first assertion: "Lambert is my poor Alfred." In fact he takes up the theme again on a mystic plane: "This devil of a book made me dream of Alfred all night long. Is it *Louis Lambert* that summoned Alfred (eight months ago I dreamed of lions, and just as I was dreaming of them, a boat carrying a menagerie was passing beneath my windows)?" In brief, he would like to imagine that the book, through some magic power, has evoked his dead friend. Nothing could demonstrate better than this disorderly letter his implicit determination to play both roles in turn or, if he can, simultaneously: he will be the sacred hermaphrodite if he is Alfred and Gustave in the dialectical unity of a single person. Or, if you like, if he is Gustave, the repository of Alfred's spirit. The last pages of *Louis Lambert* must have intoxicated him:

> The sight of Louis had some sort of sinister influence over me. I was afraid of finding myself once again in that intoxicating atmosphere where ecstasy was contagious. Any man would have felt, as I did, a longing to throw himself into the infinite, just as one soldier after another killed himself in a certain sentry box where one of their number had committed suicide in the camp at Boulogne. It is a known fact that Napoleon was forced to burn that hut down, the repository of an idea that had become a mortal infection. Louis's room may have had the same fatal effect as that sentry box. These two facts would then be additional evidence in favor of his theory of the transmission of the Will. I was conscious of strange disturbances transcending the most fantastic effects of tea, coffee, opium, of sleep and fever, mysterious agents whose terrible actions so often set our brains on fire. Perhaps I might have been able to transform into a book these fragments of thought intelligible only to certain spirits used to leaning over the edge of the abyss in the hope of seeing down to the bottom. The life of that mighty brain, which no doubt split in all directions like an empire grown too vast, should have been set forth in the narrative of this man's visions—a being incomplete for lack of strength or weakness; but I preferred to give an account of my impressions rather than to compose a more or less poetical work.
>
> Louis Lambert died at the age of twenty-eight . . . how often he had yearned to plunge proudly into the void, and to abandon there the secrets of his own life![95]

95. Balzac, 10:455–56.

In these "strange disturbances" felt in Louis's room, Flaubert will no doubt have recognized the "prodigious perceptions" he received in Alfred's death chamber. And in the narrator's temptation "to transform into a book these thoughts intelligible only to [a few] . . . ," wouldn't he have found an echo of the postscript of his letter to Maxime (7 April 1846): "I have a great desire to see you, for I have a need to say unintelligible things"?[96] In any case, he retained Balzac's conclusion: Louis-Alfred's life was a failure; the unhappy man was incomplete by default or by excess (it could only be a question of something *lacking*: too strong to be simply a man, Louis-Alfred was not strong enough to achieve angelic or superhuman status). But what certainly must have pleased Gustave was the sudden affirmation of self with which the narrator concludes: he would have been quite capable of "transforming into a book" those fragments of thought, in short, of restoring them in their integrity, of reading this mighty brain like an open book. This is what Flaubert thinks: at bottom he can take up and finish the task, and by so doing his superiority over the deceased brain is well established. The perceptions he receives are a mandate: I missed my chance, finish the job in my place. This explains the "I did not want to fall from those heights" in the letter to Laure. This is deliberately to forget that Alfred did not charge him with anything and that he held himself to be superior to art, just like Lambert who finally loses interest in even the expression of his own thought.

By incorporating Alfred's being, however, Gustave internalizes his gratuitousness. As a child, he felt himself to be superfluous; this was an obsession from which he could escape only by throwing himself into the rarely open arms of Achille-Cléophas; rejected, he retained the feeling of being *de trop* in his family and in the world—he led a life without a visa, he existed without an existence permit. By giving himself the mission of instituting Alfred, would he not have a chance to transform this being-*de-trop* into being-*de-luxe?* We shall soon see him reinstate in himself as principal virtues his dead friend's emptiness and boredom. Wasn't he himself bored, in former times: Yes, but like a plebeian: the boredom that made him "swollen" was the very taste of his contingency. Now he sees it as his passport to nobility: it is proof that his pride places him above men. But the "good worker" will not abandon his task: this emptiness is the sign of his election by the absolute end. He can think, according to his desire of the moment, that his lacunary gratuitousness is the internalization of the artistic imperative, or that it is what designates him as being a "worker in art."

96. It was this letter that informed Du Camp of Alfred's death.

We shall be struck by his new-found pride if we reread his letter to his mother of 15 December 1850: "If a man, whether of high or low degree, wishes to meddle with God's works, he must begin, if only as a healthy precaution, by putting himself in a position in which he cannot be made a fool of. You can depict wine, love, women, and glory on condition that you are not a drunkard, a lover, a husband, or a foot soldier. Meddle actively with life and you don't see it clearly: you suffer from it too much or enjoy it too much. The artist, to my way of thinking, is a monstrosity, something outside of nature."[97] Which this arrogant claim very well sums up: "We artists are God's aristocrats." This hired laborer in letters takes himself for a prince when he has a mind to. He is nothing of the sort, thank God. But there are moments when he must believe it or die. Alfred, *incorporated*, encourages his illusions: it is *the Other* in Flaubert who is princely.

Gustave's dominant personalization therefore integrates Alfred in three distinct dimensions, of which two are imaginary: the dead youth is the source of Great Desire—or infinite privation; he is instituted by his friend and within him as the *being* of the artist—that is, as his inert and noble gratuitousness of the art object. The third dimension, real or at least in the process of realization, is determined the gratuitousness of the *work to be done*. Deprived of everything, superfluous by birth, and disdainful of the necessary, Gustave *is nothing* else, in truth, but a worker of the imaginary, that is, the means of an inhuman end. It is as though at his friend's death he had decided to remain as two men in one, a couple with only one life, in short, Gustave and Alfred simultaneously. This is made easier for him by the perpetual doubling of his ego, that is, by the constant movement in him from *I* to *he*, and vice versa. Yet the disparity of the couple is undeniable, and it results from the disparity of social conditions. The path upward remains closed to the man of the necessary: Gustave knew this from 1848 on, although he hardly says so. We shall see in the third part of this work that he could escape from his class only by dropping *below it*, that is, having himself completely disqualified and discarded as an *unusable* means. He learned, then, that the path to the "superhuman" first runs below, in the realm of the submen. Be that as it may. For Gustave, the institution of Alfred makes Alfred the tutor of his pride. The survivor never stops inflating the merits of the deceased in order to inflate himself, Alfred's peer in the eyes of the world, in the esteem of others and in his own.

97. *Correspondance*, 2:268.